ALFRED KAZIN'S
AMERICA

ALFRED KAZIN'S
AMERICA

Critical and Personal Writings

———•◆•———

EDITED AND WITH
AN INTRODUCTION BY
TED SOLOTAROFF

HarperCollins*Publishers*

An extension of this copyright page follows page 540.

ALFRED KAZIN'S AMERICA. Copyright © 2003 by The Estate of Alfred Kazin and Ted Solotaroff. All rights reserved. Printed in the United States of America. No part of this book may be used or reproduced in any manner whatsoever without written permission except in the case of brief quotations embodied in critical articles and reviews. For information, address HarperCollins Publishers Inc., 10 East 53rd Street, New York, NY 10022.

HarperCollins books may be purchased for educational, business, or sales promotional use. For information, please write: Special Markets Department, HarperCollins Publishers Inc., 10 East 53rd Street, New York, NY 10022.

FIRST EDITION
Designed by Joseph Rutt
Printed on acid-free paper

Library of Congress Cataloging-in-Publication Data

Kazin, Alfred.
Alfred Kazin's America : critical and personal writings / edited and with an introduction by Ted Solotaroff.—1st ed.
p. cm.
Includes index.
ISBN 0-06-621343-6 (acid-free paper)
1. American literature—20th century—History and criticism. 2. American literature— History and criticism—Theory, etc. 3. United States—Civilization—20th century. 4. Critics—United States—Biography. 5. Kazin, Alfred. I. Title: America. II. Solotaroff, Ted. III. Title.
PS29.K38A25 2003
810.9—dc21
2003049997

03 04 05 06 07 NMSG/RRD 10 9 8 7 6 5 4 3 2 1

To Judith Dunford

All that a man has to say or do that can possibly concern mankind is in some shape or other to tell the story of his love,—to sing; and if he is fortunate and keeps alive, he will be forever in love. This alone is to be alive to the extremities.

—*Henry David Thoreau*

. . . sometimes the life seems dying out of all literature, and this enormous paper currency of Words is accepted instead. I suppose the evil may be cured by the rank-rabble party, the Jacksonism of the country, heedless of English and of all literature—a stone cut out of the ground without hands;—they may root out the hollow dilettantism of our cultivation in the coarsest way, and the newborn may begin again to frame their own world with greater advantage.

—*Ralph Waldo Emerson*

Seeking to conquer a larger liberty, man but extends the empire of necessity.

—*Herman Melville*

CONTENTS

III. THE AGE OF REALISM

IV. THE LITERARY LIFE

V. CONTEMPORARIES

VI. DEPARTED FRIENDS

VII. THE LITERARY LIFE

VIII. SUMMING UP

PREFACE

———•◆•———

When I was approached by Philip Roth, acting in behalf of the Alfred Kazin estate, to edit a collection of Kazin's writings, we decided that the best way to make it serve as a resource rather than as a monument, soon out of print, and to best bring out his significance as a critic and writer, would be to concentrate on his writings about Kazin's American subject and to include his personal as well as critical writing. The book that follows is what I have made of this approach.

Pieces from virtually all of Kazin's books have found their way into this one. They follow the general development of his oeuvre, though I have begun with some of the subsequent writing about his early life and the beginning of his career. Along with the pleasure of reading one of the best memoirists of his generation, the reader should find an added interest in the criticism that follows from having a sense where its author was coming from. I have also culled several profiles of writers from his memoirs to give the reader a taste of the literary life he led as well as his personal take on them.

As with any one-volume collection of a first-rate critic, there is much more that belongs in it than one can select. In the case of Kazin, one has the additional decision to make among the three or four different pieces and chapters that he wrote on most of the major American writers. To make the book as coherent and inclusive as possible, I have foreshortened or excerpted from several of the longer essays and cut passages from others. These places are indicated by an ellipsis at the beginning or end of a paragraph or, where the excision is more than a page, an ellipsis between the paragraphs. For the most part, I have kept or slightly varied Kazin's titles, though for material from his periodical writing I've felt free to change a title to suit my purposes, just as the editor of the review or essay likely did. In a few places I have altered the phrasing, syntax, or punctuation in the interest of clarity, and in one instance, the profile of Delmore Schwartz, have moved a climactic paragraph that seemed out of place. An appendix lists the source of each selection and its original title.

I want to thank Terry Karten, my editor at HarperCollins, for backing this approach to Kazin's legacy, for her encouragement and advice along the way, and for her astute editing of the introduction. Eugene Goodheart's strong criticism of the introduction forced me to clarify and strengthen it at various points. I am also indebted to Philip Melita for his help with Kazin's journals in the Berg Collection at the New York Public Library, and to Penny Vlagopoulos of Columbia University, who meticulously assembled and formatted most of the text and patiently put up with my vagaries of judgment. As for the writer Judith Dunford, Kazin's widow, I hardly know where to begin thanking her—she has facilitated my work at every turn and, along with Kazin himself, has been its inspiration.

Ted Solotaroff
February 17, 2003

INTRODUCTION

Major critics tend to have a major subject, one which identifies them and is, in turn, marked by their imprint. What the liberal imagination was to Lionel Trilling, social fiction to Irving Howe, modernism to Edmund Wilson, the moralist imagination to F. R. Leavis, so the American sensibility was to Alfred Kazin. From the boy on the tenement fire escape in immigrant Jewish Brownsville reading his way into the American past to the old distinguished professor in his skyscraper office at CUNY pondering God's place in it, Kazin attended to the light that came from his favorite American writers and drew close to their native and individual traits and vibrations, even to those of their terrain.

There is a story told of his reviewing a book about the American West in which he went on a bit about the majesty of its mountains and rivers, something like that. "Hey, Alfred," Philip Rahv mocked, "What's this about 'our mountains, our rivers?' " "What's this" was genuine, intensely so, starting early in his life:

> The day they took us to the Children's Museum—rain was dripping
> on the porch of that old wooden house, the halls were lined with
> Audubon prints and were hazel in the thin antique light—I was left

with the distinct impression that I had been stirring between my fingers dried earth and fallen leaves that I had found between the paving stones of some small American town.

Kazin's sense of the American spirit continued to possess this visceral attachment. His journals are full of passages such as the following:

Every once in a while some token—a sentence in a book, a voice heard—will recall for me the fresh instant delight in American landscape and culture. . . . The sentence this morning fresh as a spring wind comes from Constance Rourke's book on Audubon, on the sudden realization that his ornithology showed a national sense of scale, that like Whitman he was a great voice of American nationality.

The anecdote points up the difference between Kazin and most of the other New York Jewish writers associated with *Partisan Review* whose relation to America tended to be a position rather than a possession. In his later years Rahv, for example, became a sometime Americanist—the framer of the famous classification of our writers as Palefaces (Irving, Hawthorne, James, et al.) and Redskins (Cooper, Mark Twain, Whitman. Dreiser, et al.). But what became a literary interest to Rahv was a world to Kazin; and the Americanism that Rahv tuned into by his changing ideology and situation was to Kazin, in Henry James's phrase, a complex fate.

The complexity came partly from the implication of Rahv's question—a Jew of their generation had not grown up in our pluralist mentality, but rather in one still sharply divided by custom and suspicion and governed by a tacit mutual agreement, with a shaky tolerance clause. No matter how much one wished and dreamed otherwise, in Brownsville in the 1920s and 1930s, the feeling of being different, outside of and threatened by a society that proffered freedom and opportunity but remained exclusively Christian and mostly WASP in its culture, was inseparable from feeling Jewish, inseparable even from feeling authentic. "Why must it *always* be them and us?" young Alfred asks himself and then, typically, forecloses the issue by asserting his Jewish loyalty and solidarity.

As time went on, his anxious passage from home would take him far but not change very much, being guided by his effort to fathom, like Whitman and Dreiser before him, the good and evil of American individualism and to live out "the bitter patriotism of loving what one knows."

2

He grew up in the 1920s and early 1930s in one of the rawer ghettos—half Brooklyn, half Belz—at the end of the subway line. The firstborn of a house painter and dressmaker who had married out of immigrant loneliness and remained distant, Kazin was to be haunted by the image of his father weeping on their wedding night and by the cold barrenness between his parents that ensued, which he believed had chilled his own character until late in life. Fortunately his aunt Sophie, the family boarder, was a sultry woman of parts, a seamstress who brought books, art and music and two equally vivid friends into the house. Their Russian songs and stories at the weekly Shabbos dinner, as well as the nightly sense the boy had of ardent Sophie lying close by in her room, gave his young sensibility the compensating glow and heartfulness that went into his writing. He was to remark that "the best of whatever I knew as a child I got from this nearness to Sophie, lay in this brooding, dark, sultry arousement, this sudden brushing of wings, when I felt that it was Sophie, in her insistence on love, in the fierce sullenness with which an immigrant dress-maker no longer young lived for love, that made up the living contrast to my mother's brooding carefulness and distrust." One imagines that his favorite positive adjectives—"burning," "fiery," "blazing," "furious," and their synonyms—were a primal link to her and through her to the headstrong Russian literature that partly shaped his sense of a literary vocation.

He also had both the lift and burden of being the family "Columbus"—as greenhorn couples referred to their firstborn ("What do *we* know?" their refrain); and also "the redeemer of the constant anxiety of their existence . . . the monument of their liberation from the shame of being—what they were." From the accounts in *Walker in the City* and *Writing Was Everything,* he comes through as a socially awkward, high-strung youth who keeps to himself but on whom nothing is lost. He was also a reader with a preternatural responsiveness. At twelve, he discovered Dickens and was never to recover.

I felt I was in Dickens' head and could not get out . . . *Oliver Twist* was all around me and in me. I wanted never to get away from its effect. . . . Why was Dickens compelled to write like that, and why did it work on me like a drug? . . . That was how I started as a critic.

Walker in the City is a memoir of images and scenes rather than events, of places rather than people, of rapid observation and impressions and virtually no stories: the experience of an intense boy who has no friends worth mentioning until he is sixteen. Living on a knife edge in school between triumph and catastrophe, he developed a stammer, perfect English being part of the right answer in the New York school system of the time. Sent off to the ignominy of speech therapy, he found that his impediment disappeared as he walked the streets, fluently mouthing the riffs of his inner voice. He became a walker, the loner's sport, and a Cortés of the near world of Brooklyn, with a passion to turn it into an outdoor museum of Americana and the museums themselves into intense communions.

The center of the Kazin household was the kitchen, not only by ethnic convention but because by day and far into the evening, it was his mother's dressmaking shop. Kazin's workaholic nature (his widow, Judith Dunford, has told me that there was hardly a flat space in their apartment not covered by books, journals, or manuscripts), his anxiety, and his social discomfort appear to have come from his mother, a woman who cooked for the family but was too busy or spent to eat with them; just as the incessant whirr of her sewing machine became the rhythm and emblem of the grinding, remorseless capitalist society out there in America. "Where is the day taking us now?" Kazin, "always so near to her moods," has her asking herself as she steals a moment to stare out the window into the Brownsville dusk.

The phrase soon echoes in the boy's own inner voice after crossing Brooklyn Bridge late one afternoon. He feels himself being picked up by the great American force of acculturation, of being whisked away from dingy, backward but secure Brownsville into the Great American "Beyond," as Protestant as the austere brownstones on his journeys through Brooklyn Heights, and his mind spins with the question, "Papa, where are they taking me? Where in this beyond are they taking me?"

Also a loner and library haunter, like his son, Charles Kazin had started out in America by working his way westward. In his travels he had seen Sidney Hillman, the famous labor leader, working in a Chicago suit factory and had heard Eugene Debs speak at a rally. Taking a job painting boxcars, he had gotten as far as Omaha and been offered a homestead in Colorado. These were important events in the Kazin family romance that dictated to the boy's imagination. ("*Omaha* was the most beautiful word in the language, *homestead* the next one"), and help to explain Kazin's subsequent passion for the prairie novelists who provided a homestead of thousands of already mostly forgotten pages that he would settle in with, ten years later, to witness the dawn of American realism.

Charles Kazin was an ardent socialist; his father, Abraham, had been an early one, a pieceworker with a rented sewing machine, who had tried to organize the *"forloiryne menschen "* (lost souls) of the terrible first years of the East European immigration. He died of the effort at twenty-five or -six, another important item in the family saga. The socialist legacy was also actively transmitted to Alfred by his aunt Sophie and her co-workers at the infamous Triangle Shirtwaist Factory. As an adolescent, he loyally went to meetings at the local Labor Lyceum, where he would gaze at the large photograph of Eugene Debs, who gave American socialism its human face; he had twice gone to jail for the cause, five times run for president. "Poor Parnell!" Alfred would say to himself. "Our dead king!"—Joyce having joined the other literary/spiritual rebels—Blake and Lawrence and Whitman—who were now his personal models. Like the young Henry James, he wanted to be "just literary," but still it was socialism that he took into the street arguments of the 1930s along Pitkin Avenue where the radical factions were like the Jewish form of gang fighting. Brandishing their battle insult of "Sell out!," the Stalinists dominated the arguments, broke up the Socialist meetings, even got the girls. Opposing them in the Brownsville streets and later in the famed "alcoves" at City College, where it was always the period after Lenin's death, the right to the succession still in fierce dispute—Kazin developed his penchant for "strong argument" and the dialectical dramatics that would characterize his criticism.

His main intellectual circle once he got out of Brownsville became the high-powered anti-Stalinist, eclectic Marxist one around V. F. Calverton, the editor of the *Modern Monthly*, which Kazin helped him put out while still in his teens. This was an important phase; the polymath Calverton came to express for Kazin much of the libertarian spirit that was one of the better parts of the 1930s, as was the intellectual intensity of Calverton's milieu where Kazin witnessed at first hand the arguments between such redoubtable figures as Max Eastman and Sidney Hook. For these and other reasons, the 1930s would remain a positive part of Kazin's background as the 1960s would for his son, the labor historian Michael Kazin. He would have no need to reject its ideals along with its illusions, no need to stalk himself and other radicals into the hardline anti-communism of the 1950s and on to neoconservative Americanism.

Kazin believed that literature was too important a personal and cultural resource to be left to the modernist literati or the Popular Front. He had experienced it as the staff of the spirit and the better part of aspiration in the wretched households in Brownsville where he went as a teenager early in the Depression to discuss works like *The Waste Land* and Blake's *The Marriage of Heaven and Hell*. The virtual hovel in which his older friend David, his first writing audience, lived with a dying mother and small brother, a few sticks of furniture, the photos of lynchings and the books of the international Left— Lenin and Frederick W. Douglass, Ernst Thaelmann and Henri Barbusse— conveyed to the sixteen-year-old Kazin "some deep, brave, and awful earnestness before life itself" and a "naked freedom of thought" that he would never lose and would soon come to write out of.

Another formative experience was of the Group Theater productions of Clifford Odets's plays. Thanks to the authenticity of Odets's dramas and the revolutionary realism of this repertory company (Russian-Jewish-radical theater come into its own), Kazin discovered people occupying the stage "by as much right as if they were Hamlet or Lear." The "right" was hardly conferred by tragic stature but rather by the power of theatrical art to electrify the "crowded, tense, shabby Brooklyn life" and to present its soul while remaining faithful to its atmosphere, issues and idiom. The significance of such an experience is that it authorized as well as naturalized the sensibility young Kazin had developed in just such circumstances, giving the young writer the confidence to make use of who he actually was rather than willing a persona as many of the *Partisan Review* crowd did. It's not an accident, I think, that Kazin, Irving Howe, Paul Goodman, and Saul Bellow, its most productive members, were the ones who remained most connected to their early life.

At the end of one of the Odets performances, the exhilarated young writer from Brownsville thinks, "It was all one, as I had always known. Art and truth and hope could all come together—if a real writer was their meeting place." They indeed soon began to come together for him: the literary man's standards, the socialist aspiration, the Jewish respect for the hard facts but also for the soft ones, the working-class rebel's sense that his hour had come.

On the other hand, in every young writer there is a renegade yearning to break out into the land of otherness, all the more so in the immigrant Jewish family and community like Kazin's, whose ethos of possessiveness and solidarity made leaving it feel like a jailbreak. One looks for models, and Kazin found two of his in the Solovey couple, whose arrogance and refinement weigh like lead in the rough sea of Brownsville survival. The enigmatic Soloveys' love and doom is the major episode in *Walker*, and one can feel in Kazin's fascinated retrospect of himself with the blond, French-speaking Mrs. Solovey and her bitterly aloof intellectual husband, the inchoate passion and independence they provoked as he hung around their failing drugstore.

So, too, in the remarkable section in *Walker in the City* where one sees the beginning of an insurgent spirituality with young Alfred's breaking a taboo of the Jewish mind when he all but falls into the prose of the Gospels and discovers in his intense excitement and shame "my Yeshua: the very embodiment of everything I had waited so long to hear from a Jew. . . ." And along with Blake, Walt Whitman, and Ernest Hemingway, "another writer I can trust." Kazin's Judaism was to be a religion he used rather than practiced. He prayed to his own, often elusive God and his spirituality as well as religious learning flowed most strongly, I think, when he was writing about another writer's, such as his superb introduction to William Blake.

The compact and nuanced narrative of Mr. and Mrs. Solovey is also a testimonial to the fiction writer Kazin didn't become, but who, locked away in his heart and active in his imagination, will make him the critic he became, one who writes about writers as gifted novelists and poets do—that quick assessment of the author's character and the work's texture—the life, or lack of it, on the page—and that ability to put a hand into the prose or verse and measure the strength of the current. Kazin wrote less as a literary critic than as a writer possessed by literature as moral testimony and lived history. He was not interested in literary theory or in what nowadays is called textuality; he didn't interpret the work so much as characterize the mentality of the writer that is operating within the work and career, seeing him or her, in other words, like a character in a story or novel—an individual set against a social/moral ground or, often, two such figures to define and dramatize them against each other. "Looking at [Sherwood] Anderson and [Sinclair] Lewis together, the drowsing village mystic and the garrulous village atheist, it seemed as if they had come from the opposite end of the world (or from the same Midwestern street) to meet in the dead center of the postwar emancipation and be stopped there, wondering what came next."

3

Kazin's first work appeared in *The New Republic*, which he began writing for at the age of nineteen. He had been sent there by John Chamberlain, after he had barged into his cubicle at the *Times* to protest a review Chamberlain had written. Jewish sons in the 1930s did this sort of thing: the toughs had unionism, boxing, and crime, the sensitives education and the arts as the ladder up from the ghetto, and the reviewers' bench at *The New Republic* was crowded with them. The magazine had been founded at the height of the Progressive movement, and in the subsequent twenty years had become the leading national journal of political and social reform and innovation in the arts. Here Kazin began to develop his own tradition, to model his style on the intellectual dignity he admired in the early independent activist writers who sustained "the promise of American life," the title of a seminal book by Herbert Croly, its founding editor. The intellectual radicalism of the then Socialist Walter Lippmann, the democratic philosophy of John Dewey, the fiery reportage and social criticism of Randolph Bourne, the committed literary journalism of Edmund Wilson and Van Wyck Brooks all worked on young Kazin, inspired and authenticated his gift. During the Depression *The New Republic* was trying to restate Progessivism as Marxism—*To the Finland Station* was running in its pages when Kazin began showing up in 1934. Wilson himself was gone as literary editor, succeeded by Malcolm Cowley, who was then in his sophisticated Stalinist phase but was another brilliant practitioner as well as encourager of the review that dramatized the author and his book in the context of the times.

Young Kazin learned from him, too, but took his point of view from the less blinkered perspectives of Wilson and Brooks, whose book *America's Coming of Age* in 1919 had been the shot heard around the literary world for the next decade, a forthright indictment of America as a commercial civilization that acted like a plague on the careers of its serious writers and artists (Mark Twain and Henry James were subsequently to be his foremost examples). It was from the influence of Brooks's idealism that much of the literary ethos of the 1920s developed with its respect for craftsmanship, its resistance to "selling out," and its belief that literary criticism in America is compelled to become social criticism to preserve the human spirit.

To be sure, such a position was taken for granted during the Depression years, but the tradition of Progressivism with its positive blend of protest and faith in America, along with Kazin's own earlier socialism, would stand him in good stead by enabling him to maintain a coherent critical liberalism, like that of, say, John Kenneth Galbraith and Lewis Mumford who were also of the old *New Republic* stripe. But much as he admired Brooks, Kazin thought that in the hard times and hard light of the 1930s, Brooks's social program, derived from Ruskin and William Morris, was sentimental and anachronistic, and his style self-indulgently lyrical. Also I suspect that the young Kazin, a raw youth from Brownsville standing on the edge of the Stalinist five o'clock gin-and-lime-and-deck-tennis circle at *The New Republic*, had a lot of resistance as well as fascination. Its cantankerous former literary editor, Edmund Wilson, was a hovering absence, and it was Wilson that he yearned to emulate, particularly his immense ability to dramatize literary and intellectual history by weaving a writer's character, work, career, and times seamlessly together; and he carried in his head like a mantra the final sentence of Wilson's chapter on Proust in *Axel's Castle*:

> Proust is perhaps the last great historian of the loves, the society, the intelligence, the diplomacy, the literature and the art of the Heartbreak House of capitalist culture; and the little man with the sad appealing voice, the metaphysician's mind, the Saracen's beak, the ill-fitting dress-shirt and the great eyes that seem to see all about him like the many-faceted eyes of a fly, dominates the scene and plays host in the mansion where he is not long to be master.

4

Like everyone else, Kazin scrambled during the Depression—working as a researcher in the Federal Writers' Project and writing reviews wherever he could and anything else that paid, from vanity biographies to radio plays on WNYC based on Dickens and Poe. But though he was still writing on the kitchen table in Brownsville, the young freelancer had crossed the Brooklyn Bridge, his lifelong symbol of the linkage between his early and later self, and was beginning to make his way. One can easily sense his excitement from the momentum of the writing in his second memoir, *Starting Out in the Thirties*. *Walker* is situational—"The Kitchen," "The Neighborhood," "The Beyond"— an active reverie of the heart, the prose crackling with the tension of an anxiously venturesome young mind warmly hugged by Jewish solidarity and strongly tugged by the American prospect; *Starting Out* is relational—each chapter a year going by in rushes of mostly elated contacts, the prose picking up the beat of an eager, naive rebel who is beginning to go places—to hang out with Otis Ferguson, sort of a Pete Hamill of his day; to go to the intellectual-studded parties of V. F. Calverton and ogle Calverton's ravishing young mistress; to meet other young minority writers from the slums or the sticks on their way up—Richard Wright, William Saroyan, James T. Farrell, Robert Cantwell. Then, in 1938, came the jolt of the big opportunity that makes a career. Carl Van Doren, the literary editor of *The Nation*, casually suggested to his young reviewer that a book was needed on the history of American modernism, and all the vectors of his development came together, all the bees in his bonnet began to buzz and head into clover.

Kazin has written in several places about the rapturous three years that followed at the shiny yellow desks in Room 304, the main reading room of the New York Public Library. His own graduate school—which he shared with his friend Richard Hofstadter, who was working on *Social Darwinism in America*—the reading room was also during those years the "asylum and church of the unemployed." What better place to launch himself into the mainstream of American prose in the 1890s as it flowed strongly through another prolonged and bitter time of crisis and to do so directly at the point at which it bent widely left.

He went at it whole hog: the complete works not just of Howells and Crane, Frank Norris and Upton Sinclair, Edith Wharton and Hamlin Garland, but the whole archive of novels, stories, manifestos, studies, pamphlets by the ironic metropolitan realists, the lonely small-town individualists, the angry prairie naturalists. Kazin read them all, down to Joseph Kirkland's *Zury: The Meanest Man in Spring County*. His curiosity was ravenous, the young literary immigrant possessing his newfound land, the ambitious scholar-critic developing a background of minor writers against which to place the major ones and thereby write with the undertext of first-rate history, the silent reserves of what is left out that produce the ring of authority, the resonant hum of distinctions and implications. Finally, too, Kazin was impelled by his own shock of recognition, his felt need to do justice to these "lone protestants of their time," these "Jeffersonian hearts plagued by a strangely cold and despotic America, some of whom lacked every capacity for literature save a compelling passion to tell the truth." Fighting or mourning for their land, their distinctively American voices and "elementary nationalism" were Emerson's prophecy come true—the "rank-rabble party" who uproot genteel cultivation and prepare the ground for "the newborn to frame their own world with greater advantage."

They were also pioneers of the new democracy of American letters that went hand in hand with the new realism that was springing up all across the cultural front from down-to-earth poetry to crusading journalism; from the pragmatism of Peirce, James, and Dewey to the revisionist history of James Allen Smith and the young Charles Beard that boldly questioned the class interests of the Founding Fathers and sharply distinguished between the abstract "juristic" republic and the actual perishing one. This broadly based realism also functioned as a kind of Greek chorus pointing out and lamenting the anarchy and brutality of rampant industrial capitalism. John Jay Chapman summed it up as a railroad coming to a town and then dominating it, and as a "cruelty going on before you" that leaves the alternative of "interposing to stop it or of losing your sensibility." Liberal intellectuals and writers were made of sterner, more fighting stuff back then, and Kazin happily entered their minds and their fellowship.

With the 1930s' winds of change at his back and a whole, relatively unexplored field before him that began with Howells and ended with Faulkner; that ranged from the thought of Dewey, Steffens, Veblen, and Parrington to that of James Hunecker and Ludwig Lewisohn, Irving Babbitt, and John Crowe Ransom; from the turn-of-the-century aesthetes to the muckrakers across town; from the primitive realists and half-baked modernists to the sophisticated writers who put out *The Seven Arts* in the 1920s; from the Progressives who rose and fell with President Wilson to the Marxists and New Humanists and Fugitives and social documentarians of the 1930s—Kazin presented and evaluated them, connected them, and wrote on to the darkening end where everything came to an ominous halt as the new world war drew on.

A great story to be told. Supported by his wife, a young research bacteriologist, he had the time and stability as well as urgency to tell it, finishing it just before he received his draft notice in 1941. His heated imagination and cool judgment produced a tempered prose and a kinetic texture. The prodigious reading Kazin had done comes to seem like a great river and his capacious imagination like a hydroelectric plant steadily generating the images that bring power and light to his vast subject. And, to complete Auden's line, "a sovereign touch." The command of the subject at virtually every turn would be remarkable in a historian twice his age. Sixty years after its publication, *On Native Grounds* stands beside Perry Miller's *The New England Mind*, F. O. Matthiessen's *American Renaissance*, and Richard Chase's *The American Novel and Its Tradition* as landmarks of our literary history.

Basically, what Kazin did was lay the development of American realism and modernism as parallel tracks on which to move his history forward, and to create perspective and argument by pitting the urgencies of expression of essentially a protest literature against the exigencies of art as practiced and usually compromised by a succession of writers most of whom had virtually no native literary models. In Europe, naturalism grew out of the literary tradition as the counter movement to Romanticism; in America, naturalism was mainly a weapon to assail the trusts. With a few nods to Zola, writers like Norris and Sinclair had to make up their literary culture as they went along. Lacking a tradition other than the New England one become genteel or the frontier one become obsolete, the more imaginative writers, like Stephen Crane, Edith Wharton, Theodore Dreiser, and Willa Cather, descended deep into themselves as Joseph Conrad, another solo pioneer advised, to find the terms of their appeal. Otherwise, there were so many books that were groping rather than accomplished, so many careers that were uneven, repetitious, or brief.

Steering between the Marxists and the New Critics, Kazin early set his standard by the career and practice of Henry James—itself a pretty remarkable choice for a young radical doing his research amid the human flotsam and jetsam of a reading room in New York City during the Depression. What he drew from James was that human character, social forces, and moral implications required a relentless attention and a full consciousness of complexity as well as an artist's intuition. By means of them James's art had "fastened itself to . . . subjects, themes, qualities, events which the conventional assessment of his talents were presumably closed to . . . but which by the slow, avid pressure of his perception he conveyed with devastating lucidity." Kazin's case in point was *The Princess Casamassima*, the only American novel of its era to portray the slow incubation of the revolutionary spirit as it went on, in James's words, "irreconcilably, subversively, beneath the vast smug surface." Stoutly persisting both doctrinaire modernism and populism, the young critic held to the old Master's "standard of art—perception at the pitch of passion and expression as embracing as the air." In Fitzgerald, Cummings, Hemingway, and Dos Passos, modern America finally produced the fiction writers who had led in varying degrees of fullness the life and practice of an artist, who had stamped their writing so that it could be read like Braille, as Fitzgerald put it, and who had each written a chapter of the moral history of his age. And it is here that *On Native Grounds* reaches it own pitch of perception in Kazin's account of Fitzgerald working his way deep into himself and into 1920s America to bring forth Jay Gatsby; the remarkable surrealism of E. E. Cummings's *The Enormous Room*; of Dos Passos's slow development of his power and techniques of social observation, and of the rise and fall of Hemingway's practice of a "major art on a minor vision of life."

Still Kazin's American pride and leftist sympathy leaven the text. Despite Stephen Crane's limitations, say, as a young journalist who was still "only half a writer" and who had no experience of war, Kazin points up the originality of his horrific landscapes of the Civil War battles and also observes how *The Red Badge of Courage* anticipates the future literature of war by focusing its boredom, havoc, and horror on the common soldier. Or again, though Anderson and Lewis each had only a couple of strings to their instruments, they nonetheless caught the tone and rhythm of the heretofore unsung private life of middle Americans and helped to create the first broad audience for serious fiction. Or again, he presents Dreiser transforming the wretchedness and disrepute of his family into the morally numbing force of circumstances in the new urban society and of introducing American literature to the sexual drive. You can pretty much tell a critic's literary politics by his take on Dreiser. Lionel Trilling, who came to see the liberal imagination in America as half-empty, regarded Dreiser as mostly a pretentious brute who is dogmatically praised to show up the artificiality and irrelevance of cultivated masters such as Henry James. Kazin regards Dreiser as a great folk artist like Knut Hamsun and Gorky—"the spirits of simplicity who raise local man as they have known him to world citizenship . . . ."

The young post-immigrant radical tended to find isolation and alienation almost everywhere he looked, sometimes mistaking the novelist's necessary reclusiveness and quarrel with society for them. Also he gives short shrift to novelists like Hergesheimer and Cabell, who identified with the wrong class; he undervalues Edith Wharton's achievement because in snobbishly viewing society *haut en bas* she missed what Dreiser saw; and he faults the positivist Dewey for lacking a tragic sense of life. He writes about the literary South with a leftist brashness that makes the Fugitives into so many bitter nostalgists, if not apologists for slavery, and as excessive in their aestheticism as the Marxists were in their philistinism; and he will spend the rest of his career atoning for his underrating of Faulkner as a half-baked genius who let his social vision run wildly into rhetoric and solipsism.

Nonetheless, the literary and intellectual judgment in *On Native Grounds* is generally remarkable for its astuteness, all the more so when you remind yourself that the author was writing some of it in his early twenties. Had the book been only a study of the fiction of its fifty-year span it would have been a major achievement. What made it a lasting one was Kazin's doubling its reach and interest and the evolution of its theme of the making of the modern American spirit by including its influential thinkers and historians, social and literary critics, and providing the background for these figures by his astute accounts of the leading movements. He also brings his narrative of the rise of the democratic mentality and its adversaries to a creative and appropriate climax by steering around the dreary dead end of protest fiction in the 1930s, save for Farrell and Steinbeck, to take up the rich and various documentation through all the arts, from poetry to photography, of the "new nationalism" that emerged during the decade, as the giant nation, on its knees, struggled to clear its mind and pull itself together.

5

Kazin said that *On Native Grounds* was his easiest book to write because of the spirit of the times, his passion for the task, and the wide-openness of the field. Such favoring circumstances would not occur again in his career.

The book won him a job as literary editor of *The New Republic*, which put him in personal touch with other young Jewish prodigies such as Delmore Schwartz, Saul Bellow, Isaac Rosenfeld, and Paul Goodman, who energized him; with influential critics such as Trilling and Wilson, who certified his sudden reputation; and with such competitors as Philip Rahv and Mary McCarthy, who productively infuriated him. But *The New Republic* had fallen upon dull times during these war years, and he soon moved on to the staff of *Fortune*, which had become a sort of halfway house for disenchanted radicals who could use the money and stand the pretentiousness of Henry Luce's think tank. Rejected by the draft and eager to get overseas, Kazin ended up in England where he found a more intense social consciousness than any he had known, in reporting on the British army's effort to educate its fractious working-class troops and in absorbing on the spot, as it were, George Orwell's wide-ranging social vision and intellectual independence. He was also profoundly affected by the prophetic struggle of Kafka and then of the postwar European writers and intellectuals, notably Simone Weil, to pursue the philosophical and spiritual implications of the huge devastation of the war and its horrible aftermath of the death camps: a kind of mental ground zero after the European twin towers of enlightenment and humanism had collapsed.

On his return to the States, Kazin found himself all dressed up for crisis writing, as it were, with no place to go. Just as it had after the First World War, the United States quickly resumed its pursuit of affluence and state power, much intensified now by the Cold War and the rise of McCarthyism. Having nothing to recant, Kazin stayed clear of the Committee for Cultural Freedom and the other former radicals who were making so much of a self-regarding alarm and so much of a good thing career-wise out of their anti-communism. Dubbing them the Upper West Side Hebrew Relief Association, he devoted the most blistering pages in his third and final memoir, *New York Jew*, to them as "total arrivistes" whose new notion of American society left them undisturbed by "what was really going on at home—especially in their native home—especially in their native streets of New York"—where the drug epidemic, the massive Hispanic immigration, the flight of the middle class from the violence and crime was turning their own Upper West Side into a gilded ghetto and a violent one separated by Broadway.

Socialism being no longer even a hope to him, Kazin refrained from joining the saving remnant of it around Irving Howe's *Dissent* and went his solitary way—a progressive with a despairing sense of the future, a leftist who had gone from the deep-sea pressure radicalism of the 1930s to the thin air of liberalism in the 1950s, a humanist unhinged from his former faith in humanity by the Holocaust, a modernist who watched its rebels and iconoclasts being institutionalized by the pervasive of the New Criticism in the English departments. The literary scene was a lot thinner and blander, too, as one by one the last of the great moral historians and innovators of the first half of the century declined and departed, and instead there were two young writers of major war novels. two new and accomplished black literary artists, a sprinkling of experimental work such as *The Recognitions* and *The Lime Twig.* The scene soon came to be characterized by Augie March knocking at the door of society, Holden Caulfield rebelling against prep school and phoniness, John Cheever asking plaintively why in this "half-finished civilization, in this most prosperous, equitable and accomplished world, should everyone seem so disappointed?" There was little awareness in America about the Holocaust until 1956 when Elie Wiesel, a young survivor writing in French and living in New York, published *Night.*

These would all become subjects for Kazin, opportunities to clarify and to discriminate, to take a position that lent support or put up resistance, but he had a hard time after the war in finding his way again. The trouble with sudden worldly success, particularly if you've been raised as far from it as he was, is that it badly throws off the default settings of your character which can take a lot of time, confusion and frustration to reset to your new program. The success of *On Native Grounds* appears to have gone directly to his libido. His supportive early marriage to the gentle biologist Asya was soon smashed by an all but predictable affair with one of those alluring young Villagers who live on air and for big ideas, and sleep with anyone who has them. After the war came a love affair, also pretty much in the cards, with a daughter of the Upper East Side German-Jewish gentry that ended in a trophy marriage *à deux.* This produced a son but soon fell apart from its own weightlessness. Kazin became a Central Park weekend father as well as an uneasy participant in the literary cafe society that had replaced his cafeteria one. After finishing his *Portable Blake* he collaborated with Henri Cartier-Bresson on a piece for *Harper's Bazaar* on New York, then began to write a book about walking around Manhattan in the postwar boom. But he couldn't bring it off, his prose fitfully dazzled rather than jelled, and for the first time he entered writer's hell.

He remained there for many months. He had written, "Every time I go back to Brownsville it is as if I had never lived there"; but, recording a family visit in his journal, he changed the last two words to "been away." The floodgate opened and the deeply held experience began to generate the intense prose of *Walker in the City*.* He was back again to being the writer who would boldly title his third memoir *New York Jew*.

6

I began to read him assiduously when I was a graduate student at Chicago during the late 1950s, mostly his regular reviews in *The Reporter*. By then he was teaching at either Amherst or Smith. The contemporary having breached the ramparts of the scholarly, the doors of the English departments in prestigious places were swinging open to Jews, and in the rapid expansion of the educated class and higher education, the New York intellectuals of the 1930s and '40s, who had lived mostly on their wives' earnings, joined the professariat. For a time it didn't matter very much: whether the prose was written in Northampton or Princeton, Minneapolis or Waltham, Massachusetts, it was coming to me like literary Care packages from New York. Try to imagine a Ph.D. student writing a dull, dutiful paper on "Two Recent Views of Emerson's Oversoul," opening *The Reporter* and reading:

> "I like," said Emerson, "dry light, and hard clouds, hard expressions, and hard manners." The writers who become our saints and sages, the wise men of our tribe, they who help us to live—there is only one way by which we know them: their genius for compression. They are the ones who are always stripping life down to fundamentals and essentials, to aphorisms and parables and riddles, and if we ask what is holy about men whose life sayings often shock and hurt as much as they illuminate, the answer is that the final compression they get into their speech is a compression they have attained in their lives.

Such writing was not only sustenance but came to embody my hope that after I had done my time with academic jargon and footnotes, I would try to write like that, the higher literary journalism that communicates directly and

---

*Kazin's daily journal was the starting point of his writing day, and the principal mine of his mind. The one-volume selection he made, *A Lifetime Burning in Every Moment*, is but a small sample of the rich ore that remains to be processed.

yet broadly, that rings like a hammer on iron, that revives the dead and positions the living. The point Kazin is making here reflects back on the prose making it—the pith and edge of a compression attained by a mind that goes to the core of a career and unwinds it in 2,500 words or less of fresh description, judgment, and context. Just as a first-rate short story has the nucleus of a novel, so a review of Kazin's typically read like the concentrate of a full-length study.

As with other young literary types during this time, Kazin became one of my go-to guys—the strong, accurate point makers at any range from the distant erudite to the close-in topical. Why was Bellow the preeminent novelist of the 1950s? Because, according to Kazin, he could calibrate so well the power of resistance in things at a time when society was losing its force and shape as a subject and becoming the mere backdrop of the hungry postwar self. Also because Bellow's prose was so wired with vision that a simple situation—the Viennese-style charlatan Tamkin carrying a plate of Yankee pot roast and red cabbage, two cups of coffee, and a slice of watermelon to a cafeteria table— made one see "multiple aspects of the human condition." Finally, because Bellow, like Melville, was a metaphysical writer who "identifies man's quest with the range of the mind itself." As Kazin observed, Bellow's heroes are so pulled and harassed by their need to understand their destiny within the particular problem of human destiny that taken together they constitute "the deepest commentary I know on the social utopianism of a generation which always presumed that it could pacify life, that it could control and guide it to an innocuous social end, but which is painfully learning . . . to praise in it the divine strength which disposes of man's proposals."

All of this is in the first few pages of a review of *Henderson, the Rain King*. What was most real for a fiction writer? What did he most love ("in the artistic sense of what fully interested him")? What empowered or weakened his work? How much of our life could he lift up and inspect? What made his work morally useful or useless? What distinguished his writing or made it all too typical of the age or one of its subgenres? Reading Kazin's answers corrected or enlarged my understanding of what was both original and distinctively Jewish in the work of Malamud: (1) his language: the cryptic expressiveness of a people who lived on the rim of existence, who wrote and spoke as if "the book of life were about to close shut with a bang." And (2) his transformation of traditional

Jewish mysticism, where earth is so close to heaven and hell that the supernatural and the ordinary tweak each other. Malamud's principal limitation: the reliance on moral symbolism and allegory that make his characters less individuals than members of a depressed, mystical repertory company. Or again, what made *Prince of Darkness*, the first collection by J. F. Powers, so remarkable? His "maturity." His stories were about a world, rather than diverse social situations and "constantly yielded literary vanity to the truth and depth of this world." His art also benefited from rising out of a long cultural tradition at a time most young American writers were standing on the dime of present-mindedness. With his rapid but deft touch Kazin put his finger on Powers's distinctive voice—fusing "intelligence and compassion to come out as humor"—and his main drawback—a tendency to let his stories of the workings of grace on worldliness and mediocrity turn into a formula. Why were James Baldwin's essays more powerful than his novels? Because his novels are willed, hypothetical, meant to prove he can write them, while the more open form of the essay enabled him to give his full attention and voice to the struggle in himself between the oppressed and the responsible man "'who had become an American,'" as Kazin lets Baldwin tell it, "'by walking right into the bottomless confusion both public and private of the American republic.'"

The bottom line of Kazin's judgment remained the standard of realism; however complex and nuanced his understanding of its possibilities, he remained committed to the power of the illusion of life generated by the human struggle against the force of circumstances in a life, a society, the world. In an essay on "the aesthetics of realism" Kazin uses Dreiser's work to develop a model of what he calls "personal realism"—the assembling of the web of social images and facts spun from his varied experience and imbued with his own sense of wonder and bemusement at the strangeness of the real that both validates it and complicates it. Dreiser's personal realism achieves a depth of description that comes only to a writer whose imagination is fully inhabited by the social forces at issue, who has put himself in the way of being swept up by history, and in doing so is able to find a pattern in it that gives reverberating significance to his story. (A good current example of what he means is the topical visionary fiction in the past decade of Don DeLillo and E. L. Doctorow or the deeply witnessed recent political novels of Philip Roth, work that points up the crying need for more of it in the contemporary novel, which continues to bear out de Tocqueville's prophecy that in modern society people become more alone and more completely preoccupied with a puny object—themself.)

This was already Kazin's complaint in the 1950s. In an important essay of that time, "The Alone Generation," he attributed the narcissistic malaise of most novels to the general condition of American culture:

> Our culture is stupefyingly without support from tradition, and has become both secular and progressive in its articulation of every discontent and ambition; the individual now questions himself constantly because his own progress—measured in terms of the social norms—is his fundamental interest. The kind of person who in the nineteenth-century novel was a "character" now regards himself in twentieth-century novels as a problem; the novel becomes not a series of actions which he initiates because of who he is but a series of disclosures . . . designed to afford him the knowledge that may heal him.

He realized that this wasn't the whole story, that the "queerness," as he called it, of society after the Bomb as well as the technology-driven universal of change that made the present seem more linked with the future than with the past had made the nature of America—the go-go, mobile, complacent consumer society on the surface, the stealthy superpower behind the scenes—that much more difficult to portray than the more ponderous and naked society of Dreiser's era. Despite his general dissatisfaction, Kazin continued to move with the times, to look for and to find writers as different as Ralph Ellison, Nabokov, and Flannery O'Connor who practiced a personal realism, who asserted values as truths rather than as options, who displayed the "unforeseen possibilities of the human—even when everything seems dead set against it."

7

I first met Kazin in 1961, shortly after I began to work at *Commentary*. One of the first pieces I was given to edit was a lecture of his about the current state of literary criticism. It began by deploring the practice of teaching literature by issuing the New Criticism tool kit of tension, irony, paradox, symbol to open any text. He went on to argue for the old criticism that perceives itself as part of the general criticism of values that any humane society requires, and that is most itself when its account of a work, a writer, a career grows out of the critic's efforts to put his own thoughts and feelings about them in order, as does Randall Jarrell or F.W. Dupee. The essay concluded with the hope that criticism might yet regain the public function and force that it had had with Emerson and Matthew Arnold, Orwell and Eliot, Leavis and Trilling might join itself to contemporary writing again, and might regain the élan and transgressiveness that had made modernism what it was.

I couldn't have agreed more. I had just come away from an English department that practiced its own analytic orthodoxy and was remote from current literature—my subject, Henry James, had barely qualified as ripe enough for scholarship. Moreover, I owed my new life in New York to an enthusiastic piece I'd contributed to the *TLS* about the impact of contemporary Jewish writers and sensibility on American letters, an essay written, I thought, to the risky specifications Kazin's piece was calling for. I didn't have much to contribute editorially to his essay, but I did give it its title, "The Function of Criticism Today," an allusion to Matthew Arnold's seminal essay on the quickening effect of fresh ideas in moving literature forward again. This pleased Kazin enough to invite me downtown for a drink.

It didn't go well. He quickly let me know that my essay was exaggerated and not well-informed, and the conversation was slow to recover, at least on my side. Riding back uptown in a cab, he asked me what I was working on. I said that I was editing a collection of posthumous literary pieces by Isaac Rosenfeld. He replied, "Why are you doing that? Isaac wasn't important."

"He is to me," I said. I tried to explain why, even saying that Rosenfeld was just the kind of critic Kazin's essay was calling for. I reminded him that a famous piece of his in *Commentary* on the sexual implications of the dietary laws had almost shut down the magazine.

He said that was what he meant—the "clownish, Reichian squandering" of his gift. He had known Isaac well, he said. He had even sublet his apartment, sat in his crazy orgone box.

He was talking about someone I hadn't known personally but about someone other than the literary mensch I had read. I tried to tell him that. But as I talked, he mainly sniffed, a tic of his. Fully aggrieved by now, I said, "Okay, who do you think I should be writing about?"

"You should be writing about someone important. Like Willa Cather."

I looked hard at him. Was I being advised or insulted? Either way, his expression was deadly serious. When I got out of the cab, I took the adverb with me and let the adjective go.

That was the last time we had much to say to each other, but I continued to read and learn from him. A year or so later he brought out his major collection, *Contemporaries,* that covered the 1950s much as Edmund Wilson's *The Shores of Light* had done for the '20s and subsequent ones had for the following decades. By now Kazin had pretty much become Wilson's successor as the secretary of American letters, the one who best kept its proceedings, remembered its history, remained in touch with the outstanding writers abroad and the intellectual conditions at home, such as the sections in *Contemporaries* devoted to Freud and his influence, and to various recent books that bore on "The Puzzle of Modern Society." Part of the role Wilson passed on was that of acting as a public intellectual who brought a literary imagination to bear on American political and social issues, and in Wilson's case, according to Kazin, a character that "would be as ashamed to take the side of power as to write a bad sentence."

Kazin's judgment of Arthur Schlesinger Jr.'s history of the Roosevelt administration and of the Kennedy presidency around this time are typical of his criticism of the recurrent intellectual poverty at the center of American politics and hence the "tragedy of a diminishing democratic leadership" and the permanent crisis from the pressure of mass society, global power, and economic imperialism on an eighteenth-century system of government. Kazin regarded FDR's and JFK's extreme administrative maneuvering under the spell of personal charm and myth as a decline from the politics of Woodrow Wilson, which for all of his obstinate idealism, were still based on historical reasons and moral convictions for what he did and couldn't do and thus created a legacy of ideas for his party that none of his major democratic successors were to do. (He included FDR—rather perversely, I think—because of the meagerness of his presidential papers.) This judgment fell into place with Kazin's increasing despair of a society and culture "stupefyingly without tradition" and running more and more out of control of the immense power it generated.

My next memory of Kazin is at a public forum a few years later, following the publication of Hannah Arendt's *Eichmann in Jerusalem.* Led by Irving Howe, it had the air of an emergency meeting to deal with Arendt's thesis that the Jewish leaders collaborated in the destruction of their people. It was interesting to see so much fervor coming from several *bien pensants* who had hardly given any thought in their careers to Jewish concerns, and the rhetoric became more inflamed as each speaker tried to outdo the others in telling outrage. Finally, Howe introduced a survivor of the Holocaust and was happily translating for the audience his Yiddish testimony against Arendt when Kazin stood up, walked to the podium, and said, "That's enough, Irving. This disgraceful piling on has to stop." Something like that. He then said a few words about the great distinction of Arendt's thought and the complexity of her book and walked out.

I don't remember precisely what happened after that, except that a lot of the energy went out of the room and the meeting ended soon after. When he'd left I noticed that Kazin had the same obdurate expression on his face as when he'd told me to write about Willa Cather. So I saw that it wasn't personal, that he'd spoken his mind in both cases because he knew no other way and cared not a fig what people thought of him.

8

By the 1970s he had taken his sensibility about as far into the present culture as it cared to go with the publication of *Bright Book of Life*, his energetic and wide-ranging study of the postwar fiction writers from the later Hemingway and Faulkner to Pynchon and Nabokov and of categories such as war, Southern, and urbane social fiction (from O'Hara to Updike) as well as the new ones that had emerged, such as the contemporary Jewish novel, the absurd novel, the non-fiction novel, and the oeuvre of Nabokov, which constituted a kind of one-man genre of Euro-American fiction. As with *On Native Grounds*, whose coverage of American fiction he was bringing up to date, *Bright Book of Life* derived its strength from Kazin's ability to capture the tone and issues of an age through a writer's interaction with them and through his or her vitalizing take on life itself—the fateful operation of sin and error in Flannery O'Connor; the drifty, porous reality through which subversive fantasy streams in John Cheever's suburbia; the émigré's past-haunted self and sharpened eye for Americana in Nabokov; the antagonistic mutations of history in Pynchon; the new social mobility in Updike; the new Jewish outspokenness in Philip

Roth. The writer who preoccupies him as the most fully cognizant of the increasing anarchy of power and the most responsive to the "voraciousness of American life . . . its fury of transformation" is Norman Mailer. He appears in three separate profiles in *Bright Book*: the most politically aware and purposeful of the war novelists, the most ambitious and effective in becoming a cultural force among the Jewish ones, and the most able of the practitioners of the new journalism to impose his perceptions of the psychic effects of our multifarious age: the nuclear, space, information, racial integration, sexual liberation, and feminist age. As Kazin puts it, Mailer's characteristic vision of the shock and simultaneity of diverse new experience, of "different orders of reality to be willed together did in fact reflect the imbalance between everyone's inner life and the constant world of public threat," as well as "the seeming unlimitedness of national and personal ambition." Alluding to a well-known remark of Philip Roth's, Kazin observes that Mailer would never regard America as an embarrassment to the meagerness of one's own imagination.

What Kazin shared with Mailer was a heavy investment of psychic energy in that precarious vantage point of the mind between close attention and foreboding, from which the devil could be glimpsed at work in Washington and Watts and Vietnam, in the jockeying for advantage at the edge of mutual assured destruction, in the horrors of the century that were still alive and latent behind the scenes of multiple co-existence with the inhuman. In 1943, while he was at *The New Republic*, he had reprinted in its pages with his own commentary a letter from the *New York Times* written by Shmuel Ziegelboim, an official of the Polish government-in-exile, explaining why the continuing indifference of the West to the destruction of his people left him with no other recourse than to join them by taking his life. Heartbreaking in its calm despair, the letter lodged in Kazin's memory as the voice that personalized the 6 million, as his cousin in Poland who refused to flee and was shot dead on her doorstep personalized their image. From then on he kept close track of "the murder of my people" and found that "nothing had so unhinged me from my old 'progressivist' belief."

The Holocaust remained the abyss on whose edge he felt that we lived. But during the postwar era he found himself virtually alone among the New York intellectuals who, he said, found it easier to think about Alger Hiss and Whittaker Chambers; and he drew close to Hannah Arendt and her husband, Heinrich Bluecher, who insisted that a decisive break in human history had occurred. Later on, though he defended her at the *Dissent* meeting, he thought her thesis about Jewish responsibility was a willfully misplaced attack on the Jewish leaders that she had always scorned, like most other assimilated German intellectuals. He also regarded the lesson she drew from the Eichmann trial of the banality of evil as "appalling German intellectual swank." Nonetheless, he continued to think of her as an "everlasting consolation" because of her spiritual depth and her abiding concern for the public realm as the basis of civilized life that she adapted from classical political thought and that led her to cherish John Adams as the most tutelary of the American Founding Fathers. It was this theory of the *polis* that became the foundation of the *Origins of Totalitarianism* and enabled her to understand and dramatize the unprecedented nature of the two states that had produced the limitless European catastrophe. She and Bluecher were his most kindred spirits after Richard Hofstadter died in 1970, and the strongest influence, I think, on his thought after World War II, reinforcing his view of a new dark age of humanity and complicating his sense of himself as both a leftist and a New York Jew.

9

By 1975 he had settled down, as much as he ever did, into being a distinguished professor at CUNY and was going through the final years of a notoriously hostile marriage. I heard his beautifully apt eulogy for Josephine Herbst, and afterward went up to him to tell him it was. He gave me a perfunctory nod as if to say, What else did you expect from me? Then, toward the end of the '70s, two decades of personal obsession and strife ended for him when he met the writer Judith Dunford. Reading his journal for that year, one sees the sun finally stay out in his life:

> If Judith didn't exist, I could never invent her, ever hope for someone like her. . . . How to describe her plainness and openness of soul, the honesty, the absolute purity in the smallest details of life—the long-cherished pieces from Chaucer through Yeats to Lear always gushing out. And the fun. "Of course I look like a Latin teacher." Her letters run the blood through me, there is such a fearlessness to her loving.

"There is a God," he said immediately after meeting her for the first time, and she proved to be a godsend in the crisis years that followed through a divorce whose terms were no less upsetting and onerous than the marriage had been. Moreover, he was now in his mid-sixties and struggling with the condition in which everything begins to decline except the anxiety of ambition and the sense of the distant summons. In his journals, he observes himself turning increasingly to prayer:

> When I lie awake at night, afraid that I am walking though the valley of the shadow of death, I feel that I am still the entangled Brooklyn boy who all his life has depended on His will. . . . When I pray to You to give me some peace, to cease this endless clamor of anxiety . . . I am really asking for relief from my overstrained will, from the determination to do and even to do over what is expected of me. That is what secularism is—the triumph of the individual will, no matter what the cost to everything crying out in you for another realm of living and being.

Just a thought away from this prayer is the big book he is trying to write, having turned away from the dizzying present to travel back to the first great age of American letters before the Civil War and then come forward once again to the end of the second one in the 1920s. He envisioned *An American Procession* as the assembling of the great tradition of literary individualism and selfhood responding to a century of mounting accumulation of wealth, power, and demagogy. Or, to put it the other way around, he wanted to explore the remarkable phenomenon, often unremarked by those who didn't know America from the inside, that the most dynamic society in Western history had produced as its major characteristic writers—ones so intently concerned with the inner life, who vested so much power and truth in the self, whether Emerson or Hawthorne, Melville or William James. His main companion of this dialectical route is Henry Adams, the firsthand witness of the American dynamo, who as political scion, historian, Washington insider, and autobiographer saw the beginning and thought he saw the end of the accumulation, acceleration, and explosive dispersion of American power as a "planetary event."

An American Procession is Kazin's least coherent book. He not only places Emerson at the head of the line, as Whitman did, but seems to be sometimes under the spell of the cryptic style of Emerson's *Journals*. Instead of the prose of Kazin's literary journalism and memoirs, which generally hangs together despite the pressure of his rushes of thought and feeling, the sentences of *Procession* sometimes do not make a point so much as allusively, associatively encircle several at a time. I quote almost at random:

> Dickinson's poetry must be taken, initially, as a young woman's rebellion. There are obvious cries of frustration, a sexual kittenishness and bravado from the round corner room (her first image of "circumference") in the house on Main Street. She was very late in accepting restriction on her destiny; it was a game to make restrictions on herself when her brother, Austin, and Susan Gilbert were married and lived next door. Amherst was "old," sedate, churchy, assured. The Dickinsons were important people. The life of an unmarried young woman in the family setting was traditional. Whatever her often self-mocking cries of protest she accepted the setting and the life that came with it.

The final sentence seems to have lost touch with the first one in this very busy account. There is a kind of dispersion of Kazin's own mental energy in these staccato sentences—a mind running full tilt between objective and subjective, fact and inference, explication and implication, biography and criticism, Dickinson's mentality and Kazin's own. Previously he was personal; now he is subjective. Also the book as a whole has a curious bend in its shape and perspective that comes from Kazin's holding the material very close to himself, letting his elderly preoccupations into the design and vision of the book. Thus it begins with the Adams of 1918, an old man in his airy Washington study, warplanes flying nearby, as he contemplates with "his special dryness of heart and mockery . . . the century of improvement" that is ending in the chaos of world war. Similarly, Kazin begins the first of his two chapters on Emerson with him on his deathbed, his sonorous voice and fragmented mind still working away. The chapter on Thoreau begins with Queequeg's coffin and the chest Thoreau built himself to house the journals that had been his main residence on earth. Hawthorne, too, is first taken up in his frustrated closing years, obsessed with several "tales" he couldn't bring off. The marvelous chapter on Melville comes to rest on his mostly silent, anonymous later years as a New York customs inspector. They are presented less as the authors of specific works than as Emersonian representative men viewed at the point where their shadow lengthens into America's moral history as it resides in Kazin's mind. As such the portraits themselves have an impressionistic effect, the perspective diffused through the details and examples, comparisons and allusions, images and symbols that crowd Kazin's mind and often require a second reading and much contemplation for the figure to come together. This is a book for a patient reader prepared to do a lot of the integrating himself.

What most enables one to do so is Kazin's still unfailing instinct for the mentality of a writer and his ability to dramatize it by means of its force and crises. With Thoreau, the turning point comes when his genius for self-completeness and transcendental harmony is overtaken by the reach of the state and the gathering forces of the Civil War; instead of the inspector of snowstorms he becomes the fiery defender of John Brown and of pacifism in the war—a disconnect that can weaken and even kill a man of Thoreau's integrity, which is what Kazin feels happened. With Melville, the great metaphysician and voyager of American literature, there is the long aftermath of his disastrous career: the customs inspector in New York banking the fires of his imagination of the negative, destructive universal and of proto-American imperialism to write his lapidary poems and his final testament of the dark enigma at the heart of things for which only a code of duty provides a little direction. With Mark Twain, there is the immensely successful literary entertainer and entrepreneur turning the nineteenth-century American passion for books about larky youths (the national sentiment) into the discovery of Huckleberry Finn in himself and the recovery of his soul in the relationship of Huck and Jim.

The radical or at least progressive light that steadily fell across America in *On Native Grounds* is, for the most part, already dimming by the 1840s. Instead of the democracy that earlier was producing Emerson's brave new audience of " 'men and women of some religious culture and aspirations, young, or else mystical,' " Kazin emphasizes the Emerson who found himself, on his frequent lecture trips, surrounded by a society in which people asserted the most primitive self-interest and self-importance as "rights," and portrays him as increasingly alarmed that the "multitude have no habit of self-reliance or original action." Twenty years further along in the national destiny, he announces that "the calamity is the masses." Until the Dred Scott decision forces Emerson to think otherwise, the American problem is not slavery but mediocrity.

Emerson is hardly alone in this respect in Kazin's "great procession."

Thoreau could just barely abide his Concord neighbors, whose industry was much less apparent than their alcoholism (one of the well-kept secrets, Kazin notes, of the national mythos). Hawthorne loathed the debased taste of the popular audience. Melville had a highly developed contempt for American society in general and the New York rabble in particular. Mark Twain's view of the democratic populace is pretty much that of the cowardly, gullible crowd that Colonel Sherburne addresses in *Huckleberry Finn* and is so readily swindled in "The Man Who Corrupted Hadleyburg." And so on to Mencken's boobs and Faulkner's Snopeses, Eliot's carbuncular young man, and the aging Henry Adams's Washington insider's contempt for "the degradation of the democratic process." With the notable exception of Whitman, who identified his genius with American democracy itself, most important modern American writers, including the elder Kazin, himself, are unable to forgive it for the loss of the hopefulness it had inspired. Fitzgerald, for example, has his spokesman, Nick Carraway, turning away from his "crowded, sprawling, disordered, increasingly pointless country" to his solitary vision of "the West's last magic island before the people came."

So ends *Gatsby* and so, too, is soon to end the forward-looking direction of the public American imagination, with its waning legends of a unique and positive destiny, its faith in the individual having turned into the theology of capitalism. As Kazin concludes, the skeptical novelists of the 1940s and thereafter no longer felt the need to wrestle with the huge embracing American subject that one still finds in a writer like Thomas Wolfe; the great subject for them, as John O'Hara had advised, was no longer the rise of modern America. Even before Hiroshima, with writers like Nathanael West and Faulkner, the American dream had edged into the nightmare that anticipates the skeptical view of America as an impinging mass society like any other.

Though a good deal of the material in *An American Procession* had been pulled together and revised from earlier published essays and lectures (another reason for its unevenness), it still bears the mark of being completed during the early Reagan years, which Kazin regarded as the rock bottom of American politics, and it left him, I think, all the more under the influence of the acerb Henry Adams and his woeful/cynical view of American power rather than of Walt Whitman's democratic vistas of a progressive destiny for its people and fellowship with their poets, which had formed one of the themes of *On Native Grounds*. Or, perhaps, some of the recent exhaustion, diffuseness, and ambivalence of the post-Vietnam American spirit had crept into Kazin's own point of view, and it is hard to know whether to read his book as an American version of the "great tradition" or as a "redoing" of the themes of *On Native Grounds.*

Reviewed respectfully but quizzically—notably in *The New York Review of Books* by Denis Donoghue, who found it more moving than thought through, *Procession* did not have anything like the impact and staying power of *On Native Grounds.* Bitterly disappointed, Kazin found himself in the late-life crisis of What Then?—confronting in his four A.M. awakenings not only the terror of death but also praying "to get beyond myself, to indicate to this believing unbeliever that there is a territory beyond this bundle tied up so angrily in the night. I pray to be relieved of so much 'self,' I asked to be extended."

As his journals show, his turmoil led to the effort to think religiously as well as socially. Not so much about Judaism, though occasionally that, too, but rather about what his favorite American writers had made of religion as, in Whitehead's words, "the vision of something which stands beyond, behind, and within the passing flux of immediate things; something which is real, and yet waiting to be realized. . . ."

As such Kazin wasn't looking for faith so much as company in his own quest: his working title for his next and last major book, *God and the American Writer,* was "Absent Friends." Each of his subjects had used his or her freedom of thought to arrive at a characteristically idiosyncratic spiritual position. As Emily Dickinson, America's greatest religious poet, put it, "We thank thee for these strange minds that enamour us against Thee." At the same time, in typical fashion, Kazin pitted their religious individualism against another, opposing American tendency. America was not only the home of the free man's worship but also the nation which, as De Tocqueville saw, had effectively applied the most radical theories of eighteenth-century government, including unlimited free speech, without making any headway against the influence of religion.

Kazin began this time with Hawthorne, wanting to see the paradox *ab ovo,* as it were. In the early chapters, however, one feels from the writing that he is going mostly to his mental hard drive for his material, the text sprinkled with familiar themes, pet phrases, allusions, etc. The chapter on Hawthorne makes the interesting point that American individualism begins with the Calvinist view of man steadily fixed in God's scrutiny, but the discussion then becomes mostly an adaptation of a previous introduction to *The Scarlet Letter* and all but ignores the central biographical question it raises of why Hawthorne, who became a full-bore skeptic in his own life, should have been so haunted by the Calvinist/Puritan absolutism. One feels that the real story is being missed, that Hawthorne's preoccupation with the permanence of guilt as the core of religion derives from his own relation to the Puritan subject, which steadily drew his imagination back 150 years, when two of his ancestors, bearing his name, had been leaders of the Salem witch hunts. One feels the pressure of Hawthorne's guilt on his imagination particularly in the closing pages of the novel, when Hester, the life-force in this dismal world, returns to it after leaving her daughter in England and resumes her penitence.

It is only when Kazin gets to Lincoln that the "do-over" machinery stops and fresh biographical and spiritual insight flows in. Carefully and subtly, Kazin builds up his portrait of Lincoln the firm Unionist slowly giving way to the morally tormented Emancipator; the agnostic, proudly rationalistic lawyer—who had rejected both his parents' old-time religion and the "living Scripture" and battle hymns that both North and South drew around their cause—coming very late in his presidency to attach God's will and justice to his own mystical faith in the Union. Like Eric Auerbach in *Mimesis*, developing a paragraph or two of Machiavelli or Stendhal into a ramifying study of the writer and his age, Kazin unpacks from the Second Inaugural the mentality of Lincoln and the climax to the whole terrible course of his ordeal as president that produced the probing, humble, but positive belief that only God's own purposes could account for the horrendous cost of His justice. Thus, by the ordeal of his conscience, will, and humility was Lincoln brought to the extraordinary tone and texture of the address in which he labors both to bind up the wounds of the nation and also to rededicate it to the scourge by the Union sword of the slaveholder's lash.

Some of the same intensity of focus enters Kazin's chapter on Emily Dickinson, who domesticated the last of the Calvinist legacy and dramatized the mystery of death from the household and pew to interplanetary space. So, too, does Kazin bear down firmly and freshly on William James's use of religion that developed out of the terror of life he experienced in himself and witnessed in others. So, too, with Mark Twain, who finally canceled the last of his boyhood Methodism by giving the devil the sensible last word.

As Kazin concludes, the religious side of American writing emerged from a multiplicity of contending theologies, faiths, and sects in America, and he believes that some of the spiritual aggressiveness of its writers was owing to the contentious circumstances of their rearing as well as to the sovereign uses of the unlimited freedom that as American writers they put them to. I don't know how much direction his own spirituality received in these years he spent with his "absent friends." What does come through in his other late book, *Writing Was Everything*, is that at the close of his life the writers he seemed to draw closest to were two Europeans whose mind, like Hannah Arendt's, had gone through the fire of the "radical evil" of the age.

The first was Simone Weil, who ministered to the night sweats and lamentations of his over-driven ego by her beautiful thought, among others, that attention without object is the supreme form of prayer. The other was Czeslaw Milosz, the extraordinarily measured witness of both totalitarian regimes in Europe. Along with the Holocaust and "the captive mind," as he called it, of Communism, Milosz brought Kazin back to Blake by his book *The Land of Ulro* (1984), the name Blake had given to "the inhuman, material world," as Kazin puts it, "from which the spiritual imagination leads us to poetry, with its revelation of another order of being." There is nothing more lucid and moving in all of Kazin's writing than the closing pages of *Writing Was Everything*, when he takes Milosz's arm, so to speak, to walk together through the contemporary version of the land of Ulro—not only the poverty, racial conflict, homelessness, drug addiction, remorseless "downsizing," but also, as Milosz remarks, the "very strong feeling of opposed forces of good and evil," the moral relativism that marks "a profound change of mentality and imagination." Reading Milosz's words and Kazin's commentary, one senses the latter's profound recall of his own lived experience of what is left of faith "after credulity has vanished from our practical, issue-tormented world," abetted by "our endless defenses and explorations of the ego."

The old issue of "alienation" comes up again, though now in a different form. Where the two briefly part company is Milosz's belief that the East European writers achieved an elemental strength by virtue of their sharing and expressing the burdens of their communities, while the Western writer continues on his "alienated" course of self-involvement. Kazin now puts the matter otherwise: the contemporary writer's alienation is not from society so much as from American literary culture itself that is "content to curse dead white males and rejoice in the loss of tradition." Where they rejoin again is in the shared belief, expressed by Milosz's words: "Nothing could stifle my inner certainty that a shining point exists where all lines intersect." Nothing could be more removed from the acid vat of radical skepticism in which postmodernism immerses itself. Nothing could be more essential than their shared certainty that imaginative writing, the making of connections between the facts and the imponderables of existence, is an act of faith that can make the world shine again. What he wrote in his journal in the midst of researching his first book, he believed in to the end:

> . . . .To think of Albert Pinkham Ryder and Henry James, of Emerson and Whitman and Dickinson in the same breath, as it were, gives me extraordinary satisfaction. Makers and movers and thinkers—observers in the profoundest sense. I love to think of America as an idea, to remember the adventure and the purity, the heroism and the *salt*.

About a year before he died, there was a celebration of Kazin's career at the Center for the Humanities at CUNY. After two days of lectures and readings in his honor (he insisted that the invited writers talk about their work, not his), the event drew to an end with his appearance. As he took the podium, one settled back to receive the heartfelt, valedictory words appropriate to the occasion. There were none. As though he had just stepped out of his office, Kazin began talking about what was on his mind: the thwarted purpose of the Founding Fathers who separated church and state to protect not only the state from religion but also religious belief from the rampant politicization of it today that was riding roughshod over the separation and debasing the values of both.

That's how I best remember him now: Emerson's American scholar standing up there—civic, forthright, independent, incandescent.

ALFRED KAZIN'S
AMERICA

————•◆•————

I

HOME IS WHERE
ONE STARTS FROM

THE KITCHEN

———•◆•———

In Brownsville tenements the kitchen is always the largest room and the center of the household. As a child I felt that we lived in a kitchen to which four other rooms were annexed. My mother, a "home" dressmaker, had her workshop in the kitchen. She told me once that she had begun dressmaking in Poland at thirteen; as far back as I can remember, she was always making dresses for the local women. She had an innate sense of design, a quick eye for all the subtleties in the latest fashions, even when she despised them, and great boldness. For three or four dollars she would study the fashion magazines with a customer, go with the customer to the remnants store on Belmont Avenue to pick out the material, argue the owner down—all remnants stores, for some reason, were supposed to be shady, as if the owners dealt in stolen goods—and then for days would patiently fit and baste and sew and fit again. Our apartment was always full of women in their housedresses sitting around the kitchen table waiting for a fitting. My little bedroom next to the kitchen was the fitting room. The sewing machine, an old nut-brown Singer with golden scrolls painted along the black arm and engraved along the two tiers of little drawers massed with needles and thread on each side of the treadle, stood next to the window and the great coal-black stove which up to my last year in college was our main source of heat. By December the two outer bedrooms were closed off, and used to chill bottles of milk and cream, cold borscht, and jellied calves' feet.

The kitchen held our lives together. My mother worked in it all day long, we ate in it almost all meals except the Passover seder, I did my homework and first writing at the kitchen table, and in winter I often had a bed made up for me on three kitchen chairs near the stove. On the wall just over the table hung a long horizontal mirror that sloped to a ship's prow at each end and was lined in cherry wood. It took up the whole wall, and drew every object in the kitchen to itself. The walls were a fiercely stippled whitewash, so often rewhitened by my father in slack seasons that the paint looked as if it had been squeezed and cracked into the walls. A large electric bulb hung down the center of the kitchen at the end of a chain that had been hooked into the ceiling; the old gas ring and key still jutted out of the wall like antlers. In the corner next to the toilet was the sink at which we washed, and the square tub in which my mother did our clothes. Above it, tacked to the shelf on which were pleasantly ranged square, blue-bordered white sugar and spice jars, hung calendars from the Public National Bank on Pitkin Avenue and the Minsker Progressive Branch of the Workmen's Circle; receipts for the payment of insurance premiums, and household bills on a spindle; two little boxes engraved with Hebrew letters. One of these was for the poor, the other to buy back the Land of Israel. Each spring a bearded little man would suddenly appear in our kitchen, salute us with a hurried Hebrew blessing, empty the boxes (sometimes with a sidelong look of disdain if they were not full), hurriedly bless us again for remembering our less fortunate Jewish brothers and sisters, and so take his departure until the next spring, after vainly trying to persuade my mother to take still another box. We did occasionally remember to drop coins in the boxes, but this was usually only on the dreaded morning of "midterms" and final examinations, because my mother thought it would bring me luck. She was extremely superstitious, but embarrassed about it, and always laughed at herself whenever, on the morning of an examination, she counseled me to leave the house on my right foot. "I know it's silly," her smile seemed to say, "but what harm can it do? It may calm God down."

The kitchen gave a special character to our lives; my mother's character. All my memories of that kitchen are dominated by the nearness of my mother sitting all day long at her sewing machine, by the clacking of the treadle against the linoleum floor, by the patient twist of her right shoulder as she automatically pushed at the wheel with one hand or lifted the foot to free the needle where it had got stuck in a thick piece of material. The kitchen was her life. Year by year, as I began to take in her fantastic capacity for labor and her anxious zeal, I realized it was ourselves she kept stitched together. I can never remember a time when she was not working. She worked because the law of her life was work, work and anxiety; she worked because she would have found life meaningless without work. She read almost no English; she could read the Yiddish paper, but never felt she had time to. We were always talking of a time when I would teach her how to read, but somehow there was never time. When I awoke in the morning she was already at her machine, or in the great morning crowd of housewives at the grocery getting fresh rolls for breakfast. When I returned from school she was at her machine, or conferring over *McCall's* with some neighborhood woman who had come in pointing hopefully to an illustration—"Mrs. Kazin! Mrs. Kazin! Make me a dress like it shows here in the picture!" When my father came home from work she had somehow mysteriously interrupted herself to make supper for us, and the dishes cleared and washed, was back at her machine. When I went to bed at night, often she was still there, pounding away at the treadle, hunched over the wheel, her hands steering a piece of gauze under the needle with a finesse that always contrasted sharply with her swollen hands and broken nails. Her left hand had been pierced through when as a girl she had worked in the infamous Triangle Shirtwaist Factory on the East Side. A needle had gone straight through the palm, severing a large vein. They had sewn it up for her so clumsily that a tuft of flesh always lay folded over the palm.

The kitchen was the great machine that set our lives running; it whirred down a little only on Saturdays and holy days. From my mother's kitchen I gained my first picture of life as a white, overheated, starkly lit workshop redolent with Jewish cooking, crowded with women in housedresses, strewn with fashion magazines, patterns, dress material, spools of thread—and at whose center, so lashed to her machine that bolts of energy seemed to dance out of her hands and feet as she worked, my mother stamped the treadle hard against the floor, hard, hard, and silently, grimly at war, beat out the first rhythm of the world for me.

Every sound from the street roared and trembled at our windows—a mother feeding her child on the doorstep, the screech of the trolley cars on Rockaway Avenue, the eternal smash of a handball against the wall of our house, the clatter of "der Italyéner's" cart packed with watermelons, the singsong of the old-clothes men walking Chester Street, the cries *"Árbes! Árbes! Kinder! Kinder! Heyse gute árbes!"* All day long people streamed into our apartment as a matter of course—"customers," upstairs neighbors, downstairs neighbors, women who would stop in for a half hour's talk, salesmen, relatives, insurance agents. Usually they came in without ringing the bell—everyone knew my mother was always at home. I would hear the front door opening, the wind whistling through our front hall, and then some familiar face would appear in our kitchen with the same bland, matter-of-fact inquiring look: no need to stand on ceremony; my mother and her kitchen were available to everyone all day long.

At night the kitchen contracted around the blaze of light on the cloth, the patterns, the ironing board where the iron had burned a black border around the tear in the muslin cover; the finished dresses looked so frilly as they jostled on their wire hangers after all the work my mother had put into them. And then I would get that strangely ominous smell of tension from the dress fabrics and the burn in the cover of the ironing board—as if each piece of cloth and paper crushed with light under the naked bulb might suddenly go up in flames. Whenever I pass some small tailoring shop still lit up at night and see the owner hunched over his steam press; whenever in some poorer neighborhood of the city I see through a window some small crowded kitchen naked under the harsh light glittering in the ceiling, I still smell that fiery breath, that warning of imminent fire. I was always holding my breath. What I must have felt most about ourselves, I see now, was that we ourselves were like kindling— that all the hard-pressed pieces of ourselves and all the hard-used objects in that kitchen were like so many slivers of wood that might go up in flames if we came too near the white-blazing filaments in that naked bulb. Our tension itself was fire, we ourselves were forever burning—to live, to get down the foreboding in our souls, to make good.

Twice a year, on the anniversaries of her parents' deaths, my mother placed on top of the ice-box an ordinary kitchen glass packed with wax, the *yortsayt*, and lit the candle in it. Sitting at the kitchen table over my homework, I would look across the threshold to that mourning glass, and sense that for my mother the distance from our kitchen to *der heym*, from life to death, was only a flame's length away. Poor as we were, it was not poverty that drove my mother so hard; it was loneliness—some endless bitter brooding over all those left behind, dead or dying or soon to die; a loneliness locked up in her kitchen that dwelt every day on the hazardousness of life and the nearness of death, but still kept struggling in the lock, trying to get us through by endless labor.

With us, life started up again only on the last shore. There seemed to be no middle grounds between despair and the fury of our ambition. Whenever my mother spoke of her hopes for us, it was with such unbelievingness that the likes of us would ever come to anything, such abashed hope and readiness for pain, that I finally came to see in the flame burning on top of the ice-box death itself burning away the bones of poor Jews, burning out in us everything but courage, the blind resolution to live. In the light of that mourning-candle, there were ranged around me how many dead and dying—how many eras of pain, of exile, of dispersion, of cringing before the powers of this world!

It was always at dusk that my mother's loneliness came home most to me. Painfully alert to every shift in the light at her window, she would suddenly confess her fatigue by removing her pince-nez, and then wearily pushing aside the great mound of fabrics on her machine, would stare at the street as if to warm herself in the last of the sun. "How sad it is!" I once heard her say. "It grips me! It grips me!" Twilight was the bottommost part of the day, the chillest and loneliest time for her. Always so near to her moods, I knew she was fighting some deep inner dread, struggling against the returning tide of darkness along the streets that invariably assailed her heart with the same foreboding—Where? Where now? Where is the day taking us now?

Yet one good look at the street would revive her. I see her now, perched against the windowsill, with her face against the glass, her eyes almost asleep in enjoyment, just as she starts up with the guilty cry—"What foolishness is this in me!"—and goes to the stove to prepare supper for us: a moment, only a moment, watching the evening crowd of women gathering at the grocery for fresh bread and milk. But between my mother's pent-up face at the window and the winter sun dying in the fabrics—"Alfred, see how beautiful!"—she has drawn for me one single line of sentience.

[1951]

"BEYOND!"

———◆———

There was never enough time. The morning they led us through the Natural History Museum, under the skeletons of great whales floating dreamlike on wires from the ceiling, I had to wait afterward against the meteor in the entrance yard for my dizziness to pass. Those whales! Those whales! But that same morning they took us across Central Park to the Metropolitan, and entering through the back door in from the park, I was flung spinning in a bewilderment of delight from the Greek discus throwers to the Egyptians to the long rows of medieval knights to the breasts of Venus glistening in my eyes as she sat—some curtain drawn before her hiding the worst of her naked-ness—smiling with Mars and surrounded by their children.

The bewilderment eased, a little, when we went up many white steps directly to the American paintings. There was a long, narrow, corridor-looking room lined with the portraits of seventeenth-century merchants and divines—nothing for me there as they coldly stared at me, their faces uninter-ruptedly rosy in time. But far in the back, in an alcove near the freight elevator, hung so low and the figures so dim in the faint light that I crouched to take them in, were pictures of New York some time after the Civil War—skaters in Central Park, a red muffler flying in the wind; a gay crowd moving round and round Union Square Park; horse cars charging between the brownstones of lower Fifth Avenue at dusk. I could not believe my eyes. Room on room they had painted my city, my country—Winslow Homer's dark oblong of Union soldiers making camp in the rain, tenting tonight, tenting on the old campgrounds as I had never thought I would get to see them when we sang that song in school; Thomas Eakins's solitary sculler on the Schuylkill, resting to have his picture taken in the yellow light bright with patches of some raw spring in Pennsylvania showing on the other side of him; and most wonderful to me then, John Sloan's picture of a young girl standing in the wind on the deck of a New York ferryboat—surely to Staten Island, and just about the year of my birth?—looking out to water.

It had to be something dark, oily, glazed, faintly flaring into gaslight at dusk. Dusk in America any time after the Civil War would be the corridor back and back into that old New York under my feet that always left me half-stunned with its audible cries for recognition. The American past was gaslight and oil glaze, the figures painted dark and growing darker each year on the back walls of the Metropolitan. But they had some strange power over my mind as we went down the white steps into Fifth Avenue at the closing bell—the little Greek heralds on top of the traffic boxes gravely waving me on, my own loneliness gleaming back at me as the street lamps shone on their nude gold chests—that would haunt me anytime I ever walked down Fifth Avenue again in the first early-evening light.

  It would have to be dusk. Sitting on the fire escape warm spring afternoons over the Oliver Optics, I read them over and over because there was something about old New York in them—often the dimmest drawing in the ad on the back cover of a newsboy howling his papers as he walked past the World building in the snow—that brought back that day at the Metropolitan. I saw Park Row of a winter afternoon in the 1880s, the snow falling into the dark stone streets under Brooklyn Bridge, newsboys running under the maze of telegraph wires that darkened every street of the lower city. How those wires haunted me in every photograph I found of old New York—indescribably heavy, they sagged between the poles; the very streets seemed to sink under their weight. The past was that forest of wires hung over lower New York at five o'clock—dark, heavy, dark; of the time, surely, my parents had first stepped out on the shores of New York at Castle Garden; of the time they had built all police stations in? Walking past our police station on East New York

Avenue, I would always be stopped in my tracks by an abysmal nostalgia for the city as it had once been. The green lamps on each side of the station, the drifters along the steps that led down into the public urinals, even the wire netting in the doors of the patrol wagons whose terrifying backs squatted side by side in the yard—all plunged me so suddenly into my daylight dream of walking New York streets in the 1880s that I would wait on the corner, holding my breath, perfectly sure that my increasingly dim but still almighty Police Commissioner Theodore Roosevelt would come down the steps at any moment.

It would have to be dusk in the lower city. That steaming spring afternoon I was on my way to a lesson at the Music School Settlement, and deep in Bleecker Street could see the streaky whitewashed letters on the back walls of the tenements FLETCHER'S CASTORIA CHILDREN CRY FOR IT CHARLES S. FLETCH . . . , there was a sickening sweetness out of the fur shops, and I saw for the first time derelicts sleeping across the cellar doors—some with empty pint bottles behind their heads; some with dried blood and spittle on their cracked lips, as if they had scraped themselves with knives; some with their flies open, so that the storekeepers cooling themselves in the doorways grinned with scorn and disgust. I knew those men as strangers left over from another period, waiting for me to recognize them. The old pea jackets and caps they slept in were somehow not of the present; they were still in the work clothes they wore on the last job they had had; they bore even in their faces the New York of another century, and once I followed one up the Bowery, strangely sure that he would lead me back into my own, lost, old New York. The El over my head thundered just as it did in that early New York of the Oliver Optics; there were signs hung above the roofs, gold letters on a black field, advertising jewelry, Klein's Special Size Suits For Fat Men, pawnshops. Dusty particles of daylight fell between the tracks of the El; I had never seen anything so right; it was dusk, dusk everywhere in the lower city now all the way to Cooper Square and Bible House and Astor Place, where even the books and prints and sheet music on the stalls were dusty old, and as I went up the black stairs of the El station with the Gold Stripe silk stocking ad teasing my eye from step to step, only the cries of the old Jewish women selling salted pretzels near Union Square broke the spell.

But why that long ride home at all? Why did they live there and we always in "Brunzvil"? Why were they there, and we always here? Why was it always them and us, Gentiles and us, all rightniks and us? Beyond Brownsville was all "the city," that other land I could see for a day, but with every next day back on the block, back to the great wall behind the drugstore I relentlessly had to pound with a handball. Beyond was the strange world of Gentiles, all of them with flaxen hair, who hated Jews, especially poor Jews, had ugly names for us I could never read or hear without seeing Pilsudski's knife cold against our throats. To be a Jew meant that one's very right to existence was always being brought into question. Everyone knew this—even the Communists' summer nights on Pitkin Avenue said so, could make the most listless crowd weep with reminders of what they were doing to us in fascist Poland, Roumania, Hungary. It was what I had always heard in the great *Kol Nidre* sung in the first evening hours of the Day of Atonement, had played on my violin for them Friday evenings in the dining room whenever I felt lost and wanted to show them how much I loved them, knew them through and through, would suffer loyally with them. Jews were Jews; Gentiles were Gentiles. The line between them had been drawn for all time. What had my private walks into the city to do with anything!

[. . . .]

Now, summer by summer, when I went about Brooklyn delivering the *Eagle*; or went up and down the sands of Coney Island selling Eskimo Pies; or stopped in the Brooklyn Museum to look at the Ryders; or in front of the Library at Fifth and Forty-second, waiting for the light to change, laughed right out loud because I had just sat my first exultant hour in those long sun-filled reading rooms on the third floor; or floundered and gawked my way past Cleopatra's Needle to the back door of the Metropolitan, to take in, now, Winslow Homer's *The Gulf Stream* and Thomas Eakins's portrait of Walt Whitman in a lace collar; or with a knapsack my mother had made for me out of old laundry bags walked over the Palisades to Alpine—now, when I stopped to catch my breath under the shepherd's crook of a lamp pole in Brooklyn, the streets themselves reeled for joy, and whenever I humbly retired into the subway for the long ride home, something would automatically pull me out at Brooklyn Bridge for one last good walk across the promenade before I fell into the subway again.

For all those first summer walks into the city, all daily walks across the bridge for years afterward, when I came to leave Brownsville at last, were efforts to understand one single half hour at dusk, on a dark winter day, the year I was fourteen. There had been some school excursion that day to City Hall and the courts of lower New York, and looking up at the green dome of the *World* as we came into Park Row, I found myself separated from the class, and decided to go it across the bridge alone. I remember holding a little red volume of *The World's Greatest Selected Short Stories* in my hand as I started out under the groined arcade of the Municipal Building and the rusty green-black terminal of the El sweeping onto the bridge from Park Row—somewhere in the course of that walk across the bridge the last of those volumes got lost for all time. Evening was coming on fast, great crowds in thick black overcoats were pounding up the staircases to the El; the whole bridge seemed to shake under the furious blows of that crowd starting for home.

Rush hour above, on every side, below: the iron wheels of the El trains shooting blue-white sparks against the black, black tracks sweeping in from Chinatown and Oliver Street under the black tar roofs and fire escapes and empty window boxes along the grimy black tenements on whose sides I could see the streaky whitewashed letters CHILDREN CRY FOR IT FLETCHER'S CASTORIA CHARLES S. FLETCHER; trolley cars bounding up into the air on each side of me, their bells clanging, clanging; cars sweeping off the bridge and onto the bridge in the narrow last roadways before me.

Then a long line of naked electric bulbs hung on wires above the newsstands and hot dog stands in the arcade, raw light glittering above the flaky iron rust, newsboys selling the *Evening World*, the smell of popcorn and of frankfurters sizzling on the grill. And now up a flight of metal-edged wooden steps and into the open at last, the evening coming on faster and faster, a first few flakes of snow in the air, the lights blue and hard up one side of the transparent staircases in Wall Street, dark on another; the river black, inky black; then the long hollow boom shivering the worn wooden planks under my feet as a ship passes under the bridge.

Dusk of a dark winter's day that first hour walking Brooklyn Bridge. Suddenly I felt lost and happy as I went up another flight of steps, passed under the arches of the tower, and waited, next to a black barrel, at the railing of the observation platform. The trolleys clanged and clanged; every angry stalled car below sounded its horn as, bumper to bumper, they all poked their way along the bridge; the El trains crackled and thundered over my right shoulder. A clock across the street showed its lighted face; along the fire escapes of the building were sculptured figures of runners and baseball players, of prizefighters flexing their muscles and wearing their championship belts, just as they did in the *Police Gazette.* But from that platform under the tower the way ahead was strange. Only the electric sign of the *Jewish Daily Forward,* burning high over the tenements of the East Side, suddenly stilled the riot in my heart as I saw the cables leap up to the tower, saw those great meshed triangles leap up and up, higher and still higher—Lord my Lord, when will they cease to drive me up with them in their flight?—and then, each line singing out alone the higher it came and nearer, fly flaming into the topmost eyelets of the tower.

Somewhere below they were roasting coffee, handling spices—the odor was in the pillars, in the battered wooden planks of the promenade under my feet, in the blackness upwelling from the river. A painter's scaffold dangled down one side of the tower over a spattered canvas. Never again would I walk Brooklyn Bridge without smelling that coffee, those spices, the paint on that canvas. The trolley car clanged, clanged, clanged, taking me home that day from the bridge. Papa, where are they taking me? Where in this beyond are they taking me?

[1951]

MRS. SOLOVEY

———— • ◆ • ————

The Soloveys had been very puzzling; from the day they had come to our tenement, taking over the small, dark apartment on the ground floor next to his drugstore, no one had been able to make them out at all. Both the Soloveys had had an inaccessible air of culture that to the end had made them seem visitors among us. They had brought into our house and street the breath of another world, where parents read books, discussed ideas at the table, and displayed a quaint, cold politeness addressing each other. The Soloveys had traveled; they had lived in Palestine, France, Italy. They were "professional" people, "enlightened"—she, it was rumored, had even been a physician or "some kind of scientist," we could never discover which.

The greatest mystery was why they had come to live in Brownsville. We looked down on them for this, and suspected them. To come deliberately to Brownsville, after you had lived in France and Italy! It suggested some moral sickness, apathy, a perversion of all right feelings. The apathy alone had been enough to excite me. They were different!

Of course the Soloveys were extremely poor—how else could they even have thought of moving in among us? There were two drab little girls with Hebrew names, who went about in foreign clothes, looking so ill-nourished that my mother was indignant, and vowed to abduct them from their strange parents for an afternoon and feed them up thoroughly. Mrs. Solovey was herself so thin, shy, and gently aloof that she seemed to float away from me whenever I passed her in the hall. There was no doubt in our minds that the Soloveys had come to Brownsville at the end of their road. But what had they hoped to gain from us? If they had ever thought of making money in a Brownsville drugstore, they were soon disenchanted. The women on the block bought such drugs as they had to when illness came. But they did not go in for luxuries, and they had a hearty, familiar way of expecting credit as their natural right from a neighbor and fellow Jew that invariably made Mr. Solovey furious. That was only for the principle of the thing: he showed no interest in making money. He seemed to despise his profession, and the store soon became so clogged with dust and mothballs and camphor-smelling paper wardrobes and the shampoo ads indignantly left him by salesmen of beauty preparations, which he refused to stock, that people hated to go in. They all thought him cynical and arrogant. Although he understood well enough when someone addressed him in Yiddish, he seemed to dislike the language, and only frowned, curtly nodding his head to show that he understood. The Soloveys talked Russian to each other, and though we were impressed to hear them going on this way between themselves, everyone else disliked them for it. Not to use our familiar neighborhood speech, not even the English expected of the "educated," meant that they wanted us not to understand them.

Mr. Solovey was always abrupt and ill-tempered, and when he spoke at all, it was to throw a few words out from under his walrus mustache with an air of bitter disdain for us all. His whole manner as he stood behind his counter seemed to say: "I am here because I am here, and I may talk to you if I have to! Don't expect me to enjoy it!" His business declined steadily. Everyone else on the block was a little afraid of him, for he would look through a prescription with such surly impatience that rumors spread he was a careless and inefficient pharmacist, and probably unsafe to use. If he minded, he never showed it. There was always an open book on the counter, usually a Russian novel or a work of philosophy; he spent most of his time reading. He would sit in a greasy old wicker armchair beside the telephone booths, smoking Murads in a brown-stained celluloid holder and muttering to himself as he read. He took as little trouble to keep himself clean as he did his store, and his long, drooping mustache and black alpaca coat were always gray with cigarette ash. It looked as if he hated to be roused from his reading even to make a sale, for the slightest complaint sent him into a rage. "I'll never come back to you, Mr. Solovey!" someone would threaten. "Thanks be to God!" he would shout back. "Thanks God! Thanks God! It will be a great pleasure not to see you!" "A *meshugener*" the women on the block muttered to each other. "A real crazy one. Crazy to death."

The Soloveys had chosen to live in Brownsville when they could have lived elsewhere, and this made them mysterious. Through some unfathomable act of will, they had chosen us. But for me they were beyond all our endless gossip and speculation about them. They fascinated me simply because they were so different. There was some open madness in the Soloveys' relation to each other for which I could find no parallel, not even a clue, in the lives of our own parents. Whenever I saw the strange couple together, the gold wedding ring on his left hand as thick as hers, I felt they were still lovers. Yet the Soloveys were not rich. They were poor as we were, even poorer. I had never known anyone like them. They were weary people, strange and bereft people. I felt they had floated into Brownsville like wreckage off the ship of foreignness and "culture" and the great world outside. And there was that visible tie between them, that wedding ring even a man could wear, some deep consciousness of each other, that excited me, it seemed so illicit. And this was all the more remarkable because, though lovers, they were so obviously unhappy lovers. Had they chucked each other on the chin, had they kissed in public, they would have seemed merely idiotic. No, they seemed to hate each other, and could often be heard quarreling in their apartment, which sent every sound out into the hallway and the street. These quarrels were not like the ones we heard at home. There were no imprecations, no screams, no theatrical sobs: "You're killing me! You're plunging the knife straight into my heart! You're putting me into an early grave! May you sink ten fathoms into the earth!" Such bitter accusations were heard among us all the time, but did not mean even that someone disliked you. In Yiddish we broke all the windows to let a little air into the house.

But in the Soloveys' quarrels there was something worse than anger; it was hopelessness. I felt such despair in them, such a fantastic need to confront each other alone all day long, that they puzzled me by not sharing their feelings with their children. They alone, the gruff ne'er-do-well husband and his elusive wife, were the family. Their two little girls did not seem to count at all; the lovers, though their love had been spent, still lived only for each other. And it was this that emphasized their strangeness for me—it was as strange as Mr.

Solovey's books, as a Brownsville couple speaking Russian to each other, as strange as Mrs. Solovey's delightfully shocking blondness and the unfathomable despair that had brought them to us. In this severe dependence on each other for everything, there was a defiance of the family principle, of us, of their own poverty and apathy, that encouraged me to despise our values as crude and provincial. Only in movies and in *The Sheik* did people abandon the world for love, give themselves up to it—gladly. Yet there was nothing obviously immoral in the conduct of the Soloveys, nothing we could easily describe and condemn. It was merely that they were sufficient to each other; in their disappointment as in their love they were always alone. They left us out, they left Brownsville out; we were nothing to them. In the love despair of the Soloveys something seemed to say that our constant fight "to make sure" was childish, that we looked at life too narrowly, and that in any event, we did not count. Their loneliness went deeper than our solidarity.

And so I loved them. By now I, too, wanted to defy Brownsville. I did not know where or how to begin. I knew only that I could dream all day long while pretending to be in the world, and that my mind was full of visions as intimate with me as loneliness. I felt I was alone, that there were things I had to endure out of loyalty but could never accept, and that whenever I liked, I could swim out from the Brownsville shore to that calm and sunlit sea beyond where *great friends* came up from the deep. Every book I read restocked my mind with those great friends who lived out of Brownsville. They came into my life proud and compassionate, recognizing me by a secret sign, whispering through subterranean channels of sympathy: "Alfred! Old boy! What have they done to you!" Walking about, I learned so well to live with them that I could not always tell whether it was they or I thinking in me. As each fresh excitement faded, I felt myself being flung down from great peaks. Sometimes I was not sure which character I was on my walks, there were so many in my head at once; or how I could explain one to the other; but after an afternoon's reading in the "adults'" library on Glenmore Avenue, I would walk past the pushcarts on Belmont Avenue and the market women crying, "Oh you darlings! Oh you pretty ones! Come! Come! Eat us alive! Storm us! Devour us! Tear us apart!"—proud and alien as Othello, or dragging my clubfoot after me like the hero of *Of Human Bondage,* a book I had read to tatters in my amazement that Mr. W. Somerset Maugham knew me so well. In that daily walk from Glenmore to Pitkin to Belmont to Sutter I usually played out the life cycles of at least five imaginary characters. They did not stay in my mind very long, for I discovered new books every day; somewhere I felt them to be unreal, cut off by the sickening clean edge of the curb; but while they lived, they gave me a happiness that reverberated in my mind long after I had reached our street and had turned on the first worn step of our stoop for one last proud annihilating glance back at the block.

The Soloveys came into my life as the nearest of all the *great friends.* Everything which made them seem queer on the block deepened their beauty for me. I yearned to spend the deepest part of myself on someone close, someone I could endow directly with the radiant life of the brotherhood I joined in books. Passionately attached as I was to my parents, it had never occurred to me to ask myself what I thought of them as individuals. They were the head of the great body to which I had been joined at birth. There was nothing I could *give* them. I wanted some voluntary and delighted gift of emotion to rise up in me; something that would surprise me in the giving, that would flame directly out of me; that was not, like the obedience of our family love, a routine affair of every day. I wanted to bestow love that came from an idea. All day long in our kitchen my mother and I loved each other in measures of tribulation as well worn as the *Kol Nidre.* We looked to each other for support; we recognized each other with a mutual sympathy and irritation; each of us bore some part of the other like a guarantee that the other would never die. I stammered, she used to say, because she stammered; when she was happy, the air on the block tasted new. I could never really take it in that there had been a time, even in *der heym,* when she had been simply a woman alone, with a life in which I had no part.

Running around the block summer evenings, I always stopped in front of the Soloveys' windows and looked across the spiked iron fence above the cellar steps on the chance that I might see Mrs. Solovey moving around her kitchen. I still spent hours every afternoon hanging around the telephone; he simply refused to answer it; and sometimes I would sit in his greasy old wicker armchair outside the booths, excitedly taking in the large color picture of General Israel Putnam on his horse riding up the stone steps just ahead of the British, the hard dots that stuck out of the black stippled wallpaper, the ladies dreaming in the brilliantine ads on the counter, the mothballs and camphor and brown paper wardrobes that always smelled of something deep, secret, inside. I liked to watch Mr. Solovey as he sat there reading behind his counter, perfectly

indifferent to everyone, glowering and alone, the last wet brown inch of cigarette gripped so firmly between his teeth that I could never understand why
the smoke did not get into his eyes or burn the edges of his mustache. It
excited me just to watch someone read like that.

But now, night after night as I lay on our kitchen chairs under the quilt, I
found I could will some sudden picture of his wife, hospitable and grave in the
darkness. Everything that now made her so lustrous to me—her air of not
being quite placed in life, her gentle aloofness, her secret carnality—was missing in her husband's appearance. The store went from bad to worse, and he
seemed to plant himself more and more in the back of it like a dead tree defying us to cut him down. He never even looked at me when I sat in his wicker
armchair near the telephone booths, but barricaded himself behind his
counter, where his Russian novels lay in a mound of dust and gradually displaced the brilliantine ads and the ten-cent toilet articles. Except in emergen-
cies, or when I had someone to call to the telephone, hardly anyone now came
into the store. Most people were afraid of him, and the boys on the block took
a special delight in exasperating him by banging a handball just above his
kitchen windows. Yet there was something indomitable in his bearing, and
with it an ill-concealed contempt for us all, that made it impossible to feel
sorry for him. His blazing eyes, his dirty alpaca jacket always powdered with a
light dust of cigarette ash, the walrus mustache that drooped down the sides of
his mouth with such an expression of disgust for us, for his life—everything
seemed to say that he did not care how he lived or what we thought of him.
Having determined to fail, his whole bearing told me he had chosen *us* to
watch him; and he would fail just as he liked, shocking us as he went under,
like a man drowning before our eyes whom our cries could not save. Perhaps
he liked to shock us; perhaps our shame and incredulity at seeing him put back
so far were things he viciously enjoyed, since the whole manner of his life was
an assault on our own hopes and our plain sense of right and wrong. There
was something positive in him that had chosen to die, that mocked all our
admiration for success. We failed every day, but we fought our failure; we
hated it; we measured every action by its help in getting us around failure. Mr.
Solovey confused us. In some unspoken way, full of bitterness and scorn, he
seemed to say that success did not matter.

I alone knew his secret; I, too, was in love with his wife. I was perfectly
sure that all his misery came from the force and bafflement of his attachment

to her. The hopeless love between them had scoured them clean of normal concerns, like getting money and "making sure" and being parents. The store went to pieces, the two little girls in their foreign clothes played jacks all afternoon long on the front steps, Mr. Solovey denounced us with his eyes, and Mrs. Solovey walked among us in her dream of a better life. But alone, I used to think every time I passed their door on my way upstairs, they glided up and down in their apartment like two goldfish in the same tank. This was the way I saw them; she was the only key I had to their mystery. I based it entirely on my incredulous delight in her.

It was her dreaminess, her air of not being quite related to anything around her, that pleased me most. She floated through our lives; in most ways she was never really with us. I saw her so seldom that afterward, whenever I summoned up her face a second before dropping off to sleep, I could never actually tell whether it was her face I remembered, or the face of another woman with blond hair who had once lived in our house. Under the quilt, all women with blond hair and gold wedding rings shining from behind the lattices of a summer house soon took on the same look as they comfortably placed one hand over my back, had the same wide-open dreamy smile as the women in the brilliantine ads on the counter. Only the name I had invented for Mrs. Solovey could bring her instantly back to me. I would say it over and over under my breath, just to hear the foreign syllables ring out—Elizavéta, Elizavéta, no name they ever gave a good Jewish woman; Elizavéta, Elizavéta, I was so astonished to think of Mrs. Solovey, a Jewish woman, speaking Russian every day; Elizavéta, Elizavéta, more accessible than any character I had ever found in a book, but as pliable; more real, but as deliciously unreal. There she was, only two flights of stairs below us, someone I might pass on the block every day, yet a woman like no other I had ever seen. Her blondness flashed out in our tenement, among our somber and dogged faces, with a smiling wantonness. *Die blonde! Die blonde!* In her blondness and languor I seemed to hear the comfortable rustle of nakedness itself.

One day she came into our kitchen, looking for my mother to make a dress for her. I was alone, doing my French lesson at the table. When she spoke to me in her timid, Russian-gruff accent, I felt myself flying back to *Anna Karenina.* There was a grandeur of suffering in her face, in the spindly thinness of her body in the old-fashioned dress, that immediately sent me to that world I had heard of all my life. I was glad my mother was out; I felt I could now enjoy Mrs. Solovey alone. She stood at the kitchen door smiling uneasily, deliberating with herself whether to wait, and when I pressed her, timidly sat down on the other side of the table. I had made so much of her that seeing her so close gave me a curious feeling of alarm. How would it turn out? How did you address your shameful secret love when she walked into a kitchen, and sat down with you, and smiled, smiled nervously, never fitting herself to the great design? Looking at her there, I scorned her mean role as a wife and mother, held to the wildly unhappy husband below, to the two little girls who were always playing jacks by themselves on the front steps. She was Anna, Tolstoy's and my Anna, the sensual and kindly and aristocratically aloof heroine who was unhappily married, who bewitched men's minds, who shocked everyone in St. Petersburg by the gentle power that welled up despite her gold wedding ring. She might have just walked in from a frosty afternoon's ride with her lover on the Nevsky Prospekt, swathed in furs, a mink toque on her head, shyly impervious to the stares and whispers of the envious crowd.

"You are perhaps going to school, young man?" Mrs. Solovey asked after a long silence.

I nodded.

"Do you, uh, do you like the going to school?"

I sighed. She would understand.

"Oh!" she said doubtfully. There was another long silence. Not knowing what else to do, I made a great show of studying my book.

"What are you reading, young man, so serious young man?" she smiled.

I turned the book around.

Surprise and delight showed in her face. "You study French? You already perhaps speak it? I call it my other language! From the time I was a girl in Odessa I study it with application and pleasure. How pleasing to speak French with you as I wait for your mother! We can converse?"

"Yes, Mrs. Solovey," I fumbled. *"Il . . . il me ferait? Il me ferait très heureux."*

She laughed. *"Ferait? Pas du tout!* And you have not a suggestion of the true *ac-cent!"* Then I heard her say to me: "I suppose you are learning French only to read? The way you do everything! But that is a mistake, I can assure you! It is necessary to speak, to speak! Think how you would be happy to speak French well! To speak a foreign language is to depart from yourself. Do you not think it is tiresome to speak the same language all the time? Their language! To feel that you are in a kind of prison, where the words you speak every day are like the walls of your cell? To know with every word that you are the same, and no other, and that it is difficult to escape? But when I speak French to you I have the sensation that for a moment I have left, and I am happy."

I saw her timidly smiling at me. "Come, young man, you will repeat your lesson to me?"

I read the exercise slowly from the book. *"Plus d'argent, donc plus d'amusement. N'importe; j'aime mieux ne pas m'amuser. Je n'ai dit mot à personne, et je n'en parlerai pas de ma vie. Ni moi non plus."*

"Et vous?" she interrupted. *"Comment vous appelez-vous?"*

"Alfred."

"Al-fred! Voilà un joli nom! Un nom anglais, n'est-ce pas? En connaissez-vous l'origine?"

"What?"

She sighed. "You know the origin of your name?"

"Je pense . . . pense . . . un roi d'Angleterre?"

"Bien sûr. Et la légende des petits gâteaux?"

"What?"

She tried again, very slowly.

I shook my head.

"But what is it they teach you in this American public school?!"

"We're not up to irregular verbs."

"The old peasant woman, she asked the king to watch the cakes on the hearth. That they should not burn. But he thought and thought only of his poor country as he sat there, and he let them burn."

"La vieille paysanne . . . était . . . était . . ."

"Fâchée! Ex-cel-lent!" She was very, very displeased. *"Que c'est facile!* You must not stop now. Tell me something about yourself. *Quel âge avez-vous?"*

"Quinze."

"Vous avez quinze ans. My older girl, she is only nine. *Maintenant, dites-moi: qu'est-ce que vous aimez le mieux au monde?"*

"J'aime . . . j'aime . . ."

"You have not understood me at all! I must be more careful to speak slowly. *Quand-je-parle-comme-ceci-me-comprenez-vous?"*

"Oui."

"Bien. Qu'est-ce que vous aimez le mieux au monde?"

"Livres."

"Les livres!" She laughed. *"Quel genre de livres?"*

"Roman."

"Le roman?"

"Poésie."

"La poésie!"

"L'histoire. Les voyages."

"Tout ça? Tout? Vous êtes un peu pédant."

"What?"

She sighed. "Does your mother come back very soon?"

"Soon! Soon!"

"Let us try again. What is it not books you like? *La mer?"*

"Oui. J'aime la mer beaucoup."

"J'aime beaucoup la mer. Encore."

"J'aime beaucoup la mer."

"Et puis?"

"Les montagnes."

"Et ensuite?"

"I know what I want to say, but don't know how to say it."

"Le cinéma? Le sport? Les jeunes filles? Les jeunes filles ne vous déplaisent pas, naturellement?"

"Yes," I said. "I like some girls very much. But . . . it's on the tip of my tongue . . ."

"Pas en anglais!"

"Well," I said, "I like summer."

"Summer! And the other seasons?"

"Le printemps, l'automne, l'hiver?"

"Combien font trois fois trois?"

"Neuf."

"Combien font quarante et vingt-six?"

"Soixante-six."

"Pourquoi préférez-vous l'été?"

"La . . . la chaud?" I gave it up. "The warmth . . . the evenness."

She stared at me silently, in gratitude. I distinctly heard her say: "I understand very well. I feel sympathy with your answer! I myself come from Odessa in the south of Russia. You know of Odessa? On the Black Sea. One of the most beautiful cities in all the world, full of sun. It is really a part of Greece.

When I was a girl in Odessa, I would go down to the harbor every day and stare out across the water and imagine myself on a ship, a ship with blue sails, that would take me around the world."

"You have lived in many places."

"*Oui. Nous avons habité des pays différents. La Russie, la France, l'Italie, la Palestine.* Yes, many places."

"Why did you come here?" I asked suddenly.

She looked at me for a moment. I could not tell what she felt, or how much I had betrayed. But in some way my question wearied her. She rose, made a strange stiff little bow, and went out.

Occasionally I saw her in the street. She made no effort to continue my practice in French, and I did not know how to ask. For a long time I did not see her at all. We knew that Mr. Solovey had gone bankrupt, and was looking for someone to buy the fixtures. There were rumors on the block that once, in the middle of the night, he had beaten her so violently that people in the other tenement had been awakened by her screams. But there was nothing definite we knew about them, and after many weeks in which I vainly looked for her everywhere and once tried to get into their apartment from the yard, I almost forgot her. The store was finally sold, and Mr. Solovey became an assistant in a drugstore on Blake Avenue. They continued to live in the apartment on the ground floor. One morning, while her children were at school, and her husband was at work, Mrs. Solovey sealed all the doors and windows with adhesive tape, and sat over the open gas jets in the kitchen until she was dead. It was raining the day they buried her. Because she was a suicide, the rabbi was reluctant to say the necessary prayers inside the synagogue. But they prevailed upon him to come out on the porch, and looking down on the hearse as it waited in the street, he intoned the service over her coffin. It was wrapped in the blue-and-white flag with a Star of David at the head. There were hundreds of women in their shawls, weeping in the rain. Most of them had never seen Mrs. Solovey, but they came to weep out of pity for her children, and out of terror and awe because someone was dead. My mother was in the front line outside the synagogue, and I needed urgently to see her. But the crowd was so large that I could not find her, and I waited in the back until the service was over.

[1951]

YESHUA

———•◆•———

NOTICE: ANYONE PLACING ANY ENCUMBRANCE ON THIS BALCONY WILL BE FINED TEN DOLLARS. Now, when I sat on the fire escape evenings after work, the sky was the mirror of the book in my hand. I could have shown those open pages to the roofs and have read them back from the clouds moving over my head. From that private perch, everything in sight now loosed itself from its containing hard edges in space and came back to me as a single line of words burning across the page. Half past five on a summer day—at my back I could smell soupgreens being put into the pot—just that hour which in the tense autumn of school beginning again or in the blindness of winter at the bottom of the year is so dark, but which now brims over with light you can breathe and breathe in with the iron grit flaking off the sign on the fire escape: NOTICE: ANYONE PLACING ANY ENCUMBRANCE ON THIS BALCONY WILL BE FINED TEN DOLLARS.

Look how much light there is. It does not matter now that your bottom itches to the pebbly stone on the windowsill; that the sun is so fierce, it burns your feet on the iron planks; that when you get up to stretch your legs, the heat makes you so dizzy, you can see yourself falling down the red-painted ladders that chase each other to the street. For now a single line of English words takes you up slowly, and slowly carries you across the page to where, each time you reach its end, you have to catch your breath and look away—the pleasure is unbearable, it is so full.

> But when that which is perfect is come, then that which is in part shall be done
>   away.
> When I was a child, I spake as a child, I understood as a child, I thought as
> a child; but when I became a man, I put away childish things.
> For now we see through a glass, darkly; but then face to face: now I know in part;
>   but then shall I know even as also I am known.

The man from whom I had accepted the little blue volume on the steps of the Fifth Avenue Library had said to me in Yiddish, searching my face doubtfully: "You *are* a Jew? You will really look into it?" No, I was not really looking into it; I could not read more than two or three pages at a time without turning away in excitement and shame. Would the old women across the street ever have believed it? But how square and hardy the words looked in their even black type. Each seemed to burn separately in the sun as I nervously flipped the pages and then turned back to where the book most naturally lay flat: *For now we see through a glass, darkly.* Each time my eye fell on that square, even black type, the sentence began to move in the sun. It rose up, a smoking frame of dark glass above the highest roofs, steadily and joyfully burning, as, reading aloud to myself, I tasted the rightness of each word on my tongue.

It was like heaping my own arms with gifts. There were images I did not understand, but which fell on my mind with such slow-opening grandeur that once I distinctly heard the clean and fundamental cracking of trees. First the image, then the thing; first the word in its taste and smell and touch, then the thing it meant, when you were calm enough to look. Images were instantaneous; the meaning alone could be like the unyielding metal taste when you bit on an empty spoon. The initial shock of that language left no room in my head for anything else. But now, each day I turned back to that little blue testament, I had that same sense of instant connectedness I had already noticed in myself to the exclamation *O altitudo!* in a quotation from Sir Thomas Browne; to the chapter on the cathedral in Lawrence's *The Rainbow*; to the opening line of Henry Vaughan's "The World,"

I saw Eternity the other night

that haunted me from the day I came on it in an anthology; to Blake's

When the stars threw down their spears
And water'd heaven with their tears,
Did he smile his work to see?
Did he who made the Lamb make thee?;

to the opening lines of *A Farewell to Arms*, indescribably dry and beautiful with the light on those pebbles in the plain; to "When Lilacs Last in the Dooryard Bloom'd," where I knew as soon as I came on the line

Passing the yellow-spear'd wheat, every grain from its shroud in the dark brown
   fields uprisen.

that I had found another writer I could instinctively trust.

First the image, then the sense. First those clouds moving blue and white across the nearest roofs; and then—*O altitudo!*, the journey into that other land of *flax*, of summer, eternal summer, through which *he* had walked, wrapped in a blue-and-white prayer shawl, and, still looking back at me with the heartbreaking smile of recognition from a fellow Jew, had said: *The blind receive their sight, and the lame walk, the lepers are cleansed, and the deaf hear, the dead are raised up, and the poor have the gospel preached to them.*

And blessed is he, whosoever shall not be offended in me.

Offended in him? I had known him instantly. Surely I had been waiting for him all my life—our own Yeshua, misunderstood by his own, like me, but the very embodiment of everything I had waited so long to hear from a Jew— a great contempt for the minute daily business of the world; a deep and joyful turning back into our own spirit. It was *he*, I thought, who would resolve for me at last the ambiguity and the long ache of being a Jew—Yeshua, our own long-lost Jesus, speaking straight to the mind and heart at once. For that voice, that exultantly fiery and tender voice, there were no gaps between images and things, for constantly walking before the Lord, he remained all energy and mind, thrust his soul into every corner of the world, and passing gaily under every yoke, remained free to seek our God in His expected place.

How long I had been waiting for him, how long: like metal for a magnet to raise it. I had recognized him immediately, and all over: that exaltation; those thorny images that cut you with their overriding fervor and gave you the husk of every word along with the kernel; that furious old Jewish impatience with *Success*, with comfort, with eating, with the rich, with the whole shabby superficial fashionable world itself; that fatigue, as of a man having constantly to make his way up and down the world on foot; and then that sternness and love that gushed out of him when he turned to the others and said:

> *For verily I say unto you, Till heaven and earth pass, one jot or one tittle shall in no wise pass from the law, till all be fulfilled.*

Yeshua, my Yeshua! What had he to do with those who killed his own and worshiped him as God? Why would *they* call him only by that smooth Greek name of Jesus? He was Yeshua, my own Reb Yeshua, of whose terrible death I could never read without bursting into tears—Yeshua, our own Yeshua, the most natural of us all, the most direct, the most enchanted, and as he sprang up from the heart of poor Jews, all the dearer to me because he could now return to his own kind: *and the poor have the gospel preached to them.*

[1951]

II

THE LITERARY LIFE

BROWNSVILLE: 1931

It was to the sound of *The Waste Land* being read aloud that I met David. Whenever I got tired of flopping around the dusty streets and rang Isrolik's bell, the banister smelled of damp, the mother sat on a kitchen chair moaning against her unemployed husband as she stared at the sink, and from the city relief checks and cold family despair in that house Isrolik would start up with his glassy imperturbable poet's smile: "What an idiot! You still walking around in this heat? Come in and listen to Eliot! Everybody else is here!"

They lived on the ground floor, in a perpetual sour smell from the backyard. Wherever you sat in that house, you saw the clotheslines in the yard. On the round table in the "dining room," Isrolik's study by day and a bedroom for the four younger children at night, lay the hallowed copy of *The Waste Land* that he carried around with him wherever he went, and his regular offering of *Poetry*, *The New Masses*, squares of chocolate halvah, biscuit sandwiches filled with a soft vanilla cream beginning to run in the heat, and bottles of seltzer. Isrolik and I never took to each other, but he was the first boy I knew in Brownsville who cared for poetry, and even wrote it. So despite all my uneasiness in his house, it always astonished and excited me to sit around that table with him and David and two or three other boys who would listen gravely, munching the biscuit sandwiches and drinking seltzer as Isrolik read aloud from *The Waste Land,* and then commented on the *technique* and the *symbolism.*

I had never seen such boys before; I had not known they existed in Brownsville. There was one they privately called the *hunchback,* for his head was so enormous that it looked ready to fall of its own weight back on his spine. He was so ashamed that he never looked anyone in the face, and from time to time would mumble quotations he hoped someone would recognize and so begin to talk with him. Whenever we all went about in the evenings—to the Free Theater on East Twenty-seventh Street to see *Rosmersholm* or *Ghosts,* to the Civic Repertory to see Eva Le Gallienne in *Hedda Gabler,* to Lincoln Terrace Park to pick up a girl—he walked behind us whispering lines from *The Ballad of Reading Gaol* to see if we knew the next ones. There was another, his cheeks so pitted with acne that it was as if muddy wheels had passed over his face, who spoke every word with an Oxford accent. Whenever you sat next to him, you could hear each sharp intake of his breath like a hiss. There was still another, with a small growth of beard—they called him Ilyich, in honor of Lenin—a boy much older than the rest of us, a strange boy who lived by himself in a fur-nished room off Dumont Avenue, who had sworn never to shave until the *boss class* freed Tom Mooney. His long, matted hair and beard gave him so archaic a look that I could never take it in that he was really there with me, talking in his gently condescending voice as I stared at the clotheslines. He seemed to be someone I had remembered from a book, or perhaps even from a dream, about Russian intellectuals sitting around a hut in Siberia early in the century.

It was his feeling for poetry that held me to Isrolik's damp cluttered "study" those summer evenings. Wherever I looked, there were loose sheets of his own poems on the table, the floor, the beds, thrown in with stray issues of *Poetry,* commentaries on Eliot, and poems torn out of *The New Masses.* If Isrolik had to go into the kitchen to quiet his mother down, or to feed one of the chil-dren, or had to speak to us about anything not directly connected with poetry, he became irritable and impatient, tapped his feet, and giggled nervously in his high, thin voice until he could get back to reading from *The Waste Land,* a poem he loved with such breathless adoration that I seemed to see him sucking on each phrase like a lozenge he could not bear to swallow. Even when we tried to make money selling Eskimo Pies on the Coney Island beach, he would cry, "Shantih, shantih, shantih" as we thrashed our way through the sands.

Yet in some way that puzzled me—I was so grateful to him for living two blocks away—I felt uneasy in his presence, and whenever I listened to him reading from *The Waste Land* to the sound of the mother moaning in the kitchen, I kept expecting a scream, a blow, perhaps even a fire, to bring things to a head in that house. How grim, sour, and alone I felt as we walked around Brownsville those summer evenings arguing Keats and Shelley, Blake and Coleridge, Trotsky and Stalin. It was the second summer of the Depression: my father had not worked for nine months, and every Friday evening as we sat down to eat my mother cried out: "Better I should work all night than we should take from the city!" Spain had a republic at last, and in England Ramsay MacDonald had just stabbed the Labor Party to the heart. I remember how we stopped in a school playground off Powell Street to play one last furious game of handball in the fading light; how, in front of a cutlery store on Belmont Avenue whose windows were ablaze with light, I stood looking at all those scissors and knives as Isrolik and his friends cried "Sellouts! Sellouts!" along my right ear. I felt that loneliness that shamed me after Socialist meetings on the steps of the Labor Lyceum—a loneliness I felt even in the massed and steaming "adults'" library on Glenmore Avenue, where all the future young lawyers sat at their law books with green eye-shades fixed over their faces like a second frown of attention; and in Lincoln Terrace Park, where old men played chess in the light from the street lamps. As we sat around all night arguing France, Germany, China, Italy, Spain, I hungrily listened to the girls squealing in the grass below.

The best of that bunch was David. He was a chemist, but I understood him better than I did Isrolik. David loved Beethoven, and *The Marriage of Heaven and Hell*; he could always predict in advance the days on which Macy's would put Modern Library books up for thirty-eight cents; and though entirely devoted to chemistry and the *Negro question* and forever blinking at me uneasily from behind his thick glaring lenses, he would sit in our "dining room" every late Friday afternoon reading aloud in a clear voice the essays and poems and sketches I had written at the kitchen table that week, and from time to time say with a heartwarming smile: "That's good! That's a pretty good phrase! I really think you're improving!" Crowded summer nights in the "adults'" library on Glenmore Avenue, how good it was to run into David in the fiction section— just there, where Gogol's *Evening on a Farm Near Dikánka* seemed to me the most beautiful title I had ever seen—how good just to walk him home to East New York, singing themes from the Beethoven Violin Concerto as we went.

It was poorer at his end than where we lived; most of the houses were the oldest tenements, with wooden staircases; when you went up the street bridge that led past the railroad yards, the streets looked as if they had cracked under the hot steam and the thunder from the freight cars being shuttled below. Along the route there were old tinsmith shops in basements, little unpainted wooden synagogues so old and bent and squeezed for space that you could see the boards loose in the walls; sweatshops where they made artificial flowers and ladies' slips until late in the evening. But I preferred it there; the nearer I got to David's house, the deeper I seemed to enter into Brownsville's frankness. Here was the other border, as far as possible from the *alrightniks* on Eastern Parkway; here was the turnoff for Highland Park, the transfer point to all good things that summer I was sixteen. The minute I went up the cracked and moldy wooden steps of David's house, my heart began to race against the thunder from the railroad yards. "Go over! Go over!"

The thing I always saw first in David's dining room was the far wall solidly covered with newspaper pictures of lynchings, pickets being beaten up by the police, Ukrainian wheat fields from *Soviet Russia Today*, photographs, torn out of books, of Lenin, Toussaint L'Ouverture, Frederick W. Douglass, Henri Barbusse, and Ernst Thaelmann. On the bureau next to his chemistry texts, ranged in front of the glass so that you saw their backs reflected in the glass whenever you looked at them, were the collected works of Lenin. On the wall above hung the usual oval photographs of the grandfather and grandmother, side by side staring down at me where I had nervously caught my shoes in the holes of the dark-brown linoleum. Whenever I looked away from those pictures on the far wall of Negroes hanging from the boughs of trees in the deep South, I would see those dead grandparents gloomily taking me in, and would feel that I had come up too close to some strange stone carving in the desert and had fallen between the cracks.

On those hot summer evenings you could hear through the screens the endless charging of the freight cars in the yards. The mother, already yellow with cancer, sat silently and stiffly propped up on pillows; a young boy sat at her feet waving a palmetto fan, and whenever she cried out, would glare up at me fiercely and dash into the kitchen for another glass of water. In that house the light of the early summer evening had the same yellowness as the mother's face. She was small, with her hair oddly cut short like a boy's; and whenever I saw her, wore an old patched middy blouse; the yellowness of that room ran in sick querulous waves down into the bandages thick over her left breast. From the stale weedy garden patch in the old "private" house next door, the dusty prong of an old tree pressed against the window screen, and when the screen rattled in the sudden windy darkening of the air before a rainstorm, seemed to expel a thin layer of dust into the room.

Everything in that house looked as if it had come down to a few minimum utensils for eating, sleeping, and dying. I remember the peculiar desolation of the broken dining room chairs around the table, and how, every time I moved, my shoes seemed to catch in the holes of the linoleum. Yet far more than the poverty in that orphaned and rotting house; more, even, than the sense of impending death, it was some deep, brave, and awful earnestness before life itself I always felt there. From time to time I would even catch in the air the curious, unbelievable idea that David had stripped their life deliberately to those chemistry textbooks, the collected works of Lenin, those Negroes on the far wall hanged, castrated, and burned in darkest Georgia. I had never seen such a naked house. And that it should be lived in so indifferently; that David should walk so carelessly across the hollows in the linoleum as he went over to the bureau to seize a fresh volume of Lenin that might purge me of my *confusions* and harden me up at last; that the mother herself, whether from interest or despair, should ignore everything there but our bitter arguments as she silently looked down at us—it was just this that kept me coming back. The house was so naked, everyone in it seemed entirely free to think.

⌊1951⌋

THE NEW REPUBLIC: 1934

———— • ◆ • ————

What young writers of the Thirties wanted was to prove the literary value of our experience, to recognize the possibility of art in our own lives, to feel that we had moved the streets, the stockyards, the hiring halls into literature—to show that our radical strength could carry on the experimental impulse of modern literature. And it was because of this genuine literary ambition that the influence of Malcolm Cowley, then literary editor of *The New Republic,* was so fundamental. For Cowley had lived among the expatriates in Paris, he had just published *Exile's Return* as a chronicle of the lost generation, and each Wednesday afternoon, when I waited with other hopeful reviewers for Cowley to sail in after lunch with a tolerant smile on the face which so startlingly duplicated Hemingway's handsomeness, the sight of Cowley in the vivid stripes of his seersucker suit seemed to unite, through his love of good writing and his faith in revolution, the brilliant Twenties and the militant Thirties. The summer of 1934, that bottom summer when the first wild wave of hope under the New Deal had receded, there were so many of us edged onto the single bench in the waiting room downstairs, so many more of us than he needed for reviews, that Cowley, not knowing what else to do for the hungry faces waiting to see him, would sell the books there was no space to review and dole out the proceeds among the more desperate cases haunting him for review assignments. This kindliness was also a conscious symbol of the times. Cowley had been at Harvard in the time of Dos Passos, he had left Harvard in 1917 for service in an American ambulance unit in the time of E. E. Cummings, he had drunk in Paris with Hemingway, had fought the *flics* with Aragon, had walked the Village with Hart Crane. Just as he now lived in Connecticut (and *Exile's Return* noted when writers began moving from Greenwich Village to Connecticut), so he was unable to lift his pipe to his mouth, or to make a crack, without making one feel that he recognized the literary situation involved. He seemed always to have moved in the company of writers, literary movements, *cénacles*, to see history in terms of what writers had thought and how they had lived. When in his book he recounted his memories of the Dome and the Select, hinting at the real names of the characters in *The Sun Also Rises*, I had an image of Malcolm Cowley as a passenger in the great polished coach that was forever taking young Harvard poets to war, to the Left Bank, to the Village, to Connecticut. Wherever Cowley moved or ate, wherever he lived, he heard the bell of literary history sounding the moment and his own voice calling possibly another change in the literary weather.

Cowley had more than most the critic's love of writers and of the literary life, the need to recognize the moment, to appropriate and to share in the literary feast. And it was this feeling for movements that made Cowley redirect the literary side of *The New Republic* in the direction of a sophisticated literary Stalinism, since for Cowley "revolution" was now the new stage of development. He had the intellectual elegance of his generation, and did not indulge the Party-line hacks for the sake of ideology. In Cowley's reviews and literary essays there was no abdication from the standards of the aesthetic generation: he wrote of Baudelaire on the barricades in 1848, of Wagner the revolutionary, of Marx's own profound literary culture. Cowley was an expressive poet, and he had such a gift of clear style, he had such distinguished literary standards and associations, he had translated so many books from the French, he had known so many writers and had worked on so many magazines, that I felt in reading him that I had been led up to the most immense spread of literary tidbits. Cowley's face had kept the faint smile of defiance, the swashbuckling look and military mustache of intellectual officers in the First World War, the look of gallantry in sophistication that one connected with the heroes of Hemingway—he even resembled Hemingway in much the same way that matinee idols once resembled Clark Gable; he had an *air*. Unlike the heavy old

Germanic progressives from Wisconsin who had just lost their jobs and the professors from Oklahoma fired for liberal opinions whom I met at the *New Republic*, stiffly expectant on the waiting bench; unlike the emaciated and curious English stray who had mysteriously landed on this American beach and looked panicky, starving, wild as he stumblingly tried to get a loan out of the secretaries; unlike the "working-class" writers to whom he passed out review copies with a half-smiling air of acknowledging *their* turn in the literary tide, Cowley radiated ease and sophistication.

[. . . .]

The lead review in *The New Republic*, a single page usually written by Cowley himself, brought the week to focus for people to whom this page, breathing intellectual fight in its sharp black title and solid double-columned lines of argument, represented the most dramatically satisfying confrontation of a new book by a gifted, uncompromising critical intelligence. A time would come, in the early Forties, when Cowley could report with astonishment that a famous Broadway designer he had met on the train no longer kept up with these lead reviews; an era had passed. Cowley was the last of this era—the last *New Republic* literary editor who dominated "the back of the book," and who week after week gave a continuing authority to his judgments. Cowley made his points with unassailable *clarté* and concreteness; he *made* an article each week that one had to read and could remember. He did not have Edmund Wilson's capacity for losing himself in the complexity of a subject; Cowley was always conscious of making a point, and he summed the point up at the end of his review to make sure that the reader got it. He was shrewd, positive, plain, in the Hemingway style of artful plainness that united simplicity of manner with a certain slyness. Whenever you crossed Malcolm directly, he would sidle into his familiar role of the slow-moving and slow-talking country boy from western Pennsylvania, clear-minded and deliberate, definite as the gestures with which he tapped the last pinch of tobacco into his pipe and then looked out at you through the flame of the match as he slowly and puffingly lighted up. But, reading his reviews, I was stirred by his gift for putting the vital new books into the dramatic context of the times. During the Moscow Trials of the mid-Thirties, when his lead review of the official testimony condemned the helpless defendants accused of collaboration with Hitler and sabotage against the Soviet state, I felt that Cowley had made up his mind to attack these now-helpless figures from the Soviet past, had suppressed his natural doubts,

because he could not separate himself from the Stalinists with whom he identified the future. To Cowley everything came down to the trend, to the forces
that seemed to be in the know and in control of the time-spirit. This gave an
unforgettable vividness to his description of the peasants waiting on Silone's
door to tell him what had happened to their village of Fontamara, to his
description of the wounded Communists at the end of *Man's Fate* waiting in
what had formerly been a schoolyard to be led out by Chiang Kai-shek's soldiers and thrown into the boiler of a locomotive.

The Communist leaders in *Man's Fate* carried cyanide in the flat buckles of
their belts. The Russian, Katov, took pity upon two frightened boys waiting to
be burned, and in the darkness made equal shares of the poison and passed
them over; one of the boys was wounded and dropped them. In the darkness,
said Cowley, the condemned searched for the pellets as though "they were
looking for diamonds."

Cowley's review was an exciting concentrate of Malraux, who was himself
an intoxicating concentrate of the pride, vision, and sacrifice of those Communists from everywhere who had been burned alive in China for the greater
glory of humanity. Kyo Gisors, the hero of the book, half Japanese and half
French, "had fought for what in his time was charged with the deepest meaning and the greatest hope." The power of that meaning and that hope was now
reaching me in New York as I read a book review; exulting in the possibilities
of the human will to a better life, I could not have said what I was excited
by—the vividness of a book review suggesting the power of a book I had not
yet read, dramatizing historical events I did not fully understand. The critic
aroused the reader in behalf of the imagination that had aroused him, and
from where I stood at the moment, it looked as if the imagination of revolution and the imagination of literature were stirred by the same fiery depths.

[1965]

AT V. F. CALVERTON'S: 1936

The literary person in New York who at that time most clearly brought my two worlds together was V. F. Calverton, who died at forty in 1940. Calverton came from Baltimore, where at twenty-three he had founded his own magazine, *The Modern Quarterly*. In the New York of the Thirties it became *The Modern Monthly*; in his last years it became *The Modern Quarterly* again; and never did the still polemical word *modern* mean so much to an editor and writer as it did to Calverton. He was a round, kindly, swarthy, eager man, curiously distracted, with flowing energy, who wrote and edited and lectured indiscriminately on sex, on psychoanalysis, on American literature, on the theory of society, on anthropology. In his youth he had been a semiprofessional baseball player, and had thought of becoming a Lutheran minister. Dashing back and forth between Baltimore and New York, keeping up his magazine singlehanded, writing "social science" and literature with the same eager knowingness, as if he were really the heir of Diderot and Bernard Shaw, he nevertheless, for all his bounce, seemed plaintive and absent-minded, like a man who has unaccountably missed his goal. Calverton believed that love had to become "modern," and art, and socialism, and criticism, and all knowledge. Everything that a modern man could learn to believe was to come off the same great modern tree. . . .

[B]y the mid-Thirties, when I fell in with him, Calverton was one of the few independently active and prosleytizing Marxist intellectuals in New York who were actually at war with the Communists. He had no faction or party but those independent spirits who, like himself, had been driven off by the Communists, slandered and ostracized by the faithful, for criticizing Stalin's course. Calverton had been a boy revolutionary in Baltimore in 1918, an intellectual sympathizer with the Communists in the early Twenties, when it was still possible to think of them as rebels rather than "shock brigadiers of culture." The early days of Communism were in fact Calverton's Bohemian Period, his Left Bank and his 1920s. He was a premature Marxist. By the middle Thirties, when so many respectable and important figures were being welcomed into the United Front and Stalin was being acclaimed as the only responsible leader of the time by reformed cynics on *Collier's* and in many a New York publishing house, Calverton was out of fashion again, this time as a premature anti-Stalinist, and was feeling increasingly isolated.

It was Calverton's personal resistance to the cult of Stalin that I most admired about him; he had been shocked by the cultural authoritarianism of the Communists, and by the time of the first big Moscow Trial, August 1936, was sickened and outraged by Stalin's frame-up of his old rivals and opponents in the Party. At a time when the literary editor of *The New Republic* was urging intellectuals to accept the official verdict in the Moscow Trials, *The Modern Monthly* rallied every shade of independent opinion on the left against such submission.

Calverton's house, like Calverton's magazine, was a natural gathering place for all sorts of radicals not in the Communist fold—old Russian Mensheviks and Social Revolutionaries, German Marxists who had known Engels and [Eduard] Bernstein, American Socialists and libertarian anarchists, ex-Communists who had fallen off the train of history or had been pushed off it somewhere up the line, possibly in 1921 at the time of Kronstadt, or in 1927 at the time of Trotsky's downfall, or in 1935 with the increasing savagery of Stalin toward all former opponents and thus presumably present critics. *The New Masses* could not mention Calverton, Norman Thomas, Max Eastman, Sidney Hook, Eugene Lyons, without accusing them of literary plagiarism, sabotage against the Soviet state, poisoning little children, and any and all other crimes necessary and logical to miscreants opposed to Stalin. But there they all were busily arguing with each other at Calverton's many parties, looking rumpled and all too human against the solid walls of bookshelves, the walls and walls of books whose severe intellectual front engloomed those long and violet-dark rooms put in shadow by the tree outside the house.

The long Greenwich Village rooms humming with darkness, lighted by a few stray lamps, were full of these still separate particles, these old-fashioned scholars who had never joined it and these obstinate rebels who had been thrown off by the Communist machine, which would not tolerate anyone it could not digest. And among the European veterans and American Jews, who looked as if they had made their way to Calverton's house through a mine field, among all the sour, sedentary, guarded faces, were the characteristically lean, straight, bony Yankee individualists with ruddy faces and booming laughs, the old Harvard dissenters, leftover Abolitionists, Tolstoyans, single-taxers, Methodist ministers, Village rebels of 1912, everlasting Socialists and early psychoanalysts, who naturally turned up at George [Calverton]'s house as friends of George's own heartiness, his great and open welcome to life. Unlike the European veterans and American Jewish veterans, survivors of many ideological wars, the "Yankees" still looked as unscarred as Norman Thomas and Max Eastman—they looked, indeed, as if they had personally enjoyed resistance to their own stuffy beginnings as ministers or the sons of ministers; they looked as if they had fought down their own kind for the pleasure of fighting. With their open American faces and their frank American voices, with their lean figures and their honest old American instincts, they looked dashing and splendid, undismayed by evil and not afraid to do good. They laughed a lot; even in argument Norman Thomas's laugh could be heard from one room to another.

At Calverton's there was one horribly experienced Polish veteran of the revolutionary wars, a kindly but despairing expert on all Socialists and socialisms, Utopian, scientific, social democratic, libertarian, and dogmatic, a man with a heavy bald front and a face shaped like a stone by every obstacle in his path. He had gone through everything, that man, he had done battle in many factions and groups, and in every country. He had been through it all— the easy idealism of Socialist students, the militancy of the Syndicalists, the world-shaking mystique of the Communists just after 1917—and he could never again trust politicians of any stripe. Power corrupted everyone, and perhaps no one so much as the administrators, experts, professionals, intellectuals, who sought dictatorial powers over the working class in the name of their emancipation from capitalism. The cruelties visited upon the Russian working class in the name of socialism, the deceptions visited upon the working class in the name of solidarity, the exploitation visited upon the ruled/rulers by the ruled! All was written in the folds of that magnificent bald dome. Gentle as he was, there was nothing to ask him, to talk over, that could modify the tragedy that power represented at all times and in all places, but never so much as for the exploited who, seeking their revolutionary emancipation, had put new oppressors to rule over them from the Kremlin, the Politburo, the secret police. There was nothing to talk over. He would only shake his head. He had passed beyond all possible illusion. The Russian people had been oppressed ruthlessly under Czarism; but when they revolted, it was under the leadership of a small and arrogant elite of intellectuals, who used the destruction of the old regime to put themselves, the all-sufficient managers, into the essential places. There could be nothing in common between those who worked with their hands, to the last strength of their bodies, and those who sat at desks framing the rules and setting the pace and giving the orders. Revolution was a tragic cycle: the powerless, seeking to determine their own fate at last, gave new power over themselves to ruthless intellectuals. There could never be any bond between those who worked and those who ruled. This Polish veteran did not need the big show trials, just beginning in Moscow, to tell him what he had already seen of the corruptions made inevitable by power. He had come out of the revolutionary movement an historian of its illusions and catastrophes, its usual renegades and its few, strange saints. He was a living memorial to the futile heroism of the revolutionary movement. For him, socialism had become its past.

Yet this sad, acid detachment was an exception at Calverton's parties. Even Max Eastman, denounced by Stalin himself as "a notorious gangster" and "crook," still believed in the Revolution's positive achievements. Eastman despised dialectical materialism as the "mystical" side of Marxism; for him the Revolution represented a great effort at scientific social engineering, unfortunately diffused with the ideological cant that Marx had absorbed from Hegel. With his mane of white hair, his conscious good looks, and his easy laugh, Eastman made his admiration of Lenin's "social engineering" and his contempt for the residue of "mysticism" in Marx's system sound natural, spontaneous, "American." You felt about Eastman that he would have liked, still, to sit down with Marx and talk him out of his unfortunate German tendency to metaphysics—as indeed he had sat down many a time with Trotsky to argue *him* out of the dialectic, much to Trotsky's indignation. Eastman's argument that Marxism had a split personality, torn between its practical scientific realism and its blind Hegelian faith in the final purpose of History, made him sound psychological and therapeutic to it. I had always known of Max Eastman as a romantic poet and rebel, vaguely a male counterpart of Edna St. Vincent Millay, and was not prepared, when I saw him in action at Calverton's parties, for such a steady drumfire in behalf of science, scientific method, experimental naturalism, and scientific engineering. When it came to poetry and art he sounded, in the phrase of the time, like a technocrat. His old teacher John Dewey, it seemed, had made a greater impression on Eastman than anyone else had, and the more he saw his dream of the Russian Revolution receding from him, the more he called after Marxism to Americanize itself, to come down to earth, to be practical and sharp, direct and plain.

Was this Max Eastman the Socialist poet and rebel who had talked a jury out of convicting him in 1918? Eastman's vision of the Revolution had been the most intense poetic act of his life, and the more he saw the curtain of fear coming down on all the rebels and poets and intellectuals in Russia like himself, so many of whom had been his friends and intimate comrades, the more desperately he tried to make the Russian Revolution sensible, to separate the positive social achievements of eighteen years from the ominous Stalinist terror. It was his last effort; within a year Eastman would be writing in total rejection of the Revolution that he had gone with uplifted heart to describe for his friends on the old *Masses* and the *Liberator.* Yet the fascination of the Revolution was still great; the wild hope of a totally new society that it had inspired in the minds of people like Eastman was dying hard. For these thinkers and scholars at Calverton's house, natural opponents of Stalin the despot and philistine, there was still more belief in the Revolution than not; its positive value was not yet in doubt. Like Trotsky himself, they would not believe that "socialism in one country" meant what it said; the October Revolution, that nucleus exploding into the twentieth century, could not be slowed down and its magnificent world-shaking energies checked that easily! Over their heads at Calverton's house hung the shadow of the impending Moscow Trials, the destruction of the revolutionary intellectuals, the ferocious terror designed to whip all elements of the population into perfect obedience to the State and its Leader: by official decree, in 1935, minors from the age of twelve could be sentenced to death. Yet obstinately and with ready charm, as if charm could give added backing to his "scientific" arguments, Eastman argued, still, that the Revolution was to be defended, that good sense might yet prevail, if only the expertise of the "professional revolutionary" Lenin could prevail over the messianic side of Marx.

In *The Modern Monthly* there had been a bitter dispute for years between Eastman and Sidney Hook on the scientific value of Marxism. Both trained in philosophy, both disciples of John Dewey, both exponents of "experimental method" and "scientific inquiry," both intensely committed to the practical and moral necessity of socialism, they disagreed bitterly as to the scientific nature of Marxism. Eastman, deploring the "cant" of the dialectic and the "animism" that in his opinion impeded the "scientific straight thinking" of the Marxist analysis of society, ran full tilt into Sidney Hook, who expounded Marxism as a thoroughly scientific, sensibly naturalistic philosophy and a startling anticipation of American pragmatism at its best. Far from wishing to disencumber Marxism of the "metaphysical" idealism that Eastman saw in it, Hook found Marxism an up-to-date and satisfactory philosophy. He approved of it as experimental, naturalistic, thoroughly instrumentalist, and against Eastman's disapproval of the dialectic brought such unsparing accusations of incompetence and of unacknowledged indebtedness to his own more solid studies in Marx's debt to Hegel that before long the two philosophers, the two disciples of John Dewey, were insulting each other up and down the columns of *The Modern Monthly.*

Eastman, almost twenty years older than Hook and over the years distracted from the strict practice of philosophy by poetry, Freudianism, travel, friendship and other pleasures of sense, did not argue as well as Hook. No one ever did. When it came to close argument, Hook was unbeatable; one saw that he could not imagine himself defeated in argument. The concentration of all his intellectual forces upon the point at issue was overwhelming, the proofs of inconsistency on the part of his opponents were unanswerable; to watch Hook in argument was to watch him moving in for the kill. Socrates may have persuaded his opponents, but Hook invariably shamed them. He was the most devastating logician the world would ever see, and as he had no doubt devastated his teachers at City College, so he was now, at Calverton's house, devastating many an independent radical like himself. Eastman was perhaps not so far off in castigating as "metaphysical" the blind faith in historical progress that Marx had carried over from Hegel; in the years to come, certainly, Hook was to blame on the Communist dictatorship a good deal of what Stalin had been able, for his own purposes, to exploit in the name of inevitable progress. But even at this moment it was clear that Hook had turned Marxism into his own kind of philosophy, that he found it acceptably scientific, logical, experimental, and naturalistic because he could not uphold anything that was not scientific, logical, experimental and naturalistic. Hook did not see anything in Freud, he did not see anything in religion, he did not see that any imaginative knowledge could be dependably gained from art. What you needed was the philosophy of John Dewey and of Karl Marx, both of which so clearly supported each other in the mind of Sidney Hook; you needed only his kind of rationalism. So the choice was easy. Hook won all the arguments, but since he always had to be right, he did not persuade one that Marx was scientific and rational because Hook said he was.

It was not Hook's logic that impressed me, for it was always partisan reasoning in behalf of Dewey or Marx or other men's ideas; it was his intellectual passion for these ideas. He was humorless, but never petty; obstinate, but not malicious; domineering, but not self-centered. He did not yield to momentary delights and human appeals, as Eastman did. It was his commitment that impressed me. He was a believer. He wanted to change society totally, to overturn disproven ways of thought, to discard all the encrusted superstitions, to give mankind the new chance that it hungered for. When he contrasted the superstitions represented by the old philosophy and the oppressions inherent in capitalism with the instrumentalism that could be the new knowledge and the cooperativeness (through the application of intelligence alone) that could be the new society, he made the choice stark and the issue dramatic. He put clearly before you the logical choice of scientific intelligence over religious superstition, of planning over confusion, of pragmatism over Thomism, of Dewey over Freud. Here was logic, here was science, here was experimentalism. Here were instruments of social analysis that exposed all the contradictions in capitalist society and could give men all they needed for creating a society practical, sensible, harmonious, and just. His method, wholly and entirely rational, would become the lever of the revolution. How could one not grasp it? Hook saw every situation so clearly that he concentrated his whole personality into the force of his logic—then wondered why his opponents were so *dumb*, and no doubt honestly regretted that they were.

[. . . .]

For Calverton I was just the sort of literary apprentice, of unimpeachably radical origin, who would share his socialism and help on *The Modern Monthly.* But while I shared some of the opinions and enjoyed working for the magazine, Calverton's real charm for me was the open, direct way in which he exposed his life to me. There was never a time when Calverton, always hard-pressed and working as if he knew he would die in a few years, would not get up from his desk to talk things over. Even when he complained about the Stalinists who were slandering him, there was some surprise in his face and voice that he could have been so mistaken in people. He worked with such impatience that I once saw him composing the first draft of a novel with carbon paper already in the machine. There were all those anthologies, histories, critiques, lectures on sex, on the newer spirit, on socialism. Yet though his books already seemed to me mechanical, Calverton's accessibility and openness were a gift. He concealed nothing, and one of the greatest charms of those long, picturesquely dark Village rooms with a filigree-iron balcony overlooking the street, the apartment pervaded by a steady blue twilight from the walls of books and the great tree outside, was the deliciously lissome lady who presided officially over Calverton's establishment as his mistress.

I had never met a *mistress* before, and Calverton's crusading books on sex and "sexology" impressed me much less than did the sight of his marvelously curved and supple girl, who had a faint touch of a model's hauteur. One winter day, when I arrived at Calverton's "studio" to read proof of his magazine, I found her draped on a couch at the center of the room—she had a cold—and the sight of her in that room at the back looking out on the frozen little New York garden outside, of the winter light from the backyard turning everything steely and gray into my vision of Paris, of the proud girl lying there in perfect serenity, was the most rewarding experience I ever had reading proof in Calverton's house. There was an odor of herbs from the kitchen preparatory to some "French" dish, there was Calverton writing another book at his desk, there was I doing editorial chores, and there was the girl. Calverton's life was all before me, and I was grateful to be sharing so much of it. Everything about the girl immediately suggested a delicate offering, a subtle power to give pleasure, that contrasted sharply with the steady dates that were the rule in our neighborhood.

[1965]

III

———•◆•———

THE AGE OF REALISM

PREFACE TO
ON NATIVE GROUNDS

———— •◆• ————

Twenty or thirty years ago, when all the birds began to sing (almost, as it seemed, in chorus), the emergence of modern American literature after a period of dark ignorance and repressive Victorian gentility was regarded as the world's eighth wonder, a proof that America had at last "come of age." Today we no longer marvel over it; though that literature has become an established fact in our national civilization, we may even wonder a little uneasily at times how deeply we possess it, or what it is we do possess.

This book had its starting point in my conviction that a kind of historic complacency had settled upon American studies of that literature, and that while the usual explanation of it as a revolt against gentility and repression had the root of the matter in it, it did not tell us enough, and that it had even become a litany. It spoke of opportunities and freedoms won; it did not always tell us how they had been used, or whether literature had come with the freedom. It marked off the timidities of the older writers from the needs of the new; we were left to suppose that William Dean Howells was somehow inferior to James Branch Cabell. It made for so arrogant and limited a time sense that it virtually dated our modern writing from the day of John S. Sumner's collapse. It wrote the history of our early modern literature as a war to the death between Henry Van Dyke and Theodore Dreiser, or between

H. L. Mencken and the forces of darkness. It applied mechanically Santayana's well-worn phrase, the "Genteel Tradition," to everything Mencken's iconoclastic generation disliked in late nineteenth-century life. It allowed young people to suppose that *Jurgen* was somehow a great book because it had once been suppressed. It was a serviceable formula, the signature in pride of men who had often fought valiantly and alone for the creation of a free modern literature in America. But just as it dated time from 1920, the beginning of wisdom from the onslaught against "Comstockery," and confused Mencken with Voltaire, so it too often left out that larger story in which Mencken's great services were only one chapter—a story hardly limited to the historic modern struggle against "Puritanism," the rejection of the old prohibitions, and the attainment of a contemporary sophistication.

Our modern literature in America is at bottom only the expression of our modern life in America. That literature did not begin with the discovery of sex alone, with the freedom to attack ugliness and provincialism, or with the need to bring our culture into the international modern stream. Everything contributed to its formation, but it was rooted in nothing less than the transformation of our society in the great seminal years after the Civil War. It was rooted in that moving and perhaps inexpressible moral transformation of American life, thought, and manners under the impact of industrial capitalism and science, whose first great recorder was not Dreiser, but Howells—the Howells who, for all his prodigious limitations, was so alive to the forces remaking society in his time that he "foresaw no literature for the twentieth century except under Socialism, and said so"; the Howells who was so misinterpreted for my generation by some of the light-bringers of 1920—they saw only his prudery—that we have forgotten that for him, as for Tolstoy, morality meant also the relation of man to his society. Our modern literature was rooted in those dark years of the 1880s and 1890s, when all America stood suddenly between one moral order and another, and the sense of impending change became oppressive in its vividness. It was rooted in the drift to the new world of factories and cities, with their dissolution of old faiths; in the emergence of the metropolitan culture that was to dominate the literature of the new period; in the Populists who raised their voices against the domineering new plutocracy in the East and gave so much of their bitterness to the literature of protest rising out of the West; in the sense of surprise and shock that led to the crudely expectant Utopian literature of the eighties and nineties, the largest single body of Utopian writing in modern times, and the most transparent in its nostalgia. But above all was it rooted in the need to learn what the reality of life was in the modern era.

In a word, our modern literature came out of those great critical years of the late nineteenth century which saw the emergence of modern America, and was molded in its struggles. It is upon this elementary and visible truth—almost too elementary and visible, so close are we still to its crucible—that this book is based; and it was the implications following upon it that gave me some clue to the patterns of the writing that came after. It was my sense from the first of a literature growing out of a period of confused change, growing out of the conflict between two worlds of the spirit, that led me to begin the book with what is for me the great symbolic episode in the early history of American realism—the move from Boston to New York of William Dean Howells, the Brahmins' favorite child but the first great champion of the new writers. And it was this same conviction that American "modernism" grew principally out of its surprise before the forces making a new world that led me to understand a little better what is for me the greatest single fact about our modern American writing—our writers' absorption in every last detail of their American world together with their deep and subtle alienation from it.

There is a terrible estrangement in this writing, a yearning for a world no one ever really possessed, that rises above the skills our writers have mastered and the famous repeated liberations they have won to speak out plainly about the life men lead in America. All modern writers, it may be, have known that alienation equally well, and for all the reasons that make up the history of the modern spirit; have known it and learned to live with it as men learn to live with what they have and what they are. But what interested me here was our alienation *on* native grounds—the interwoven story of our need to take up our life on our own grounds, and the irony of our possession. To speak of modern American writing as a revolt against the Genteel Tradition alone, against Victorianism alone, against even the dominance of the state by special groups, does not explain why our liberations have often proved so empty; it does not tell us why the light-bringers brought us light and live themselves in darkness. To speak of it only as a struggle toward the modern emancipation—and it was that—does not even hint at the lean, tragic strain in our modern American writing, that sense of tragedy which is not Aristotle's, not even Nathaniel Hawthorne's, but a clutching violence, and from Dreiser to Faulkner, an often great depth of suffering. Nor does it tell us why our modern writers have had to discover and rediscover and chart the country in every generation, rewriting Emerson's *The American Scholar* in every generation (and the generations are many in modern American writing, so many), but must still cry America! America! as if we had never known America. As perhaps we have not.

No one has told us the whole story; no one can yet weave into it all the many different factors, the rhythms of growth, the subtle effects of our American landscape, the necessary sensibility to what it has meant to be a modern writer in America at all. No one can yet tell us all that F. Scott Fitzgerald meant when he said that "there are no second acts in American lives," or why we have been so oppressed by the sense of time, or why our triumphs have been so brittle. We can only feel the need of a fuller truth than we possess, and bring in our fragment, and wait. So is this book only a panel in the larger story, and not merely because it is limited to prose. It is in part an effort at moral history, which is greater than literary history, and is needed to illuminate it. For the rest, I am deeply conscious of how much I have left out, of how much there is to say that I have not been able to say. It is an intrusion on a living literature, and as tentative as anything in life. But it is clear to me that we have reached a definite climax in that literature, as in so much of our modern liberal culture, and that with a whole civilization in the balance, we may attempt some comprehensive judgment on the formation of our modern American literature.

A few words on critical method. In my study in chapter 13 of the twin fanaticisms that have sought to dominate criticism in America since 1930—the sociological and the textual-"aesthetic" approach—I have traced some of the underlying causes for the aridity and sheer human insensitiveness that have weighed down much serious criticism in our day. It may be sufficient to say here that I have never been able to understand why the study of literature in relation to society should be divorced from a full devotion to what literature is in itself, or why those who seek to analyze literary texts should cut off the act of writing from its irreducible sources in the life of men. We are all bound up in society, but we can never forget that literature is not produced by "society," but by a succession of individuals and out of individual sensibility and knowledge and craft. It has been given to our day in America, however, to see criticism—so basic a communication between men—made into either a scholastic technique or a political weapon. We have seen the relation of the writer to society either ignored or simplified, though it can never be ignored and is never simple. We have seen the life taken out of criticism, the human grace, the simple all-enveloping knowledge that there are no separate "uses" in literature, but only its relevance to the whole life of man. We have been oppressed by the anemic bookmen, the special propagandists, the scientists of metaphor. Inevitably—see only Van Wyck Brooks's *The Opinions of Oliver Allston*—there has been a reaction through sentimentality, a confusion of the complex relations that must persist between the good of society and the life of art.

True criticism only begins with books, but can never be removed from their textures. It begins with workmanship, talent, craft, but is nothing if it does not go beyond them. An affront when it is not sane, a mere game if it is not absorbed in that which gives it being and is greater than itself—greater even than the world of literature it studies—it can yet speak to men, if it will speak *to* them, and humbly. It wants nothing less than to understand men through a study of tools. In a letter to a young reviewer who had condescended to like one of his last novels, Sherwood Anderson wrote: "You do not blame me too much for not knowing all the answers." Criticism can never blame anyone too much for not knowing all the answers; it needs first and always to prove itself. . . .

[1942]

THE OPENING STRUGGLE
FOR REALISM

———— •◆• ————

They will have seen the new truth in larger and larger degree; and
when it shall have become the old truth, they will perhaps see it all.
—*W. D. Howells*

When, early in December of 1891, William Dean Howells surprised his
friends and himself by taking over the editorship of the failing *Cosmopolitan* in
New York, he thought it necessary to explain his decision to one of the few
friends of his early years surviving in Cambridge, Charles Eliot Norton.

> Dear Friend: I fancy that it must have been with something like a
> shock you learned of the last step I have taken, in becoming editor of
> this magazine. . . . The offer came unexpectedly about the beginning
> of this month, and in such form that I could not well refuse it, when
> I had thought it over. It promised me freedom from the anxiety of
> placing my stories and chaffering about prices, and relief from the
> necessity of making quantity. . . . I mean to conduct the magazine so
> that you will be willing to print something of your own in it. I am to
> be associated with the owner, a man of generous ideals, who will leave
> me absolute control in literature.

Lowell, for whom Howells had been "Dear Boy" even at fifty, and who
had corrected his Ohio ways with gentle patronizing humor down the years—
though no one could have become more the Bostonian than Howells—had

died that year, and Howells now requested from Norton, as Lowell's executor, a poem on Grant. Six months later Howells suddenly resigned. The experience had proved an unhappy one. It was the climax to a series of publishing ventures and experiments through which he had passed ever since he had left *The Atlantic Monthly* in 1881 and taken the literary center of the country with him, as people said, from Boston to New York.

For ten years after leaving Boston—and Howells was perfectly aware of the symbolic effect of his leaving—he had flitted in and out of New York, writing for the *Century* and *Scribner's*, conducting a column in *Harper's*, supporting himself in part by lectures, and growing older and more embittered than his friends and family had ever remembered him. Leaving Boston had been the second greatest decision of his life, as going to Cambridge in 1866 had been the first; and it had not been easy to tear up his roots in the New England world which had given him his chance and beamed upon his aptitudes and his growing fame. Now he could no longer return to that world even to accept the hallowed chair once occupied by Longfellow and Lowell, though it was pleasant to be asked and exhilarating to learn that the self-educated Ohio printer and journalist had become so commanding a figure in American letters. New York excited and saddened him at once; he once wrote to Henry James that it reminded him of a young girl, "and sometimes an old girl, but wild and shy and womanly sweet, always, with a sort of Unitarian optimism in its air." He clung to the city distractedly. "New York's immensely interesting," he had written to a Cambridge friend in 1888, "but I don't know whether I shall manage it; I'm now fifty-one, you know. There are lots of interesting young painting and writing fellows, and the place is lordly free, with foreign touches of all kinds all thro' its abounding Americanism: Boston seems of another planet." To James, whose every letter evoked the great days in Cambridge in the 1870s when they had dreamed of conquering the modern novel together, he wrote that he found it droll that he should be in New York at all. "But why not?" The weird, noisy, ebullient city, which in his novels of this period resounded to the clamor of elevated trains and street-car strikes, nevertheless suggested the quality of youth; and Howells, old at fifty, delighted in the Bowery, walks on Mott Street, Washington Square, and Italian restaurants. He had strange friends—Henry George lived a street or two away, and they saw each other often; he went to Socialist meetings and listened, as he said, to "hard facts"; he even entertained Russian nihilists. Indeed, he now called himself a Socialist, a "theoretical Socialist and a practical aristocrat." To his father he wrote, in 1890, "But it is a comfort to be right theoretically and to be ashamed of one-self practically."

A great change had come over Howells. The 1880s, difficult enough years for Americans learning to live in the tumultuous new world of industrial capi-talism, had come upon Howells as a series of personal and social disasters. The genial, sunny, conventional writer who had always taken such delight in the cheerful and commonplace life of the American middle class now found him-self rootless in spirit at the height of his career. *Facile princeps* in the popular esti-mation, the inspiration of countless young writers—was he not a proof that the self-made artist in America was the noblest type of success?—financially secure, he found that he had lost that calm and almost complacent pleasure in his countrymen that had always been so abundant a source of his art and the con-dition of its familiar success. To James he could now joke that they were both in exile from America, but acknowledged that for himself it was "the most grotesquely illogical thing under the sun; and I suppose I love America less because it won't let me love it more. I should hardly like to trust pen and ink with all the audacity of my social ideas; but after fifty years of optimistic con-tent with 'civilization' and its ability to come out all right in the end, I now abhor it, and feel that it is coming out all wrong in the end, unless it bases itself anew on a real equality." Never before had he missed that equality in American life; raised upon a casual egalitarianism and a Swedenborgian doctrine in his village childhood whose supernaturalism he had abandoned early for a religion of goodness, he had always taken the endless promise of American life for granted. His own career was the best proof of it, for he had always had to make his own way, and had begun setting type at eight. Now, despite his winning sweetness and famous patience, the capacity for good in himself which had always encouraged him to see good everywhere, his tender conscience and instinctive sympathy for humanity pricked him into an uncomfortably sharp awareness of the gigantic new forces remaking American life. Deep in Tolstoy—"I can never again see life in the way I saw it before I knew him"—he wrote to his sister Anne in November 1887 that even the fashionable hotel at which he was then staying in Buffalo caused him distress. "Elinor and I both no longer care for the world's life, and would like to be settled somewhere very humbly and simply, where we could be socially identified with the principles of progress and sympathy for the struggling mass. I can only excuse our present movement as temporary. The last two months have been full of heartache and horror for me, on account of the civic murder committed last Friday at Chicago."

The "civic murder"—stronger words than Howells had ever used on any subject—was the hanging of Albert Parsons, Adolf Fischer, George Engle, and August Spies in the Haymarket case. They had been found guilty in an atmosphere of virulent hysteria not—as the presiding justice readily admitted—because any proof had been submitted of their guilt or conspiracy, but because their Anarchist propaganda in Chicago had presumably incited the unknown assassin to throw the bomb that killed several policemen and wounded several more. Howells, who was perhaps as astonished that there were Anarchists in America as he was that legal machinery and public opinion could be mobilized to kill them, exerted himself passionately in their defense. He sought the aid of Whittier and George William Curtis, offered himself to the defendants' counsel, and published a plea for them in *The New York Tribune* on November 4, 1887. But without avail. "The thing forever damnable before God and abominable to civilized men," as he described the execution to a New York editor, shocked him into furious anger and disappointment. In letter after letter of this period, he poured out his vexation and incredulity. To his father he wrote, soon after the execution: "All is over now, except the judgment that begins at once for every unjust and evil deed, and goes on forever. The historical perspective is that this free Republic has killed five men for their opinions." To his sister, a week later: "Annie, it's all been an atrocious piece of frenzy and cruelty, for which we must stand ashamed forever before history. . . . Someday I hope to do justice to these irreparably wronged men." A year later Hamlin Garland, Howells's young Populistic disciple, could joke that Howells had become more radical than he. Garland, who was enthusiastic about Henry George and the single tax, noticed that Howells was lukewarm to it because he did not think it went deep enough. A year after the Haymarket executions, Howells was writing in deep solemnity of the "new commonwealth." "The new commonwealth must be founded in justice even to the unjust, in generosity to the unjust rather than anything less than justice. . . . I don't know yet what is best; but I am reading and thinking about questions that carry me beyond myself and my miserable literary idolatries of the past."

Abused by the pack for his stand in behalf of the Anarchists, Howells suddenly found himself in disfavor for other reasons. In those fateful years,

1886–92, when his social views were brought to a pitch of indignation and sympathy he had never known before and was certainly not to retain after 1900, he was conducting a campaign for the realistic novel in the "Editor's Study" column of *Harper's*. Realism had been his literary faith from his earliest days, his characteristic faith ever since he had known that his profession lay in the commonplace and the average. "Unconsciously I have always been," he wrote once, "as much of a realist as I could." He had absorbed realism from a dozen different sources—the eighteenth-century Italian dramatist Goldoni, the Spanish novelists Benito Galdós and A. Palacio Valdés, Turgenev and Tolstoy, Jane Austen (along with Tolstoy a prime favorite), Daudet, Mark Twain, and Henry James. He had been a practicing, virtually an instinctive, realist long before the word had come into popular usage in America—was he not the Champfleury of the novel in America?—and he could say with perfect confidence that realism was nothing more or less than the truthful treatment of material. Bred to a simple, industrious way of life that accepted candor and simplicity and detestation of the highfalutin as elementary principles of democratic life and conduct, he had applied himself happily for twenty years to the portraiture of a happy and democratic society.

Howells had, as Van Wyck Brooks has said, a suspicion of all romantic tendencies, including his own; his interest in sex was always so timid, his prudishness and modesty so compulsive, that he was as incapable of the romanticist's inflation of sex as he was unconcerned with the naturalist's "scientific" interest in it. His interest was in the domesticities of society, homely scenes and values, people meeting on trains, ships, and at summer hotels, lovers on honeymoon, friendly dinners, the furrows of homespun character, housekeeping as a principle of existence, and the ubiquitous *jeune fille* who radiated a vernal freshness in so many of his early novels and whose dictation of American literary taste he accepted, since men notoriously no longer read novels. Howells had therefore no reason to think of realism as other than simplicity, Americanism, and truth. Painters like Tom Eakins and his friend George Fuller—Howells had a strong feeling for painters, architects, mechanics, careful craftsmen of all types—worked in that spirit and wrought what they saw. Could American writers do any less? Was realism any less exciting for working in the commonplace, or less moving? Like Miss Emily Dickinson of Amherst, Massachusetts, another Yankee craftsman, Howells might have said, "Truth is so rare, it's delightful to tell it." When Matthew Arnold visited America on a celebrated lecture tour to pronounce America lacking in distinction and "uninteresting," William James laughed—"Think of *interesting* used as an absolute term!" Howells, characteristically, accepted the term gladly. What greater distinction was there than fidelity to the facts of one's lack of "distinction," to the savor and quality and worth of what was abiding and true?

Now, as Howells's views on society deepened, his allegiance to realism, his characteristic feeling for it, took on a new significance. The novel had swiftly and unmistakably, from the late seventies on, become the principal literary genre, and in the wave of renewed interest in the novel which filled the back columns of the serious magazines, Howells's sharp and stubborn defense of realism, seen in the light of his own social novels of this period, made him a storm center. His most ambitious works were disparaged by the romanticists, his judgments as a reviewer ridiculed, and his reputation seriously challenged. Zola, whom Howells had always espoused with lukewarm enthusiasm, could by the middle eighties claim for his work in America a certain tolerance, even a grudging admiration; but Howells, infinitely less dangerous, who never quite understood naturalism and had to the end of his life a pronounced distaste for it, was subjected to extraordinary abuse. One fashionable literary sheet, *The Literary World*, said as late as 1891 that many of Howells's realistic dicta were "as entertaining and instructive as that of a Pawnee brave in the Louvre." When Howells pleaded with young novelists to stick to life in America as they knew it, Maurice Thompson, a leader of the "romanticists," charged that Howells had said that mediocrity alone was interesting, and "a mild sort of vulgarity the living truth in the character of men and women.... All this worship of the vulgar, the commonplace, and the insignificant," Mr. Thompson declared, "is the last stage of vulgarity, hopelessness, and decadence."

One reader wrote to the *Atlantic Monthly* in 1892 that to read the books Howells recommended was "gratuitously to weaken one's vitality, which the mere fact of living does for most of us in such measure that what we need is tonic treatment, and views of life that tend to hopefulness, not gloom." Eminent critics of the nineties wrote bitterly that they were tired of fiction which wrestled with all the problems of life. F. Marion Crawford, the most successful, intelligent, and cynical of the romanticists, laughed that realists are expected "to be omniscient, to understand the construction of the telephone, the latest theories concerning the cholera microbe, the mysteries of hypnotism, the Russian language, and the nautical dictionary. We are supposed to be intimately acquainted with the writings of Macrobius, the music of Wagner, and the Impressionist school of painting." Howells, who did not know that the attacks upon him were more often attacks upon the naturalism to which his disposition was equally alien, was stung when the romanticists in full pack accused him of triviality and dullness. In November 1889, he wrote bitterly in *Harper's:*

> When you have portrayed "passion" instead of feeling, and used "power" instead of common sense, and shown yourself a "genius" instead of an artist, the applause is so prompt and the glory so cheap that really anything else seems wickedly wasteful of one's time. One may not make the reader enjoy or suffer nobly, but one may give him the kind of pleasure that arises from conjuring, or from a puppet show, or a modern stage play, and leave him, if he is an old fool, in the sort of stupor that comes from hitting the pipe.

As his popularity decreased, Howells found himself caught between two forces. The young realists and naturalists whom he befriended even when he did not enjoy them—Garland, Stephen Crane, Frank Norris—had made his exquisite cameo studies an anachronism; and by the nineties, when realism had won its first victory, it was being submerged by historical romanticism and Stevensonian gush. Realism had passed silently into naturalism, and had become less a method than a metaphysics. To those younger friends of Howells for whom he found publishers and wrote friendly reviews, but whom he could not fully understand; to the novelists of the Middle Border writing out in silent bitterness a way of life compounded of drought, domestic hysteria, and twelve-cent corn; to the metropolitan aesthetes nourished on Flaubert and Zola—to these realism was no longer an experiment or a claim to defend against gentility; it was the indispensable struggle against the brutality and anarchy of contemporary existence. In the first great manifesto of the American naturalists, *Crumbling Idols,* Hamlin Garland wrote exultantly: "We are about to enter the dark. We need a light. This flaming thought from Whitman will do for the search-light of the profound deeps. All that the past was not, the future will be." Yet with the exception of Frank Norris, the younger men were not even interested in the *theory of* naturalism, in the scientific jargon out of Claude Bernard, Darwin, and Taine with which Zola and his school bedecked *le roman expérimental.* Provincial and gawky even in their rebel-lion (a decade after Henry James had finally and devastatingly disposed of the "moral" purpose of fiction, young Garland was still tormented by it), lacking any cohesive purpose or even mutual sympathy, the young naturalists who had drawn the iron of American realism out of social discontent and the rebellion of their generation were united only in their indifference to the simpering ene-mies of realism and the forces of academic reaction. They loved Howells even if they did not always appreciate him, and like a hundred American critics of the future, regarded him as something of an old woman. They thought of Henry James (if they thought of him at all) as an old woman, too; but James, the greatest critic of his generation—and theirs—conducted his campaign for the novel on a plane they would never reach. Howells, never too strong in crit-ical theory, at least defended realism in terms the young men out of the West could assess, develop, or reject.

Yet what the naturalists missed in Howells, as so many others were to miss it for almost half a century after them, was that his delight in reality and his repugnance to romanticism clearly encouraged them to work at the reality they themselves knew. Whatever his personal limitations of taste and the prudery that was so obsessive that it does not seem altogether a quality of his age, Howells's service was to stimulate others and to lend the dignity of his spirit to their quest. Whatever the fatuousness or parochialism that could label "three-fifths of the literature commonly called classic . . . filthy trash" and set Daudet above Zola because the latter wrote of "the rather brutish pursuit of a woman by a man which seems to be the chief end of the French novelist," his insistence that young writers be true to life as they saw it—"that is the right American stuff"—was tonic. For if he was philosophically thin, he could be spiritually intense; he imparted a shy moral splendor to the via media, and though the range of his belief was often narrow, he suffered profoundly for it.*

---

*To Brander Matthews he wrote in 1902: "*The Kentons* has been fairly killed by the stupid and stupefying cry of commonplace people. I shall not live long enough to live this down, but possibly my books may. I confess that I am disheartened. I had hoped that I was helping my people know themselves in the delicate beauty of their everyday lives, and to find cause for pride in the loveliness of an apparently homely average, but they don't want it. They bray at my flowers picked from the fruitful fields of our common life, and turn aside among the thistles with keen appetites for the false and impossible."

Yet despite a disposition to the conventional that was so essential a part of his quality, the amiable old-fashionedness that he displayed from his earliest days, he was wonderfully shrewd, and he could hit hard. "These worthy persons are not to blame," he once wrote of the gentility opposed to realism. "It is part of their intellectual mission to represent the purification of taste, and to preserve an image of a smaller and cruder and emptier world than we now live in, a world which was feeling its way towards the simple, the natural, the honest, but was a good deal 'amused and misled' by lights no longer mistakable for heavenly luminaries." Never less pretentious than in his criticism, Howells could say with perfect justice that the nineteenth century, which had opened on the Romantic revolution, was now closing with equal splendor on the revolution of realism, since romanticism had plainly exhausted itself. "It remained for realism to assert that fidelity to experience and probability of motive are essential conditions of a great imaginative literature." Thus, with all its failings, *Criticism and Fiction,* Howells's little manifesto in behalf of realism, had the ring of leadership in it, and the aging novelist whose tender shoot of rebellion was his last great creative act had a wonderful eagerness for the future. The enemies of realism sigh over every advance, he smiled, but let them be comforted. "They will have seen the new truth in larger and larger degree; and when it shall have become the old truth, they will perhaps see it all."

[1942]

Nor did he ever live it down. His reputation, which began to sink in the middle eighties, reached its nadir soon after. Five years before his death in 1920, he wrote to Henry James: "I am comparatively a dead cult with my statues cut down and the grass growing over them in the pale moonlight."

TWO EDUCATIONS:
EDITH WHARTON AND
THEODORE DREISER

———— • ◆ • ————

Did you, too, O friend, suppose democracy was only for elections,
for politics, and for a party name?
                                    —*Whitman*, Democratic Vistas

Out of the "arrested energies" of the nineties, that great seminal period in
modern American life, there now emerged two distinguished novelists whose
careers, precisely because they were so diametrically opposed, help to illuminate the spirit of American experience and literature after 1900. Though both
did not receive appropriate recognition until the 1920s, when modern literature received its official "liberation," their best work was largely done by the
First World War, and the full significance of their work becomes clear only
when considered against the drift of American life between 1895 and 1914.

The society into which Edith Wharton was born was still, in the 1860s, the
predominant American aristocracy. Established in New York behind its plas-
ter cast of Washington, its Gibbon and its Hoppner, its Stuart and its
Washington Irving, it was a snug and gracious world of gentlewomen and
lawyers who stemmed in a direct line from the colonial aristocracy. Though it
was republican by habit where its eighteenth-century grandfathers had been
revolutionary by necessity, it was still a colonial society, a society superbly
indifferent to the tumultuous life of the frontier, supercilious in its breeding,

complacent in its inherited wealth. It was a society so eminently contented with itself that it had long since become nerveless, for with its pictures, its "gentlemen's libraries," its possession of Fifth Avenue and Beacon Hill, its elaborate manners, its fine contempt for trade, it found authority in its own history and the meaning of life in its own conventions.

To a writer's mind it was a museum world, delicately laid out on exhibition and impeccable in its sanctuary. To Edith Wharton that society gave a culture compounded equally of purity and snobbery. If no one soared above the conventions, only bounders sought to degrade them. Its gentility boasted no eagles of the spirit and suffered no fanatics. The young Edith Newbold Jones accepted it from the first and admired its chivalry to the end. Its kindliness, its precision of taste, its amenability, were stamped on her. She was educated to a world where leisure ruled and good conversation was considered fundamental. Even in New York, a city already committed to a commercial destiny, ladies and gentlemen of the ancien régime gathered for elaborate luncheon parties. "Never talk about money," her mother taught her, "and think about it as little as possible." The acquisition of wealth had ceased to interest her class. They looked down not in fear but with an amusement touched by repulsion upon the bustling new world of frontiersmen who were grabbing the West, building its railroads, and bellowing down the stock exchange. The revolution in Edith Wharton's world, characteristically a revolution of manners, came when the vulgarians of the new capitalism moved in upon Fifth Avenue. For to the aristocracy of New York, still occupying the seats of splendor in the sixties and seventies, the quiet and shaded region just above Washington Square was the citadel of power. There one lived soundlessly and in impeccable taste, the years filtering through a thousand ceremonial dinners, whispering conspiracies, and mandarin gossip. One visited in one's circle; one left one's card; one read the works of Mr. Hawthorne, Mr. Irving, Mr. Edward Bulwer-Lytton. Even as an old woman Edith Wharton was to fill her autobiography with the fondled memory of the great dishes eaten in her childhood, the exquisite tattle, the elaborate service, the births and marriages and deaths of slim patrician uncles and aunts and cousins bestriding time. It was the way of a people, as its not too rebellious daughter described it in *The Age of Innocence,* "who dreaded scandal more than disease, who placed decency above courage, and who considered that nothing was more ill bred than 'scenes,' except the behavior of those who gave rise to them." There were standards: the word *standard*, she confessed later, gave her the clue her writer's mind needed to the world in which she was bred. Bad manners were the supreme offense; it would have been bad manners to speak bad English, to nag servants. Edith Wharton's first literary effort, the work of her eleventh year, was a novel which began: " 'Oh, how do you do, Mrs. Brown?' said Mrs. Tompkins. 'If only I had known you were going to call I should have tidied up the drawing-room.' " Her mother returned it coldly, saying, "Drawing-rooms are always tidy."

Edith Wharton became a writer not because she revolted against her native society, but because she was bored with it; and that restlessness of the spirit was a primary achievement in such a world as hers. Whatever its graciousness, its almost classic sense of the past, its mildewed chivalry, the gentility which a colonial culture must always impose with exaggerated fervor and weight excluded women from every function save the cultivation of the home. Its distrust of the creative intelligence was as profound and significant as its devotion to the appurtenances of culture and the domestic elevation of library sets and vellum manuscripts. It worshiped literature as it worshiped ancestors, for the politeness of society; and if it distrusted the passions of literature, this was not because its taste was conscious and superior. It had not even that generous contempt for literature so marked in the boorish patronage of the arts by the industrial tycoons of the Gilded Age; it rejected what it could not understand because the creative elan affronted its chill, thin soul. It had already become a lifeless class, rigidly and bitterly conservative, filling its days with the desire to keep hold, to sit tight, to say nothing bold, to keep away from innovation and scandal and restless minds. There was no air in it, nothing to elevate an intellectual spirit; even its pleasures had become entirely ceremonial. To judge it in the light of the new world of industrial capitalism was to discriminate against it, for it offered no possibilities of growth.

By becoming a writer Edith Wharton did discriminate against it; but in the effort she liberated only her judgment, never her desire. She became a writer because she wanted to live; it was her liberation. But what it was she wanted to live for as a writer, she did not know. Unlike her master, Henry James, she did not begin with the conviction of a métier, the sense of craftsmanship and art; she did not even begin with that artist's curiosity which mediates between cultures, that passionate interest in ideas and the world's experiences which stimulates and nourishes the energy of art. She asked only to be a Writer, to adopt a career and enjoy a freedom; she offered nothing in exchange.

Even Edith Wharton's marriage, which might in other circumstances have liberated and matured her, repressed her. Her husband, as she confessed with remarkable candor in her autobiography—and the intensity and poignance of that confession was itself significant in so reticent and essentially trivial a record—was a conventional banker and sportsman of her own class, without the slightest interest in ideas and humiliatingly indifferent to her aspirations. Her greatest desire in youth had been to meet writers, not some particular master, but Writers; her marriage forced her into a life of impossible frivolity and dullness. It was a period in the middle Eighties when the younger generation of American aristocracy challenged the vulgar nouveaux riches by emulating their pleasures but soon came to admire them; the aspirant young novelist who had been married off at twenty-three in peremptory aristocratic fashion now found herself dreaming of literary conquests amidst a distracting and exasperating round of luncheons, parties, yachting trips, and ballroom dinners. "The people about me were so indifferent to everything I really cared for," she wrote in later life, "that complying with the tastes of others had become a habit, and it was only some years later, when I had written several books, that I finally rebelled and pleaded for the right to something better." In her earliest years her family had discouraged her; her husband and his friends now ridiculed her. They evidently spoke to her of her work only to disparage it; the young society woman had now to endure the crowning humiliation of pursuing even spasmodically a career which her immediate circle thought disgraceful and ridiculous. Then her husband became ill and remained so for a good many years. It was not a pleasant illness, and it diverted her from literature. Significantly enough, it was not until she was able to arrange for his care by others that she moved to Paris—her true home, as she always thought of it—where she lived until her death.

2

It is easy to say now that Edith Wharton's great subject should have been the biography of her own class, for her education and training had given her alone in her literary generation the best access to it. But the very significance of that education was her inability to transcend and use it. Since she could do no other, she chose instead to write, in various forms and with unequal success, the one story she knew best, the story that constituted her basic experience— her own. Her great theme, like that of her friend Henry James, became the plight of the young and innocent in a world of greater intricacy than they were accustomed to. But where James was obsessed by the moral complexity of that theme and devoted his career to the evaluation and dramatization of opposing cultures, Edith Wharton specialized in tales of victimization. To James the emotional problems of his characters were the representative expression of a larger world of speech, manners, and instinct—whose significance was psycho-logical and universal. He saw his work as a body of problems that tested the novelist's capacity for difficulty and responsibility. To Edith Wharton, whose very career as a novelist was the tenuous product of so many personal malad-justments, the novel became an involuted expression of self.

She was too cultivated, too much the patrician all her days, to vulgarize or even to simplify the obvious relations between her life and her work; she was too fastidious an artist even in her constricted sphere to yield to that obvious romanticism which fulfills itself in explicit confession. But fundamentally she had to fall back upon herself, since she was never, as she well knew, to rise above the personal difficulties that attended her career. She escaped the tedium and mediocrity to which her class had condemned her, but the very motivation of that escape was to become a great artist, to attain by the extension of her pow-ers the liberation she needed as a woman; and a great artist, even a completely devoted artist, she never became. James, who gave her friendship, could encour-age but not instruct her. Actually, it was not to become such a writer as he, but to become a writer, that she struggled; what he had to give her—precision of motive, cultivation of taste, the sense of style—she possessed by disposition and training. James's need of art was urgent, but its urgency was of the life of the spirit; Edith Wharton's was desperate, and by a curious irony she escaped that excessive refinement and almost abstract mathematical passion for art that encumbered James. She could speak out plainly with a force he could never muster; her own alienation and loneliness gave her a sympathy for erratic spir-its and "illicit" emotions that was unique in its time. It has been forgotten how much Edith Wharton contributed to the plain-speaking traditions of American realism. Women wrote to her indignantly asking if she had known respectable women; Charles Eliot Norton once even warned her that "no great work of the imagination has ever been based on illicit passion."

The greater consequence of Edith Wharton's failure to fulfill herself in art was its deepening of her innate disposition to tragedy. She was conscious of that failure even when she was most successful, and in the gap between her resolution and her achievement she had recourse to a classical myth, the pursuing Eumenides who will not let Lily Bart—or Edith Wharton—rest. She was among the few in her generation to attain the sense of tragedy, even the sense of the world as pure evil, and it found expression in the biting edge of her novels and the superficially genial fatalism of their drama. "Life is the saddest thing," she wrote once, "next to death," and the very simplicity and purity of that knowledge set her off in a literary generation to whom morality signified the fervor of the muckrakers and for whom death as a philosophical issue had no meaning. Spiritually, indeed, Edith Wharton was possessed of resources so much finer than any contemporary American novelist could muster that even the few superior novelists of her time seem gross by comparison. It was a service—even though, like so many artistic services, it was an unconscious one—to talk the language of the soul at a time when the best energies in American prose were devoted to the complex new world of industrial capitalism.

Yet what a subject lay before Edith Wharton in that world, if only she had been able, or willing, to use it! Her class was dying slowly but not painfully, and it was passing on into another existence. To write that story she would have had to tell bluntly how her class had yielded to the *novi homines* of the Gilded Age, how it had sold itself joyfully, given over its houses, married off its acquiescent daughters, and in the end—like all bourgeois aristocracies—asserted itself in the new dominion of power under the old standard of family and caste. It would have been the immemorial tale of aristocrat and merchant in a capitalist society, their mating, their mutual accommodation, their reconciliation. Edith Wharton knew that story well enough; its significance had sundered the only world she knew, and its victims were to crowd her novels. The fastidious college lawyers who had scorned the methods of a Daniel Drew in the seventies would do the work of a Carnegie in the nineties; the Newport settled first by the Whartons and their friends was now to become the great summer resort of the frontier-bred plutocracy; the New York that had crystallized around the houses and reputations of the Livingstons, the Crugers, the Schuylers, the Waltons, now gave room to the Vanderbilts, whose family crest might properly have been the prow of a ferryboat on a field gilded with Erie Railroad bonds, with the imperishable boast of its Commodore founder for a motto: "Law! What do I care about law? Hain't I got the power?" So had the eighteenth-century Dukes of Nottingham developed the mines on their hereditary estates; so would the seedy marquises of France under the Third Republic marry American sewing-machine heiresses. Howells had said it perfectly: the archetype of the new era was "the man who has risen." To tell that story as Edith Wharton might have told it would have involved the creation of a monumental tragicomedy, for was not the aristocracy from which she stemmed as fundamentally middle-class as the rising tide of capitalists out of the West it was prepared to resist?

Edith Wharton knew well enough that one dynasty had succeeded another in American life; the consequences of that succession became the great subject of her best novels. But she was not so much interested in the accession of the new class as she was in the destruction of her own, in the eclipse of its finest spirits. Like Lily Bart, Ellen Olenska, Ralph Marvell, she too was one of its fine spirits; and she translated effortlessly and pointedly the difficulties of her own career into the difficulties of young aristocrats amidst a hostile and alien culture. It is the aristocrat yielding, the aristocrat suffering, who bestrides her best novels: the sensitive cultivated castaways who are either destroyed by their own class or tied by marriage or need to the vulgar nouveaux riches. Henry James could write of revolutionaries and nobility, painters and politicians, albeit all talked the Jamesian language with the same aerial remoteness from plain speech; Edith Wharton's imagination was obsessed by the fellow spirits of her youth. Though she had been hurt by her class and had made her career by escaping its fundamental obligations, she could not, despite all her fertile powers of invention, conceive of any character who was not either descended from that class or placed in some obvious and dramatic relation to it. At bottom she could love only those who, like herself, had undergone a profound alienation but were inextricably bound to native loyalties and taste. Indeed, their very weakness endeared them to her: to rise in the industrial-capitalist order was to succumb to its degradations. "Why do we call our generous ideas illusions, and the mean ones truths?" cries Lawrence Selden in *The House of Mirth.* It was Edith Wharton's stricken cry. She had accepted all the conditions of servitude to the vulgar new order save the obligation to respect its values. Yet it was in the very nature of things that she should rebel not by adopting a new set of values or by interesting herself in a new society, but by resigning herself to soundless heroism. Thus she could read in the defeat of her characters the last proud affirmation of the caste quality. If failure was the destiny of superior men and women in the modern world, failure was the mark of spiritual victory. For that is what Edith Wharton's sense of tragedy came to in the end; she could conceive of no society but her own, she could not live with what she had. Doom waited for the pure in heart; and it was better so.

Is not that the theme of *Ethan Frome* as well as of *The House of Mirth*? Ethan, like Lily Bart or Ralph Marvell, fails because he is spiritually superior and materially useless; he has been loyal to one set of values, one conception of happiness, but powerless before the obligations of his society. It was not a New England story and certainly not the granite "folktale" of New England in essence its admirers have claimed it to be. She knew little of the New England common world, and perhaps cared even less; the story was begun as an exercise in French while she was living in Lenox, Massachusetts, and she wanted a simple frame and "simple" characters. The world of the Frome tragedy is abstract. She never knew how the poor lived in Paris or London; she knew even less of how they lived in the New England villages where she spent an occasional summer. There is indeed nothing in any of her work, save per-haps the one notable story she wrote of people who work for a living, *The Bunner Sisters*, to indicate that she had any conception of the tensions and responsibilities of even the most genteel middle-class poverty. Sympathy she possessed by the very impulse of her imagination, but it was a curious sympa-thy which assumed that if life in her own class was often dreary, the world "below" must be even more so. Whenever she wrote of that world, darkness and revulsion routinely entered her work. She thought of the poor not as a class but as a condition; the qualities she automatically ascribed to the poor—drabness, meanness, anguish—became another manifestation of the futility of human effort.

Edith Wharton was not confined to that darkness; she could hate, and hate hard, but the object of her hatred was the emerging new class of brokers and industrialists, the makers and promoters of the industrial era who were beginning to expropriate and supplant her own class. She disliked them no less fiercely than did the rebellious novelists of the muckrake era—the Robert Herricks, the David Graham Phillipses, the Upton Sinclairs; but where these novelists saw in the brokers and industrialists a new and supreme condition in

American society, Edith Wharton seemed to be personally affronted by them. It is the grande dame, not the objective novelist, who speaks out in her caricatures of Rosedale and Undine Spragg. To the women of the new class she gave names like Looty Arlington and Indiana Frusk; to their native habitats, names like Pruneville, Nebraska, and Hallelujah, Missouri. She had no conception of America as a unified and dynamic economy, or even as a single culture. There was old New York, the great house in Lenox (from which she gazed down upon Ethan Frome), and the sprawling wilderness that called itself the Middle West, a land of graceless manners, hoary jests, businessmen, and ridiculous provincial speech. It was a condescending resignation that evoked in her the crackling irony that smarted in her prose; it was the biting old dowager of American letters who snapped at her lower-class characters and insulted them so roundly that her very disgust was comic. As the world about her changed beyond all recognition, she ignored the parvenu altogether and sought refuge in nostalgia. Her social views, never too liberal or expansive, now solidified themselves into the traditional views of reaction. After 1920, when she had fulfilled her debt to the past with *The Age of Innocence*, she lost even that interest in the craft of fiction which had singled her out over the years, and with mechanical energy poured out a series of cheap novels which, with their tired and forlorn courtesy, their smooth rendering of the smooth problems of women's magazine fiction, suggest that Edith Wharton exhausted herself periodically, and then finally, because she had so quickly exhausted the need that drove her to literature.

If it is curious to remember that she always suggested more distinction than she possessed, it is even more curious to see how the interests of the American novel have since passed her by. James has the recurrent power to excite the literary mind. Edith Wharton, who believed so passionately in the life of art that she staked her life upon it, remains not a great artist but an unusual American, one who brought the weight of her personal experience to bear upon a modern American literature to which she was spiritually alien.

3

The fortunes of literature can reverse the fortunes of life. The luxury that nourished Edith Wharton and gave her the opportunities of a gentlewoman cheated her as a novelist. It kept her from what was crucial to the world in which she lived; seeking its manners, she missed its passion. Theodore Dreiser had no such handicap to overcome. From the first he was so oppressed by suffering, by the spectacle of men struggling aimlessly and alone in society, that he was prepared to understand the very society that rejected him. The cruelty and squalor of the life to which he was born suggested the theme of existence; the pattern of American life was identified as the figure of destiny. It was life, it was immemorial, it was as palpable as hunger or the caprice of God. And Dreiser accepted it as the common victim of life accepts it, because he knows no other, because this one summons all his resources.

Winter, Dreiser wrote in his autobiography, had always given him a physical sense of suffering.

> Any form of distress—a wretched, down-at-heels neighborhood, a poor farm, an asylum, a jail, or an individual or group of individuals anywhere that seemed to be lacking in the means of subsistence or to be devoid of the normal comforts of life—was sufficient to set up in me thoughts and emotions which had a close kinship to actual and severe physical pain.

He grew up in the friendly Indiana countryside of the eighties, in the very "Valley of Democracy" to be rhapsodized by Booth Tarkington and Meredith Nicholson; but he never shared its legendary happiness. His father, a crippled mill superintendent who was unable to provide for the family of fifteen, was a rigidly devout Catholic. The family separated periodically, the father going to Chicago to pick up work, the mother and younger children living in one small town after another. The bugaboo of social disapproval and scandal followed them insistently; at one time the mother kept a boardinghouse and a sister furnished the village gossips with a first-rate scandal. The family poverty was such that the town prostitute, his brother Paul's mistress, once sent them food and clothes, and even arranged for their removal to another city.

Dreiser grew up hating the shabby and threadbare rationale of the poor as only their sensitive sons learn to hate it; he hated his father as much for his repellent narrowness of belief as for his improvidence, and pitied his mother because she seemed so ineffectual in the face of disaster. The shining success in the family was his brother Paul, who became a popular vaudeville artist and composer. It was a painful, brooding boyhood, whose livid scars were to go into the first chapters of *An American Tragedy;* a boyhood touched by the lonely joys of wallowing in Ouida and *Tom Jones,* but seared by the perennial separations of the family and its grim and helpless decline. There was stamped upon Dreiser from the first a sense of the necessity, the brutal and clumsy dispensation of fate, that imposed itself upon the weak. He hated something nameless, for nothing in his education had prepared him to select events and causes; he hated the paraphernalia of fate—ill luck, the shadowy and inscrutable pattern of things that grounds effort into the dust. He did not rebel against it as one who knows what the evil is and how it may be destroyed; he was so overpowered by suffering that he came to see in it a universal principle.

As Dreiser wandered disconsolately through the Nineties, a reporter and magazine writer in New York and Chicago, St. Louis and Pittsburgh and Toledo, he began to read the pronouncements of nineteenth-century mechanism in Darwin and Spencer, in Tyndall and Huxley. They gave him not a new insight but the authority to uphold what he had long suspected. They taught him to call a human life a "chemism," but they did not teach him the chemical nature of life; they suggested that man was an "underling," a particle of protoplasm on a minor planet whirling aimlessly in the solar system, which for such a mind as Dreiser's was an excellent way of calling man what Dreiser had from his earliest days known man to be—a poor blind fool. The survival of the fittest was not a lesson in biology to be gathered in Darwin; it was the spectacle of the nineties as Dreiser watched and brooded over it in the great industrial cities that had within the memory of a single generation transformed the American landscape. For whatever the middle-class environment of his boyhood had given him, it was not its laissez-faire theology. Capitalism had denied the young Dreiser its prizes, but it had not blinded him to its deceptions. All about him in the convulsive Nineties, with their railroad strikes and Populist riots, Dreiser saw American society expanding as if to burst, wealth rising like mercury in the glass, the bitter shambles of revolt, the fight for power. While Robert Herrick was peering anxiously through his academic window and Edith Wharton was tasting the pleasures of Rome and Paris, while David Graham Phillips was reporting the stale scandals of New York high society for Pulitzer and Frank Norris was eagerly devouring the history of California for *The Octopus,* Dreiser was walking the streets of Chicago, the dynamic, symbolic city which contained all that was aggressive and intoxicating in the new frontier world that lived for the mad pace of bull markets and the orgiastic joys of accumulation. He was not of that world, but he understood it. Who could resist the yearning to get rich, to scatter champagne, to live in lobster palaces, to sport the gaudy clothes of the new rich? It was easy enough for those who had made a religion of their desire; it was easier still for a poor young writer who had been so hurt by poverty and the poor that the call of power was the call of life.

What Dreiser learned from that world was that men on different levels of belief and custom were bound together in a single community of desire. It was not the plunder that excited him, the cheating and lying, the ruthlessness and the pious excuses; it was the obsession with the material. A subtler mind, or a less ambitious one, might have cackled in derision; but Dreiser was swept away by the sheer intensity of the passion for accumulation. In *The Titan* he was to introduce a staggering procession of Chicago buccaneers on "Change" with the same frowning, slow, heavy earnestness with which Abraham might have presented his flocks to God. He was fascinated by the spectacular career of Charles T. Yerkes, the most dazzling financier of his day, whose reckless energy and demoniac thirst for money spelled the highest ambition of his culture. Power had become not an instrument but a way of life. The self-conscious tycoons sat a little insecurely before their gold plate, their huge and obvious pictures, giggled perhaps in rare moments at their ostentatious and overdressed wives; but to Dreiser they represented the common soul's most passionate hopes made flesh. The symbols of power had become monumental: stocks and bonds blown feverishly into imitation French chateaux, the luxury of yachts, and conquerors' trips to Europe.

These evidences of success were something Dreiser could neither approve nor disapprove. Secretly, perhaps, he may have admired them for taking the American dream out of the literary testaments and crowning it with a silk hat; but what caught him was the human impulse that stole through the worst show of greed and gave it as natural and simple a character as local pride or family affection. As he wrote the story of Frank Algernon Cowperwood (Yerkes himself) in *The Financier* and *The Titan*, his plan was to build by tireless research and monumental detail a record of the industrial-commercial ethic. Though both novels were published at the height of the Progressive agitation, they have nothing in common with the superficial distaste that ruled David Graham Phillips's books, or with the sensitive homilies of Robert Herrick's.

For the muckraking novel of the Theodore Roosevelt era assumed as its first premise that the society it excoriated was a passing condition; the novelists of the period based their values either on the traditional individualism and amenity of an agricultural and small owner's way of life (which was the ideal of the Progressive movement), or on the ideal society of Socialism, as did London and Sinclair. Dreiser would neither tinker with that society nor reject it. It was the only society he knew, the only society he had been allowed to understand; it was rooted in the same rock with poverty and mischance, strength and valor; it was life in which, as he wrote, "nothing is proved, all is permitted."

It was this very acceptance that gave him his strength. Since he could conceive of no other society, he lavished his whole spirit upon the spectacle of the present. Where the other novelists of his time saw the evils of capitalism in terms of political or economic causation, Dreiser saw only the hand of fate. Necessity was the sovereign principle. "We suffer for our temperaments, which we did not make," he once wrote, "and for our weaknesses and lacks, which are no part of our willing or doing." There was in nature "no such thing as the right to do, or the right not to do." The strong went forward as their instinct compelled them to; the weak either perished or bore life as best they could. Courage was one man's fortune and weakness another man's incapacity.

In a lesser novelist this very dependence upon fate as a central idea might have been disastrous; it would have displayed not an all-encompassing intensity but mere ignorance. Dreiser rose to the top on the strength of it. He raised Cowperwood-Yerkes to the level of destiny, where another might have debased him below the level of society. Cowperwood becomes another Tamburlane; and as one remembers not the cities that Tamburlane sacked but the character that drove him to conquest and the Oriental world that made that character possible, so one sees Cowperwood as the highest expression of the acquisitive society in which he rules so commandingly. His very spirit may seem repulsive; his ostentation, his multitudinous adulteries, his diabolism, his Gothic pile in Philadelphia and Renaissance palace in New York, merely a display of animalism. But we do not indict him for his ruthlessness and cunning; we despise his rivals because they envy him the very brutality with which he destroys them. When Cowperwood slackens (it cannot be said that he ever fails), it is not because his jungle world has proved too much for him, but because it is not enough. He has exhausted it by despoiling it, as he has exhausted his wives, his partners, his friends, and the sycophantic ingenuity of the architects to the rich. One remembers that poignant episode in which Cowperwood confesses to Stephanie Platow that his hunger for life increases with age but that men have begun to judge him at their own value. He must accept less from life because he has surged beyond its traditional limitations.

4

It was by a curious irony that Dreiser's early career became the battleground of naturalism in America. He stumbled into the naturalist novel as he has stumbled through life. It is doubtful that he would have become a novelist if the fight for realism in American letters had not been won before he arrived on the scene; but when he did, he assumed as a matter of course that a tragic novel so indifferent to conventional shibboleths as *Sister Carrie* was possible. Frank Norris became a naturalist out of his admiration for Zola; Stephen Crane, because the ferocious pessimism of naturalism suited his temperament exactly. Naturalism was Dreiser's instinctive response to life; it linked him with the great primitive novelists of the modern era, like Hamsun and Gorky, who found in the boundless freedom and unparalleled range of naturalism the only approximation of a life that is essentially brutal and disorderly. For naturalism has always been divided between those who know its drab environment from personal experience, to whom writing is always a form of autobiographical discourse, and those who employ it as a literary idea. The French naturalists, and even their early disciples in America, found in its clinical method, its climate of disillusion, their best answer to romantic emotion and the romantic ideal. Naturalism was the classicism of the nineteenth century. Flaubert, Zola, Stephen Crane, and Frank Norris were all suckled in the romantic tradition; they turned to naturalism to disown romantic expansiveness, lavishness of color, and the inherent belief that man is capable of molding his own destiny. To a Flaubert and a Stephen Crane the design became all; it was the mark of fatality in human life rather than life as a seamless web of imponderable forces that interested them. Much as Pope proclaimed in *An Essay on Man* that

> *In human works, though laboured on with pain,*
> *A thousand movements scarce one purpose gain . . .*

So Man, who here seems principal alone,
Perhaps acts second to some sphere unknown,

so the classic naturalists furnished case histories of suffering to describe the precise conditions under which, as a citizen of the urban industrial world, modern man plans his life, fumbles in the void, and dies.

What Dreiser gave to the cause of American naturalism was a unique contribution. By exploding in the face of the Genteel Tradition, *Sister Carrie* made possible a new frankness in the American novel. It performed its function in literary history by giving the "new" morality of the nineties the example of solid expression; but it liberated that morality quite undeliberately. The young Dreiser, as John Chamberlain has put it, "had not been accepted by Puritan-commercial folk; therefore he was not loaded down in childhood with hampering theories of the correct way in which to live and act and write." The same formless apprenticeship and labored self-education which kept him from the stakes of modern society shielded him from its restrictions. He had no desire to shock; he was not perhaps even conscious that he would shock the few people who read *Sister Carrie* in 1900 with consternation. It would never have occurred to Dreiser that in writing the story of Hurstwood's decline he was sapping the foundations of the genteel. With his flash, his loud talk and fine linen, his rings and his animal intelligence, Hurstwood was such a man as Dreiser had seen over and over again in Chicago. The sleek and high-powered man of affairs automatically became Dreiser's favorite hero. To tell his story was to match reality; and the grossness and poignance of that reality Dreiser has known better than any other novelist of our time.

Dreiser's craftsmanship has never been copied, as innumerable writers have copied from Stephen Crane or even from Jack London. There has been nothing one could copy. With his proverbial slovenliness, the barbarisms and incongruities whose notoriety has preceded him into history, the bad grammar, the breathless and painful clutching at words, the vocabulary dotted with "trig" and "artistic" that may sound like a salesman's effort to impress, the outrageous solecisms that give his novels the flavor of sand, he has seemed the unique example of a writer who remains great despite himself. It is by now an established part of our folklore that Theodore Dreiser lacks everything except genius. Those who have celebrated him most still blush a little for him; he has become as much a symbol of a certain fundamental rawness in American life as Spanish villas on Main Street and Billy Sunday.

Yet by grudging complete homage to him, Americans have innocently revealed the nature of the genius that has moved them. As one thinks of his career, with its painful preparation for literature and its removal from any literary tradition, it seems remarkable not that he has been recognized slowly and dimly, but that he has been recognized at all. It is because he has spoken for Americans with an emotion equivalent to their own emotion, in a speech as broken and blindly searching as common speech, that we have responded to him with the dawning realization that he is stronger than all the others of his time, and at the same time more poignant; greater than the world he has described, but as significant as the people in it. To have accepted America as he has accepted it, to immerse oneself in something one can neither escape nor relinquish, to yield to what has been true and to yearn over what has seemed inexorable, has been Dreiser's fate and the secret of his victory.

An artist creates form out of what he needs; the function compels the form. Dreiser has been one of the great folk writers, as Homer, the author of *Piers Ploughman*, and Whitman were folk writers—the spirits of simplicity who raise local man as they have known him to world citizenship because their love for him is their knowledge of him. "It was wonderful to discover America," Dreiser repeated once after another, "but it would have been more wonderful to lose it." No other writer has shared that bitterness, for no other has affirmed so doggedly that life as America has symbolized it is what life really is. He has had what only Whitman in all the history of the American imagination had before him—the desire to give voice to the Manifest Destiny of the spirit, to preserve and to fulfill the bitter patriotism of loving what one knows. All the rest have been appendages to fate.

[1942]

AN INSURGENT SCHOLAR: THORSTEIN VEBLEN

———•◆•———

In 1919, when he had come to New York to lecture at the New School for Social Research and to write editorials for *The Dial*, Thorstein Veblen published a characteristic little essay in a professional journal in which he expressed the hope that the Jews would never form a nationalistic movement of their own, since that would be a loss to world culture.

> It appears to be only when the gifted Jew escapes from the cultural environment created and fed by the particular genius of his own people, only when he falls into the alien lines of Gentile inquiry and becomes a naturalized, though hyphenate, citizen in the Gentile republic of learning, that he comes into his own as a creative leader in the world's intellectual enterprise. It is by loss of allegiance, or at the best by force of a divided allegiance to the people of his origin, that he finds himself in the vanguard of modern inquiry.

For the first requisite for constructive work in modern science, Veblen continued, is skepticism; the Jew, lost between the native tradition he has discarded and the Gentile world he can never fully accept, is a skeptic by force of circumstances over which he has no control. . . . He becomes a disturber of the intellectual peace, but only at the cost of becoming an intellectual wayfaring man, a wanderer in the intellectual no-man's-land, seeking another place to rest, farther along the road, somewhere over the horizon.

It was one of Veblen's rare self-portraits. He put the matter a little portentously, as he did everything, half in jest, half because he could not help it (a later generation, discovering that he often affected a witty pomposity, would think his prose nothing but elaborate impersonation); but he exposed the austerity and poignance of his intellectual career as few of his exegetes and literary admirers ever have. He was, in truth, an "intellectual wayfaring man and a disturber of the intellectual peace." His own generation thought him ridiculous or vaguely dangerous, when it did not ignore him; a later generation, having heard that his economic heresies have become commonplace, thinks of him chiefly as an economist who spent most of his time parodying the official prose of other economists and designing lugubrious epigrams for clever intellectuals. As a phrasemonger for critics of the established order, Veblen has become a hero of the intelligentsia. As a Cassandra foretelling the collapse of the economic order in 1929, a satirist of the status quo and the conduct of the middle class, he has even appeared to be one of the most substantial figures in the development of a native radicalism. But that is another phase of Veblen's public reputation and the public legend which delights in his domestic eccentricities and has forgotten that he was one of the most extraordinary and tragic figures in the history of the American imagination.

Professionally Veblen was a leading figure in the destruction of classical economics in America and a post-Darwinian who adapted evolutionary insights and methods in every available social study to institutional economics. But he was also a Western writer with an agrarian background who belonged to Hamlin Garland's generation and shared the problems of Theodore Dreiser's. He was a Norwegian farmer's son who, like so many of his background, was half-destroyed by the struggle to attain self-liberation in the endless conflict with the hostile dominating culture. Veblen was an alien twice over, for he was by every instinct estranged not only from the "pecuniary culture" of the East, but also from the native tradition and speech of his neighbors. He was not Norwegian, but his imaginative sympathies were linked to the parental culture; he was an American scholar and trained exclusively in America, but he spoke English always with a slight accent and wrote it always with more difficulty than his subsequent literary admirers were to know. Until he went to school, English had been a foreign language, and the young Norskie who scandalized the denominational world of Carleton College, Minnesota, in the Eighties by championing Bjornson and Ibsen (and the Greenbackers) spent a good part of his life pottering at a translation of the great Norwegian Laxdaela Saga.

The conflicts in modern society which Veblen was later to describe so mordantly made themselves felt in the tensions of his own life and personality from the first. He was a solitary in every sense: an immigrant farmer's son who was prodigiously brilliant but could not find his way; a child of the equalitarian and Populist ideas of his time and region who had no great love for farmers and only a vast contempt for contemporary provincial ignorance. He was not of the Gentile world of bourgeois culture and intellectual prestige, but he belonged in it; and it was already clear that he would not get too many of the Gentiles' prizes. He was arrogant, lonely, curious, and difficult.

When he went to Yale in the late eighties for his doctorate, he saw that the culture he needed was not a culture he could believe in. President Noah Porter, under whom he studied, was intellectually feudal, the exponent of a tradition that seemed irrelevant to Veblen's absorbed study of the industrial culture that he had already learned to regard as the enemy of his mind and fortune. Yet when William Graham Sumner, under whom Veblen also studied, railed against Porter's Greco-Latin conception of a gentlemanly leisure-class education, he could not have known that to Veblen the authentic leisure class was the rising business class whose needs Sumner preached so warmly.

For seven years after receiving his degree, Veblen searched fruitlessly for an academic post and lived among farmers in the Middle West. At thirty-five, after serving as a fellow at Cornell, he was engaged by J. Laurence Laughlin to teach at the Rockefeller-endowed University of Chicago. Like Fuller, Dreiser, Herrick, and so many others of his realistic generation, Veblen had finally made his way to the "cliff-city," the great apex of the commercial spirit in America that was to furnish him with so many notes on the institutional habits of a profit society. The newly opened university gave Veblen his chance and introduced him to a gifted group that included Albert Michelson, John Dewey, Jacques Loeb, and George H. Mead, among others. With its "oil blessings" from Rockefeller, its Baptist heritage, its gift of an observatory from the notorious traction magnate Charles T. Yerkes (Dreiser's Cowperwood), it was also an abundant source of evidence for a mind like Veblen's. To deck out his university, President Harper had robbed the academic halls of America of their best brains and most illustrious reputations; and with his shambling gait, his inscrutable but mocking foreignisms, his air of failure, Veblen was a dubious asset. He was, as the Veblenians forget, a very bad and frequently inaudible teacher; but it is a matter of record that when a friend urged Veblen's promotion (at forty-two he had barely attained the rank of instructor), President Harper replied that Veblen might leave if he wished; he "did not advertise the university." It was not for nothing that when Veblen came to write *The Higher Learning in America* (subtitled *A Memorandum on the Conduct of Universities by Business Men*), he should have written of the relation of university teachers to the businessman: "They have eaten his bread and it is for them to do his bidding." Veblen's bitterness and frustration were now to enter into the composition of his work. It was at Chicago that he composed his first great portrait, written in fury and sardonic contempt, of the business culture, *The Theory of the Leisure Class.*

2

Significantly, the book was immediately picked up by literary people; it was Howells who wrote the review that helped to make it famous. No other economist would have thought of writing the book; not too many economists at the moment troubled to read it. Yet for all its rhetorical tricks and ambitious literary manner, it was a purely professional work from Veblen's own point of view. In his earliest essays, notably, "Why Is Economics Not an Evolutionary Science?" he had attacked classical economics on the grounds that it was pre-evolutionary in its method, artificial in its logic, and a "system of economic taxonomy." Drawing upon the radical psychological studies of William James, Jacques Loeb, and John Dewey, which had already destroyed the mechanical antiquated psychology that buttressed classical economics, Veblen had become the principal exponent of a modern and genetic economics. Economics had too long been a pseudo-metaphysical study of Manchester "natural law." At this time he wrote:

In so far as it is a science in the current sense of the term, any science, such as economics, which has to do with human conduct, becomes a

genetic inquiry into the human scheme of life; and where, as in economics, the subject of inquiry is the conduct of man in his dealings
with the material means of life, the science is necessarily an inquiry
into the life-history of material civilization, on a more or less
extended or restricted plan.... Like all human culture this material
civilization is a scheme of institutions—institutional fabric and institutional growth.

It was this insight into the need for an economics that would constitute an
"inquiry into the life-history of material civilization" that gave a design to *The
Theory of the Leisure Class* and suggested the imaginative range and depth of
Veblen's mind. He had always been an omnivorous student of anthropology
and social psychology, of folk habit and language (he had once seriously
thought of devoting himself to philology). As an evolutionary economist, a
student of contemporary material civilization in all its complexity, he could
now freely study the bourgeois Americanus with impunity and in the interests
of a modern institutional economics. For as an anthropologist of the contemporary, an anatomist of society, an evolutionist who had synthesized the social
studies, he could now legitimately describe his interpretation of the history of
civilization—in his eyes a history of predation, conquest, and ostentatious
leisure. Later, in books like *The Theory of Business Enterprise* and *The Instinct of
Workmanship*, this theory would develop into his famous doctrine that the
industrial skill that runs modern technology is opposed to those who draw
their profits from it; that there is an inveterate conflict between engineers and
businessmen, efficiency and the profit system, the Veblens of this world and
university trustees in general.

The Veblen who had always been the great outsider, who as a cultural and
social alien had always been obsessed by cultural differences, now found that
he could investigate them with propriety. The Veblen who "loved to play with
the feelings of people not less than he loved to play with ideas" could now
adapt his contempt and hatred for the pecuniary culture to a playful "scientific" scrutiny. As an evolutionist, Veblen could now prove, as Alvin Johnson
once put it, that "the pirate chieftain of one epoch becomes the captain of
industry of another; the robber baron levying upon peaceful trade becomes the
financial magnate." The introduction to *The Theory of the Leisure Class* featured a
solemn study of leisure-class habits among Eskimos and Japanese and Pacific

islanders; the subject was Dreiser's Cowperwood and Norris's *Octopus* and David Graham Phillips's *Reign of Gilt.*

Veblen was, at bottom, not an anthropologist at all, and possibly not as learned as his display of neolithic data seemed to indicate; but he could use anthropology as a form of malicious genealogy and ethnology as a medium of "protective coloration." He had no direct interest in the past; he always despaired of the future; but the material civilization of the present was his subject, even his obsession, and he made the most of it. His great insight, and the one on which he literally deployed his fantastic erudition, was the realization that in the process of human evolution the businessman had become the archetype of modern Christendom. His learning became a series of illustrations by which to "prove" that the warrior of barbarism had given way to the priest and noble of feudalism only to yield in turn to the trader, the financier, and the industrialist. Beneath the ferocious solemnity of manner and the humor that was only an exaggeration of a psychic habit, Veblen could now vent his hatred of modern capitalism on a study of the materialism that sustained it and the elaborate pattern of manners, dress, ritual, education, that illustrated its vulgarity and its greed.

The satiric element in Veblen's book is almost pyrotechnical in its elaboration; but the art in his prose has often been exaggerated. The Veblen legend of a great prose craftsman stems from the fact that Veblen wrote a prose aesthetically more interesting than most economists in America (not to forget literary historians, political scientists, and philosophers) have ever written or seem likely to; it has even thrived on the delightful irony that he must always seem imaginatively superior to many American novelists and critics. But the fact remains that he was as much the victim of his material as he was the master of it, and that the pains he took with his prose should not obscure the pain he can still inflict on his readers. If he sought at times to outrage deliberately, he succeeded too often without premeditation; though he loved to parody academic solemnity, it was his natural element. For though Veblen was an extraordinary phrase-maker and even an epigrammatist of superb wit, he was, as John Chamberlain once said, not a good sentence-maker. The peculiar quality of his prose lies, like Dreiser's, in the use he made of a naturally cumbersome and (despite its polysyllabic sophistication) primitive medium. The ironist in Veblen, occasionally mad and often delightful, was always a little ponderous. He succeeded too often, as in his famous passage on "the taxonomy of a monocotyledonous wage-system," by wringing academic jargon to death; but the humor was monstrously grotesque. Veblen's trickery as a writer lay in his use of the "grand" style, but he did not choose it; it chose him.

For Veblen *was* an alien; and like so many alien writers, he had a compensatory need (as he would have said) for formality. The deracinated always exaggerate the official tone of the race among whom they are living at the moment, and to no one could dignified circumlocutions have been so natural in the nineties as to a Norwegian farmer's son moving in the company of academic intellectuals who did not accept him. Veblen had that certain pompousness of style, largely undeliberate, which has not yet ceased to be the mark of the professional scholar in America; in his early years it was an article of clothing like the Prince Albert coat, and in many respects resembled it. In a day when wild-eyed Populists wrote like senators, and senators talked like Shakespeare's Romans, purity of style demanded a compelling direct interest in diction and rhythm, which Veblen did not have. He often parodied the academic style, but with a suffering mischievousness that betrays the intensity of his exasperation. His leading ideas were brilliant intuitions, but he developed their implications slowly, so that the quality of his prose is often characterized by insensitiveness to proportion. Every style is an accumulation of psychic habits and records some organic personal rhythm; the Veblen who mumbled in the classroom those "long spiral sentences, reiterative like the Eddas," as John Dos Passos called them, also mumbled in his book.

From this point of view Veblen's celebrated irony and prose devices do not appear any less skillful and amusing than worshipful admirers of his style have claimed them to be; they are merely one phase of his temperament and his powers as a writer. He used devices and played with grotesque phrases; he startled the reader into an awareness of the ties that exist everywhere in modern "material civilization" between new institutions and the use men make of them, between habits of work and prejudices of thought. But his style was not, as such, a pullover satiric style like Swift's or the one Goldsmith employed in his Chinese letters. A satiric style is a dramatic characterization, an impersonation; Veblen's verbosity was often painfully ingenuous. When he was ironic, as in a famous passage in *The Theory of the Leisure Class* in which he disclaimed any invidious use of the word *invidious*, the humor was almost too palpable for comfort. "In making use of the term 'invidious,' it may perhaps be unnecessary to remark, there is no intention to extol or deprecate, or to commend or deplore.... The term is used in a technical sense as describing a comparison of persons with a view to rating and grading them in respect of relative worth or value..." and so forth. This type of bearish pleasantry appeared in his definition of leisure as connoting "non-productive consumption of time," which was a hit, a very palpable hit indeed at the jargon of economists, and one that pointed up his satiric interpretation of leisure in modern bourgeois society.

It may be true that Veblen's solemnity of style was a medium of concealing his contempt for the pecuniary culture; but he did not conceal it, and it is an extremely simple and even sentimental criticism which can suppose that Veblen did nothing but play the comedian for thirty years in a world that he found excruciatingly wretched. He had, admittedly, a masquerade; but it was a projection of desperation as well as a disguise. The native self, and the native prolixity, often stole through. For all his labor, he seems to have had a lurking cynicism toward his own work, as if it were only another aspiration that had been disappointed. Veblen's view of the world was not only mordant, it was densely, even profoundly, tragic. As a satirist in *The Theory of the Leisure Class* he could write with almost cheerful irony of the "peaceful," the "sedentary," the "poor," whose "most notable trait" was a "certain amiable inefficiency when confronted with force or fraud"; but his obsession with the forms and honors of property did not, in later books, conceal his despair at their supremacy.

No one before Veblen had realized with such acuteness the monstrous conflict between what he called the instinct of workmanship and the profit motive; the conflict became the design he saw in modern life. In his mind the conflict was not between capital and labor, but between capital and the intellectual élite which ran the profit system for capital and sacrificed itself for capital. He was never interested in the Marxian dream of a revolution by the working class; he had a certain contempt for Marxism, and thought of it as romantic and, in one sense, even unintelligible. The tragedy of that other class struggle, as Veblen saw it, was that it could never be resolved. The engineers, the symbolic protagonists of a harmonious new world, could do nothing about it. In Veblen's view, as Max Lerner has expounded it, "man finds himself ever farther away from the sense of economy and workmanship and social order that his primitive instincts called for. And as if to deepen the irony of his position, every attempt that he makes to adjust himself rationally to the new conditions of life is doomed by the nature of his own institutions." This dilemma had the ruthless severity of Greek tragedy, in which man, like

Prometheus, has brought light to the world but must suffer for it. The interests of profit and the community, of industry and business, of skill and greed, were diverse. "Gain may come to" the business classes, Veblen wrote in *The Theory of Business Enterprise,* "whether the disturbance makes for heightened facility or for widespread hardship." Modern life had become petrified in institutional habits of waste and greed. Like Henry Adams, Veblen had a bitter respect for the machine process, but he did not regard it as a literary symbol; it had become the focus of the modern tragedy. The machine, as Veblen was among the first to show, had its own rhythm, which it dictated to men and compelled them to live by. The will rebelled, the machine persisted; the critical mind might quarrel with it, the body acquiesced.

Only a thinker who had so pressing a need of social change could have brought so much passion to the doubt of its realization. Veblen's distinction as an American writer of his time was thus uniquely tragic. He saw what so few in his generation could ever see; yet he affirmed nothing and promised nothing. Lonely all through a fairly long life plagued by poverty, alienation, ill health, he suffered even more deeply from the austere honesty of his vision. Applauded by Marxists for his attacks upon the status quo, he laughed at their optimism; he threw the whole weight of his life into his examination of the pecuniary culture, but bolstered its institutional vanity. He was a naturalist, a more tragic-minded and finely conscious spirit than any American novelist of the naturalist generation; his final view of life was of an insane mechanism, of a perpetual and fruitless struggle between man and the forces that destroy him. Yet though he had what Dreiser and Crane and Norris seemed to lack, he was not their equal as an artist. He knew the rationale of everything where Dreiser, for example, has known only how to identify all life with the poignant gracelessness of his own mind; but he did not have the ultimate humility or enjoy the necessary peace. Veblen was an alien to the end, and the torment of his alienation is forever to be felt in his prose.

[1942]

THE NEW REALISM:
SHERWOOD ANDERSON AND
SINCLAIR LEWIS

Though no two novelists were to prove more different than Lewis and Anderson, it was with them, as with that whole group of modern realists who now came into the Twenties—writers so diverse as Floyd Dell, Zona Gale, and Ring Lardner—that the way was opened for the kind of realism that was to dominate American fiction, a realism that neither apologized for itself nor submitted to the despairs of naturalism, a realism that took itself for granted and swept at will over every sector of American life. No longer did the American realist have to storm the heavens, or in the grimness of creation build his books with massive blocks of stone. Realism had become familiar and absorbed in the world of familiarity; it had become a series of homely fabliaux, like the stories grasped out of common life that men had told one another in the Middle Ages; it had become the normal circuit. And though Anderson, and he alone among these realists, was later to learn from Gertrude Stein's literary ateliers in Paris—the learning process did not last very long— the new realists were essentially indifferent to the old dream of a perfect "work of art." For these writers did not usually think of themselves as "artists" in the European sense. They were participants in a common experience, newly liberated from what the young Sinclair Lewis called the "village virus" and writing for others like them. They had no desire to erect artistic monuments as such. They had emerged from the farms, the village seminaries, newspaper desks, with a fierce desire to assert their freedom and to describe the life they knew, and they wrote with the brisk or careless competence—Anderson sometimes did not seem interested in *writing* at all—that was necessary to their exploration of the national scene.

What this meant also, however, was that the new realists, by their very example and instinctive interests, gave the American novel over to the widest possible democracy of subject and theme. It was the homely average type—Sinclair Lewis's Babbitts and Chum Frinkleys, his Rotarians and business-ridden little men and Wheatsylvania farmers; Ring Lardner's dumb baseball players and Broadway producers and Long Island socialites; Zona Gale's unhappy young village couples; Sherwood Anderson's gallery of village librarians, horse-trainers, yearning young poets; even Edgar Lee Masters's farmers—it was these who now brought the savor and pain of common life back into the novel. Where Crane and Norris had gone to the depths to prove their realism, where Dreiser's naturalism had led him to massive realistic characters who were the embodiment of his profound sense of tragedy, the new realists brought into the novel the walking show of American life. For whether they wrote with the photographic exactness of Lewis, the often inchoate exultation of Anderson, or the harsh, glazed coldness of Lardner, they had a compelling interest in people, American people, of all varieties, sizes, temperaments, standards; and the interest was always direct.

It was this feeling for common talk and appreciation of common ways, so marked even in Lardner—perhaps especially in Lardner, though he seemed to hate everything he touched—that gave the new realists their hold over the popular imagination and made them so significant a cultural influence. Indeed, far from having to fight their public, the new realists often seemed to be associated with their readers in a certain camaraderie of taste and humor. Sinclair Lewis, as Constance Rourke said in her *American Humor*, could even in one sense be considered the first American novelist, for in his unflagging absorption of detail and his grasp of the life about him, Lewis caught the tone, the speech, of the pervasive American existence; and it was significant that in his sharp attention to American speech—did anyone before him ever catch the American "uh"?—he brought back the comic and affectionate mimicry of the old frontier humor. There had been nothing of that humor in Dreiser, Crane, and Norris; and for all their superior weight, their more profound grasp of human life, nothing of the discovery of American fellowship that made for so significant a bond between novelist and reader in the new novels of the twenties. And even when he seemed to be groping under the surface of life, to be perplexingly "mystical" like Anderson, the new realist made his readers share in the pride of discovering the poignance and the concealed depths to be found in so many prosaic American examples. Anderson more than the others, in fact, gave to a younger generation growing up in the twenties a sense of curiosity, an unashamed acceptance of their difficulties and yearnings, that was to remain with them long after he had come to seem a curiously repetitive and even confused figure. For whatever else men like Anderson and Lewis may have lacked, they gave back, out of their candid and often bitter penetration of American life, a confidence to those who saw in their books the mirror of a common American existence. It was not an impersonal "America" that had stepped finally out onto the world's stage; it was Americans, millions of them—all the Americans who snickered at Babbitt yet knew him for their own; all the Americans who knew how authentic and tender was the world Sherwood Anderson illuminated in *Winesburg, Ohio*; all the Americans who knew that if Carol Kennicott was not as great a creation as Emma Bovary, she was certainly more real to them, and lived next door. The American was here; he belonged; he was a character in the gallery of the world's great characters even if he did nothing more than sell Ford cars and live in a clapboard house. Even Babbitt inspired a kind of pride by his vividness; even the mean despotic village enemy in Chum Frinkley; and particularly all those Lincolnesque ghosts out of so many different Spoon River anthologies in the novel, village grocers and spinster aunts and thwarted farmers' wives, who addressed themselves so roundly to history, and so well.

2

Under these circumstances it mattered perhaps less that the new realists had turned to explore the national life with a sharp bitterness than that they were the spokesmen of a new liberation. Even a classic of postwar emotion like Masters's *Spoon River Anthology*, which was perhaps not so much a portrait of a representative town as an image of Masters's own bitterness and frustration, posited a new freedom. To know the truth of American life was to rise in some fashion above its prohibitions; to recognize the tragedy so often ignored in commonplace lives was to lead to a healthy self-knowledge. Reveling in the commonplace, the new realists felt that with them the modern novel in America had at last come to grips with the essentials, and the vigor with which they described the mean narrowness and sterility of their world had in it a kind of exuberance. Thus even a writer like Zona Gale, whose early stories up to 1918 had seemed so sentimental, now suddenly burst out with novels like *Birth* and *Miss Lulu Bett* that were almost intolerably intense parodies of everyday American existence. The tone of *Miss Lulu Bett* particularly, in fact, suggested a concentrated dreariness, a high-spirited savagery, that was almost inconceivable in terms of Zona Gale's strong affection for all the small Wisconsin towns represented. Yet the evidence of a sudden disaffection was there, as in Willa Cather's stories of this period; and both of Miss Gale's novels were so harshly written that it was as if concealed depths of repulsion and bitterness in her had suddenly been brought to light.

It was this sense of a personal quest in realism, particularly marked at a time when so many young writers seemed to have endured life in a hundred different Spoon Rivers for the sole purpose of declaring their liberation in their novels, that so clearly distinguished these books from the dark night world of naturalism. And it was this same insistence on personal liberation that made Sherwood Anderson the evangel of the postwar deliverance. For Anderson, so often described as a "naturalist" at a time when any effort at realism was still associated with Dreiser's dour massive objectivity, even appeared to be inadequately conscious of objective reality. His great subject always was personal freedom, the yearning for freedom, the delight in freedom; and out of it he made a kind of left-handed mysticism, a groping for the unnamed and unrealized ecstasy immanent in human relations, that seemed the sudden revelation of the lives Americans led in secret. If Sinclair Lewis dramatized the new realism by making the novel an exact and mimetic transcription of American life, Anderson was fascinated by the undersurface of that life and became the voice of its terrors and exultations. Lewis turned the novel into a kind of higher journalism; Anderson turned fiction into a substitute for poetry and religion, and never ceased to wonder at what he had wrought. He had more intensity than a revival meeting and more tenderness than God; he wept, he chanted, he loved indescribably. There was freedom in the air, and he would summon all Americans to share in it; there was confusion and mystery on the earth, and he would summon all Americans to wonder at it. He was clumsy and sentimental; he could even write at times as if he were finger-painting; but at the moment it seemed as if he had sounded the depths of common American experience as no one else could.

[. . . .]

"I have come to think," he wrote in *A Story-Teller's Story*, "that the true history of life is but a history of moments. It is only at rare moments that we live." In those early days it was as if a whole subterranean world of the spirit were speaking in and through Anderson, a spirit imploring men to live frankly and fully by their own need of liberation, and pointing the way to a tender and surpassing comradeship. He had left his own business and family to go to Chicago—"there was a queer kind of stoppage of something at the center of myself"—and he would dream, in the tenement-house rooms where he wrote *Winesburg*, after working as a laborer or an advertising writer, of the life that went on in those houses, a life that could be heard through thin partitions. "I had thought, then, on such evenings," he wrote twenty-five years later in nostalgia, "that I could tell all of the stories of all the people of America. I would get them all, understand them, get their stories told." Out of his wandering experiences at soldiering and laboring jobs, at following the racehorses he loved and the business career he hated, he had become "at last a writer, a writer whose sympathy went out most to the little frame houses, on often mean enough streets in American towns, to defeated people, often with thwarted lives." Were there not people, people everywhere, just people and their stories to tell? Were there not questions about them always to be asked—the endless wonderment, the groping out toward them, the special "moments" to be remembered?

Living in the heart of the "Robin's-Egg Renaissance" in Chicago, as he called it later, it even seemed to Anderson that hardly anyone had ever before him in America asked the questions he needed to ask about people. The novels he knew did not tell their story; their creators were afraid, as the New England writers who had written too many of the first American stories before Dreiser were afraid. Between the people he saw and the books he read, Anderson saw the terrible chasm of fear in America—the fear of sex, the fear of telling the truth about the hypocrisy of those businessmen with whom he too had reached for "the bitch-goddess of success"; the fear, even, of making stories the exact tonal equivalent of their lives; the fear of restoring to books the slackness and the disturbed rhythms of life. For Anderson was not only reaching for the truth about people and "the terrible importance of the flesh in human relations"; he was reaching at the same time for a new kind of medium in fiction. As he confessed explicitly later on, he even felt that "the novel form does not fit an American writer, that it is a form which had been brought in. What is wanted is a new looseness; and in *Winesburg* I had made my own form." Significantly enough, even such warm friends of the new realism as Floyd Dell and H. L. Mencken did not think the *Winesburg* stories stories at all; but Anderson, who had revolted against what he now saw as the false heroic note in his first work, knew better, and he was to make the new readers see it his way.

For if "the true history of life was but a history of moments," it followed that the dream of life could be captured only in a fiction that broke with rules of structure literally to embody moments, to suggest the endless halts and starts, the dreamlike passiveness and groping of life. What Gertrude Stein had for fifteen years, working alone in Paris, learned out of her devotion to the independent vision of modern French painting, Anderson now realized by the simple stratagem of following the very instincts of his character, by groping through to the slow realization of his characters on the strength of his conviction that all life itself was only a process of groping. The difference between them (it was a difference that Gertrude Stein's pupil, Ernest Hemingway, felt so deeply that he had to write a parody of Anderson's style, *The Torrents of Spring*, to express his revulsion and contempt) was that where Miss Stein and Hemingway both had resolved their break with the "rules" into a formal iconoclastic technique, a conscious principle of design, Anderson had no sense of design at all save as life afforded him one. Although he later listened humbly enough to Gertrude Stein in Paris—she had proclaimed him one of the few Americans who could write acceptable sentences—he could never make one principle of craft, least of all those "perfect sentences" that she tried so hard to write, the foundation of his work. Anderson was, in fact, rather like an older kind of artisan in the American tradition—such as Whitman and Albert Pinkham Ryder—artisans who worked by sudden visions rather than by any sense of style, artisans whose work was the living grammar of their stubborn belief in their own visions. Hemingway's bitterness against Anderson, it may be, was as much a recognition of the older man's advantage in his awkwardness

as it was a revulsion against his self-indulgence and groping; but it is significant that it was just Hemingway's need of style and a deliberate esthetic in the
novel that separated them.

Anderson did not merely live for the special "moments" in experience; he
wrote, by his own testimony, by sudden realizations, by the kind of apprehension of a mood, a place, a character, that brought everything to a moment's
special illumination and stopped short there, content with the fumbling
ecstasy it brought. It was this that gave him his interest in the "sex drive" as a
force in human life (it had so long been left out), yet always touched that
interest with a bold, awkward innocence. He was among the first American
writers to bring the unconscious into the novel, yet when one thinks of how
writers like Dorothy Richardson, Virginia Woolf, and James Joyce pursued the
unconscious and tried to trace some pattern in the fathomless psychic history
of men and women, it is clear that Anderson was not interested in contribut-
ing to the postwar epic of the unconscious at all. What did interest him was
sex as a disturbance in consciousness, the kind of disturbance that drove so
many of his heroes out of the world of constraint; but once he had got them
out of their houses, freed them from convention and repression, their liberation was on a plane with their usually simultaneous liberation from the world
of business. It was their loneliness that gave them significance in Anderson's
mind, the lies that they told themselves and each other to keep the desperate
fictions of conventionality; and it was inevitably the shattering of that loneliness, the emergence out of that uneasy twilit darkness in which his characters
always lived, that made their triumph and, in his best moments, Anderson's
own.

The triumph, yes; and the agony. It is a terrible thing for a visionary to remain
a minor figure; where the other minor figures can at least work out a minor
success, the visionary who has not the means equal to his vision crumbles into
fragments. Anderson was a minor figure, as he himself knew so well; and that
was his tragedy. For the significance of his whole career is that though he could
catch, as no one else could, the inexpressible grandeur of those special
moments in experience, he was himself caught between them. Life was a succession of moments on which everything else was strung; but the moments
never came together, and the world itself never came together for him. It was
not his "mysticism" that was at fault, for without it he would have been noth-

ing; nor was it his special way of groping for people, of reaching for the grotesques in life, the homely truths that seemed to him so beautiful, since that was what he had most to give—and did give so imperishably in *Winesburg*, in stories like "I'm a Fool," in parts of *Poor White* and *Dark Laughter*, and in the autobiographical *Tar.* It was rather that Anderson had nothing else in him that was equal to his revelations, his tenderness, his groping. He was like a concentration of everything that had been missed before him in modern American writing, and once his impact was felt, the stammering exultation he brought became all. That was Anderson's real humiliation, the humiliation that perhaps only those who see so much more deeply than most men can feel; and he knew it best of all.

> *I should be sitting on a bench like a tailor.*
> *I should be weaving warm cloth out of the threads of thought.*
> *I am a helpless man—my hands tremble.*
> *The tales should be clothed.*
>
> *They are freezing on the doorstep of the house of my mind.*

"If you love in a loveless world," he wrote in *Many Marriages*, "you face others with the sin of not loving." He had that knowledge; he brought it in, and looked at it as his characters looked at each other; but he could only point to it and wonder. "There is something that separates people, curiously, persistently, in America," he wrote in his last novel, *Kit Brandon*. He ended on that note as he had begun on it twenty-five years before, when Windy McPherson's son wondered why he could never get what he wanted, and Beaut McGregor led the marching men marching, marching nowhere. The brooding was there, the aimless perpetual reaching, that indefinable note Anderson always struck; but though no writer had written so much of liberation, no writer seemed less free. He was a Prospero who had charmed himself to sleep and lost his wand; and as the years went on Anderson seemed more and more bereft, a minor visionary whose perpetual air of wonder became a trance and whose prose disintegrated helplessly from book to book. Yet knowing himself so well, he could smile over those who were so ready to tell him that it was his ignorance of "reality" and of "real people" that crippled his books. What was it but the reality that was almost too oppressively real, the reality beyond the visible surface world, the reality of all those lives that so many did lead in secret, that he had brought into American fiction? It was not his vision that was at fault, no; it was that poignant human situation embodied in him, that story he told over and again because it was his only story—of the groping that broke forth out of the prison house of life and . . . went on groping; of the search for freedom that made all its substance out of that search, and in the end left all the supplicators brooding, suffering, and overwhelmed. Yet if he had not sought so much, he could not have been humiliated so deeply. It was always the measure of his reach that gave others the measure of his failure.

3

[. . . .]

For Anderson, at least, this sense of anticlimax after his first important books in the early twenties was almost a private matter between Anderson and his kind of vision—a private failure to sustain what he had to give. There was always a failure of will in Anderson's books, a slow decomposition that had its source in some fatal stagnancy. But Lewis, who enjoyed from the first a sense of public domination such as few novelists have ever known, suffered a different kind of humiliation. For there was nothing obviously "lacking" in him, as in Anderson. All the energy, the hard, bright wisdom, the tireless curiosity, that were in him reached maximum expression; all the public favor and understanding a writer could want he had. Far more than Anderson, far more than any other contemporary novelist, in fact, he had welded himself inextricably into the American scene. But Lewis had done his work so well, fitted the times so perfectly, that he became almost invisible *in* that scene; he had worked over the surface world so thoroughly, and with so contagious a wit and skepticism, that he became part of that surface. A more profound writer would not have had so assured a success; a less skillful one would not have been so influential in his success. But Lewis hit a certain average in art perfectly, as he hit off the native average—or what Americans like to think is the native average—so well in his characters; and that was at once his advantage and his misfortune. As his characters became public symbols, he came to seem more a public influence than a novelist; as his jokes against the old American ways became new American ways themselves, the barrier between his books and life in America came down altogether. George F. Babbitt had entered as completely into the national imagination as Daniel Boone, but with his emergence, as with every new archetype of American life Lewis brought in, some part of Lewis's usefulness seemed to be over.

To say this would seem to pay only the necessary tribute to Lewis's extraordinary place in modern American life and manners; but to define that success is at the same time to define his position as a writer and the resources he brought to the novel. For there is a certain irony in Lewis's career that is now impossible to miss, and one that illuminates it as a whole. Here was the bright modern satirist who wrote each of his early books as an assault on American smugness, provincialism, ignorance, and bigotry; and ended up by finding himself not an enemy, not a danger, but the folksiest and most comradely of American novelists. Here was the young rebel who had begun *Main Street* as his spiritual autobiography, who even wrote dashingly in his foreword that it preached "alien" doctrine and who painted that whole world of endless Main Streets where "dullness is made God"—and found that people merely chortled with delight over how well he had hit off the village butcher, the somnolent afternoons on Main Street, the hysterical Sunday-night suppers, and the genteel moneylender's wife, with her "bleached cheeks, bleached hair, bleached voice, and a bleached manner." Here was the crusading satirist who spared none of the hypocrisies by which Babbitt and his group lived, least of all their big and little cruelties, and gave Babbitt back to his people as a friendly, browbeaten, noisy good fellow. Here was the indignant critic of commercialism in science who portrayed the tragedy of Max Gottlieb in *Arrowsmith* and the struggles of Martin Arrowsmith against those who threatened his disinterested worship of truth, yet succeeded even more significantly in making out of Arrowsmith a gangling romantic American hero. Here was the topical novelist, with his genius for public opinion, who tried to describe the nightmare coming of fascism to America in *It Can't Happen Here*, but really described his own American optimism in the affectionate portrait of Doremus Jessup, that good American small-town liberal.

In the first flush of his triumph in the twenties, when Lewis did seem to be the bad boy breaking out of school, the iconoclast who was Mencken's companion in breaking all the traditional American commandments, it was easy enough to enjoy his satiric bitterness and regard him as a purely irreverent figure. But today, when his characters have entered so completely into the national life and his iconoclasm has become so tedious and safe, it is impossible to look back at Lewis himself without seeing how much native fellowship he brought into the novel and how deeply he has always depended on the common life he satirized. The caricature will always be there, and the ugly terror that Babbitt felt when he tried to break away for a moment from the conventional life of his society. There is indeed more significant terror of a kind in Lewis's novels than in a writer like Faulkner or the hard-boiled novelists, for it is the terror immanent in the commonplace, the terror that arises out of the repressions, the meannesses, the hard jokes of the world Lewis had soaked into his pores. But in a larger sense his whole significance as a writer rests on just his absorption of all those commonplaces, for Lewis has seemed not merely to live on the surface of public reality but for it. It was this that so many critics have felt when they have accused him of living intellectually from hand to mouth, and what T. K. Whipple meant when he so cleverly compared Lewis to a Red Indian stalking the country of his enemies. For Lewis has always led so mimetic an existence that his works have even come to seem an uncanny reproduction of surface reality. Not so much revelations of life as brilliant equivalents of it, his books have really given back to Americans a perfect symbolic myth, the central image of what they have believed themselves to be; and it is this which has always been the source of his raucous charm and his boisterous good-fellowship with the very people and ideas he has caricatured.

For what is it about Lewis that strikes one today but how deeply he has always enjoyed people in America? What is it but the proud gusto and pleasure behind his caricatures that have always made them so funny—and so comfortable? Only a novelist fundamentally uncritical of American life could have brought so much zest to its mechanics; only a novelist anxious not to surmount the visible scene, but to give it back brilliantly, could have presented so vivid an image of what Americans are or believe themselves to be. It was the satire that always gave Lewis's books their design, but the life that streamed out of them impressed people most by giving them a final *happy* recognition. Lewis caught the vulgarity and the perpetual salesmanship, and caught it as effortlessly as he caught the sights and sounds, the exact sound of a Ford car being cranked on a summer morning in Zenith in 1922, the exact resemblance of Chum Frinkley to Eddie Guest and of Sharon Falconer to Aimee Semple McPherson. But he caught also, as almost no one did before him, the boyish helplessness of a Babbitt, the stammering romance of a Martin Arrowsmith on his first day at the McGurk Institute, the loneliness of a great Sam Dodsworth before all those Europeans in Paris. Even his novel on fascism reminded Americans that when an exiled American Hitler like Buzz Windrip goes to Paris, he yearns only for Lucky Strikes and the smoking-car jokes of his pals. Even his assault on small-town ignorance and bigotry in *Main Street* suggested that if Carol Kennicott was heroically unhappy on Main Street, she was just a little silly with her passion for uplift.

Yes, and for all their sharp thrusts and irritable mutterings, his books also confirmed in Americans the legend of their democratic humility, the suspicion that every stuffed shirt conceals a quaking heart, and the need of an industrial magnate like Sam Dodsworth or a scientist like Martin Arrowsmith to translate the most momentous problems of his craft into the jargon of a manly American fellowship. Lewis's men are boys at heart, living in a world in which boys are perpetually stealing through their disguise as men, and glad to know that a certain boyishness in the native atmosphere will always sustain them. Businessmen, scientists, clergymen, newspapermen, they are forever surprised at their attainment of status and seek a happiness that will encourage them to believe that they are important. They are frontiersmen suddenly ushered into the modern inheritance, and can giggle at themselves, as John Jay Chapman did on his grand tour of Europe in the eighties, by remembering all the derisive ancestors who stand behind them—"Dear old Grandpa, with his old cotton socks; wouldn't he be proud if he could see me hee-hawing and chaw-chawing with Roman princes!" But if Lewis's natives are boys, the Europeans in his books—Max Gottlieb, Bruno Zechlin, Fran Dodsworth's cousins in Berlin—though they are usually crushed by the native barbarians, are older than the rocks on which they sit, older and wiser than life, the sage miracle men of some ancient world of light and beauty and culture. Old Gottlieb in *Arrowsmith*, for example, was not merely a European scientist; he was *the* European scientist, the very incarnation of that indescribable cultivation and fathomless European wisdom—a man on speaking terms with Leonardo, Brahms, and Nietzsche; a scientist whose classic work on immunology only seven men in all the world could understand; a cosmopolitan who advised—sneeringly—his students to read *Marius the Epicurean* for "laboratory calmness," and could prepare exotic little sandwiches for his grubby coworkers.

Martin Arrowsmith himself, be it remembered, had no such skills. In fact, it was not until he came to Chicago (that halfway station to Europe?), shedding the provincialisms of Wheatsylvania and even Zenith, that he heard

Mischa Elman, saw a Russian play, and—"learned to flirt without childishness." The Europeans in Lewis's novels never flirted with childishness; they had all the learning of the world at their fingertips; and as Gottlieb, or Bruno Zechlin in *Elmer Gantry,* proved by their inevitable humiliation and fall, they were almost too good to live in the parched American wilderness. Here was only one American folklore legend that Lewis made his own, a legend based on a conviction of native inferiority and subservience to Europe; and nowhere did it show so clearly as in Sam Dodsworth's encounter with Europe, a Europe that was the negation of Gottlieb's, yet cut out of the same cloth—a Europe too charming, too learned, treacherous and sly, Henry James's favorite story of American innocence abroad came back here with a vengeance. Yet it is interesting to note that a character like Gottlieb succeeded so brilliantly because he was so sentimentally realized a type. Gottlieb suggested so abundantly for Lewis just what many Americans would have supposed a German-Jewish scientist in Winnemac to be that he lived, as it were, precisely because he was a stock figure; lived because in him banality had been raised to the rank of creation.

Lewis's characters have often been criticized as "types," and they are, partly because he memorialized some of them as such, gave people in George F. Babbitt what seemed the central portrait of a businessman. But what is really significant in his use of types is that his mind moved creatively in their channels. With his ability to approximate American opinion, his lightning adaptability to the prejudices, the fears, the very tonal mood, as it were, of the contemporary American moment, Lewis has always been able to invest his tintypes with a careless energy that other writers would not have been able to understand, much less share, since they did not work so close to the surface. Lewis restored life; he did not create it. Yet what that means is that for him the creative process lay in the brilliance of that restoration—the ability to restore one Pickerbaugh, with his "he-males" and "she-males," out of the fledgling Pickerbaughs all over the American scene; the ability to set his villains or bores—Elmer Gantry, Chum Frinkley, especially Lowell Schmaltz—so to talking that though they were incredible, they attained a fantastic representative quality. It is doubtful, in fact, whether Lewis even wished to make Lowell Schmaltz credible in that long monologue, *The Man Who Knew Coolidge.* He wished only to hit him off perfectly, to make Lowell a kind of monstrous incarnate average, just as he wished to make Elmer Gantry an accumulative

symbol of all the phoniness he hated in American life. With his lonely suffering rebels, however—Frank Shallard, Erik Valborg, Paul Reisling, Gottlieb,
and Zechlin—he attained not an average type but an average myth. For they
are the protestants, the victims of the national life in which his other characters survive as a matter of course; and though Lewis admired them and suffered with them, the characters he gives them are just those which the
artist-rebels, the men who are "different," would seem to possess by average
standards.

Just as Lewis has always worked from type to type, embodying in them
now the cruelty, now the sentimentality, now the high high jinks, now the
high-pressure salesmanship of one aspect of the national life after another, so
he has always moved in his books from one topic to another, covering one sector of American life after another—the small town, Rotary, business, medicine, the smoking car, travel, religion, social work. More than any other
American novelist since Frank Norris, he felt from the first the need to go
from subject to subject that would lead him to cover the entire national scene.
He knew that scene in all its range and could characteristically work up any
subject; he had concentrated his whole ambition in the national life, and could
hit the perfect moment again and again. In fact, like a sailor hitting ducks in a
shooting gallery, Lewis gave the impression that he had only to level his aim,
seize a new idea, a new flash of life in the American sector, and go after it. Yet
this could work only up to a certain point, as the steady decline of his novels
after *Dodsworth*, reaching a really abysmal low in *The Prodigal Parents*, has proved.
For the ducks in the American shooting gallery soon stopped moving in con-
venient rotation. In a sense Lewis depended on an America in equilibrium, a
young postwar America anxious to know itself, careless and indulgent to his
friendly jokes against it, ambitious even to improve its provincial manners in
the light of his criticism; but when that America lost its easy, comfortable self-
consciousness, Lewis's nervous mimicry merely brushed off against it.

It followed also from Lewis's whole conception of the novel that his brisk
mimetic energy would become a trick repeating itself long after he had lost his
sense of design and purpose. In some of the early brilliant descriptions in *Ann
Vickers*, he seemed to be blocking out perfect scene after perfect scene that led
to nothing; there is a forlorn flashiness about them that reveals Lewis running
over his old technique even when he had little to say. In Lewis's first works his
verve had always been able to light up an inconsequential book like *Elmer*

Gantry with dozens of hilarious scenes, or, as in *The Man Who Knew Coolidge*, even to make one long monologue out of it; but now, with nothing more substantial to write about than Barney Dolphin in *Ann Vickers*, Ora Weagle in *Work of Art*, or Fred Cornplow in *The Prodigal Parents*, he could keep on bringing in his "trick," his special gift and charm, while the books merely sagged. They were tired, evasively sentimental books, and full of a hard surface irritability and uncertainty. Even *It Can't Happen Here*, for all its attempt to cover the imaginary coming of fascism to America, was not a really ambitious book and certainly not a careful and deeply imagined one. Responding to the public terror that filled the air out of Hitler Germany as he had responded to a certain public mood he had known so well in the twenties, Lewis could catch only the surface terror, the surface violence; and they erupted mechanically in his book. But he could not really imagine Fascism in America, he had not really tried to; he had tried to hit the bell in 1936 as he hit it in 1920 with *Main Street* and in 1922 with *Babbitt*, to sound off a surface alarm and strike the public consciousness.

What these later works also signified, however, was not only Lewis's growing carelessness and fatigue, but an irritable formal recognition of his relation to American life. Far from even attempting iconoclastic satire, he wrote these books as moralities for a new time; and his new heroes—Ora Weagle, the poetic hotel keeper; Doremus Jessup, the amiable and cautious liberal; Fred Cornplow, the good, solid husband and father betrayed by his erring children— were the final symbols of everything Lewis had always loved best. He had lampooned Babbittry easily enough; but when the Babbitts themselves were threatened, he rushed forward to defend them. From his own point of view, indeed, there were no Babbitts now, or at least nothing to lampoon in them— Fred Cornplow was the mainstay of the times and Doremus Jessup a representative American hero.

[1942]

WILLA CATHER'S ELEGY

————•◆•————

It's memory: the memory that goes with the vocation.
—Willa Cather on Sarah Orne Jewett

Willa Cather and Nebraska grew up together. Born in Virginia, she was taken at eight to a country moving in the first great floodtide of Western migration in the eighties. Within a single decade half a million people—Yankee settlers, sod-house pioneers out of the Lincoln country, Danes, Norwegians, Germans, Bohemians, Poles—pulled up stakes or emigrated from the farms of northern and eastern Europe to settle on the plains of a region that had been "a state before there were people in it." Nebraska was the first of the great settlements beyond the Mississippi after the Civil War, and the pace of its settlement and the polyglot character of its people were such that they seemed to mark a whole new society in flower. The successive stages of economic and social development were leaped quickly, but not too quickly; as late as 1885 the state was mostly raw prairie, and for the children of the first pioneers, history began with the railroad age roaring in from the East. Nebraska was a society in itself, a bristling new society, proud of its progress and of values and a morality consciously its own. The prairie aristocracy that was to play as triumphant and even didactic a role in Willa Cather's novels as the colonial aristocracy had played in Edith Wharton's may have been composed out of the welter of emigration; but it was a founding class, and Willa Cather never forgot it.

Her enduring values were the values of this society, but they were not merely pioneer and agrarian values. There was a touch of Europe in Nebraska everywhere during her girlhood, and much of her distinctive literary culture was to be drawn from it. The early population numbered so many Europeans among it that as a young girl she would spend Sundays listening to sermons in French, Norwegian, and Danish. There was a Prague in Nebraska as well as in Bohemia. Europe had given many brilliant and restless young men to the West. Amiel wrote letters to a nephew who died among the Nebraska farmers; Knut Hamsun worked on a farm just across the state line in South Dakota; a cousin of Camille Saint-Saëns lived nearby in Kansas. One could walk along the streets of a county seat like Wilber and not hear a word of English all day long. It was in this world, with its accumulation of many cultures, a world full of memories of Grieg and Liszt, of neighbors who taught her Latin and two grandmothers at home with whom she read the English classics, that Willa Cather learned to appreciate Henry James and at the same time to see in the pioneer society of the West a culture and distinction of its own. Her first two years there, she wrote later, were the most important to her as a writer.

All through her youth the West was moving perpetually onward, but it seemed anything but rootless to her; it suggested a distinctive sense of permanence in the midst of change, a prairie culture that imparted to her education a tender vividness. Unconsciously, perhaps, the immigrants came to symbolize a tradition, and that tradition anchored her and gave her an almost religious belief in its sanctity. Growing up in a period of violent disruption and social change, she was thus brought up at the same time to a native and homely traditionalism. Later she was to elegize it, as all contemporary America was to elegize the tradition of pioneer energy and virtue and hardihood; but only because it gave her mind an abiding image of order and—what so few have associated with the pioneer tradition—of humanism. Her love for the West grew from a simple affection for her own kind into a reverence for the qualities they represented; from a patriotism of things and place-names into a patriotism of ideas. What she loved in the pioneer tradition was human qualities rather than institutions—the qualities of Antonia Shimerda and Thea Kronberg, Alexandra Bergson and Godfrey St. Peter—but as those qualities seemed to disappear from the national life, she began to think of them as something more than personal traits; they became the principles which she was to oppose to contemporary dissolution.

Willa Cather's traditionalism was thus anything but the arbitrary or patronizing opposition to contemporary ways which Irving Babbitt personified. It was a candid and philosophical nostalgia, a conviction and a standard possible only to a writer whose remembrance of the world of her childhood and the people in it was so overwhelming that everything after it seemed drab and more than a little cheap. Her distinction was not merely one of cultivation and sensibility; it was a kind of spiritual clarity possible only to those who suffer their loneliness as an act of the imagination and the will. It was as if the pervasive and incommunicable sense of loss felt by a whole modern American generation had suddenly become a theme rather than a passing emotion, a disassociation which one had to suffer as well as report. The others were lost in the new materialism, satirized or bewailed it; she seceded, as only a very rare and exquisite integrity could secede with dignity. Later, as it seemed, she became merely sentimental, and her direct criticism of contemporary types and manners was often petulant and intolerant. But the very intensity of her nostalgia had from the first led her beyond nostalgia; it had given her the conviction that the values of the world she had lost were the primary values, and everything else merely their degradation.

It was this conflict, a conflict that went beyond classes and could be represented only as a struggle between grandeur and meanness, the two poles of her world, that became the great theme of her novels. She did not celebrate the pioneer as such; she sought his image in all creative spirits—explorers and artists, lovers and saints, who seemed to live by a purity of aspiration, an integrity or passion or skill, that represented everything that had gone out of life or had to fight a losing battle for survival in it. "O Eagle of Eagles!" she apostrophized in *The Song of the Lark.* "Endeavor, desire, glorious striving of human art!" The world of her first important novels—*O Pioneers!, The Song of the Lark, My Ántonia*—was unique in its serenity and happiness. Its secret was the individual discovery of power, the joy of fulfilling oneself in the satisfaction of an appointed destiny. The material Alexandra Bergson and Thea Kronberg worked with was like the naked prairies Jim Burden saw in *My Ántonia* on the night ride to his grandparents' farm. "There was nothing but land: not a country at all, but the material out of which countries are made." It was always the same material and always the same creative greatness impressed upon it. Ántonia was a peasant and Thea a singer, but both felt the same need of a great and positive achievement; Alexandra was a farmer, but her feeling for the land was like Thea's feeling for music. The tenacious ownership of the land, the endless search of its possibilities, became the very poetry of her character; the need to assert oneself proudly had become a triumphant acceptance of life.

Yet even as Willa Cather's pale first novel, *Alexander's Bridge*, had been a legend of creative desire and its inevitable frustration, so in these novels the ideal of greatness had been subtly transformed into a lesson of endurance. Even in *My Ántonia*, the earliest and purest of her elegies, the significance of achievement had become only a rigid determination to see one's life through. The exultation was there, but it was already a little sad. Her heroines were all pioneers, pioneers on the land and pioneers of the spirit, but something small, cantankerous, and bitter had stolen in. The pioneer quality had thinned, as the pioneer zest had vanished. Ántonia might go on, as Thea might flee to the adobe deserts and cliff cities of the Southwest for refuge, but the new race of pioneers consisted of thousands of farm women suffering alone in their kitchens, living in a strange world amidst familiar scenes, wearing their lives out with endless chores and fears.

> On starlight nights I used to pace up and down those long, cold streets, scowling at the little sleeping porches on either side, with their storm-windows and covered back porches. They were flimsy shelters, most of them poorly built of light wood, with spindle porch-posts horribly mutilated by the turning-lathe. Yet for all their frailness, how much jealousy and envy and unhappiness some of them managed to contain! The life that went on in them seemed to me made up of evasions and negations; shifts to save cooking, to save washing and cleaning, devices to propitiate the tongue of gossip.

By 1920, the stories in *Youth and the Bright Medusa* hinted at a growing petulance, and in stories like "A Wagner Matinée" and "The Sculptor's Funeral" there was nothing to indicate that Willa Cather thought any better of small-town life than did Zona Gale or Sinclair Lewis. Yet by their very bitterness, so much more graphic than the dreary tonelessness of *Miss Lulu Bett*, these stories revealed how sharp her disillusionment had been, and when she developed the theme of small-town boorishness in *One of Ours* into the proverbial story of the sensitive young man, she could only repeat herself lamely. She was writing about an enemy—the oppressively narrow village world—which seemed only one of the many enemies of the creative spirit, but she did not have Zona Gale's inverted sentimentality, or anything like the spirit of Lewis's folksy and fundamentally affectionate satire. *One of Ours* was a temporary position for an artist whose need of an austere ideal was so compelling. Claude Wheeler was only the Midwest *révolté*; her authentic heroes were something more than sensitive young men who "could not see the use of working for money when money brought nothing one wanted. Mrs. Ehrlich said it brought security. Sometimes he thought that this security was what was the matter with everybody: that only perfect safety was required to kill all the best qualities in people and develop the mean ones." The farmer's wife in "A Wagner Matinée" had felt something deeper when, after her few moments of exultation at the concert, she turned and cried:

> "I don't want to go, Clark. I don't want to go!" Outside the concert hall lay the black pond with the cattle-tracked bluffs; the tall, unpainted house with weather-curled boards, naked as a tower; the crook-backed ash seedlings where the dish-cloths hung to dry; the gaunt moulting turkeys picking up refuse about the kitchen door.

The climax in Willa Cather's career came with two short novels she published between 1923 and 1925, *A Lost Lady* and *The Professor's House.* They were parables of the decline and fall of the great tradition, her own great tradition; and they were both so serenely and artfully written that they suggested that she could at last commemorate it quietly and even a little ironically. The primary values had gone, if not the bitterness she felt at their going; but where she had once written with a naively surging affection, or a rankling irritation, she now possessed a cultivated irony, a consummate poise, that could express regret without rancor or the sense of irretrievable loss without anguish. She had, in a sense, finally resigned herself to the physical and moral destruction of her ideal in the modern world, but only because she was soon to turn her back on that world entirely in novels like *Death Comes for the Archbishop* and *Shadows on the Rock.* In the person of a Captain Forrester dreaming railroads across the prairies, of a Godfrey St. Peter welding his whole spirit into a magnificent history of the Spanish explorers in America, she recaptured the enduring qualities she loved in terms of the world she had at last been forced to accept. These were the last of her pioneers, the last of her great failures; and the story she was now to tell was how they, like all their line, would go down in defeat before commerce and family ties and human pettiness.

Only once in *A Lost Lady* did her submerged bitterness break through, in her portrait of Ivy Peters, the perfect bourgeois:

> Now all this vast territory they had won was to be at the mercy of men like Ivy Peters, who had never dared anything, never risked anything. They would drink up the mirage, dispel the morning freshness, root out the great brooding spirit of freedom, the generous, easy life of the great landholders. The space, the colour, the princely carelessness of the pioneer they would destroy and cut up into profitable bits, as the match factory splinters the primeval forest. All the way from Missouri to the mountains this generation of shrewd young men, trained to petty economies by hard times, would do exactly what Ivy Peters had done.

The theme was corruption, as it was to be the theme of *The Professor's House*. It was as explicit as Marian Forrester's dependence on her husband's frontier strength and integrity, as brutal as Ivy Peter's acquisition of Marian Forrester herself. And at the very moment that Willa Cather recognized that corruption in all its social implications, gave its name and source, she resigned herself to it. It had been her distinction from the first to lament what others had never missed; she now became frankly the elegist of the defeated, the Amiel of the novel. The conflict between grandeur and meanness, ardor and greed, was more than ever before the great interest of her mind; but where she had once propounded that conflict, she now saw nothing but failure in it and submitted her art almost rejoicingly to the subtle exploration of failure. In any other novelist this would have made for sickliness and preciosity; now that she was no longer afraid of failure as a spiritual fact, or restive under it, her work gained a new strength and an almost radiant craftsmanship.

The significance of this new phase in Willa Cather's work is best seen in *The Professor's House*, which has been the most persistently underrated of her novels. Actually it is one of those imperfect and ambitious works whose very imperfections illuminate the quality of an imagination. The story of Godfrey St. Peter is at once the barest and the most elaborately symbolic version of the story of heroic failure she told over and over again, the keenest in insight and the most hauntingly suggestive. The violence with which she broke the book in half to tell the long and discursive narrative of Tom Outland's boyhood in the Southwest was a technical mistake that has damned the book, but the work as a whole is the most brilliant statement of her endeavor as an artist. For St. Peter is at once the archetype of all her characters and the embodiment of her own beliefs. He is not merely the scholar as artist, the son of pioneer parents who has carried the pioneer passion into the world of art and thought; he is what Willa Cather herself has always been or hoped to be—a pioneer in mind, a Catholic by instinct, French by inclination, a spiritual aristocrat with democratic manners.

The tragedy of St. Peter, though it seems nothing more than a domestic tragedy, is thus the most signal and illuminating of all Willa Cather's tragedies. The enemy she saw in Ivy Peters—the new trading, grasping class—has here stolen into St. Peter's home; it is reflected in the vulgar ambition of his wife and eldest daughter, the lucrative commercial use his son-in-law has made of the invention Tom Outland had developed in scholarly research, the genteel but acquisitive people around him. St. Peter's own passion, so pure and subtle a pioneer passion, had been for the life of the mind. In the long and exhaustive research for his great history, in the writing of it in the attic of his old house, he had known something of the physical exultation that had gone into the explorations he described. As a young man in France, studying for his doctorate, he had looked up from a skiff in the Mediterranean and seen the design of his lifework reflected in the ranges of the Sierra Nevada, "unfolded in the air above him." Now, after twenty years of toil, that history was finished; the money he had won for it had gone into the making of a new and pretentious house. The great creative phase of his life was over. To hold on to the last symbol of his endeavor, St. Peter determined to retain his old house against the shocked protests of his family. It was a pathetic symbol, but he needed some last refuge in a world wearing him out by slow attrition.

In this light, the long middle section of the novel, describing Tom Outland's boyhood in the desert, is not a curious interlude in the novel; it becomes the parable of St. Peter's own longing for that remote world of the

Southwest which he had described so triumphantly in his book. Willa Cather, too, was moving toward the South, as all her books do: always toward the more primitive in nature and the more traditional in belief. Tom Outland's desert life was thus the ultimate symbol of a forgotten freedom and harmony that could be realized only by a frank and even romantic submission to the past, to the Catholic order and doctrine, and the deserts of California and New Mexico in which the two priests of *Death Comes for the Archbishop* lived with such quiet and radiant perfection. Her characters no longer had to submit to failure; they lived in a charming and almost antediluvian world of their own. They had withdrawn, as Willa Cather now withdrew; and if her world became increasingly recollective and abstract, it was because she had fought a losing battle that no one of her spirit could hope to win. It was a long way from the Catholic Bohemian farmers of Nebraska to the eighteenth-century Catholicism of the Southwest, but she had made her choice, and she accepted it with an almost haughty serenity. As early as 1922, in "The Novel *Démeublé*," her essay on fiction, she had defined her rejection of modern industrial culture explicitly, and had asked for a pure novel that would throw the "social furniture" out of fiction. Even a social novelist like Balzac, she had insisted, wrote about subjects unworthy of him; for the modern social novelists she had only a very gracious and superior contempt. "Are the banking system and the Stock Exchange worth being written about at all?" she asked. She thought not, and itemized the "social furniture" that had to be thrown out of the novel, among them the factory and a whole realm of "physical sensations." It was now but a step from the colonial New Mexico of *Death Comes for the Archbishop* to old Quebec in *Shadows on the Rock* and the lavender and old lace of *Lucy Gayheart*. Her secession was complete.

The significance of Willa Cather's exquisitely futile values was often slurred over or sentimentalized; the felicity of her art was never ignored. Her importance to the older generation—a generation that was now to make room for Hemingway—was a simple and moving one: she was its consummate artist. To critics sated with the folksy satire or bitterness of the village revolt, she suggested a preoccupation with the larger motives; to critics weary of the meretriciousness of Cabell and Hergesheimer, she personified a rich and poised integrity; to critics impatient with the unkempt naturalism of Dreiser and Anderson, she offered purity of style. As an indigenous and finished craftsman, she seemed so native, and in her own way so complete, that she restored confidence to the novel in America. There was no need to apologize for her or to "place" her; she had made a place for herself, carved out a subtle and interesting world of her own. If that world became increasingly elegiac and soft, it was riches in a little room.

[1942]

ALL THE LOST GENERATIONS

————•◆•————

"What do you think happens to people who aren't artists? What do you think people who aren't artists become?"

"I feel they don't become: I feel nothing happens to them; I feel negation becomes of them."

—*E. E. Cummings, introduction to*
The Enormous Room

All right we are two nations.

—*John Dos Passos,* U.S.A.

When Paul Elmer More denounced one of John Dos Passos's early novels, *Manhattan Transfer*, as "an explosion in a cesspool," he was yielding to his familiar rage against the whole trend of realism and naturalism in America rather than expressing a judgment on Dos Passos. Yet as the tradition of that realism, so uniformly abominable to More and his fellows, passed on to the younger writers of Dos Passos's own generation, it became clear that it was not uniform at all, and that with these writers, for whom life and literature had begun with the war, a fateful new influence had entered American writing.

In 1920 and 1921 their first novels, *This Side of Paradise* and *Three Soldiers*, had been among the leading testaments of contemporary revolt and had come in with the stream of new novels like *Winesburg, Main Street, Jurgen,* and *My Ántonia.* The Hemingway character dominated the imagination of the twenties as easily as the Mencken irreverence, and the "flapper generation" which found its historian in F. Scott Fitzgerald was the most obvious of postwar phenomena. But where the writers of the "middle generation," like Lewis and Anderson, Cabell and Mencken, had been released by the new current of freedom after the war, had been given opportunities and themes in the postwar scene, the young writers who had been through the war made it and its aftermath their very substance. Born in the middle nineties, when modern American writing was just beginning to emerge as a positive force, they arrived on the scene just at the moment of triumph; and they seemed from the first not merely the concentration of all that the modern revolution had brought to America, but its climax. Standing at the center of the whole modern literary experience in America, writers like Fitzgerald, Hemingway, and Dos Passos were significantly the evangels of what had been most tragically felt in the American war experience. They were "the sad young men," the very disillusioned and brilliant young men, "the beautiful and the damned," and counterparts of all those other sad and brilliant young men in Europe, Aldous Huxley and Louis Aragon, Ernst Toller and Wilfred Owen, who wrote out of the bitterness of a shattered Europe and the palpable demoralization of Western society. Between Hemingway and Sherwood Anderson, between Fitzgerald and Sinclair Lewis, there was as wide and deep a gulf as there had been between Stephen Crane and Howells. And it was in that gulf, something more for these young writers than the familiar disassociation of the American generations, that they lived and wrote—proud and stricken in the consciousness of their difference from their predecessors, from all those who had not shared their intimacy with disaster, from all those who spoke out of an innocence the young writers no longer knew, or through a style that seemed to them conventional.

It was primarily the war, of course, that had made that difference, even for a writer like Scott Fitzgerald, who had not been abroad to the war at all, and had written the first of the lost-generation novels, *This Side of Paradise*, under army lanterns at an officers' training camp. The war had dislodged them from their homes and the old restraints, given them an unexpected and disillusioning education, and left them entirely rootless. They were—in the slogan Gertrude Stein gave to Hemingway—the lost generation, the branded victims, the generation that had been uprooted and betrayed, a generation cast, as one of them wrote, "into the dark maw of violence." Life had begun with war for them and would forever after be shadowed by violence and death. "The only place where you could see life and death, i.e., violent death now that the wars were over, was in the bull ring and I wanted very much to go to Spain where I could study it." But it was not only the war that had at once isolated them and given them their prominence; it was also their sense of an artistic mission. Alone in their disenchantment and famous for it, they were at the same time the appointed heirs of modernism, the new American pilgrims of art, closer to

James Joyce than to Mencken, and more familiar with Gertrude Stein's revelations than with Warren G. Harding's blunders. It was their enforced education in the international community of war and art, their impatience with an art that did not express *them*, that separated them so persistently from the older writers who had become famous in the twenties with them. They had leaped at one bound from the midwestern world of their childhood into the world of Caporetto, of Dada, of Picasso and Gertrude Stein, and their detachment from the native traditions now became their own first tradition.

Mencken and Lewis and Cabell spoke for them in the sense that they spoke for all young people after the war, but in the greater sense they did not speak for them at all. What had Hemingway, the Hemingway who, it is said, had been left for dead on the Italian front and was now dreaming away in Verlaine's old room in Paris of a new style, to learn from the older writers save Sherwood Anderson's honest simplicity? What had Scott Fitzgerald, the golden boy of the twenties who moved through them like a disenchanted child, to learn from the complacent satirists of a society that he at once enjoyed more lustily and held more cheaply than they? What had the very sensitive and romantic and conscientious Dos Passos to learn from writers who could mock everything save the essential cruelty and indignity of the industrial culture he hated? In its own mind the lost generation was not merely lost in the world; it was lost from all the other generations in America. It was a fateful loss and perhaps a willing loss, no tragedy for them there; but it was part of the general sense of loss, the conviction by which they wrote (and experienced the world, as with different senses), which gave them so epic a self-consciousness.

Lost and forever writing the history of their loss, they became specialists in anguish; and as they sentimentalized themselves, so they were easily sentimentalized. "It was given to Hawthorne to dramatize the human soul," John Peale Bishop once wrote. "In our time Hemingway wrote the drama of its disappearance." No other literary generation could have commented on itself with such careless grandeur. Had Hemingway really recorded the disappearance of the human soul "in our time"? Had Dos Passos's America, so symmetrical a series of hell pits, as much correspondence to America as his inclusive ambition promised? No: but what was so significant about these writers from the first was that they were able to convince others that in writing the story of their generation, they were in some sense describing the situation of contemporary humanity. It was the positiveness of their disinheritance, the very glitter of their disillusionment, the surface perfection of a disbelief that was like the texture of Hemingway's novels, that made them so magnetic an influence, in manners as well as in literature. They had a special charm—the Byronic charm, the charm of the specially damned; they had seized the contemporary moment and made it their own; and as they stood among the ruins, calling the ruins the world, they seemed so authoritative in their dispossession, seemed to bring so much craft to its elucidation, that it was easy to believe that all the roads really had led up to them—that a Hemingway could record "the disappearance of the human soul in our time."

Indeed, it was even easy to believe that they were not merely a group of brilliantly talented young writers enjoying a special prominence, but major voices, major artists.

2

Beyond this point, of course, these writers differed very strikingly. Hemingway and Dos Passos were as essentially unlike each other as two contemporaries sharing in a common situation can ever be. Fitzgerald, who never underwent the European apprenticeship that others did, always stood rather apart from them, though he was the historian of his generation and for a long time its most famous symbol. For Fitzgerald never had to create a lost-generation legend or apply it to literature—the exile, the pilgrimage to Gertrude Stein, the bullfighters at the extremity of the world, the carefully molded style, the carefully molded disgust. The legend actually was his life, as he was its most native voice and signal victim; and his own career was one of its great stories, perhaps its central story. From the first he lived in and for the world of his youth, the glittering and heartbroken postwar world from which his career was so indistinguishable. Living by it, he became for many not so much the profoundly gifted, tragic, and erratic writer that he was, a writer in some ways inherently more interesting than any other in his generation, but a marvelous, disappointed, and disappointing child—"a kind of king of our American youth" who had long since lost his kingdom and was staggering in a void. He became too much a legend in himself, too easily a fragment of history rather than a contributor to it. And when he died in his early forties, the "snuffed-out candle," dead in that Hollywood that was his last extremity, with even one of his greatest books, *The Last Tycoon*, unfinished like his life, glittering with promise like his life, he served the legend in death as he had served it by his whole life. *Eheu fugaces!* Scott Fitzgerald was dead; the twenties were really over; the waste and folly had gone with him.

It was almost impossible, of course, not to discount Fitzgerald in some such spirit, for he was as much a part of the twenties as Calvin Coolidge, and like Coolidge, represented something in the twenties almost too graphically. He had announced the lost generation with *This Side of Paradise* in 1920, or at least the home guard of the international rebellion of postwar youth, and the restiveness of youth at home found an apostle in him, since he was the younger generation's first authentic novelist. Flippant, ironic, chastely sentimental, he spoke for all those who felt, as one youth wrote in 1920, that "the old generation had certainly pretty well ruined this world before passing it on to us. They give us this thing, knocked to pieces, leaky, red-hot, threatening to blow up; and then they are surprised that we don't accept it with the same attitude of pretty, decorous enthusiasm with which they received it, way back in the eighties." As the flapper supplanted the suffragette, the cake-eater the earnest young uplifter of 1913, Fitzgerald came in with the modernism that flew in on short skirts, puffed audaciously at its cigarette, evinced a frantic interest in sport and sex, in drinking prohibited liquor, and in defying the ancient traditions. In 1920 he was not so much a novelist as a new generation speaking; but it did not matter. He sounded all the fashionable new lamentations; he gave the inchoate protests of his generation a slogan, a character, a definitive tone. Like Rudolph Valentino, he became one of the supreme personalities of the new day; and when his dashingly handsome hero, Amory Blaine, having survived Princeton, the war, and one tempestuous love affair, stood out at the end of the novel as a man who had conquered all the illusions and was now waiting on a lonely road to be conquered in turn, it seemed as if a generation ambitious for a sense of tragedy had really found a tragic hero.

Like Alfred de Musset's Rolla, Fitzgerald might now have said: *Je suis venu trop tard dans un monde trop vieux pour moi*—and he did, in all the variants of undergraduate solemnity and bright wisdom. With its flip and elaborately self-conscious prose, *The Side of Paradise* was a record of the younger generation's victory over *all* the illusions. The war, Amory Blaine confesses, had no great effect on him, but it certainly ruined the old backgrounds. Sort of killed individual-ism out of our whole generation. . . . I'm not sure it didn't kill it out of the whole world. Oh, Lord, what a pleasure it used to be to dream I might be a really great dictator or writer or religious or political leader—and now even a Leonardo da Vinci or Lorenzo de Medici couldn't be a real old-fashioned bolt in the world.

Knocking loudly and portentously at the locked doors of convention, Fitzgerald had already become the voice of "all the sad young men." With a sly flourish, he announced that "none of the Victorian mothers—and most of the mothers were Victorian—had any idea how casually their daughters were accustomed to be kissed." Mothers swooned and legislators orated; Fitzgerald continued to report the existence of such depravity and cynicism as they had never dreamed of. The shock was delivered; Fitzgerald became part of the postwar atmosphere of shock. But though it was inconsequential enough, *This Side of Paradise* had a taste of the poignance that was to flood all Fitzgerald's other books. To tell all was now the fashion; flaming youth was lighting up behind every barn; but of what use was it? Behind the trivial irony of Fitzgerald's novel, its heroic pose, its grandiose dramatizations ("Amory was alone—he had escaped from a small enclosure into a great labyrinth. He was where Goethe was when he began 'Faust'; he was where Conrad was when he wrote 'Almayer's Folly' "), lay a terrible fear of the contemporary world, a world young men had never made. Freedom had come, but only as a medium of expression; while some of the young men licked their war wounds, others sought certainty. "We *want* to believe, but we can't." The problem was there for all men to ponder, and for "the beautiful and the damned" to suffer. But how did one learn to believe? What was there to believe in?

Fitzgerald never found the answer, yet he did not mock those who had. In those first years he did not seek answers; perhaps he never did. As Glenway Wescott said in his tribute at the end, he "always suffered from an extreme environmental sense." He commented on the world, swam in it as self-contentedly as the new rich, and understood it sagely—when he wanted to; he had no innerness. His senses always opened outward to the world, and the world was full of Long Island Sundays. This was what he knew and was steeped in, the procession and glitter that he loved without the statement of love, and he had the touch for it—the light yet jeweled style, careless and knowing and affable; the easiness that was never facility; the holiday lights, the holiday splendor, the twenties in their golden bowl, whose crack he knew so well. He was innocent without living in innocence and delighted in the external forms and colors without being taken in by them; but he was preeminently a part of the world his mind was always disowning. The extravagance and carnival of the times had laid a charm on him, and he caught the carnival of the world of his youth, and its welling inaudible sadness, as no one else did—the world of Japanese lanterns and tea dances, the hot summer afternoons in *The Great Gatsby,* the dazzle and sudden violence, the colored Easter eggs whose tints got into his prose, the blare of the saxophones "while a hundred pairs of golden and silver slippers shuffled the shining dust. At the gray tea hour there were always rooms that throbbed incessantly with this low, sweet fever, while fresh faces drifted here and there like rose petals blown by the sad horns around the floor."

Inevitably, there was a persistent tension in Fitzgerald between what his mind knew and what his spirit adhered to; between his disillusionment and his irrevocable respect for the power and the glory of the world he described. "Let me tell you about the very rich," he wrote in *All the Sad Young Men.*

> They are different from you and me. They possess and enjoy early, and it does something to them, makes them soft where we are hard, and cynical where we are trustful, in a way that, unless you were born rich, it is very difficult to understand. They think, deep in their hearts, that they are better than we are because we had to discover the compensations and refuges of life for ourselves. . . . They are different.

He was fascinated by that difference, where a writer like Joseph Hergesheimer merely imitated it; none of the others in his generation felt the fascination of the American success story as did Fitzgerald, or made so much of it. ("The rich are not as we are," he once said to Hemingway. "No," Hemingway replied. "They have more money.") This was the stuff of life to him, the American achievement he could recognize, and hate a little, and be forever absorbed by. And from Amory Blaine's education to Monroe Stahr's Hollywood in *The Last Tycoon,* Fitzgerald's world did radiate the Cartier jewel glints of the twenties— the diamond mountain in "The Diamond as Big as the Ritz," Anson Hunter in "The Rich Boy," Jay Gatsby's mansion and dream, the prep-school princelings who swagger through so many of his stories, the luxurious self-waste of the last expatriates in *Tender Is the Night*, and finally Monroe Stahr, the Hollywood king, "who had looked on all the kingdoms, with the kind of eyes that can stare straight into the sun."

Fitzgerald did not worship riches or the rich; he merely lived in their golden eye. They were "different"; they were what the writer who lived forever in the world of his youth really knew; and they became for him what war became for Hemingway, or the anarchy of modern society for Dos Passos—the pattern of human existence, the artist's medium of understanding. His people were kings; they were imperious even in their desolation. They were always the last of their line, always damned, always the death-seekers (there are no second generations in Fitzgerald). Yet they were glamorous to the end, as the futilitarians in *Tender Is the Night* and Monroe Stahr were iridescent with death. For Fitzgerald always saw life as glamour, even though he could pierce that glamour to write one of the most moving of American tragedies in *The Great Gatsby*. Something of a child always, with a child's sudden and unexpected wisdom, he could play with the subtle agonies of the leisure class as with a brilliant toy; and the glamour always remained there, even when it was touched with death. In one sense, as a magazine writer once put it, his books were "prose movies," and nothing was more characteristic of his mind than his final obsession with Hollywood. In the same way much of his writing always hovered on the verge of fantasy and shimmered with all the colors of the world. Just as the world swam through his senses without being defined by him, so he could catch all its lights and tones in his prismatic style without having to understand them too consciously. What saved his style from extravagance was Fitzgerald's special grace, his pride in his craft; but it was the style of a man profoundly absorbed in the romance of glamour, the style of a craftsman for whom life was a fairy world to the end.

To understand this absorption on Fitzgerald's part is to understand the achievement of *The Great Gatsby*, the work by which his name will always live. In most of his other work he merely gave shallow reports on the pleasures and self-doubts of his class, glittered with its glitter. He tended to think of his art as a well-oiled machine, and he trusted to luck. Rather like Stephen Crane, whom he so much resembled in spirit, the only thing he could be sure of was his special gift, his way of transfusing everything with words, the consciousness of craft; and like Crane he made it serve for knowledge. But like Crane in another respect, he was one of those writers who make their work out of a conflict that would paralyze others—out of their tragic moodiness, their troubled, intuitive, and curiously half-conscious penetration of the things before them. And it is this moodiness at the pitch of genius that lights up *The Great Gatsby.* For Fitzgerald was supremely a part of the world he there described, weary of it but not removed from it, and his achievement was of a kind possible only to one who so belonged to it. No revolutionary writer could have written it, or even hinted at its inexpressible poignance; no one, perhaps, who was even too consciously skeptical of the wealth and power Jay Gatsby thought would make him happy. But for Fitzgerald the tragedy unfolded there, the tragedy that has become for so many one of the great revelations of what it has meant to be an American at all, was possible only because it was so profound a burst of self-understanding.

To have approached Gatsby from the outside would have meant a sacrifice of Gatsby himself—a knowledge of everything in Gatsby's world save Gatsby. But the tragedy here is pure confession, a supplication complete in the human note it strikes. Fitzgerald could sound the depths of Gatsby's life because he himself could not conceive any other. Out of his own weariness and fascination with damnation he caught Gatsby's damnation, caught it as only someone so profoundly attentive to Gatsby's dream could have pierced to the self-lie behind it. The book has no real scale; it does not rest on any commanding vision, nor is it in any sense a major tragedy. But it is a great flooding moment, a moment's intimation and penetration; and as Gatsby's disillusion becomes felt at the end, it strikes like a chime through the mind. It was as if Fitzgerald, the playboy moving with increasing despair through this tinsel world of Gatsby's, had reached that perfect moment, before the break of darkness and death, when the mind does really and absolutely know itself—a moment when only those who have lived by Gatsby's great illusion, lived by the tinsel and the glamour, can feel the terrible force of self-betrayal. This was the playboy's rare apotheosis, and one all the more moving precisely because all of Gatsby's life was summed up in it, precisely because his decline and death gave a meaning to his life that it had not in itself possessed.

Here was the chagrin, the waste of the American success story in the twenties: here, in a story that was a moment's revelation. Yet think, Fitzgerald seems to say to us, of how little Gatsby wanted at bottom—not to understand society, but to ape it; not to compel the world, but to live in it. His own dream of wealth meant nothing in itself; he merely wanted to buy back the happiness he had lost—Daisy, now the rich man's wife—when he had gone away to war. So the great Gatsby house at West Egg glittered with all the lights of the twenties, and there were always parties, and always Gatsby's supplicating hand, reaching out to make out of glamour what he had lost by the cruelty of chance. "Gatsby believed in the green light, the orgiastic future that year by year recedes before us. It eluded us then, but that's no matter—tomorrow we will run faster, stretch out our arms farther. . . . And one fine morning—" So the great Gatsby house, Gatsby having failed in his dream, now went out with all its lights, save for that last unexpected and uninvited guest whom Nick heard at the closed Gatsby door one night, the guest "who had been away at the ends of the earth and didn't know that the party was over." And now there was only the wry memory of Gatsby's dream, left in that boyhood schedule of September 12, 1906, with its promise of industry and self-development—"Rise from bed. . . . Study electricity . . . work. . . . Practice elocution and how to attain it. . . . Read one improving book or magazine per week." So all the lights of Fitzgerald's golden time went out with Jay Gatsby—Gatsby, the flower of the republic, the bootlegger who made the American dream his own, and died by it. "So we beat on, boats against the current, borne back ceaselessly into the past."

Gatsby's was Fitzgerald's apotheosis, too. As the haunting promise of *The Last Tycoon* testifies, he did not lose his skill; there is a grim poetic power in his unraveling of Monroe Stahr greater in itself than anything else in his work. But something in Fitzgerald died concurrently with the dying of his world. His fairy world decomposed slowly, lingeringly; and he lived with its glitter, paler and paler, to the end. Writing what he himself called "the novel of deterioration" in *Tender Is the Night*, he kept to the glow, the almost hereditary grace, that was so natural for him. But he lavished it upon a world of pure emptiness there; he was working away in the pure mathematics of sensation. The subtlety of his last books was a fever glow, a neurotic subtlety. He had always to return to the ancient dream of youth and power, the kings who always died in his work but were kings nevertheless—the dominating men, the ornate men, the imperials in whose light he lived because they were the romantic magnifications of the world of his youth. And reading that painful confession of his own collapse, the essay smuggled away in *Esquire* which he called "The Crack-Up," one felt how fantastic it was, as Glenway Westcott put it in his tender tribute to Fitzgerald, "that a man who is dying or at least done with living—one who has had practically all that the world affords, fame and prosperity, work and play, love and friendship, and lost practically all—should still think seriously of so much fiddledeedee of boyhood." But Fitzgerald was a boy, the most startlingly gifted and self-destructive of all the lost boys, to the end. There is an intense brooding wisdom, all Fitzgerald's keen sense of craft raised and burnished to new power, in *The Last Tycoon* that is unforgettable. To see how he could manipulate the emergence of Stahr's power and sadness, the scene of the airplane flight from New York to Hollywood and the moment when the earthquake trembled in Hollywood, is to appreciate how much closer Fitzgerald could come than most modern American novelists to fulfillment, of a kind. But what is Monroe Stahr—the Hollywood producer "who had looked on all the kingdoms," who died so slowly and glitteringly all through the book as Fitzgerald did in life—but the last, the most feverishly concentrated of Fitzgerald's fairy-world characters in that Hollywood that was the final expression of the only world Fitzgerald ever knew? Fitzgerald could penetrate Hollywood superbly; he could turn his gift with the easiest possible dexterity on anything he touched. But he did not touch very much. With all his skill (it is odd to think that where he was once too easily passed off as the desperate Punch of his generation, he may now be rated as a master craftsman in a day worshipful of craftsmanship), Fitzgerald's world is a little one, a superior boy's world—precocious in its wisdom, precocious in its tragedy, but the fitful glaring world of Jay Gatsby's dream, and of Jay Gatsby's failure, to the end.

3

After Fitzgerald, much of the story of his lost generation is the story of the war he never saw, the craftsmanship which became so great an ideal for his generation, and the blistering world of the thirties and early forties in which he died.

In 1922, two years after F. Scott Fitzgerald had first propounded the idea of the lost generation in *This Side of Paradise*, a young artist and poet, Edward Estlin Cummings, published the record of his unique war experience in a narrative entitled *The Enormous Room*. It was not the first of the American war novels—John Dos Passos, like Cummings a Harvard graduate and a volunteer in the Norton-Harjes Ambulance Service, had already published *One Man's Initiation* in 1921 and the better-known *Three Soldiers* in 1921—but it showed a new kind of sensibility, as *This Side of Paradise* had announced a generation. Unlike Fitzgerald, Cummings had seen the war at first hand, and his book was something more than Fitzgerald's defense of a generation that "had grown up to find all Gods dead, all wars fought, all faiths in men shaken." *The Enormous Room* was one of those works that break so completely with one tradition that they mechanically inaugurate another. The book seemed to be an exercise in violence; it rumbled with an indignation that was as livid as the experience it described. Its language, more radical in spirit than the buck-sergeant profanity of *What Price Glory?*, was less obvious, and suggested a philosophy of war compounded equally of resignation, hatred for all authority, and an almost abstract cynicism. America had possessed no Barbusse or Sassoon or Wilfred Owen during the war; the irreverence of its war literature, like its bitter reaction against the war spirit, came much later. Cummings's harsh book was thus almost the very first to express for America the emotions of those artists, writers, students, and middle-class intellectuals who were to constitute the postmortem war generation, and whose war experience was to transform their conception of life and art.

Cummings's war experience had not been typical. Serving as a volunteer in the gentlemanly Norton-Harjes Ambulance Service, he had been arrested by French military police because of some indiscreet letters written by his friend Slater Brown. Jaded with the war spirit, he gave flippant answers at his hearing and was shipped off to a foul and barnlike "preliminary" prison in the south of France, where he spent months in the company of international spies and suspects, thieves, eccentric vagrants from every corner in Europe, prostitutes, and profiteers. The enormous room was his theater of war: he fought no battles, followed the progress of the war through rumor, and spent most of his time trying to keep sane, to get a little food, and to escape. Yet huddled together with the flotsam of war, living on the grudging patronage of a government too busy with routine to be kind, and too suspicious of its prisoners to be fair, Cummings experienced the brutality and the mechanical cruelties of war as a personal disaster. He lived the war through on a lower level, where the slogans seemed farcical, the reality more oppressive, and the great movements of the armies almost unreal. The enormous room concentrated the war. Living on dirty mattresses, humbled by a succession of punishments and insults, deprived of freedom though not confined to "jail," thrown together without common loyalties or even a common purpose, its inmates consciously parodied the war ideals and the war mind. They lived in a perpetual state of mutiny, but there was nothing to protest except life and the French state, no one outrage on which to fix their indignation save the general outrageousness of existence. The enormous room, by its very remoteness from war, mirrored and intensified war's inherent meaninglessness; it became a maze in which men clawed each other to escape or to keep their reason. And the central theme of their imprisonment was chaos.

The enormous room was a cell-like sliver torn from life, and its character, as Cummings saw it, was sheer monstrousness. It was a world so profoundly irrational that anger was wasted on it. It was so atrocious that it was comic; it mingled a perverse horror with hysterical exaltation. It was like a surrealist vision of the universe, for it seemed to caricature the conventional dimensions and emotions with such a contempt for order that the very effort to express its horror ended in jollity. *"C'est de la blague."* "Who is Marshal Foch?" the Dadaists used to ask in 1921. "Who is Woodrow Wilson? What is war? Don't know, don't know, don't know." War, Cummings proclaimed in this spirit, was the history of decomposition. It was reflected in the tubercular German girl, interned for the greater protection of the French Republic, who was choking to death in solitary. It was the tragic life of Jean Le Nègre, the great dumb beast playing with war as a child plays with blocks. It was the living corpses on their mattresses, the gamblers of European stakes, the lechery and the gossip.

> The doors opened with an uncanny bang and in the bang stood a fragile minute queer figure, remotely suggesting an old man. The chief characteristic of the apparition was a certain disagreeable nudity which resulted from its complete lack of all the accepted appurtenances and prerogatives of old age. Its little stooping body, helpless and brittle, bore with extraordinary difficulty a head of absurd largeness, yet which moved on the fleshless neck with a horrible agility. Dull eyes sat in the clean-shaven wrinkles of a face neatly hopeless. At the knees a pair of hands hung, infantile in their smallness. In the

loose mouth a tiny cigarette had perched and was solemnly smoking itself.

The enormous room was a Black Bourse of all the war emotions.

To describe this procession of horrors, Cummings needed a prose that was as nervously mobile as jazz, as portentously formal as a document, and as crisp and precise as his own poetry. He developed a style as far removed from declamation as possible, but one that parodied the pompous undertones of declamation, a style that took its pace and weight and diction from the unspoken resources of war cynicism. The essential character of this prose was its self-conscious originality. In a world nerve-lacerated by the prevailing sense of defeat, riddled with pretensions that were grisly in their unconscious irony, it offered none of the conventional courtesy that a young writer can tender to standard rhetoric. And though it scattered its effects carelessly, the motive behind it was austere: Cummings's great desire was for a prose that should be, beyond everything else, completely and inexorably true; a prose that would express, as Hemingway later said in a celebrated statement of his own purpose, "the truth about his own feelings at the moment when they exist." It was to be a prose as ruthless, as impolite, as sharp, as consciously and even elaborately bitter, as the world it described. It was to be a prose so contemptuous of conventional standards that no one could doubt the depth of the experience behind it.

Cummings's prose was not the hard and deliberately plain prose which Hemingway and later Dos Passos established as their own. Like theirs, it was a prose of inverted lyricism, but more frankly emotional and self-assertive. What he had rejected in his novel was the tonelessness, the machinelike patter, of conventional writing, its implicit submission to the objective world and its lack of personal force. With the same passionate individualism that he was soon to bring to his poetry—an individualism not unrelated, as some critics have observed, to the Emersonian and New England tradition that has always been so strong in Cummings—he sought to impose a new conception of reality. Like so many in his generation, he had returned to an elemental writing, as writers often do in periods of social crisis; but his "simplicity" was a form of grotesquerie and not, like Wordsworth's realism or Whitman's, a serene faith that his fellow men would approve a democratic language and purpose. As Cummings saw it, the world was composed of brutal sensations and endured only by a fiercely desperate courage and love; it was so anarchical that all attempts to impose order were motivated by either ignorance or chicanery. What remained to the artist, who was always the special victim of this world, was the pride of individual self-knowledge and the skill that went beyond all the revolutionary and sentimental illusions of a possible fraternity among men and gave all its devotion to the integrity of art.

A parallel code of fatalism developed in Ernest Hemingway's hands into the freshest and most deliberate art of the day. What Cummings had suggested in his embittered war autobiography was that the postwar individual, first as soldier and citizen, now as artist, was the special butt of the universe. As Wyndham Lewis wrote later of the typical Hemingway hero, he was the man "things are done to." To Hemingway life became supremely the task of preserving oneself by preserving and refining one's art. Art was the ultimate, as it was perhaps the only, defense. In a society that served only to prey upon the individual, endurance was possible only by retaining one's identity and thereby proclaiming one's valor. Writing was not a recreation, it was a way of life; it was born of desperation and enmity and took its insights from a militant suffering. Yet it could exist only as it purified itself; it had meaning only as it served to tell the truth. A writer succeeded by proving himself superior to circumstance; his significance as an artist lay in his honesty, his courage, and the will to endure. Hemingway's vision of life, as John Peale Bishop put it, was thus one of perpetual annihilation. "Since the will can do nothing against circumstance, choice is precluded; those things are good which the senses report good; and beyond their brief record there is only the remorseless devaluation of nature."

The remarkable thing about Hemingway from the first was that he did not grow up to this rigid sense of tragedy, or would not admit that he had. The background of his first stories, *In Our Time*, was the last frontier of his Michigan boyhood, a mountainous region of forests and lakes against which he appeared as the inquisitive but tight-lipped youth—hard, curt, and already a little sad. With its carefully cultivated brutality and austerity, the sullen boy in *In Our Time* revealed a mind fixed in its groove. These stories of his youth— set against the superb evocation of war monotony and horror, elaborately contrived to give the violence of the Michigan woods and the violence of war an equal value in the reader's mind—summarized Hemingway's education. Their significance lay in the number of things the young Hemingway had already taken for granted; they were a youth's stricken responses to a brutal environment, and the responses seemed to become all. Just as the war in *A Farewell to Arms* was to seem less important than the sensations it provoked, so the landscape of *In Our Time* had meaning only as the youth had learned from it. For Hemingway in his early twenties, the criticism of society had gone so deep that life seemed an abstraction; it was something one discounted by instinct and distrusted by habit. It was a sequence of violent actions and mechanical impulses: the brutality of men in the Michigan woods, the Indian husband who cut his throat after watching his wife undergo a Caesarean with a jack-knife, adolescent loneliness and exaltation, a punch-drunk boxer on the road. And always below that level of native memories, interspersed with passing sketches of gangsters and bullfights, lay the war.

> Nick sat against the wall of the church where they had dragged him to be clear of machine-gun fire in the street. Both legs stuck out awkwardly. He had been hit in the spine. His face was sweaty and dirty. The sun shone on his face. The day was very hot. . . . Two Austrian dead lay in the rubble in the shade of the house. Up the street were other dead. . . . Nick turned his head carefully and looked at Rinaldi. "Senta Rinaldi. Senta. You and me we've made a separate peace."

The glazed face of the Hemingway hero, which in its various phases was to become, like Al Capone's, the face of a decade and to appear on a succession of soldiers, bullfighters, explorers, gangsters, and unhappy revolutionaries, emerged slowly but definitively in *In Our Time*. The hero's first reaction was surprise, to be followed immediately by stupor; life, like the war, is in its first phase heavy, graceless, sullen; the theme is sounded in the rape of Liz Coates by the hired man. Then the war became comic, a series of incongruities. "Everybody was drunk. The whole battery was drunk going along the road in the dark. . . . The lieutenant kept riding his horse out into the fields and saying to him: 'I'm drunk, I tell you, *mon vieux*. Oh, I am so soused.' . . . It was funny going along that road." Then the whole affair became merely sordid, a huddle of refugees in the mud, the empty and perpetual flow of rain, a woman bearing

her child on the road. "It rained all through the evacuation." By the sheer accumulation of horrors, the final phase was reached, and the end was a deceptive
callousness.

> We were in a garden at Mons. Young Buckley came in with his patrol
> from across the river. The first German I saw climbed up over the gar-
> den wall. We waited till he got one leg over and then potted him. He
> had so much equipment on and looked awfully surprised and fell
> down into the garden. Then three more came over further down the
> wall. We shot them. They all came just like that.

Hemingway's own values were stated explicitly in the story called "Soldier's
Home," where he wrote that "Krebs acquired the nausea in regard to experience
that is the result of untruth or exaggeration." The Hemingway archetype had
begun by contrasting life and war, devaluating one in terms of the other. Now life
became only another manifestation of war; the Hemingway world is in a state of
perpetual war. The soldier gives way to the bullfighter, the slacker to the tired revolutionary, the greed of war is identified with the corruption and violence of
sport. Nothing remains but the individual's fierce, unassailable pride in his pride,
the will to go on, the need to write without "untruth or exaggeration." As a soldier, he had preserved his sanity by rebelling quietly and alone; he had made the
separate peace. Mutiny was the last refuge of the individual caught in the trap of
war; chronic mutiny now remains the safeguard of the individual in that state of
implicit belligerence between wars that the world calls peace. The epos of death
has become life's fundamental narrative; the new hero is the matador in chapter 12
of *In Our Time.* "When he started to kill it was all in the same rush. The bull looking at him straight in front, hating. He drew out the sword from the folds of the
muleta and sighted with the same movement and called to the bull, *Toro! Toro!* and
the bull charged and Villalta charged and just for a moment they became one."
The casual grace of the bullfighter, which at its best is an aesthetic passion, is all.
And even that grace may become pitiful, as in the saga of the aging matador in
"The Undefeated." For the rest, defeat and corruption and exhaustion lie everywhere: marriage in "Cross-Country Snow," sport in "My Old Man" ("Seems like
when they get started they don't leave a guy nothing"), the gangrene of fascism in
"Che Ti Dice la Patria?" The climax of that first exercise in disillusion is reached
in the terse and bitter narrative called "The Revolutionist," the story of the young

boy who had been tortured by the Whites in Budapest when the Soviet collapsed, and who found Italy in 1919 beautiful. "In spite of Hungary, he believed altogether in the world revolution."

"But how is the movement going in Italy?" he asked.
"Very badly," I said.
"But it will go better," he said. "You have everything here. It is the one country that everyone is sure of. It will be the starting point of everything."

4

When Hemingway published those first stories in 1925, he was twenty-seven years old, and the rising star—"the surest future there," Lincoln Steffens recalled in his autobiography—in the American literary colony in Paris. Unlike most of the writers in the "lost generation," he had not gone to a university; after completing a round of private schools he had gone to work, still in his teens, for the *Kansas City Star,* a paper famous for its literary reporters. He had driven an ambulance on the Italian front before America entered the war, been wounded gloriously enough to receive the Croce di Guerra, and after 1921 had traveled extensively as a foreign correspondent. "In writing for a newspaper," he reported seventeen years later in the rambling prose of *Death in the Afternoon,* "you told what happened, and with one trick or another, you communicated the emotion aided by the element of timeliness which gives a certain emotion to any account of something that has happened on that day. But the real thing, the sequence of motion and fact which made the emotion and which would be as valid in a year or ten years or, with luck and if you stated it purely enough, always, was beyond me and I was working very hard to get it."

Hemingway's intense search for "the real thing" had already singled him out in Paris before he published *In Our Time.* In those early years, guided by his interest in poetry and his experiences as a reporter of the European debacle, he seemed to be feeling his way toward a new prose, a prose that would be not only absolutely true to the events reported and to the accent of common speech, but would demand of itself an original evocativeness and plasticity.

What he wanted, as he said later in *Death in the Afternoon,* was a prose more intensely precise than conventional prose, and hence capable of effects not yet achieved. He wanted to see "how far prose can be carried if anyone is serious enough and has luck. There is a fourth and fifth dimension that can be gotten. . . . It is much more difficult than poetry. It is prose that has never been written. But it can be written without tricks and without cheating. With nothing that will go bad afterwards." Yet what he was aiming at in one sense, F. O. Matthiessen has pointed out, was the perfect yet poetic naturalness of a Thoreau. Hemingway's surface affiliations as a prose craftsman were with his first teachers, Gertrude Stein and Sherwood Anderson, who taught him the requisite simplicity and fidelity and—Gertrude Stein more than Anderson— an ear for the natural rhythms of speech. But his deeper associations went beyond them, beyond even the Flaubertian tradition of discipline and *le mot juste.* He did not want to write "artistic prose," and Gertrude Stein and Anderson, equally joined in their hatred of display and their search for an inner truth in prose, had certainly taught him not to. But he wanted not merely to tell "the truth about his own feelings at the moment when they exist"; he wanted to aim at that luminous and imaginative truth which a writer like Thoreau, on the strength of a muscular integrity and passion for nature very like his own, had created out of fidelity to the details of life as he saw them. What he wanted was that sense of grace, that "sequence of motion and fact" held at unwavering pitch, that could convey, as nothing else could, the secret fluid symbolism in the facts touched and recorded.

It was this that separated him essentially from Gertrude Stein and Anderson. Anderson was not fundamentally interested in *writing;* Gertrude Stein, who could help everyone in the world but herself, was interested in nothing else. The Hemingway legend, which Hemingway himself fostered in the twenties, encouraged the belief that he was only a pure nihilist and coldly assimilative, even brutish, in imagination. But nothing could have been more false. He brought a major art to a minor vision of life, and it is as important to measure the vision as it is to appreciate the art. But his seeming naïveté was really an exemplary straightforwardness and a remarkable capacity for learning from every possible source. As a practicing artist he had the ability to assimilate the lessons of others so brilliantly that he seemed to impart a definitive modern emotion to everything he touched. He learned so brilliantly, indeed, that the extent of his borrowing has often been exaggerated. What is significant in Hemingway's literary education is not that he learned prose rhythm from the Gertrude Stein of *Three Lives*, the uses of simplicity from Sherwood Anderson, the sense of discipline from Ezra Pound, and the cosmopolitan literary ateliers of postwar Paris, but that they gave him the authority to be himself. Despite his indebtedness to Mark Twain's *Huckleberry Finn*—the greatest book in all American writing for him—he had no basic relation to any prewar culture. Byron learned from Pope, but Hemingway learned to write in a literary environment that could not remember 1913. Even the literary revolution that found its appointed heir in him, an avant-garde forever posing under its Picasso and talking modernism with a midwestern accent, could not long claim him. Once Hemingway had learned the principles and tricks of his art, made a literary personality out of the midwestern athlete, soldier, and foreign correspondent, created a new hero for the times in the romantically disillusioned postwar dandy, he went his own way in his search for "the real thing."

It was in his unceasing quest of a conscious perfection through style that Hemingway proclaimed his distinction. To tell what had happened, as he wrote later, one used "one trick or another," dialogue being the supreme trick. But "the real thing," the pulse of his art, was to Hemingway from the first that perfect blending of fact into symbol, that perfect conversion of natural rhythm into an evocation of the necessary emotion that would fuse the various phases of contemporary existence—love, war, sport—and give them a collective grace. And it was here that style and experience came together for him. Man endured the cruelty and terror of life only by the sufferance of his senses and his occasional enjoyment of them; but in that sufferance and enjoyment, if only he could convey them perfectly, lay the artist's special triumph. He could rise above the dull submissive sense of outrage which most men felt in the face of events. By giving a new dimension to the description of natural fact, he could gain a refuge from that confusion which was half the terror of living. What this meant was brilliantly illustrated in the association of the worlds of peace and war in *In Our Time*; the theme of universal loneliness in the midst of war that was sounded in the very first paragraph of *A Farewell to Arms* and attained its classic expression in the retreat at Caporetto, where the flowing river, the long grumbling line of soldiers, the officers who are being shot together by the carabinieri, seem to melt together in the darkness; the extraordinary scene in *The Sun Also Rises* where Robert Cohn, sitting with Jake and his friends at the bullfight, is humiliated a moment before the steer is gored in the ring. In each case the animal in man has found its parallel and key in some event around it; the emotion has become the fact.

If "the real thing" could not always be won, or retained after it had been won, there were other forms of grace—the pleasures of drinking and making love, the stabbing matador dancing nervously before his bull, the piercing cry of the hunt, the passionate awareness that would allow a man to write a sentence like "In shooting quail you must not get between them, or when they flush they will come pouring at you, some rising steep, some skimming by your ears, whirring into a size you have never seen them in the air as they pass." If art was an expression of fortitude, fortitude at its best had the quality of art. Beyond fortitude, which even in *For Whom the Bell Tolls* is the pride of a professional integrity and skill, there was the sense of nature paralyzed, nature frozen into loneliness or terror. No nature writer in all American literature save Thoreau has had Hemingway's sensitiveness to color, to climate, to the knowledge of physical energy under heat or cold, that knowledge of the body thinking and moving through a landscape: what Edmund Wilson, in another connection, has called Hemingway's "barometric accuracy." That accuracy was the joy of the huntsman and the artist; beyond that and its corresponding gratifications, Hemingway seemed to attach no value to anything else. There were only absolute values or absolute degradations.

The very intensity of Hemingway's "nihilism" in his first stories and novels proved, however, that his need for an ideal expression in art was the mark of a passionate romanticist who had been profoundly disappointed. The anguish of his characters was too dramatic, too flawless; it was too transparent an inversion. The symbols Hemingway employed to convey his sense of the world's futility and horror were always more significant than the characters who personified them, and they so often seemed personified emotions that the emotions became all. The gallery of expatriates in *The Sun Also Rises* were always subsidiary to the theme their lives enforced; the lovers in *A Farewell to Arms* were, as Edmund Wilson has said, the abstractions of a lyric emotion. Hemingway had created a world of his own more brilliant than life, but he was not writing about people living in a real world; he was dealing in absolute values again, driving his characters between the two poles of an absolute exaltation and an absolute frustration, invoking the specter of their damnation.

After that, *Death in the Afternoon* and the Hemingway legend. There had always been a Hemingway legend, and with good reason; like Byron, he was in part the creation of his own reputation. But the legend became ominous and even cheap only when Hemingway chose to treat it as a guide to personal conduct and belief; when, in truth, he became not only one of his own characters but his own hero. After *Death in the Afternoon*, Hemingway's work became an expression of the legend, where the legend had once been a measure of the world's response to his work. The sense of shock, the stricken malaise of his first stories, were now transformed into a loud and cynical rhetoric. "Madame, all our words from loose using have lost their edge," Hemingway tells the Old Lady in *Death in the Afternoon*; and proves it by his own example. "Have you no remedy then?" she asks. "Madame, there is no remedy for anything in life." The pose, pretentious in one scene, becomes merely gluttonous in another. The high jinks of the wastrels in *The Sun Also Rises* had suggested a tragic self-knowledge, an affirmation of life as they saw it; Hemingway's own tone was now giggly and a little frantic. "So far, about morals, I know only that what is moral is what you feel good after and what is immoral is what you feel bad after." It was on a plane with the famous parody of Marx in "The Gambler, The Nun, and the Radio":

Religion is the opium of the people.... Yes, and music is the opium of the people.... And now economics is the opium of the people; along with patriotism the opium of the people in Italy and Germany. What about sexual intercourse; was that an opium of the people? Of some of the people. Of some of the best of the people. But drink was a sovereign opium of the people, oh, an excellent opium. Although some prefer the radio, another opium of the people.... Along with these went gambling, an opium of the people if there ever was one.... Ambition was another, an opium of the people, along with a belief in any new form of government.

As the years went by, one grew accustomed to Hemingway standing like Tarzan against a backdrop labeled Nature; or, as the tedious sportsman of *Green Hills of Africa*, grinning over the innumerable beasts he had slain, while the famous style became more mechanical, the sentences more invertebrate, the

philosophy more self-conscious, the head shaking over a circumscribed eternity more painful. Most of the lost generation had already departed to other
spheres of interest; Hemingway seemed to have taken up a last refuge behind
the clothing advertisements in *Esquire,* writing essays in which he mixed his
fishing reports with querulous pronouncements on style and the good life.
Then, eight years after the publication of *A Farewell to Arms,* when the
Hemingway legend had already lost its luster with the disappearance of the
world that had encouraged that legend with emulation and empty flattery,
Hemingway wrote *To Have and Have Not.* It was a frantically written novel,
revealing a new tension and uncertainty in Hemingway; but for all its melodrama, it was not cheap, and it was strange to note that it was the first novel he
had written about America. The dry crackle of the boozed cosmopolitans eating their hearts out in unison, the perpetual shift of scene to Malaga or Paris
or the African jungle, seemed to have been left behind him. The America of *To
Have and Have Not* was Key West, like the Paris of 1925 an outpost of a culture
and its symbol. It was by Key West that Hemingway had come home, and it
was Key West, apparently, that became a working symbol of America for him,
a cross section: the shabby, deeply moving rancor of all those human wrecks,
the fishermen and the Cuban revolutionaries, the veterans and the alcoholics,
the gilt-edged snobs and the hungry natives, the great white stretch of beach
promising everything and leading nowhere.

The Hemingway of *To Have and Have Not* was not a "new" Hemingway; he
was an angry and confused writer who had been too profoundly disturbed by
the social and economic crisis to be indifferent, but could find no clue in his
education by which to understand it. Inevitably, he lapsed into melodrama and
sick violence. To the Hemingway who had gained his conception of life from
the First World War only to crash into the Second by way of international
panic and the Spanish Civil War, mass suffering had always been a backdrop
against which the Hemingway hero persisted by dint of his Byronic pride, his
sense of grace. But this new crisis had to be endured with something more
than artistic fortitude; every generation was caught up in it, every phase of
contemporary culture and manners was transformed by it, as even his beloved
Spain was being devastated by it. It was like Hemingway, of course, to pick for
his new hero in the thirties the pirate of *To Have and Have Not* and the international secret agent of *The Fifth Column:* the two men left in the era from Black

Friday* to Munich who could remain casual about annihilation! He was reaching for something in these two productions that he could not identify satisfactorily or project with confidence, and it was inevitable that both Harry Morgan and Philip should represent a tormented individualism eager for human fellowship and contemptuous of it. The Hemingway hero was now a composite exaggeration of all the Hemingway heroes, yet nothing in himself. He was the *Esquire* fisherman and an OGPU agent in Spain who found that he had to choose between the Spanish Republic and a Vassar girl; he was a murdering gangster who killed only because Hemingway wanted to kill something at the moment, and a sentimental sophisticate who, when he heard the militia sing "Bandera Rossa" downstairs in the shell-battered Hotel Florida, cried: "The best people I ever knew died for that song." Yet Philip in *The Fifth Column* was not one of the best people; he was Jake Barnes making up for his impotence by murdering Fascists, and the Fascists were as unreal as the sick wisdom he and the perennial Lady Brett mumbled at each other in the midst of a civil war that was shaking Western society.

Whatever it was Hemingway tried to reach, however, he found in some measure in Spain; and he found it first in an extraordinary little story, "Old Man at the Bridge," which he cabled from Barcelona in April 1938. "It will take many plays and novels to present the nobility and dignity of the cause of the Spanish people," he wrote in his preface to *The Fifth Column*, "and the best ones will be written after the war is over." "Old Man at the Bridge" was more than an introduction to the retrospective wisdom of *For Whom the Bell Tolls*; it was a record of the better things Hemingway had learned in Spain, an intimation of a Hemingway who had found the thwarted ideal clear and radiant again through the martyrdom of the Spanish masses. In the retreat of the Loyalist forces a Spanish officer encounters the last refugee from San Carlos, an old man who has been taking care of eight pigeons, two goats, and a cat, but has been separated from them and from his own people by the advancing Fascist armies. "And you have no family?" the Loyalist officer asks. "No," replies the old man, "only the animals I stated. The cat, of course, will be all right. A cat can look out for itself, but I cannot think what will become of the others."

---

*The collapse of the stock market in October 1929 [ed.].

"What politics have you?" the officer asks. "I am without politics," replies the old man. "I am seventy-six years old. I have come twelve kilometers now and I think now I can go no further."

It was in something of this spirit that Hemingway wrote *For Whom the Bell Tolls*, the work of a profound romanticist who had at last come to terms with the ideal, and who had torn down the old charnel house with such ardor that his portrait of the Spanish war was less a study of the Spanish people than a study in epic courage and compassion. The idealism that had always been so frozen in inversion, so gnawing and self-mocking, had now become an unabashed lyricism that enveloped the love of Robert Jordan and Maria, the strength of Pilar, the courage and devotion of the guerrillas, the richness and wit of Spanish speech, in a hymn of fellowship. "All mankind is of one Author, and is one volume. . . . No man is an Island, intire of it selfe." Nothing could have been more purely romantic than the love story of Robert and Maria, and no love story ever seemed so appropriate an expression of a writer's confidence in life and his overwhelming joy in it. Hemingway had apparently gained a new respect for humanity in Spain, an appreciation of the collectivity that binds all men together; and in the spirit of the Catholic devotion by John Donne which gave him his title, it seemed as if his long quest for an intense unity, the pure absolute fortitude and grace, had become a joyous unison of action and battle and love.

Yet *For Whom the Bell Tolls* is among the least of Hemingway's works. Its leading characters are totally unreal; as a record of the human and social drama that was the Spanish Civil War, it is florid and never very deep. And if one compares this work of his ambitious conversion—with its eloquence, its calculation and its romantic inflation—with the extraordinarily brilliant story of this late period, "The Snows of Kilimanjaro," it is clear that the attempted affirmation of life in the novel, while passionate enough, is moving only in itself, while the concentrated study of waste and death in the story is perfectly dramatic, perfectly Hemingway's own. Hemingway's world is a world of death still, even in *For Whom the Bell Tolls*; and the great things in it, like the battle scenes or the pillage of the Fascist town, flow with a carefully contrived violence and brutality from him. But the Spanish war is essentially only Robert Jordan's education—"It's part of one's education. It will be quite an education when it's finished." The Hemingway "I" is still the center of existence, as only he could alternate between the war and Maria in the sleeping bag so easily; as only he could seem less a man entering into the experience of others than the familiarly damned, lost-generation Byron playing a part beside them. Yes, and the Hemingway hero is still "the man things are done to"—the war is something happening to Robert Jordan—still the brilliant young man counting the costs of his own life among the ruins. *For Whom the Bell Tolls* is thus an unsatisfactory novel, certainly unsatisfactory for Hemingway, because it is a strained and involuntary application of his essentially anarchical individualism, his brilliant half-vision of life, to a new world of war and struggle too big for Hemingway's sense of scale and one that can make that half-vision seem significantly sentimental.

The will is there, the reaching hope; nothing could be more false than the familiar superstition that Hemingway wanted to go round and round in the old nihilist circle. But as Robert Jordan lived and fought the war so curiously alone, so he dies alone, waiting for the enemy to come—the Hemingway guerrilla dying a separate death as once he made a separate peace, the last of the Hemingway heroes enjoying the final abnegation, and now the least impressive. That separate death and abnegation were all there before, and they were very good before. Good when the hunter was alone in the hills, the matador before his bull, the quail skimming through the air. Good when Gertrude Stein could teach a young man fresh from war to write perfect sentences, and the triumph of art was equal to the negation of life. Good when the world could seem like a Hemingway novel; and the "I" was the emblem of all the disillusionment and fierce pride in a world so brilliant in its sickness; and the sentences were so perfect, spanning the darkness. It did not matter then that the art could be so fresh and brilliant, the life below its superb texture so arid and dark. For Hemingway's is one of the great half-triumphs of literature; he proved himself the triumphal modern artist come to America, and within his range and means, one of the most interesting creators in the history of the American imagination. But if it did not matter then, it matters now—not because what is supremely good in Hemingway is in any way perishable, but because his work is a stationary half-triumph, because there is no real continuity in him, nothing of the essential greatness of spirit which his own artistic success has always called for. It matters now that Hemingway's influence has in itself become a matter of history. It will always matter, particularly to those who appreciate what he brought to American writing, and who, with that distinction in mind, can realize that Hemingway's is a tactile contemporary American

success; who can realize, with respect and sympathy, that it is a triumph in and
of a narrow, local, and violent world—and never superior to it.

5

Technically and even morally Hemingway was to have a profound influence on
the writing of the thirties. As a stylist and craftsman, his example was magnetic on younger men who came after him; as the progenitor of the new and
distinctively American cult of violence, he stands out as the greatest single
influence on the hard-boiled novel of the thirties, and certainly affected the
social and left-wing fiction of the period more than some of its writers could
easily admit. No one save Dreiser in an earlier period had anything like
Hemingway's dominance over modern American fiction, yet even Dreiser
meant largely an example of courage and frankness during the struggle for realism, not a standard of craftsmanship and a persuasive conception of life, like
Hemingway's. Hemingway is the bronze god of the whole contemporary literary experience in America. Yet in a sense he marks an end as clearly as he once
marked a beginning. If we consider how the whole lost-generation conception
of art and society reached its climax in him, and how much that conception
was the brilliant and narrow concentration of the individualism and alienation
from society felt by the artist in the twenties, it is clear that Hemingway's stubbornly atomic view of life is the highest expression of the postwar sequence,
not a bridge to the future. Despite his will and formal conversion to "the
interests of humanity," the "I" and society do not meet imaginatively for him.
The writing that came after him in the thirties had only the surface of his brilliance, when it had that at all; but by its absorption in the larger concerns of
society, its conviction that no man is alone today, it reveals a departure from
Hemingway as much as its toughness reveals his association with it.

A chapter in the moral history of modern American writing does come to an
end with Hemingway and the lost generation, and nowhere can this be more
clearly seen than in the work of John Dos Passos, who rounds out the story of
that generation and carries its values into the social novel of the thirties. For
what is so significant about Dos Passos is that though he is a direct link
between the postwar decade and the crisis novel of the Depression period, the
defeatism of the lost generation has been slowly and subtly transferred by him

from persons to society itself. It is society that becomes the hero of his work, society that suffers the anguish and impending sense of damnation that the lost-generation individualists had suffered alone before. For him the lost generation becomes all the lost generations from the beginning of modern time in America—all who have known themselves to be lost in the fires of war or struggling up the icy slopes of modern capitalism. The tragic "I" has become the tragic inclusive "we" of modern society; the pace of sport, of the separate peace and the separate death, has become the pounding rhythm of the industrial machine. The central beliefs of his generation, though they have a different source in Dos Passos and a different expression, remain hauntingly the same. Working in politics and technology as Fitzgerald worked in the high world and Hemingway in war and sport, Dos Passos comes out with all his equations zero. They are almost too perfectly zero, and always uneasy and reluctantly defeatist. But the record of his novels from *One Man's Initiation* to *Adventures of a Young Man*, whatever the new faith revealed in his hymn to the American democratic tradition in *The Grounds We Stand On*, is the last essential testimony of his generation, and in many respects the most embittered.

Dos Passos's zero is not the "nada hail nada full of nada" of Hemingway's most famous period, the poetically felt nihilism and immersion in nothingness; nor is it the moody and ambiguous searching of Fitzgerald. The conviction of tragedy that rises out of his work is the steady protest of a sensitive democratic conscience against the tyranny and the ugliness of society, against the failure of a complete human development under industrial capitalism; it is the protest of a man who can participate formally in the struggles of society as Hemingway and Fitzgerald never do. To understand Dos Passos's social interests is to appreciate how much he differs from the others of his generation, and yet how far removed he is from the Socialist crusader certain Marxist critics once saw in him. For what is central in Dos Passos is not merely the fascination with the total operations of society, but his unyielding opposition to all its degradations. He cannot separate the "I" and society absolutely from each other, like Hemingway, for though he is essentially even less fraternal in spirit, he is too much the conscious political citizen. But the "I" remains as spectator and victim, and it is that conscientious intellectual self that one hears in all his work, up to the shy and elusive autobiography in the "Camera Eye" sections of *U.S.A.* That human self in Dos Passos is the Emersonian individual, not Hemingway's agonist; he is the arbiter of existence, always a little chill, a little withdrawn (everything in Dos Passos radiates around the scrutiny of the camera eye), not the sentient, suffering center of it. He is man believing and trusting in the Emersonian "self-trust" when all else fails him, man taking his stand on individual integrity against the pressures of society. But he is not Hemingway's poetic man. What Emerson once said of himself in his journal is particularly true of Dos Passos: he likes Man, not men.

Dos Passos certainly came closer to socialism than most artists in his generation; yet it is significant that no novelist in America has written more somberly of the dangers to individual integrity in a centrally controlled society. Spain before the war had meant for Hemingway the bullfighters, Pamplona, the golden wine; for Dos Passos it had meant the Spanish Anarchists and the Quixotic dream he described so affectionately in his early travel book, *Rosinante to the Road Again*. Yet where Hemingway found his "new hope" in the Spanish Civil War, Dos Passos saw in that war not merely the struggle into which his mind had entered as a matter of course, the agony of the Spain with which he had always felt spiritual ties, but the symbolic martyrdom of Glenn Spotswood, the disillusioned former Communist, at the hands of the OGPU in Spain in *Adventures of a Young Man*. Hemingway could at least write *For Whom the Bell Tolls* as the story of Robert Jordan's education; Dos Passos had to write his Spanish novel as the story of Glenn Spotswood's martyrdom. And what is so significant in Dos Passos's work always is individual judgment and martyrdom, the judgment that no fear can prevent his heroes from making on society, the martyrdom that always waits for them at its hands. That last despairing cry of Glenn Spotswood's in the prison of the Loyalists—"I, Glenn Spotswood, being of sound mind and emprisoned body, do bequeath to the international working-class my hope of a better world"— is exactly like the cry of the poilu in Dos Passos's callow first novel, *One Man's Initiation*—"Oh, the lies, the lies, the lies, the lies that life is smothered in! We must strike once more for freedom, for the sake of the dignity of man. Hopelessly, cynically, ruthlessly, we must rise and show at least that we are not taken in; that we are slaves but not willing slaves." From Martin Howe to Glenn Spotswood, the Dos Passos hero is the young man who fails and is broken by society, but is never taken in. Whatever else he loses—and the Dos Passos characters invariably lose, if they have ever possessed, almost everything that is life to most people—he is not taken in. Hemingway has "grace under pressure," and the drama in his work is always the inherently passionate need of life: the terrible insistence on the individual's need of survival, the drumming fear that he may not survive. Dos Passos, though he has so intense an imagination, has not Hemingway's grace, his need to make so dark and tonal a poetry of defeat; he centers everything around the inviolability of the individual, his sanctity. The separation of the individual from society in Hemingway may be irrevocable, but it is tragically felt; his cynicism can seem so flawless only because it mocks itself. In Dos Passos that separation is organic and self-willed: the mind has made its refusal, and the fraternity that it seeks and denies in the same voice can never enter into it.

It is in this concern with the primacy of the individual, with his need to save the individual from society rather than to establish him in or over it, that one can trace the conflict that runs all through Dos Passos's work—between his aestheticism and strong social interests; his profound absorption in the total operations of modern society and his overscrupulous withdrawal from all of them; the iron, satirical prose he hammered out in *U.S.A.* (a machine prose for a machine world) and the youthful, stammering lyricism that pulses under it. Constitutionally a rebel and an outsider, in much of his work up to *U.S.A.* a pale and self-conscious aesthete, Dos Passos is at once the most precious of the lost-generation writers and the first of the American "technological" novelists, the first to bring the novel squarely into the Machine Age and to use its rhythms, its stockpiles of tools and people, in his books.

Dos Passos has never reached the dramatic balance of Hemingway's great period, the ability to concentrate all resources of his sensibility at one particular point. The world is always a gray horror, and it is forever coming undone; his mind is forever quarreling with itself. It is only because he has never been able to accept a mass society that he has always found so morbid a fascination with it. The modern equation cancels out to zero, everything comes undone, the heroes are always broken, and the last figure in *U.S.A.*, brooding like Dos Passos himself over that epic of failure, is a starving and homeless boy walking alone up the American highway. Oppression and inequity have to be named and protested, as the democratic conscience in Dos Passos always does go on protesting to the end. Yet what he said of Thorstein Veblen in one of the most brilliantly written biographies in *U.S.A.* is particularly true of himself: he can "never get his mouth round the essential yes." The protest is never a Socialist protest, because that will substitute one collectivity for another; nor is it poetic or religious, because Dos Passos's mind, while sensitive and brilliant in inquiry, is steeped in materialism. It is a radical protest, but it is the protest against the status quo of a mind groping for more than it can define to itself, the protest of a mind whose opposition to capitalism is no greater than his suspicion of all societies.

In Dos Passos's early work, so much of which is trivial and merely preparatory to the one important work of his career, *U.S.A.*, this conflict meant the conflict between the aesthete and the world even in broadly social novels like *Three Soldiers* and *Manhattan Transfer*. But under the surface of preciosity that covers those early novels, there is always the story of John Roderigo Dos Passos, grandson of a Portuguese immigrant, and like Thorstein Veblen—whose mordant insights even more than Marx's revolutionary critique give a base in social philosophy to *U.S.A.*—an outsider. Growing up with all the advantages of upper-middle-class education and travel that his own father could provide for him, Dos Passos nevertheless could not help growing up with the sense of difference which even the sensitive grandsons of immigrants can feel in America. He went to Choate and to Harvard; he was soon to graduate into the most distinguished of all the lost generation's finishing schools, the Norton-Harjes Ambulance Service subsidized by a Morgan partner; but he was out of the main line, out just enough in his own mind to make the difference that can make men what they are.

It is not strange that Dos Passos has always felt such intimate ties with the Hispanic tradition and community, or that in his very revealing little travel book, *Rosinante to the Road Again,* he mounted Don Quixote's nag and named himself Telemachus, as if to indicate that his postwar pilgrimage in Spain was, like Telemachus's search for Ulysses, a search for his own father-principle, the continuity he needed to find in Hispania. It was in Spain and in Latin America that Dos Passos learned to prize men like the Mexican revolutionary Zapata and the libertarian Anarchists of Spain. As his travel diaries and particularly the biographical sketches that loom over the narrative in *U.S.A.* tell us, Dos Passos's heart has always gone out to the men who are lonely and human in their rebellion, not to the victors and the politicians in the social struggle, but to the great defeated—the impractical but humane Spanish Anarchists, the Veblens, the good Mexicans, the Populists and the Wobblies, the Bob La Follettes, the Jack Reeds, the Randolph Bournes, all defeated and uncontrolled to the last, most of them men distrustful of too much power, of centralization, of the glib revolutionary morality which begins with hatred and terror and believes it can end with fraternity. So even the first figure in *U.S.A.*, the itinerant Fenian McCreary, "Mac," and the last, "Vag," are essentially Wobblies and "working stiffs"; so even Mary French, the most admirable character in the whole trilogy, is a defeated Bolshevik. And it is only the defeated Bolsheviks whom Dos Passos ever really likes. The undefeated seem really to defeat themselves.

The grandson of the Portuguese immigrant was also, however, the boy who entered college, as Malcolm Cowley has pointed out, "at the beginning of a period which was later known as that of the Harvard aesthetes." The intellectual atmosphere there was that of "young men who read Pater and 'The Hill of Dreams,' who argued about St. Thomas in sporting houses, and who wandered through the slums of South Boston with dull eyes for 'the long rain slanting on black walls' and eager eyes for the face of an Italian woman who, in the midst of this squalor, suggested the Virgin in Botticelli's *Annunciation*." Dos Passos went to the slums; and he could find the Botticelli Virgin there. [...]

By 1921, with *Three Soldiers*, the aesthete had become something more of the social novelist. The rhetorical petulance of *One Man's Initiation* had given way to a dull, gritty hatred. [...] He was a realist whose odyssey of three buck privates—Fuselli from the West, Christfield from the South, John Andrews the musician from New York—was an attempt to tell in miniature the national story of the A.E.F. Yet for all the grimness of *Three Soldiers*, the sounding in it of the characteristically terse and mocking tone of Dos Passos's later social novels, it was essentially as flaky and self-consciously romantic as *One Man's Initiation*. There are three protagonists in the book, but only one hero, John Andrews; and it is his humiliation and agony in war that finally dominate the book. It is interesting to note that in this first important novel Dos Passos had already shown that interest in the type, the mass as central protagonist, that would distinguish *U.S.A.*; and certainly nothing is so good in the book as his ability to suggest the gray anonymity, the treadmill, the repeated shocks and probings of the private's experience, the hysterical barroom jokes and convulsive brothel loves, the boredom and weariness. [...]

Thirteen years after he had completed *Three Soldiers*, Dos Passos wrote that it was a book that had looked forward to the future. For all its bitterness, he had written it as an epilogue to the war from which men in 1919 seemed to be turning to reconstruction or even revolution. "Currents of energy seemed breaking out everywhere as young guys climbed out of their uniforms ... in every direction the countries of the world stretched out starving and angry, ready for anything turbulent and new." He himself had gone on to Spain, Telemachus looking for the father and teasing himself because he was so callow. Spain was where the old romantic castles still remained; Spain had been neutral during the war; in Spain one might even be free of the generation "to which excess is a synonym for beauty." In Spain there were the Anarchists, and tranquility without resignation, and the kind of life that would develop a Pio Baroja, physician and baker and novelist of revolution. "It's always death," cries the friend in *Rosinante to the Road Again*, "but we must go on. . . . Many years ago I should have set out to right wrong—for no one but a man, an individual alone, can right a wrong; organization merely substitutes one wrong for another—but now . . ." But now Telemachus is listening to Pio Baroja, whose characters, as he describes them, are so much like the characters in *Manhattan Transfer* and *U.S.A.*—"men whose nerve has failed, who live furtively on the outskirts, snatching a little joy here and there, drugging their hunger with gorgeous mirages." Baroja is a revolutionary novelist as Dos Passos only seems to be, but as Dos Passos reports Baroja's conception of the middle-class intellectual, one can see his own self-portrait:

> He has not undergone the discipline which can only come from common slavery in the industrial machine, necessary for a builder. His slavery has been an isolated slavery which has unfitted him forever from becoming truly part of a community. He can use the vast power of knowledge which training has given him only in one way. His great mission is to put the acid test to existing institutions, and to strip the veils off them.

By 1925, when he published *Manhattan Transfer*, Dos Passos had come to a critical turn in his career. He had been uprooted by the war, he had fled from the peace; but he could not resolve himself in flight. More than any other American novelist of the contemporary generation, Dos Passos was fascinated by the phenomenon of a mass society in itself; but his mind had not yet begun to study seriously the configuration of social forces, the naturalism and social history, which were to become his great subject in *U.S.A.* Like so much that he wrote up to 1930, *Manhattan Transfer* is only a preparation for *U.S.A.*, and like so many of those early works, it is a mediocre, weakly written book. He had as yet no real style of his own; he has not even in *Manhattan Transfer.* But he was reaching in that book for a style and method distinctively his own; and just as the Sacco-Vanzetti case was two years later to crystallize the antagonism to American capitalist society that is the base of *U.S.A.*, so the experimental form of *Manhattan Transfer*, its attempt to play on the shuttle of the great city's life dozens of human stories representative of the mass scene (and, for Dos Passos, the mass agony), was to lead straight into the brilliantly original technique of *U.S.A.*

Yet the achievement in style and technique of *Manhattan Transfer* is curiously inconclusive and muddy. The book seems to flicker in the gaslight of Dos Passos's own confusion. Out of the endlessly changing patterns of metropolitan life he drew an image that was collective. He was all through this period working in expressionist drama, as plays like *The Garbage Man, Airways, Inc.,* and *Fortune Heights* testify; and as in the expressionist plays of Georg Kaiser and Ernst Toller, he sketched out in his novel a tragic ballet to the accompaniment of the city's music and its mass chorus. Most significantly, he was working out a kind of doggerel prose style completely removed from his early lushness, full of the slangy rhythms he had picked up in *Three Soldiers* by reproducing soldier speech, and yet suggestive of a wry and dim poetry. This new style Dos Passos evidently owed in part to contemporary poetry, and like his trick of liquefying scenes together as if in a dream sequence and fusing words to bring out their exact tonal reverberation in the mind, to James Joyce. But what this meant in *Manhattan Transfer* was that the romantic poet, the creator and double of Martin Howe and John Andrews and the novel's Jimmy Herf, had become fascinated with a kind of mass and pictorial ugliness. The book was like a perverse aesthetic geometry in which all the colors of the city's scenes were daubed together madly, and all its frames jumbled. What one saw in *Manhattan Transfer* was not the broad city pattern at all, but a wistful absorption in monstrousness. The poet-aesthete still stood against the world, and rejected it completely. Characteristically, even the book's hero (*U.S.A.* was to have no heroes, only symbols), Jimmy Herf, moons through it only to walk out into the dawn after a last party in Greenwich Village, bareheaded and alone, to proclaim his complete disgust with the megalopolis of which he was, as the Dos Passos poet-heroes always are, the victim.

So Dos Passos himself, though torn between what he had learned from Pio Baroja and his need to take refuge in "the aesthete's cell," was ready to flee again. The conflict all through his experience between the self and the world, the conflict that he had been portraying with growing irony and yet so passionately in all his works, was coming to a head. And now the social insights he had been gathering from his own personal sense of isolation, from his bitterness against the war, and from Spain, were kindled by the martyrdom of Sacco and Vanzetti. More perhaps than any other American writer who fought to obtain their freedom, Dos Passos was really educated and toughened, affected as an artist, by the long and dreary months he spent working for them outside Charlestown Prison. For many writers the Sacco-Vanzetti case was at most a shock to their acquiescent liberalism or indifference; for Dos Passos it provided immediately the catalyst (he had never been acquiescent or indifferent) his work had needed, the catalyst that made *U.S.A.* possible. It transformed his growingly irritable but persistently romantic obsession with the poet's struggle against the world into a use of the class struggle as his base in art. The Sacco-Vanzetti case gave him, in a word, the beginnings of a formal conception of society; and out of the bitter realization that this society—the society Martin Howe had mocked, that John Andrews had been crushed by, that Jimmy Herf had escaped—could grind two poor Italian Anarchists to death for their opinions, came the conception of the two nations, the two Americas, that is the scaffolding of *U.S.A.*

Dos Passos knew where he stood now: the old romantic polarity had become a social polarity, and America lay irrevocably split in his mind between the owners and the dispossessed, between those who wielded the police power and the great masses of people. He began to write *The 42nd Parallel*, the first volume in *U.S.A.*, after the Sacco-Vanzetti case; and the trilogy itself draws to its end after Mary French's return from their execution in *The Big Money*. The most deeply felt writing in all of *U.S.A.* is Dos Passos's own commentary on the Sacco-Vanzetti case in the "Camera Eye," where he speaks in his own person, an eloquent hymn of compassion and rage that is strikingly different from the low-toned stream-of-consciousness prose that is usually found in the "Camera Eye" sections, and which lifts it for a moment above the studied terseness and coldness of the whole work.

they have clubbed us off the streets they are stronger they are rich they
hire and fire the politicians the newspapereditors the old judges the
small men with reputations the collegepresidents the wardheelers (lis-

ten businessmen collegepresidents judges America will not forget her betrayers) they hire the men with guns the uniforms the policecars the patrolwagons

all right you have won you will kill the brave men our friends tonight

America our nation has been beaten by strangers who have turned our language inside out who have taken the clean words our fathers spoke and made them slimy and foul

their hired men sit on the judge's bench they sit back with their feet on the tables under the dome of the State House they are ignorant of our beliefs they have the dollars the guns the armed forces the powerplants

they have built the electricchair and hired the executioner to throw the switch

all right we are two nations

All right we are two nations. It is the two nations that compose the story of *U.S.A.* But it was the destruction of two individuals, symbolic as they were, that brought out this polarity in Dos Passos's mind, their individual martyrdom that called the book out. From first to last, Dos Passos is primarily concerned with the sanctity of the individual, and the trilogy proper ends with Mary French's defeat and growing disillusionment, with the homeless boy "Vag" alone on the road. It is not Marx's two classes and Marx's optimism that speak in *U.S.A.* at the end; it is Thorstein Veblen, who like Pio Baroja could "put the acid test to existing institutions and strip the veils off them," but "couldn't get his mouth round the essential yes." And no more can Dos Passos. *U.S.A.* is a study in the history of modern society, of its social struggles and great masses; but it is a history of defeat. There are no flags for the spirit in it, and no victory save the mind's silent victory that integrity can acknowledge to itself. It is one of the saddest books ever written by an American.

6

Technically *U.S.A.* is one of the great achievements of the modern novel, yet what that achievement is can easily be confused with its elaborate formal structure. For the success of Dos Passos's method does not rest primarily on his schematization of the novel into four panels, four levels of American experience—the narrative proper, the "Camera Eye," the "Biographies," and the "Newsreel." That arrangement, while original enough, is the most obvious thing in the book and soon becomes the most mechanical. The book lives by its narrative style, the wonderfully concrete yet elliptical prose which bears along and winds around the life stories in the book like a conveyor belt carrying Americans through some vast Ford plant of the human spirit. *U.S.A.* is a national epic, the first great national epic of its kind in the modern American novel; and its triumph is not the pyrotechnical display that the shuttling between the various devices seems to suggest, but Dos Passos's power to weave so many different lives together in narrative. It is possible that the narrative sections would lose much of that power if they were not so craftily built into the elaborate framework of the book. But if the framework holds the book together and encloses it, the narrative makes it. The "Newsreel," the "Camera Eye," and even the very vivid and often brilliant "Biographies" are meant to lie a little outside the book; they speak with the formal and ironic voice of History. The "Newsreel" sounds the time; the "Biographies" stand above time, chanting the stories of American leaders; the "Camera Eye" moralizes shyly in a lyric stammer upon them. But the great thing about *U.S.A.* is that though it sweeps up so many human lives together and intones their waste and illusion and defeat so steadily, we seem to be swept along with them and to see each life perfectly at the moment it passes by us.

The brilliance of the structure lies therefore not so much in its external surface design as in its internal one, in the manifold rhythms of the narrative. Each of the various narrative sections has its dominant musical mode, as it were; each of the characters is encased in his characteristic prose. Thus at the very beginning of *The 42nd Parallel,* when the "Newsreel" blares in a welcome to the new century, while General Miles falls off his horse and Senator Beveridge's toast to the new imperialist America is heard, the story of Fenian McCreary, "Mac," begins with the smell of whale-oil soap in the printer's house in Middletown. That smell, the clatter of the presses, the political arguments, the muddy streets and saloons, give the tone of Mac's life from the first, as his life—Wobbly, tramp, working stiff—sounds the emergence of labor as a dominant force in the new century. So the story of Eleanor Stoddard begins with "When she was small she hated everything," a sentence that calls up the thin-lipped rebellion and superciliousness, the artiness and desperation, of her loveless life before we have gone into it. *The 42nd Parallel* is a study in youth, of the youth of the new century, the "new America," and of all the human beings who figure in it; and it is in the world of Mac's bookselling and life on freights, of Eleanor Stoddard's rebellion against her father and Janey Williams's picnic near the falls at Georgetown, of J. Ward Moorehouse's Wilmington and the railroad boardinghouse Charley Anderson's mother kept in North Dakota, that we move. The narrator behind his "Camera Eye" is a little boy holding to his mother's hand, listening to his father's boasts (at the end of the book he will be on his way to France); the "Newsreel" sings out the headlines and popular songs of 1900–16; the "Biographies" are of the magnates (Minor C. Keith, Carnegie), the wonder men of the new century (Steinmetz, Edison, Burbank), the rebels (Bryan, Debs, Bob La Follette, Big Bill Haywood).

We have just left the world of childhood behind us in *The 42nd Parallel,* but we can already hear the clatter of the conveyor belt pushing all these lives along. Everyone is sparring hard for position; the fences of life are going up. There is no expectancy in this youth, not even the sentimental poetry of adolescence. The "Newsreel" singing the lush ballads of 1906 already seems very far away; the "Biographies" are effigies in stone. The life in the narrative has become dominant; the endless pulsing drowns everything else out. Everything is hard, dry, and already a little outrageous. Johnny Moorehouse falls in love only to learn that the socially prominent girl whom he needs for his ambition is a whore. When Eleanor Stoddard's father announces his plan to marry again, he tells her it will be to a "Mrs. O'Toole, a widow with five children who kept a boardinghouse out Elsden way." Mac, after his bitterly hard youth, leaves the Wobblies with whom he has found comradeship and the joy of battle to marry a girl who drives him almost insane; then leaves her and is thrown into the Mexican revolutions of the period. Janey Williams's life has already taken on the gray color of the offices in which she will spend her life. There are no refuges in this world, no evasions, and above all no second starts. The clamps have been laid down early, and for all time.

Yet we can feel the toneless terror of all these lives, the oppression and joylessness that seem to beat down upon us from the first, only because every narrative section is so concrete and every sentence, as Delmore Schwartz pointed out, "can expand in the reader's mind to include a whole context of experience." *U.S.A.* is perhaps the first great naturalistic novel that is primarily a triumph of style. Everything that lives in the book is wound up on the spool of that style; from the fragments of popular songs in the "Newsreel" and the clean verse structure of the "Biographies" down to the pounding beat of the narrative, the book seems to be propelled by one dynamic rhythm. The Dos Passos prose, once so uncertain and self-conscious, has here been whittled down to a sharpness that can kill; but it has by no means lost its old wistful rhetoric, which is particularly conspicuous in the impressionist "Camera Eye" sections, and generally gives a kind of secret and mischievous color to the severely reportorial prose. Scrubby, slangy, with a kind of grim straightforwardness, it is the style of a very cunning artisan who seems to be working in these human materials as another might work in stone or wood—forever carving away, forever whittling, but never without subtle turns and a loving sense of design. It is never a "distinguished" style, beautiful in its own right; never as prismatic as Fitzgerald's or as delicately molded as Hemingway's, and there is always something fundamentally mechanical about it. But it is the style Dos Passos needs to turn the motor of the conveyor belt; it is the reportorial and satiric style needed to push along and circumscribe all these lives. With *The 42nd Parallel* we have entered into a machine world in which the rhythm of the machine has become the primal beat of all the people in it; and Dos Passos's hard, lean, mocking prose, forever sounding that beat, calling them to their deaths, has become the supreme expression of his conception of them.

Perhaps nowhere in the trilogy, save in the descending spiral of Charley Anderson's life in the first half of *The Big Money*, is Dos Passos's use of symbolic rhythm so brilliant as in the story of Joe Williams in *1919*. For Joe, Janey Williams's sailor brother, is the leading protagonist of the war and the early postwar period, as J. Ward Moorehouse's ambitiousness marked the pattern of *The 42nd Parallel*. Joe's endless shuttling between the continents on rotting freighters has become the migration and rootlessness of the young American generation whom we saw growing up in *The 42nd Parallel*; and the growing stupor and meaninglessness of his life became the leitmotif of the waste and death that hold everyone in the book as in a ghostly vise. The theme of death, of the false optimism immediately after the Armistice, are sounded immediately by the narrator behind his "Camera Eye," reporting the death of his mother and the notation on the coming of peace—"tomorrow I hoped would be the first day of the first month of the first year." The "Biographies" are all studies in death and defeat, from Randolph Bourne to Wesley Everest, mutilated and lynched after the Centralia shootings in Washington in 1919; from the prose poem commemorating the dozens of lives the Unknown Soldier might have led to the death's-head portrait of J. P. Morgan ("Wars and panics on the stock exchange,/ machinegunfire and arson/ . . . starvation, lice, cholera, and typhus"). The "Camera Eye" can detect only "the almond smell of high explosives sending singing éclats through the sweetish puking grandiloquence of the rotting dead." And sounding its steady beat under the public surface of war is the story of Joe Williams hurled between the continents— Joe, the supreme Dos Passos cipher and victim and symbol, suffering his life with dumb unconsciousness of how outrageous his life is, and continually loaded and dropped from one ship to another like a piece of cargo.

> Twentyfive days at sea on the steamer *Argyle*, Glasgow, Captain Thompson, loaded with hides, chipping rust, daubing red lead on steel plates that were sizzling hot griddles in the sun, painting the stack from dawn to dark, pitching and rolling in the heavy dirty swell; bedbugs in the bunks in the stinking focastle, slumgullion for grub, with potatoes full of eyes and mouldy beans.

All through *1919* one can hear death being sounded. Every life in it, even J. Ward Moorehouse's, has become a corrosion, a slow descent. Richard Ellsworth Savage goes back on his early idealism and becomes a cynical but willing abetter in Moorehouse's schemes. Eveline Hutchins and Eleanor Stoddard lose all their genteel pretense to art and grapple for Moorehouse's favor. "Daughter," the Texas girl Savage has betrayed, falls to her death in an airplane. Even Ben Compton, the New York radical, soon finds himself rotting away in prison. The war for almost all of them has become an endless round of drink and travel; they have brought nothing to it and learned nothing from it save a growing consciousness of their futility. And when they all slip into the twenties and the boom with *The Big Money*, the story of Charley Anderson's precipitate rise and fall becomes the last mad parable of their existence, a carnival of greed and corruption. Beginning with Dick Savage's life on ambulances and trains over France and Italy in 1919, the pace of the trilogy has become faster and faster; now, as the war world empties into the pleasure world of *The Big Money*—New York and Detroit, Hollywood and Miami at the height of the boom—it has become a death ride. There is money in the air, money and power for Charley Anderson and Margo Dowling and Dick Savage; but as they come closer to this material triumph, their American dream, the machine has begun to spin them too rapidly. Charley Anderson can kiss the bright new century notes in his wallet, Margo can rise higher and higher in Hollywood, Dick Savage, having sold out completely, can enjoy his power at the hands of J. Ward Moorehouse; the machine has begun to strangle them; there is no joy here for anyone. All through *The Big Money* we wait for the balloon to collapse, for the death cry we hear in that last drunken drive of Charley Anderson's and his smashup.

What Waldo Frank said of Mencken is particularly relevant to Dos Passos: he brings energy to despair. Not merely does the writing in the trilogy become richer and firmer as the characters descend into the pit, but Dos Passos himself seems so imbued with an almost mystical conviction of failure that he rises to new heights in those last sections of *The Big Money* which depict the last futile efforts of the liberals and radicals to save Sacco and Vanzetti, and their later internecine quarrels. The most moving scene in all of *U.S.A.* is the scene in which Mary French, the only counterpoise to the selfishness of the other characters in *The Big Money*, becomes so exhausted by her labors for Sacco and Vanzetti that when she goes to bed she dreams that her whole world is forever coming apart, that she is climbing up a shaky hillside "among black gutted-looking houses pitching at crazy angles where steelworkers lived" and being thrown back. The conflicting hopes of Mary French, who wanted Socialism, and of Charley Anderson, who wanted the big money, have brought two different kinds of failure; but it is failure that broods over them and over everyone else in *U.S.A.* in the end—over the pompous fakes like J. Ward Moorehouse, the radicals like Ben Compton, the grasping little animals like Eleanor Stoddard and Eveline Hutchins, the opportunists like Richard Ellsworth Savage. The two survivors are Margo Dowling, supreme for the moment in Hollywood, and the homeless boy "Vag," who stands alone on the Lincoln Highway, gazing up at the transcontinental plane winging its way west, the plane full of solid and well-fed citizens glittering in the American sun, the American dream. *All right, we are two nations.* And like the scaffolding of hell in *The Divine Comedy*, they are frozen into eternity; for Dos Passos there is nothing else, save the integrity of the camera eye that must see this truth and report it, the integrity and sanctity of the individual locked up in the machine world of modern society.

With *The Big Money*, published at the height of the 1930s, the story of the twenties comes to a close; but even more does it bring the story of the lost generation to a close, that generation which has stood at the peak of modern time in America as no other has. Here in *U.S.A.*, in the most ambitious of all its works, is its measure of the national life, its conception of history—and it is a history of struggle that is vain, of failure that is irrevocable, and of final despair. There is strength in *U.S.A.*, Dos Passos's own strength, the strength of the craft that can weld so many lives together and make them live so intensely before us as they pass. But for the rest it is a brilliant hecatomb, and one of the coldest and most mechanical of tragic novels. By the time we have come to the end of *U.S.A.* we begin to feel what Edmund Wilson could detect in Dos Passos before it appeared, that "his disapproval of capitalistic society becomes a distaste for all the human beings who compose it." The protest, the lost-generation "I," has taken all of them into his vision; he has given us his truth. Yet if it intones anything affirmative in the end, it is the pronouncement of young Orestes Brownson—"There is no such thing as reforming the mass without reforming the individuals who compose it." It is this conviction, rising to a bitter crescendo in *Adventures of a Young Man*, this unyielding protest against modern society on the part of a writer who has now turned back to the roots of "our storybook democracy" in works like *The Grounds We Stand On* and his projected life of Thomas Jefferson, that separates Dos Passos from so many of the social novelists who follow after him in the thirties. Where he speaks of sanctity, they speak of survival; where he lives by the truth of the camera eye, they live *in* the vortex of that society which Dos Passos has always been able to measure, with hatred but not in panic, from the outside. Dos Passos is the first of the new naturalists, and *U.S.A.* is the dominant social novel of the thirties; but it is not merely a vanished social period that it commemorates: it is an individualism, a protestantism, a power of personal disassociation, that seem almost to speak from another world.

[1942]

IV

—◆—

THE LITERARY LIFE

PROVINCETOWN, 1940: BERTRAM WOLFE, MARY MCCARTHY, PHILIP RAHV

———— ◆ ————

Our closest friends in Provincetown were a middle-aged radical couple, childless, austere, extraordinarily sweet, among the few survivors of the original idealistic core of the American Communist movement, who had lived in Russia, Spain, Mexico, and had now settled into a small radical sect, really a company of friends, wistfully seeking to stave off American entry into the war.

The Wolfes lived over a wobbly staircase on Commercial Street, in two little rooms, with the same austerity, intellectual faith, the same lovingness toward each other and their trusted friends, that they had shown in Spain, Russia, Mexico. With the little Mexican rugs and pots that they carried with them, the battered suitcases that contained their manuscripts and their favorite books, they looked like the traditionally "pure" couple of radical theory joined by devotion to a common ideal. In their relations with us they were kindly, generous, altogether loving, as in their political thinking they were fiercely separatist from most people in the United States [....]

Bert[ram] Wolfe was almost the last of his breed, and sitting with him at the end of Provincetown pier, I listened gratefully to his stories of the original Communist International, of John Reed and Angelica Balabanov, Bukharin and Lunacharsky and Trotsky, in those legendary days of the 1920s, when the new Communist movement had been led by revolutionary intellectuals,

Doctrinaire and fanatical as they had been, they had honestly considered imperatives of the intellect. Stalin did not like intellectuals with that much conviction. Stalin could do something about his jealousies and dislikes. Bert had once heard Stalin, trying to bully members of the American opposition back into line, gleefully boast, case by case, of what he had done to his opponents, rivals, and detractors. This had been in the late twenties, before these same men were brought up in the show trials to accuse themselves of plotting with Hitler against the Soviet state. The victim was usually a revolutionary intellectual of the old type, a "Westerner" who had lived abroad, often a Jew, brought down by the sly and venomous Georgian who, from a rage for unlimited power that could finally be sated only with blood, had killed the theorists, the intellectuals who still embodied the *élan* of the Russian Revolution. Looking at Bert Wolfe's long, thin, scholarly frame always ready to leap into discussion, the Bert whom I saw every day with his medicine bottle, his newspaper clippings, his Marxist texts, sitting before a typewriter in his hot little room just under the roof, tapping out fresh polemics in defense of his radical sect, still trying to nail down some disputed point about Soviet history that would bolster his "scientifically" related argument about America's need to stay out of the war, I saw the belief in the "laws" of history that had brought Bert and his friends to become the victims of those who in the name of these "laws" operated as professional sadists, terrorists, inquisitors, and policemen. Bert and his wife, who never seemed to speak ill of anyone personally, who had come to value their revolutionary integrity over their very chances of survival, had finally acquired the innocent self-approval which in threadbare clergymen and their wives insulates them against a skeptical world. The very impersonality and loftiness of their principles expressed itself in this refusal to judge persons too closely. Social forces, impersonal as the stars in their courses, made it unnecessary to look sharply at people's personal failings. The Wolfes, by the high-principled kindness with which they accepted us, silently left the implication that any further probing would have been undignified. But when, through them, I met in Provincetown young radical intellectuals and writers of the *Partisan Review* group, notably Mary McCarthy, I noticed this reproach they would never speak, the reproach of their old-fashioned socialist abstemiousness against those who had already passed through the radical movement as if it were a bohemian experience.

I met Mary McCarthy through Wolfe, and all the time she spoke to some friends with her fluent style and her nervous laugh, inching her way from personality to personality over boulders of well-chosen words, Wolfe watched her, his mouth open, as if he would never be able to express his amazement. Wolfe and his wife, on principle, avoided personalities; Mary McCarthy dealt in nothing else. She had, I thought, a wholly destructive critical mind, shown in her unerring ability to spot the hidden weakness or inconsistency in any literary effort and every person. To this weakness she instinctively leaped with cries of pleasure—surprised that her victim, as he lay torn and bleeding, did not applaud her perspicacity. She seemed to regard her intelligence as essentially impersonal; truth, in the person of this sharply handsome twenty-eight-year-old Vassar graduate, had come to pass judgment on the damned in Provincetown. Though she was often right enough about the small specific absurdities that she felt compelled to point out about themselves to her friends, she despised the world in which she moved; her judgment represented that insignificant display of cleverness which a cynical society photographer might use in emphasizing a double chin and the dribble from an open mouth.

Mary McCarthy was the first writer of my generation who made me realize that it would now be possible to be a radical without any idealism whatsoever. I was reading Sainte-Beuve that summer in Provincetown, and I was struck by his saying that in France people remain Catholics long after they have ceased to be Christians. Even in conversation, practicing those portraits of familiars who in two years would be expected to recognize themselves in *The Company She Keeps*, she showed that her moving principle was that bleak, unsparing, suspicious view of human nature which is so much admired by reactionaries because it leaves the lower classes so little reason to rebel. Mary was to be stimulated to literary production by the habit of seeing other people as fools. She operated on all her old radical friends, reserving indulgence only for herself. Without the growing conviction of meaninglessness in the air, she might never have felt any authority at all. But bewilderment in the "movement" now set her up exactly as the pathos of the "emancipated" woman of the twenties had made a world for Dorothy Parker. Among disillusioned radicals, Mary served as governess in the new correctness toward which they were moving. She reminded them of the classical learning they had never acquired, the niceties of style they had despised, the social lapses they could no longer overlook. Herself an orphan, with none of the pusillanimous dependence on family love that was the besetting weakness of so many anxious intellectuals, she turned the very outrageousness of her judgments into a social virtue. She operated on her circle in Provincetown and New York with open scorn and impressed them—they who were so solemn—with her power to make them ridiculous. The crispness, hardness, shininess of her performance was the *examen de conscience* to which the sick, deluded ex-utopians, so long victims of their easy credulity, would have to submit. The wretches who had so long believed in revolutionary progress now cowered before the crisp Vassar girl with the Irish jaw who proclaimed the endless treacheries of the human heart—proclaimed it with a discipline of style, a show of classical severity and subtler manners than their own, that pointed up her right to take such a large bite of her victim.

The readiness to total skepticism, to the spirit of comedy, would have been fruitful in an imaginative dramatist or novelist; but the inner group of *Partisan Review* did not value imagination. "Who's in it?" I once heard the editor Philip Rahv ask a writer who submitted a story to him. The *Partisan Review* group were interested in the people around them to the point of ecstasy; in this world nothing interested them so much as the personalities of their friends. The ability to analyze a friend, a trend, a shift in the politico-personal balance of power, was for them the greatest possible sign of intellectual power. Creative imagination they unconsciously disdained as simple-minded—except if it came from the Continent, and thus could be an analogy to their kind of intelligence. This boundless belief in criticism was actually their passport to the postwar world, for as society became more complex and intellectuals more consciously an elite, the old literary radicals were among the few, in an age of academic criticism, who understood the relation of literature to institutions. Some of these writers even became the favorite intellectuals of the mass media, and presiding over the cultural rites of television and the slicks, delighted their most eager readers by insulting them to their faces as the mass audience, the conformists, the herd. The intellectuals who had failed at revolution were to succeed as intellectual arbiters. They had passion. They would never feel that they had compromised, for they believed in alienation and would forever try to outdo conventional opinion even when they agreed with it. They were intellectuals, and the new age of American power that was to come with the war was to be more and more indulgent to intellectuals. But though they were fated to make brilliant careers in the elitist society that was coming, they would not be happy. The *élan* of their lives, revolutionary faith in the future, was missing. "... it is possible to be atheist, it is possible not to know whether God exists or why and yet believe that man does not live in a state of nature but in history," Nikolai Nikolaievitch, an unfrocked priest, was to say in Pasternak's *Doctor Zhivago.* A Soviet diplomat who committed suicide in 1927 in order to protest Trotsky's expulsion from the Party wrote in his farewell letter, "... human life has sense only insofar as it is spent in the service of the infinite—and for us mankind is the infinite. To work for any finite purpose—and everything else is finite—is meaningless. ... Anything accomplished in our time for mankind's benefit will in some way survive into future ages; and through this our existence acquires the only significance it can possess." History was now a tangle of meanings without clear-cut issue. Meanings there were always plenty of; a critic had only to read a significant book to feel that his inner world was expanding with meaning. But where was the great transformation, which, Marx had promised, would do away with all other faiths? Where was the meaning that had enchanted the poor and intoxicated their visionary and millennial leaders? "There is much suffering in the world," André Malraux one day in New York said in behalf of Spain. "But there is one kind of suffering which it is a privilege to endure, the suffering of those who endure because they want to make a world worthy of man. ... The life of culture depends less on those who inherit it than on those who desire it. Let each man choose his own way of alleviating this suffering, relieve it he must. That is our responsibility to man's destiny, and perhaps to our own hearts."

Critical intelligence, the old-fashioned kind based on solid moral conceptions, on history as the record of man's progress, was what dominated these ex-radicals; but they no longer identified their ideas with anything but personal strength of mind. They were sour outsiders analyzing a situation which they could neither join nor control. They were fixed in the habit of intellectual influence, but the influence did not determine the future to which they were dedicated as their own creation. In the years to come, they would shift back and forth amid the ideologies like a fevered patient trying to find a cool place in bed; they would accept any position for a time, no matter how shocking; they would flirt with the most nationalistic and aggressively "realistic" positions. None of these excursions changed them; they would always remain radi-

cal intellectuals dedicated to the better world that only intellectuals had imagined to be possible in practice. After the war, when concrete political issues
exploded again, the radical tradition was to become more dynamic than it
looked in 1940, in the depths of our defeat. But what would never come back
in this most political of ages—not even in Russia—was the faith in a wholly
new society that had been implicit in the revolutionary ideal.

There were many ways of taking this. For people like the *Partisan Review*
editor Philip Rahv, nothing had happened but that they were out of their natural period, abandoned by their proper Zeitgeist. It was impossible to believe
that Mary McCarthy had ever been a believing Socialist; she could belong to a
radical movement only when it was in decay and objectively ridiculous. Rahv,
on the other hand, was an intellectual in the pure Russian style. He would have
been happy with Belinsky in 1834, with Chernishevsky in 1861, with Trotsky in
1905; he was not happy with many of his friends after 1936. He was naturally a
talker rather than a writer, a pamphleteer, a polemicist, an intellectual master
of ceremonies and dominator who just escaped being entirely absorbed in parties, gossip, and talk by his genuine absorption in issues and ideas. Even the
homely pleasant shreds of Russian accent left over in his speech made him
more fascinating as a controversialist than he could ever be as a writer. To listen to Rahv talk with so much passion and scorn, the syllables crunching in
his speech with biting Russian sincerity, was to realize that radicalism was
Rahv's destiny, his character, his fulfillment. Even when he was most awful in
the *Partisan Revew* style of personal attack, deliberately outrageous, burying his
victim in hot sand up to his neck and smearing his face with honey, you felt
that with all the pleasure he took in denouncing wrongdoers, miscreants, bear-
ers of intellectual error, he still looked on people as carriers of ideas, symbols
of moral policy, that his fundamental concern was a vision of history and not
gossip.

Though Rahv was inherently one of the narrowest men I knew, he was
vividly authentic and stimulating as a critic of literature in society. Rahv was so
much of a Russian intellectual in the positive, absorbed, evangelical old style,
he lived his ideas in conversation; he lived them almost too publicly. I saw him
always in a crowd, his impatient, burry accent driving down confused and friv-
olous people with a force that evoked admiration as well as submission. He
was already, in 1940, the Doctor Johnson of his small group of radical intellectuals.

In the years to come the social standards of this group became increasingly more sophisticated and demanding, but it did not seem to me that the everlasting atmosphere of the group, the party, the clique, the coterie in which he always moved—that this essential setting had changed at all, or that he functioned at all apart from it. For Rahv a piece of writing was not real unless it appeared in the immediate social setting of a magazine and evoked an immediate social response in conversation, rebuttal, polemic. Literature for him came out of social tension, and to social tension it had to contribute literature as the product of social debate—and Rahv's idea was to add to it. This could be overdone, and there was much in Rahv's circle, where people seemed to sit for a long evening glued to each other in fascination with the weaknesses that could be turned to immediate account, that was cruel but comic. This avant-garde gnawed on each other, lived on each other. Yet though the very basis of the association that *Partisan Review* editors and writers had with each other was a kind of group identification, these people saw themselves as loyal to a great cultural tradition. It was my tradition. We shared a fundamental realism about our society and obstinate hopes for mankind that were to be conspicuously missing from the intellectual scene as America went to war again.

[1965]

DELMORE SCHWARTZ

———◆———

There were explosive days [at *The New Republic*] when Delmore Schwartz happened in out of the elevator. Delmore never just came in. He spilled out in a reedy voice a headlong rush of words that seemed to engage every muscle in his face as he twisted and spat in the rage of his opinions. On the days when Delmore erupted into the office to get a book for review and to berate me for something I had just published, he conversed in a style of great bitterness that nevertheless tried to be classical and impersonal in its reasoning. Since he could write without rage and always with a great show of reasoning, a certain classical outlook—he had been trained in philosophy—was the style of his terribly proper, intellectual poems and profound early stories. The contrast was even physical. He moved heavily, his head turning with some uneasiness. He seemed to see his life as a clash between gravity, heaviness, depression, and poetry, which was the absolute, the truth, elusive as "the lip of snow on the windowsill." I would look at his amazingly wide, stone white, sweaty brow, knotted with intellectual indignation as with ropes. I would grow properly frightened, Delmore was such a prophecy of the last literary generation to believe in the authority of culture, the logic of tradition. There was this belief, which not even Hitler would destroy in some of us, that there *was* a reason behind all frightfulness. Of course, every political season the reason changed.

Once it was "imperialism." When the killing began, it was "human nature," or the devil in us. Delmore was already the poet on the cross of culture, every muscle contorted; Brooklyn's best, nailed down. But from his cross he shrieked the most brilliant things, the most scathing things, excitedly analyzing a passage by "my king, James Joyce," and, like a mad shuttlecock, flying at anyone who saw less beauty in his favorite texts than he did.

His face could be marvelous even in his most manic flights. It had a way of withdrawing into lonely thought that somehow transcended every angry occasion. His body nobly represented him even when he was throwing words at people he did not trust. Although he was bitterly witty in his mysterious fashion—"Europe is still the biggest thing in North America"—storming up against people with the same passionate logic with which he argued for or against certain books, his face was as remarkable in a relaxed moment as the first time I had seen him, in a train going up to Boston. I had been struck by the immense intellectual devotion in it, the fine distraction, the obstinate love behind the familiarly Jewish frantic manner.

In those first days he looked what he was—obsessive, unable to let go on anyone or about anything, but more gifted than anyone else, not petty, full of the excited discoveries he was then making as a teacher of composition at Harvard. He looked, as a friend said, "our poet." No writer of my generation, typically lamented by a Communist poet as "caught between the wars, with all the streetlights out," knew so well from the inside what literature was and what a poet should aim at. He looked proud. He still had a young authority. He had come on the scene in his early twenties with stories and poems that astonished everyone by being impeccably formally *right* in the prevailing Eliot tradition— emotional ingenuity tuned to perfect pitch by gravity of manner. Although he talked fast and masticated his words, he could grow marvelously possessed between gulps of argument and boyish smiles. There was the unmistakable look of the poet speaking from his own depths. He stood for something, and he knew it.

The single most beautiful thing he was ever to write, the classic story of the Jewish son unable to escape the history represented by his family, was the highly charged personal fantasy "In Dreams Begin Responsibilities." The narrator imagines himself in the darkness of a movie theater watching his father walk down the quiet shaded streets of Brooklyn to court his mother. The light is bad, the film is patchy, and from time to time the young writer, watching his own unhappy destiny being prepared in the bad temper of his father and the quarrels of his parents-to-be, cries out from the darkness of the theater against the ill-fated marriage. At one point he stands up and tells the figures on the screen not to marry. "Don't do it! It's not too late to change your minds, both of you. Nothing good will come of it, only remorse, hatred, scandal, and two children whose characters are monstrous."

"In Dreams Begin Responsibilities" was straight, beautiful, haunting. It was a little masterpiece that used up a man's whole life even before he had lived it. It was the greatest fable I was ever to read of "our experience." It was the one work of Delmore Schwartz's life that had the power of a dream, and it remains with me as if I had dreamed it myself. Delmore was never again to bring out with such precision what it was to be a marked man, under a curse and wolfishly alone. We used to laugh at the story that Delmore's mother had appropriated his name from a delicatessen, though "Delmore" was not more innocently pretentious than Lionel, Clifton, Clifford, Hilton, Leslie, Walt Whitman.* But with his terrible belief in working things out intellectually, Delmore saw in his mother's innocent cultural pretension "a wound like circumcision." He would be a clown with an urgent message to deliver. Delmore's tortured personal epics, *Shenandoah* and *Genesis . . .* , showed him struggling with ridiculous names for himself like Shenandoah Fish and Hershey Green. The friends he put into his stories were also cruelly tagged by fate. Poor Shenandoah, poor Hershey, poor Rudyard Bell, Edmund Kish, Ferdinand Harrap, Francis French, and Mortimer London, poor Algernon. Poor Von Humboldt Fleisher, a final sacrifice to his famous self-laceration! Such names piled on each other became funnier than Groucho's J. Worthington Silverstein. Delmore could not laugh anything off. He practiced "irony" as if this famous literary strategy of the time was a Jew's only defense. Of course he could not see the joke. He was the drama.

"A poet shouldn't be that unhappy," Auden said with derision, looking at the photograph on Delmore's book *Summer Knowledge.* The eyes looked almost blind in their sick, milky introspection; the face that had once moved me by its independent devotion was now furrowed and creased with unimaginable pain. Less than ever now was he looking *at* anything. But anyone who understood Delmore's mind knew that he was finally drowning in his own blood. He was

*As in Walt Whitman Rostow [ed.].

hopelessly caught up in the logical web, still trying to prove the injustice that was everywhere being practiced against him. *This* was his lifelong dilemma. The worse things got, the more actively, frantically, outragedly he *argued* against them. He was a terrifying and terrified rationalist, a prisoner of his superb intellectual training. The great philosophers and poets were always in his mind, training him into a victim of the logic he loved more than himself. He would never come to believe in the "absurd" that filled the decade in which he died. His end was "absurd" enough to please the exuberant chaos around him, but it was absurd in Delmore's own desperate style.

He had surely predicted it. He was, more than the rest of us, expert in anguish. Even when impaled on his favorite theme, betrayal, he lacked the saving grace of madness. He was the prisoner of culture, and could never be distracted from its supposed truth. He would never lose himself in that dream of a totally other world that becomes to the eye of genius the only real world. Delmore could be maddening, but he never relaxed into the full madness of art. He would never lose his faith in the rationality of the world.

Delmore talked with his whole face. The hopeless intensity of every feeling was there the last time I saw him. It was a few years before his terrible death, in 1966, in a sleazy Broadway hotel, after which his body lay around Bellevue unknown and unclaimed. He was railing against his friend Saul Bellow. Bellow was returning the fund he had collected for Delmore's treatment. Delmore did not think he needed treatment. He thought of the fund as his personal property. He was in a squalid box of a room on Greenwich Street near the river. It was a room that only long practice in disaster could have discovered. He was buried up to his fine eyes in accusations of "betrayal," unbearably sicker than in the forties, not so much talking as accusing, erupting, plotting, demanding, suffering. Everything was vehement and tragic at once. You could not leave him without hating yourself.

[1978]

SAUL BELLOW AND
LIONEL TRILLING

———— •◆• ————

Through the Chicago writer Isaac Rosenfeld—whose wife, Vasiliki, was my secretary—I met Saul Bellow, who was also just in from Chicago, and who carried around with him a sense of his destiny as a novelist that excited everyone around him. Bellow was the first writer of my generation—we had been born ten days apart—who talked of Lawrence and Joyce, Hemingway and Fitzgerald, not as books in the library but as fellow operators in the same business. As I walked him across Brooklyn Bridge and around my favorite streets in Brooklyn Heights, he looked my city over with great detachment. He had the gift—without warning, it would follow a séance of brooding Jewish introspection—of making you see the most microscopic event in the street because *he* happened to be seeing it. In the course of some startling observations on the future of the war, the pain of Nazism, the neurotic effects of apartment-house living on his friends in New York (Chicago was different; it was a *good* thing to grow up in Chicago), he thought up some very funny jokes, puns, and double entendres. It was sometimes difficult to catch the punch line, he laughed so fast with hearty pleasure at things so well said. And they were well said, in a voice that already shaped its words with careful public clarity. He explained, as casually as if he were in a ballpark faulting a pitcher, that Fitzgerald was weak, but Dreiser strong in the right places. He examined

Hemingway's style like a surgeon pondering another surgeon's stitches. Then, familiarly calling on the D. H. Lawrence we all loved as our particular brother in arms, he pointed to the bilious and smoke-dirty sky over the Squibb factory on Columbia Heights. Like Lawrence, he wanted no "umbrella" between him and the essential mystery. He wanted direct contact with everything in the universe around him.

Bellow had not yet published a novel; he was known for his stories and evident brilliance only to intellectuals around *Partisan Review* and the University of Chicago. Yet walking the unfamiliar Brooklyn streets, he seemed to be measuring the hidden strength of all things in the universe, from the industrial grime surrounding Brooklyn Bridge to the prima donnas of the American novel, from the lasting effects of Hitler to the mass tensions of New York. He was measuring the world's power to resist *him*, he was putting himself up as a contender. Although he was friendly, unpretentious, and funny, he was ambitious and dedicated in a style I had never seen in an urban Jewish intellectual; he expected the world to come to him. He had pledged himself to a great destiny. He was going to take on more than the rest of us were.

It was bracing to meet someone exactly my age and background who looked at life with this loftiness, this proud sense of vocation. "And being a novelist," Lawrence said, "I consider myself superior to the saint, the scientist, the philosopher, and the poet, who are all great masters of different bits of man alive, but never get the whole hog." To be a novelist! To take on anything and everything! As Bellow talked, I had an image of a wrestler in the old Greek style, an agonist contending in the games for the prize. Life was dramatically as well as emotionally a contest to him. In some way I could not define, he seemed to be always training for it. And he was wary—eager, sardonic, and wary.

For a man with such a range of interests, Bellow talked with great austerity. He addressed himself to the strength of life hidden in people. An anthropologist by training, he liked to estimate other people's physical capacity, the thickness of their skins, the strength in their hands, the force in their chests. He talked like a Darwinian, calculating the power of survival hidden in the species. There was nothing idle or showy about his observations; he did not talk for effect. His definitions, epigrams, were of a formal plainness that went right to the point and stopped. That was the victory he wanted. There was not the slightest verbal inflation in anything he said. Yet his observations were direct and penetrating; they took on the elegance of achieved thought. When he considered something, his eyes slightly set as if studying its power to deceive him, one realized how formidable he was on topics generally exhausted by ideology or neglected by intellectuals too fine to consider them. Suddenly everything tiresomely grievous came alive in the focus of this man's unfamiliar imagination.

Listening to Bellow, I became intellectually happy—an effect he was soon to have on a great many other writers of our generation. We were coming through. There seemed nothing deliberate about Bellow's sense of destiny. He was proud in a laconic way, like an old Jew who feels himself closer to God than anybody else was. He could be unbearable in his unresting image of himself, but he was never smug and could be as openly vulnerable as anyone I ever met. Then he would nail with quiet ferocity someone who had astonished him by offering the mildest criticism.

The proud novelist-to-be, like the young Joseph in the Bible, airily confided his dreams of greatness to his brothers; he would be quick to divide the world into allies and enemies. I believed in him as a novelist because, like his strength in being a Jew, *this* was a sealed treasure undamaged by his many anxieties. Saul was clearly a man chosen by talent, like those Jewish virtuosos—Heifetz, Rubinstein, Milstein, Horowitz—who had been shaped into slim and elegant men of the world by talent alone. Even his conscious good looks were those of a coming celebrity. But the great thing was Saul's talent for the literature of direct experience. Every day, I saw intellectuals clever enough to make the world over, who indeed had made the world over many times. Yet Bellow, who had been brought up in the same utopianism and was himself a nimble adept of the University of Chicago style, full of the Great Books and jokes from Aristophanes, would obviously be first and last a novelist, a storyteller, creating new myths out of himself and every other intellectual he had ever known, fought, loved, hated. This loosened the bonds of ideology for the rest of us. It was refreshing to be with a man who disposed of so many pedantic distinctions. It seemed to have something to do with his love of Yiddish and Jewish jokes, his affection for big-city low life, his sense of himself as a *creative* Jew. Saul was the first Jewish writer I met who seemed as clever about every side of life as a businessman. He was in touch.

I lived my life among brilliant intellectuals, and would soon encounter Lionel Trilling, who had very warmly reviewed *On Native Grounds* and one day came into the *New Republic* office to discuss some possible pieces with Bliven. Trilling was an intense intellectual admiration of mine, but we were not fated to have much conversation. Ten years older than I, the first Jew in recorded history to get tenure in a Columbia English Department as crowded with three-barreled Anglican names as the House of Bishops, Trilling in his middle thirties was fascinating, subtle, and careful. "We have room for only one Jew," the English chairman had told Clifton Fadiman at their graduation, "and we have chosen Mr. Trilling." Those ten years between us reinforced my impression of Trilling as a writer who had absorbed the casual, more gentlemanly style of the twenties much as Bellow and I had absorbed the social angers of the abrasive lower-class thirties.

Trilling already had his distinguished white hair over a handsome face that seemed to be furrowed, hooded, closed up with constant thought. The life was all within, despite his debonair practiced easiness of manner. With his look of consciously occupying an important place, his already worn face, his brilliant discriminations as we talked, he quietly defended himself from the many things he had left behind. He seemed to feel more than the usual literary connection to things English, and proudly told me that his mother had been born in England. Victorian England would be his intellectual motherland. During the heyday of Marxist criticism, I had been grateful to him for writing against the spirit of the age and for the intense devotion behind his wonderful book on Matthew Arnold. He still believed in culture as a guide to society. In person, there was immense and even cavernous subtlety to the man, along with much timidity, a self-protectiveness as elegant as a fencer's; my first meetings with Trilling were just too awesome. With the deep-sunk colored pouches under his eyes, the cigarette always in hand like an intellectual gesture, an air that combined weariness, vanity, and immense caution, he was already a personage. He seemed intent on not diminishing his career by a single word. At our very first meeting in the *New Republic*, when I brought him into Bliven's office so as to stress the importance of his writing for us, Trilling astonished me by saying, very firmly, that he would not write anything that did not "promote my reputation." Bliven gave every assurance that Trilling would not have to write anything that did not promote his reputation. Although I found so much solemnity about one's reputation hilarious, I was impressed by the tight-lipped seriousness with which Trilling said "my reputation." It seemed to resemble an expensive picture on view. "My reputation" was to be nursed along like money in the bank. It was capital. I had never encountered a Jewish intellectual so conscious of social position, so full of adopted finery in his conversation: "I should scarcely have believed that."

[. . . .]

The sudden emergence of Jews as literary figures was certainly due to their improved status in an economy liberated by the war and catapulted by war into domination of the "free world." Immensely subtle and learned authorities on Matthew Arnold, Henry James, James Joyce, Paul Cézanne could hardly be identified with Depression novels out of the tenements like *Jews Without Money; Haunch, Paunch, and Jowl; Call It Sleep, The Old Bunch.* Speculative by nature, sophisticated in the lore of modern literature and painting, even the novelists and poets among these new writers were intellectuals and university teachers who respected nothing in this world so much as a great new world idea. They put all their zeal for social revolution into the purer and perhaps more lasting revolution of modern literature and art. They would soon be the intellectual style setters, the cultural leaders and gurus of a modernism that would replace old academic orthodoxies. Kafka might be obliterated in all the German-language countries under the influence of Hitler; Babel and Mandelstam might perish in Stalin's camps; *Finnegans Wake* and Picasso's latest might still be a joke to fat European burghers. But Kafka, Babel, Joyce, Picasso—not to forget Malraux, Sartre, Italo Svevo, Stravinsky, Schönberg—were the gods of this world to those intellectuals who wanted to be both established and advanced, and soon were.

They were still outsiders for all their inside knowledge of the modern. The "accommodation to America" did not keep Jewish intellectuals like the Trillings from criticizing their own liberalism. They saw with the eyes of great twentieth-century masters, Eliot, Yeats, Mann, who were conservative and even aristocratic. To be a Jew and yet not Jewish; to be of course a liberal, yet to see everything that was wrong with the "imagination of liberalism"; to be Freudian and a master of propriety; academic and yet intellectually avant-garde—this produced the tension, the necessary intellectual ordeal, that was soon to make Trilling the particular voice of intellectuals superior to liberalism. Freud said that "being a Jew, I would always be in the opposition." A master of distinctions, Trilling was to perform with particular subtlety as a critic of liberalism and radicalism who could not be tied down to any conservative position. The fascination of his work to the many ex-liberals and post-radicals in his audience was that he made every distinction, touched every base, without finding himself stranded on any. No one could have been more discerning, and less involved.

One night at the Trillings' the conversation came around to Paul Goodman. Goodman in 1942 was still the *enfant terrible*, the homemade avant-gardist with a dozen books to his credit who could interest no commercial publisher. He had not yet attained fame as a loving analyst of the young, or as an anarchist setting out community schemes. But he was already A Figure—if only in the Village—with a deep apostolic sense of himself, his bisexual life, his fate, his homelessness, his early orphan roamings on the sidewalks of New York. He seemed to press his self-declared difference as a writer and his bold-ness as a lover into everything he said and wrote. He was as assertive as Robespierre, Napoleon, Trotsky. Anything I picked up of his always seemed to me as roughly written as a leaflet. But he fascinated—or intimidated—because with all his ferocious conceit as novelist, poet, philosopher-at-large, writing was a way of living to a desperate man whose theme was love; looking for love. He was open about his pickups, his hopes and disasters, his love for boys; I was awed by his hungry searching and the unashamed naïve egomania with which he celebrated his desires as the privilege of his gifts as writer and oracle.

That night at the Trillings', still basking in the warmth of Lionel's review of my book, I had innocently brought myself and some of my recent essays in a state of respectful homage—and discovered that despite Lionel's guarded amiability, I was distinctly persona non grata with his wife. Diana had been writing book reviews for *The New Republic* before my accession and, on her most recent appearance in the paper, had without my knowledge been described in the contributors' box as "the wife of Lionel Trilling." Despite all my efforts to explain away this stupidity and to make amends, Diana fixed me with an unforgiving stare that was to last forever. She was a dogged woman and looked it, with a passion for polemic against all possible dupes of the Soviet Union that in the McCarthy era and the heyday of the American Committee for Cultural Freedom was to make her the scourge of all mistaken ill-thinking "anti-anti-Communists." She was tirelessly attentive to the intellectuals—a class that included some writers (by no means just any writers), and was often referred to by both Trillings, with great disappointment, as "our educated classes," our "enlightened" classes. Her favorite literary genre seemed to be the letter to the editor. Sometimes she wrote in to criticize an unfavorable review of a book for not being unfavorable enough.

With this seething sense of her intellectual-political righteousness, Diana always seemed more alert to the wrongdoing of other intellectuals than to the beauty of creative art. And I was young, and despite my admiration for her husband's subtle intelligence, distinctly not one of his humble imitators at Columbia. I must have irritated her profoundly. Her anxieties were soon all astir. The evening wore on slowly and heavily, my heart sinking fast at every glacial stare and exasperated grunt from Diana as I beseechingly offered up cultural conversation first to both of them, and on being steadily cold-shouldered by her, to him alone. Did Professor Trilling, uh, care for the novels of Henry Green? Was he as fond as I was of the Glyndebourne Festival recording of *The Marriage of Figaro* I had seen lying atop their phonograph? And what, if I might venture the question, did Professor Trilling think of that famous bad boy Paul Goodman?

To my relief and surprise, Trilling and I found ourselves agreeing, with the little furtive smile of such heavily proper people as ourselves, that we rather *envied* Paul Goodman his "scandalous" reputation. Here we were, two eminently right-thinking, heavily moral literary critics, both in the very flower of life, who had to confess that we rather envied this street gamin, this bohemian, the intense amorousness of his Village life!

Trilling opened up surprisingly on the topic of Goodman, lost his ceremonially guarded air. Smiling happily, he gave rein to some ancient fantasies about tearing off into the wild blue yonder. With a grin he admitted that he had once been fired from Columbia for being a "Marxist and a Freudian." He had actually gone off for a year to teach way out there—he waved his arm—at the University of Wisconsin. I understood him completely. New York was a great adventure for *them*, not for the likes of us. I was beginning to understand why Freud so much occupied Trilling's mind. What a price one paid for "culture"! Suddenly "the wife of Lionel Trilling," as irritated with him as she was contemptuous of me, tore into both of us as "hopeless romantics." Paul Goodman?! Paul Goodman?! I hurriedly took my leave and was never again to see the Trillings at home.

For Trilling I would always be "too Jewish," too full of my lower-class experience. He would always defend himself from the things he had left behind. This would go on and on for thirty years; it was *the* barrier, like his fondness for the words "scarcely," "modulation," "our educated classes." I had scarcely enough modulation. Even when Trilling came to praise a novel of "low life" like *The Adventures of Augie March* (he drove Bellow wild by withdrawing his approval in a second article), the abstract diction Trilling favored, his nerveless compromised accents, explained why our friend Harold Rosenberg muttered: "When I first encountered the style of Lionel Trilling, I looked for the joke and discovered there wasn't any":

> The extent of Mr. Bellow's success in these pages may be judged from the familiarity of the matter upon which he exercises his talents. The life of the slums and the near-slums of Chicago or some other great city has established itself over the last thirty years as a canonical subject in our literature. It is a good subject; it has its own implicit richness; one can almost say that if a writer comes to it with honesty and painstakingness, he can scarcely fail to make something good of it.
>
> We have, then, a prose which is articulate to the last degree, very fluent and rapid, yet thick with metaphor and epithet.
>
> For all its human richness, it is a novel of specific moral, intellectual intention—that intention being, as it happens, the demonstration of how to achieve and celebrate human richness—and it must be allowed the resolution and relaxation that comes with the sense of something learned....

I felt more at home with Bellow's attitude toward experience. He was always peering under the covers of our vaunted culture, thinking ahead of the general line. Chicago seemed to explain his self-confidence. New York was so big and "important" that no novelist had ever done the whole city as Dreiser had done Chicago. What made the New York intellectual's life a perpetual culture show was no help to the novelist. The speculative directness of Bellow and his friend Isaac Rosenfeld, who addressed experience with every possible question, seemed to me a product of Chicago itself—the city created, a Chicago novelist said at the end of the nineteenth century, expressly for the purpose of making money. Chicago gave people the midwestern openness, a sense of being at home in America. It had so clearly been *made* that a writer could still take it all on. Even the lofty Great Books curriculum at Robert Maynard Hutchins's University of Chicago sharpened perspective on so much contemporary reality.

[1978]

V

CONTEMPORARIES

THE FASCINATION AND TERROR OF EZRA POUND

———•◆•———

In the museum of modern literature no figure commands more space than Ezra Pound. Born in 1885 and dying at the ripe age of eighty-seven in 1972, he published his first book of poems, *A Lume Spento,* in Venice in 1908. My packed shelves hold almost thirty volumes of his writings—the early collected poems in *Personae,* the final one-volume collected *Cantos* of 1970, Pound on *The Spirit of Romance,* on *Kulchur,* on Joyce, on the classic Noh theater of Japan and the Confucian odes; Pound on *How to Read, Make It New,* the *ABC of Reading;* Pound's literary essays and letters, his translations from the Anglo-Saxon, Chinese, French, Greek, Hindi, Italian, Japanese, Latin, love poems from ancient Egypt, Sophocles' *Women of Trachis.* There are many more in general circulation.

Not in general circulation these days are the "money pamphlets" Pound wrote in Italian during the war and that were published in London by Peter Russell in 1950. *An Introduction to the Economic Nature of the United States. Gold and Labour. What Is Money For? A Visiting Card. Social Credit: An Impact. America, Roosevelt, and the Causes of the Present War.* These are full of fascinating material you are not likely to find elsewhere. Abraham Lincoln was assassinated after making a statement on the currency. Franklin D. Roosevelt was "a kind of malignant tumor . . . an unclean exponent of something less circumscribed than his own evil personal existence.... His political life ought to be brought *sub judice.*" Less difficult of access but definitely not in print is *Jefferson and/or Mussolini; L'Idea Statale; Fascism as I Have Seen It* (1935). The Government Printing Office put out the speeches in behalf of the Axis that Pound delivered before and after Pearl Harbor on the Italian radio for transmission to the United States. In 1973 Pound's estate threatened legal action against me for quoting from these speeches in a magazine article, but they have been published by Leonard W. Doob as *Ezra Pound Speaking.*

The literature on Pound is enormous and swells every month. Much of it explains and justifies the *Cantos* by annotating them and reminds me of Joyce saying that he would be immortal because *Ulysses* had given the professors work for more than a century. Pound's fellow poets from Yeats through Tate and Auden to Lowell and Jarrell were often indifferent to the *Cantos.* Yeats was baffled and irritated. Professors have no trouble. I write surrounded not only by reminiscences of Pound by H.D. and William Carlos Williams, by the letters exchanged with his future wife Dorothy Shakespear, by old biographies and a recent one, Dr. E. Fuller Torrey's *The Roots of Treason: Ezra Pound and the Secret of St. Elizabeth's,* by a book on Pound's "distinguished American roots," but also by a spate of still more critical studies. *The Dance of the Intellect: Studies in the Poetry of the Pound Tradition. Blossoms from the East: The China Cantos. Pound and Twentieth-Century Thought. Pound, Vorticism, and Wyndham Lewis. Translation after Pound. Pound and Dante. Pound and John Adams. Fugue and Fresco in Pound's Cantos.* And Hugh Kenner's doctoral thesis, *The Poetry of Ezra Pound,* republished with a preface detailing how hard it was once to get people to read Pound intelligently.

Whether people now read Pound more "intelligently" is less certain than that modernism, which used to make history, has passed into history. It is indeed a museum, every scrap of which is now necessary to "Kulchur." Pound was determined to be famous as soon as he reached Europe in 1908. He is now one of the dominating names in the history of the century. Artistic progress is measured in the academy by modernist canons.

Modernism was a historical moment from the end of the "bourgeois" nineteenth century to its collapse in the era of totalitarianism. It was not so much a movement as an upsurge of related energies in those wonderful years of illusion just before World War I. Pound, constantly telling his generation to

"Make It New," called it a disturbance and persuaded us that he was the center of it. From time to time he allowed the "Reverend Eliot" to share the limelight. When still in London just before the First World War, he mocked "the *deah* English public for not understanding that a troika of Americans"—the third was Robert Frost—"were making all the trouble." Later he identified modernism as a fundamental revolution in consciousness whose social correlatives were fascism to the end and bolshevism in its beginnings.

Pound saw parallels between his avant-garde activity and that of Lenin and Mussolini in the political realm. Mussolini and Hitler described themselves as artists who performed on history; the masses were their raw material. Pound said in 1927:

> Lenin is more interesting than any surviving stylist. He probably never wrote a brilliant sentence; he quite possibly never wrote anything an academic would consider a "good sentence," but he invented or very nearly invented a new medium, something between speech and action (language as cathode ray) which is worth any writer's study.

In *Jefferson and/or Mussolini* (1935), his homage to Mussolini as the perfect ruler, he assigns Lenin to a secondary place only because, Russia not having had a classical civilization, Lenin was not able to conceive fascism. Being an artist "in a new medium, something between speech and action," was Pound's role when modernism lost its vital energy in the thirties and the war. Pound, still the "disturber," plumped for social credit and fascism. His own conviction, never shaken in extreme isolation, was that he knew many things outside of art because he was an artist.

If ever man looked The Poet as antagonist of bourgeois civilization (especially in Latin countries, where the beard, the wide-brimmed black hat, the open collar, the walking stick, and the defiant look were familiar at anarchist congresses), it was Pound in the course of a career always full of uproar. There is very little of Pound's personal life in his poetry; from it you would never guess his relations with Dorothy Shakespear and Olga Rudge. But his self-proclaimed persona is all over it. In a film, *Ezra Pound: American Odyssey*, centered around him not long before his death, he is picturesque as ever sitting in a gondola, still in his classic getup, replete with walking stick. Venice frames him exactly as he frames himself in Canto III sitting on the steps of the custom house on his arrival in 1908.

When you are not looking at Pound himself in this film, you are looking at Italy, its sunbaked towers and layers of terraces—Italy the classic land before Christianity which Pound invoked and celebrated so many times that Italy now seems more an extension of Pound than does his birthplace in Idaho or his youth on the mainline near Philadelphia. Pound always took all his associations along with him; that was his genius. He was a natural taker-over; when his mind didn't, his will did. When Pound and Italy are not on the screen they are replaced by lyric passages from his work. The effect is extraordinary. Pound's silky lyrics move across the screen as if they came straight from his mind. Filaments, fragments "opaline," as he liked to say in their perfection, vibrant as air, give back the shock of the natural world in language that offers its homage to a world that will always transcend and elude language. This, though it is the story of Pound's life, he of course did not believe until it was too late.

> Bright gods and Tuscan, back before dew was shed.
> Light: and the first light, before ever dew was fallen.
> Panisks, and from the oak, dryas,
> And from the apple, maelid,
> Through all the wood, and the leaves are full of voices,
> A-whisper, and the clouds bowe over the lake,
> And there are gods upon them,
> And in the water, the almond-white swimmers.

A genius not least in his American gift for appropriating land not his own, gods distinctly not in the Protestant tradition, a language so far out of time that his very need to impersonate it is as impressive as his ability to do so. He recorded his translation of the Anglo-Saxon "Sea-farer." You hear a cultivated, deeply musical American voice trilling his *r*'s in the upper-class style of Theodore Roosevelt—an affectation that died out about the time Pound left for Europe. He recites his poem to the pounding of a drum at appropriate intervals, and is understandably intense. The wall-shaped alliterative consonants following each other in Indian file are themselves

Bitter breast-cares have I abided,
Known on my keel many a care's hold,
And dire sea-surge, and there I oft spent
Narrow nightwatch nigh the ship's head
While she tossed close to cliffs . . .

Here, as always when Pound is the lyric poet in a state of grace—not repeating the same anecdote in the *Cantos* about Jacques Maritain, not bitching about the failure of the English to appreciate him, not railing at the fall of civilizations that would not have fallen if they had read Confucius and John Adams and the autobiography of Martin Van Buren—you feel, as you do when watching Pound's lacy lines streaming across the screen, that his real genius was to identify with poetry itself, poetry without which men once never went to war, poetry as primal element, kin to nature as prose can never be.

No one of Pound's generation in English, the modernists born in the "failure" of the last century and determined to remake the next, caught so rapturously as Pound did, from within, poetry's genius for summoning up the beginning of things, the archaic as inception, the childhood of the race, the ability to look at the world as Homer did, for the wonder of creation:

God-sleight then, god-sleight:
Ship stock fast in sea-swirl,
Ivy upon the oars, King Pentheus,
grapes with no seed but sea-foam,
Ivy in scupper hole.
Aye, I, Acoetes, stood there,
and the god stood by me,
Water cutting under the keel,
Sea-break from stern forrads,
wake running off from the bow,
And where was gunwale, there now was vine-trunk,
And thenthril where cordage had been,
grape-leaves on the rowlocks,
Heavy vine on the oarshafts,
And, out of nothing, a breathing,
hot breath on my ankles. . . .

Seeing but especially *hearing* such words, one gets charged up, relieved for the moment from the unfelt emotions so often proclaimed in poetry, poetry too often written by people to whom, evidently, nothing very much has happened. The force of Pound's lyricism suggests an extraordinary ability to possess and incarnate his classical reading. From this ability to assimilate, he has imagined as actions words he has taken off the page.

Pound did something amazing: he turned himself into a mythical creature, the poet from ancient times. The bard, the "singer of tales," which Pound in his genius for sound felt himself to be, has an understandable affinity with war as his element. Pound was unable to understand a society that had lost all contact with poetry as its great tradition. It actually declined to credit Pound with the sagacity he attributed to *il gran poeta.* As he grew more isolated abroad, especially after his removal to Fascist Italy in 1924, Pound's talent for seeing life as literary myth augmented each year. He finally understood the vast indifference around him: a malignant conspiracy threatened civilization itself. As the crisis of the thirties broke, Mussolini assumed a role in Europe he never could have assumed before. Pound rallied to him with the same pretentiousness and demonstrated a capacity for intellectual hatred that was his only intemperance. As he was himself a natural hero-worshiper, so he attracted acolytes by the force of his gift and his total fearlessness in instructing the "bullet-headed many" how to read, what to think.

What spellbound the acolytes were feats of association; they set up reverberations in his readers and replaced contemporary realities with a web of learning. There was an extraordinary energy, a driving impulse; poetry was assuming powers lost in the nineteenth century to the great novelists. The forever bristling Pound style in the *Cantos*—the Browning version he learned early—and his zeal for violent types from Malatesta to Mussolini in the heroic mold, condottieri, reflected Pound's harkening back to martial associations with poetry. These were certainly not in the minds of poets contained by personal anguish like Matthew Arnold and T. S. Eliot. Arnold thought that the future of poetry was "immense" because it would ease the shock of Europe's de-Christianization. Eliot in his journey from Prufrock's conflict of the self to the healing by sacred places in *Four Quartets* practiced poetry as a medium of personal salvation.

Pound never understood such agony. He was no Christian. Poetry could still be primitive because "the gods have never left us." With this he helped to establish modernism as a position marked by fascination with the archaic and the unconscious, disdain for the mass, a view of industrial society as nothing but a matter of mechanization. He was spellbound by the vision of an earlier world, supposedly more charged and radiant than ours, truer to the hieratic world identified with art by conservatives and sought for society by fascists. Pound boasted of his "American roots" that he "could write the whole social history of the U.S. from his family annals." From Italy in 1944 he defended Hitler and Mussolini by writing, "In 1878 my grandfather said the same things I'm saying now, but the memory of his efforts has been obliterated."

Pound was unyielding in his scorn for those outside the magic circle of poetry. The force of his rejections was irresistible to some southern conservatives before they became Texas Republicans and to literary critics who had enough to do explaining Pound's allusions to students who thought Virgil was some American's first name. Katherine Anne Porter: "That falling world between 1850 and 1950. We have been falling for a century or more, and Ezra Pound came along at just the right time to see what was happening." Hugh Kenner:

> To give over all that: to recover the gods, Pound had called it, or to free (said [Wyndham] Lewis) faculties "older than the fish," to achieve (Eliot) "the new, the really new," which should be fit company for an Altamira bison, these had been the intentions of their vortex, dragging a dark world up into the light, forging an ecumenical reality where all times could meet without the romance of time, as jewelry perhaps Helen's had hung around Sophie Schliemann's neck for a photograph to be made by daylight, like Dublin daylight. An exactness of perception like an archaeologist's. . . .

It is funny now to think of how resolutely antimodern (in spirit) high modernism felt itself to be—while it expressed itself, as Pound did, in telescoped history and in formally disconnected images that were distinctly novel. Modernism arrived with the conquest of space by steamers, wireless, automobiles, airplanes, the appropriation of Africa and Asia by Western powers. If in 1853 Commodore Perry had not anchored his armed squadron in Tokyo Bay, Ernest Fenollosa would not have spent the twelve years teaching in Japan that left his literary executor Ezra Pound with an addiction to the Chinese written character. The acceleration that Henry Adams saw as the essence of modern history has defied all attempts at a science of history. Speedup is the motor of our century. It seems unbelievable now that the horse was still a basic means of locomotion and transport when the airplane was being invented.

Historical drive had by 1890 led William James in his *Principles of Psychology* to recognize a stream of consciousness. The obsession with consciousness as a basic flow intermixing non-successive periods in a person's memory made it possible for "artists"—Dr. James was distinctly one of them—to record images of the external world as a personal recreation from within oneself. The crucial words are in James's chapter 9, "The Stream of Thought":

> Remembrance is like direct feeling; its object is suffused with a warmth and intimacy to which no object of mere conception ever attains. . . . So sure as this present is me, is mine, it says, so sure is any- thing else that comes with the same warmth and intimacy and imme- diacy, me and mine.

A student of the *Cantos* may well think that William James was reading Pound's mind when he described such imperial confidence in anything that comes to mind. Actually William James was reading his own troubled mind, trying to liberate himself by accepting the flow as well as the data of con- sciousness.

The stream of consciousness gave privilege to the person immersed in that stream. Cubism's juxtapositions justified themselves as rhythmic design. Myth ceased to be folklore personifying natural forces, became the past buried in the artist. Rilke: "Poetry is the past that breaks out in our hearts." Eliot: "In using myth, in manipulating a continuous parallel between contemporaneity and antiquity," Joyce's method in *Ulysses* was "simply a way of controlling, of order- ing, of giving a shape and significance to the immense panorama of futility and anarchy which is contemporary history."

Modernism was a summoning up, a way of establishing order, with pecu- liarly up-to-the-minute tools that were too much in the spirit of the age to be recognized as such by those fleeing Pound's "half-savage country" for "the spirit of romance." Pound's tool he still called poetry. Dante was always in his mind: the unifying figure whose journey through hell and purgatory up to paradise Pound saw as a model for his epic journey in the *Cantos* even when he forgot that it was supposed to make a similar point. Behind Dante was Virgil, behind Virgil Homer. Epic was a book as action (always a hope to Pound) unifying a race through the chronicle of its wars, sacred places, gods.

Did Pound begin the *Cantos* thinking he had the qualifications? Not altogether, but he felt *himself* to embody this affinity with poetry, with its fundamental tonality as a separate medium of speech. *Poetry* was literature. In the novel he could recognize only those who prized style above everything else, had strictness of intention like Flaubert, James, Joyce. The social application of the modern novel meant nothing to him. The great voices were authority. "With a day's reading a man may have the key in his hand." In treating the novel purely as art object, he was projecting poetic epic as the only true history.

This he failed to prove in his inordinate subjectivism. The fascination of Pound's *Cantos* was to lie in its reflection of Pound's mind; not what he brought together but what he was capable of thinking of from line to line. We are never so much in the *Cantos* as we are observing a performance. We join Pound's mental flight even when we don't follow his matter. As for the "matter," his intentions are no help whatever. Pound's mind was not structural in details but assimilative, lyrical, impatient. After some great passage he was always breaking off to introduce something he had read. Early on he told his father that the *Cantos* would constitute a *"commedia agnostica"* as against the *commedia divina.* He liked to stress the work's analogy to musical structure, and its parallels with the "subject and response and counter subject in fugue." There were to be three principal elements: "Live man goes down into the world of Dead. The 'repeat in history.' The 'magic moment' or moment of metamorphosis, but through from quotidian into 'divine or permanent world,' Gods etc." (I like that "Gods etc.") He hoped that "out of the three main climaxes of themes, permanent, recurrent, and casual (or haphazard), a hierarchy of values should emerge."

This was to be a *modern* epic, "a poem including history" that "encompasses not only the world's literature but its art, architecture, myths, economics, the lives of historical figures—in effect, block letters, THE TALE OF

THE TRIBE." En route it would take in sixteenth-century Italian architecture, Provençal lyrics, Confucian politics, medieval economic history—almost a dozen languages. Pound was going to show "ideas in action" and "things explaining themselves by the company they keep."

[. . . .]

Pound's genius for the sound and arrangement of words that bring out the *inherency* of poetry did not extend to ideas. In his intellectual rage he was incapable of making the most elementary distinctions. Jefferson as president was forced to declare an embargo on American shipping during the Napoleonic wars in order to keep us from getting embroiled with both England and France. This measure was so unpopular in New England that secession was considered. Fascist Italy had so many unemployed that Mussolini attempted an embargo on emigration from the country. Pound likened Mussolini to Jefferson because both employed an embargo.

Pound was rapturous about leadership, thought everything he saw in Europe the great museum came from the top down. And so *inter alia* he enthroned the Adamses as the emblem of administrative genius. Details about the American experience escaped him. Rapallo is a very pretty town on the water but not in the main line even of European communications. Pound built up William Woodward's biography of Washington and Catherine Drinker Bowen's biography of John Adams as the last word on their subjects. He thought that the autobiography of Martin Van Buren had been deliberately kept from the people, and never understood that its eventual publication by the American Historical Association was a pious gesture toward an ex-president who was one of the shiftiest politicians of his day. Pound mistakenly conflated Jefferson with the Adamses, bitter antagonists for the most part. He thought the *Diary of John Quincy Adams,* the longest diary ever kept by a public man in America, had never been reprinted because of Adams's views on the currency.

Given Pound's equation of the *Führer-Prinzip* with wisdom and his being so far from home, it now seems inevitable that he should have fallen for Mussolini. Every Italian wall proclaimed *Mussolini ha sempre ragione.* Pound must have been the only inhabitant of Fascist Italy who thought Mussolini always self-possessed. "The Boss," as Pound calls him because that is what his entourage did, opens XLI. This is based on Pound's interview with the Boss, who affably responds to some bright sally *Ma questo è divertente*. Pound seems to have had better luck with the great man than other foreign visitors had. His office above Piazza Venezia was so vast that everyone had to walk an enormous distance to where *Il Duce* awaited you with folded arms and the famous scowl of mastership.

But he was the Boss, "catching the point before the aesthetes had got there." What point Pound made is not disclosed: he shifts to

> *Having drained off the muck by Vada*
> *From the marshes, by Circeo, where no one else wd. have drained it.*
> *Waited 2000 years, ate grain from the marshes;*
> *Water supply for ten million, another one million "vani"*
> *that is rooms for people to live in.*

The social achievements of Italian fascism existed mostly on paper. Thanks to the gifted engineer Arrigo Serpieri, the marshes were drained and wheat planted. This was urgent because there were so many unemployed that Mussolini had no trouble employing thousands for some fifteen years. This triumph is followed by a story of land speculators put in prison by the Boss, a story told by someone half Jewish, a *"mezzo-yit"* who is presumably one of the speculators. And now " *'Noi ci facciam sgannar per Mussolini'* said [t]he commandante della piazza." This is euphemistically turned around to mean "We would die for Mussolini." That they certainly did. In the twenties Pound admitted in a letter to Ford Maddox Ford:

> I tried a smoother presentation and lost the Metamorphosis, got to be hurley burley, or no one believes in the change of the ship. Hence mess of tails, feet, etc. . . .
> Re the double words, and rep. of cadence. The suffering reader is supposed to have waded through seven cantos already; MUST BANG THE BIG BAZOO a bit, I mean rhythm must strengthen here if he is to be kept going.

The "Big Bazoo," in the world crisis of the thirties ending in war, turned out to be *usura* and the Jews. Allen Tate was unfair when he said that the *Cantos* were not *about* anything. But to "include history," Pound's famous postulate for an epic, is not necessarily to describe it. The fascination of the *Cantos,* circling around golden bits of lyric landscape, lies in the journey up and down Pound's mind, which for great stretches shows mostly his reading. . . .

What Emperor Alexander said to John Quincy Adams along the Neva . . . Sir Basil Zaharoff the arms salesman becomes "Metevsky" . . . then we have Joyce, Marconi, Jimmy Walker . . . August Belmont comes to America to represent the Rothschilds . . . Field Marshal Hindenburg at a concert is annoyed by the music of Mozart. Better not to ask why Charles Francis Adams appears as Charles H. Adams. Then, since Pound is never out for the count, the great passage, and very beautiful it is, in XLV:

> **With Usura**
> *With usura hath no man a house of good stone*
> *each block cut smooth and well fitting*
> *that design might cover their face,*
> *with usura*
> *hath no man a painted paradise on his church wall*
> *. . .*
> *with usura, sin against nature,*
> *is thy bread ever more of stale rags*
> *is thy bread dry as paper,*
> *with no mountain wheat, no strong flour*
> *with usura the line grows thick*
> *with usura is no clear demarcation*
> *and no man can find site for his dwelling.*

My pleasure in these powerfully felt and beautifully structured lines is somewhat diminished by Pound's fond belief that usury is always a conspiracy against the public by alien forces. In the United States of America, state legislatures have been abolishing anti-usury statutes at the behest of banks in the credit-card business; these offer employment to states that formerly prohibited banks from operating across state lines. Ordinary economic history interested Pound as little as the fact that Mussolini, despite vast numbers of the unemployed, wanted a 22 percent expansion of the population in order to give Fascist Italy more muscle in the rivalries of the century.

Pound in the midst of his campaign against *usura* did not forget the rivalries of poetry. Canto XLVI opens with the sour admission that Pound's tale of usury will not get through to the boobs, and if you think it will,

> . . . *or that the Reverend Eliot*
> *has found a more natural language . . .*
> *you who think you will*
> *get through hell in a hurry. . . .*

But we are in hell, for enter the Jews, Canto LII, sound the drums. Pound has been told that the Hebrew word for usury is *neschek (neshekh)*. We cannot make out whose names have been blacked out on page 257 of the final collected cantos. But it is clear that somebody whose name ends in "sin" is "drawing vengeance, poor yitts . . . paying for a few big jews' vendetta on goyim." This is Pound's response to Hitler, whom he was to praise in his broadcasts as having "ended bad manners in Germany."

"Neschek" for usury, "yitt" for yid. Someone told him that the Hebrew language contains a word for weapons, *chazims*, which Pound took to mean knives. Rabbi Ben Ezra, as Conrad Aiken called him, never could resist sound clusters in a foreign language. Pound in this section manages to cover Gertrude Bell, the famous traveler in the Near East writing to her mama about England's need to keep its pledge to the Arabs in Palestine. "Thus we lived on through sanctions," refers to the League of Nations' farcical protest against Mussolini's rape of Ethiopia. And so on to

> *through Stalin*
> *Litvinof, gold brokers made profit*
> *rocked the exchange against gold. . . .*

This refers to Maxim Litvinof, the Jewish foreign secretary of the Soviet Union in the thirties, long out of favor even before Stalin made his pact with Hitler. In his last years, reports his English wife Ivy Low, Litvinof expected arrest and slept with a gun under his pillow.

Through "Stalin Litvinof" (presumably the same person)

> . . . *gold brokers made profit*
> *rocked the exchange against gold*

Before which entrefaites remarked Johnnie Adams (the elder)
IGNORANCE, sheer ignorance ov the natr ov money
sheer ignorance of credit and circulation.
Remarked Ben: better keep out the jews
or yr / grand children will curse you
jews, real jews, chazims and neschek
also super-neschek or the international racket. . . .

(The rest of this section is blacked out.)
A dozen or more lines down Pound eases into one of his beautiful lyrics,

The green frog lifts up his voice
and the white latex is in flower.

But when Pound's mind operated at full steam under the pressure of his many hatreds, he uttered one of the most frightful lies yet perpetrated about the Holocaust. The "poor yitts" dismissed, exiled, imprisoned, tortured, massacred in Germany, Italy, France, Belgium, Holland, Greece, Norway, Denmark—are paying for the crimes of Jewish bankers. Hitler told the Reichstag in 1939 that the Jews would be massacred if "they" started the war. Pound pretends to sympathy for the "poor yitts," but, unlike Hitler, he believes his own atrocity stories.

And now we have arrived at the *Pisan Cantos.* The war is over, and Pound in his cage is sorrowing over

The enormous tragedy of the dream in the peasant's bent shoulders
Manes! manes was tanned and stuffed,
Thus Ben and la Clara a Milano by the heels at Milano
That maggots shd / eat the dead bullock
DIGONOS, . . . but the twice crucified where in history will you find it?

At this point it would be funny to play Professor X and confront "this text for itself alone," history being extraneous to literature (still!), except that literature like Pound's itself writes history. But we cannot depend on Pound to describe rationally Mussolini's ruin and his own as he sits in a cage at the U.S.

Army's disciplinary barracks outside Pisa writing these lines on a table made for him by a black soldier awaiting execution.

Piero della Francesca included "their" landscape in his portraits of the duke and duchess of Urbino. How I wish someone could have painted Pound against the Italian landscape 1943–1945 as he sat writing that beautiful, much-cited passage,

> *What thou lovest well remains,*
> *the rest is dross*
> *What thou lov'st well is thy true heritage*
> *Whose world, or mine or theirs*
> *or is it of none?*

What a landscape with figure that would have been! Italy in ruins, hundreds of thousands of soldiers dead in Sicily, Calabria, Crete, Greece, Russia. Of the 50,000 Italian Jews before the war (one for every thousand Italians), and this in the least anti-Semitic country in Europe, among people who still called Jews *Ebrei* (Hebrews), 13 percent have emigrated, 12 percent have accepted conversion (often the price for being harbored by the Vatican). Out of the 8,360 deported to Auschwitz, 7,740 are dead. Fewer than thirty thousand will be found in Italy at war's end. Among Italy's leading exiles: Toscanini, Salvemini, Silone, Modigliano. Matteotti was murdered early in the regime, Gramsci allowed to leave prison for a clinic because he was dying. Mussolini: "This brain must be stopped from working."

Europe, Pound's great good place, everywhere in ruins. Yet Pound until his capture was blissfully out of it. He visited Mussolini's "Republic of Salò" on Lake Garda, ringed by the Nazis who delivered him from a penal island. Pound even spouted his economic nostrums to Italian Fascists who must have thought him totally nuts not to be aware that the "social republic" was a joke and Mussolini doomed by the hatred of his people. Of course we are dealing here with some remarkably self-centered types. Mussolini was pouting that he would never go back to Rome so as to punish the ungrateful people for celebrating his ouster from office in 1943. Pound, despite warnings from friends, insisted on broadcasting Axis propaganda after Pearl Harbor, and, says Dr. Torrey in his book on Pound in St. Elizabeth's, volunteered to broadcast in

Hitler's Germany. He never understood—or did he?—that what from his mouth would be excused by other writers could be understood by ordinary folk as encouragement to murder. At one point, said George Orwell, Pound chortled about "fresh meat on the Russian steppes." On April 3, 1942, he called in a broadcast for "a pogrom at the top. . . . But on the whole, legal measures are preferable. The sixty kikes who started this war might be sent to St. Helena as a measure of world prophylaxis, and some hyper-kikes or non-Jewish kikes along with them."

In St. Elizabeth's, talking to Allen Ginsberg and invoking his old friendship with Louis Zukofsky, Pound charmed his audience with the disclosure that his anti-Semitism was "a suburban prejudice." Bewitched by words as usual, he also explained that no one named Ezra could really be an anti-Semite. Whether or not he always knew what he was saying—clearly impossible in such a lifetime's flood of words—Pound was dishonest, and so were his defenders, when he finally claimed insanity as a reason for his actions. He got away with it.

Pound was a convinced fascist. The cruelty and death of fascism are an essential part of his epic and cannot be shrugged away in judging his work. Pound recognized his epic hero in Mussolini because fascism, like Ezra Pound, had few abiding social roots and was based on an impersonation, like Pound's, of a mythic personage. Pound was a racist, a defender of racial persecution, indifferent to the obliteration of fellow artists. These were not personal aberrations but part of hierarchic beliefs into which he grew through long years of alienation from his country and from the people around him. Pound was a fascist in a period when everything turned against the humane spirit of pre-1914 Europe in which modernism began.

The growing tendency of our century is against that spirit. Nowhere is it more striking than in the museum of modern literature—where the curators of the modernist classics replay their authors as Pound replayed the epic poets.

In the masterpiece of the Pound industry, *The Pound Era*, Hugh Kenner offers a defense of Pound's anti-Jewish writings and activity along the following lines. The Rothschilds defeated Napoleon. They were despised outsiders who sought to dominate and use those who had snubbed them. Such Jews resemble Sir Basil Zaharoff, the international arms salesman born in Turkey of Greek-Russian parentage, who is said to have hated the British all his life because a Britisher kicked him in Constantinople. (Strangely, Zaharoff established a chair at Oxford and was knighted.) "Hitler jailed no Rothschilds."

I have never been as interested in the Rothschilds as Pound was, but Pound's suggestion that "poor yitts" were paying for the crimes of the Rothschilds, which Hugh Kenner picks up, led me to look up the history of the family during Hitler's war. Elie and Alain de Rothschild were on the Maginot Line and became prisoners of war. Louis de Rothschild was a hostage. Guy fought with the Free French. Philippe was arrested by Vichy at the request of the Nazis and eventually made his way to Spain, climbed the Pyrenees to join the Free French. Edmund was an artillery major in the Italian and North African campaigns. Colonel Victor Rothschild was an intrepid bomb-removal expert whose work earned him the George Medal from England, the U.S. Bronze Star, and the U.S. Legion of Merit.

Pound, in the words of Professor Kenner, thought that "the poor Jews whom German resentment drove into concentration camps were suffering for the sins of their inaccessible religionists." Pound's usual name for a Rothschild was Stinkschuld. This charming name has been blacked out at the opening of Canto LII.

> ———sin drawing vengeance,
> poor yitts paying for———
> paying for a few big jews' vendetta on goyim.

This lunatic thesis is Pound's. But what is Professor Kenner up to?

It is a pity Pound's distinction between the financiers and the rest of Jewry was not allowed to be emphasized while he was still in the habit of making it. Correctly or not, it attempted a diagnosis, and one tending rather to decrease than to encourage anti-Semitism.

Kenner then defends Pound on the grounds that in 1938, when Pound wrote those passages, the concentration camps were "not yet committed to a policy of extermination. News of that policy, when it was instituted, no more reached Rapallo than it did most of Germany."

To mark the fortieth anniversary of V-E Day, the president of the German Federal Republic, Richard von Weizsäcker (his father was indicted for war crimes) addressed the Bundestag on the subject of "Hitler's Legacy":

At the root of the tyranny was Hitler's immeasurable hatred against our Jewish compatriots. Hitler had never concealed this hatred from the public, but had made the entire nation a tool of it. Only a day before Hitler died on April 30, 1945, he concluded his so-called will with the words, "Above all, I call upon the leaders of the nation and their followers to observe painstakingly the race laws and to oppose ruthlessly the poisoners of all nations: international Jewry." Hardly any country has in its history always remained free from blame for war or violence. The genocide of the Jews, however, is unparalleled in history.

The perpetration of this crime was in the hands of a few people. It was concealed from the eyes of the public, but every German was able to experience what his Jewish compatriots had to suffer, ranging from plain apathy and hidden intolerance to outright hatred. Who could remain unsuspecting after the burning of the synagogues, the plundering, the stigmatization with the Star of David, the deprivation of rights, the ceaseless violation of human dignity? Whoever opened his eyes and ears and sought information could not fail to notice that Jews were being deported. The nature and scope of the destruction may have exceeded human imagination. But in reality there was, apart from the crime itself, the attempt by too many people, including those of my generation, not to take notice of what was happening. There were many ways of not burdening one's conscience, of shunning responsibility, looking away, keeping mum. When the unspeakable truth of the Holocaust then became known at the end of the war, all too many of us claimed that they had not known anything about it or even suspected anything.

The contrast between what History knows and what Pound thought he knew threatens the integrity of literary study if it reduces itself to apologia and to vicarious scorn for what the modernist masters scorned. Ever since modernism became academically respectable, it has threatened to take over the curriculum. Eliot's prescription, that past literature should constantly be assimilated to the taste of the present, has led to a steady omission and distortion of actual history. Modernism must not become the only writer of its history, especially when puffed up with the antidemocratic and racist views of

Ezra Pound. Modernism is not our only tradition. The museum of modern literature, like all museums these days enshrining the first half of the twentieth century, cannot show us all that we leave out and even deform in the name of art.

[1986]

WILLIAM FAULKNER:
THE SOUND AND THE FURY

———•◆•———

Dreiser was a novelist Faulkner once praised. He may have found Dreiser easier to praise than he did his contemporary and rival Hemingway, like himself a product of the modern literary revolution.* But he found Hemingway narrow. When Faulkner, to his great surprise, became a world figure in the 1950s, he told an interviewer in Japan:

> I thought that he [Hemingway] found out early what he could do and stayed inside of that. He never did try to get outside the boundary of what he really could do and risk failure. He did what he really could do marvelously well, first rate, but to me that is not success but failure ... failure to me is the best. To try something you can't do, because it's too much [to hope for] but still to try it and fail, then try it again. That to me is success.

"Failure" was a condition that Faulkner, the descendant of "governors

---

*Dreiser wrote as if there were no other novelists. In the bleak period following *Sister Carrie*, he told himself in his diary to read some current novels, for he might want to write another novel some day.

and generals" (the embittered Jason Compson in *The Sound and the Fury* is always throwing the past at his sorry family), was used to. He made failure a condition of the South in his fiction and of the human condition—despite all ready-made American propaganda to the contrary. "Count no account," folks called the young Faulkner in Oxford, Mississippi.

Failure was more habitual in the South than elsewhere for most of the eighty years (1865–1945) before "the old unreconstructed had died off." This was the period that Faulkner (born in 1897) shared with survivors and memories of the Confederacy. In his long chronicle, it ended only with the Second World War and the rascally poor white Snopeses taking over from the once high and mighty Compsons, Sartorises—and Faulkners. Those eighty years were also continuous in Faulkner's mind with the Highlander who with just his tartan and claymore had barely escaped to the South from the English hunting-down of survivors of the last Jacobite campaign. His descendant crossed the Appalachians to the last southern frontier—the delta country owned by Chickasaws. The Compsons acquired their land from Indians who kept Negro slaves (and buried them with their master when the master died). In his "appendix" to *The Sound and the Fury,* written seventeen years after the novel in an effort to clear away Compson history over three centuries, Faulkner introduced the Chickasaw chief Ikkemotubbe, "a dispossessed American king," who merrily changed what the French called him, "de l'homme," to "Doom,"

> who granted out of his vast lost domain a solid square mile of virgin North Mississippi dirt as truly angled as the four corners of a card-table top (forested then because these were the old days before 1833 when the stars fell and Jefferson Mississippi was one long rambling onestorey mudchinked log building housing the Chickasaw Agent and his tradingpost store) to the grandson of a Scottish refugee who had lost his own birthright by casting his lot with a king who himself had been dispossessed.

The Chickasaws went on "to the wild western land presently to be called Oklahoma; not knowing then about the oil." In one compendious sentence Faulkner filled up two and a half centuries. Since he was a bit of southern history himself, one who traced "my own little postage stamp of native soil" from the Chickasaws to the Snopeses, that period (vast for an American) belonged to him. The crucial eighty years marked the last time when the South could claim to be separate in culture and memory.

Given his South, his family, his class, the breaking down that coincided with Faulkner's life and became his life, it is evident that history opened up to Faulkner with his name. "Whether he wanted it or not," Faulkner liked to say. He was steeped in legends of the Highlanders, reports by old hunters of the original wilderness, the primitive isolation of Mississippi before "the Wawh," the violent separation of the races ordained by God. The "old forces" were part of him. From his earliest days Faulkner still lived the heroic and defiant past—though its decay mocked the oratory with which southerners celebrated it. Faulkner lived with sacred history like a character in the Bible. Yet God's promise to His people had been withdrawn. Forced to live in the past, southerners were kept from prolonging it. What remained was the "imperishable" story, one that Faulkner felt condemned and privileged to write. Only by writing could he save his awareness and extend it. Among so many failed and desperate southerners in the "silent South," he was isolated by being a writer. He was to project his menaced sensibility onto many defeated and violent southerners. Oxford did not like his stubborn refusal to be absorbed elsewhere.

Faulkner's sharpest characteristic as a person and as a "poet," as he first called himself, was his concealment of his idiosyncrasy, his protection of his privacy. He was one with the South in its history, but he knew it well enough to be afraid. Many a writer emerging in the twenties was glad to escape his established family. Faulkner, growing up in the poorest state in the Union, in a regressive family and an impoverished culture, started cutting ties as soon as he could. He hated school, left high school without graduating, enjoyed being a roustabout and playing the local eccentric. He enlisted in the Royal Canadian Flying Corps in 1918 but never flew. He was a special student at the University of Mississippi because of his interest in French; he worked at a bookstore in New York, where he met Elizabeth Prall, Sherwood Anderson's future wife. Anderson's slovenly independence from literary convention was a decided influence when Faulkner lived near Anderson in New Orleans's French Quarter and wrote sketches for *The Double Dealer* and other publications that were meant to deliver the South from Mencken's "cultural swamp." Anderson said he would get Faulkner's first novel, *Soldiers' Pay* (1926), published as long as he did not have to read it himself, and he was as good as his word.

Faulkner, always hard up, was an assistant postmaster at the university, where he was fired because he neglected the customers. (He did not want to be at the mercy of every son of a bitch who needed a two-cent stamp.) After publishing a first book of poems, *The Marble Faun* (1924), *Soldiers' Pay,* and *Mosquitoes* (1927), he worked as a carpenter, a painter, a paperhanger, and was a coal heaver in Oxford's power plant. From 1932, the year he published one of his greatest novels, *Light in August,* to 1946, the year he was finally "recognized," he spent half of every year writing film scripts in Hollywood in order to be able to devote himself to his own work the rest of the time.

In the twenties the New South (as it was optimistically called) saw the emergence of a typically American middle class. Local businessmen and lawyers were not displeased by the descent from glory of proud families like the Faulkners. Faulkner was disliked for rejecting all virtuous paths to prosperity, mocked for drinking himself (sometimes literally) into the gutter. The tensions that racked him were not easily relieved by whiskey, but whiskey helped to relieve them in passionately inclusive one-sentence paragraphs. In *The Sound and the Fury* (originally called *Twilight*) the Compsons have come down to a father who died of drink, a self-pitying mother who has given up on everything to become a professional invalid, a sister cast off by her husband for marrying him when she was pregnant by another man, a brother who commits suicide because he is hopelessly in love with his sister. The baby of the family is an idiot who has been castrated after frightening a little girl. Jason Lycurgus Compson IV, who has blackmailed his sister and stolen the money sent for her daughter's care, says bitterly (after he has had his idiot brother, Benjy, sent to the state asylum in Jackson), "Blood, I says, governors and generals. It's a damn good thing we never had any kings and presidents; we'd all be down there at Jackson chasing butterflies."

In one respect Faulkner in Oxford was beyond censure. A writer was generally ignored. This may have been his good fortune. Faulkner agreed with critics that his style might have been less fervid if he had had other writers around for him to talk to and compare notes with; he described his writing as "oratory out of solitude." But there was no way for Faulkner to develop except on his own lines—and Mississippi made this easy. The South even in its palmiest days before the Civil War had never seen any use for local writers. William Gilmore Simms of South Carolina, though eager to espouse the "code," was told by the plantation owners who alone could afford to buy books that they were satisfied to get their reading matter from England. Their favorite author was Sir Walter Scott. Romance consoled the defeated South until the 1920s. The premature realist George Washington Cable had had to flee to Massachusetts because of his outlandish views on the "Negro Question."

Faulkner was an exception even among southern writers in the twenties, when the affected style and giggly double entendres of *Jurgen* passed for naughtiness from James Branch Cabell's Virginia. In some way that can be accounted for only by instinct, Faulkner (as Ezra Pound was to say of the young T. S. Eliot) had modernized himself on his own. Eliot had enjoyed "advantages" in St. Louis, had studied at Harvard, Marburg, Oxford. Faulkner did not find his stride even with his third novel, *Sartoris* (1929), though it took up the waiting theme of the failed "aristocracy." Its working title was *Flags in the Dust*, it was rejected by twelve publishers, and the published text was carved out of an enormous manuscript that everyone thought hopeless. Yet astonishingly, Faulkner's masterpiece, *The Sound and the Fury*, was published the same year. Looking back from it, one can see in all Faulkner's early work, not least in the New Orleans sketches, a jaunty need to make experiments, a wish to try himself to the limit, that prepare one for the imaginative abandon of *The Sound and the Fury*. He felt bound to certain themes but was always shifting his point of view.

Faulkner's deep sense of locale and his total involvement in its history often suggest Hawthorne. But his constant growth within himself and his particular gift for locating every narrative within the rush and beat of some embattled single voice have only one analogue in American writing. Melville was a self-educated wanderer who first wandered within each book, then from book to book. He constantly shifted and transformed himself; the motion of the sea became his image of truth. Faulkner did not continue to experiment after the extraordinary series—*Sartoris, The Sound and the Fury, As I Lay Dying, Sanctuary, Light in August, Absalom! Absalom!*—was produced in just seven years, 1929–36. In the 1950s, when he had become a world figure, Faulkner recalled of this time:

I think there's a period in a writer's life when he, well, simply for lack of any word, is fertile and he just produces. Later on, his blood slows, his bones get a little more brittle, his muscles get a little stiff, he gets perhaps other interests, but I think there's one time in his life when he writes at the top of his talent plus his speed, too. Later the speed slows; the talent doesn't necessarily have to fade at the same time. But there's a time in his life, one matchless time, when they are matched completely. The speed, and the power and the talent, they're all there and then he is . . . "hot."

The Sound and the Fury is certainly hot. Something like Melville's incessancy of thought and commanding rhetoric, marking the proud wanderer (within his own mind) who despises the progress of society, stamps *The Sound and the Fury* with Faulkner's fundamental image—life as a perpetual breaking down. In Benjy's mind, the bottommost layer and residue of Compson family history with which the novel opens, the world is all phenomenon, things-are-just-happening. In this beginning Benjy is incapable of explaining why they are happening. He just reverberates to every call of "Caddy!" from the golf course . . . and every glint from the fireplace that brings back the memory of his absent sister, Candace ("Caddy"), warming him in winter.

Only as we ascend from Benjy's mind to Quentin's monologue on the day of his death, recounting *his* love for his sister; from Quentin to Jason, the maddened survivor spewing out all his bitterness; from Jason to Faulkner himself, taking over the last section, are we put into the light. We are given every why and when that have produced the downfall of the Compsons, interlocked by so much passion and rage. The novel ends in the light of Easter Sunday and the unspoken triumph (if that is the word for those who merely "endured") of Dilsey, still a slave to these degenerate whites whom she and her family will survive. But the last word and the last cry out of the book belong not only to Benjy, who bellows in protest when Dilsey's grandson drives him the "wrong" way around the Confederate monument in the center of town, but to Faulkner's wonderfully sustaining style. The whole book recounts in the most passionate detail life as phenomenon, a descent into breakdown. In the end we are saved and exhilarated by Faulkner's reconstituting all this in the speed and heat of his art.

What the novel owed to the Freudian emphasis on the interior consciousness and to the already inescapable influence of *Ulysses* (1922) is obvious.
Theodore Dreiser was so awed studying the case histories in an early book
explaining psychoanalysis that he exclaimed: "I feel as though I were walking in
great halls and witnessing tremendous scenes." But Clyde Griffiths's tormented
dialogues with himself, though they go to the bottom of his character, could
have come out of a novel by Zola or Hardy. Dreiser's strength lay in the all-or-
nothing determinism of the nineteenth century.

James Joyce was a great originator. *Ulysses,* like the classical epic it absorbs
into a single day, is by now a fundamental reference to our civilization. But as a
great epic will be, it is a labored synthesis, more demonstrative of Joyce's fabulous powers than of the Dublin that remains a project in Joyce's mind. *The
Sound and the Fury* is a greater *novel,* more dramatic, more universally representative through the interior life of everyone in it. We do not know just what
Faulkner owed Joyce. Joyce in the twenties affected other writers like the
weather. Eliot heralded *Ulysses:* "Mr. Joyce is pursuing a method which others
must pursue after him." Faulkner was not that interested in becoming a
founder. It is a mistake to assume that in scrambling so many different periods
of time (especially in the "Benjy" section) Faulkner wished to mystify and
even to "test" his readers. But Faulkner was telling the truth when he said that
he had originally written a lot and even sent it off before he realized that people would actually read it. He was certainly having *his* joke when he explained
that there were four different voices in his book because each of the first three
had proved insufficient. What rings true to readers of *The Sound and the Fury* is
Faulkner's admission that the novel began as a story in a vision. Faulkner
"saw" a little girl with muddied drawers sitting in a tree, reporting to her
brothers below what she could see through a window of their grandmother's
funeral in the house across the way.

In another report of how the novel had begun, Faulkner said that the little
girl had muddied her drawers when she had sneaked under the barbed wire
dividing the Compson property. The little girl became Candace, "Caddy." The
land on the other side of the fence, the future golf course, was sold to send
Quentin Compson to Harvard. A fence separates the Compsons from their
past.

Intimate family details lock together in the novel so that every repetition is
heard in a different register, widening and deepening its effect on the reader as

it does on the Compsons themselves. We share every flicker of their minds. In the concluding section, "The clock tick-tocked, solemn and profound. It might have been the dry pulse of the decaying house itself; after a while it whirred and cleared its throat six times." Everything belonging to this family makes itself heard, over and over, like the sound of that clock. There is soon no "mystery" to the book, no pedantry of the kind that makes *Ulysses* so formidable; we get so caught up by the Compsons that one of the many pleasures of the book is that everything long stored up in everyone is intoned by a different character so as to advance the action. Caddy, not directly present for most of the book, is so intensely visualized by her brothers that she dominates their lives. Every sensation in Benjy's fractured mind reminds him of her. Her brother Quentin, preparing to drown himself in the Charles River, walks about Cambridge reliving every precipitous scene that he (more than she) botched at the last minute. Jason is magnetized by her, but his resentment of her freedom will not permit him to admit that he is jealous.

The charming but usually sodden father of this tumultuously incestuous family, Jason Lycurgus Compson III, a classical scholar, had long before given up and retired to his dog-eared Horace and his whiskey decanter. When his son Quentin departed for Harvard, he gave him (as cynical farewell) his ancient watch. Quentin twists its hands off in the morning of the day that will end with his suicide. But like the dead son, the idiot son, the absent daughter, the father is a constant infliction to his son and namesake, Jason. Nothing that ever happened in this family is forgotten; every offense, anything appropriated by one Compson at the expense of another, everything taken by the world to the shame of the Compsons in general, is endlessly (but variously) repeated. Finally, because their history has ended, the novel can begin—in the splintered, hopelessly yearning mind of Benjy.

Many novelists have claimed that any family can become a novel. This novel succeeds beyond all others of its time and place because the Compsons *live* time, they do not just live in it, which makes them as real as our family makes time real to us. Time is entirely fluid in the book, not an external measure against which people move. It assumes so many shapes because the force of memory plays on many people.

Any action—Quentin buying weights to keep his body down after he has jumped into the river, or Jason hysterically running after his niece Quentin after she has stolen the money that he had stolen from her care—interrupts a dream scene of reminiscence. The daughter's name "Quentin"—the departing sister's salute to the self-lacerating brother who died for love of her—itself reflects the sameness and repetition that are a constant in every family. The rapid shifts in time that Benjy lives successively, and that at first are bewildering to the reader, are soon enjoyed as the fragments that surprise our waiting consciousness. What makes Benjy so poignant is that he experiences nothing but sensations—Caddy shielding him from the cold, Caddy bringing him to the fire, Caddy crying "Stomp, Benjy! Stomp!" when they put on his galoshes. This family is in decay, but everything we see of them is bright with life, thrilling in its actuality. Dilsey near the end intones, "I seed de beginnin, en now I sees de endin." That refers to the Compsons themselves, over whom she waits in judgment without knowing that she does. But for the reader hypnotized by so much life on the page, nothing has ended. As it never ended for Faulkner, who when asked to supply an appendix clearing up the difficulties, went back to 1699 and forward to 1945 to fill in the Compson history. He spilled the book out in such ecstasy and freedom that he rewrote it as if he could not bear to leave it. He said that the book "caused me the most grief and anguish, as the mother loves the child who became the thief or murderer more than the one who became the priest. I wrote it five separate times, trying to tell the story which would continue to anguish me until I did."

Because of the war and the uncertainty of everything in sight, the twenties lived with a sharp, baleful sense of time. Secular man had supposedly triumphed, since he was ready to pay the cost of an existence totally without illusion. The hero of Dreiser's anachronistic novel [*An American Tragedy*] had nothing to say about the circumstances that drew him down. The "sentinel" trees around the lake were still the old gods. The brave new world *entre les deux guerres* gave a demonstrative radiance to style in *Ulysses, In Our Time, Voyage au bout de la nuit, The Great Gatsby, Mrs. Dalloway.* Style was heightened consciousness, the only defense against the fatal ordering of things, our true Prometheus. Style now proclaimed the Everlasting No. In *The Sound and the Fury,* consciousness never stops addressing itself or the absent loves and foes of one's own household. Sharpened to a scream—to a murder that is never accomplished, except by brother Quentin against himself—Jason curses the world as he frantically chases after his niece, then cries, "And damn You, too. See if You can stop me." Benjy without knowing it has become nothing but style, in the voice he cannot hear as his own.

Quentin is so full of his moony, overburdened style that he cannot get relief from it or from himself (he is all too conscious of *his* style) this side of the river. Jason's hatred is so expressive that, terrible as he is, we come to love his *fluency* (certainly not him) for never letting up.

In the fourth section, where Faulkner takes over to conclude the novel, there is a good deal of charged writing, as there is in Quentin's reveries. (Quentin is grandiloquent enough to be a parody of Edgar Allan Poe on *his* last day in Baltimore.) Faulkner compares the little black preacher at the Easter morning service to "a worn small rock whelmed by the successive waves of his voice.

> With his body he seemed to feed the voice that, succubus-like, had fleshed its teeth in him. And the congregation seemed to watch with its own eyes while the voice consumed him, until he was nothing and they were nothing and there was not even a voice but instead their hearts were speaking to one another in chanting measures beyond the need for words, so that when he came to rest against the reading desk, his monkey face lifted and his whole attitude that of a serene, tortured crucifix that transcended its shabbiness and insignificance and made it of no moment, a long moaning expulsion of breath rose from them, and a woman's single soprano: "Yes, Jesus!"

The blacks in *The Sound and the Fury* do not speak for themselves. The Compsons live in such echoing transmission from one mind to another that by the time we get to see them on stage in the final section, *we* are helping to complete the design. They have been in our ears all along; now we *see* them. But Dilsey must be seen first, and nothing in the prose fiction of our time could be more satisfying than her entrance, it is so much the proof of what is already in our minds.

> The day dawned bleak and chill, a moving wall of grey light out of the northeast which, instead of dissolving into moisture, seemed to disintegrate into minute and venomous particles, like dust that, when Dilsey opened the door of the cabin and emerged, needled laterally into her flesh, precipitating not so much a moisture as a substance partaking of the quality of thin, not quite congealed oil. She wore a

stiff black straw hat perched upon her turban, and a maroon velvet cape with a border of mangy and anonymous fur above a dress of purple silk, and she stood in the door for awhile with her myriad and sunken face lifted to the weather, and one gaunt hand flac-soled as the belly of a fish, then she moved the cape aside and examined the bosom of her gown.

We never feel in these charged-up passages, as we do in Faulkner's later writing, that he is elaborating his text and even commenting on it. In *The Sound and the Fury* everything about this family—especially those whose servitude makes them a part of it—already fits together, so that when Faulkner comes to describe them, the inherent design is rounded out in words as charged as these lives. Faulkner also needed to take over at the end and to put his particular stamp on the book. He liked to say that his ambition was to put everything, "the world," into one sentence. Our extraordinary view of Dilsey was composed under that spell. There was a stunning contractedness that followed from Faulkner's calling himself a failed poet. "Maybe every novelist wants to write poetry first, finds he can't, and then tries the short story, which is the most demanding form of poetry. And, failing at that, only then does he take up novel writing."

It was nice of Faulkner to say that "every novelist" was like him. He could be generous to the competition, for they never got in his way. His need to pile everything on his "little postage stamp of native soil" was his tribute to style. "Art is simpler than people think because there is so little to write about." The material is all so elemental, obvious, and foreclosed that one has constantly to bring a different perspective to it, which is style. But Faulkner liked to add, "I'm still trying to put it all on one pinhead. I don't know how to do it. All I know to do is to keep trying in a new way."

The "trying" was central to Faulkner's style; he saw the novelist not as an artist capable of finishing anything but as a gambler playing for higher and higher stakes. The Compsons, he said in his appendix to *The Sound and the Fury*, were gamblers; they were wrecked as a family, out of the running in the South (except for Jason, who, as Faulkner admitted with astonished admiration, was still running). Their claim on the past was like their ancestor's claim on the future when he entered the Mississippi wilderness. Man's desire was always in inverse proportion to himself. He had to gamble everything he had—little enough—against time's closing in on him. There was "one anonymous chance to perform something passionate and brave and austere not just in but into man's enduring chronicle . . . in gratitude for the gift of time in it."

Life to Faulkner was "this pointless chronicle." "Though the one I know is probably as good as another, life is a phenomenon but not a novelty, the same frantic steeplechase toward nothing everywhere and man stinks the same stink no matter where in time." We are moved about by what Faulkner in both *The Sound and the Fury* and *Light in August* called "the Player." We seem to be without help when matched against this figure. Faulkner's "Christ figures" are an idiot castrated in *The Sound and the Fury* because he frightened some little girls (and had a sadistic brother), and the murderer Joe Christmas in *Light in August,* pursued all his life because he *may* be a "nigger." (He is finally run to earth, castrated, and bled to death by a Ku Kluxer.) In *A Fable* (1954) the illiterate French corporal who leads the mutiny against the war obviously represents Christ; he has twelve followers. After rejecting the temptation offered by the "Supreme Commander," he is shot and falls into barbed wire that crowns his head with thorns.

A Fable is more allegory than fiction. By the 1950s Faulkner was editorializing over "fables" written in his "one matchless time." Faulkner's "Christ figures" are such only in their power of suffering. One of the most wonderful touches in the conclusion of *The Sound and the Fury* shows blond Benjy with eyes the color of sunflowers sitting next to Dilsey in the Negro church. "In the midst of the voices and the hands Ben sat, rapt in his sweet blue gaze." What Faulkner evidently wanted to say in *A Fable* was that his corporal was for the salvation of the world gambling his own life against the greater power represented by Satan, the "Supreme Commander." He lost. The essence of Christ for Faulkner in the twenties, that period of great skepticism, was that we are not savable.

The potent and redemptive figure in Faulkner's mythology is the novelist. The novelist gambles his talent against the silence surrounding us. He pits himself against vacancy and unreality, replacing the silence with a world organized by himself alone. Words must somehow exceed themselves through an effort that ultimately becomes the writer's signature, his style. The failure of a class, a tradition, a way of life, was the haunting subject. Failure entered the writer's attempted grasp of a *comédie humaine* often beyond language. "I don't know how to do it. All I know to do is to keep trying in a new way."

Faulkner liked the word *immortality*. He meant the novel that lasts, Ezra Pound's "literature is news that stays news." It was an ambition still fundamental to writers of the twenties, who could not conceive of immortality anywhere else. Faulkner was amazing. The novelist was his hero. He meant *the novelist*, not himself.

[1984]

SOUTHERN ISOLATES: FLANNERY O'CONNOR AND WALKER PERCY

———— • ◆ • ————

In Flannery O'Connor's fiction we start beyond the line of sexual love; it is never an issue. The characters are recurrently the Mother, the Child, the Brother, and other totally angry people. There are so many angry people, especially if they are landowners burdened by tenant farmers, that the stock elements of human nature—more real to O'Connor than "personalities"— cohere by conflict. What is at once feminine and Southern about her fiction—the original and originating element—is her trust in her own fatalistic truth. Hers is not a world of people made lonely by their freakishness, not simply a rural world that turns people fanatical, but one that subsists on the belief that human beings are absolutely limited.

All people in this uniform condition of silence seem to be the same age. Her stories—more effective in this than her two novels, *Wise Blood* and *The Violent Bear It Away*, which make the same point at greater length—are of a crazy human disposition to error. These stories are as amazing in their stoic self-sufficiency as Stephen Crane's. Their significant fault, rising from the South's intellectual moralism, the need to show that the same legend or fable operates at the heart of everything, is that they are too much alike. The recurrent situation is our fatal disposition to turn petty issues into the greatest possible mistake. Mr. Fortune, an old man who wildly loves his granddaughter, who thinks her the only person at all like himself, tries to absorb her will entirely into his own. He kills her in an hysterical protest against an obstinacy just like his own. A young boy, away from his sophisticated parents in the company of a madly religious baby-sitter, gets baptized. "Where he lived everything was a joke. From the preacher's face, he knew immediately that nothing the preacher said or did was a joke." He returns home but has to get back to the river. "He intended not to fool with preachers any more but to Baptize himself and to keep on going this time until he found the Kingdom of Christ in the river." In "Everything That Rises Must Converge," a liberal on the race question, hopelessly irritated by his mother's obtuse prejudices, finds after a short bus ride that life has come to a complete stop. His mother collapses on the street after being pushed out of the way by a powerfully built, angry Negro woman to whose child she loftily tried to offer a penny. "The lights drifted farther away the faster he ran and his feet moved numbly as if they carried him nowhere. The tide of darkness seemed to sweep him back to her, postponing from moment to moment his entry into the world of guilt and sorrow." In "Greenleaf," Mrs. May's outrageously inefficient tenant farmer can never keep the bull penned in. She is finally gored to death through a carelessness on Greenleaf's part that is total hostility.

> She looked back and saw that the bull, his head lowered, was racing toward her. She remained perfectly still, not in fright, but in a freezing unbelief. She stared at the violent black streak bounding toward her as if she had no sense of distance, as if she could not decide at once what his intention was, and the bull had buried his head in her lap, like a wild tormented lover, before her expression had changed. One of his horns sank until it pierced her heart and the other curved around her side and held her in an unbreakable grip. She continued to stare straight ahead but the entire scene in front of her had changed—the tree line was a dark wound in a world that was nothing but sky—and she had the look of a person whose sight has been suddenly restored but who finds the light unbearable.

Flannery O'Connor's dryness rises to eloquence only in the death-throe. The Pascalian perfection of her phrasing takes us out of time into the last possible thought before death. There is an intense sense of the immediate scenery but the place has been stamped by the South into a universal extract of itself. The place is simply that which backs up this recurrent fault in ourselves, this abysmal disposition to do the wrong thing, to *be* wrong. Her characters are souls in the wrong world, creatures totally resentful, who must express themselves in these ominous silences and ragged figures. Many Southern writers have been grateful for original sin as an explanation of the "guilt" of slavery; Flannery O'Connor really believed in it. She reminds me of that fiercest of all Catholics, Joseph de Maistre, who said that only the executioner keeps man's total untrustworthiness from turning society into chaos.

The fascinations of Flannery O'Connor's work to me are many. She is one of the few Catholic writers of fiction in our day—I omit the convert Evelyn Waugh as being too ideological—who managed to fuse a thorough orthodoxy with the greatest possible independence and sophistication as an artist. Her parish priest in Milledgeville once told me that she was constantly berating him for admiring conventional fiction. Yet her stories show that the Church— which as an institution she used rarely in her work, and then in a relaxed mood of satire at her own expense—was so supreme in her mind as to be invisible. The world of "guilt and sorrow," the light that has been restored but is unbearable—these ultimates are almost Platonic in their severity. The "real" world is the Bible Belt, an allegory. Reality is sin and error, multiplied by hillbilly fanaticism.

No wonder that the situations are hypnotic, the characters synonymous, the time of the drama anytime. The place is the bull that kills, the river in which you drown, not a place you remember for its tragicomic unsuitability to grace, like the rectories in J. F. Powers's quietly brilliant stories of American priests. Flannery O'Connor's severity is an intrinsic view of the world, the style by which she sees. Her stories remain in your mind as inflexible moral equations. The drama is made up of the short distance between the first intimations of conflict and the catastrophe. They are souls driven into this world and so forced to crash. They rush to their fate in the few pages needed to get them going at all. I am fascinated by O'Connor's severity—by its authority, its consistency, and wonder at its personal source. She inherited the dread circulatory disease of lupus, died of it before she was forty, knew she had it from the time she began to write. Her short career was a progress by dying—the sourness, the unsparingness, the constant sense of human weakness in her work may not need as many translations into theology as they get in contemporary American criticism. As Josephine Hendin pointed out in *The World of Flannery O'Connor*, there was an unreal and even comic gentility to her upbringing in Milledgeville that must have given O'Connor a wry sense of her aloneness as a woman, artist, and southerner who happened to be an Irish Catholic. The local Daughters of the Confederacy liked to babify her as one of Milledgeville's authors, but probably would not have enjoyed her real views about human nature or her mystical, not merely Irish, sense of her isolation as a Catholic in the Bible Belt.

On the other hand, she was so locked up in her body that one can understand why life as well as her faith made her think of *this is my body, this is my blood.* Christianity was sunk into her own flesh. She was a doomed young woman who had nothing to do in her short life but write fiction. There are recurrent examples of the Mother and the precocious, peculiarly neutral figure of the Child who so early sees all, knows all, and forgives no one. The psychological sources of her fiction are so neglected by her closest friends that one might think that Flannery O'Connor wrote fiction only to explain the true religion to the heathen. Yet these are less important than the criticism she makes—as a woman more reduced to inaction than most women, as a southerner even more suspicious of "America" than most southerners—of power.

She links power, ownership, authority to violence. People move into violence by a disposition to treat the world as entirely theirs. What Flannery O'Connor is most severe about is the uselessness of mere doing—she is severe about the illusion, not just the traditional male vanity, involved in the despotic show of will. Again and again her stories turn on fights over land and children. People go mad with temper trying to sustain ownership that is supreme—in their own minds. Often the characteristically resentful protagonist is a widow alone in middle age, whose dream is the preservation of property as her authority. The illusion ends in physical smashup. The human quality, at once dull and savage, is as expectable as the animals to which O'Connor goes for her characteristic similes. But what people are most is their disproportion to the world. Human beings are nothing but their moral natures, which sit in them like sacks waiting to be emptied into the world of action. The world is necessarily an empty place for O'Connor; the external is just a trigger. Her art is unhistorical. The only real issue is the primal fault. What people *do* is always grotesque.

To see life with such detachment from the bustling all-consuming power world, the world that dominates and so often hypnotizes the American novel-ist, is not to satirize the power but to turn one's back on it. Only a Southerner born to the tradition of being "different," off the main road of American progress, could have faced so much relinquishment. In the face of so much glut after 1945, only a woman of an austerity so scriptural as by our present stan-dards to seem mad could have done it. Perhaps Flannery O'Connor owed this "madness" to her sense of many disadvantages. To herself, certainly not to us, she felt like an afterthought even in the most brilliant period of southern writ-ing. (As she said of Faulkner's presence.) "Nobody wants his mule and wagon stalled on the same track the Dixie Limited is roaring down."

2

Faulkner ceased to be an influence on southern novelists when the South at last had its own worldliness to satirize. All modern images of the South had been of the poverty, differentness, resistance with which a writer could iden-tify; suddenly there was a South of stockbrokers and corporation executives who could make a Walker Percy feel as marginal as a Negro or Jew. When Percy's *The Moviegoer* unexpectedly won the National Book Award for fiction in 1962, the agitation over the prize in New York—Percy's own publisher had barely heard of the book—was in sharp contrast with Walker Percy himself and with *The Moviegoer*—a sardonic, essentially philosophical novel about the spiritual solitude of a young stockbroker in the New Orleans suburb of Gentilly who eventually marries a tragically vulnerable young woman to whom he is distantly related. *The Moviegoer* was a first novel by an unknown writer in Covington, Louisiana, who was a doctor of medicine but had never practiced. The book had not been launched with any great expectations and was indeed published only because one editor had stuck with it and with the author through four drafts.

The Moviegoer was certainly not a book to rouse the usually bored reviewers of "other fiction," or those editors of Sunday book supplements to whom any book on public affairs now seems more immediately newsworthy than any novel not left by Hemingway in a bank vault. By the early 1960s, the onset of the Kennedy years, the Vietnam War, the perpetual crisis at home that made this "intellectual" president's fondness for reading history altogether character-istic of the period, "mere fiction" was getting written off with dismaying ease.

The Moviegoer was in any event a book difficult to place. It was a lean, tartly written, subtle, not very dramatic attack on the wholly bourgeois way of life and thinking in a "gracious" and "historic" part of the South. But instead of becoming merely a satire on the South's retreat from its traditions, it was, for all the narrator's bantering light tone, an altogether tragic and curiously noble study in the loneliness of necessary human perceptions.

The narrator and protagonist—John Bickerson Bolling, "Binx"—cleverly increases his income every year and carries on in a mechanical way with one of his secretaries after another. But he has become obsessed with the meaningless-ness of everything he is just beginning to *see*, with the despair whose specific character, said Kierkegaard, is that it is unaware of being despair. His father, a doctor, perished during the war; Binx has a distinct sense of fatherlessness, of traditions he is supposed to carry on that he cannot locate or justify in the cozy ways around him. In the secrecy of his own mind he is excited by the pos-sibility of newly looking at life with the special, hallucinated feeling of discov-ery that he gives to the movies, where he spends many evenings. He has become an enraptured observer of the human face, a man who is training him-self to look steadily at the most commonplace things in his path. He has found some tiny chink in the wall of his despair—the act of looking, of seeing and discovering. He is a man who can look and listen, in a world where most people don't. His real life, one might say, is dominated by the excitement of conversion. There is a newness in his life. He is a spiritual voyeur, a seeker after the nearest but most unfathomable places of the human heart. He can lis-ten to the tortured girl Kate, who has a powerful attraction to death and belabors him—his ability to give her all his attention constitutes the love between them. He has become the one man around him who seems to want nothing for himself but to look, to be a spectator in the dark. This clinician and diagnostician of the soul trains himself in the movies. The enlarged, bril-liantly lighted and concentrated figures upon the screen have taught him how to focus on the secret human places.

The Moviegoer, essentially a sophisticated search of the search for faith in a world that seems almost bent on destroying faith, was not calculated to win great popularity. It was not exactly about going to the movies. It was a brilliant novel about our abandonment, our *Verworfenheit,* as the existentialists used to say—our cast-off state. Yet Binx the narrator and presiding figure was so tart and intractable in tone that one had to be sympathetic to the mind behind it, not impatient with the lack of action, in order to respond. It was, in fact, a book about an outsider for outsiders. Southerners used to call themselves outsiders in respect to the United States because they came from the rural, underdeveloped, old-fashioned, defeated South. But as Binx shows, in every passage of his involvement with the sophisticated upper middle class in New Orleans, it is the South *itself* that today makes outsiders of its people, breeds a despair that will never know it is despair.

The Moviegoer was an odd, haunting, unseizable sort of book. It was not "eccentric," did not overplay tone and incident in any current style—it was as decorous as an old-fashioned comedy of manners. But it was evidently and deeply the expression of some inner struggle. The author himself seemed in some fundamentals to feel himself in the wrong, to be an outsider in relation to his society. In *The Moviegoer* Gentilly, New Orleans, the South, had become the representative examples of an America in which people no longer knew how to *look* at anything, did not know how or what to look for. They lived with only the most distant intimations of their own pain. One man would have to learn to *see* (as if for the first time) with only the minimum chance of saving himself at all. His bride-to-be, Kate, they both know he cannot save.

The author of *The Moviegoer* was a Percy, of the "aristocratic" Mississippi clan that might have stepped out of Faulkner's novels. The Percys were Confederate leaders, southern planters, lawyers, gentlemen. A Senator Percy was driven out of office by one of those demagogues after whom the Snopeses used to name their even more horrible children. This senator's son, William Alexander Percy, was a lawyer and poet, brought up the orphaned Walker Percy and his brothers, fought the Ku Klux Klan in Greenville, was a friend of Faulkner—and a believer in the traditions of his class. William Alexander Percy romanticized the South in a way that his cousin Walker has never been tempted to do. In his autobiography, *Lanterns on the Levee*, William Alexander Percy said of the old slaveholders, the landed gentry, the governing class: "Though they have gone, they were not sterile; they have their descendants, whose evaluation of life approximates theirs." In 1965, writing on Mississippi as "The Fallen Paradise," Walker Percy wrote:

> The bravest Mississippians in recent years have not been Confederates or the sons of Confederates, but rather two Negroes, James Meredith and Medgar Evers.... No ex-Mississippian is enti-

tled to write of the tragedy which has overtaken his former state with any sense of moral superiority. . . . He strongly suspects that he would not have been counted among the handful . . . who not only did not keep silent but fought hard. . . . The Gavin Stevenses have disappeared and the Snopeses have won. . . . Not even Faulkner foresaw the ironic denouement of the tragedy: that the Compsons and Sartorises should not only be defeated by the Snopeses but that in the end they should join them.

William Alexander Percy, who went to Sewanee and had the social views of Donald Davidson, Allen Tate, Andrew Lytle, and Robert Penn Warren (before Warren became a brilliantly sympathetic student of the Negro movement in the sixties), wrote that Negroes had "an obliterating genius for living in the present. . . . [The Negro] neither remembers nor plans. The white man does little else; to him the present is the one great unreality." Walker Percy graduated from the College of Physicians and Surgeons at Columbia, and as an intern caught pulmonary tuberculosis from one of the many bodies on which he performed autopsies. America was just entering the war. While waiting to be admitted to the famous Trudeau sanitarium in Saranac Lake, Percy lived in a boardinghouse, all alone, reading and beginning to write. He says now, "TB liberated me." His illness, the enforced absence from his family, the solitariness all seem to have brought out in him one of those religious personalities whom William James called the "twice-born." His real life, his spiritual and intellectual life, his vocation as a writer, above all his concern with the "sick souls" who haunt his fiction—all this began when he found himself cut off from the career he had planned, from the war that was to be decisive for his generation, from the South that on Percy Street in Greenville he had taken for granted. Typically, it was the religious existentialists Kierkegaard and Dostoevsky, not Faulkner the Southern genius, who influenced him. He became a Catholic. This was one of his many actual "conversions": he underwent an unusually significant personal change, a change of faith within his change of profession. Although he is a natural writer, downright, subtle, mischievous, his novels seem to be essentially the self-determination of a religious personality, of a seeker who after being ejected from the expected and conventional order of things has come to himself as a stranger in the world.

A disposition to look at things in a radically new way is very much what happens in *The Moviegoer, The Last Gentleman, Love in the Ruins.* The violence of southern history—the violence you can feel in the streets of Greenville today, where stores advertise "Guns and Ammo," where every truck driver seems to have a rifle with him—is in *Love in the Ruins* projected into the future—when the whole country has gone mad with violence. It is not in *The Moviegoer* and a much murkier book, *The Last Gentleman.* But in all three novels the protagonist is someone who feels himself in the grip of a profound disorder, and who as a result cultivates from outside the art of looking. Binx in *The Moviegoer* says that "I am more Jewish than the Jews I know. They are more at home than I am. I accept my exile." Binx is not really in the world he seems to be thriving in. "What are generally considered to be the best of times are for me the worst of times, and that worst of times was one of the best. . . ." The mental refusal, the silent spiritual opposition, the effort to make some countervailing gesture are those of a man who seems to be *here,* with us, but is really out *there,* all by himself.

> Today is my thirtieth birthday . . . and knowing less than I ever knew before, having learned only to recognize *merde* when I see it, having inherited no more from Father than a good nose for *merde,* for every species of shit that flies . . .

This contrast of the here and the there, of the "regular" American world that can never understand the panic it breeds and the self training itself to face despair, to become a microscopist of salvation, gives *The Moviegoer* its special wry charm. Binx does see things in a special light—like the light on a movie screen, the light of hallucination, excessive concentration, obsession, that is given to those who at least turn their faces in the right direction. The southern writer's secret is still to believe that the world is moral, historical, meaningful.

[1971]

ARTHUR SCHLESINGER JR.: THE HISTORIAN AT THE CENTER

———— • • ————

Some years ago, during the Truman era, when Arthur Schlesinger Jr. began thinking of *The Age of Roosevelt,* he understandably felt that it was a bad time to be writing about Roosevelt. Whatever Truman's endearing personal qualities, his administration certainly did not add to the reputation of the New Deal; and Truman's weaknesses as the heir of the Roosevelt administration so quickly made him the sacrificial goat when the Republicans in the McCarthy period came up with their retrospectively long knives that Schlesinger must have felt that he was writing dead against the spirit of the times. Moreover, Eisenhower, at least in those now far-off first months when he seemed to be coherent and occasionally even sage, offered up so powerful a glamour in opposition to F.D.R.'s that it intensified the disenchantment with Roosevelt that had set in with Stalin's obvious exploitation of Allied victory.

But a work of history takes so long to produce that it sometimes sees changes—either in the public taste or in the historian himself—that make for an ironic reversal of expectations. The Truman era may have been a bad time to begin *The Age of Roosevelt,* but the last years of Eisenhower's have certainly made it a good time for publishing it. By 1957, when Schlesinger published his first volume, *The Crisis of the Old Order,* it was impossible not to see parallels on every hand between the obstinacy of Hoover and the obtuseness of Eisenhower.

No wonder Schlesinger's account of how the first New Deal emerged has proved so unexpectedly rousing. Not only was the Depression the most significant social experience of the generation now increasingly in the ascendancy; it so colored its experience of the war that anyone who came of age in the 1930s recognized not only that war is politics carried on by other means but that the war was in some sense an extension of the Depression. Everything since 1933 has taken place outside the domain of the "normal," the traditionally hopeful American experience. The increasing weakness of middle-class standards and traditions, of the faith in progress and of the habitual insistence on freedom; the increasing frivolity of popular culture; the political nihilism and cynicism of which McCarthy was the largest postwar symbol—all this had its beginnings in the bitterness of the Depression and the intellectual bankruptcy of business leadership. It is the great merit of Schlesinger's history that he describes the breakdown of public order, then the first excitement of the New Deal and the hoped-for revival of the national faith, with complete emotional authenticity.

This is because Schlesinger really believes in the New Deal as a tradition, a political idea, a historical legacy. He believes that it was one of the great expressions in our time of historical intelligence and moderation, that it symbolizes the vitality still possible at the center. Schlesinger believes in the New Deal even more than do most of the New Dealers, for whom it represented a whole series of inconclusive compromises. He is sure that as a philosophy the New Deal has coherence and that as a national tradition it has distinct shape. This, while historically debatable, is so deeply felt a conviction that he includes among the dramatis personae of the New Deal the ancestral figures of many American social philosophers with whom Roosevelt had no intellectual connection.

Schlesinger has conviction, and what among so many historians is merely a liberal prejudice is for Schlesinger a way of separating all sheep from all goats. Very few American historians have a real point of view. The amorphous liberalism of so many intellectuals works with particularly numbing force on historians who are so full of American history (i.e., *modern* history) that they are too much a part of what they are writing about to describe it with required force and edge and interest. American historians are deficient in ideas. Whether their lack of perspective is due to their lack of general historical interests or whether it is the other way around, they need a gimmick, a tool, a formula. (No wonder that the conservative and Catholic de Tocqueville is always invoked by American historians; he knew what he thought.) But the gospels are all contradictory—de Tocqueville, Turner, Beard, Marx, Freud, and now Riesman. Schlesinger, whose ease embodies some of the characteristic glibnesses of the present historical guild, certainly has a point of view. It was this, in a period when few historians will try a "big" book, in the grand style, that led him to attempt the whole age of Roosevelt. One reason for this is his evident wish to re-create, as an intellectual tradition, the New Deal for the Democratic Party. But even more, Schlesinger's book represents an interest in history as seen from the top, from the inside, among the policy makers—and it is this, actually, that gives the book its old-fashioned *literary* interest, for the great nineteenth-century historians also wrote as if they were operating from the center of things.

2

Schlesinger's notable sense of literary organization and drama, his ability to describe the Washington scene and the New Dealers as episodes in a historical drama—these have distinct literary overtones (there is even a reminiscence of John Dos Passos's style in the early portrait of Hoover's childhood) and literary value. Because Schlesinger writes as a partisan, with enormous confidence in his cause, he lacks the literary freedom of a Van Wyck Brooks or Edmund Wilson; but he is also free from the mawkish and desperate psychologizing of the academic historian who feels that he writes from the outside, far from the centers of power. Schlesinger's history embodies the admiration of an American intellectual, who feels himself part of a new elite outside the business ethos, for the one great recent American leader who was also outside it. Radicals are usually interested in ideology, not politics; liberals tend to see themselves as sympathizers, not leaders. Schlesinger has reversed this pattern among American historians, just as he believes that F.D.R. reversed it in government.

It was Roosevelt the "country squire," who was patrician in tradition and in fact undistinguished at both law and business, who became the idol of all those people in this country—minorities, labor, southern peons and southern aristocrats, intellectuals—who also felt themselves outside the business community as an activity and a tradition. In particular, Roosevelt gave new sanction to those academic intellectuals and theorists who, until the New Deal came along, had always been baffled by their inability to make use of, even to test, their explicit analysis of modern society. The more the businessmen hated Roosevelt because, as they correctly thought, he despised business as a way of life, the more the intellectuals and academicians clung to him. They had all been thrown together by their common exclusion from "normal," commercial, American experience. The Roosevelt haters were wrong when they charged that Roosevelt hated business because he had failed in it. Schlesinger quotes a remarkable letter Roosevelt once sent to a Harvard dean: he really thought business "absurd." It was this freedom from the most powerful tendency in American life that gave Roosevelt his inner freedom; it is this, surely, that gave him his sense of the dramatic, of the "forward" movement in American life at a time when the old order, in Schlesinger's phrase, was not merely in crisis but had actually collapsed.

Schlesinger's first volume, *The Crisis of the Old Order*, though highly partisan and sometimes downright unfair in its black-and-white scheme of values, was exciting because it represented the actual drama in the passing of the old order. *The Coming of the New Deal* is far more technical in its detail and minutely carries the history of the administration up to the 1934 elections. It is not merely his sense of historical responsibility, it is his New Deal mystique, as it were, that has made Schlesinger in this volume stick so closely to the inner history of the new reform agencies—the AAA, the NRA, the PWA, and all the rest. Yet the image of Roosevelt is always in the reader's mind, obviously because it is in the author's. The book concludes with a character study of Roosevelt in office that is an extension of the biography of Roosevelt with which the first volume ended; I suspect that future volumes in *The Age of Roosevelt* are likely to close on this same magnetic human image.

3

The administrative point of view, I have suggested, is a brilliant literary and dramatic device that gives the reader the old-fashioned sense of commanding history as a drama and a spectacle. The conflict of administrators, the sensitivities of Henry Wallace, the prickliness of Harold Ickes—all these become problems of policy, as they must have been to Roosevelt; and, like Roosevelt, we feel ourselves to be patient, sage, endlessly resourceful. The trouble with this is that while it gives us a sense of being at the center and almost in command of things, it tempts Schlesinger into sacrificing the truth that cannot be fitted in, the jagged edges that would detract from the straight frame and the smooth design. From the center of the administrative web, all things appear in relation to itself. The historian in this position, like the president, gets a sense of the whole that is exciting, but some things look flatter to him than they need to; he must cover too much in a hurry; he cannot help being a little condescending and mechanical. Just as Roosevelt said "my old friend" too easily, so Schlesinger is a little offhand in describing a New Deal politician as "irresistible and penetrating."

More serious is the intellectual unctuousness that comes from thinking inside the position of power. It is true, as Schlesinger says in his moving portrait of Roosevelt, that "the American system remained essentially a presidential system; in the end, all things came to the man in the White House." But the White House is more likely to hear of things than it is to initiate or even to understand them, and here Roosevelt's famous "pragmatism," his lack of ideas, has turned out to be far more sterile and even dangerous than Schlesinger's account of Roosevelt in his favorite image of himself—the "quarterback," the shifting center of operation—suggests. Roosevelt's freedom from the business ethos was more an accident of birth and a quality of personality than a matter of personal philosophy. When one recognizes the intellectual poverty and spiritual thinness with which he defended democracy during the war—has there ever been so notable an American leader whose public papers are so insignificant as political literature?—and remembers how Wilson, by contrast, always had historical reasons for what he did and recognized the historical tragedy of what he was forced to do, one sees the tragedy of a diminishing democratic leadership that Schlesinger, who sees F.D.R. always in winning human terms, does not bother with. Wilson, demonstrably a failure in his own terms, a "foolish" and obstinate idealist, nevertheless left behind him concepts that the Democratic Party could think about. The use of a political philosophy, after all, is that it be carried on. Roosevelt's pragmatism, which his enemies thought opportunism and which in Schlesinger's book becomes an exciting democratic vitalism and pluralism, was in fact conducted so far beyond the limits of "normal" politics that it signified neither the bankruptcy that his enemies saw nor the inspired common sense that Schlesinger sees. It represented the extreme of administrative maneuvering, Roosevelt's only knowledge, in a world in which—as with Stalin at Yalta—gestures and smiles and personal charm deceived the actor far more than they did his audience. It had been Roosevelt's great good luck that he was socially an anachronism, but by the end of the war he was really one politically: only his growing inaccessibility inside the web permitted him not to realize that stratagems had replaced principles.

The New Deal did not destroy the old order. Like all modern revolutions, it came in after the old order had collapsed. It operated, as all governments must operate nowadays, under the shadow of extremes, in a world of improvised solutions. But Roosevelt could not know how much he had gone beyond the traditional morality, the clear sense of good and evil, that at least left Woodrow Wilson historically lucid.

It is this failure to show the growing uncontrol within and behind the New Deal, the hidden dimension of moral extremism, that I object to in Schlesinger's new book. He writes as if, by recounting on so minute a scale the first year of the New Deal, he were reporting from some irrefutable center the established truth. Actually, it has become increasingly clear that the New Deal represented, against the will and sometimes without the knowledge of many people who participated in it, a series of adventures in a void that was created by the decay of tradition.

When Roosevelt was asked once for his philosophy, he replied testily: "I am a Christian and a Democrat." This was the legacy passed on to him, and was purely personal; it was not one he could hand on to his successors. And in fact, he has no disciples, only admirers. Since, in Schlesinger's total argument, the New Deal represents a philosophy of moderation, a middle way between laissez-faire and the Communist specter, I think that one clear intention of his book—to create a canon, to show the New Deal as a viable tradition—is an illusion. What makes his volumes so notable is really their literary sense, their dramatic organization, their feeling for the personalities of administrators who were swept up by the times as by a tidal wave. It is in such pages that Schlesinger shows his awareness of the plight of democracy, of the increasing pressure of mass society on the eighteenth-century machinery of American government. Schlesinger's book, which becomes thin in its complacent New Deal references, is actually exciting and moving whenever, in seeking to render the facts, it hints of the permanent crisis that is the truth of our times.

[1959]

PRESIDENT KENNEDY AND
OTHER INTELLECTUALS

———•◆•———

Some years ago, when Sherman Adams was still grand vizier of the Eisenhower administration, a famous American poet and longtime friend of Adams's, while sitting in his office in the White House, expressed a desire to meet the president. Adams went in and came out again and tactfully explained that the president was not curious to meet the famous poet.

That same poet, however, was prominently displayed at the inauguration of John F. Kennedy. And although many of us who admire Robert Frost's poetry and enjoy Robert Frost's conversation and have not shared his political views may well be surprised to hear that he has *returned* to the Democratic fold, Frost's enthusiasm says a good deal about Kennedy's charm for some of the most interesting minds in the United States. During the campaign and afterward, Kennedy certainly never hid his allegiance to the fundamental principles of the New Deal—which Robert Frost has always detested. Yet no sooner did the New Frontier get itself named (somewhat mechanically) than Robert Frost heralded "an Augustan age of poetry and power, with the emphasis on power." [...]

Norman Mailer at Los Angeles, preparing the article that *Esquire* was to insist on calling "Superman Comes to the Supermart," was staggered on interviewing Kennedy when the candidate said he had read "*The Deer Park* ... and the others." The conventional remark on meeting Mailer is, of course, that one has read "*The Naked and the Dead* . . . and the others." But Kennedy, happily, was not conventional. The man who was very possibly the next president of the United States had read the scandalous hip novel about Hollywood doings in Palm Springs that had enraged and disgusted so many publishers and critics. Mailer's brilliant if overwritten article expressed the same hope for Kennedy that in their different ways Lippmann and Rovere and Kempton and even Robert Frost had openly felt. Given the "vacancy" in American life, as Lippmann had put it during the last days of the Eisenhower administration, the increasing divorce between private thought and the public realm, could it be that here at last was one of the "creative innovators" in politics, one man with brains and vision enough to pull our people to world reality, away from business as usual? Could it be, dared one hope, that with this rich, handsome, literate, and courageous young man the sickening cycle of underground life and public inanity had at last been cut? *Esquire*, more hip than Mailer himself, advertised his article as "The Outlaw's Mind Appraises the Heroes' Dilemmas." But what Mailer said, with moving hope as well as concern, was that perhaps, with Kennedy, there might at last be some positive awareness of the ever-growing disrespect of intellectuals for politics. Too long, as he said, had politics quarantined us from history, and too long had we left politics to those who "are in the game not to make history but to be diverted from the history which is being made." Although the convention at Los Angeles was actually dull, full of seedy machine politicians, "the man it nominated was unlike any politician who had ever run for president in the history of the land, and if elected he would come to power in a year when America was in danger of drifting into a profound decline."

Mailer was stirred enough to romanticize Kennedy with faintly derisory analogies to Marlon Brando. Yet whatever is Mailer's personal symbol of an American hero, what he said was no more than what so many intellectuals felt. "It was a hero America needed, a hero central to his time, a man whose personality might suggest contradictions and miseries which could reach into the alienated circuits of the underground, because only a hero can capture the secret imagination of a people, and so be good for the vitality of his nation. . . ."

And just recently there has come to hand the most moving expression of the wretchedness and the positive sense of unreality that political alienation can suggest to a sensitive mind. It is the brilliant excerpt, recently published in *Esquire*, from Saul Bellow's new novel, *Herzog*. The hero is a university teacher and writer, racked by the collapse of his marriage and by his spiritual loneliness, who wildly scribbles in his notebook letters to public leaders as well as to private individuals. At the end of this excerpt, he suddenly writes a letter to President Eisenhower, and this defines not only the grounds of his private unhappiness but his feeling that it has a public source:

> . . . it seems a long time since chief executives and private citizens had any contact. The President is briefed by experts or informed by committees on the problems of the nation. That is too bad. Sometimes obscure citizens are wildly intelligent, without the disabilities of special training. But we have to recognize that intelligent people without influence have a certain contempt for themselves. This partly reflects the contempt the powerful have for them, but mainly it comes from the contrast between strength of mind or imagination and social weakness or political impotence. . . . It seems to them that society lets them think everything, do nothing. The private resentment and nihilism that result are due to a private sense of failure which possibly comes from the intellectual's faulty definition of himself and his prospects. What should his thought do? What power ought he to have from it?

The Russians speak of many disaffected and silent people in their country as "internal *émigrés*"; increasingly it has become natural for many American writers and scholars and intellectuals to think of themselves as "internal *émigrés*." In the very thirties that now seem to some young people an unrecapturable time of *engagement* and public responsibility, Nathanael West said that we have no outer life, only an inner one, "and that by necessity." By the 1960 presidential campaign, it was perfectly possible for writers like Robert Frost and Norman Mailer (who, whatever the outer life, are not so hilariously divergent as they seem) to herald, with varying tones of enthusiasm and private distrust, what Frost called "a new Augustan age" and Mailer an end to the "alienated circuits of the underground." I grant that writers welcome an audience in high places, that "the new Augustan age" is pure rhetoric—much more so (whatever the phrase) than Mailer's felt and even obsessive feeling that now there are "alienated circuits of the underground." But if the writer is good, even his egotistical affections are intelligent. And of course one reason for this pro-Kennedy feeling was the contrast he made with the General and the General's Westerns and the General's sentences—to say nothing of the General's party, which a year after the campaign announced a major new campaign to enlist "the specialized knowledge and experience of the nation's intellectuals," which has now drawn plans in every state "to facilitate the utilization of friendly academicians in party affairs at all levels."

Truman, even more than Eisenhower, showed himself to be intemperate in denouncing "advanced" American pictures that had been selected by museum officials for exhibition abroad, while F.D.R., whatever his spontaneous shrewdness in answering to immediate situations, had the landed gentleman's repugnance to excessive intellectual labor. No wonder that so many writers and scholars have felt that they can at least *talk* to Kennedy. He reads, he reads endlessly, his reading is constantly an amazement in a country where the strongest minds often on principle declare a positive contempt for the reading of serious books. Addressing a newspaper publishers' convention, the president of the United States recalled that Karl Marx had been correspondent for the *New York Tribune.* Before leaving for his talks with De Gaulle and Khrushchev, the president at his birthday dinner in Boston quoted William Lloyd Garrison's famous thunder cry from the opening number of the *Liberator.* When he was welcomed to Paris by De Gaulle, the president graciously replied by invoking Jefferson's love for France and Franklin's popularity in the *salons.* When Hemingway died, the president quickly issued a tribute in which he made reference to Paris in the 1920s, the lost generation and the fact that Hemingway had helped to end the old provincialism of American letters. The president, as James Reston has said, takes printer's ink for breakfast, and by now his bookishness and intellectual sophistication are so well known that one is no longer surprised to hear that C. P. Snow has been invited to the White House and that E. E. Cummings has been to tea, or that at a certain juncture Kennedy alone, of all his intellectual entourage, knew the title of Churchill's first book. It did not seem at all pretentious to me that the First Lady, interviewed on her plans for redecorating the White House, should have spoken of her interest in antique furniture as natural to the wife of a "historian." Not only has history been the president's strongest intellectual interest, but so far as he has been trained to any profession, it has been to the study and the writing of history.

The son of the American ambassador to Great Britain in 1940 had positive reasons to remember that during the Civil War the son of the American ambassador to Great Britain was Henry Adams, and there learned a great deal that was to be important to the life of politics and the writing of history. President Kennedy, who before the war thought of becoming a newspaperman, reminds me, in the range of his sophistication, of a great many "intellectual" newsmen and editors. The author of *Why England Slept* and *Profiles in Courage,* the president whose favorite book has been given out as Lord David Cecil's *Melbourne* and favorite novel as Stendhal's *The Red and the Black* is in his personal interests alone far more of a "historian" than many who teach history rather than learn it.

Now it is also true that President Kennedy's anecdotes from American history tend to be trotted out rather irrelevantly to formal occasions, and that the punch line quoted in Paris from Samuel Adams is unaccountably accredited in Vienna to someone else. And if he cited a little-known detail from Karl Marx's biography to an audience of publishers, it was to joke that Marx had vainly asked the *New York Tribune* for a raise—look, said the President, what you fellows may get us all into by not giving a correspondent a raise! William Lloyd Garrison's "I will not equivocate and I will be heard!" is in excess of what a birthday dinner among Massachusetts politicians, even on the eve of his going to Europe to meet Khrushchev, seems to call for. And *Profiles in Courage,* perhaps because it was indubitably *written* by the author himself (as he replied to reviewers who doubted it), is certainly far more interesting for its personal emphasis on "courage," courage by *anybody* in the United States, whether Taft or Norris, than for any significant political ideas of his own. *Profiles in Courage* always reminds me of those little anecdotes from the lives of great men that are found in the *Reader's Digest,* Sunday supplements, and the journal of the American Legion. It is the kind of book that reads like a series of excerpts even when you read it through; and indeed it seems composed of excerpts—excerpts of reading, excerpts of anecdote. Nor, quite apart from his conventional public statements, am I impressed with the tales of a voracious reading that seems to be concerned largely with getting the "facts," the highly separable material and statistical facts that can be shoveled into the executive mind. And with everything that has been said about Kennedy's being a Catholic, almost nothing, so far as I can tell, has emerged about the personal and intellectual side of his Catholicism. Unlike Senator Eugene McCarthy and other American politicians whose thoughtfulness and sense of philosophical principles owe so much to the traditional teachings of their church, John F. Kennedy seems to have been more aware of Catholics as a source of political support than of the Church as a source of intellectual inspiration. And although Kennedy's narrow victory, which owes so much to Catholics, has caused many Catholic writers and intellectuals to rally almost defensively around him, some of them, before Kennedy was nominated, were positively bitter about his political exploitation of Catholic support.

Yet with all these limitations and conventionalities and sales tricks, it is interesting to see how much of an "intellectual" Kennedy wants to be and how eagerly his bookishness, his flair and sophistication, his very relish for the company of intellectual specialists, have been advertised to the public without any fear that it might dismay a people so notoriously suspicious of these qualities in others. Obviously in Kennedy's case an "intellectual" taste does not suggest a fastidious withdrawal from anything—not even normal passion. Adlai Stevenson in his two campaigns seemed to be running not only against the bluff, smiling General, but against the General's philistine supporters. It is interesting to learn from the autobiography of T. S. Matthews that when Matthews warned Stevenson against "Ohio" (meaning the Yahoos), Stevenson's advisers just stared at him, while Stevenson smiled and went back to work. The extraordinary identification that so many American intellectuals make with Stevenson has often struck me as loyalty not to a lost cause but to lostness as a cause. I have never been sure just how much of an "intellectual" Adlai Stevenson is, but he has certainly been cherished among intellectuals more for his obvious sensitivity than for the strength of his ideas. In 1956 even more than in 1952, and at Los Angeles in 1960 even more than in 1956, he seemed the peerless leader of intellectuals who boasted that they had never had a candidate before—and who warned that if he were counted out for positively the last time, they could never be that much concerned again: they would have suffered just too much. And since Stevenson's public style seemed to combine self-demeaning wit and vulnerability to such a degree that some of his closest friends condoled with him on having to face the public at all, perhaps it is no wonder that the candidate who publicly yearned that the cup might pass from him was defeated by the General who listens with particular respect to the head of any large American corporation.

By contrast, of course, Kennedy has not only surrounded himself with many of the liberal historians, economists, and political scientists who were reputedly such a liability to Stevenson, but despite certain necessary political favors to be paid back, he has made a point of appointing as ambassador to Japan a professor of Japanese history, as ambassador to India a John Kenneth Galbraith, as secretary of the National Security Council the former dean of the Faculty of Arts and Sciences at Harvard, as one of his immediate advisers the author of a scholarly study of presidential power, as another adviser a young man in his twenties who was first in his law class at Harvard. Although the secretary of state obviously was chosen to be one of a team, it is interesting that his last previous job should have been as president of the Rockefeller Foundation; although the secretary of defense was president of the Ford Motor Company, he came to Ford and rose at Ford because he was a brilliant statistician; although the secretary of the interior necessarily comes from the West, the present one really is crazy about Robert Frost. Even the postmaster general in this administration has written a novel; even the new military adviser to the President has written a superb book on American defenses. No wonder that Arthur Miller and John Steinbeck and W. H. Auden were asked to the inauguration as publicly declared assets of the republic; that even the Kennedys' French chef is felt to be a compliment to their good taste rather than to their wealth—to say nothing of the *fête champêtre* thrown for the Pakistan president at Mount Vernon, which (it is safe to guess) irritated some congressmen not because of its reputed cost, but because, with its announced links to classic entertainments in the past, it represented a bit of intellectual swagger that not all Americans are likely to admire.

In short, the president has gladly let it be known that he is in fact a highbrow, an intellectual, an omnivorous reader. There was once a Tammany mayor of New York who, in private, talking with a favorite magazine reporter, confided that he indeed knew and enjoyed Joyce's *Ulysses.* But this was a secret, not a boast. President Kennedy's acquaintance with some minor details in the life of Karl Marx is rather more a boast than a secret, like his open espousal of Robert Frost, his invocation of William Lloyd Garrison in Boston and of Jefferson in Paris; all these and more are attempts to form his public style. As has often been said, Kennedy is the most "intellectual" president since Woodrow Wilson—some even say since Theodore Roosevelt. Hoover may have been a brilliant mining engineer on three continents and with his wife he did translate a medieval Latin treatise on mining; but in public he gave the appearance of suffering fools miserably, and stimulated no one. Wilson had been a political scientist and had written books; but he, too, tended rather to patronize and to moralize, and at Versailles in 1918 was hopelessly outclassed in wit and learning, to say nothing of his not knowing a single blessed word of French. (President Kennedy's French is primitive, but even on a state visit to Canada he was able to make a virtue of his limitations by likening it to Prime Minister Diefenbaker's.) Like Theodore Roosevelt (also trained to no profession but that of "historian"), Kennedy has cultivated as his public style the bookman-in-office. Although Kennedy has not yet publicly found jobs for poets (as T.R. did for Edwin Arlington Robinson), he, like Roosevelt, has praised the strenuous life as if he were promoting a historical revival and, like T.R. again, he lets his literary opinions be known. He has helped to establish taste. And it is just this cultivation of the highbrow world as an executive taste and presidential style, his turning the poor old suffering American egghead into something better than a martyr to popular culture, that I find most suggestive about Kennedy-as-intellectual. If during the campaign he grew on many thoughtful observers who distrusted his family background and despised his failure to say a single word about McCarthy, so in his first weeks, at least, he was able to persuade many cool observers that his was the necessary style of administration in these times—like Churchill, like De Gaulle. Before Cuba, one English joke was that Kennedy talked like Churchill but acted like Chamberlain; even after Cuba, it was said that there had been an *unaccountable* lapse of his dominant executive style. But Cuba apart for the moment, it is obvious that Kennedy's reputation as an "intellectual" has been an asset to him at a time when government operates on a scale of such complexity, requires so deft an ability at least to show a nodding acquaintance with many subjects. It has often been said that Kennedy turned the tide in his first television debate with Nixon by the precise answers he was able to supply to questions raised from so many different fields. Before his nomination, says Theodore H. White in *The Making of the President, 1960*, Kennedy astonished his own staff by analyzing without notes his chances in every single state of the union, and, in the "honeymoon" weeks of the administration, Vice President Johnson let it be known that he was positively awestruck by the president's ready handling of so many different subjects.

This smooth and easy assimilation of fact, this air of overall sophistication, is what Americans have learned more and more to admire in journalism, in business, in conversation, and on television quiz shows—whether the man in the dock is Charles Van Doren or the president of the United States being questioned mercilessly (and pointlessly) about everything from Laos to Tammany. The quiz show did not die out with the exposure that the contestants had been briefed; the candidates in the 1960 campaign were also briefed, as is the president of the United States today, and the show goes on. If the reporters sometimes act as if they wanted to trip the president up, the president knows that he can impress the country by way of the reporters. This overall style, so much like the division of even the arts and sciences into departments of *Time* magazine, became a "research" style among the military during the war, and it has now invaded the big universities and "scientific research and development." It is our national style, *intellect-wise.* We now admire it—when it comes unaccompanied by personal stress. A recent article in a liberal weekly on "The Mind of John F. Kennedy" turns out to be an entirely admiring study of Kennedy's range as an administrator. This vocational or psychological use of the word *mind* is so typical of our time and place that it probably never even occurred to the author to extend the word to cover "beliefs." Instead we are told that Kennedy's "marshaling of related considerations" defines Kennedy's mind "as political in the most all-encompassing sense. The whole of politics, in other words, is to such a mind a seamless fabric, in which a handshaking session with a delegation of women is an exercise directly related to hearing a report from a task force on Laos." And this ability to assimilate on the jump necessary quantities of fact, to get statements of a problem that carry "action consequences"—this is what we have come to value as the quality of intellectual all-roundedness or savvy. It is a style that depends always on research done by other people, on a swift and agile reaction to the statement of the problem *set* by other people, on the professional politician's total recall for names and faces, the professional communicator's ability to wham the effective phrase right down the mass media to the great audience. The more complex and insoluble the problems become, the more intellectuals are needed to pile up research on them; the incoming trays are piled higher, ever higher, with Freedom Riders, Latin American poverty, education bills, recalcitrant congressmen, the Congo, obstinate Englishmen, and offended Nigerian diplomats who were refused a cup of tea in a Maryland restaurant. The professors who coasted along on two courses and one committee now work from eight-to-eight before they go out to the big dinner every night: "I don't have time to put my shoes on in the morning." Since the boss is the man who takes his problems home with him, the boss proves that he is the boss by a certain air of tense vigilance and unsleeping physical resiliency and readiness. Never in any administration have we been told so constantly how little sleep the president gets.

The boss nowadays does not have to be an expert himself; in the normal course of nature he cannot be one and boss, too. But he has to know who the experts are. So much is this executive style—with its dependency on batteries of advisers, experts, "researchers"—the admired "intellectual" style because it works with intellectuals, that the president of this nation of boastful pragmatists, in a public tribute to Robert Frost, told the story of a mother's writing the principal of a school, "Don't teach my boy poetry; he's going to run for Congress"—and affirmed: "I've never taken the view that the world of politics and the world of poetry are so far apart." No wonder that some who suffered with Stevenson in 1956 for being too good for the American public felt with Kennedy in 1960 that intellect was at last in touch with power. He had read the essential books; and the essential names, the principal formulae, the intellectual shorthand, were at his disposal. No wonder that, conversing with certain Kennedy advisers in March, one felt about them the glow of those who have not merely conceived a great work but are in a position to finish it. The boss *understood*; he was just as savvy as anyone else, but less "sensitive" (meaning destructible). It took half the time to explain highly technical problems to Kennedy that it had to Stevenson, and it turned out, too, that Stevenson actually wasn't much of a reader. During the Eisenhower administration, I heard a famous scientist say with some satisfaction that the president was "actually very intelligent." And Robert Frost, when he finally did get to an Eisenhower stag dinner at the White House, made a point of saying afterward that President Eisenhower was extremely intelligent. I understood. When a really good mind, suffering from the natural loneliness of really good minds, gets the ear of a man smart enough to make his way to the very top, even to make the topmost pinnacle an attribute of himself, there is a natural sense of satisfaction. For when all is said and done, action is the natural sphere of a mind sane and hopeful, eager to revive the classic center of man's public activity. To real intellectuals, power means not Caesarism but right influence; and it must be said that the type of Henry Adams, who wants to be near power so that he can deride it but feels that he is too intelligent to influence it, is really the prisoner of his own despairing rationality. Adams did not want his private obsessions interrupted by any new dimension of experience. And while the *quality* of mind is not necessarily better among those who are more "healthy-minded," it is a fact that the capacity of certain intellectuals to wield influence, the belief that they not only can but that they should, is interpreted maliciously by those who are so alienated from the body politic (to say nothing of politics) that they must explain everything as self seeking.

2

I would suggest that what drew certain historians, political scientists, economists, and lawyers to Kennedy was the fact that he, too, was outside the business community, had grown up independent of the main influence, and that Kennedy's very adroitness and eagerness of mind, his sense that there were deeper sources which he could employ, pleased them as the style of a politician no more limited by the business ethos than they are. In many ways the current intellectual style brings together people who have nothing in common but their indifference to the conventional values. It is the style of labor lawyers from immigrant families; of university administrators with a family tradition of diplomacy and liberal Republicanism in the tradition of Stimson, not the shabby rhetoric of "free enterprise" set up by professional demagogues; of professors themselves brought up in professors' families; of economists who remember with bitterness what young men with brains had to fight in the way of prejudice and snobbery when they first made their way up the university ladder. Such figures, whether their background was too patrician or too scholarly or too radical or too foreign for the majority view, represent the accelerating war of the "specialists" (or the "engineers," as Veblen called them) with the "price system." They have grown up on ideas, they have made their way up on ideas, they live on ideas. And in some way that must be both exciting to them and yet frustrating, Kennedy is also not limited to business and by business. He shares with his advisers a certain intellectual freedom from the dominant prejudices and shibboleths. But what for them is often a positive article of belief may, for him, be only freedom from vulgar prejudice—and it is exactly here that Kennedy's use of his advisers has already proved so much more significant than their influence on him.

About Kennedy one *has* to make psychological guesses, for unlike his advisers, one does not know what he thinks by reading him—nor even by talking to him. His most essential quality, I would think, is that of the man who is always making and remaking himself. He is the final product of a fanatical job of self-remodeling. He grew up rich and favored enough not to make obvious mistakes or to fall for the obvious—he has been saved from the provincial and self-pitying judgments that so many talented Americans break their teeth on. He has been saved, not merely from the conventional but from wasting his time on it. Even now there is an absence in him of the petty conceit of the second rate, and a freshness of curiosity behind which one feels not merely his quickness to utilize all his advantages but also his ability to turn this curiosity on himself. He turns things over very quickly in his own mind; he gets the angle. Yet all the while he stands outside, like a sculptor surveying his work. He is what a certain time has made, has raised highest, and he can see himself in perspective in a way that perhaps only Americans can—since only they have *made* so much of themselves. The father made a killing in liquor and even as ambassador managed to sound like a district boss; the son has as many European "connections" as royalty. The father worked it so that each of his children would have at least a million dollars; the son, starting out high above the economic motive, asked advice of fatherly gentlemen in New England as if he had all the world to choose from. The grandfathers in Boston still had to look at *No Irish Need Apply;* their grandson, as the attorney general of the United States said with grim pride when he urged Negroes to fight more for their *political* rights, is now president of the United States. He is president of the United States, he is a millionaire, he has the sex appeal of a movie hero, the naturalness of a newspaperman and as much savvy as a Harvard professor— and whereas you and I would be scared even to imagine ourselves taking on such responsibilities as face them every moment of the day and night, the highest office is what he wanted, this is what he went straight for, this is what he has. He has learned so continuously, so brilliantly, even so greedily, that one observer, noting that the author of *Profiles in Courage* didn't show his profile on the McCarthy issue, dryly wonders "if the book didn't, on some very private level, instruct him in what to avoid." The determination to succeed, the guardedness against vulnerability of any sort, the constant vigilance not to show himself wanting (his health has been the only admitted "weakness")—this is so sharp that another writer has brilliantly compared Kennedy to the type of Whig who in the eighteenth century entered the rising House of Commons:

"of large and comparatively recent fortune, intelligent, elegant, tremendously determined to make a place for himself, desiring above all to be effective and to succeed, contemptuous of the aristocratic condescensions and concerned not to be condescended to."

But unlike those Whigs, it is to be doubted that Kennedy represents a definite social interest. What has given him his influence, even over the "brain power," as he describes this resource passingly in *The Strategy of Peace*, is his sophisticated freedom from conventional prejudice. When one adviser, submitting a memorandum on Latin American problems, noted that certain recommendations could be highly irritating to American business, Kennedy waved the hypothetical objection aside. This elasticity makes him exciting to work for, and to pass from so detached a mind to the endless analysis of itself that Washington goes in for might well make an intellectual in Washington feel that "brain power" is at the center of things again, that the few have again the chance to do well by the many.

3

Yet as this is being written, nothing stands out so clearly about the Kennedy administration as its frustrations. The occasion is piled higher with difficulty than ever before, and "the most intellectual and idea-seeking president since Woodrow Wilson" must find it as hard to remember some of the ideas he came in with as it is to promote some he has acquired since. Only in the White House, it may be, will Kennedy know the "contradictions and miseries" that other men have always lived with. And perhaps it is only in the White House, too, that the intellectual advisers who have gone smoothly from academic success to academic success may for the first time experience rebuff, defeat, obloquy. The "decisions" get more and more "educated," to use the president's interesting word, but they do not grow more decisive. And when I think of the increasing ugliness of American "conservatives," the political stalemate that Kennedy is faced with by Russia, the impossible difficulty of getting Americans to limit their smallest economic privileges enough to create a new social sense in this country, the conflicting views of so many different groups of advisers who were meant to counteract each other but who can produce administrative chaos, I anticipate that so restless and so ambitious a man as Kennedy will want to cut through the ever-deepening morass.

The most striking side of the Cuban disaster, to me, was the virtually official apologia that since Kennedy inherited the invasion scheme from Eisenhower and found that the C.I.A. had been arming and training an invasion army that could no longer be "contained," the technical approval by the Joint Chiefs of Staff and the approval of a majority of his advisers were enough to make him approve not merely an immoral but an impractical scheme to invade Cuba. Even a literary man reading up on Castro and his revolution could guess that Castro was much too popular to be overthrown from a small landing at the Bay of Pigs. Yet, faced by so many conflicting and in a sense mutually canceling bodies of advice, Kennedy allowed the gun to go off. And nothing has been said by him since, or by his advisers, that indicates it was anything but the *failure* of the Cuban invasion that they regret. It has given a "bad mark" to the administration that wants so much to succeed. What is immoral and downright stupid about the invasion, what represents not merely faithlessness to our traditions but an executive temperament restless, tricky, irritable—this has not been understood by the administration and its advisers. And seeking out Hoover and MacArthur at the Waldorf in an effort to make a show of national unity at the first sign of national dismay! The only defense that I have heard against the frightening impatience displayed in the Cuban adventure has been that so-and-so wasn't in on the decision, and that intellectuals on the outside never recognize how many important decisions are improvised and uncalculated. Where, then, is the meaningful relation of intellectuals to power? Is it only to write memoranda, to "educate" the decisions that others make? History will not absolve them that cheaply. What troubled me about the Cuban adventure was that although its failure was attributed to "erroneous" advice, the essential philosophy behind it was perhaps uttered by the adviser who, when asked for a show of hands, said "Let 'er rip," and by another who said pompously that it was time to come to a power confrontation with communism in this hemisphere. (Stewart Alsop reporting.) In short, actions may be excused as "improvised," but is the essential philosophy a longing to come to a power "confrontation" in this hemisphere? Is it possible that the very freedom from conventionality that I interpret as the essential mark of Kennedy's intellectuals and of his receptivity to them—that this may yet create an abstract and virtually ideological conception of American power?

The famous State Department "White Paper" on Castro, published before the invasion attempt, listed many distinguished Cuban liberals, democrats, intellectuals, who had fled from Castro after being part of the 26 July revolutionary movement against Batista. Various pro-Castro "progressives" in this country noted that the White Paper quite conveniently omitted mention of any of the privileges lost by American business in Cuba. But although it is not for me to prove this, I suspect that in the mind of the author of the White Paper was not so much the desire to overlook the resentment of American business against Castro as the intellectual bitterness of an American liberal Democrat against a political adventurer (Castro), who began as a "reformer" and has since shown himself a cynical and dangerous ally of totalitarianism. Perhaps business just did not come into it for the principal author of the White Paper. Hard as it is for pro-Castro intellectuals in this country to take this, I believe that economic determinism appears to explain as little of our bellicosity as it does Russian bellicosity. Anyone who has studied Castro's political development can see that his gravitation toward totalitarianism has had nothing whatever to do with American economic policies in Cuba. Khrushchev's stated belief to Walter Lippmann that Kennedy takes orders from "Rockefeller" is as mechanical a piece of Communist rhetoric as Stalin's stated belief that Hitler's policies were dictated by German capitalists. Indeed, the Russian Revolution itself, launched entirely by intellectuals whose historic dissociation from the great mass of the Russian people explains the very structure of the Communists as a party of intellectual managers, offers the most devastating proof that, especially in our times of centralization, history is made not for material interest but out of intellectual fanaticism often divorced from the most elementary social interest.

After the invasion attempt against Cuba, Kennedy replied to Khrushchev's professed indignation by cautioning him not to support Castro militarily. He ended his message with this emphatic burst: "I believe, Mr. Chairman, that you should recognize that free people in all parts of the world do not accept the claim of historical inevitability for the Communist revolution. What your government believes is its own business; what it does in the world is the world's business. The great revolution in the history of man, past, present, and future, is the revolution of those determined to be free." This is stirring language quite different from the usual muddle of Eisenhower's public statements. But I find it hard to believe that for Kennedy the Soviet government's philosophy is "its own business"; I find it also hard to believe Khrushchev when he says (on alternate Tuesdays) that he himself does not plan to attack the socially backward nations and explains that the well-known law of Marxist development will take care of that. Of course Kennedy is not driven by a fanatical creed of political messianism that is taken as the only universal law of history; nor is he as driven as Russians have been by a profound resentment of the creeds and relative good fortune of the West. But to the extent that Kennedy has been liberated by his own good fortune from the intellectual torpidity of American business, he may have been thrown back on the intellectual's natural outlet in causes. And the most significant side of Kennedy-as-intellectual seems to lie, not in his public cultivation of the "intellectual" style that is now admired in the highest echelons, but in the fact that, as a would-be intellectual who happens to be president of the United States, his natural tendency may be to identify the United States with a crusade, a cause, with "liberty." It was exactly this accessibility to causes that now constitutes, retrospectively, the disagreeable and even false side of Theodore Roosevelt. Similarly, what one fears about Kennedy is the other side of what one admired and was prepared to admire more in him—that he has been left free by his immense power to adopt a cause forged out of his energy and the depths of his restless ambition. Hard as it is for most of us to imagine ourselves arguing the fate of humanity with Khrushchev, it does not seem to bother Kennedy. And when I ask myself, as I increasingly must, what it is in Kennedy's ambition to be an "intellectual" statesman that steels him for his awesome responsibility, what in his *convictions* can carry him over the sea of troubles awaiting all of us, I have to answer that I do not know. At this juncture, Kennedy's shrewd awareness of what intellectuals can do, even his undoubted inner respect for certain writers, scholars, and thinkers, is irrelevant to the tragic issues and contributes nothing to their solution. To be an "intellectual" is the latest style in American success, the mark of our manipulatable society.

[1961]

PROFESSIONAL OBSERVERS: CHEEVER, SALINGER, AND UPDIKE

———— ·◆· ————

John Cheever found in suburbsville almost as many cruel social differences as [John] O'Hara had always known in Gibbsville. But the overwhelming sensation that a reader got from Cheever's special performance of the short story was of a form that no longer spoke for itself. It was not even a "slice of life," as O'Hara's stories were, but had become a demonstration of the amazing sadness, futility, and evanescence of life among the settled, moneyed, seemingly altogether domesticated people in Proxmire Manor. As Cheever said in two different pieces of fiction, Why, in this "half-finished civilization, in this most prosperous, equitable, and accomplished world, should everyone seem so disappointed?" It is a question that earlier writers of "*The New Yorker* story" would not have asked openly, with so much expectation of being agreed with, and twice. But Cheever's brightly comic, charming, heartbreaking performances always came out as direct points made about "the quality of life in the United States," or "How We Live Now."

Cheever—Salinger and Updike were to be like him in this respect—began and somehow has remained a startlingly precocious, provocatively "youthful" writer. But unlike Salinger and Updike, he was to seem more identifiable with the rest of *The New Yorker*, just as his complaint about American life was more concrete and his fiction more expectable. His stories regularly became a form of social lament—writing never hard to take. What they said, and Cheever openly said it, was that America was still a dream, a fantasy; America did not look lived in, Americans were not really settled in. In their own minds they were still on their way to the Promised Land. In story after story Cheever's characters, guiltily, secretly disillusioned and disabused with their famous "way of life" (always something that could be put into words and therefore promised, advertised, and demonstrated), suddenly acted out their inner subversion. They became "eccentrics," crazily swimming from pool to pool, good husbands who fell in love with the baby-sitter. Sometimes, like "Aunt Justina," they even died in the living room and could not be moved because of the health laws and restriction by the zoning law on any funeral parlors in the neighborhood.

Acting out one's loneliness, one's death wish—any sudden eccentricity embarrassing everybody in the neighborhood—these make for situation comedy. Life is turning one's "normal" self inside out at a party. The subject of Cheever's stories is regularly a situation that betrays the basic "unreality" of some character's life. It is a trying-out of freedom in the shape of the extreme, the unmentionable. Crossing the social line is one aspect of comedy, and Cheever demonstrates it by giving a social shape to the most insubstantial and private longings. Loneliness is the dirty little secret, a personal drive so urgent and confusing that it comes out a vice. But the pathetic escapade never lasts very long. We are not at home here, says Cheever. But there is no other place for us to feel that we are not at home.

In these terms the short story becomes not the compression of an actual defeat but the anecdote of a temporary crisis. The crisis is the trying-out of sin, escape, the abyss, and is described by Cheever with radiant attention: *there is* the only new world his characters ever reach. "... They flew into a white cloud of such density that it reflected the exhaust fires. The color of the cloud darkened to gray, and the plane began to rock.... The stewardess announced that they were going to make an emergency landing. All but the children saw in their minds the spreading wings of the Angel of Death. The pilot could be heard singing faintly, 'I've got sixpence, jolly, jolly sixpence. I've got sixpence to last me all my life....'" The "country husband" in this most brilliant of Cheever's stories returns home to find that his brush with death is not of the slightest interest to his family, so he falls in love with the baby-sitter. He does not get very far with the baby-sitter, so he goes to a therapist who prescribes woodworking. The story ends derisively on the brainwashed husband who will no longer stray from home. But who cares about this fellow? It is Cheever's clever, showy handling of the husband's "craziness," sentence by sentence, that engages us. Each sentence is a miniature of Cheever's narrative style, and each sentence makes the point that Cheever is mastering his material, and comes back to the mystery of why, in this half-finished civilization, this most prosperous, equitable, and accomplished world, everyone should seem so disappointed. So there is no mastery in Cheever's story except Cheever's. It is Cheever one watches in the story, Cheever who moves us, literally, by the shape of his effort in every line, by the significance he gives to every inflection, and finally by the cruel lucidity he brings to this most prosperous, equitable, and accomplished world as a breaking of the heart.

My deepest feeling about Cheever is that his marvelous brightness is an effort to cheer himself up. His is the only impressive energy in a perhaps too equitable and prosperous suburban world whose subject is internal depression, the Saturday-night party, and the post-martini bitterness. Feeling alone is the air his characters breathe. Just as his characters have no feeling of achievement in their work, so they never collide with or have to fight a society which is actually America in allegory. All conflict is in the head. People just disappear, as from a party. Cheever's novels—*The Wapshot Chronicle, The Wapshot Scandal, Bullet Park*—tend to muffle his characters in meaning even more than the short stories do. Cheever is such an accomplished performer of the short story that the foreshortening of effect has become second nature with him. There is the shortest possible bridge between cause and effect. *The New Yorker* column is still the inch of ivory on which he writes. Cheever writes always about "America." He is an intellectual. The Wapshot novels are wholly allegories of place showing the degeneration of the old New England village, "St. Botolph's," into the symbolic (but spreading) suburb that is "Proxmire Manor."

When last heard from—in *The New Yorker* for June 19, 1965—J. D. Salinger gave the impression that he had withdrawn into the godhead of Seymour Glass. In "Hapworth 16, 1924," Seymour Glass is seven years old. But writing to his parents from camp, he displays (to a degree not preposterous only if you already know Seymour Glass) the religious and literary superiority to other people that in 1948, at thirty-one years of age, while on his honeymoon, was to lead him to commit suicide right in front of the sleeping figure of his bride. He had called her "Miss Spiritual Tramp of 1948."

Salinger's evident obsession with Seymour the dead brother, Seymour the artist, saint, spiritual teacher, had taken over his writing ever since "Franny and Zooey." The Glass family had become a chorus ecstatically living in memory of Seymour. It lived by reciting his great deeds of love and perception. Seymour Glass had in fact become, in death, the charisma behind a new religion,* the Glass religion. All Glasses were Seymour's worshipers. Buddy Glass (explicitly J. D. Salinger himself) is the apostle to whom it was left to put the sacred words down. Whether the obsession with Seymour became so extensive that it proved too much for Salinger, or whether Salinger's contempt for the profane non-Glass world became unbearable to himself, is not for the outsider to say. Salinger is outraged by the very act of criticism, wants only readers who are faithful, loving friends, like his editors at *The New Yorker* and the armies of young people who gratefully recognized themselves in *The Catcher in the Rye.* He would rather be silent at the moment than see his imaginative world profaned by criticism.

Salinger's extraordinary stories—extraordinary in their residual pain and obsession, extraordinary as fiction—are dominated by the idea of the Glass family as exceptional beings. In a world too plainly made "absurd" by our inability to love it, the Glasses are loved by their relative and creator, J. D. Salinger, every inexhaustible cherished inch of their lives. His microscopic love for them compels them into our field of vision; we see them through the absoluteness of Salinger's love and grief. And non-Glasses are spiritual trash. One recognizes in Salinger's stories a disturbing death wish, a sympathy with extinction, the final silence tempting to absolutists of feeling. This pertained so long to the unworthy non-Glass world that it may have turned on Salinger himself.

Yet for all this eerie devaluation of everyone outside the Glass family, the

---

*Even the bride, who reports to her mother that Seymour called her "Miss Spiritual Tramp of 1948," is drawn to the man who disapproves of her to the point of (his) death. Only Salinger's belief in Seymour's greatness explains his bride's devotion to the man who publicly skipped out of marrying her in "Raise High the Roofbeam, Carpenters," and after she finally eloped with him, scorned her in "A Perfect Day for Bananafish" for not reading Rilke *in German* and punished her for his mistake in marrying him by shooting himself right in front of her.

whole charm of Salinger's fiction lies in his gift for comedy, his ability to represent society as it is, for telltale gestures and social manners. In what is probably his best story, "Raise High the Roofbeam, Carpenters"—the beautifully spun-out account of what happened among the wedding guests when the bridegroom failed to show up, the meticulous telling of every detail, the light ironic allusions to the contrasts of the shifting social groupings, in the obviously but not explicitly Jewish bourgeoisie, are somehow held together by the intense self-consciousness of brother, Buddy Glass, the narrator. In the heat of the midsummer afternoon, in a bedraggled uniform, and barely over an attack of pleurisy, he somehow manages to describe completely the external human *performance* of every guest at this fiasco of a wedding.

Salinger's great gift was always comic, Chaplinesque, in his ability to project a world of social types from a fumbling, theatrically awkward observer and narrator, Buddy Glass the English instructor and as yet unpublished writer, who is confessedly a failure and somehow ridiculous in his excessive feelings of alienation. Buddy's special thing was to create sympathy for his pratfalls and fumbling, for his own unachieved gestures, that then lighted up other people's gestures and fumbling as a way of life. No American fiction writer in recent memory has given so much value, by way of his hypnotized attention, to the little things that light up character in every social exchange. Salinger has been the great pantomimist in our contemporary fiction. One of his favorite characters is obviously the deaf-mute uncle in "Raise High the Roofbeam, Carpenters," whose mysteriously stiff movements Buddy, as usual, describes with infinite patience and loving curiosity. In "Franny" "the boys who had been keeping themselves warm began to come out to meet the train, most of them giving the impression of having at least three lighted cigarettes in each hand. . . . It was a station-platform kiss—spontaneous enough to begin with, but rather inhibited in the follow-through, and with something of a forehead-bumping aspect." In "Raise High the Roofbeam, Carpenters," Buddy reads Seymour's diary in the bathroom (there is no other place to hide):

> I . . . sat for several minutes with the diary under one arm, until I became conscious of a certain discomfort from having sat so long on the side of the bathtub. When I stood up, I found I was perspiring more profusely than I had all day, as though I had just got out of a tub, rather than just sitting on the side of one. I went over to the laun-

dry hamper, raised the lid, and, with an almost vicious wrist movement, literally threw Seymour's diary into some sheets and pillowcases that were on the bottom of the hamper. Then, for want of a better, more constructive idea, I went back and sat down on the side of the bathtub again.

Salinger has a genius for capturing the emotional giveaway. Love is isolating. The fact that his love necessitates so much disdain shows how much social comedy springs from coldness toward the *world*. Salinger gives his hypnotized attention to every "enemy" gesture as well as to Seymour's saintly touch, which leaves stigmata. "I have scars on my hands from touching certain people," Seymour modestly confesses in his diary. This attentiveness, charging the front line of Salinger's fiction, is the beleaguered animal's need to know the ways of the hunter. The whole scheme of values in Salinger's fiction is to give the highest marks to the individual made exceptional by a sensitivity to society that is fear of it. Holden Caulfield endeared himself to the anti-socializers of all ages because he went right into the lion's cage—all those phonies!—without liking *anything* of what he relentlessly described.

The same marginality is expressed in the purely contemplative Oriental poetry that usually serves as the scripture of Seymour's sacredness and in the cult of non-action that places the highest value on a tender, loving, *religious* attentiveness to the littlest things of this world. To notice every seeming triviality (Seymour protests that he loves, loves, loves everything and everyone in his path) is to respect the creation—and gives Salinger's fiction its dense social texture. Extreme importance is given to things made hallucinatory by the Glass family's cherishing. Attention is compulsively fixed, as in a dream, on any item separated from its normal connections—a letter kept in the middle of a manuscript, where the stapling is *tightest.* Yet as each Glass story elongated, as these magical, disrelated, hysterically overstressed gestures, letters, camp memories formed themselves into the cult of Seymour, the reader could not help noticing that all this was founded on an idolatry of certain *persons* altogether unusual in contemporary fiction.

Salinger is an oddity, an obsessive, who commands respect because certain of his characters are so important to him. The Glass stories are not another family chronicle; Salinger's emotions are too selective and even arbitrary. But they do display, to the point of anguish, a sense that *some* people are more

important than anything else in the world. So much regard for individual personality (incestuous as the particular case may be) makes Salinger's Holy
Family stand out from the great mass of unvalued, unregarded, and unde-
scribed individuals in contemporary fiction. *His* people will last.

Salinger, so self-limiting, "special," fanatical, making his American comedy of
manners out of desperate love for his own, now makes a deceptively pathetic
contrast with John Updike, a virtuoso who seems able to make up stories
about anything that interests him intellectually, morally, pictorially. Salinger is
of course reporting to someone. His work is pervaded by a filial piety that
reminds one of the pilgrim on his knees, with hands uplifted in prayer, who
puts himself into a corner of his own painting of Seymour Glass's crucifixion.
Even his intellectual loves are those of a worshiper; nothing Oriental and quietist may ever be questioned. Updike writes as if there were no greater pleasure
than reconstituting the world by writing—writing is mind exercising itself,
rejoicing in its gifts. Reading him, one is always conscious of Updike the
Gifted, Updike the Stylist, Updike the Concerned Roguish Novelist. Updike
is always so much Updike that it is the highest tribute to this gifted and serious writer that the omnipresence of Updike in all his writing finally seems not
a hindrance but a trademark, youth's charming flourish of itself. This is a
writer confidently personal but not subjective—who indeed pleases his busy
imagination, his sense of play, by looking steadily at the contradiction within
every human display.

A prime fact about Updike is that he was born in 1932, went to Harvard
when there was still a great literary tradition for an undergraduate to join himself to, then felt himself the most fortunate of men when he became part of
The New Yorker and its still debonair literary tradition. Precocious, original, distinctly not a loner, a writer in the postwar suburban style who associated himself with families, townships, churches, citizens' committees, Updike became a
novelist of "society" in the fifties, the age of postwar plenty and unchallenged
domesticity for both sexes when many once-poor Americans, moving to the
suburbs, felt they were at last coming into their reward.* Domesticity is a
dominant subject of Updike's world—and so is the unavailing struggle against
it, as in one of his best novels, *Rabbit, Run*. But there is in even the lucid emo-

---

*"He thinks we've made a church of each other." (*Couples*)

tions of *Rabbit, Run*, in the filial tenderness of *The Centaur*, a kind of brilliant actionlessness, a wholly mental atmosphere. Updike, thanks not least to the marvelous movement within postwar society and its unprecedented interchange of classes, backgrounds, social information, is an extremely adroit and knowledgeable observer of society and its customs. He likes to put presidents into his work as a way of showing that President Buchanan (ancient history) and President Kennedy (the sixties) are the real landmarks.* But such historic moments just serve to date the personal mythology in his characters' minds; they are never forces. There is no struggle with American society; its character is fixed, though nothing else is.

Updike's characters represent many things to him; he glosses all his own novels. And because Updike fancies them as many-sided and intellectual designs, they are unusually distinct and memorable among characters in contemporary fiction. They always *mean*. Updike's fiction is distinguished by an unusually close interest in every character he writes about. But these characters who represent so much never struggle with anything except the reflections in their minds of a circumscribing reality that seems unalterable. Updike is a novelist of society who sees society entirely as a fable. It stands still for him to paint its picture; it never starts anything. On the other hand, it is always there to say "American," now and in the future—Updike's first novel, *The Poorhouse Fair*, started with the future as tyranny, institutions that are there to say that institutions always take over.

The older American novelists of society were not this much used to it. Scott Fitzgerald, who loved its color, its prodigality, profoundly distrusted it and thought it would revenge itself on its critics. Updike, who persistently recalls Fitzgerald's ability to show society as a dream, has accommodated himself to its dominating possessiveness. Where there are no alternatives, even in one's memory, the proliferating surfaces encourage myths, transferable symbols—a sense of situation, not opposition. Updike is in the best sense of the

---

*INTERVIEWER: Let's turn from myth to history. You have indicated a desire to write about President Buchanan. Yet so far as I can see, American history is normally absent from your work. UPDIKE: Not so; quite the contrary. In each of my novels, a precise year is given and a president reigns: *The Centaur* is distinctly a Truman book, and *Rabbit, Run* an Eisenhower one. *Couples* could have taken place only under Kennedy; the social currents it traces are as specific to those years as flowers in a meadow are to their moment of summer. (*Paris Review*, interview, Winter, 1968)

word an intellectual novelist, a novelist of paradox, tension, and complexity who as a college wit in the fifties learned that we are all symbols and inhabit symbols. His easy mastery of social detail never includes any sense of American society as itself a peculiar institution, itself the dynamo, the aggressor, the maker of other people's lives. Society is just a set of characteristics. Society— our present fate!—shows itself in marvelously shifting mental colors and shapes. Brightness falls from the air, thanks to the God on whose absence we sharpen our minds. But Updike's own bright images of human perception fall along a horizontal line, metaphors of observation that connect only with each other. The world is all metaphor. We are not sure *who* is thinking these brilliant images in *Rabbit, Run*. Need Updike's fine mind be so much in evidence?

> His day had been bothered by God: Ruth mocking, Eccles blinking— why did they teach you such things if no one believed them? It seems plain, standing here, that if there is this floor, there is a ceiling, that the true space in which we live is upward space. Someone is dying. In this great stretch of bridge someone is dying. The thought comes from nowhere: simple percentages. Someone in some house along these streets, if not this minute then the next, dies; and in that suddenly stone chest the heart of this flat prostrate rose seems to him to be. He moves his eyes to find the spot; perhaps he can see a cancer-blackened soul of an old man mount through the blue like a monkey on a spring. . . .

Updike is indeed a great mental traveler through the many lands of American possibility. Though *The Poorhouse Fair, The Olinger Stories, The Centaur,* and others of his best works deal with the southeasternmost corner of Pennsylvania he comes from, he no more judges the rest of America by it than puts America into it—as O'Hara put everything he knew into his corner of Pennsylvania. Updike has nothing of the primitive attachment to early beginnings that made a whole generation of American realists once describe the big city as a total dislodgement. As a believer in tradition rediscovered, he can weave a surpassingly tender novel about his father, *The Centaur,* into a set of mythological associations and identifications that in other hands would have academicized the novel to death. *The Centaur* is one of his best books. In *Rabbit, Run* he wrote the marriage novel of a period marked by an increasing disbelief in marriage as the foundation of everything. At the end of *Rabbit, Run* the over-size Harry Angstrom ran away from his mopey wife, Janice, who while drunk had accidentally drowned their baby, and from the unfathomable insatiable domesticity of the "tranquilized fifties," as Robert Lowell calls them.

Rabbit Redux of course opens on the day in 1969 that saw the first manned American flight to the moon, "leaving the rest of us here." Harry was once too young and is now mysteriously too old. He is now a decaying man in an American city typically running down, is proud to support the Vietnam War when everybody else has seen through it, and in order to provide the reader with a glibly topical symposium, suddenly finds himself sharing his house with Jill, a wild young hippie runaway from her family, and her sometime lover and drug supply, Skeeter, a young black Vietnam veteran who has jumped bail. Yet even an inferior novel like *Couples*—the book of suburban marriage and its now conventional adulteries that shows Updike exercising his gifts and putting up his usual intellectual-religious scaffolding with somewhat too bountiful ease—is *not* a document, for Updike is happily a novelist excited by his charac-ters. In *Bech*, Updike not only takes on the Jewish novelist—a subject that has long fascinated and provoked him because "the Jewish novelist" is so much a fact of our times, so important a social category and rival, the most striking sudden success in a society of sudden successes—he even manages to show the comedy in Bech, a failure.

Everything seems possible to Updike; everything *has* been possible. He knows his way around, in every sense, without being superficial about it. His real subject—the dead hand of "society," the fixity of institutions—has gone hand in hand with the only vision of freedom as the *individual's* recognition of God. This is a period when, as Updike says, "God has killed the churches." There is no nemesis: just an empty space between those untouching circles, society and the individual. Updike has managed to be an intellectual without becoming abstract; in an era of boundless personal confusion, he has been a moralist without rejecting the mores. If poise is a gift, Updike is a genius. If to be "cool" is not just a social grace but awareness unlimited, Updike is the best of this cool world. All he lacks is that capacity for making you identify, for summoning up affection in the reader, which Salinger (now "poor Salinger") expressed when in *The Catcher in the Rye* he had Holden Caulfield reserve his praise for authors who make you want to call them up.

[1971]

THE EARTHLY CITY OF
THE JEWS: BELLOW,
MALAMUD, AND ROTH

———— •◆• ————

When John Updike brilliantly conceived Henry Bech, who was in everything he did, and especially in what he couldn't do, "the Jew as contemporary American novelist," Updike was having his fun with that once unlikely but now well-known American product, Bellow-Malamud-Roth. Bellow said that the constant linking of these names reminded him of Hart, Schaffner, and Marx. But irritating as it might be to one proudly gifted and much-honored novelist to be linked with other *Jewish* names, Bellow more than any other American novelist of his ability used the modern Jewish experience in his work.

Most of Bellow's characters were Jews, his non-Jewish characters (rare enough) were, like Allbee in *The Victim*, obsessed with Jews or, like Henderson, clamorously produced wittily agonized definitions of human existence remarkably like those of the Jewish protagonists in Bellow's novels—Joseph in *Dangling Man*, Asa Leventhal in *The Victim*, Tommy Wilhelm in *Seize the Day*, Augie March, Herzog, Mr. Sammler. Over and again in Bellow's novels there were the parents who to tyrants in eastern Europe had been nothing but Jews, and in the slums of Montreal and Chicago saw nothing but their own experience reflected back from the neighborhood. There was a natural, enchanted repetition of the Jewish neighborhood, the Jewish family circle, the Jew as college intellectual, radical, dreamer, explorer of lowlife—the Jew discovering worlds new to him. "Look at me going everywhere!" Augie March cries out after pages devoted principally to the emancipation and enlightenment of Augie's senses—"Why, I am a sort of Columbus of those near-at-hand!" More than anyone else, Bellow connected one novel after another with a representative Jew in order to represent Jewish experience itself.

This emphasis on one people's collective idiosyncratic experience, an emphasis so intense that it seems to follow from some deep cut in Bellow's mind, is nevertheless intense in attention rather than partisan. Bellow is positively hypnotized by the part of human life he knows best, as a novelist should be, and he sees everything else in this focus. But without being detached and "impartial" about the long Jewish struggle for survival, he is fascinated and held by the texture of Jewish experience as it becomes, as it can become, the day-to-day life of people one has created. This is very different from writing about people one names as Jews but who, no matter how one feels about them, are just names on the page. Texture is life relived, *life* on the page, beyond praise or blame. In Bellow's first novel, *Dangling Man* (1944), the hero writes of himself: ". . . To him judgment is second to wonder, to speculation on men, drugged and clear, jealous, ambitious, good, tempted, curious, each in his own time and with his customs and motives, and bearing the imprint of strangeness in the world." To Asa Leventhal in *The Victim*, crossing over to Staten Island,

> the towers on the shore rose up in huge blocks, scorched, smoky gray. . . . The notion brushed Leventhal's mind that the light over them and over the water was akin to the yellow revealed in the eye of a wild animal, say a lion, something inhuman that didn't care about anything human and yet was implanted in every human being too, one speck of it, and formed a part of him that responded to the heat and the glare . . . even to freezing, salty things, harsh things, all things difficult to stand.

In *Seize the Day*, where the Upper West Side of New York is the most living, throbbing character, Tommy Wilhelm, trying to make a confident appearance with a hat and a cigar, feels that the day is getting away from him: ". . . the cigar was out and the hat did not defend him . . . the peculiar burden of his existence lay upon him like an accretion . . . his entire chest ached . . . as though tightly tied with ropes. He smelled the salt odor of tears in his eyes. . . ." In the sunshine of upper Broadway there was "a false air of gas visible at eye level as it spurted from the bursting buses."

This air of having lived, of experiencing the big city in every pore, of being on the spot, is the great thing about Bellow's fiction. It is this living, acrid style—in the suddenly chastened, too glibly precise, peculiarly assertive bitterness of postwar American writing, with its hallucinated clarity about details, its oversized sense of our existence, of too many objects all around (what desolation amidst wonders!)—that made us realize Bellow as an original. He is a key to something that would emerge in all the American writing of this period about cities, the "mass," the common life. This was not the "minority" writing of the poignant, circumscribed novels of the 1930s. Even in the best of them, like Daniel Fuchs's *Low Company, Summer in Williamsburg, Homage to Blenholt,* one had been aware that "Jewish" equals ghetto. Bellow had come out of a ghetto in Montreal, the Napoleon Street that makes one of the deeper sections of *Herzog.* But what made him suddenly vivid, beginning with what was later to seem the put-on of *The Adventures of Augie March* (1953), was his command of a situation peculiarly American, founded on mass experience, that was as far from the metaphysical wit in Kafka as it was from the too conscious pathos of the Depression novels. With Bellow an American of any experience could feel that he was in the midst of the life he knew.

What was perhaps most "American" about it was the fact that despite all the crisis psychology in *The Victim, Seize the Day, Herzog,* there was a burning belief in commanding one's own experience, in putting it right by thought. Each of these narratives was a kind of survival kit for a period in which survival became all too real a question for many Americans. The Jewish experience on that subject—and what else had the experience been?—seemed exemplary to Americans, especially when it came armed with jokes. Good-bye to Henry Roth and how many other gifted, stunted, devastated Jewish novelists of the Thirties. In book after book Bellow went about the business of ordering life, seeing it through, working it out. He was intimate with the heights-and-abyss experience of so many intellectual Jews, the alternating experience of humiliation and the paradise of intellectual illumination. And it was this depiction of life as incessant mental struggle, of heaven and hell in the same Jewish head, that made Bellow's readers recognize a world the reverse of the provincial, a quality of thought somber, tonic, bracing, that was now actual to American experience yet lent itself to Bellow's fascinatedly personal sense of things.

In all of this Bellow became a style-setter for those many writers emerging in the fifties who found in him a kind of paradigm for taking hold, for getting in there, for being on top of the desperate situation. And indeed no one was more impressed by this angle on life, this sense of command, this ability to be *imaginatively* in charge, than Bellow himself, whose books, one after another, were usually founded on a protagonist who was the nearest possible spokesman for himself. Just as the success story of American Jews "making it" was represented by a bewildering succession of changes in their lives, so Bellow's novels, each registering a different state of awareness but all coming together as successive chapters of the same personal epic, made the nearest and best literary expression of the disbelief behind a Jewish ascent that was also haunted by the Holocaust. Bellow expressed both the American facts and the disbelief.

Here was an American Jewish writer who had a powerful sense of his own experience as imaginative, yet could beat other Jewish intellectuals at putting the universe into a sentence. He was as clever as a businessman but racked by a sense of responsibility to his "soul." Bellow underwent all these phases in his fiction. But at the center of each narrative was always a hero, a single mind and conscience, adventurous but forever counting the cost of existence. Above all, the Bellow persona was a hallucinated observer of what Sartre called the "hell that is other people"—he brilliantly sized up the strength in other people's arms, lives, faces, seeing what they had to say to the predominating self's vision at the heart of each Bellow novel. The man had been an anthropologist, a traveler, a musician, an editor of the University of Chicago's "great books"; he was a teacher, a lover, a liberated Jewish male and the most watchful of Jewish sons; he had found a way through the thickets of the big-city ghetto, the big-city university, the Depression, the merchant marine during the war; he had been a left radical, a welfare investigator; he was soon to become the sternest of Jewish moralists. And in all this Bellow influenced himself far more than others ever did, which is why book after book added up to what he had experienced and learned. The key belief was that right thinking is virtue and can leave you in charge of the life that is so outrageous to live.

The process of self-teaching thus becomes the heart of Bellow's novels, and the key to their instructiveness for others. One could compile from Bellow's novels a whole commonplace book of wisdom in the crisis era that has been Bellow's subject and opportunity. His novels are successively novels of instruction as well as existential adventure tales. The story as a whole tells, as the best Jewish stories always do, of the unreality of this world as opposed to God's. The hero struggles in a world not his own, a world run by strangers. The Jewish son has indeed lost the paradise that in childhood was within his grasp. In scripture this world is God's world; Jews must be grateful and obedient for being allowed to share it. In Jewish fiction this world is always someone else's world, though it is one in which Jews call themselves Jews and remain Jews. The so-called Jewish novel (there really is one, though only a few Jews have written it, and those who write it are not always Jews) takes place in a world that is unreal, never *our* world. The heart of the world is Jewish (said John Jay Chapman) but in Bellow's novels only one's mother and father have a heart. Bellow is in magnetized relation to the big-city environment, to the vertigo and clamor of New York, to the opulent yet sortable detail. But his is not a world in which a Jew feels at home. The Jew is always in some uneasy relation to "them"—he is a newcomer, parvenu, displaced person whose self-ordering becomes the issue in each book. In his humanist attack on anti-Semitism in France, *Jew and Anti-Semite,* Jean-Paul Sartre defined a Jew as someone whom others regard as a Jew. This understandably provoked Bellow by its lack of knowledge. When even "a prince of European philosophy" knows so little about them, Jews may wonder if this is their world. And so the Jew in Bellow's novels is a "stranger" because he really is one—not, like Camus's "*étranger,*" because he is free of other people's opinions to the point of total indifference. This representative Jew is involved in a catch-as-catch-can relationship to the world, that famous anchor of the old bourgeois novel, that keeps him lightly suspended just above the earth.

But the vitality of Bellow's fiction comes from the importance of being a Jewish son, a figure of importance; this may be hidden from everyone but himself. The Bellow hero, though often distraught, has the powerful ego of Joseph relating his dreams to his jealous brothers. This hero is so all-dominating that other males tend to become distinct only if they are intellectuals who personify *wrong ideas.* Non-intellectuals, like the women in the later novels, tend to become "reality instructors," opaque emblems of the distrusted world. The central figure is the only pilgrim who makes any progress. From Joseph in *Dangling Man* to old Mr. Sammler, each of Bellow's heroes represents the same desperate struggle for life—by which he means a more refined consciousness.

It is a concentrated example of the age-old Jewish belief that salvation is in thinking well—to go to the root of things, to become a kind of scientist of morals, to seek the ultimate forces that rule us.

Thinking is for Bellow the most accessible form of virtue. The "reality instructors" have become indistinguishable from the worldliness with which they are clotted. Bellow's recurrent hero, by contrast, is so concerned with thinking well that the imbalance between the hero and his fellows becomes an imbalance between the hero's thinking and the mere *activity* of others. Bellow is not a very dramatic novelist, and unexpected actions tend to be dragged into his novels—like Herzog's halfhearted attempt to kill his wife's lover—as a way of interrupting the hero's reflections. But evidently Bellow's personae attain their interest for *him* by their ability to express the right opinions. And not surprisingly, the protagonists of Bellow's novels are the voices of his intellectual evolution. A Bellow anthology would take the form of a breviary, an intellectual testament gathered from diaries, letters to public men and famous philosophers that were never mailed, arias to the reader à la Augie March, the thoughts of Artur Sammler that are neural events in the privacy of one's consciousness because they cannot be expressed to others—they are too severe, too disapproving.

Bellow has found fascinating narrative forms for the urgency of his many thoughts. He has been clever in finding a distinct *style* for so much silent thinking—from Joseph's diaries in *Dangling Man* to Herzog's equally incessant meditations and finally old Mr. Sammler's haughty soliloquies, where the style is one of the lightest, featheriest, mental penciling, an intellectual shorthand (here involving brusque images of the city) that answers to the traditional contractedness of Jewish thought. The favorite form for Jewish sages has always been the shortest, and Bellow's best fictions are his shortest. V. S. Pritchett, who admires Bellow for powerful descriptions of city life rare among "intellectual" novelists, thinks that in his long books Bellow "becomes too personal. There is a failure to cut the umbilical cord." Bellow's more lasting fictions will probably be those whose personae are not *exactly* as intelligent as he is—*The Victim* and *Seize the Day*.

In these books the weight of the world's irrationality, which is its injustice, falls heavily upon human beings who win us by their inability to understand all that is happening to them and why it is happening to *them*. Asa Leventhal at the end of *The Victim*, having been persecuted, exploited, terrified by a Gentile who accuses the Jew of having persecuted *him*, ends up innocently saying to his tormentor—"Wait a minute, what's your idea of who runs things?" Tommy Wilhelm in *Seize the Day*, who in one day realizes that he has lost wife, mistress, father, money, God, confronts the depths of his suffering only by identifying with a stranger into whose funeral he has stumbled by accident. These incomprehensions are truly evocative of the "existential situation" in contemporary fiction—that of individuals who are never up to their own suffering, who cannot fully take it in, who have learned only that their suffering has its reasons of which reason knows nothing.

Artur Sammler, on the other hand, is so openly Bellow's mind now, in its most minute qualifications, that one can admire the man's intellectual austerity and yet be amazed that Bellow's hero should be so intelligent about everything except his relation with other human beings. Sammler is an old man, a widower, with only one eye left to him by the Nazis; his wife was shot to death in the same Polish pit from which he managed to escape past so many dead bodies (the fable that haunts Jewish writers). Sammler is old, experienced, intelligent, cultivated. But none of these things accounts for the fact that Artur Sammler disapproves of everything he sees and everyone he knows except a vague kinsman, a doctor who got him to America and supports him. He dislikes all the women especially. The evident fact is that Mr. Sammler is the Jew who, after Hitler, cannot forgive the world, for he recognizes that its exterminations may be more pleasurable to it than its lusts. He has decided, not as the rabbis have decided but as Jewish novelists have decided in this first era of fiction by many Jews, that the "world" is a very bad place indeed. In God's absence human consciousness becomes the world; then the only thing for us, *Mr. Sammler's Planet* ends, is to know and to admit that we know.

The unsatisfactory thing about Mr. Sammler—a "collector" indeed, but of wisdom—is that he is always right while other people are usually wrong—sinfully so. More than most Jewish intellectuals, Artur Sammler is right and has to be right all the time. The Jewish passion for ideological moralism, for ratiocination as the only passion that doesn't wear out (and is supposed not to interfere with the other passions)—that passion has never been "done" in our fiction. There is no precedent for its peculiar self-assertiveness, so different from luxuriating in one's ego as a cultural tradition in the style of Stephen Dedalus. In Bellow's novel, insistently moralistic and world-weary, the hero is totally identified with his own thought. His total rejection of other people because of *their* thought sets up a lack of incident, an invitation to symbolic politics, like the now celebrated scene in which a Negro pickpocket follows old, delicate Mr. Sammler to his apartment house and exposes an intimidating penis, or the corollary scene in which Mr. Sammler's mad Israeli son-in-law—a sculptor carrying a bag of metal pieces—beats the same Negro almost to death near Lincoln Center.

Bellow's intellectual at-homeness with Sammler's thought is so assured that over and again one has the Blakean experience of reading thoughts expressed as sensations. But what is certainly not Blakean are the austere, dismissive jeremiads, the open contempt for the women in the book as crazy fantasists, improvident, gross careless sexpots, "birds of prey." There is a brilliantly immediate, unsparing knowledge of other people's appearance and limitations which in its moral haughtiness becomes as audible to the reader as sniffing, and is indeed that. There is so strong a sense of physical disgust with all one's distended, mad-eyed, pushing neighbors on the West Side that there seems nothing in the book to love but one's opinions.

So much self-assertion is a problem among contemporary American novelists, not least among Jewish writers who have been released into the novel under the comic guise of getting clinically close to their own minds. Jewishness as the novelist's material (which can be quite different from the individual material of Jews writing fiction) is constructed folklore. It is usually comic, or at least humorous; the characters are always ready to tell a joke on themselves. With their bizarre names, their accents, *their* language, they are jokes on themselves. And so they become "Jewish" material, which expresses not the predicament of the individual who knows himself to be an exception, but a piece of the folk, of "Jewishness" as a style of life and a point of view.

This sense of a whole folk to write about is indeed what Yiddish fiction began with late in the nineteenth century, and folklore remains a style, a manner, an attitude to life among many Jewish entertainers. But the appearance of this subject in the fiction of Bernard Malamud is so arch and clever a transposition into serious literature, a conscious piece of artifice, that one becomes aware of "Jewishness" in Malamud's language and style as the play within the play. The characters are all of a piece and of a tribe; they all speak with vigor the same depressed-sounding dialect, giving a Yiddish cadence to New York English that is pure Malamud and that makes his characters so aware of and dependent on each other that they have become a stock company ready to play any parts so long as they can keep their accents. In "Take Pity," a story that takes place in the next world (and is just as grubby), a recording angel or "census taker, Davidov, sour-faced, flipped through

> the closely scrawled pages of his notebook until he found a clean one. He attempted to scratch in a word with his fountain pen but it had run dry, so he fished a pencil stub out of his vest pocket and sharpened it with a cracked razor.

Rosen, a new arrival, tells the story of a refugee whose pitiful little grocery store is failing:

> He was talking to me how bitter was his life, and he touched me on the sleeve to say something else, but the next minute his face got small and he fell down dead, the wife screaming, the little girls crying that it made in my heart pain. I am myself a sick man and when I saw him laying on the floor, I said to myself, "Rosen, say goodbye, this guy is finished!" So I said it.

The all-dominating poverty in the Malamud world and of any Malamud character reduces everything to the simplicity of a single tabletop, chair, carrot. No matter where the Malamud characters are—Brooklyn, Rome, or a collapsible hall bedroom in the next world—they are "luftmenschen," so poor that they live on air, and are certainly not rooted in the earth. In one of the "Fidelman" stories, a young art historian who finally makes his way to Rome encounters and is ultimately defeated by Susskind, a refugee from every country—in Israel he could not stand "the suspense." Poverty as a total human style is so all-dominating an aesthetic medium in Malamud, coloring everything with its woebegone utensils, its stubborn immigrant English, its all-circulating despair, that one is not surprised that several of Malamud's characters seem to travel by levitation. They live not only on air but in it, one jump ahead of the BMT. All forms of travel and communication are foreshortened, contracted, made picturesque, as it were. Malamud has found a sweetly humorous dialect for the insularity of his characters. The outside world, which for Jews can be "another," does not even reach the consciousness of Malamud's Jews. They exist for each other, depend on each other, suffer each other and from each other with an unawareness of the "world" that *is* the definitive and humorously original element—and for which Malamud has found a narrative language whose tone derives from the characters' unawareness of any world but their own. Turning the tables on those who fear that the son of Yiddish-speaking immigrants might not be "proper" in his English, Malamud adopted a style essentially make-believe and fanciful, a style so patently invented by Malamud in tribute to the vitality of the real thing that the real humor of it is that someone made it up.

Malamud has always been an artificer. Even his first and only "non-Jewish" novel, *The Natural*, is a baseball with a deceiving drop in every curve. But from the time that Malamud left his native New York to teach in Oregon, and in what was distinctly a "new life" for him finessed his detachment and whimsicality into an operational set of characters and a terrain distinctly "Jewish," Malamud's own voice became that artfully dissonant irony that says in every turn: Reader, something out of your usual experience is trying to reach you.

Thus Malamud will describe in *The Assistant* Helen Bober reflecting on the life of the utterly spent man, the grocer who is her father: "He was Morris Bober and could be nobody more fortunate. With that name you had no sure sense of property, as if it were in your blood and history not to possess, or if by some miracle to own something, to do so on the verge of loss." The Bobers do not "live": they "eke out an existence." But though they address each other in the same toneless style, as if each word were their last,

> "Why do I cry? I cry for the world. I cry for my life that it went away wasted. I cry for you—"

the truth of this cadence, in its perfect fall of the voice, is so natural yet "made" that it takes us straight to Malamud's own wit behind the voice we hear. Of American Jewish writers, only Clifford Odets, in those plays whose original voice is now unrecognized (probably because it is assumed that all Jews talked this way during the Depression), took the same pleasure in creating this art-language from Yiddish roots. But Malamud is always wry, detached, a straightforward performer, who enjoys spinning some of this speech for the pleasure of seeing whether, with his odd freight, he can make it over to the other side. Gruber the outraged landlord in "The Mourners" says to the old tenant whom he cannot get rid of, "That's a helluva chutzpah. Gimme the keys. . . . Don't monkey with my blood pressure. If you're not out by the fifteenth, I will personally throw you out on your bony ass." Malamud is in fact so much of a "humorist" trying out situations and lines of dialogue for their immediate effect that Bellow once objected to the artifice of the last scene in "The Mourners," where the old tenant says Kaddish for the landlord who has been so cruel to him. "It struck him with a terrible force that the mourner was mourning him; it was he who was dead." Malamud's usual material, however, is so much about the violation of Jews, about actual physical deprivation and suffering, that obviously Malamud has returned the compliment to life, to the repeated violation of Jewish existence, by a kind of literary "violation," a studied contraction, in himself.

Certainly much of Malamud's humor as a writer lies in his conscious attitude of dissonance, his own wry "handling" of situations. What was oppressively pathetic in life becomes surreal, overcolored, picturesque, illustrative of a folk culture in the Chagall style rather than about Jews as fully grown individuals. His characters are all Malamud's children. Yet by the same logic of detachment, Malamud almost absently tends to turn his protagonists into emblems of "Jewish" goodness and sacrifice. In the best of Malamud's novels, *The Assistant*, which in the thoroughness of its workmanship, its fidelity to the lived facts of experience, its lack of smartness and facile allegorizing, is also the most satisfactory single Jewish novel of this period, even Morris Bober apostolically says what no Jew would ever say to a man taunting him, "What do you suffer for, Morris?" "I suffer for you." Morris Bober might live by this without thinking of it one way or the other. He would certainly be too absorbed in the struggle for existence to say grandly to an enemy, "I suffer for you." But *The Assistant* works all the time and all the way, it convinces, because of the tenacity with which Malamud has captured the texture of Morris Bober's grinding slavery to his store, his lack of energy, his lack of money, the terrible hours from six in the morning to late at night. It is the total poverty of the grocer that gives *The Assistant* the rigor of a great argument. (Malamud's stories sometimes tend to be picturesque and highly colored.) In *The Assistant* Malamud's strength is his total intuition of the folk idiosyncrasy involved.

The sacrifice of Morris Bober is meaningful because he does not know to what he has been sacrificed.

Malamud's almost automatic identification of suffering with goodness, his old-fashioned affection for Jews as the people of poverty and virtue, is in any event a tribute to *his* past. It does not reflect the world Malamud has lived in since his own rise from the world in which Morris Bober rose in the dark every winter morning to sell the "Poilesheh" an onion roll for three cents. The hold of the past on Bellow and Malamud—of the immigrant parents, the slum childhood, the Hitler years that inevitably summed up the martyrdom of Jewish history—is in contrast with the experience of the "new" Jewish novelists, whose aggressively satiric star is Philip Roth.

Roth's natural subject is the self-conscious Jew, newly middle-class, the Jew whose "identity," though never in doubt, is a problem to himself, and so makes himself a setup for ridicule, especially to his son. The Jewish son now sees himself not as a favorite but as a buffer state. Far from identifying any of his characters with the legendary virtues and pieties of Jewish tradition, Roth dislikes them as a group for an unconscious submission that takes the form of hysteria. His first work, *Goodbye, Columbus,* builds up from dislikable outward attributes of the we-have-made-it Patimkin family out of Newark, the suburb to which they have escaped; the coarse, sentimental father; the shrewish, hostile mother; the dumb athletic brother; the brattish kid sister. Even Brenda Patimkin, girlfriend to the sensitive narrator, Neil—an assistant in the Newark Public Library who is defined by his lack of status and his friendliness to a little Negro boy out of the slums who regularly visits the library to stare with ignorant wonder at a book of Gauguin reproductions—exists to betray him. Roth is so quick here to define people by their social place, and to reject them, that he does not always grant a personal trait to their intelligence. Brenda Patimkin seems more Sweet Briar than Radcliffe, just as the narrator Neil Klugman would not necessarily become a Newark public librarian just because *he* did not go to Harvard.

Yet what made Roth stand out—there was now a rut of "Jewish novelists"—was his toughness, the power of decision and the ability to stand moral isolation that is the subject of his story "Defender of the Faith." There was the refusal of a merely sentimental Jewish solidarity. At a time when the wounds inflicted by Hitler made it almost too easy to express feelings one did not have to account for, but when Jews in America were becoming almost entirely middle-class, Roth emphasized all the bourgeois traits that he found. He cast a cold eye on Jews as a group; he insisted—by the conscious briskness of his style and his full inventory of the exaggerated, injurious, sordid, hysterical—that *he* was free. In story after story, in the contrasting voices of his long novels and his short, in his derisions, satires, lampoons, Roth called attention to the self-declared aloofness of his fictional intelligence by the way he worried surprising details and emphasized odd facts in people's behavior. Nathan Zuckerman, the narrator of the story "Courting Disaster," recounts his childhood habit, when given puzzles and arithmetic problems, of dwelling on points different from those he was expected to notice. This "seemingly irrelevant speculation of an imaginary nature" was to become in Roth's own work a stress on his thoughtfulness as an observer. But the marked overstress of oddities was Roth's way of focusing on his real subject, social style. The *show* of any extreme, opened to the aroused fine eye of Roth as narrator, became his way of grasping people fictionally. Harriet in *Goodbye, Columbus*, about to marry into the Patimkin family,

> "impressed me as a young lady singularly unconscious of a motive in others or herself. All was surfaces, and seemed a perfect match for Ron, and too for the Patimkins. . . . She nodded her head insistently whenever anyone spoke. Sometimes she would even say the last few words of your sentence with you. . . ."

Roth wrote from sharpness as his center, his safety. Yet in a period when many young Jewish writers became almost too fond of "absurdity" as a style, and saw fiction as a series of throwaway lines, Roth—no Lenny Bruce even if he sometimes mimed like one—was notable for his moral lucidity and compactness. He had this ability to figure out a situation stylistically: the style of something was both its comedy and its allegory. Each of the stories in *Goodbye, Columbus* made a point; each defined a social situation without any waste and extended it to evident issues. Even when Roth, in his 1961 lecture "Writing American Fiction," found America "absurd," he insisted on defining the absurdity head-on, made it a problem to be solved, above all established its neatly laid-out *comic* reality. Two teenage sisters in Chicago, Pattie and Babs Grimes, had disappeared, were rumored dead. It turned out that they had been living with two tramps in a flophouse. The mother gave interviews to the Chicago press and basked in her sudden fame. Roth found in this episode the kind of scandalousness, disorder all around, which he was always to take with the greatest possible seriousness, even when he mockingly imitated it:

> The American writer in the middle of the 20th century has his hands full in trying to describe, and then to make credible, much of the American reality. It stupefies, it sickens, it infuriates, and finally it is even a kind of embarrassment to one's own meager imagination. The actuality is continually outdoing our talents, and the culture tosses up figures almost daily that are the envy of any novelist. Who, for example, could have invented Charles Van Doren? Roy Cohn and David Schine? Sherman Adams and Bernard Goldfine? Dwight David Eisenhower?

Roth seemed willing to meet the problem. But though the 1960s closed on more public disorder than Roth could have dreamed of, he did not become the novelist of this disorder, or even the journalist of it, as Mailer did. Roth significantly scored his first popular success with *Portnoy's Complaint,* which succeeded as a comic monologue with baleful overtones, very much in the style of a stand-up Jewish comic. The exactitude and fury of memory, the omnivorous detail going back to the most infantile rejections and resentments, captured perfectly a generation psyche which was more anchored on family, and more resentful of it, than any other. Now its novelists found the analyst's couch, the confession, the psychoanalytical recital, the litany of complaint, its most serviceable literary form.

In *Portnoy* the Jewish son had his revenge, as in Bellow's novels the Jewish son had his apotheosis. A whole middle class of sons and daughters, turning and turning within the gyre of the nuclear Jewish family—nucleus indeed of the Jewish experience and the first scenario of the psychoanalytic drama—found in *Portnoy* its own fascination with the details of childhood. It was this emphasis on the unmentionable, Roth's gift for zanily working out usually inaccessible details to the most improbable climax, like Portnoy masturbating into a piece of liver, that was the farce element so necessary to Roth's anger. There was the calculated profanation of mother, father, the most intimate offices of the body—a profanation by now altogether healthy to those therapeutized members of the professional middle class to whom everything about the body had become, like the possibility of universal destruction through the Bomb, small talk at the dinner table. Portnoy's howls of rage, love, and anguish were so concentrated that this made them funny. Some of the incidents were so improbable that this alone made them necessary. Ronald Nimkin, the young pianist, hanged himself in the bathtub. Portnoy reminisces:

> My favorite detail from the Ronald Nimkin suicide: even as he is swinging from the shower head, there is a note pinned to the dead young pianist's short-sleeved shirt:—"Mrs. Blumenthal called. Please bring your mah-jongg rules to the game tonight. Ronald."

In any event, the Jewish mother had by now become such a piece of American folklore—I'll make fun of my ethnic if you'll make fun of yours—that *Portnoy's* success may be attributed to the fact that Roth was the first writer so obsessed with the Jewish family as to remove all the mystery from the Jewish experience. Roth secularized it all to the last micrometer of stained underwear, yet gave it his own "hard," fanatically enumerative quality. Whom do *you* suffer for, Alex Portnoy? I suffer for me. To be Jewish is to resent. What made Roth interesting in all this was that, with all his comic animosity, he was still glued to the Jewish family romance and depended on an "emancipated" Jewish audience as much as he depended on Jews for his best material. "Your book has so many readers!" I once heard an admirer say to Roth. "Why," she continued enthusiastically, "you must have at least six million readers!"

[1971]

THE IMAGINATION OF FACT:
CAPOTE AND MAILER

———— •◆• ————

When Truman Capote explained, on the publication in 1965 of *In Cold Blood: The True Account of a Multiple Murder and Its Consequences*, that the book was really a "nonfiction novel," it was natural to take his praise of his meticulously factual and extraordinarily industrious record of research as the alibi of a novelist whose last novel, *Breakfast at Tiffany's*, had been slight, and who was evidently between novels. Capote clearly hungered to remain in the big league of novelists, so many of whom are unprofitable to everyone, even if he was now the author of a bestselling true thriller whose success was being arranged through every possible "medium" of American publicity. Capote is a novelist, novelists tend to be discouraged by the many current discourtesies to fiction. Clearly Capote wanted to keep his novelist's prestige but to rise above the novelist's struggle for survival. *In Cold Blood*, before one read it, promised by the nature of the American literary market to be another wow, a trick, a slick transposition from one realm to another, like the inevitable musical to be made out of the Sacco-Vanzetti case.

What struck me most in Capote's labeling his book a "nonfiction novel" was his honoring the profession of novelist. Novels seem more expendable these days than ever, but *novelist* is still any writer's notion of original talent.

What interested me most about *In Cold Blood* after two readings—first in *The New Yorker* and then as a book—was that though it *was* journalism and soon gave away all its secrets, it had the ingenuity of fiction and it was fiction except for its ambition to be documentary. *In Cold Blood* brought to focus for me the problem of "fact writing" and its "treatment." There is a lot of "treatment" behind the vast amount of social fact that we get in a time of perpetual crisis. These books dramatize and add to the crisis, and we turn to them because they give a theme to the pervasive social anxiety, the concrete human instance that makes "literature."

In *Cold Blood* is an extremely stylized book that has a palpable design on our emotions. It works on us as a merely factual account never had to. It is so shapely and its revelations are so well timed that it becomes a "novel" in the form of fact. But how many great novels of crime and punishment are expressly based on fact without lapsing into "history"! *The Possessed* is based on the Nechayev case, *An American Tragedy* on the Chester Gillette case. What makes *In Cold Blood* formally a work of record rather than of invention? Because formally, at least, it is a documentary; based on six years of research and six thousand pages of notes, it retains this research in the text. Victims, murderers, witnesses, and law officials appear under their own names and as their attested identities, in an actual or, as we say now, "real" Kansas town.

Why, then, did Capote honor himself by calling the book in any sense a "novel"? Why bring up the word at all? Because Capote depended on the record, was proud of his prodigious research, but was not content to make a work of record. After all, most readers of *In Cold Blood* know nothing about the case except what Capote tells us. Capote wanted his "truthful account" to become "a work of art," and he knew he could accomplish this, quite apart from the literary expertness behind the book, through a certain intimacy between himself and "his" characters. Capote wanted, ultimately, to turn the perpetually defeated, negative Eros that is behind *Other Voices, Other Rooms* into an emblematic situation for our time. As Norman Mailer said when running for mayor, "Until you see what your ideas lead to, you know nothing." Through his feeling for the Clutter family *and* its murderers, Capote was able to relate them—a thought that would have occurred to no one else.

Fiction as the most intensely selective creation of mood, tone, atmosphere, has always been Capote's natural aim as a writer. In *In Cold Blood* he practices this as a union of art and sympathy. His book, like so many "nonfiction" novels of our day, is saturated in sexual emotion. But unlike Mailer's reportage, Capote's "truthful account" is sympathetic to everyone, transparent in its affections to a degree—abstractly loving to Nancy Clutter, that all-American girl; respectfully amazed by Mr. Clutter, the prototype of what Middle America would like to be; helplessly sorry for Mrs. Clutter, a victim of the "square" morality directed at her without her knowing it. None of these people Capote knew—but he thought he did. Capote became extremely involved with the murderers, Perry Smith and Dick Hickock, whom he interviewed in prison endlessly for his book and came to know as we know people who fascinate us. He unconsciously made himself *seem* responsible for them. Kenneth Tynan drew blood when, with the glibness which knows that "society" is always to blame, Tynan entered into the spirit of the book completely enough to denounce Capote for not doing everything possible to save his friends Perry and Dick.

This fascinated sympathy with characters whom Capote visited sixty times in jail, whom he interviewed within an inch of their lives, up to the scaffold, is one of many powerful emotions on Capote's part that keeps the book "true" even when it most becomes a "novel." Capote shows himself deeply related to Alvin Dewey of the Kansas Bureau of Investigation, who more than any other agent on the case brought the murderers in. And as a result of *In Cold Blood* Capote, who had so successfully advertised his appearance on the jacket of *Other Voices, Other Rooms* in 1948, had by 1969 become an authority on crime and punishment and an adviser to law-and-order men like Governor Reagan. Capote was a natural celebrity from the moment he published his first book. *In Cold Blood* gave him the chance to instruct his countrymen on the depths of American disorder.

Yet with all these effects of *In Cold Blood* on Capote, the book itself goes back to the strains behind all Capote's work: a home and family destroyed within a context of hidden corruption, alienation, and loneliness. Reading *In Cold Blood*, one remembers the Gypsy children left hungry and homeless in *The Grass Harp*; the orphans in *A Tree of Night, The Thanksgiving Visitor*, and *A Christmas Memory*; the wild gropings of Holly Golightly in *Breakfast at Tiffany's* toward the "pastures of the sky." One remembers Capote himself in his personal pieces and stories in *Local Color* searching for a home in New Orleans, Brooklyn,

Hollywood, Haiti, Paris, Tangier, and Spain—then returning to Brooklyn again in "A House on the Heights":

> Twenty yards ahead, then ten, five, then none, the yellow house on Willow Street. Home! And happy to be.

The victims in *In Cold Blood* were originally the Clutters, but by the time the crime is traced to the killers and they are imprisoned, all seem equally victims. As in any novel, innocent and guilty require the same mental consideration from the author. In any event, innocence in our America is always tragic and in some sense to blame, as Mr. Clutter is, for incarnating a stability that now seems an "act." Capote is always sympathetic to Nancy Clutter, who laid out her best dress for the morrow just before she got murdered, and Nancy is the fragile incarnation of some distant feminine goodness, of all that might have been, who gets our automatic sympathy. But despite Capote's novelistic interest in building up Mr. Clutter as the archetypal square and Mrs. Clutter as a victim of the rigid lifestyle surrounding her, Capote's more urgent relationship is of course with "Perry and Dick." Almost to the end one feels that they might have been saved and their souls repaired.

This felt interest in "Perry and Dick" as persons whom Capote knew makes the book too personal for fiction but establishes it as a casebook for our time. The background of the tale is entirely one of damaged persons who wreak worse damage on others, but the surface couldn't be more banal. Perry is the "natural killer" selected by Dick for the job, and Dick's father can say to Agent Nye of the Kansas Bureau of Investigation:

> Was nothing wrong with my boy, Mr. Nye, ... an outstanding athlete, always on the first team at school. Basketball! Basketball! Dick was always the star player. A pretty good student, too ...

Terror can break out anywhere. The world is beyond reason but the imagination of fact, the particular detail, alone establishes credibility. It all happened, and it happened only this way. The emotion pervading the book is our helpless fascinated horror; there is a factuality with nothing beyond it in Perry's dwarfish legs, the similar imbalance in Dick's outwardly normal masculinity and his actual destructiveness. On what morsels of unexpected fact, summoned out of seeming nowhere by the author's digging alone, is *our* terror founded! On the way to rob the Clutters, Dick says:

> "Let's count on eight, or even twelve. The only sure thing is every one
> of them has got to go. Ain't that what I promised you, honey—plenty
> of hair on them-those walls?"

The Clutters are stabbed, shot, strangled, between mawkish first-name American "friendliness" and bouncy identification with one another's weaknesses. Nancy couldn't be sweeter to her killers, Perry worries that Dick may rape her, Kenyon asks Perry not to harm his new chest by putting the knife on it. All this "understanding" between "insecure" people makes the crime all the more terrifying. It is the psychic weakness that removes so many people, taking their "weakness" for themselves, from any sense of justice. So much fluency of self-centered emotion makes crime central to our fear of each other today.

We may all have passing dreams of killing. But here are two who killed perversely, wantonly, pointlessly, yet with a horrid self-reference in the pitiful comforts they offered their victims that establishes their cringing viciousness. And the crime, like the greatest crimes of our time, is on record but remains enigmatic, "purposeless," self-defeating. The will to destroy is founded on what we insist are personal weaknesses, but which we cannot relate to what has been done. Even before the Hitler war was over, there were Nazis who said, "At least we have made others suffer." The fascination of Capote's book, the seeming truthfulness of it all, is that it brings us close, very close, to the victims, to the murderers, to the crime itself, as psychic evidence. Killing becomes the primal scene of our "feelings" that with all the timing of a clever novelist and all the emphatic detail brought in from thousands of interview hours by a prodigious listener, Capote presents to us as a case study of "truth" we can hold, study, understand.

As a novelist, dramatist, travel writer, memoirist, Capote had always been rather a specialist in internal mood, tone, "feeling"; now an action, the most terrible, was the center around which everything in his "truthful account" moved. He was ahead of his usual literary self, and the artfulness of the book is that it gets everyone to realize, possess, and dominate this murder as a case of the seemingly psychological malignity behind so many crimes in our day. The book aims to give us this mental control over the frightening example of what is most uncontrolled in human nature.

Technically, this is accomplished by the four-part structure that takes us from the apparently pointless murder of four people to the hanging of the killers in the corner of a warehouse. The book is designed as a suspense story—why did Perry and Dick ever seek out the Clutters at all?—to which the author alone holds the answer. This comes only in Part III, when the book is more than half over. Each of the four sections is divided into cinematically visual scenes. There are eighty-six in the book as a whole; some are "shots" only a few lines long. Each of these scenes is a focusing, movie fashion, designed to put us visually as close as possible now to the Clutters, now to Perry and Dick, until the unexplained juncture between them is explained in Part III. Until then, we are shifted to many different times and places in which we see Perry and Dick suspended, as it were, in a world without meaning, for we are not yet up to the explanation that Capote has reserved in order to keep up novelistic interest. Yet this explanation—in jail a pal had put the future killers on to the Clutters and the supposed wealth in the house—is actually, when it comes, meant to anchor the book all the more firmly in the world of "fact"—of the public world expressed as documented conflict between symbolic individuals. It was the unbelievable squareness of the Clutters as a family that aroused and fascinated the murderers. The book opens on Kansas as home and family, ends on Alvin Dewey at the family graveside,

> Then, starting home, he walked toward the trees, and under them leaving behind him the big sky, the whisper of wind voices in the wind-bent wheat.

The circle of illusory stability (which we have *seen* destroyed) has closed in on itself again.

Capote's book raises many questions about its presumption as a whole, for many of the "fact" scenes in it are as vivid as single shots in a movie can be—and that make us wonder about the meaning of so much easy expert coverage by the writer-as-camera. ("A movie pours into us," John Updike has said. "It fills us like milk being poured into a glass.") One of the best bits is when the jurors, looking at photographs of the torn bodies and tortured faces of the

Clutters, for the first time come into possession of the horror, find themselves focusing on it in the very courtroom where the boyishness and diffidence of the defendants and the boringly circular protocol of a trial have kept up the jurors' distance from the crime.

There is a continuing unreality about the murder of the four Clutters that Capote all through his book labored to eliminate by touch after touch of precious fact. He is our only guide through this sweetly smiling massacre. He is proud of every harrowing or grotesque detail he can dredge up—Perry unbelievably tries to buy for a face mask black stockings from a nun, remembers that after the attack on Mr. Clutter he handed a knife to Dick and said, "Finish him. You'll feel better." The labor after so many facts emphasizes the world of conflict, social bitterness, freakishness, the "criminal" world, the underworld for which Capote asks compassion in the epigraph from Villon's "Ballade des pendus":

> Frères humains, qui après nous vivez,
> N'ayez les cueurs contre nous endurcis,
> Car, si pitié de nous povres avez,
> Dieu en aura plus tost de vous mercis.

—But now, "real" or "unreal," this murder is public. Closeness is the key. The hope of the book is to get us close, closer, to what occurred in the heart of Middle America and occurs every day now. There is in us, as well as in the Clutters' neighbors, "a shallow horror sensation that cold springs of personal fear swiftly deepened."

The horror is now in the nature of the "fact" material. What can be reconstructed as fact from actual events may take the form of a cinematic "treatment" and easily use many shifts of time and place. But it makes our participation in the story more narrow and helpless than a real novel does. The attempt at closeness is all through Capote's work; he attempts to induce it here by identifying us with "real" people we may think we know better than we do—victims and murderers both.

The reason for the "nonfiction novel" (and documentary plays, movies, artworks) is that it reproduces events that cannot be discharged through one artist's imagination. Tragedy exists in order to be assimilated by us as individual fate, for we can identify with another's death. Death in round numbers is by definition the death of strangers, and that is one of the outrages to the human imagination in the killing after killing which we "know all about," and to which we cannot respond. Capote worked so long on this case—"his" case—because to the "fact writer" reporting is a way of showing that *he knows*. The killing of the Clutter family was not "personal," as even Gatsby could have admitted about *his* murderer's mistake in killing him. History is more and more an example of "accident." The Clutters were there just for their killers to kill them.

"The event" is fascinatingly inscrutable though it is in the public light— just one of many killings in our time by people who did not know their victims. As with so many mass murders, many witnesses and documents are needed to reconstruct the true history of the crime. But irony more than truth is the motif of such fact books, for the point made is that there is no "sense" to the crime. This is what relieves the liberal imagination of responsibility and keeps it as spectator. In a "real" novel—one that changes our minds—a single Raskolnikov or Clyde Griffiths commits a singular crime (and is usually pursued by a single law-enforcer who has no other crime to uncover). The resolution of the crime—murder is the primal fault—gave the moral scheme back to us. But as Joan Didion said when she decided not to do a "fact" book around the taped memories by Linda Casabian of living in the Charles Manson "family," there was nothing she could *learn* by writing such a book.

In the many gratuitous murders that have soundlessly bounced off the imagination of our time, murderers and victims remain in every retrospect forever strange to each other. Apart from "war crimes" like Auschwitz, Hiroshima, Dresden, My Lai, the dropping of Viet Cong prisoners on villages from American helicopters, the torture, confessions and executions of whole masses of people as "enemies of the state," there are the murders by Detroit policemen (described by John Hersey in *The Algiers Motel Incident*) of three Negroes just because they have been found in a motel with white women, the killing of parents and children on a Kansas farm by two not abnormally rootless American boys of whom we know enough to know (even if they do talk of killing as "scoring") that we don't know them, the murder of eight-months-pregnant Sharon Tate and six other people by members of the Charles Manson "family."

[. . . .]

Subject—the "situation," the accident, the raid, the murder—is so primary in these novelized special cases that the only force apparently able to do justice to extreme experiences is the writer's myth of himself as an agent for change. The world and the battered author, the revolutionary demonstration and the ego, the crime and the reporter, the moon and me!

These are the now chilling polarities in Norman Mailer's brilliantly literary but evanescent descriptions of the 1967 march on the Pentagon, the 1960 and 1968 national conventions, the first landing of American know-how on the moon. They move us out of the inherent consistency and exhaustive human relationships of the novel onto the great TV screen of contemporary history, and Mailer's illusion is that he is somehow helping to change history. Mailer is the greatest historical actor in his own books, but they do not convey any action of his own. They are efforts to rise above the Americanness that he loves to profane, but which fascinates him into brilliance. The nonfiction novel exists in order *not* to change the American situation that makes possible so much literary aggression against it.

Mailer's tracts are histrionic blows against the system. They are fascinating in their torrential orchestration of so many personal impulses. Everything goes into it on the same level. So they end up as Mailer's special urgency, that quest for salvation through demonstration of the writer's intelligence, realism, courage, that is to be effected by making oneself a gladiator in the center of the ring, a moviemaker breathing his dreams into the camera.

Yet the theme of Mailer's reportage is the unprecedented world now, rushing off to its mad rendezvous with the outermost spaces of blind progress. Mailer's reportage responds excitedly to great public demonstrations, conventions, crowds, coordinations of technological skill. He has carried over from his fiction many sensory equivalents for the sound and weight of crowds, for physical tension, anxiety, conflict, for the many different kinds of happenings that his mind can register as he watches Jack Kennedy arriving in Los Angeles in 1960, senses the Florida cracker's feeling that *he* has made it as the Saturn booster goes up from its Florida pad in 1969. Mailer has both lived and written his life with the greatest possible appetite for the power and satisfaction open to successful Americans since 1945; but his reportage has become steadily more baleful and apocalyptic—not least because his subjects soon lose their interest for everybody but himself.

One aim of his highly colored style has been to find new images for energy, for savoring the last possible tingle of orgasm, for life among the managers, for the sexual power and thrust (sex as thought, thought as sex) inseparable from the experience of self-representative American males. But a new reason for so much style is to keep the zing in his subjects. Mailer has been the hungriest child at the American feast, directly in the line of those realistic novelists for whom John O'Hara spoke when he said that the development of the United States during the first half of the twentieth century was the greatest possible subject for a novelist.

But clearly Mailer's reportage represents his dilemma as an artist forced back on too many "ideas"—a superbly gifted writer too good for this genre. *Of a Fire on the Moon* is a book of such brilliance, and of such sadness in trying to keep different things together, that like a rocket indeed, it has been set off by forces that at every moment threaten to explode it. Proust says somewhere that notes are fantasies. But in Mailer it is precisely with his fantasies, the greatest of which is that he can bring to some portentous world-historical consummation the battle in himself between so many loves and so many Spenglerian despairs, that he has written his moon book. It is not *exactly* a book about the journey of the Apollo 11, not exactly a book about the "WASP" types who fascinate him by their bureaucratized steadiness, or all those dumb other reporters, the computer age.... It is a book about a novelist trying to write instant history.

Of course we all have a sense these days of being ridden down by history, and want to do something about it. Never has there been such a concerted consciousness, in the name of history, of how little history is leaving our minds and our souls. Never have there been so many techniques for circulating facts and dramatizing them. Real history, partisan history, and commercial history are so thick a part of contemporary writing that it is as if History had come back to revenge itself on its upstart rival, Fiction. But not without Fiction's own techniques, as one can see nowhere better than in Mailer's allegory of *himself* as history. The effort sprouts more coils around Mailer himself than the serpents did around Laocoön and his sons. With one breath he must say yes! serpents are of the essence and I can take anything! with the next make a mighty heave to get the damned things off him, two Americans to the moon, and the book to the publisher.

Such ambition, such imagination, such wrath, such sadness, such cleverness, so many ideas! The flames licking Saturn-Apollo on its way up had nothing on this. It is as if Mailer were sketching the possibilities of one brilliant novel after another. The dreaming, longing, simulating—of masterpieces—give the reader the sense that Mailer was really dreaming of other books all the time he was writing this one. The giveaway at crucial passages of philosophizing—and that was another reason for taking on the assignment; it was like asking Hamlet to give a lecture on Monarchs I Have Known—is that with the whole universe to travel up and down on his typewriter, Mailer cannot help fudging the world-historical bit; he is not always clear to himself, and damn well knows it. Rather than dramatize the American contradictions that are eating him up, he tries to keep them all in eloquent bursts that stagger you with ideas, but that leave you uneasy. The performance is not of the moon but of the effort to talk about it.

Journalism will no more diminish than will the "communications industry," but the new art-journalism, journalism as a private form, has already had its day. It went through a whole cycle in the sixties, and no longer astonishes. Issues die on it as fast as last week's issue of *Time*, and while the professional reporter can still depend on a bored downgrading of human nature, Mailer depended for his best "pieces," like *The Prisoner of Sex*, on challenges to his manhood that not even the Kate Milletts will always provide. Mailer identified creative vitality in his best tract, *The Armies of the Night: History as a Novel: The Novel as History* with his revolutionary élan. But America has worn out the revolutionary in Mailer; the historical blues are more a problem to the novelist-as-reporter than to the novelist or reporter as such. Mailer in *Of a Fire on the Moon* describes the lifting of the Saturn-Apollo in language born in the envy of *Moby-Dick* and manifest destiny—language that somehow suggests there may yet be political hope in so much mechanical energy. Some transformation of minds may yet take place in outer space!

But the possibility of doom is just as strong in Mailer's own moon trip as in his enthusiasm for a technical wizardry of which, in the end, he knows less than he does about doom. With so many agonies of contradiction in himself, the brilliant novelist's lesser rhetoric won't do—that just passes out symbols like party hats to *surprise*—but the patience and depth of fiction itself, dramatic imagination, the world reconstructed in that personal sense of time about which space centers, sex movements, and all other plurals know nothing, but which is a writer's secret treasure. Despite all our rapture about them now, the great nineteenth-century novels were not and certainly are not the "world." The world is a world, dumb as nature, not a novel. The world as our common experience is one that only the journalist feels entirely able to set down. It is a confidence that those who stick to fiction do not feel, for if the "world" is not an experience in common, still less is it a concept on which all can agree. It is not even as close as we think. As Patrick White, the Australian novelist, says in one of his books—"Why is the world which seems so near so hard to get hold of?"

[1971]

THE "SINGLE VOICE" OF RALPH ELLISON

———— ◆ ————

Ralph Ellison's *Invisible Man*, published in 1952, has proved the most believable of the many current novels of the embattled self's journey through an American reality defined as inherently "absurd." Certainly more than any other black writer, Ellison achieved as dramatic fact, as a rounded whole, beyond dreamy soliloquy or angry assertion, a demonstration of the lunatic hatred that American can offer, on every facet of its society, to a black man. This irrationality is more real, more solidly grounded to blacks writing out of actual oppression than is the *idea* of an irrational society to white writers dislocated in the country they used to take for granted and who now find so much of America "meaningless."

The hatred that society shows to an actual victim of racist hatred is not the same thing as "meaninglessness," which is a middle-class state of mind, a temporary fatigue, that represents the sometimes frolicsome despondency of intellectuals who see no great place for their moral influence—for changing things—in a future laid out in advance by technology. "Meaninglessness" is an intellectual conceit in all senses of the word; it is not something that one lives, as the nameless and somehow generic "hero" of *Invisible Man* must live the absurdity of a life that is constant contradiction to his words. He has a gift for "eloquence," for beautifully saying the expected, and is constantly promised a greater share of life by the white (and black) authorities over him while he is actually a "nigger" whom they "keep running."

Ellison's book is about the art of survival, a subject that has made tragic comedians out of many ordinary blokes in the literature of our time. And it turns on the self-deceptions of eloquence—a problem among all oppressed people, a special resource of blacks, and a problem-theme in all Ellison's work: "God's trombone" is the phrase for a masterful Negro preacher in a published fragment from his work-in-progress. But eloquence is the seat of all contradiction, the gift that is the hero's only chance for life but that also works against itself in the life of Ellison's "invisible man." And this complex use of eloquence comes out of a tradition of monologue—American, nineteenth-century, frontier-revivalist, musical—that reflects Ellison's passion for the trumpet as much as it does the famous "single voice" in Melville, Mark Twain, Faulkner, that gave Ellison the courage to discover an Oklahoma black's affinity with them.

Monologue, as it happens, has become the favorite free form for comic fiction about the world's irrationality. The clownish single voice heard in so many contemporary American novels may be the natural vehicle of those many writers who see man near the end of the twentieth century as a hilariously futile creature, trying by repeated rituals to save himself in a world that majestically ignores him. The schlemiel hero, the nonhero, the antihero, are all easy riders of despair; in their fluently disenchanted Romantic prose they mark the end of the Romantic faith that perception will yet unite man with a world that once waited for him to give it meaning. The function of the contemporary hero is to cancel the affirmations but to keep the setting of what once made him feel like a god.

Ellison's *Invisible Man* does not use the monologue form lightly or capriciously in the interests of personal fantasy. It is an old-fashioned storytelling device that owes to Ishmael and Huck Finn and Faulkner's unstoppable voice in *The Bear* the ability to get people into view through rumination. Whenever the hero-narrator of *Invisible Man* tries to report dreamlike material and the headiness of pure association under the influence of pot, he is less interesting than when he is simply *there* to bring in the succession of characters who "keep this nigger running." The voice is in that specific tradition of anecdote, rhapsody, sermonizing, yarn-spilling, that Ellison learned to recognize as his tradition from reading Constance Rourke's beautiful book, *American Humor*, which demonstrated the primacy of the monologuist's art in American writing. "I was to dream of a prose," said Ellison, "which was flexible, and swift as American change is swift."

Constance Rourke was one influence on Ellison by way of the critic Stanley Edgar Hyman, who was strong on myth and folklore; Hyman also led Ellison to Lord Raglan's *The Hero*, which taught him that a myth is always "a narrative linked with a rite, and that it celebrates a god's death, travels through the underworld, and eventual rebirth." But *Invisible Man* is founded essentially on eloquence as redemption through art and as a snare to the ambushed minority man—who in this case finally flees a Harlem mob and the New York cops into a manhole, and then takes up residence in the Harlem cellar from which he addresses us and recites his life.

To talk well, to "make an impression" on the audience, to talk so well that finally one talks only to invigorate oneself—this is indeed to be a clown who cannot respect his role nor get out of it. This is the literal absurdity of the artist who even at his peak must doubt that his performance refers to anything more than himself. The hero begins by being a "good boy" who can say all the expected right things to the Negro college president and to the white businessmen, doctors, preachers. He is so good and dutiful that he is less an individual than the service Negro putting off all feelings of his own in order to get approval. He is the nobody, the nothing man who believes all the slogans sold him by the Establishment. His gift for mouthing these in public with the requisite "sincerity" inevitably makes him the creature of the Negro college's president, Bledsoe. Bledsoe, having no reason to suspect him of anything, has him drive the white, spare, thin-blooded New England trustee, Norton, around the countryside. Norton is a parody of Emerson, and reflects a special aim on the part of a writer who shares Melville's distrust of Emerson and who is named Ralph Waldo Ellison.

Our hero ignorantly drives Norton to the old slave quarters, where a shabby old Negro tenant farmer named Trueblood, in one of the great comic episodes in American fiction, relates the story of how he got his daughter as well as his wife with child. They were all bundled up against the cold in the same bed, and Trueblood was a powerful dreamer. "But once a man gits hisself in a tight spot like that there ain't much he can do. It ain't up to him no longer.

There I was, tryin' to git away with all my might, yet having to move *without* movin'."

Norton collapses on hearing the full story, and in an effort to get medical aid, the hero inevitably tangles Norton up with some mad Negro war veterans. He has a totally unconscious gift for putting himself in the wrong with everyone in the book. This is his real craftiness, his "authenticity," the negation of his famous innocence. In the early nightmarish scenes in which he is blindfolded and led into a prize ring before the boozed-up white Establishment of the town to battle with other blindfolded black boys, he finds that the "coins" tossed into the ring give off an electric shock. But "ignoring the shock by laughing, as I brushed the coins off quickly, I discovered that I could contain the electricity—a contradiction, but it works."

Ellison was working consciously with so many literary symbols and rituals in the book that he clearly thought less about making the hero's character complex than he did about putting into his book his lessons in the symbol-hunting fashionable literary criticism of the time. He has explained that "each section begins with a sheet of paper; each piece of paper is exchanged for another and contains a definition of his identity, or the social role he is to play as defined for him." Similarly, the prize of a briefcase, presented to him early in the book by the whites in town after he has made his first ridiculously self-demeaning speech, accompanies him everywhere, like the piece of an old slave manacle given him by his secretly anti-white grandfather. But the hero's innocence is so amazingly overdone that his delightful mistakes—like speaking to the assembled whites of social "equality" when he means to say "responsibilities," or his driving Norton to hear Trueblood's helpless tale of a winter night, or his getting the colors mixed up in a paint factory—are of course the best thing about him. He is shown as a man of unwitting guile and finally of profound gifts of self-protection in his flight from all opinion not his own. Yet Ellison felt that he could manipulate his nonhero into a devastating example of the absurdity, the self-contradiction, that a man always in trouble must feel about his existence when he remembers his goodness, helplessness, innocence.

Whatever else Ellison's nonhero or antihero may be, he is not a complex, rounded, subtle figure. He is not flexible in the least. That seems to be a condition of all "novels of the absurd." Although Ellison's tale is told in monologue and emphasizes the rhetorical variety possible to the single voice, the protagonist is audibly manipulated by a novelist who is fascinated by "elo-quence." Ellison, when interviewed by Robert Penn Warren for a book of indi-vidual testimony called *Who Speaks for the Negro?*, said:

> One of the advantages of being a Negro is that we have always had the freedom to choose or to select and to affirm those traits, those values, those cultural forms, which we have taken from any and every-body. . . . We probably have more freedom than anyone; we only need to become more conscious of it and use it to protect ourselves from some of the more tawdry American values.

This is a freedom to choose roles, to borrow personalities—a point that has often been made by whites, whether compassionately or contemptuously, about the Negro's lack of roots. Ellison's protagonist is "free" in his imagina-tion only at the end of his tale, when he is ready to begin writing it. But the very point of *Invisible Man* is that while Ralph Ellison may now be "free" as writers are, his unhero certainly isn't. This lack of self-direction in his life makes the book tragicomic, as true comedy must be. He *always* looks for what is not there. He approves of his feelings, and recognizes nothing else.

This sense of society as grindingly, continuously, *totally* against us is some-thing new in fiction, for those who have experienced total rejection by a "mas-ter race" have just begun to describe it. But Ellison escapes the trumped-up farcical tone of so many would-be comic novels about the horrors of being an American—as he escapes the confines of his symbolism—by his natural sense of event. His protagonist gets stretched out on every possible betrayal, humili-ation, and pratfall. We get from *Invisible Man* a sense of real experience, real suf-fering, the mad repetitions of the outsider's efforts to get a foothold and the resonances of his failure. Talking to us from the coal cellar to which he has just escaped ahead of the police and everyone else, he exists by and in his voice—a voice that at the beginning and at the end of his journey finds its true analogy in Louis Armstrong's uplifted horn and the quavery sound "What did I do / To be so black and blue?" By contrast, the teller of this tale sees all around him in Harlem:

> birds of passage who were too obscure for learned classification, too silent for the most ambiguous words, and too distinct from the cen-

ters of historical decision to sign or even to applaud the signers of historical documents. We who write no novels, histories, or other books.

The vibration of this voice has been lasting. It is a voice powerfully urgent but not aggressive; full of the wistful seeking to be more than one's feelings and of the contradictions inherent in anyone's picture of himself as an innocent seeker. The voice is never an imposture, something I do feel about the professionally enraged black nationalist, already satirized in *Invisible Man* as Ras the Destroyer shouting at the hero from a Harlem street corner. Ellison still believes in the sufficiency of art. His own voice in *Invisible Man* conveys his faith in the tradition, from *Benito Cereno* to *Light in August*, that race differences have made the strongest writing in this country. *Our* mythology is based on nature, hardship, and the struggle between people who may have nothing and everything in common by being Americans. The hero's grandfather, before dying, dropped his Uncle Tom mask and called himself "a spy in the enemy's country ever since I give my gun back to the Reconstruction." The grandfather instructs him to play a part. "I want you to overcome 'em with yeses, undermine 'em with grins, agree 'em to death and destruction, let 'em swoller you till they vomit or bust wide open." But the hero does not really believe this or practice it. He emerges from the anonymity of Negro experience only through his gift for getting rushed to the platform, where he makes speeches held together by emotions expected of him. President Bledsoe is never anything but crafty, and the white Establishment is so sadistic that the hero's naïveté can be taken only for the continuing effects of slavery. And in fact he goes on to the North and stays dumb even in the Communist "Brotherhood" as a Chaplinesque figure whose mad gift for rousing a crowd relates only to his own loneliness. The hero's voice in the book—first innocently, then mordantly—reproduces many other voices; finally it tunes out all voices but its own. At the end he just barely saves himself by holing in from everything. But his last words are still an effort to connect: "Who knows but that, on the lower frequencies, I speak for you?"

In terms of the old tradition—the Negro as stooge, clown, sacrificial victim—he does. And in the course of the novel itself this generic figure does go on, in one of the many silent shifts of the book, to become an artist. At the end of the book he recalls the solitary figure in that half-light of the frontier that Faulkner caught in *The Bear*, for the best American writing is still a raid on the primitive. Ellison did not know how much he believed in the American frontier—in art's necessary struggle with history and nature as hardship—until he had achieved *Invisible Man*. Since 1952, faced with the problem of transcending his triumphant first book, Ellison has been too often embattled, first with Jewish literary critics who in the 1960s tried to interest him in their pro-black militancy, later with black militants who are interested in literature as exhortation. Ellison has become a solitary and wistful exhorter himself—of High Art.

But *Invisible Man* endures because it is representative, truthful, "real." It came just before the great age of derision. So much of the whole modern urban Negro experience is included in the life cycle of the hero! The believable element of absurdity—of a life situation thoroughly presented in all its con-tradictions to human sense—does not lie in the histrionic shifts of conscious-ness portrayed at the beginning (where the whipped-up Negro sermons remind one too much of famous sermons in *Moby-Dick* and *The Sound and the Fury*), or in the hallucinations and "illuminations" of the hero as he talks to us from his cellar while all that stolen electric light tapped from every circuit within reach makes a hideously bright operating room for us to stare right into his mind. It lies in the rushed total coverage of the book, which steams through so many improbabilities-as-actualities that the reader gets as trapped in the lunacies of history as the hero does.

Where to go from here? What to do? In the lobby of the YMCA the hero (just now in overalls) looks around him and ticks off, one after another, the counterfeits of middle-class success—the would-be gentlemen, the self-imagined businessmen, the janitors and messengers "who spent most of their wages on clothing such as was fashionable among Wall Street brokers, with their Brooks Brothers suits and bowler hats, English umbrellas, black calfskin shoes and yellow gloves...." By the end of the book, the hero has also exhausted the possibilities in the Communist Party, in the Black Nationalist movement of Ras the Exhorter (now Ras the Destroyer), and in trying to burn Harlem down. Chased by the police into a manhole and there cursed by them and left for dead, he feels that he has also exhausted even the eloquence in hatred and must now wait life out in his hole.

[1971]

TWO CASSANDRAS:
JOAN DIDION AND
JOYCE CAROL OATES

———— • ✦ • ————

"I come from California, come from a family, or a congeries of families, that has always been in the Sacramento Valley." Some native Californians think that Joan Didion is sentimental about that "always" bit, that the place was never as much "Eden"—as she likes to describe it—before the aerospace industries and the supermarkets came in. But Joan Didion's professional sense of style in all things—she has several times done a perfect piece around the fear of a nervous breakdown, and not had one—gives a smooth literary fervor to the constant theme of decline and fall. The story between the lines of *Slouching Towards Bethlehem* is surely not so much "California" as it is her ability to make us share her passionate sense of it. And her own reportorial voice carried very clearly indeed even at a time when "the article as art" was being more noisily promulgated by Norman Mailer and Tom Wolfe. *Slouching Towards Bethlehem* established itself extraordinarily well for a collection of "pieces"; her novel *Play It as It Lays,* though it definitely made its mark as a picture of a woman's despair within the total *nada* of the Hollywood scene, seemed to one of her editors "depressing" and less valuable than her reportage.

Living in Malibu, overlooking the Pacific Ocean, Joan Didion has described how, when the hills were on fire, the young surfers in the water would look up and go on with their surfing. Obviously only a very gifted writer with a particular eye for the harsh, inhuman, even antihuman extremes that surround our still fragile settlement on this continent would have brought into conversation the typical Joan Didion picture—Hell as Sunny California—the hills on fire in Malibu and the surfers joyfully sporting below. But Joan Didion constantly presents such moral symbols in her work with a sense of style that is both brilliant and inert, as befits a very vulnerable, defensive young novelist whose style in all things is somehow to keep the world off, to keep it from eating her up, and who describes southern California in terms of fire, rattlesnakes, cave-ins, earthquakes, the indifference to other people's disasters, and the terrible wind called the Santa Ana. With that inescapable sense of style that seems to cry "Danger!" she writes in "Los Angeles Notebook":

> The city burning is Los Angeles's deepest image of itself: Nathanael West perceived that, in *The Day of the Locust;* and at the time of the 1965 Watts riots what struck the imagination most indelibly were the fires. For days one could drive the Harbor Freeway and see the city on fire, just as we had always known it would be in the end. Los Angeles weather is the weather of catastrophe, of apocalypse... the violence and the unpredictability of the Santa Ana affect the entire quality of life in Los Angeles, accentuate its impermanence, its unreliability. The wind shows us how close to the edge we are.

Everything Joan Didion writes seems attuned to some physical anxiety surrounding her in the atmosphere of southern California. She is so responsive to the insecure surface of California that the inescapably alarmed fragility of the woman helps to explain the impending sense of catastrophe that informs so much of her work, the smartly written but brooding sense of nemesis that is the insistent theme of *Play It as It Lays.* One woman reviewer said that the book was not merely *about* nothingness, but that there was a "nothing" to the book's heroine, a movie actress who sees doom, falsehood, and violence everywhere in the Sunny West. Maria Wyeth gives herself at request to several moneyed Hollywood hoodlums, but seems to take no pleasure in her body.

Silence as a form and fear of imminent breakdown are significant elements in both Joan Didion's reportage and fiction. There are also a good many silences between her written sentences, which have a look of getting freshly loaded before they hit you. She refers often to her fragility in *Slouching Towards Bethlehem,* and she writes about her panics with a deliberation that is not merely disarming but that always makes a point, in perfect style, about something other than herself.

> I went to San Francisco because I had not been able to work in some months, had been paralyzed by the conviction that writing was an irrelevant act, that the world as I had understood it no longer existed. If I was to work again at all, it would be necessary for me to come to terms with disorder. . . .

The most striking feature of her spare, tight, histrionically desolate one-line sentences in *Play It as It Lays* is that, as in her reportage, all personal damage reflects cultural sickness. What Rough Beast Does Slouch Towards Bethlehem? When a visitor asked her to define the "evil" she sees on every hand, she replied: "The absence of seriousness." The lady is a moralist in an old-fashioned tradition. She feels "intellectually," she lays it all out, and somehow it is all so mod, empty, American, that you feel for *her.* Children in Haight-Ashbury on drugs. Abortions. Children with brain damage. An actor making love to Maria in Vegas who suddenly breaks open a popper of amyl nitrate to intensify his orgasm.

Hell now exists, as real as you and I; but in Joan Didion's fiction, as in her articles, it always has a name, a location, weather, the California specific to itself—"oil scum on the sand, a red tide on the flaccid surf and mounds of kelp at the waterline. The kelp hummed with flies." In *Play It as It Lays* Maria unbelievably opens the novel with: " 'What makes Iago evil?' some people ask. I never ask." The novel gives us inner devastation matched by fire in the California hills, husbands and wives who cannot feel anything, former lovers who return only to inflict pain, a homosexual who persuades Maria to hold his hand as he commits suicide. All this despair positively insists on saying, in the ready phrase of the homosexual's wife, "Everything is shit" and describes itself as a feature of the local life as well known as the casting couch.

Hannah Arendt once remarked that she had never seen in Europe such unexplained personal suffering as she saw here. In Joan Didion's work the names given to physical threats and devastation, the brilliantly ominous details to present life in California, are meant to explain this suffering, but they don't.

The young woman who went about everywhere as a reporter with "a pervasive sense of loss" was to give this to *all* her heroines, including Joan Didion. But the vague, haunted Lily McClellan in *Run River*—my favorite among the three Didion books—makes us feel that her sleeping with various men she does not care for is the expression of a deep personal fright, and not a judgment on her husband Everett McClellan's futile belief that "order" must be kept up at all costs. "The easiest lay in the room, I can always spot them, something scared in their eyes," a drunk at a party says about Lily. Sometimes female "fright" says more about despair than what happened to Sacramento.

In *Play It as It Lays* Maria Wyeth, a movie star separated and soon casually divorced from a husband who once directed her in a gang-bang picture, comes from Silver Wells, Nevada. There she had a solid sort of old-fashioned gambler for a father, a perfect straight shooter of a mother. It is all gone now—the real Old West is gone, and Maria is numb, utterly numb, with a sense of the "nothing" all around her. After a felt but entirely furtive affair with a married man, she has an abortion. The go-between on the drive to the abortionist's:

> "You may have noticed, I drive a Cadillac. Eldorado. Eats gas but I like it, like the feel of it. . . . If I decided to get rid of the Cad, I might pick myself up a little Camaro. Maybe that sounds like a step down, a Cad to a Camaro, but I've got my eye on this particular Camaro, exact model of the pace car in the Indianapolis 500."

This is typically brilliant, but all is symbol, every character is a *statement* that evil reigns, as real as sunshine. The center is not holding. Everyone in the book except Maria acts the pimp, the stud, the call girl, the pervert, the decadent hairdresser, the orgiast, the suicide. It is all shit, evil as what Joan Didion calls a "deprivation of seriousness," all money, sex, private terror. The assignations are as coldly calculated as tax deals.

What made *Play It as It Lays* unusually interesting, gave it an attention few new novels get nowadays, is the graphic readability it makes of our "condition." The book proceeds by a succession of rapid closeups, scenes often just a short chapter, a tattoo of one-line exchanges that does everything to wing its message to the reader. There are intense descriptive scenes of Maria wildly driving the frightening California freeways to show that she can manage them, at Hoover Dam registering the throb of the turbines in her body. The book is a film that gets its rhythm from the most relentless cutting, and the silence between the curt scenes is calculated, disturbing. The book is so cunning in its rapid-fire rhythm that all sorts of questions about the characters get over-looked under the spell of its intimacy with dread.

Joan Didion is too much in control throughout the book, literally the director-*auteur,* as they now say in cinema circles. Maria would hardly ask, "Why should a coral snake need two glands of neurotoxic poison to survive while a king snake, *so similarly marked,* needs none. Where is the Darwinian logic there...." Joan Didion is so professional a moralist that the message emerges, hypnotic but unbelievable: Nothingness is the medium in which we live. She is almost too skillful a demonstrator of the widespread lack of confidence among middle-class Americans that makes them shocking to themselves. Her real subject is the individual woman who is mysteriously a torment to herself, and it is her loyalty to this subject rather than her nostalgia for some mythical past California that makes her understand the American smartness and know-ingness from which no writer so smoothly professional and acceptable is free.

What interests me most in her writing is what, from her woman's point of view, renders the world incommunicable. *Run River,* a first book much less smart than her next two but evocative of Lily Knight McClellan's mysterious-ness to herself, has an emotional depth that I much prefer to the brilliant jour-nalism of *Slouching Towards Bethlehem* or the evasive sentimentality behind the rapid-fire technique of *Play It as It Lays.* Lily McClellan is one of the few women left in contemporary American fiction who *don't* know what life is all about, who move through their days with the full gravity of being alive. Lily's moral and physical fragility, her *not* knowing, her *not* being on top of things, her almost accidental love affairs, give her an authenticity, all around, missing in Maria Wyeth. In the midst of all that California light and space, we get the existential feeling of what it was like to be alive in the Great Valley.[...]

Lily's husband, Everett McClellan, is somewhat dim and unreal, as the men in Joan Didion's two novels generally tend to be. Perhaps this is because, as his sister Martha says about Everett to his wife, Lily: "All Everett wants is a little order."

"I guess that's what everybody wants."

Martha lay down again. "Maybe everybody wants it. But most people don't want it more than anything else in the world. The way

Everett does. You might want it, I might want it. But when the opportunity to *have* it practically hits us over the head, we just knock ourselves out getting out of the way." She paused. "Take you for
example."

I am sure that in Joan Didion's deliberate mind, *Run River* is a novel about
decline and fall in the Sacramento River Valley, and that the "pervasive sense
of loss" she remembers from earliest childhood has been steadily translated
into the many symbols—the disaster of the McClellans' marriage, Lily
McClellan as a lost lady, the decline of a "certain pride"—that have made her
almost too professional a writer about our moral condition. But the involuntary unacknowledged strength of her sensibility, the really arresting thing, is
seen not in the clear cold eye, the writer's famous detachment, the "perfect"
sentences, the amusing social cattiness about arrivistes and kept women and
the huddled mob life of New York—but in the sense of fright, of something
deeply wrong. No, the center is not holding. But the center is not the proprietary middle class that was in Sacramento, or the Establishment that tells us
where the bodies have been buried after more powerful people have disposed
of them. The "center" is that inner space, that moral realm, where, as Mark
Schorer said in his review of *Play It as It Lays*, the question that keeps nagging
is: "What makes us hurt so much? You have to be more than merely skillful
with the little knives and so on to get away with it."

2

So the days pass, and I ask myself whether one is not hypnotised, as
a child by a silver globe, by life; and whether this is living.
                                            —*Virginia Woolf*
                                         Diary, *28 November 1928*

A "sense of fright, of something deeply wrong." In Joyce Carol Oates's most
notable novel, *them*, this seemed to express itself as a particular sensitivity to
individual lives helplessly flying off the wheel of American giantism. While
writing *them* (a novel which ends with the 1967 eruption of Detroit's Blacks),
she said that Detroit was "all melodrama." There a man can get shot by the
brother of the woman he is lying next to in bed, and the body will be disposed

of by a friendly policeman. The brother himself pops up later in the sister's life not as a "murderer," but as a genially obtuse and merely wistful fellow. Nothing of this is satirized or moralized as once it would have been. It is what happens every day now; there are too many people for murders to count. There are too many murderers about for the murderer to take murder that seriously.

Joyce Carol Oates seemed, more than most women writers, entirely open to *social* turmoil, to the frighteningly undirected and misapplied force of the American powerhouse. She plainly had an instinct for the social menace packed up in Detroit, waiting to explode, that at the end of the nineteenth century Dreiser felt about Chicago and Stephen Crane about New York. The sheer rich chaos of American life, to say nothing of its staggering armies of poor, outraged, by no means peaceful, people, pressed upon her. It is rare to find a woman writer so externally unconcerned with form. After teaching at the University of Detroit from 1962 to 1967, she remarked that Detroit is a city "so transparent, you can hear it ticking." What one woman critic in a general attack on Oates called "Violence in the Head," could also be taken as her inability to blink social violence as the language in which a great many "lower-class" Americans naturally deal with each other.

Joyce Carol Oates is, however, a "social novelist" of a peculiar kind. She is concerned not with demonstrating power relationships but with the struggle of people nowadays to express their fate in terms that are cruelly changeable. Reading her, one sees the real tragedy of so many Americans today, unable to find a language for what is happening to them. The drama of society was once seen by American social novelists as the shifting line between the individual and the mass into which he was helplessly falling. It has now become the free-floating mythology about "them" which each person carries around with him, an idea of causation unconnected to cause. There is no longer a fixed point within people's thinking. In the American social novels earlier in the century, the novelist was a pathfinder and the characters were betrayed as blind, helpless victims of their fate, like Hurstwood in *Sister Carrie* or virtually everybody in Dos Passos's *U.S.A.* Joyce Carol Oates is not particularly ahead of the people she writes about. Since her prime concern is to see people in the terms they present to themselves, she is able to present consciousness as a person, a crazily unaccountable thing. The human mind, as she says in the title of a recent novel, is simply "wonderland." And the significance of that "wonderland" to the social melodrama that is America today is that they collide but do not connect.

Praising Harriette Arnow's strong, little-known novel about southern mountain folk, *The Dollmaker*, Joyce Oates said:

> It seems to me that the greatest works of literature deal with the human soul caught in the stampede of time, unable to gauge the profundity of what passes over it, like the characters of Yeats who live through terrifying events but who cannot understand them; in this way history passes over most of us. Society is caught in a convulsion, whether of growth or of death, and ordinary people are destroyed. They do not, however, understand that they are "destroyed."

This view of literature as silent tragedy is a central description of what interests Joyce Oates in the writing of fiction. Her own characters move through a world that seems to be wholly physical and even full of global eruption, yet the violence, as Elizabeth Dalton said, is in their own heads—and is no less real for that. They touch us by frightening us, like disembodied souls calling to us from the other world. They live through terrifying events but cannot understand them. This is what makes Oates a new element in our fiction, involuntarily disturbing.

She does not understand why she is disturbing. She takes the convulsion of society for granted, and so a writer born in 1938 regularly "returns" to the 1930s in her work. *A Garden of Earthly Delights* begins with the birth on the highway of a migrant worker's child after the truck transporting the workers has been in a collision. Obviously she is unlike many women writers in her feeling for the pressure, mass, density of violence in American experience not always shared by the professional middle class. "The greatest realities," she has said, "are physical and economic; all the subtleties of life come afterward." Yet the central thing in her work is the teeming private consciousness, a "wonderland" that to her is reality in action—but without definition and without boundary.

Joyce Oates is peculiarly and painfully open to other minds, so possessed by them that in an author's note to *them* she says of the student who became the "Maureen Wendall" of the novel, "Her various problems and complexities overwhelmed me.... My initial feeling about her life was, 'This must be fiction, this can't be real!' My more permanent feeling was, 'This is the only kind of fiction that is real.' " Her ability to get occupied by another consciousness makes even *them*, her best novel to date, a sometimes impenetrably voluminous history of emotions, emotions, emotions. You feel that you are turning thousands of pages, that her world is as harshly overpopulated as a sleepless mind, that you cannot make out the individual features of anyone within this clamor of everyone's existence.

This is obviously related to the ease with which Joyce Oates transfers the many situations in her head straight onto paper. I sense an extraordinary and tumultuous amount of purely mental existence locked up behind her schoolgirl's face. She once told an interviewer that she is always writing about

> love . . . and it takes many different forms, many different social levels. . . . I think I write about love in an unconscious way. I look back upon the novels I've written, and I say, yes, this was my subject. But at the time I'm writing I'm not really conscious of that. I'm writing about a certain person who does this and that and comes to a certain end.

She herself is the most unyielding lover in her books, as witness the force with which she follows so many people through every trace of their feeling, thinking, moving. She is obsessive in her patience with the sheer factuality of contemporary existence. This evident love for the scene we Americans make, for the incredible profusion of life in America, also troubles Joyce Carol Oates. Every writer knows himself to be a little crazy, but her feeling of her own absurdity is probably intensified by the dreamlike ease with which her works are produced. It must indeed trouble her that this looks like glibness, when in point of fact her dogged feeling that she writes out of love is based on the fact that she is utterly hypnotized, positively drugged, by other people's experiences. The social violence so marked in her work is like the sheer density of detail—this and this and this is what is happening to people. She is attached to life by well-founded apprehension that nothing lasts, nothing is safe, nothing is all around us. In *them* Maureen Wendall thinks:

> Maybe the book with her money in it, and the money so greedily saved, and the idea of the money, maybe these things weren't real either. What would happen if everything broke into pieces? It was queer how you felt, instinctively, that a certain space of time was real and not a dream,

and you gave your life to it, all your energy and faith, believing it to be real. But how could you tell what would last and what wouldn't? Marriages ended. Love ended. Money could be stolen, found out and taken . . . or it might disappear by itself, like that secretary's notebook. Objects disappeared, slipped through cracks, devoured, kicked aside, knocked under the bed or into the trash, lost. Her clearest memory of the men she'd been with was their moving away from her. They were all body then, completed.

The details in Oates's fiction follow each other with a humble truthfulness that make you wonder where she is taking you; this is sometimes disorienting, for she is all attention to the unconscious reactions of her characters. She needs a lot of space, which is why her short stories tend to read like scenarios for novels. The amount of *listening* this involves is certainly singular. My deepest feeling about her is that her mind is unbelievably crowded with psychic existences, with such a mass of stories that she lives by being wholly submissive to "them." She is too attentive to their mysterious clamor to *want* to be an artist, to make the right and well-fitting structure. Much of her fiction seems written to relieve her mind of the people who haunt it, not to create something that will live.

So many inroads on the suddenly frightening American situation is indeed a problem in our fiction just now; the age of high and proud art has yielded to the climate of crisis. Joyce Oates's many stories resemble a card index of situations; they are not the deeply plotted stories that we return to as perfect little dramas; her novels, though they involve the reader through the author's intense connection with her material, tend as incident to fade out of our minds. Too much happens. Indeed, hers are altogether strange books, haunting rather than "successful," because the mind behind them is primarily concerned with a kind of Darwinian struggle for existence between minds, with the truth of some limitless human struggle. We miss the perfectly suggestive shapes that modern art and fiction have taught us to venerate. Oates is another Cassandra bewitched by her private oracle. But it is not disaster that is most on her mind; it is the recognition of each person as the center of the coming disturbance. And this disturbance, as Pascal said of his God, has its center everywhere and its circumference nowhere.

So her characters are opaque, ungiving, uncharming; they have the taciturn qualities that come with the kind of people they are—heavy, hallucinated, out-side the chatty middle class. Society speaks in them, but *they* are not articulate. They do not yet feel themselves to be emancipated persons. They are caught up in the social convulsion and move unheedingly, compulsively, blindly, through the paces assigned to them by the power god.

That is exactly what Oates's work expresses just now: a sense that American life is taking some of us by the throat. "Too much" is happening; many will disappear. Above all, and most ominously, hers is a world in which our own people, and not just peasants in Vietnam, get "wasted." There is a constant sense of drift, deterioration, the end of things, that contrasts violently with the era of "high art" and the once-fond belief in immortality through art. Oates is someone plainly caught up in this "avalanche" of time.

[1973]

JAMES WRIGHT:
THE GIFT OF FEELING

———•◆•———

Anyone who has so much as looked into James Wright's poetry knows that he did not consider himself a lucky man. Like so many gifted literary children of working-class parents, he grew up feeling apart from a beloved father—this father toiled fifty years in the Hazel Atlas Glass Company in Ohio. At the same time Wright felt that his father's patient, stoic, laborious life had imparted to that life a virtue and dignity which the son, with the febrile idealism of American scholar-intellectuals, did not associate with the academy or the intense rivalries of poetry.

Wright, who was born in 1927 and died this year, knew the guilt at having departed Martin's Ferry and the industrial quagmire of the Ohio River. He was unable to love "Ohio" (a central term in his poetry that did not always require further description), yet was unable to remember anything else so vividly. All this fed a sense of uneasiness that made Wright as a poet hearken to the now scorned example of Edwin Arlington Robinson as well as the straightforward personal style of Hardy and the lyrical riddles of Frost. When Wright began his career after World War II, the going style was mandarin, heavy with symbolism, decorative, on the model of Robert Lowell's "Lord Weary's Castle" and of Lowell's mentor, Allen Tate. This was an upper-class poetry, quasi-Catholic though never as serenely devotional in the late Eliot manner as it wanted to be. It was not what Wright set his heart on—a style more like "sweet Roethke," as he called him, fiercely stoic Frost, crabbedly mournful but brightly plain Hardy.

These were poets who felt themselves under a curse—whether of godlessness or of the lovelessness that has less to do with one's personal fortunes in love than with a universe obviously born by accident, riddled with mistakes. Wright was as plain as Hardy and Frost, if not so bold in asserting the accursed time in which he was born to set it right, the obvious disparity between the universe and one's own sacred *me*. The total unrelation between them is the anguish of a godless universe. But personal unluckiness, as so many feel it despite a world that enchants us with the "supreme fiction" of poetry, stayed with Wright to the end. Poetry made the world habitable but poetry did not lighten or redeem it. (In a time when our immediate environment, the political world, seems so totally out of our control, it is startling to find that ever-busy factory called the American university absorbed in the idealization of poetry, especially of a difficult, putatively religious poetry that fascinates students brought up on the junk food of their daily commercial culture.)

Wright's poetry was obstinately plain—not in feeling certainly, where it could be sly, elusive, heartbroken, and sardonic in the same flat, Ohio voice, but plain in phrase, line, syntax, imagery. His poetry was a subdued cry of homelessness, longing, guilt, of fraternity with migrants, criminals, the murderers Caryl Chessman and George Doty, gnarled old Ohio and West Virginia factory workers and farmers. One particular feature of Wright's poetry (in this he reminds me of what the miner's son D. H. Lawrence was able to do with the surroundings of Nottingham) is the way in which a poet coming out of the blasted countryside of industrial America was still able to join the glass and tire factories to what is left of rural Ohio. That mad industrial vortex was once the barrier between industrial North and rural South; toxified as it now may be, the Ohio Valley evoked in "Three Sentences for a Dead Swan" the American mythology of a lost world:

1.
There they are now,
The wings,
And I heard them beginning to starve
Between two cold white shadows,

But I dreamed they would rise
Together,
My black Ohioan swan.

2.

Now one after another I let the black scales fall
From the beautiful black spine
Of this lonesome dragon that is born on the earth at last,
My black fire,
Ovoid of my darkness,
Machine-gunned and shattered hillsides of yellow trees
In the autumn of my blood where the apples
Purse their wild lips and smirk knowingly
That my love is dead.

3.

Here, carry his splintered bones
Slowly, slowly
Back into the
Tar and chemical strangled tomb,
The strange water, the
Ohio River, that is no tomb to
Rise from the dead
From.

The naked feeling of Wright's poetry! The modesty, the tormented quietness that holds it together as much as the metric frame! The wandering, the ever-present loneliness, a poetry essentially without "personae" yet where the poet's own cry is never glibly one of self. There is the last stanza of "The Minneapolis Poem":

I want to be lifted up
By some great white bird unknown to the police,
And soar for a thousand miles and be carefully hidden
Modest and golden as one last corn grain,
Stored with the secrets of the wheat and the mysterious lives
Of the unnamed poor.

So much ever-present feeling is not in everybody and is not for everybody, whatever generous Jim Wright with his natural American feeling for vox populi may have thought. Feeling is a gift. It was distinctively Wright's gift. Even when he added himself to the long, long American list of writer-drinkers, it was clear that he drank not, as so many American bores do, to make themselves interesting to themselves, but to lift himself out of the pit. Then he could make fun of the hangover—which neither Hart Crane nor Dylan Thomas could—as not just penitential but a stage of new perceptions. In "Two Hangovers" (from *The Branch Will Not Break*), he carefully notes:

I still feel half drunk,
And all of those old women beyond my window,
Are hunching toward the graveyard.
Drunk, mumbling Hungarian,
The sun staggers in,
And his big stupid face pitches
Into the stove.
For two hours I have been dreaming
Of green butterflies searching for diamonds
In coal seams;
And children chasing each other for a game
Through the hills of fresh graves.
But the sun has come home from the sea,
And a sparrow outside
Sings of the Hanna Coal Co. and the dead moon.
The filaments of cold light bulbs tremble
In music like delicate birds.
Ah, turn it off.

To be in one body like that and to dream of another is to have a delicious sense of irony. Wright's most famous pieces, like his "Two Poems" about his fellow Buckeye Warren Gamaliel Harding, show what delighted so many of his students at Hunter College, where he taught for many years, and turned them to poetry as a mode of thinking more lasting than the usual subjection to a subjective emotion. Only a truly witty poet could have described Harding in the 1920 campaign as having "the vaguely stunned smile/ Of a lucky man."

And only a youth saturated in Ohio folklore could have written, forty years after Harding:

> How many honey locusts have fallen,
> Pitched rootlong into the open graves of strip mines,
> Since the First World War ended
> And Wilson the gaunt deacon jogged sullenly
> Into silence?
> Tonight,
> The cancerous ghosts of old con men
> Shed their leaves,
> For a proud man,
> Lost between the turnpike near Cleveland
> And the chiropractors' signs looming among dead mulberry trees,
> There is no place left to go
> But home.
>
> "Warren lacks mentality," one of his friends said.
> Yet he was beautiful, he was the snowfall
> Turned to white stallions standing still
> Under dark elm trees.
>
> He died in public. He claimed the secret right
> To be ashamed.

This is poetry that goes straight to my heart and mind, the interweaving of the old mischievous American plainness with poetry's genius for the unexpected, all in the flat Ohio voice that can be heard in adjoining West Virginia as the laconic mountaineer's voice. (Wright's people were southerners, and fought for the Confederacy.) His obstinate plainness of style served cleverly in translation to bring out the variety of highly charged poets from Goethe to Georg Trakl and César Vallejo.

Wright's life was not an easy one; it had enormous pools of suffering in it, and he was unlucky even in his slow strangulation from throat cancer. But there was a characteristic unwillingness to let go; he was working on a new book up to the moment he lost consciousness.

[1980]

VI

———◆———

DEPARTED FRIENDS

THE INTOXICATING
SENSE OF POSSIBILITY:
THOMAS JEFFERSON AT
MONTICELLO

—— ·◆· ——

By the end of 1781 the long-drawn-out war for American independence had finally come to an end on a battlefield in Virginia overlooking the Atlantic Ocean. "There is something absurd in supposing a continent to be governed by an island," Thomas Paine wrote. Thomas Jefferson, more aware than any other leader of the Revolution that his country was indeed a continent, would soon be going abroad for the young republic. But because a secretary to the French Legation in Philadelphia had passed a series of questions "relating to the laws, institutions, geography, climate, flora, and fauna" of Mr. Jefferson's native state, he took time to write the one book he would publish in his tumultuously crowded life, *Notes on the State of Virginia.*

At Monticello, his "little mountain," the hilltop mansion he had designed and helped to build overlooking the Blue Ridge Mountains to the west, Jefferson now summed up all the knowledge available about a province that was believed in its founding charter (1609) to extend "from sea to sea." In 1781 it actually extended from the Atlantic to the Appalachians, and included what are now West Virginia and Kentucky, a roughly triangular area that Jefferson too generously thought a third larger than Great Britain plus Ireland. He proudly called it "My Country." In twenty-three chapters he described Virginia's boundaries, rivers, seaports, mountains, cascades, aborigines, laws, manners.

Nor did he overlook "proceedings as to Tories." For him the war against England was a war against the old order prevailing everywhere in Europe.

Serenely neoclassical Monticello owes much to the Renaissance architect Palladio, more to Thomas Jefferson. It awes visitors as a triumph of taste, but it was built to serve the boundless curiosity and activity of Thomas Jefferson—architect, inventor and experimenter extraordinary, agriculturist, natural philosopher, political philosopher, bibliophile, musician, lawyer, wartime governor, soon to be minister to France, secretary of state, vice president, and third president of the United States.

Monticello, stately as it looks, an eighteenth-century "picture" of a great landowner's benevolent authority, was a plantation seat that had to double as the workshop of a universal savant who lived in the middle of a great forest. Planning his own house, laying out its grounds, inventing appliances and creature comforts unthinkable to primitive Virginia, Jefferson on a grand scale was playing Adam, Prospero, Robinson Crusoe—owner and master of everything he surveyed, the first man on the place. This almost biblical sense of authority was to lead him as president to send out Lewis and Clark on a "scientific" survey of the land from the Missouri River to the Pacific, preparing its inevitable absorption into the continental United States. He drew into tiers the map of new states in the Midwest and gave names to ten of them.

The great dome over the mansion at Monticello can make a visitor think that Jefferson's intellect is still presiding over the estate he laid out in every particular. He put a similar dome over his favorite creation, the University of Virginia, one even over his modest summer retreat at Poplar Forest. He was the proprietor of Monticello, 10,000 acres, and a hundred slaves: many were trained to carpentry, cabinetmaking, housebuilding, weaving, tailoring, shoemaking. He imported the first threshing machine known in Virginia, invented the first scientific plow. Along the way he was a prime inventor of the United States. Of course it was Jefferson who wrote the Declaration of Independence. No country had deliberately created itself before. No such separation of church and state had been known in any country before Jefferson wrote the Virginia Statute of Religious Freedom. If Washington, the nation's capital, reflects the power of the United States in its solid mass of cold white Roman "temples," Monticello will always reflect the intoxicating sense of possibility on which the nation was founded.

Jefferson's biographer, Dumas Malone, notes that no one before Jefferson had thought of setting a plantation at such a height. The woods were thick, grading had to be done in stubborn soil, and everything had to be carried up a mountain. But Jefferson

> had not disciplined his mind to the loss of imagination. . . . His eye, like his mind, sought an extended view. From this spot he could see to the eastward an expanse of forested country, rolling like the sea: and to the westward he could look across the treetops to a mountain wall of lavender and blue. . . . The country was little marred by the hand of man as yet and the prospect was majestic.

On the estate, the open grounds to the west seemed to call for shrubbery: Jefferson wanted it to remain an asylum for wild animals, excepting only beasts of prey. He thought of procuring a buck elk to be monarch of the wood.

Notes on the State of Virginia, written to satisfy the curiosity of the Old World, is alive with the glow Jefferson felt in reporting everything available about that new situation in the West. "My Country." He modified Palladio to make more window space and terraced roofs looking out to the Blue Ridge. Although he had studied at the College of William and Mary and had trained as a lawyer in the old colonial capital of Williamsburg on the coast, Jefferson was by birth and inclination a product of the Piedmont and what another southern writer, William Faulkner, would call the "unstoried wilderness." Monticello was the creation of a patrician who was more a political visionary and a practical observer than any other Virginian of his class. Jefferson identified himself not with the English institutions at the tidewater but with the mountain country and beyond.

In *Notes on the State of Virginia* he listed not only the great rivers of Virginia that rush down to Chesapeake Bay—the Rappahannock, the York, the James, the Potomac—but also the Ohio, "the most beautiful river on earth, the periodically flooded Mississippi, the muddy Missouri, the gentle Illinois, the lovely Wabash, and a dozen other streams." Much that went into the building of Monticello Jefferson devised and helped to manufacture himself, as was natural to pioneer country. His prime sense of being a new man in a new country imparted a certain rapture to the political argument behind the Declaration of Independence. It appealed to "self-evident" truths, such as are proclaimed by Nature. When it became necessary for one people to dissolve the political band connecting them with another, they could "assume among the powers of the earth the separate and equal station to which the Laws of Nature and of Nature's God entitle them." Abraham Lincoln formed his political philosophy around the Declaration of Independence. It was to encourage many an American visionary to find on the frontier "self-evident" justification for his political actions.

One of these visionaries was John Brown, who in 1859 tried to stir up a slave insurrection by attacking the United States arsenal at Harpers Ferry in the Blue Ridge Mountains at the confluence of the Potomac and Shenandoah Rivers. Long before this extraordinary site was called Harpers Ferry and before the slavery issue became "the fireball in the night" that frightened Jefferson into the realization that "this government, the world's best hope," might not last, *Notes on the State of Virginia* described it as if no one had been there before Thomas Jefferson:

> The passage of the Potomac through the Blue Ridge is, perhaps, one of the most stupendous scenes in nature. You stand in a very high point of land. On your right comes up the Shenandoah, having ranged along the foot of the mountain an hundred miles to seek a vent. On your left approaches the Potomac, in quest of a passage also. In the moment of their junction they rush together against the mountain, render it asunder and pass off to the sea. The first glance of this scene hurries our senses into the opinion that this earth has been created in time, that the mountains were formed first, that the rivers began to flow afterwards, that in this place, particularly, they have been dammed up by the Blue Ridge of mountains, and have formed an ocean which filled the whole valley; that continuing to rise they have at length broken over at this spot, and have torn the mountain down from its summit to its base. . . .
>
> The distinct finishing which nature has given to the picture is of a very different character. . . . For the mountain being cloven asunder, she presents to your eye, through the cleft, a small catch of smooth blue horizon, at an infinite distance in the plain country, inviting you, as it were, from the riot and tumult roaring around, to pass through the breach and participate of the calm below. Here the eye ultimately composes itself. . . . You cross the Potomac above the junction, pass

along its side through the base of the mountain for three miles, its terrible precipices hanging in fragments over you, and within about twenty miles reach Frederictown and the fine country around that. This scene is worth a voyage across the Atlantic. . . .

Jefferson, like a good American, takes it for granted that [in Bishop Berkeley's words] "the Force of Art by Nature seems outdone." What excites him is Nature charging about, erupting and breaking through the expected, on land very near his own. Nothing could be less like the experience of an eighteenth-century Englishman on the Grand Tour. This is "Nature's Nation," and Jefferson's very own.[. . .]

The characteristically American note in Jefferson's description of the rivers meeting at the Blue Ridge, rendering the mountain "asunder" is one that dominates all early descriptions of western landscape. Astonishment, pride, "God's own country." But deeper and actually more lasting has been the sense of creation in the making. Jefferson exults in a sight for the eyes that is a continuous force. Jefferson the natural philosopher investigated Nature for his own survival as well as for curiosity's sake. But in recognizing from "the first glance of this scene . . . that this earth has been created in time, that the mountains were formed first, that the rivers began to flow afterwards," he offers us the process of creation made visible. Nothing about the New World was to put such a spell on writers, whether they saw America or not, as the fond belief that it represented the oldest world, pristine. It was the beginning of things, without man to sully the picture.

John Locke, who never saw it but needed the metaphor, roundly declared in 1690, "Thus in the beginning all the world was America, for nothing like money was known." America as perfect archaism, the world still showing its origins, was to haunt Europeans and Americans alike. "That naked country," as Charles II indifferently called it on the occasion of an early colony's rebellion against a royal governor, opened up sites for exploration that united geology to natural religion in a way especially pleasing to deism—God reduced to mere process. There was a myth about America before it had a name and was a definite place—it was what lay beyond the known world. It somehow remained beyond the known world to many who uneasily settled on its "nakedness." The Mexican writer Carlos Fuentes said that the Old World discovered the New but then had been unable to imagine it.

The world-transforming role Jefferson assigned to the "American experiment" was duplicated by the transformation in Nature he could see going on in the mountains of Virginia. *Notes on the State of Virginia* breathes the excitement of some fabulous first encounter. This recurrent thrill of discovery was to be the secret of the prime American books, from *Walden* and *Leaves of Grass* and *Moby-Dick* to *Huckleberry Finn*. Thoreau, visiting Maine in 1846, saw "the raw materials of a planet."

> Perhaps I most fully realized that this was primeval, untamed, and forever untamable *Nature*, or whatever else men call it, while coming down this part of the mountain. We were passing over "Burnt Lands," burnt by lightning, perchance, though they showed no recent marks of fire, hardly so much as a charred stump. . . . When I reflected what man, what brother or sister or kinsman of our race made it and claimed it, I expected the proprietor to rise up and dispute my passage. It is difficult to conceive of a region uninhabited by man. We habitually presume his presence and influence everywhere. And yet we have not seen pure Nature, unless we have seen her thus vast and drear and unhuman, though in the midst of cities. Nature was here something savage and awful, though beautiful. I looked with awe at the grounds I trod on, to see what the Powers had made there. . . . This was that Earth of which we have heard, made out of Chaos and Old Night. . . . Man was not to be associated with it. It was Matter, vast, terrific—not this Mother Earth that we have heard of.

Nothing like this had ever been seen before! And Jefferson on his acres all the time looking west to the Blue Ridge was (as William Faulkner liked to say of his imaginary creation Yoknapatawpha County) the sole owner and proprietor. Jefferson's " 'own country,' " says Dumas Malone, "was almost the only scene of his activity until he had entered into middle life, and if he did not know more about it than anybody else, he described it in his *Notes on the State of Virginia* more fully than anyone else had ever done." He was happy to depend on a map of Virginia that his own father had drawn. The sober tone of the book (Jefferson had been invited to write the article on the United States for Diderot's great *Encyclopédie*) reveals a man who has become enamored of his subject by possessing it.

Whitman, unrolling the American scene before him in *Song of Myself,* was to say, "*I am the man, I suffer'd, I was there.*" Jefferson describing Virginia is certainly "there." The book is full of Jefferson's glee in being able to describe a wholly new world no one before him has so thoroughly enumerated, classified, documented in the most systematic up-to-the-minute way, with all the scientific and statistical resources of the day open to him.

America as enduring myth, a second chance for mankind, was not lost on the president-philosopher who in his first inaugural address (1800) was to describe the United States as "the world's best hope. . . . Kindly separated by nature and a wide ocean from the exterminating havoc of one-quarter of the globe . . . a chosen country, with room enough for our descendants to the thousandth and thousandth generation. . . ." But Jefferson's belief that, in the New World, Nature gladly yielded its secrets transcended every myth; he incorporated the native landscape into his passion for science.[. . .]

[1988]

EMERSON: THE PRIEST DEPARTS, THE DIVINE LITERATUS COMES

———•◆•———

[. . . .]

On September 9, 1832, the twenty-nine-year-old minister of Second Church in Boston preached to his regretful congregation a farewell sermon in which he explained why he could not regard the communion service as ordained by scripture. The Lord's Supper was nothing more than the Jewish Passover feast. Emerson then resigned his pastorate. By the end of the year he was off to Europe; like Melville's Ahab, he sailed on a Christmas Day. When he returned almost a year later, he was ready to publish his first book, *Nature*. Emerson's real ministry had just begun.

The formal grounds on which Emerson resigned his pastorate were hardly enough to explain his leaving the church *and* the ministry. He had really left all formal religion behind him. Emerson was beginning to understand that total "self-reliance"—from his innermost spiritual promptings—would be his career and his fate. The death from tuberculosis of his wife, Ellen, at nineteen, after less than two years of marriage, had increased his intellectual isolation and downright boredom as he went his clerical rounds. He, too, had been in danger from tuberculosis, the New England calamity of the time that was to kill two of his brothers. He and Ellen had loved each other wildly amid her many frightening "scaldings" of blood. He never got over Ellen. Losing her made him even more impatient with his old way of life, destroyed many clerical cautions.

Emerson always maintained a preacher's professional unction, but any established creed he found intolerable. Remote and a shade too literary as he often seemed, he awed a majority of his congregation. They pressed him to stay, kept putting off acceptance of his resignation; for a year after he left he continued to receive his salary. Emerson was always to have a positive effect on people who did not know what he was talking about.

If it was hard for Second Church to let its minister go, he also recognized his going as strange. The rumor in Boston was that he had gone mad. The former president John Quincy Adams was to charge that

a young man named Ralph Waldo Emerson . . . after failing in the every-day vocations of a Unitarian preacher and schoolmaster, starts a new doctrine of transcendentalism, declares all the old revelations superannuated and worn out, and announces the approach of new revelations and prophecies. Garrison and the non-resistant abolitionists, Brownson and the Marat democrats, phrenology and animal magnetism, all come in, furnishing each some plausible rascality as an ingredient for the bubbling cauldron of religion and politics.

No one had ever been more truly born to the ministry than Emerson, and when had an Emerson not been in the ministry? For nine successive generations in New England, Emersons had been ministers. To go over the formal record of Emerson's leaving—his farewell sermon on the Lord's Supper, the affectionate letter of resignation, the reluctant vote to accept the resignation— is to summon up the departure scene on an old Greek frieze. A young man is leaving his family; they hold out their hands to him; though already on his way, he looks back to them. Even after Emerson's resignation had been accepted he was occasionally to appear in his old pulpit and many another. "I like a church; I like a cowl," he was to begin a famous poem in 1839. "Yet not for all his faith can see/Would I that cowlèd churchman be."

"In Massachusetts," Emerson wrote in 1839, "a number of young and adult persons are at this moment the subject of a revolution."

Not in churches, or in courts, or in large assemblies; not in solemn holidays, where men were met in festal dress, have these pledged themselves to new life, but in lonely and obscure places, in servitude, in solitude, in solitary compunctions and shames and fears, in disappointments, in diseases, trudging beside the team in the dusty road, or drudging, a hireling in other men's cornfields, schoolmasters who teach a few children rudiments for a pittance, ministers of small parishes of the obscurer sects, lone women in dependent condition, matrons and young maidens, rich and poor, beautiful and hard-favored, without conceit or proclamation of any kind, have silently given in their several adherence to a new hope.

These people were Christians who no longer needed a church—moralists and pietists, earnestly independent souls in the oldest Protestant tradition of the "priesthood of all believers." They were not wholly emancipated, like the George Sand of whom Emerson noted enviously that she "owes to her birth in France her entire freedom from the cant and snuffle of our dead Christianity." Emerson was not the first and certainly not the last minister to make conscience and imagination his church. He was simply more gifted, startlingly the literatus—unlike George Ripley, who was to establish Brook Farm and later become *The New York Tribune*'s literary critic under Horace Greeley, or the passionate reformer Theodore Parker, who was for the most part excluded from the churches. Emerson's marked literary grace in the pulpit had created a bond between him and the congregation. This accord was based more on the man's extraordinary presence than on an understanding of his mind; it foretells the respect his lecture audiences were to feel for the "mystic" who impressed them by talking over their heads. After he had spoken for the first time on the West Coast in a San Francisco church, a paper reported, "All left the church feeling that an elegant tribute had been paid to the creative genius of the Great First Cause, and that a masterly use of the English language had contributed to that end."

Emerson's estrangement from doctrinal Christianity was absolute. All his teaching as a sage-at-large and the exaltation that can still be felt behind the style of *Nature, The American Scholar,* the Divinity School Address, "Self-Reliance," "The Poet," reflect the "dignity" that impressed even a hostile T. S. Eliot and that rests on the minister's revelation that he did not need a church. Not "God" was dead but the church! And since the church was the Past, it was really only the Past that was "dead." Freed from obedience to superstition, dogma, hierarchy, and Sunday routine, man on the crest of his inborn faith would find in himself all that men had ever meant by God and thereby become more-than-man-had-ever-been: types of Prometheus and Zarathustra and, from the mountaintop of the Superman or Hero, deliverers of mankind.

New England as a society had been founded on the church. Pilgrims and Puritans had arrived as bodies of organized belief. Amidst the solitude and fright of the wild western shore, it was always to the church, the essential "body" of believers, the church as emblem, justification, release, that Emerson's ancestors had clung. The minister was their visible connection to the faith. Wherever radical Protestantism returned to the austerity and directness of the Gospels, it identified the whole people as the "Lord's People." The preacher reinforced this identity. By giving out the Word to his people, he assured continuity to their spiritual life, became the teacher of his tribe, a "vessel" to all those dependent on his soul-restoring eloquence.

Emerson looked as if he had been born to this role. His remoteness assured him of success even on the lecture platform. The classic New England minister was not a sweaty actor like Henry Ward Beecher but, like Hawthorne's Dimmesdale, an oracle suitably distant from the souls he never ceased to instruct. Emerson lamented his inability to reach people easily but was not downcast by this traditional failing. He looked the Puritan minister in his "lofty" bearing, his very leanness—the Yankee leanness which someone said made him look like a scruple. The photographs of him in his prime show a face so assured that it now looks archaic. William James eventually came to adore and even to "represent" Emerson in the succession of American thinkers. But in 1874 he wrote that Emerson's "refined idiocy seems as if it must be affectation." The contribution of spirituality to so much self-respect was widely noted. Condescension toward those lacking in grace was also marked. The serenity famous in every decade seemed impermeable to admirers and suspicious critics. "O you man without a handle!" the elder Henry James burst out. "Shall one never be able to help himself out of you, according to his needs, and be dependent only upon your fitful tippings-up?" An inhuman equanimity continued into his letters, which always tried to correct the general impression of his remoteness. Every report of his conversation is surprising—he is cagey, clever, unweariedly performing.

Emerson was to have the greatest possible influence on his contemporaries, on other writers, on the myth of the American as being uniquely free. Whitman was eventually let down by Emerson's prudish objections to *Leaves of Grass*, but he would have been nothing without Emerson's presence in the American picture. He sized up Emerson's temperament as "almost ideal." Talking to Horace Traubel in Camden, the old man appreciated in Emerson a "transparency" properly mysterious.

> His quality, his meaning has the quality of the light of day, which startles nobody. You cannot put your finger upon it yet there is nothing more palpable, nothing more wonderful, nothing more vital and refreshing. There are some things in the expression of this philosoph, this poet, that are full mates of the best, the perennial masters, and will so stand in fame and the centuries. America in the future, in her long train of poets and writers, while knowing more vehement and luxuriant ones, will, I think, acknowledge nothing nearer [than] this man, the actual beginner of the whole procession—and certainly nothing purer, cleaner, sweeter, more canny, none, after all, more thoroughly her own and native. The most exquisite taste and caution are in him, always saving his feet from passing beyond the limits, for he is transcendental of limits, and you see underneath the rest a secret proclivity, American maybe, to dare and violate and make escapades.

Emerson left the church because he was happy with his mind as it was. He could subsist outside the church because, living on his mind and being responsive to its every prompting, he was satisfied that the "active soul" was an actual mirror of the world. The Greeks may have discovered that the "world" replicates the human mind; Emerson lived this fact without philosophy's sense that perception can be duplicitous. The "soul" or "mind" had for him such total access to reality that it virtually replaced it. Nature is there to serve man. Mind is everywhere the master. The soul as pure perception, pathway into All Things, became for Emerson the *universe* as an "open secret." Once he discovered this secret, he saw that there was no secret. The soul was not just the perfect knower but the real medium of existence. We live in disembodied consciousness as God does. No wonder that John Jay Chapman, who thought Emerson the last barrier to the mob spirit, admitted that if an inhabitant of another planet should visit the earth, he would receive, on the whole, a truer notion of human life by attending an Italian opera than he would by reading Emerson's volumes. He would learn from the Italian opera that there were two sexes; and this, after all, is probably the fact with which the education of such a stranger ought to begin.

The French biologist Jacques Monod attributed the success of religion to the fact that it makes it possible for us to love the world. Emerson, by placing the world at the disposal of our "ripe perceptive powers," certainly made it lovable.

This was a creative mind's sweet illusion—the world is forever moving in the direction of our thought. For Emerson everything came back to the personal sense of power that seized the universe at large as its corollary and friend. "Nature," everything outside of us, waiting on us alone, perceived and possessed by us alone, easily makes itself known. God speaks through us alone, so He must be in us. We share His power. Even to radical Protestantism, whose hope for emancipation from worldly institutions like the church was finally achieved (and perhaps terminated) in Emerson, his insistence on "the infinitude of the private mind" ("the only doctrine I have ever taught") was understandably shocking. In his intoxication with the religious sufficiency of his creative powers Emerson paraded before all men a doctrine sufficient only to great creative talent. The farmers and shopkeepers at his lectures were no doubt glad to hear that the individual in America had no limit but the sky.

Emerson aroused something more specific in creative minds from Matthew Arnold to Nietzsche. In America, Thoreau and Whitman, reverberating to Emerson's revelation, were the nearest to him, the most gifted and lasting in the American line that took the unlimited self as its greatest resource. Thoreau told Moncure Conway that he found in Emerson "the same perfection as the objects he studied in external nature, his ideals real and exact." Matthew Arnold was moved to write on the flyleaf of Emerson's *Essays:*

Strong is Soul, and wise, and beautiful:
The seeds of godlike power are in us still:
Gods are we, Bards, Saints, Heroes, if we will—

(Only Melville among American writers would have thought of Arnold's next line: "Dumb judges, answer, truth or mockery?")

Emerson naturally associated his gospel with a great Protestant tradition of independence. He would have associated himself gladly with Keats's letter of May 3, 1818, on the peculiarly Protestant virtues of Milton and Wordsworth:

> In [Milton's] time Englishmen were just emancipated from a great superstition and Men had got hold of certain points and resting places in reasoning which were too newly born to be doubted, and too much opposed by the Mass of Europe not to be thought etherial and authentically divine.... The Reformation produced such immediate and great benefits, that Protestantism was considered under the immediate eye of heaven....

And Emerson would have sniffed at T. S. Eliot's condemnation of D. H. Lawrence (a rebel against the Congregationalist Church, like so many New Englanders):

> We are not concerned with the author's beliefs, but with the orthodoxy of sensibility and with the vast sense of tradition.... And Lawrence is, for my purposes, an almost perfect example of the heretic.... The point is that Lawrence started life wholly free from any restriction of tradition or institution, that he had no guidance except the Inner Light, the most untrustworthy and deceitful guide that ever offered itself to wandering humanity.

Emerson, relying on a broad tradition of religious independence, may have carried it so far as to end its connection with religion. His revelation—which became his aesthetic as well as his religion—was that the important things come easily to the man who just waits for them. God is easy to achieve—"It," the "Over-Soul," the "First Cause." Lawrence, though he recognized the "inrushes" Emerson got from his God, laughed that Emerson was connected only on "the Ideal phone." This may explain Emerson's hold on skeptics.

Emerson provided relief from the commercial round and from the most politicized society of the nineteenth century. His appeal, like that of so many rare spirits in the history of religion, was that he was altogether exceptional. Neither Thoreau nor Whitman, nor any one of his many acolytes and admirers, resembles Emerson in his gift of total conviction. William James in a positivist climate had great trouble finding objective reasons for his religious promptings. He was to conclude in *The Varieties of Religious Experience* (1902) that such promptings must not be denied as evidence of God's existence. From despising Emerson's attitude of fixed benevolence, James came to admire him, even to envy him. Religiously, Dr. William James the professional scientist could never go the whole way. Emerson began with such an absolute of personal conviction that he left himself no room in which to develop.

Emerson's God-intoxication was communicated to most people without his performing miracles. Emerson never admitted—he never understood—that so much belief in the soul is a gift. He never doubted that his conviction must pass into his audience and become the gospel of a New World. But was it "religion" or the "word" that he imparted? Was he more the evangel or the always immaculate stylist? Near the end of the twentieth century the rebellious Catholic theologian Hans Kung was to concede that if his was the church of the sacraments, Protestantism was "the church of the word." Emerson would have liked that. "Golden sentences" came out of his mouth even when he was dying. He had been trained in pulpit eloquence, of course, but his innate artist's sense of elegance and discrimination, rhetorical strategy and effect, gave him a particular taste for prophetic upwelling and scriptural cut and thrust. He confidently assumed that "soul" is the same as style, for he was so natural a stylist that conventional writers could be put down as conventional souls. No one can miss in the "saintly" Emerson the immodesty of a superb artist on familiar terms with inspiration and thus with "God": "The maker of a sentence, like the other artist, launches out into the infinite and builds a road into Chaos and Old Night, and is followed by those who hear him with something of a wild, creative delight."

How spontaneously Emerson reported the explosion of spirit behind his appearance of restraint. The connection between faith and creativity is now so dim that we jealously wonder what Yeats meant when he said that "belief makes the mind abundant." Emerson himself no longer fortifies a free personal religion. God is dead even for Allen Ginsberg. Emerson may have helped to kill "self-reliance" in religion by dispensing it too confidently from his own subjectivity. But he did recognize himself as a revenant from early ages of faith—a primordial, "aboriginal" kind of early Christian, thoroughly tuned in to his unconscious, who knew how to awaken dead souls, to *strike*, as only the God-intoxicated can.

"I like," he wrote in his journal, "dry light, and hard clouds, hard expressions, and hard manners." If Emerson looked and sounded the sage (the wise man of the American tribe who showed his ever more secular countrymen where to look for faith), it was because of his genius for compression. He reduced his style, like his life, to fundamentals. Unlike his literary son Thoreau, he did not train himself to live the absolute. Emerson lived in his study and in mild walks around Concord farms. Thoreau constantly dared himself to invade and master inhospitable country. Thoreau showed a lifelong need to *live* nature, to roll himself up in it, to enjoy "to the full" woods and fields as his erotic complement. He carried everywhere—even in Concord village, where he despised his neighbors for not being spiritual enough—the myth so dear to the American heart. The solitary man is the virtuous man as well as the more curious explorer of existence. A key sentence in Thoreau's lifelong journal: "The world appears to me uninhabited." Another: "It was not always dry land where we dwell." Emerson gave Thoreau and Whitman the satisfaction—so strange to the European mind—of being not merely an original but the incarnation of originality.

Even Whitman, so amazed by his gifts that he pretended he had invented them—even Whitman, with his posturing and his need to sell himself—made use of the American penchant for turning oneself into Adam. In America, Adam was not just the first man but sometimes the only man, the true God-man, Osiris and Christ and other masquerades for Whitman in his gallery. We know that Whitman was original, for his own literary culture resembles a musty secondhand bookstore. (Whatever is not firsthand in Whitman is fake.) His greatest lines are truly "a song of myself."

Emerson's compound of ideas—taken from Plato and neo-Platonists, Kant, Coleridge, Wordsworth, Carlyle—could have made him just another New England minister in the "ice house of Unitarianism" trying to keep up an intellectual front in the face of religious doubt. In fact Emerson impressed even the most hostile critics by his lonely certitude. Originality of thought Emerson did not claim or even want. Nor was it authority of style, which he took for granted, that made Emerson the teacher of the tribe and "the actual beginner of the whole procession." It was his paramount discovery that in an increasingly faithless world he possessed the gift of faith. Belief was something else, formal, a creed; belief usually owed everything to someone else. It was secondary to the heart's natural loyalties. Though Emerson's fame and influence came from the joyous ease with which he imparted the "open secret of the universe," the nature of his appeal, attested even by people who did not claim to understand him, was that it was himself he was imparting. He was the enraptured realization that no one *now* was in this original relation to nature and a new country.

Emerson as an eponym for freshness, discovery, openness, for all that was hopeful in his country and his century, has survived his actual message because people can still take from him the cardinal theme: a brave beginning. And no one can read *Nature* or his early essays and journals without sharing his thrill that in this great, intelligent, sensual, and avaricious America, "glad to the brink of fear," he recognized in himself a vessel of the Holy Spirit. The thrill, the positive exultation in all the early writings, lies not in any delusion of intellectual originality but in the primacy that he shared with Nature and America itself.

America itself was the original. The confrontation with it by even the most seasoned men—explorers, missionaries, worldly philosophers, and cynics—made things new. When John Locke said, "In the beginning all things were America," that was a figure of speech. But the constant raid on the vast emptiness made a person of Nature for even the practical and superstitious. Nature was wild but waiting to be exploited; as Emerson noted contentedly, it exists to serve. Many men were to make practical use of the unique opportunity; many more, expecting bonanza, fell by the wayside. (It was also typical of the Yankee Emerson to note that the actual founders of small towns in the West invariably failed.) But the first men of literary genius—Emerson, Thoreau, Whitman, and Melville—characteristically turned *their* raid on Nature into a book, the world at large into a fable. In their own mythology they acted out the role of primal man. Emerson in his journal, 1840: "I dreamed that I floated at will in the great Ether, and I saw this world floating also not far off, but diminished to the size of an apple. Then an angel took it in his hand and brought it to me and said, 'This must thou eat.' And I ate the world."

The genius of primitive Christianity lent itself to Emerson's belief that his soul was the center of a cosmic drama. John Milton seems to have infused his spacious mind into American Puritans whose influence over their new country he could not have predicted. Emerson certainly felt himself to be of the greatest possible importance to the cosmos. Which may be why he conceived of empty nature surrounding him as the unutterable stretches of space through which Satan fell. The American as "first man" was a hero of this drama because of all that he could lay his hand to. The gift of conviction that made a new age possible occurred for Emerson in the instant connection between faith and the word. The word alighting in his mind was more than a signal and symbol of faith; it was evidence that his faith was real, that it lived in the word as well as by the word. By the word he passed out faith. And in this century of the word, when literature was still central to thinking men, the word was open to all.

Emerson's sense of his own authority—so strong that one can hardly miss the exultation behind it—has been dismissed by conservative critics who charge that Transcendentalists in the age of Jackson felt themselves to be superfluous. In fact they were simply out of touch with the hard new boisterous times of democratic emergence. Emerson's contempt for the organized church still gives offense; one churchly literary critic was capable of saying in the 1950s that Emerson was responsible for Hitler. Not to see that Emerson's life work began in a religious crisis that he shared with the age, that the stream of his writings began because by leaving the church he felt that he also had a solution for others, is to miss Emerson's central need to overcome *all* skepticism.

As there was God before the church existed, so God might be rediscovered by striking out on one's own. The Kingdom of God is within you or it is nowhere. Tolstoy as a young officer during the Crimean War wrote:

> A conversation about Divinity and Faith has suggested to me a great, stupendous idea, to the realization of which I feel capable of devoting my life. That idea is the founding of a new religion corresponding to the present stage of mankind: the religion of Christ but purged of dogmas and absolutism—a practical religion, not promising future bliss but giving bliss on earth.

[1984]

THOREAU AND
AMERICAN POWER

———•◆•———

[....]

Thoreau was always a young man until he deteriorated suddenly in his late thirties. He was certainly oriented, as Thornton Wilder put it, to childhood. All transcendentalists had a way of peaking and then fading. Perhaps Thoreau anticipated this when he addressed his most famous book to "poor students." *Walden* is read mostly in schools, and Thoreau's most admiring readers, young or missing their youth, respond to the inner feeling of youth in its pages—the restlessness, the peremptory impatience with authority, the expectation of some different world just over the horizon. Students recognize in Thoreau a classic who is near their own age and condition. All his feelings are absolutes, as his political ideas will be. There is none of that mocking subtlety, that winning ability to live with contradiction, that one finds in Emerson. Thoreau in 1851 admitted that

> no experience which I have today comes up to, or is comparable with, the experiences of my boyhood.... As far back as I can remember I have unconsciously referred to the experiences of a previous state of existence.... Formerly, methought, nature developed as I developed, and grew up with me. My life was ecstasy. In youth, before I lost any

of my senses, I can remember that I was all alive, and inhabited my body with inexpressible satisfaction.

This glow is what Thoreau's readers will always turn to him for—it is that special consonance of feeling that exists between the pilgrim and his landscape. Ecstasy was not so much achieved as rewritten; whatever the moment was, his expression of it was forged, fabricated, worked over, soldered from fragmentary responses, to make those single sentences that created Thoreau's reputation as aphorist and fostered the myth that in such cleverness a man could live.

> I should not talk so much about myself if there were anybody else whom I knew as well. . . . I have travelled a good deal in Concord; and everywhere, in shops, and offices, and fields, the inhabitants have appeared to me to be doing penance in a thousand remarkable ways. . . . I see young men, my townsmen, whose misfortune it is to have inherited farms, houses, barns, cattle, and farming tools; for these are more easily acquired than got rid of. . . . Who made them serfs of the soil? Why should they eat their sixty acres, when man is condemned to eat only his peck of dirt? Why should they begin digging their graves as soon as they are born?

Each of Thoreau's famous sentences in *Walden* is a culmination of his life, the fruit of his all-too-perfect attachment to his local world. Each was a precious particle of existence, existence pure, the life of Thoreau at the very heart. Each was victory over the long unconscious loneliness—and how many people, with far more happiness in others than Thoreau ever expected or wanted, can say that their life is all victory? In the end was the word, only the word:

> When I was four years old, as I well remember, I was brought from Boston to this my native town, through these very woods and this field, to the pond. It is one of the oldest scenes stamped on my memory. And now tonight my flute has waked the echoes over that very water. The pines still stand here older than I; or, if some have fallen, I have cooked my supper with their stumps, and a new growth is rising all around, preparing another aspect for new infant eyes. Almost the

same johnswort springs from the same perennial root in this pasture, and even I have at length helped to clothe that fabulous landscape of my infant dreams, and one of the results of my presence and influence is seen in these bean leaves, corn blades, and potato vines.

The details in this key passage are so intimate, woven out of Thoreau's ardor, that the rhythms—"and even I have at length helped to clothe that fabulous landscape of my infant dreams"—seem as inevitable as a man talking in his sleep. A student once wrote about Thoreau: "This man searched to exhaustion a scene that sometimes appeared empty." Years later another student, as if to answer the first, noted that after writing *Walden*, Thoreau could look about him (as we do today when we visit Walden Pond amid a litter of beer cans) with the feeling that he had produced the place. Thoreau did create Walden Pond; the hut along its shores became, as Ellery Channing said, the wooden inkstand in which he lived. The attachment to Walden became as total and single in its all-absorbing attentiveness as that of a baby to its mother, a prisoner to his cell. *Walden* records a love blind to everything but the force of its own will. That is why we recognize in *Walden* the beauty of youthful feeling that is haunted by doom but not by tragedy—the feeling that death seems easier than any defeat from the social compact.

For youth the center of the world is always itself, and the center is bright with the excitement of the will. There is no drama like that of being young, for then each experience can be overwhelming. Thoreau knew how to be young. He knew how to live deep and how to suck all the marrow out of life. "I went to the woods because I wished to live deliberately, to front only the essential facts of life, and see if I could not learn what it had to teach, and not, when I came to die, discover that I had not lived. I did not wish to live what was not life, living is so dear; nor did I wish to practice resignation, unless it was quite necessary."

That is youth speaking; only youth thinks that it can "live deliberately," that a man's whole life can be planned like a day off, that perfect satisfaction can be maintained without friction, without friends, without sexual love, with a God who is only and always the perfect friend—and all this in relation to a piece of land and a body of water on whose shores one practices the gospel of perfection. Only the individual in the most private accesses of his experience knows what a "perfect" moment is—a unit too small for history, too precious for society. It belongs to the private consciousness. And Thoreau's predominating aim was to save his life, not to spend it; he wanted to be as economical about his life as his maiden aunts were about the sugar in the boardinghouse they ran (they kept the sugar spoon damp so that sugar would cling to it). He wanted to live, to live supremely, and always on his own terms, saving his life for still higher things.

Enter the State and the coming of modern times.[...] The State, represented by men whose overreaching frightened him, was to become the Other that he could not domesticate as he did nature. In the eighth chapter of *Walden*, "The Village," he describes his arrest in July 1846, as he was on his way to the cobbler's. He was arrested for not paying the poll tax that was still exacted by the State in behalf of the church. Thoreau's father had been enrolled in the church; Henry's name should not have been on the roll. He spent one peaceful, dreamy night in jail. In "Civil Disobedience" he reports that "the night in prison was novel and interesting enough. . . . It was like travelling into a far country, such as I had never expected to behold, to lie there for one night. . . . It was to see my native village in the light of the Middle Ages, and our Concord was turned into a Rhine stream, and visions of knights and castles passed before me."[...]

In *Walden* Thoreau was to say of his prison experience that it showed the inability of society to stand "odd fellows" like himself. In "Civil Disobedience" he said in a most superior way that the State supposed "I was mere flesh and blood and bones, to be locked up," and since it could not recognize that his immortal spirit was free, "I saw that the State was half-witted, that it was timid as a lone woman with her silver spoons . . . and I lost all my remaining respect for it, and pitied it."

What gives "Civil Disobedience" its urgency is that between 1845, when Thoreau was arrested for a tax he should have paid in 1840, and 1848, when he wrote the essay, the State had ceased to be his friend—the Concord sheriff, Sam Staples, who had so pleasantly taken him off to the local hoosegow—and had become the United States government. Under the leadership of the imperialist president James Polk and southern planters determined to add new land for their cotton culture, it was making war on Mexico and would take away half its territory in the form of California, Texas, Arizona, New Mexico, and parts of Colorado and Wyoming. The Mexican War was notoriously one for plunder, as Congressman Abraham Lincoln and many other Americans charged. But the war was the first significant shock to Thoreau's complacent position that the individual can be as free as he likes, in and for himself—especially when he has persuaded his neighbors to think him odd.

Oddity was no longer enough to sustain total independence from society. Despite Thoreau's opposition to slavery in principle, he knew no Negroes and had never experienced the slightest oppression. As a radical individualist he was very well able to support this privilege in Concord; he was not confined by his share in the family's pencil and graphite business, and he was indeed free as air—free to walk about all day long as he pleased, free to build himself a shack on Walden Pond and there to prepare to write a book, free to walk home any night for supper at the family boardinghouse. Up to the Mexican War—and more urgently, the Fugitive Slave Act of 1850, the act of 1854 permitting "squatter sovereignty" [with regard to slavery] in Kansas and Nebraska, and John Brown's raid on Harpers Ferry in 1859—Thoreau's only social antagonist was the disapproval, mockery, or indifference of his Concord neighbors. He never knew what the struggle of modern politics can mean for people who identify and associate with each other. Thoreau was a pure idealist, living on principle: typical of New England in his scorn for Irish immigrants, properly indignant about slavery in far-off Mississippi, but otherwise, as he wrote *Walden* to prove, a man who proposed to teach others to be as free of society as himself.

"Civil Disobedience" stirs us by the urgency of its personal morality. As is usual with Thoreau, he seems to be putting his whole soul into the protest against the injustice committed by the State. He affirms the absolute right of the individual to obey his own conscience in defiance of an unknown law. But despite his compelling personal heat, he tends to moralize all political relationships and to make them not really serious. He turns the State into a wholly ridiculous object, its demands on him into a pure affront, and then archly tells it to stop being so overbearing and please to disappear.

Thoreau's creed is refreshing. But anyone who thinks it a guide to political action at the end of the twentieth century will have to defend the total literary anarchism that lies behind it. Gandhi used "Civil Disobedience" a century ago because, as a young leader of the oppressed Indians in South Africa, he was looking for immediate tactics with which to sidestep a totally repressive regime. There were no laws to protect the Indians. Thoreau's essay is a noble, ringing reiteration of the highest religious individualism as a self-evident social principle. The absolute freedom of the individual is his highest good, and the State is not so much the oppressor of this individual as his rival. How Dare This Power Get In My Way? For Thoreau the problem is simply one of putting the highest possible value on himself rather than on the State. This is essential: We are all individuals first, and at many junctures it may be necessary to obey oneself rather than the State. Thoreau never shows he is aware that the individual's problem may be how to resist the State when he is already so much bound up with it (he can hardly just turn his back on what he involuntarily depends on). Thoreau denied that he owed *anything* to community, state, country.

The significantly political passages in the essay have to do with what Thoreau calls "slavery in Massachusetts." He of all people could not grant that property is the greatest passion and the root of most social conflicts and wars. Yet he insisted "that if one thousand, if one hundred, if ten men whom I could name—if ten *honest* men only—ay, if *one* honest man, in this State of Massachusetts, *ceasing to hold slaves,* were actually to withdraw from this co-partnership, and be locked up in the county jail therefor, it would be the abolition of slavery in America." With his marvelous instinct for justice, for pure Christianity, for the deep-rooted rights of the individual soul, he said: "Under a government which imprisons any unjustly, the true place for a just man is also a prison." Morally invigorating as this is, it would perhaps not have helped the fugitive slave, or the Mexican prisoner on parole, or the Indian come to plead the wrongs of his race when, as Thoreau said, they came to the prison and found the best spirits of Massachusetts there. Thoreau estimated the power of individual example to be beyond any other device in politics, but he did not explain how the usefulness of example could communicate itself to people who were in fact slaves and were not free.

The fury of the coming war could already be felt in Massachusetts. The Kansas-Nebraska Act made Thoreau explode. "There is not one slave in Nebraska; there are perhaps a million slaves in Massachusetts." But he still attacked every possible expediency connected with politics. "They who have been bred in the school of politics fail now and always to face the facts. They put off the day of settlement indefinitely, and meanwhile, the debt accumulates." The "idea of turning a man into a sausage"—the purpose of slavery—is not worse than to obey the Fugitive Slave Act. In the pulsations of a prose no longer idyllic or smugly ironic, he pounded away at the State, the Press, the Church—institutions all leagued, he felt, by the infamous conspiracy to send runaway slaves back to their masters. He mimicked the timorous, law-obeying Massachusetts citizen:

> Do what you will, O Government! with my wife and children, my mother and brother, my father and sister, I will obey your commands to the letter. It will indeed grieve me if you hurt them, if you deliver them to overseers to be hunted by hounds or to be whipped to death; but nevertheless, I will peaceably pursue my chosen calling on this fair earth, until perchance, one day, when I have put on mourning for them dead, I shall have persuaded you to relent.

Each sentence is, as usual with Thoreau, an absolute in itself; each is a distillation of the most powerful feelings. The violence inextricable from the slavery issue—even in Concord—was taking over the quietist who in Maine was shocked by his cousin George Thatcher's killing a cow moose. "The afternoon's tragedy, and my share in it, as it affected the innocence, destroyed the pleasure of my adventure." The killing suggested "how base or coarse are the motives which commonly carry men into the wilderness. . . . Our life should be lived as tenderly and daintily as one would pluck a flower."

Now John Brown brought to the surface what had long been buried in the soul of Henry David Thoreau. The most passionate single utterance of his life was "A Plea for Captain John Brown," delivered in the Concord Town Hall on the evening of October 30, 1859. (Brown had attacked Harpers Ferry on October 16; he would be hanged on December 2.) Emerson's son Edward heard Thoreau read the speech as if it "burned" him. There is nothing so inflamed elsewhere in Thoreau's work. All the dammed-up violence of the man's life came out in sympathy with Brown's violence. Brown's attack on Harpers Ferry clearly roused in Thoreau a powerful sense of identification. Apocalypse had come.

John Brown's favorite maxim was, "Without the shedding of blood there is no remission of sins." Brown's raid was exactly the kind of mad, wild, desperate, and headlong attack on the authority of the United States, on the support it gave to the slave system, that Thoreau's ecstatic individualism sympathized with. It was too violent an act for Thoreau himself to have committed; he had long since given up the use of firearms and was more or less a vegetarian. But Brown represented in the most convulsively personal way the hatred of injustice that was Thoreau's most significant political passion—and this was literally a *hatred*, more so than he could acknowledge to himself, a hatred of anyone as well as anything that marred the perfect design of his moral principles.

All his life Thoreau had been saying that there are only two realms. One is the realm of grace, which is a gift and so belongs only to the gifted; the other is the realm of mediocrity. One is of freedom, which is the absolute value because only the gifted can follow it into the infinite, where its beauty is made fully manifest; the other is of acquiescence and conformism, another word for which is stupidity. One is of God, whom His elect, the most gifted, know as no one else can ever know Him; the other is of the tyranny exacted by the mediocre in society. John Brown, whom all leading historians, judges, lawyers, and respectable people have always solidly denounced as mad, John Brown, who indeed had so much madness in his background, nevertheless represented to Thoreau the gifted man's, the ideal Puritan's, outraged inability to compromise between these two realms. Even worse than evil is the toleration of it, thought John Brown, so he tried to strike at evil itself. To Thoreau, this directness proved Brown's moral genius. Then, as the state of Virginia and the government of the United States rallied all their forces to crush this man and to hang him, it turned out, to Thoreau's horror, that another exceptional man was not understood. The State, which would do nothing to respect the slave's human rights, and had in deference to southern opinion acknowledged its duty to send back every runaway slave, would indeed obliterate John Brown with an energy that it had never shown in the defense of helpless blacks.

It was this that roused Thoreau to the burning exaltation that fills "A Plea for Captain John Brown." He had found his hero in the man of action who proclaimed that action was only the force of the highest principles. Thoreau's "plea" indeed pleads principle as the irresistible force. The pure, vehement personalism that had been Thoreau's life, in words, now sees itself turning into deeds. The pure love of Christ, striking against obstinately uncomprehending, resisting human heads, turns into pure wrath. God has certain appointed souls to speak and fight for Him, and that is the secret of New England.

> We aspire to be something more than stupid and timid chattels, pretending to read history and our Bibles, but desecrating every house and every day we breathe in. . . . At least a million of the free inhabitants of the United States would have rejoiced if [his last act] had succeeded. . . . Though we wear no crape, the thought of that man's position and probable fate is spoiling many a man's day here at the North for other thinking. If any one who has seen him here can pursue successfully any other train of thought, I do not know what he is made of. If there is any such who gets his usual allowance of sleep, I will warrant him to fatten easily under any circumstances which do not touch his body or purse.

For himself, Thoreau added, "I put a piece of paper and a pencil under my pillow, and when I could not sleep I wrote in the dark."

He wrote in the dark. Writing was what he had lived for, lived by, lived in. And now, when his unseen friend was being hanged in Charlestown prison, he could only speak for him. The word was the light, the word was the church, and now the word was the deed. This was Thoreau's only contribution to the struggle that was not for John Brown's body but for righteousness. He called the compromisers "mere figureheads upon a hulk, with livers in the place of hearts." He said of the organized church that it always "excommunicates Christ while it exists." He called the government this most *hypocritical* and *diabolical* government, and he mimicked it, saying to protesters like himself, "What do you assault me for? Am I not an honest man? Cease agitation on this subject, or I will make a slave of you, too, or else hang you." He said, "I am here to plead his cause with you. I plead not for his life, but for his character—his immortal life; and so it becomes your cause wholly, and is not his in the least. Some eighteen hundred years ago Christ was crucified; this morning, perchance, Captain Brown was hung. These are the two ends of a chain which is not without its links."

There was nothing Thoreau could do except to *say* these things. Brown, who was quite a sayer himself, had said to the court:

Had I so interfered in behalf of the rich, the powerful, the intelligent, the so-called great . . . it would have been all right. . . . I am yet too young to understand that God is any respecter of persons. I believe that to have interfered as I have done—as I have always freely admitted I have done—in defense of His despised poor, was not wrong but right.

Yet we in our day cannot forget that Brown was punished for a direct assault on the government, for attempting insurrection. Melville, putting his dispassionate elegy on John Brown at the head of his poems of the Civil War, *Battle-Pieces,* called Brown "The Portent."

Hidden in the cap
Is the anguish none can draw;
So your future veils its face,
Shenandoah!
But the streaming beard is shown
(Weird John Brown),
The meteor of the war.

Brown did as much as any one man did to bring about the Civil War—which Thoreau rejected as immoral. Concord snickered at his inconsistency. Of course he was already ill when the war broke out (he was to be dead in a year). If Thoreau died of the war as well as of the terrible struggles with himself that hastened his disease, he did not die a martyr. "The cost of a thing is the amount of what I will call life which is required to be exchanged for it, immediately or in the long run." By that test Thoreau paid much to become the writer he was. But the cost of nonviolence—which Thoreau returned to as his gospel—is so great in the face of the all-powerful twentieth-century state that Thoreau, who once in his life was astonished by power that was not his individual spiritual power, does not help us in the face of the state power which we supplicate for the general "welfare" and dread for snooping into our lives.

Thoreau did not anticipate the modern state. He distrusted all government and understood it far less than did Jesus when he counseled the Jews under the Roman heel, "Render unto Caesar the things that are Caesar's."

When the Civil War broke out, Thoreau advised an abolitionist friend to ignore Fort Sumter. "Be ye perfect, even as your Father in Heaven is perfect." That was the only power Thoreau knew and believed in—outside the writer's power that made him a life. He would not have believed it possible that the United States could become a superpower, a superstate, and that young people in this state would be reading and "imitating" Thoreau in order *not* to do anything about the government.

[1984]

HAWTHORNE:
THE GHOST SENSE

———•◆•———

When Nathaniel Hawthorne died in 1864, the most distinguished man of letters in New England, his neighbor in Concord, Ralph Waldo Emerson, had nothing positive to say: "I thought there was a tragic element in the event, that might be more fully rendered—in the painful solitude of the man which, I suppose, could no longer be endured, and he died of it." How much Emerson himself contributed to that solitude he never knew, for he could not read fiction, did not understand its dramatic necessity, regularly attributed the faults of the worst novelists to the best. Whenever he condescended to say anything about the fiction of his time, he wrote about it with a stealthy insight into its weaknesses that was used to support his moralistic distaste for fiction. [...]

What the Puritan tradition had left New England in the 1830s and 1840s, when American literature really began, was a faith that literature could still be scripture. The writer was seen as an oracle, orator, and teacher who could give out the word that connected the people of God with God. Everything in nature manifested God's presence, and every word that the gifted prophet-poet could find in his heart was a symbol of the divine truth. The Church was unnecessary, for God was everywhere, especially in the imagination of Transcendentalists. There could be no anxiety or strain as to the meaning of the creation, for all symbols found in nature easily reflected God as clear and perfect truth.

Thus Emerson was right to think that there was a painful solitude to Hawthorne, a tragic element that might be more fully rendered. For Hawthorne was a storyteller, a romancer, a fantasist in a culture still dry with religious literalism, one that had managed in literary quarters to replace the old church rigor with an insistency on its own moral certainties, born only of intuition. I have deliberately chosen archaic and approximate terms like storyteller, romancer, fantasist, in order to point up the lack of accepted terms for the profession in which Hawthorne found himself. Hawthorne, who was always calling himself a "romancer" in those prefaces to his books that were apologies for his strange calling and attempts to bridge the gap between himself and his audience, felt himself to be an oddity in choosing to be a "mere writer of tales." As a storyteller, choosing to represent psychic situations rather than to explain them, Hawthorne found himself suggesting uncertainties where there had always been God's truth, drawing shadows and hinting at abysses where there had always been clarity, straining to find images of the imponderable, the blackness and the vagueness, even the terror that waits in what he called "the dim region beyond the daylight of our perfect consciousness."

Hawthorne is the most interesting artist in fiction whom New England has produced—he is the only New England artist in fiction whose works constitute a profound imaginative world of their own, the only one who represents more than some phase of New England history. The passage that he achieved, from literature as scripture to literature as fiction, may seem ordinary and unastonishing when we think about it in bulk, as cultural history. But when we concentrate on it as the achievement of a single artist, one who had to claim as his subject the very ordeal by religion from which he emancipated himself as an artist, we can see why Henry James said: "The fine thing in Hawthorne is that he cared for the deeper psychology and that, in his own way, he tried to become familiar with it." T. S. Eliot said that Hawthorne had "the ghost sense." It is always the sense of another world; it is a peculiar saturation in something present to the human mind but not visible.

Everyone recognizes that whatever is most profound in American literature is somehow bound up with Puritanism. In Hawthorne we see an artist's natural emancipation from it but also a turning back to it as the materials of legend, as an allegory of the human heart. The incessant moralizing of the New England mind, the sententiousness of its intellectual manner, the consciousness of being God's elect, above all the overcharged and often mystical symbolism which so many Puritans attached to their experiences in primitive New England—these were turned into fanciful, elusive, symbolic elements of human nature. Hawthorne, surrounded by so many moralists who thought they commanded the reality principle, created more memorably than he did anything else a sense of the *unreality* of existence, of its doubleness, its dreaminess, its unrealizability by anything less profound than the symbolic tale. It was this that made a remarkable writer, who thought of himself as archaic, so haunting to the James of the last unfinished works like *The Sense of the Past*; to the Eliot who in 1916, when James died, could best define James's achievement as a sense of the past like Hawthorne's; to Robert Lowell, who in his play *The Old Glory* dramatized some of Hawthorne's best stories, especially "My Kinsman, Major Molineux," as if these episodes had all been dreamed in common by Hawthorne's readers. Of all the great American writers, Hawthorne is still the standard for those readers who think that a piece of writing should have the mysterious authenticity and the self-sufficient form of a dream.

It is an odd fact—to those who do not know America from within—that this extraordinarily powerful, seemingly wholly modern society, should have produced as its sweetest, rarest, profoundest literary artists, writers most concerned with the inner life, with many strange symbols for mental consciousness. Although our best writers have naturally found their subject in society, the operating force on them has been the struggle with ancestral symbols. Many ghosts have always haunted the American mind precisely because it has been so open to every secular experience. Hawthorne became a kind of virtuoso in fiction of the inner life—the only novelist from New England as subtle as its poets—because he was able to show as a human style the extraordinary burden on the New England mind of the past, of its moral introspection, its unending self-confrontation and self-examination.

It is this side of Hawthorne's fiction, in all its modest provincialism, that often makes the same impression on us as do Joyce's stories and Kafka's parables—the restrictiveness of the setting has forced the characters into a wholly mental existence. In Hawthorne people talk more to themselves than they do to other people, they talk to others only to report on what they have already told themselves, they talk to others as if they were talking to themselves. This is of course not what novelists between 1890 and 1920 were to develop as the stream of consciousness; it is not unconscious imagery and unformulated speech, but literally a communing of the self with the self in a world where the individual is more real to himself than anything else is. The "public" speech of Hawthorne's characters resembles the operatic monologues of characters in Balzac and Stendhal; it is intensely formal, as indeed everything pertaining to style is in Hawthorne. But what makes American fiction different in this period from English and Continental fiction is that, with the Americans, there is so little *public* world—so few institutions, especially the English kind that young Henry James missed in Hawthorne and thought essential to the modern social novel. New England put the greatest possible strain on the individual, for by the Puritan scheme of things he was convinced of the total depravity of mankind, yet had to find some tiny chink in this darkness, some outlet to salvation, in the report of worthiness that his own heart gave back to itself. This self-communing remained the dramatic center of Hawthorne's work forcing the individual to pursue a shadowy existence in pursuit of himself. The old Henry James, struggling to finish *The Sense of the Past*, was to find an ancestral ghost of his own in Hawthorne. James did all he could with the realistic novel, and then found himself in old age back in a world like Hawthorne's, where the human mind must pursue itself as the external world gets more and more unstuck.

This is the situation portrayed over and again in Hawthorne's fiction—as it is in so many stories out of Catholic Ireland and in so many European Jewish writers brought up to find their material in orthodoxy. All perceptions have become troubling. Where everything was once confidently an image of God's omnipresence, commonplace things show the rule of strangeness. Hawthorne's use of masks and veils, of emblems, shadows, ruins, blackness, his need of fiction machinery involving a lost inheritance, the missing will, the bloody footprint left on the stair of the rotting house, the scaffold, the pillory, the forest, show how instinctively he thought in terms of obstructions to be cleared, of disguises and secrets, of claims upon the past that could never be satisfied. Past generations, said Marx, lie like an incubus upon the living. Hawthorne, a strikingly uncooperative imagination in a "new" country, thought that men could never discharge ancestors from their minds, for the past contained the one secret they were always looking for.

Hawthorne's New England is as black as Joyce's old Dublin and Kafka's old Prague, his haunting, creepily echolalic stories, collected under demure titles like *Twice Told Tales, Mosses from an Old Manse*, affect us like music box tunes that slide into dissonance. A minister walks about with a black veil over his face, never to have it off even in his coffin. Young Goodman Brown, newly married, leaves his bride, Faith, to consort with the Devil and friends in the forest. The Devil looks like his father, the blasphemy of the communion service is attended by the most respectable people in town. " 'Welcome, my children,' said the dark figure, 'to the communion of your race. You have found thus your nature and your destiny. By the sympathy of your human hearts for sin ye shall scent out all the places. . . . Evil is the nature of mankind. Evil must be your only happiness.' " Goodman Brown is dazzled by the enthusiasm with which the villagers throw off their moral pretensions; he can never trust himself or anyone else after he has returned to his bride. In "Rappaccini's Daughter," a mad Italian botanist who breeds poisonous flowers has so trained his daughter to serve his arrogant will that his pride destroys her. In "The Birthmark" an eminent medical scientist, made equally destructive by his terrible pride, involuntarily kills his wife when he endeavors to remove a faint birthmark that is the only blemish on her beauty.

The figure of the insanely proud and thus destructive genius, which recurs in "Doctor Heidegger's Experiment" and as Chillingworth in *The Scarlet Letter*, is of course a type of the perilous self-sufficiency that Hawthorne saw as the tragic element in our isolated human nature. But to summarize Hawthorne's fictions is to conventionalize them, to make them seem more moralistic than they are. As in the case of his most famous book, *The Scarlet Letter*, Hawthorne tended to draw his situations from historic legend, or to work them up from explicitly symbolic episodes doggedly reported in his notebooks. He was deceptively obvious in announcing his themes. But what makes the charm and elusive suggestiveness of his fictions is the atmosphere he creates. He was a symbolist, an extraordinarily delicate colorist, for whom the human fancy made all necessary connections. In "Rappaccini's Daughter," where the most prominent character is really the poison garden itself, it is the extraordinary touch that Hawthorne can give his materials, not the "meaning" of the tale but the tale turning on its enigmatic surface, that brings home Hawthorne's origi-nality of vision. He was above all else a painter in words, a Piranesi of the oddly picturesque ruins that New England presented to his imaginative eye, a Georges de la Tour of light playing on the human face as it studies itself in the mirror—a situation that recurs in the stories and in *The Scarlet Letter.* What one takes away most from "Rappaccini's Daughter" is the treacherous beauty of the over-colored flowers; from "Young Goodman Brown," the black shadows in the forest and then the horridly burning brand lighting up the Devil's face as he welcomes the villagers to the "communion of their race"; from "The Minister's Black Veil," the blackness covering the minister's face; from "The Maypole of Merry Mount," the would-be pagans in New England masquerad-ing as stags, wolves, he-goats, bears; from "My Kinsman, Major Molineux," the extraordinary darkness of the approach to Boston as the young boy crosses the river; from *The Blithedale Romance,* the flower in Zenobia's hair.

Hawthorne fastened on color and on light; he lived in dim, bleak, crabbed New England; was an artist starved for Europe, for the great world, for sensu-ous possibility. But his recourse to graphic detail, to painters as characters and to portraits as emblems, was basically rooted in his need to describe every human scene in and for itself alone, to create a *picture:* make of it what you will. This passion to contract unsayable moral meanings into pictures was to become a ruling motive with Henry James and his disciple Joseph Conrad, both of whom rested the highest claims of their fiction on their ability to make the reader *see.* But until he went to Europe in 1853, Hawthorne could have seen few pictures—certainly few interesting ones. His imagination had already cast the New England scene into a deeper historical perspective than any other American novelist would know. What Hawthorne had to do was not merely to see the literally "dark" past with his own eyes but to create a picture that would on many planes and in many shades reveal the tension between freedom and law, the living struggle in the soul between the truth of private feeling and the institutionalized dogmas that represented moral certainty.

It is Hawthorne's ability to create moral tension in the form of surface picture that from the opening lines of *The Scarlet Letter* introduces us to the plastic imagination behind the book. It opens at the prison door where Hester Prynne is soon to appear wearing the scarlet letter embroidered on her dress. "A throng of bearded men, in sad-colored garments, and gray, steeple-crowned hats, intermixed with women, some wearing hoods and others bare-headed, was assembled in front of a wooden edifice, the door of which was heavily timbered with oak, and studded with iron spikes." This wooden jail is already marked with weather stains and other indications of age which gave yet a deeper aspect to its beetle-browed and gloomy front. There is rust on the ponderous ironwork of the oaken door, and everything in this new world is harsh, crude, unnaturally old; yet on one side of the portal is a wild rose-bush flaming in the June sunlight. And when Hester appears at the prison door with her infant in her arms, the elaborate embroidery and fantastic flourishes with which she has worked the letter A into the breast of her gown immediately suggests the luxurious and sensuous woman in Puritan dress who holds our imagination in a blaze of scarlet. The tension that is sex, the tension that sets up the moral drama of sex in the restrictive world, the tension that is the inner life struggling against the cage of the visible world, the tension that is the predicament of human knowledge trying to realize itself in the world—which in our time fiction has only just consciously begun to contend with as the *problem* of knowledge—this tension is what is so vibrantly realized in Hawthorne's constant visual contrast of dark and light, of heights and depths, of the pillory and the street, of the mirror and the lamp. It is this [manifold tension] that gives such an achieved, finished, truly made quality to *The Scarlet Letter,* a book that conceals many enigmas in the perfection of its surface.

Hawthorne was never able to capture this formal perfection again, although each of his other three completed novels, *The House of the Seven Gables, The Blithedale Romance, The Marble Faun,* is full of his marvelously delicate suggestion that the strange essences of which the human heart is composed become externalized forces that play about our lives. Indeed, all three books, and the several unfinished "romances" he left at the end of his life, show how increasingly hard he struggled to find the dramatic machinery by which to convey the impact of hidden human nature. In *The Scarlet Letter* the necessary means lay in the starkness of the scene and the harshness of the Puritan nature. Both of these, we feel as we read his book, he did not have to invent, but indeed recollected from memory as if they were the ancestral forces that made him up.

Hawthorne told his publisher that "*The Scarlet Letter* being all in one tone, I had only to get my pitch, and could then go on interminably." The book was delivered wholly from within, all in one piece; this is why it is fascinatingly enigmatic, like an art object. It exists like a stained-glass window that is different every hour, like a sculpture that changes as you move around it. Hawthorne said with surprise that the book was "positively a hell-fired story, into which it is almost impossible to throw any light." Hawthorne had to show the incalculable effect of a single lovemaking on his three protagonists; he had to show the tragedy inseparable from moral choice. He had to show the passion that was Puritanism and the passion that protested it; he had to present the ritual of punishment and worship, the ceremony at the scaffold and in the church into which the emotional life of the people is gathered up.

The three chief actors, the beautiful young wife, the too-saintly minister who was her lover, the old husband who with fiendish psychological intelligence now seeks to exact his revenge, are all locked up between the sea and the forest as each is locked in by feelings that he cannot explain to the others. In thought they confront one another, for they are chained by the "dark necessity" which their theology attributes to all human actions. Everything is woven so tight in the book, scene follows scene with such logic, that people's obsessions become as real as their faces. As the old husband, the pernicious doctor seeking revenge, says in wonder of his own failure—"We dream in our waking moments, and walk in our sleep."

This is our experience as we read *The Scarlet Letter.* The book is one of the few novels which, like great dramatic poetry, successfully express the inmost mind in its encounter with external society. No novelist was ever less consciously an innovator than Hawthorne was. But by trying to give dramatic form and dignity to the trauma of Puritanism, by emphasizing the uncertainty and ambiguity that are attached to human relations, he incorporated into his fictions the strangeness, the ultimate causelessness, which we attribute to human nature as the subject of literature.

[1968]

"MELVILLE IS DWELLING SOMEWHERE IN NEW YORK"

———•◆•———

[. . . .]

Melville's New York long ago vanished from New York. Even as Melville was forced back into the city, his own New York was eroded as a physical landscape and as a society. New York's aristocracy before the Gilded Age had consisted of solid old-fashioned merchants, preferably with some Dutch ancestry. It would soon be replaced by Society—the ostentatious new-rich of the Four Hundred. If Melville's father, in the business on lower Broadway of importing fine French dry goods, had not failed and then died of the shock (his son was fourteen), Melville would never have gone to sea. Like his well-placed relatives and in-laws, like George Templeton Strong and the father of Theodore Roosevelt, he might have become another of those weighty New Yorkers whom Edith Wharton would portray in all their external wealth and private melancholy. Melville looked on his literary career as an accident—which did not lighten his grim humor at becoming a slave to it. He saw himself more pursued by chance than Moby-Dick was by Captain Ahab—into a world without precedents and rules.

New York's top layer was disappearing, becoming what Melville's fellow New Yorker Henry James would in horror call the "swarm." This, along with the immigrant masses who found Tammany a benevolent despot, already meant the money-men. Wall Street came to represent New York just when

Melville, by living in New York, vanished from sight. He ignored all external change in his native city. A minor sketch, "Jimmy Rose," describes a bon vivant turned bankrupt. Melville's own New York does not exist in his works. They are an allegory of his life in his most familiar roles: orphan, castaway, renegade from orthodox Christianity and the West, "isolato," the white savage driven out by his society and contemptuous of it. With his old-fashioned merchant's sense of honor, the bankrupt father had died of shame. The desperate son would find his positive ideal in men older and more harmonious than himself: the Englishman Jack Chase, captain of the maintop on the navy vessel that brought Melville home in 1844, and Nathaniel Hawthorne. But like the lonely killer Ahab, Melville could not believe that anyone had authority over this world—or within it. Heroes were such through strength of will. They had no objective ideal, only the magnetism of being superior persons. There was no father in heaven and only the resentful memory of one on earth.

The bereaved family broke up. Maria Gansevoort Melville wrote to the jurist Lemuel Shaw, one day to be Melville's father-in-law, that her husband's family had "deserted" her eight children. The loans advanced to Allan Melville during his lifetime were charged against the children.

At sixteen Herman was a clerk in Albany; at seventeen, a teacher in a country school; nearing twenty, he shipped as a cabin boy to Liverpool. In *Redburn* (1849), the record of this voyage, he described a customs officer in Liverpool. "A man of fine feelings, altogether above his situation; a most inglorious one, indeed; worse than driving geese to water." At twenty-one he shipped out in a New Bedford whaler, the *Acushnet*, for the South Seas. New Bedford whaling captains were the worst slave drivers on the seven seas.

2

Now began Melville's grand initiation: the three-and-a-half-year voyage that never left him and became his imaginative life. To read Melville is to go round and round the earth in magnified and mythified versions of that voyage. It took him from New England round Cape Horn to the lunar-looking but "enchanted" Galápagos six years after Darwin, exploring them, had been struck by the subtle variations that led certain birds and animals to thrive when others did not and to develop into new species. Melville already knew all he needed to know about the struggle for existence at sea and in the horrible fo'c'sle of an American ship—a byword for hardship, oppression, and desperate characters from all nations who would not have been employed elsewhere. American ships were known as floating jails.

In the Marquesas Melville deserted, became the "white man who lived among the cannibals" (for a month), was taken off by an Australian whaler, went to Tahiti, mutinied with other hardbitten types, was briefly and farcically jailed. After further escapades in the company of deserters, drifters, drunks, castaways, "mongrel renegades . . . and cannibals," he ended up in Honolulu as a clerk, as a pinboy in a bowling alley, before returning home on an American man-of-war, the *United States.* Melville's record of the return voyage is *White-Jacket*, half documentary and half lampoon. His biting description of flogging is supposed to have ended the practice in the American navy. The captain is incompetent and a martinet, the surgeon a sadist, the midshipmen "terrible little boys." The American navy provided "evils which, like the suppressed domestic drama of Horace Walpole, will neither bear representing, nor reading, and will hardly bear thinking of." But in the captain of the maintop he found his ideal man—bluff, hearty, poetry-spouting Jack Chase.

Melville's three-and-a-half-year voyage made him see Western man in confrontation (his favorite activity) with the primitive in society, the elemental in nature. His underlying antagonist was the conventional in white middle-class America and its Christianity. The great voyage furnished material for a lifetime. *Billy Budd*, Melville's last work, written in the last years of his life and not discovered until 1919, was "Dedicated to Jack Chase, Englishman, Wherever that great heart may now be, here on Earth or harbored in Paradise, Captain of the Maintop in the year 1843 in the U.S. Frigate *United States.*"

So central and dominating for the rest of his life was Melville's great voyage that his prototype became a wanderer, an exile, a sailor, while his work takes us on an endless journey. It leads to South Sea islands and prisons; to the gigantic tortoises and reptiles of "The Encantadas"; to Liverpool in *Redburn*, where in the desolate cellars off the docks the poor die under the eyes of the indifferent police; to the slums of London, where Israel Potter spends most of his life trying vainly to get home; to the waters off the coast of Chile, where Benito Cereno is held prisoner by rebellious slaves who dupe the kindly American Captain Delano into thinking that Cereno still has authority; to the seamy streets of old New York in *Pierre* and the desolation of Wall Street on

Sunday in "Bartleby the Scrivener"; to the Mississippi in *The Confidence Man*; to Egypt and Palestine in Melville's extraordinary *Journal up the Straits* and his narrative poem *Clarel*; to ancient Italy in the virgin astronomer's passionate lament over wasted womanhood in the monologue "After the Pleasure Party."

This narrative journey, the most imaginative single span of the earth in American writing, ends in midocean with the sacramental crucifixion in *Billy Budd* of a son by his father.

"Heureux qui, comme Ulysse, a fait un beau voyage," wrote the Renaissance poet Joachim du Bellay. "Happy the man who, like Ulysses, made a good journey," and then came home full of experience and wisdom to live out his life among his family! No other significant writer of his time and place came anywhere near Melville's absorption of the imperial midcentury world in which New England whalers and cargo ships made portions of the Pacific an American preserve. New England devised the clipper ships that traded with China and newly opened Japan. New England whalers stripped Japan's seas of whales in the 1830s and 1840s. America first went to Japan in Commodore Matthew Perry's "black ships" in 1852–54, opening a reluctant, fearful country to the outside world after centuries of seclusion. (Perry's aim, Japanese scholars say, was to obtain water and coaling stations for American whalers.)

Melville had reason to become jeeringly skeptical of Western civilization and Protestant moralism; he had seen the missionaries at work. Because young gentlemen sometimes developed trouble with their eyes and had to leave Harvard for a spell, Richard Henry Dana had gone to sea and produced that superbly healthy and objective record of life at sea and in California before it was American, *Two Years Before the Mast*. But Melville cannot be relied on to give us straight facts. Conrad, asked in 1907 to write a preface to *Moby-Dick*, refused. "It struck me as a rather strained rhapsody with whaling for a subject and not a single sincere line in the 3 vols of it." Melville's significant imagination captured well the highs and lows of manifest destiny in its time: the exuberance of discovering the "world" and the disgust of sharing in the imperial grab that made Melville's great voyage possible. No other American writer served such an apprenticeship. Melville never forgot the human flotsam and jetsam around him. American literature was still captive to "high culture," was self-consciously genteel, and, in the fading of authentic belief, was replacing religion with moralism. The literary class was still homogeneous and unaware that it lacked muscle. Social power was in other hands. Melville on reading Emerson: "To one who has weathered Cape Horn as a common sailor what stuff all this is."

Melville's experience before he was twenty-five not only gave him material for a lifetime, it created his basic image: the inconclusive nature of reality, man forever driven back on himself as he seeks a fixed point. Melville's linked orphanage and "fall" from status, his sense of social injury and his maritime world of wonders, were urgent symbols to the ex-sailor who became a great reader only after discovering that he was a writer. He was never to write one of his semidocumentary novels without other men's voyages at his side.

Of all the many surprises in his life, probably none was so startling to Melville as his need of books and his passion for ideas. He proudly said that he "swam through whole libraries" to write *Moby-Dick*. He borrowed other men's narrative experiences in *Typee*, *Redburn*, *White-Jacket*, *Moby-Dick*; this was necessary not only to his extensive imagination but to his need to parody other writers' limitations. A corrosive humor became as important to his pride as his assertion of mental homelessness. And so did his sense of the ferocity of life at sea—"I have had to do with whales with these visible hands." He was a Darwinian by intuition. As he was to say, "Luther's day had expanded into Darwin's year." Original sin was behind natural selection. Predestination was in the genes as well as in the "soul."

Melville was unlike the gentle Darwin, who resisted his own awareness of the killer instinct in nature and was often made ill by the conclusive evidence he piled up. A year before the *Origin of Species* appeared, Darwin wrote: "It is difficult to believe in the dreadful but quiet war of organic beings going on in the peaceful woods and smiling fields." "It is like confessing a murder," Darwin wrote to the botanist Joseph Hooker, confiding his suspicion that species are not immutable. Ten miles outside Pittsfield, Melville was living in the Berkshires' peaceful woods and smiling fields when he produced Ahab's hymn to the killer instinct in nature. He was remembering his youth at sea. Killers cannot help themselves:

> By heaven, man, we are turned round and round in this world, like yonder windlass, and Fate is the handspike. And all the time, lo! that smiling sky, and this unsounded sea! Look! see yon Albicore! who put it into him to chase and fang that flying-fish? Where do murderers go, man! Who's to doom, when the judge himself is dragged to the bar?

Melville's "Darwinism" brought to his books a complex sense that human beings were futile yet heroic. His career was an example. The man who wrote in *Mardi*, "Oh, believe me, God's creatures fighting fin for fin a thousand miles from land, and with the round horizon for an arena, is no ignoble subject for a masterpiece," jauntily wrote to Hawthorne: "Genius is full of trash." A significant side of Melville is the scorn he developed for his early fame. Just before he landed in England in 1849, to sell *White-Jacket*, he derisively noted in his diary that ten years before he had sailed there as a common sailor; now he was "H. M., the author of Pee-Dee, Hullabaloo and Pog-Dog."

Melville was "posthumous" by the time he finished *Moby-Dick*. He was thirty-two. The problem was his incessant development after leaving the sea— a wholly personal matter not to be correlated with worldly success. He confessed his premonitions to Hawthorne as he was completing *Moby-Dick*.

> My development has been all within a few years past. I am like one of those seeds taken out of the Egyptian pyramids, which, after being three thousand years a seed and nothing but a seed, being planted in English soil, it developed itself, grew to greenness, and then fell to mould. So I. Until I was twenty-five, I had no development at all. From my twenty-fifth year I date my life. Three weeks have scarcely passed, at any time between then and now, that I have not unfolded within myself. But I feel that I am now come to the inmost leaf of the bulb, and that shortly the flower must fall to the mould.

The restlessness, the *interminability* of his personal quest, saw truth only in the sea's maddening beat. "Poor Rover!" cries Pip the cabin boy when he jumps out of the boat in fright and goes mad, "will ye never have done with all this weary roving? where go ye now?" "Annihilation" for Herman Melville meant never to be done voyaging, searching; never to lose the heart's dissatisfaction and the mind's inconclusiveness. We hear this in *Moby-Dick* from the frantic preparations for the voyage: "All betokening that new cruises were on the start; that one most perilous and long voyage ended, only begins a third, and so on, for ever and for aye. Such is the endlessness, yea, the intolerableness of all earthly effort."

"Annihilation" appears in book after book. The killer instinct that is so strong in *Moby-Dick* is first of all annihilation of the known limits, of the land, of the familiar self. Waiting for the *Pequod* to get off and meet its destiny, Ishmael senses the design [in] which, like another Ulysses forever roaming the world, he is caught:

> The port would fain give succor; the port is pitiful; in the port is safety, comfort, hearthstone, supper, warm blankets, friends, a's kind to our mortalities. But in that gale, the port, the land, is that ship's direst jeopardy; she must fly all hospitality; one touch of land, though it but graze the keel, would make her shudder through and through. With all her might she crowds all sail off shore; in so doing, fights against the very winds that fain would blow her homeward; seeks all the lashed sea's landlessness again; for refuge's sake forlornly rushing into peril; her only friend her bitterest foe!

Moby-Dick is the product of a powerfully crossed mind—imitating the bursting century, expanding America, the manifest destiny out of which it came. It is an epic of mixed motives, of unyielding contradictions. And it is always histrionic. Ahab's dream of perfect freedom demands total mastership. Yet he admits himself subject to predestination in all things. It is "Nature's decree." Man and Nature must fight each other up and down the watery waste. Although Melville finds "linked analogies" in every observation—in this he is a good American of the Transcendentalist church—Nature for Melville is not Emerson's word for man's *moral* nature. The great beasts of the sea—and the sea is the greatest beast—give the rule of things. They are the first and last of the earth. The antediluvian world is still with us, frightening, and in perpetual creation. The animal kingdom, the sea kingdom, is totally itself and aboriginal. It cares nothing for death. Nature was the killer from the beginning.

But now it is confronted by the ironic, weary, expectant mind of the nineteenth century. There are two principal voices in *Moby-Dick:* the excessively assertive Faust from Nantucket who pursues the sperm whale that bit his leg off and the passively contemplative, quietist, all-enduring survivor. He is the lost son and eternal wanderer Ishmael, whom his father Abraham ordered with his concubine mother Hagar into the wilderness—where, Genesis tells us, he became an archer.

Moby-Dick is the most memorable confrontation we have had in America between Nature—as it was in the beginning, without man, God's world alone—and man, forever and uselessly dashing himself against it. It is a confrontation peculiarly American and of the nineteenth century, for it connects the still-present "wilderness," the ferocity of brute creation, with the anxiously searching mind that has lost its father in heaven. *Moby-Dick* is full of symbols that unlike those of Emerson and Thoreau do not exhaust the natural facts from which they are extracted. The power of the book, the rolling, endlessly conjunctive style rushing to do justice to all this hunting, gashing, killing, devouring—and sexual cannibalism—gives us the full measure, brimming over in Melville's prose, of what the narrator's mind brings to the primordial scene.

The detachment essential to storytelling does not confine Melville's style. He certainly lacked Emerson's doubt of the final sufficiency of language. Melville luxuriates in language, looks to "Vesuvius for an inkwell," a "condor's wing" to write with. The extraordinary rhythm of the book is the wavelike pull, forward and back, between the expansive human will and the contraction of necessity. Freedom and necessity battle throughout the book. The mind naturally thinks itself free, but necessity is the deeper rhythm of things. Nature's "tiger heart" is just beneath the surface while, at his ease in the masthead, Ishmael "takes the mystic ocean at his feet for the visible image of that deep, blue, bottomless soul, pervading mankind and nature."

Like Carlyle, Melville shows sexual abandon in fitting his language to his subject matter. His shipmates address whales with a harpoon, Ishmael with a pen. The "fiery hunt" of the mightiest beast demands a style that from the opening of *Moby-Dick* conveys a sense of abundance that is easy, full, peculiarly rich in suggestion of the universal fable in the background and the epic stretching the narrative line. If ever there was a style that belonged to America's own age of discovery, a style innocently imperialist, romantic, visionary, drunk on symbols, full of the American brag, this is it. We come to feel that there is some shattering magnitude of theme before Melville as he writes. He has been called to a heroic destiny:

> But it is a ponderous task; no ordinary letter-sorter in the Postoffice is equal to it. To grope down into the bottom of the sea after them; to have one's hands among the unspeakable foundations, ribs, and very pelvis of the world; this is a fearful thing. What am I that I should

essay to hook the nose of this Leviathan! The awful tauntings in Job might well appall me. "Will he make a covenant with thee? Behold the hope of him is vain!" But I have swum through libraries and sailed through oceans; I have had to do with whales with these visible hands; I am in earnest; and I will try.

Moby-Dick is the greatest epic we have of the predatory thrill. Long before Americans completed their conquest of a continent and its aborigines, they had reached out to the Orient. But the savages the white man replaced entered into his soul—and they are all present on the *Pequod.* Power in every human guise is the norm in *Moby-Dick.* Ahab's dream of absolute power wrecks everything and almost everyone. The book overpowers by an uncontainable force, an appropriation that is instinctive and unashamed. It is a hymn to the unequaled thrust that lifted America to the first rank, and it is equally a hymn to the contemplativeness that was left to its literary men, its sensitive consciences, its lonely metaphysicals and seekers after God. It is at once Ahab's book, fiercely masculine, yet from the beginning rooted in Ishmael's passive, wonder-struck gaze. The reader is caught up by these different sides of Melville—the androgyny that American writing suffers in respect to American power. Ishmael constantly reports Ahab but never seems to meet him. There is no confrontation between the daemonic father and the lost son. There will be none between Captain Vere and Billy in *Billy Budd,* where Isaac *praises* his father Abraham for loving the law more than he loves his son. If there *is* a father, he is a disaster to Melville; yet Melville's despairing sense of "God" is that "God-like" minds are without a God. So his love and adoration for Hawthorne ended in the suspicion that he was writing to a father figure who was not really there.

Moby-Dick is *the* book of nineteenth-century American capitalism carried to the uttermost. Yet everything is encompassed by the dreaming mind of Ishmael, the last Transcendentalist. Ishmael has no power whatever; but he thinks and thinks because he is the residue of a Calvinism that has emptied itself out into as much dread as wonder. It is not God who is absolute sovereign but the whale. "Though in many of its aspects this visible world seems formed in love, the invisible spheres were formed in fright."

No wonder that the missionary papers disliked the book, or that Melville never quite recovered from the effort his "mighty" theme required. His struggle was not with the "daemonic" elements in the book, Ahab's "deliriously howling" as he baptized his harpoon "*in nomine diaboli.*" The devil stuff in the book is imitation Gothic, boring and melodramatic; the only significance of Fedellah and the Parsee crew is the "exotic" tinge they give to Melville's determinism. The real struggle of the book was to create a great body of fact, learning, and humor around a theme ultimately nihilist. Melville admitted that his book "is not a piece of fine feminine Spitalfields silk—but it is of the horrible texture of a fabric that should be woven of ships' cables & hawsers. A Polar wind blows through it, & birds of prey hover over it." It is also a celebration of American enterprise and a grand joke on the ultimate futility of so much energy, will, and death-dealing bravado in the face of "eternal fates." Between Ahab as the maddened Faust seeking to exert his will and the indifferent beast-God he chases around the world only to sting him into contemptuous retribution, lies the sea, even more indifferently waiting to receive us all. But if there were no beast or God to pursue, there would be nothing. The sea in itself to human eyes is nothing. And nothingness is the "fright" behind the book.

3

Without Nathaniel Hawthorne, *Moby-Dick* might have remained the whaling yarn Melville started out to write. Hawthorne became the greatest, most direct inspiration in Melville's literary life; he was the only other man of genius in the neighborhood. Between the summer of 1850, when the Melvilles moved to Pittsfield, and November 1851, when the Hawthornes left Lenox, Melville rose to the height of his power as an artist, to all possible fervor as a man. But after the failure of the book coincided with the Hawthornes' leaving, Melville could never be sure that there had been a Hawthorne in his life.

It was not Hawthorne's fault that Melville came to think of him as being absent. Absence, vacancy, the "divine inert," the nothingness which a human being must constantly assail in "the now egotistical sky; in the now unhaunted hill," was forever in Melville's mind. Ahab *is* his greatest character, despite the bombast crowding this wholly literary, all-too-willed characterization, because Ahab is not so much a person as an idea—pursuing an idea. The "fiery hunt" carries no hope that there is anything out there; it is just the essential human effort. The great beast is from the beginning a metaphor by which we challenge ourselves. Moby-Dick (to the great delight of twentieth-century readers brought up on symbolism) is a pretext for Ahab's fanaticism. The "God-like" presence that finally emerges, in all his "Jove-like" beauty, is—like so many things in the book—unrelated to the abstraction Ahab first summons his crew to hunt: "Sometimes I think there's naught beyond. But 'tis enough. He tasks me; he heaps me; I see in him outrageous strength, with an inscrutable malice sinewing it. That inscrutable thing is chiefly what I hate."

The *Pequod* is condemned by Ahab to sail up and down the world in search of a symbol. And everyone but the necessary narrator will die in the attempt; such is the burden on the mind seeking an Other in our narcissistic existence. The "world" seems to be easy to grasp but never is. Man continually mounts the world in its appearance as Nature but never really joins it. The failure is what torments us. It kills the illusion that we are part of what we see.

Hawthorne, just by being there for Melville at the crux of his life, gave Melville the bliss of meeting a genius. Hawthorne filled the vacancy that had been Melville's residual image of the father, of the "divine inert"—and of the hopeless chase for fame and money that was the literary career in America. Melville could not believe his luck—his letters run over with jubilant surprise: "Whence come you, Hawthorne? By what right do you drink from my flagon of life? And when I put it to my lips—lo, they are yours and not mine. I feel that the Godhead is broken up like the bread at the Supper, and that we are the pieces. Hence this infinite fraternity of feeling."

Melville heartily joined himself to his century's easy belief in genius. Like Carlyle, he advanced a high and mighty idea of the writer as hero. But where the secret nihilist Carlyle shouted at a world it was too late to redeem, Melville was overcome by the discovery of his own gifts. In the tumbling, rhapsodic letters he wrote to Hawthorne during their brief acquaintance, he constantly projects his own literary temperament. Melville to the conservative, resigned, decidedly non-thundering Hawthorne:

> There is the grand truth about Nathaniel Hawthorne. He says No! in thunder; but the Devil himself cannot make him say *yes.* For all men who say *yes,* lie; and all men who say *no,*—why, they are in the happy condition of judicious, unincumbered travellers in Europe; they cross the frontiers into Eternity with nothing but a carpet-bag,—that is to

say, the Ego. Whereas those *yes*-gentry, they travel with heaps of baggage, and, damn them! They will never get through the Custom House. What's the reason, Mr. Hawthorne, that in the last stages of metaphysics a fellow always falls to *swearing* so? I could rip an hour.

Hawthorne was not Melville. Melville's response was to raise Hawthorne to royalty, out of *everyone's* reach. Hawthorne's own image of himself was that of a spy, a peeping Tom, lurking everywhere without being discovered. "The most desirable mode of existence," he wrote in "Sights from a Steeple," "might be that of a spiritualized Paul Pry, hovering invisible round man and woman, witnessing their deeds, searching into their hearts, borrowing brightness from their felicity, and shade from their sorrow, and retaining no emotion peculiar to himself."

Julian Hawthorne said his father always reflected the person he was with, was a mixture of

a subtle sympathy . . . and a cold intellectual insight . . . the real man stood aloof and observant. . . . Seeing his congenial aspect towards their little rounds of habits and belief, [other people] would leap to the conclusion that he was no more and no less than one of themselves; whereas they formed but a tiny arc in the great circle of his comprehension.

Sophia Hawthorne, who idolized her husband, probably reflected something of Hawthorne's opinion of Melville as well as her own limitations when she wrote to her sister Elizabeth Peabody that Melville's gushing tributes to Hawthorne on *The House of the Seven Gables* showed Melville

a boy in opinion—having settled nothing as yet—unformed—ingenue—& it would betray him to make public his confessions & efforts to grasp,—because they would be considered perhaps impious, if one did not take in the whole scope of the case. Nothing pleases me better than to sit & hear this growing man dash his tumultuous waves of thought up against Mr. Hawthorne's great, genial, comprehending silences. . . . Yet such a love & reverence & admiration for Mr. Hawthorne as is really beautiful to witness—& without doing any thing on his own part, except merely doing, it is astonishing how people make him their innermost Father Confessor.

4

In 1883 Julian Hawthorne, in search of his father's letters for the biography he was writing of his parents, called on Melville "in a quiet side street in New York, where he was living almost alone." Melville said with a melancholy gesture that Hawthorne's letters to him

> had all been destroyed long since, as if implying that the less said or preserved, the better!... He said, with agitation, that he had kept nothing; if any such letters had existed, he had scrupulously destroyed them.... When I tried to revive memories in him of the red-cottage days—red-letter days too for him—he merely shook his head.

Julian Hawthorne did not feel that he had learned much from the visit. He did give us a rare view of the "forgotten" Melville in New York:

> He seemed nervous, and every few minutes would rise to open and then to shut again the window opening on the court yard.... He was convinced Hawthorne had all his life concealed some great secret, which would, were it known, explain all the mysteries of his career ... some secret in my father's life which had never been revealed, and which accounted for the gloomy passages in his books. It was characteristic in him to imagine so; there were many secrets untold in his own career.

Melville's bitterness was to come out in his poem "Monody."

To have known him, to have loved him
After loneness long;
And then to be estranged in life,
And neither in the wrong;

And now for death to set his seal—
Ease me, a little ease, my song!

Melville probably considered this the final word—it was his only word—
on his relation to Hawthorne. But the writer resurrected in the 1920s was in
for a surprise. A great many people turned out to know so much about
Melville's "secret" that it also became Hawthorne's "secret." In a poem celebrating Melville, W. H. Auden explained that "Nathaniel had been shy
because his love was selfish."

5

In the late 1850s, as his wife revealed, Melville had "taken to writing poetry." If,
as one reviewer complained about *Moby-Dick*, its expansive prose was "so much
trash belonging to the worst school of Bedlam literature," poetry was certainly
Melville's way of contracting his style by enclosing himself. But more than ever
would he argue with himself. Even the prose fiction he wrote after *Moby-
Dick*—the sometimes hysterical parody of the genteel style in *Pierre*, the stories
and reveries he collected in *The Piazza Tales*, the shut-in terseness of *The
Confidence Man*—show a restless waywardness of form, an exasperated need to
try anything at hand, that finally came to rest in poetry privately published,
poetry in which and for which he did not have to answer to anyone.

This was to be true of the posthumous *Billy Budd*, which Melville left
unfinished, perhaps not wanting to see it finished and published. When it was
discovered in 1919 by Raymond Weaver, who was tracking down Melville for
the first biography, *Mariner and Mystic*, it was in a confusing state in Melville's
most crabbed hand. Concealed in a tin breadbox, says Melville's great-
grandson Paul Metcalf, it had to be "dug loose from the tight seaweed of
Melville's heirs and descendants."

"Crabbed" is the word for Melville's poetry—and for the peculiar syntac-
tical complexity of style in *Billy Budd*, which for all its drama betrays an instrument long unused as well as the grave slowness and quizzicality into which
Melville's youthful force had subsided in "retirement."

The poetry is in every sense occasional. Even his most unforced, his easiest poem, "Billy in the Darbies," which concludes *Billy Budd* and in its humorous stoicism at the approach of death sums up Melville's work (and life) with

all his old grace, answers to a kind of occasion: April 19, 1891, the date Melville added to "End of Book." "Billy in the Darbies" is a truly personal poem, "dramatic" in its monologue, since it is Billy speaking from his last night on earth. So many of Melville's poems—about history, vaguely historic personages, "fruits of travel long ago," Melville's burrowing in historical myths—proceed from some grave meditative center. By contrast with "Billy in the Darbies,"

> *But me they'll lash in hammock, drop me deep.*
> *Fathoms down, fathoms down, how I'll dream fast asleep . . .*

most of Melville's poems are altogether too "philosophic," too far above the battles that composed Melville's life and formed the strenuousness of his mind.

Reading Melville's verse, one cannot help picturing him, evening after evening, wreathed in cigar smoke as he measures his way from line to line, rhyme to rhyme. In one of his *Battle-Pieces,* "Commemorative of a Naval Victory," he was surely thinking of himself when he wrote:

> *But seldom the laurel wreath is seen*
> *   Unmixed with pensive pansies dark;*
> *There's a light and a shadow on every man*
> *   Who at last attains his lifted mark—*
> *   Nursing through night the ethereal spark.*
> *Elate he never can be;*
> *He feels that spirit which glad had hailed his worth,*
> *   Sleep in oblivion.—The shark*
> *Glides white through the phosphorous sea.*

"The shark / Glides white through the phosphorous sea" certainly breaks up the evening labor wreathed in cigar smoke; Melville is full of wonderful lines.

There are no outcries from this long-haunted man like the middle passages of baffled love in "After the Pleasure Party." "Amor threatening," he calls it in this remarkable piece about a woman astronomer in ancient Italy who suddenly awakens to the cost of her virginal existence. This is an unusually *felt* monologue. With the sudden brilliance that can flash across a Melville poem, his preoccupation with sexual ambiguity now asserts itself in urgent tones.

> Could I remake me! or set free
> This sexless bound in sex, then plunge
> Deeper than Sappho, in a lunge
> Piercing Pan's paramount mystery!
> For, Nature, in no shallow surge
> Against thee either sex may urge,
> Why hast thou made us but in halves—
> Co-relatives? This makes us slaves.
> If these co-relatives never meet
> Self-hood itself seems incomplete.
> And such the dicing of blind fate
> Few matching halves here meet and mate.
> What Cosmic jest or Anarch blunder
> The human integral clove asunder
> And shied the fractions through life's gate?

The weary, inexperienced poet was his old self, if not his once-Promethean self: he still took on big "historical" themes. But they were now occasions for reflection, not scenes of action. The requisite subject after 1865 was the Civil War, which stirred Melville to write *Battle-Pieces* out of a sense of national tragedy rather than patriotism. In "America"

> Valor with Valor strove, and died:
> Fierce was Despair, and cruel was Pride;
> And the lorn Mother speechless stood,
> Pale at the fury of her brood.

The end of slavery stirred him less than the deaths of "young collegians." But even Melville's serial portraits of America's slaughtered youth, like many poems in *Battle-Pieces* commemorating battles and leaders of the Civil War, seem composed in a gray light. They lack the involvement (real or hoped) that Whitman brought to *Drum-Taps*. Melville's noble compassion for both sides shows no strong political resolve in response to America's finest hour and ever-lasting hurt.

The great exception is "The House-top," Melville's bitter response to the July 1863 anti-draft riots; it jolts the reader after so many shadowy genre paintings of war. Melville as Coriolanus, standing on the roof of his house in New York, describes with the most concentrated contempt for the mob its "Atheist roar of riot." The poem voices an embittered Toryism that is not altogether surprising. In his early works Melville's most obvious political reflex was a jeer at conventional Western values; missionary repressiveness and pettiness in the South Seas appalled him, as the natives certainly did not. He is disgusted by the city's "new democracy," its masses, and scornful of

> . . . the Republic's faith implied,
> Which holds that Man is naturally good,
> And—more—is Nature's Roman, never to be scourged.
> He says with gritted teeth that
> The Town is taken by its rats—ship-rats
> And rats of the wharves. All civil charms
> And priestly spells which late held hearts in awe—
> Fear-bound, subjected to a better sway
> Than sway of self; these like a dream dissolve,
> And man rebounds whole aeons back in nature.

In "The Conflict of Convictions," a poem about the anxious "secession winter" of 1860–61, Melville obviously remembers his futile efforts, in sight of the unfinished Capitol dome, to obtain a consular appointment from the Lincoln administration. But the irrepressible conflict has turned his personal failure into political bleakness. His disenchantment, as in "The House-top," laments the vanished dream of the Founders:

> Power unanointed may come—
> Dominion (unsought by the free)
> And the Iron Dome,
> Stronger for stress and strain,
> Fling her huge shadow athwart the main;
> But the Founders' dream shall flee.

Age after age shall be
As age after age has been,
(From man's changeless heart their way they win);
And death be busy with all who strive—
Death, with silent negative.

6

Why did Melville turn to poetry? It was not just because his novels had failed; or, as soft-minded critics once thought, because Melville's "subjective" and "intellectual" side had become "excessive." He had been willing to try any form, sometimes within a single "novel," because his greatest literary need was to express contraries. As Hawthorne noticed, Melville never tired of "wandering to and fro" over "intellectual deserts." The condensation of thought that poetry makes possible now appealed to a strenuous if no longer frantic thinker. He was aging, he was "retired," in just that drop of American idealism after the Civil War that saw—nowhere more sharply than in Herman Melville—a reversal of the Enlightenment. Verse offered the increasingly conservative ex-novelist the possibility that life could be contained as epigram. He anticipated at the end of "The Conflict of Convictions" (and in capital letters) the kind of jeering little "lines" that Stephen Crane called poetry:

YEA AND NAY—
EACH HATH HIS SAY;
BUT GOD HE KEEPS THE MIDDLE WAY.
NONE WAS BY
WHEN HE SPREAD THE SKY;
WISDOM IS VAIN, AND PROPHESY.

Melville offered a riposte to Blake in a poem from *Timoleon*, "Fragments of a Lost Gnostic Poem of the 12th Century."

Indolence is heaven's ally here,
And energy the child of hell:
The Good Man pouring from his pitcher clear,
But brims the poisoned well.

Melville in the long evening of his life needed such terseness as he came to the end of his roaming. His long search within himself and his need to elude the fate of Narcissus had ended in a reconciliation with certain fundamentals.* What could not have changed was the need to storm "the axis of reality." As an exuberant young author just in from the Pacific, Melville had sought to transcend limits, to escape confines, to find in the heroic age of his young country the last undiscovered place. As a fugitive from the great American marketplace, Melville then "reduced" himself to stories for magazines, to soliloquies in his travel notes on Egypt and Palestine, to the contemptuous "masquerade" of The Confidence Man, to octosyllabics in his long narrative poem Clarel. In his last three years he was to reduce himself to the anonymity of Billy Budd and its theme, the father's compliance in the death of the son.

In the wild flight of writing Moby-Dick, Melville had praised himself (while praising Hawthorne) for embodying "a certain tragic phase of humanity. . . . We mean the tragedies of human thought in its own unbiassed, native, and profounder workings . . . the apprehension of the absolute condition of present things as they strike the eye of the man who fears them not, though they do their worst to him."

Melville the great American agonist, forever trying to recapture his belief in the God-given unity of all things, was a thinker unmistakably in search of the elemental. In his first, romantic books, this quest made him go to the ends of the earth. In the triumphant moment of his life, when he was finishing Moby-Dick, he avowed to Hawthorne that his own deepest concern was with the beginning and end of things. As a sailor he had had the merest glimpse of the Galápagos, but in the marvelous sketches and tales of "The Encantadas" Melville recreated a biblical scene—the first days of creation. In his journal of Egypt and Palestine, the intensity of his lifelong association with the Bible led him to put his impressions into the starkest personal shorthand.

Pyramids still loom before me—something vast, indefinite, incomprehensible, and awful. Line of desert & verdure, plain as line between

---

*"And still deeper the meaning of that story of Narcissus, who because he could not grasp the tormenting, mild image he saw in the fountain, plunged into it and was drowned. But that same image, we ourselves see in all rivers and oceans. It is the image of the ungraspable phantom of life; and this is the key to it all." (Moby-Dick, "Loomings")

good and evil. A long billow of desert forever hovers as in act of breaking, upon the verdure of Egypt. Grass near the pyramids, but will not touch them. Desert more fearful to look at than ocean. Theory of design of pyramids. Defense against desert. A line of them. Absurd. Might have been created with the creation.

Ride over mouldy plaine to Dead Sea—Mountains on both sides—Lake George—all but verdure——foam on beach & pebbles like slaver of mad dog—smarting bitter of the water,—carried the bitter in my mouth all day—bitterness of life—thought of all bitter things—Bitter is it to be poor & bitter, to be reviled, & Oh bitter are these waters of Death, thought I—Old boughs tossed up by water—relics of pick-nick—nought to eat but bitumen & Ashes with desert of Sodom apples washed down with water of Dead Sea.—Must bring your own provisions, as well, too, for mind as body—for all is barren.

Melville *had* to make his way to the Holy Land after his nervous crisis of the 1850s, just as when a young man, "having little or no money in my purse, and nothing particular to interest me on shore, I thought I would sail about a little and see the watery part of the world." Melville's instinct made him sink the *Pequod* in the deepest waters of the Pacific. With like instinct he sought nature in its most savage aloofness from man. Yet even in the Holy Land, "the issues there but mind," as he wrote at the end of *Clarel*, he betrayed his truly "metaphysical anguish," his thirst for conclusiveness. The summing up, however, was in East Twenty-sixth Street, where this wanderer in thought was hidden by the frantic busyness of New York.

Melville retreating to New York regarded himself as a private thinker, nearly anonymous. The anonymity was parallel to the theme at the heart of all his work. Was there a home for thought, unavailing, unending thought, in this world of indifference? Ahab's assault on the white whale was not more dogged than Melville's on the looming nothingness that invades his style with endless play on words ending in "less"—*homeless, landless, formless, speechless*—on images of extreme personal will—*furious*—on different names for blockage—*verge, wall, pyramid*. The beast always in view is emptiness, the deception inherent in the mere appearance of things. The harpooner rising to "strike" gets caught from "behind," is snagged and twisted in the rope whose coiled force catapults him into the sea. Dream and electric bitterness, strength and abjection, give us the polarities of Melville's life and work. No other "isolato" (he made up the word) in American writing communicates so fervently a writer's looking for a place to put his mind.

Emptiness! In the New York of the Gilded Age and the Brown Decades, the landlocked sailor was more than ever alone with himself. It was his nature to rebound on himself as the desperate quest. But his strangest association with New York was that living *there* did not matter.* Still, Melville did have his roots, and more besides, in this "Babylonish brick-kiln." New York from the 1860s to Melville's death in 1891 was the money city that the expatriate Edith Wharton would return to in her last, unfinished novel, *The Buccaneers.* It would soon be the city that another New Yorker, Henry James, would confront in 1904 as the most "extravagant" of international cities. To think of Melville back in New York is to remember Edith Wharton's complaint that "he was qualified by birth to figure in the best society," for he was a cousin of the Van Rensselaers. Alas, she "never heard his name mentioned."

We can imagine what the rich and bossy Edith Wharton (Henry James complained that she regularly "swooped" down on him even when he welcomed the discovery of the world from her "motor") would have made of a descendant of the best society working as a customs inspector at three dollars and sixty cents a day. Bright prophetic Britishers and Canadians wrote Melville of their admiration for him and their inability to procure all his books. They wanted to see him. Robert Buchanan in New York complained that "no one seemed to know anything of the one great imaginative writer fit to stand shoulder to shoulder with Whitman on that continent." All that the reigning literary mediocrity of the day, the stockbroker-poet Edmund Clarence Stedman, could tell him was that "Melville is dwelling somewhere in New York."

Melville had no assurance of tenure in his "political" job. He was so much in danger of losing it that his brother-in-law John Hoadley wrote to the secretary of the treasury

---

*Melville had taken the measure of "society" in *The Confidence Man* (1857), unmistakably the work of an extraordinary mind obsessed with the falsity of appearances. As a satire on a trickster's society, it repeats itself claustrophobically—Melville's depression is all over the book like a fog[...]There is no conflict, no crisis, no development. Man here is entirely static—not a comfortable stance for Melville's energy.

to ask you, if you can, to do or say anything in the proper quarter to secure him permanently, or at present, the undisturbed enjoyment of his modest, hard-earned salary, as deputy inspector of the Customs in the City of New York,—Herman Melville. Proud, shy, sensitively honorable—he had much to overcome, and has much to endure; but he strives earnestly to so perform his duties as to make the slightest censure, reprimand, or even reminder,—impossible from any superior. Surrounded by low venality, he puts it all quietly aside, quietly returning money which has been thrust into his pockets behind his back, avoiding offence alike to the corrupting merchants and their clerks and runners, who think that all men can be bought, and to the corrupt swarms who shamelessly seek their price; quietly, steadfastly doing his duty, and happy in retaining his own self-respect.

This glimpse of Melville during the Iron Age (when New York became the great exchange place for money and money-making) can fascinate a New Yorker in search of Melville the New Yorker. He is still easy to imagine in old New York—the lower city. In the eighties, when he had retired from his nineteen years on the docks, he sometimes dropped in on John Anderson's bookstore in Nassau Street—and he is rumored to have bought copies of his books in the Financial District, where Bartleby did his scrivening. His genially uncomprehending employer was a Wall Street lawyer:

> I placed his desk close up to a small side-window in that part of the room, a window which originally had afforded a lateral view of certain grimy backyards and bricks, but which, owing to subsequent erections, commanded at present no view at all, though it gave some light. Within three feet of the panes was a wall, and the light came down from far above, between two lofty buildings, as from a very small opening in a dome. Still further to a satisfactory arrangement, I procured a high green folding screen, which might entirely isolate Bartleby from my sight.

Melville himself flashes into animation when he can report

"a ship on my district from Girgate—Where's that? Why, in Sicily—
the ancient Agrigentum. . . . I have not succeeded in seeing the captain
yet—have only seen the mate—but hear that he has in possession
some stones from these magnificent Grecian ruins, and I am going to
try to get a fragment, however small, if possible."

The altogether proper, nobly stoical resident on East Twenty-sixth Street
returned each evening to the bust of Antinoüs on a stand in the hall, the little
white sails in the Bay of Naples on the wall, the oversized desk in his bedroom.
On Sundays he walked with his grandchildren in the park. "At my years, and
with my disposition," he wrote to John Hoadley, "one gets to care less and less
for everything except downright good feeling." Home he is and taken his wages.
Surely his feelings were those he had confessed to Hawthorne in the exultation
of finishing *Moby-Dick*—"Am I now not at peace? Is not my supper good?"

But if Melville was "peaceful" (the Melville family motto was "Heaven at
Last" and Melville may still have had longings in that direction), the resurrected Melville, the Melville who surfaced posthumously with *Billy Budd* (and
much more besides), seemed anything but peaceful, was still endlessly dramatic. Melville may have been ditched by his own century; he became important to the next because he stood for the triumph of expression over the most
cutting sense of disaster, negation, and even the most ferociously unfavorable
view of modern society in classical American literature. Melville to many
another "isolato" in the next century represented the triumph of a prisoner
over his cell, of a desperado over his own philosophy. There is in Melville the
peculiar bitterness of a man who has lost everything except the will to survive
by writing—and who is acid yet clamorous in a style that reminds us more of
Rimbaud and Beckett than of the stoic acceptances of Hardy and Conrad.
Melville's protagonist and hero is thematically the deserter, the shipwrecked
sailor, the castaway, the tramp, the mad author, the criminal—and most centrally, the iconoclast who does not escape retribution from society by becoming a murderer.

7

On September 13, 1971, more than a thousand New York State troopers
stormed the Attica State Correctional Facility, where 1,200 inmates held

thirty-eight guards hostage, thereby ending a four-day rebellion in the maximum-security prison. Many of the troopers shouted "White power!" as they broke into the prison yard. Nine hostages and twenty-eight convicts were killed. One of the dead was Sam Melville, known as the Mad Bomber, a leader of radical groups in the 1960s who had adopted his last name because of his total veneration of a writer he identified with revolution. Carl Oglesby, another radical leader in the sixties, said in an article on "Literature as Revolution":

> Our abiding contemporary Melville posed in effect the following question: "Given these historical origins and social sources, these current grounds of spirit and pathways of hope, how might we secure the faith that our imperial-minded republic, unlike its ancient homologues, will not commit its energies in immense genocidal gulps at the expense, one time or another, of all the major colors, types, and varieties of mankind?"

Melville, eclipsing his idol Hawthorne, became a hero to all who found a mirror image in Melville's expansiveness and "ambiguities." "Call Me Ishmael," said the poet Charles Olson in an excited little book most important for documenting Melville's debt to Shakespeare. "Call me Billy Budd," thought many a young man fascinated by the beauty and pathos of Melville's last work. In the 1920s Melville fascinated Hart Crane, Lewis Mumford, Jean Giono; was soon to fascinate W. H. Auden, Cesare Pavese, E. M. Forster, Benjamin Britten. He became such an obsession for highbrow opinion that the best-selling novelist John Marquand jealously attacked him. In the postwar reaction against the Popular Front liberalism of the 1930s, Melville even became a totem to neoconservatives in academe. In death as in life, Melville was like no other American "classic"; he divided bitter political loyalties.

Which of his many books speaks for him *now*? Which had the last word? From *Billy Budd*, certainly his last work, the secret work of his old age, it is easy to assume that Melville had found a solution to his long search for truth past the chimera of this world. The solution is law, or authority. In the great debate over Billy Budd's fate, between Captain Vere and the young officers of the court-martial trying Billy for the "accidental" killing of Claggart, Vere drives them to hang someone who is possibly his own son.

"How can we adjudge to summary and shameful death a fellow creature innocent before God, and whom we feel to be so?—Does that
state it aright? You sign sad assent. Well, I too feel that, the full force
of that. It is Nature. But do these buttons that we wear attest that our
allegiance is to Nature? No, to the King. Though the ocean, which is
inviolate Nature primeval, though this be the element where we move
and have our being as sailors, yet as the King's officers lies our duty in
a sphere correspondingly natural? So little is that true, that in receiving our commissions we in the most important regards ceased to be
natural free agents. . . . Our vowed responsibility is in this: That however pitilessly that law may operate in any instances, we nevertheless
adhere to it and administer it."

Perhaps it was not "resignation" to which Melville gave "assent" at the
end; it may have been "authority." This may have been his way out of the
total anarchy of appearances in *The Confidence Man*, that nihilistic babel of
voices from an unmoving ship on an unbelievable river. No one is going anywhere in that book. But in the ever-growing contempt for American profes-
sions of honesty, *The Confidence Man* became what one anxious scholar called
"Melville as Scripture." So the drama of his many changes went on, as it had
for so long gone on within Melville himself, each book seeming to cancel the
one before.

It was Melville's capacious intellectual personality that drew so many people to the different images he now presents. But the tormented subjectivism
behind all his work shows the same problem—to find truth that would not
disappear from voyage to voyage, book to book.

Where is the foundling's father hidden?
    Where do murderers go, man! Who's to doom, when the judge
himself is dragged to the bar?

By vast pains we mine into the pyramid; by horrible gropings we
come to the central room; with joy we espy the sarcophagus; but we
lift the lid—and no body is there!—appallingly vacant as vast is the
soul of man.

Melville's "tales of terror told in words of mirth" were wonderful enough. But his assault on the "axis of reality," driven by the most consummate doubt of where reality finally lay, pointed to lustful contradictions that only the future would relish. And that the future would not untangle or replace.

[1984]

WALT WHITMAN:
I AM THE MAN

———◆———

You have waited, you always wait, you dumb, beautiful ministers,
We receive you with free sense at last, and are insatiate henceforward.
　　　　　　　—*Walt Whitman*, "Crossing Brooklyn
　　　　　　　Ferry"

The priest departs, the divine literatus comes.
　　　　　　　—*Walt Whitman*, Democratic Vistas

When Walt Whitman, age thirty-six, a former "jour-printer," delivered himself of "Song of Myself" (1855)—of course no other date would do for this but the Fourth of July—only he knew that American individualism, American strut and brag, American egocentricity, American triumphalism in all departments, had just found in him their most extreme and shameless expression.

Although there was no author's name on the cover, deep in the poem the author described himself as "Walt Whitman, an American, one of the roughs, a kosmos." The book opened on a portrait of the author. Who else? Those who have had access to the original edition report that this was an engraved daguerreotype of a bearded man in his middle thirties. He is slouching under a wide-brimmed and high-crowned black felt hat that has "a rakish kind of slant," the engraver said later, "like the mast of a schooner." "His right hand," Malcolm Cowley reported,

> is resting nonchalantly on his hip; the left is hidden in the pocket of his coarse-woven trousers. He wears no coat or waist-coat, and his shirt is thrown wide open at the collar to reveal a burly neck and the top of what seems to be a red-flannel undershirt. It is the portrait of

a devil-may-care American workingman, one who might be taken as a somewhat idealized figure in almost any crowd.

There was also a long, madly assertive preface, announcing the oncoming presence of a great native poetry that would be equal to the significance of the United States in history. It is so rhapsodic that William Everson has arranged it as verse, which does not keep it from being a series of inflamed declarations. There is no need to look for a coherent argument. The voice is everything here, and nothing like that voice had been heard before in American poetry. Whitman was replaying the nationalist orations he had been giving as a radical Democrat in Brooklyn:

> The Americans of all nations at any time upon the earth have proba-bly the fullest poetical nature. The United States themselves are essentially the greatest poem. In the history of the earth hitherto the largest and most stirring appear tame and orderly to their ampler largeness and stir. Here at last is something in the doings of man that corresponds with the broadcast doings of the day and night.

The tone of the preface is pitched very high. It makes many claims (and rhap-sodically repeats them) line after line about the greatness of the United States and the hovering greatness of the poetry that is natural to such a creation as the United States. To be rhapsodic in this defiant voice the writer has clearly had to gather himself together as he never has before. He is plainly determined to force something on the reader—and it's not just these "states," or the "com-mon people," or the promise that "the American poets are to enclose old and new." Whitman celebrates himself as an individual personifying all he sees and honors, from the common street life to the incipient poets entwined with the country that has made it all possible. To write on such a scale and in such a voice is to thrust oneself upon the world. He is "one of the roughs, a kosmos." He is like nothing and no one else.

"Of all mankind the great poet is the equable man." One doesn't argue with that, or with the man capable of saying that. One bows to the power of personality that enables him to dominate wherever he situates himself, to play so many roles that add up to one—Walt Whitman. Although the preface to the 1855 poems is so insistently general, and has nothing of what makes "Song of Myself" "work"—America in its variousness, the love play, the tenderness mixed with a view of human existence projected onto the universe at large—it prepares us for Whitman the truly representative man as he made himself. "I am the man. . . . I suffer'd. . . . I was there."

Nevertheless, the preface is suffused with religion as a great fact about this society that mounts an even greater hope. Whitman has written the great psalm of the Republic in singable lines.

The largeness of nature or the nation were monstrous
Without a corresponding largeness and generosity
Of the spirit of the citizen.

A live nation can always cut a deep mark
And can have the best authority the cheapest . . .
Namely from its own soul. This is the sum
Of the profitable uses of individuals and states.

Nothing too close, nothing too far off . . .
The stars not too far off.

As he sees the farthest he has the most faith.
His thoughts are the hymns of the praise of things.
In the talk on the soul and eternity and God off of his equal plane
He is silent.
He sees eternity less like a play with a prologue and denouement.

Dismiss whatever insults your own soul.

Did you suppose there could be only one Supreme?
We affirm there can be unnumbered Supremes,
And that one does not countervail the other.

There is no one supreme Deity, no hierarchy, no heaven. It is here on earth and nowhere else that we live out the divine in ourselves to which we are called. We are as gods when we recognize all things as one. Spiritually, we are sovereign—entirely—thanks to our culture of freedom. As we dismiss whatever offends our own souls, so we can trust our own souls for knowledge of the infinite.

So Whitman played companion to all the gods from Osiris to Christ, and tied God to the ecstasy of sexual love. Everything human was on an equal plane. In the first 1855 edition of "Song of Myself" he equated the passing "influx" of divinity with God as "a loving bedfellow, the perfect provider night and morning. Mon semblable, mon frère!"

> *I am satisfied. . . . I see, dance, laugh, sing;*
> *As God comes a loving bedfellow and sleeps at my side all night and close on the peep*
>   *of the day,*
> *And leaves for me baskets covered with white towels bulging the house with their*
>   *plenty,*
> *Shall I postpone my acceptation and realization and scream at my eyes,*
> *That they turn from gazing after and down the road,*
> *And forthwith cipher and show me to a cent,*
> *Exactly the contents of one, and exactly the contents of two, and which is ahead?*

Like so many of his countrymen in the nineteenth century, Whitman was drenched in religion; he positively swam in it, without having to believe in much of it. There was no personal God. He was not a Christian. He was to add nothing to the many public "revivals" of faith storming around him. Even in his childhood among Long Island Quakers, he owed his spiritual aloofness, his independence from orthodoxy, to his father's admiration for Tom Paine and the father's adherence to Elias Hicks, whose belief in the sufficiency of the "inner light" separated him from most Quakers. On the other hand, Whitman *fils* was no eighteenth-century Deist; in his easy embrace of the universe (and of its diverse creeds) he was the most fervid example imaginable of what Whitehead meant when he said that "Romanticism is spilled religion." "Religion" was in Whitman's blood, as in all his American generation (and after), but it was not central to his attempt to incarnate himself as the "divine literatus" (as he would call himself in *Democratic Vistas*)—the poet as world-embracing witness to all that was now profane in America but still sacred because of the limitless progress it embodied. Whitman, personifying this American optimism, presented himself at the center of everything material and "spiritual." In old age, when he was still fighting for recognition, he called religion essential to the ultimate design of *Leaves of Grass.*

There would be wholeness but no intended "design" to his final edition. Everything in Whitman's thirties followed from personal appetite, ambition, and the strident radicalism of both his political and religious background, which promoted the faith in universal benevolence that carries one along in "Song of Myself"—Here Comes Everybody! This was before the Civil War, before the Gilded Age, and before the worship of a few heated disciples cast him in his last role—as "the Good Gray Poet," the elegist of Lincoln and of the democracy that had never recognized him as its most fervent apostle. But "young" or old—and as a writer he made the most of both—he never had as much interest in "God" as he did in replacing conventional religion with himself as all-seeing poet. "The priest departs, the divine literatus comes."

Why "divine" and why "literatus"? Because, lordly as Whitman paraded himself in "Song of Myself," the metaphor that opens the poem, insinuates itself everywhere back into the poem, and recurs at the end—leads to a conclusion perfect in tenderness:

> Failing to fetch me at first keep encouraged,
> Missing me one place search another,
> I stop some where waiting for you.

When Whitman says "I," there is always another in wait. He said it in the most comprehensive way, the most loving. There is never a direct reference to the other he seeks, loves, is making love to. The "nigh young men" who boisterously, familiarly greet him in the street remain just that. In the unusually intimate poem "Out of the Cradle Endlessly Rocking" the boy on the beach recognizes himself as a poet-to-be, "uniter of here and hereafter," in the mating songs of "Two feather'd guests from Alabama, two together." But one disappears, forsakes the other, so that it must be in loss and loneliness, the boy weeping yet ecstatic, that the emerging poet recognizes

> Now in a moment I know what I am for, I awake,
> And already a thousand singers, a thousand songs, clearer, louder and more
>   sorrowful than yours,
> A thousand warbling echoes have started to life within me, never to die.
> O you singer solitary, singing by yourself, projecting me,

Whitman in "Song of Myself," guardedly, evasively describing intercourse and hinting at fellatio, was never so true, for once truly personal, as when he ended the "solitary singer" passage with

Never more shall I escape, never more the reverberations,
Never more the cries of unsatisfied love be absent from me,
O solitary me listening, never more shall I cease perpetuating you.
Never again leave me to be the peaceful child I was before what there in the night,
By the sea under the yellow and sagging moon,
The messenger there arous'd, the fire, the sweet hell within,
The unknown want, the destiny of me.

That first arousal is backed up by the mother-sea, "the fierce old mother incessantly moaning," and the maternal breasts represented by "The yellow half-moon enlarged, sagging down, drooping, the face of the sea almost touching." The mother as the everlasting sea, the sorrowfully "moaning" sea, is the only other human person—represented as a force of nature—in the poem. One wonders if, after all the parading of his masculine charms, Whitman as *seeker* of love was not more real than the lover he portrays as so publicly irresistible that

I am satisfied. . . . I see, dance, laugh, sing;
As God comes a loving bedfellow and sleeps at my side all night and close on the peep
*   of the day.*

However that was, Whitman the lover in general was at first sufficiently recognized by Emerson when he said that Whitman's book "has the best merits, namely of fortifying and encouraging." Emerson turned his back on Whitman when it became clear with "Children of Adam" and "Calamus" that the poet was "fortifying," all right, but not in the direction that Concord thought worthy of public print. "It was as if the beasts spoke," said Thoreau (who was charged up by the book for reasons his purity did not recognize). In Amherst, Emily Dickinson, who never saw a line by Whitman, was told he was "disgraceful." It was all too early for anyone to tell her that some of her poems, silently seething in her bedroom drawer, were in a sense more "sexual" than his, since they were fed by a direct passion for one particular man after another. It was more *natural* for Whitman (not just more discreet) to embrace the universe. To name a "hugging and loving bedfellow" as "God."

In the 1881 version of "Song of Myself" "God" got replaced by someone we know as little—"the hugging and loving bedfellow sleeps at my side through the night, and withdraws at the peep of the day with stealthy tread." Whitman in the overflowing heedless spontaneity of the first version (before "Song of Myself" became so overladen an epic journey through America that the original sexual connection was submerged in inventory) was in such rapture of self-creation that "God" was just as lovable and nameable as anything else. Perhaps that is the real point of naming God, including God in his many personae. The whole world of existent phenomena is open to Whitman's general lovingness, which is boundless affirmation. Nothing may be excluded; nothing is higher or lower than anything else. He is the perfect democrat, in religion as in love and politics. There is no hierarchy in his determination to love everything and everyone in one full sweep.

The essential point is that almost despite himself, Whitman made something infinitely precious of *Leaves of Grass*. The essence of it is a call for infinite harmony, harmony relating all things to the poet at the center. It is remarkable: every great Whitman poem grows out of itself, *on* itself as nature does. What runs through *Leaves of Grass* and turns a collection of poems into a *book* (a word Whitman always insisted on; it was his American testament) is his genius for evoking love, sympathy, "comradeship" and for receiving them in turn. Starting with the acceptance of homosexual love for himself, he transformed individual love into a love for everything natural that finally made not "God" sacred but the world.

The most beautiful expression of this is in "Crossing Brooklyn Ferry," with its vision of the future in the present. T. S. Eliot would not have agreed that Whitman on the East River (of all people and of all places!) anticipated the lines with which "Burnt Norton" opens *Four Quartets:*

Time present and time past
Are both perhaps present in time future,
And time future contained in time past.
If all time is eternally present
All time is unredeemable.

Whitman positively embraced the future to show that all times joined in being equally human. His "indiscriminate" love of life made this possible:

The impalpable sustenance of me from all things at all hours of the day,
The simple, compact, well-join'd scheme, myself disintegrated, every one disintegrated
yet part of the scheme,
The similitudes of the past and those of the future,
The glories strung like beads on my smallest sights and hearings, on the walk in the
street and the passage over the river.

This interweaving of different worlds in time is radiant *and* secular. It is our ability to imagine a future that gives permanence to what surrounds our temporal existence. We die, the world does not. Hence the lasting appeal of

Closer yet I approach you,
What thought you have of me now, I had as much of you—I laid in my stores in
advance,
I consider'd long and seriously of you before you were born.

Who was to know what should come home to me?
Who knows but I am enjoying this?
Who knows, for all the distance, but I am as good as looking at you now, for all you
cannot see me?

The sum of it is a love of the world that imparts sacredness to objects and people connected to us by the future. For Eliot time is circular in a way that would have shocked Whitman the radical democrat. The past, he liked to say in praise of his native land, was "feudal." It was exactly his own past in St. Louis along the Mississippi and summers off the Atlantic that entranced Eliot in the personal memories that pervade *Four Quartets*. To bring back the past was to transcend it into the larger circle of God's will that crowned belief in the Incarnation (another interweaving of past and future, based on the union of spirit and flesh).

Nevertheless, Whitman and Eliot are characteristically American in thinking of time as a promise, of something to be fulfilled. They can't wait "to get on with it." They both look forward to a world made secure by their imagination. "Little Gidding" ends *Four Quartets* with

We shall not cease from exploration
And the end of all our exploring
Will be to arrive where we started
And know the place for the first time.

Whitman would have laughed, "Tom, *I* never left—have been here all the time!" Eliot says "we" because he regards himself as a Christian speaking for Christians. Whitman can say "I" because he is in touch with everything he sees. Loves it all. How wonderful to see "glories strung like beads on my smallest sights and hearings, on the walk in the street and the passage over the river." It is this love that carries him into the future:

It avails not, time nor place—distance avails not,
I am with you, you men and women of a generation, or ever so many generations
    hence,
Just as you feel when you look on the river and sky, so I felt,
Just as any one of you is one of a living crowd, I was one of a living crowd.

By identifying with the "living crowd," Whitman really enters into the future—of a people's America crowded with men and women no different from himself. By admitting that "I too felt the curious abrupt questionings stir within me," he gains our trust—our love—he is talking about us—a century and a half yet to come! It is his constant call to himself to "merge and merge again"—by no means just as a lover—that has won me all my life to Whitman's rapture here. "Crossing Brooklyn Ferry" brings together earth, water, and sky into a wonder of space that alternates time now and time future like the tidal rise and fall of the East River. As the future awaits the present, so there is something in *looking* that enables us to recognize our own soul. This is what Emerson did for Whitman. This is what we can at last call proof of an American religion. It matters not that poets in Europe were also "transcendental." This was from Brooklyn, on a ferryboat, 1856.

You have waited, you always wait, you dumb, beautiful ministers,
Not you any more shall be able to foil us, or withhold yourselves from us,
We use you, and do not cast you aside—we plant you permanently within us,
We fathom you not—we love you—there is perfection in you also,

We receive you with free sense at last, and are insatiate henceforward,
You furnish your parts toward eternity,
Great or small, you furnish your parts toward the soul.

The very homeliness of this went to make Whitman lovable. The response to Whitman, creating an aura, went right into his work. One did not need to posit a supernatural Deity—Whitman did not—to be a "religious" poet. It was enough to *become* a religion. The more in his time he languished for attention as a poet, the more he presented himself as a unique example, the prophet of a wholly new age to come, an American of Americans. A "screamer" as he might be to the Establishment, something vaguely sacred, a touch of authority clung to someone who was, as a poet, so many things at once. Perhaps the "nigh young men" he describes in "Crossing Brooklyn Ferry" flirtatiously calling to him as he crossed Broadway helped form his idea of himself as irresistible. But crucial as liberated sex was to his self-developing legend, it was only a prelude to the comprehensive "vision" he gained from sex:

Swiftly arose and spread around me the peace and joy and knowledge that pass all the
  art and argument of the earth;
And I know that the hand of God is the elder hand of my own,
And I know that the spirit of God is the eldest brother of my own,
And that all the men ever born are also my brothers . . .
And the women my sisters and lovers,
And that a kelson of the creation is love;
And limitless are leaves stiff or drooping in the fields,
And brown ants in the little wells beneath them,
And mossy scabs of the worm fence, and heaped stones, and elder and mullen and
  pokeweed.

Pokeweed! A perennial herb better than its name, but it was a name that only a truly folk poet would have come up with to conclude the most exalted passage in "Song of Myself." So the rough earth and true personal spirituality (our American genius) came together. Not altogether, even in Whitman's old age. No other American writer made such a thing of being "old" at forty-six. With his great beard and the various slouches to which he put his hat, he was such a favorite of photographers that he was virtually a professional model. He willingly posed holding a "butterfly" on one finger. (It was wood, a contraption.)

Of course the "average" Americans Whitman was always calling to paid no attention. Nothing was farther from the reality of Whitman's emerging reputation than the resounding conclusion of his preface to *Leaves of Grass*.

> The soul of the largest and wealthiest and proudest nation may well go half-way to meet that of its poets. The signs are effectual. There is no fear of mistake. If the one is true the other is true. The proof of a poet is that his country absorbs him as affectionately as he has absorbed it.

Whitman's appeal was to the young, to rebels and "progressives," the sexually liberated, the freethinkers and socialist Utopians (especially in Germany) who anticipated that the twentieth century would at last be "theirs." He was admired in England by Tennyson, Swinburne, Hopkins, Edward Dowden, W. M. Rossetti, Edward Carpenter, and John Addington Symonds, and in Germany by young radicals and poets who were fated to die in the "Great War" with pocket editions of Whitman in their uniforms. Of course the "real" Whitman had to tell the German Jewish socialist Horace Traubel, who in 1873 became an intimate friend [...] and who meticulously recorded every last thought of the great man after 1888 in the six volumes of *With Walt Whitman in Camden*, "Be radical, be radical, be not too damned radical!"

But Whitman happily agreed with everything his admirers and disciples said about him. His time had come, his life was finally crowned. By 1872, summing up his career in "As a Strong Bird on Pinions Free," he generously admitted that in his poetry "one deep purpose underlay the others, and has underlain it and its execution ever since—and that has been the religious purpose." "Purpose" was certainly yielding to convention in a way that undercut the actual subtlety of his "purpose" as an *artist*. And he did not have to declare his faith in "immortality" when all his greatest poems, especially his one triumph as a truly "old" man, "Passage to India," made "immortality" less a password than a vision:

> *All these hearts as of fretted children shall be sooth'd,*
> *All affection shall be fully responded to, the secret shall be told,*

All these separations and gaps shall be taken up and hook'd and link'd together,
The whole earth, this cold, impassive, voiceless earth, shall be completely justified,
Trinitas divine shall be gloriously accomplish'd and compacted by the true son of
    God, the poet. . . .
Nature and Man shall be disjoin'd and diffused no more,
The true son of God shall absolutely fuse them.

Of course the poetry was not enough for those who wanted to be not admirers but disciples. How Whitman, the supposedly broken and half-paralyzed Whitman in Camden, actually furthered his legend as a cosmic figure is shown in the way he took over the adoring biography of him by the Canadian alienist Dr. Richard Maurice Bucke. Bucke, on encountering *Leaves of Grass* in 1867, became an instant "convert," thanks to the divine capabilities he saw in Whitman. Bucke's *Walt Whitman* (1883) is so rapturous in celebrating *Leaves of Grass* as "revealer and herald" of a religious era not yet reached that one sees in its most enthusiastic form the Romantic belief that poetry would rescue religion by replacing it.

> With the incoming moral states to which it belongs, certain cherished social and religious forms and usages are incompatible; hence the deep instinctive aversion and dread with which it is regarded by the ultra-conventional and conservative. Just so, in their far-back times, was Zoroastrianism, Buddhism, Mohammedanism, Christianity, and every new birth received. . . . So also our church-going, bible-reading, creeds, and prayers, will appear from its vantage-grounds mere make-believes of religion. . . . *Leaves of Grass* . . . is the preface and creator of a new era. . . . What the Vedas were to Brahmanism, the Law and the Prophets to Judaism, the Avesta and Zend to Zoroastrianism, the Kings to Confucianism and Taoism, the Pitakas to Buddhism, the Quran to Mohammedanism, will *Leaves of Grass* be to the future of American civilization.

Whitman, after his best work was done, never tired of summing up self and career, interpreting both in weary but friendly new perspectives. He never tired of self-portraits, especially when he discovered readers who thought him as wondrous as he did himself. A year before his death he wrote to Dr. Bucke likening himself to Lear as he went over the complete *Leaves of Grass* once again.

> From my own point of view I accept without demur its spurty (old Lear's irascibility)—its off-handedness, even evidence of decrepitdue & old fisherman's seine character as part of the *artism* (from my point of view) & as adherent as the determined cartoon of personality that dominates or rather stands behind all of *L. of G.* like the unseen master & director of the show.
>
> W. W.

Not without his blessing, he became a church. In Bolton, Lancashire, a group of "adherents" met weekly to read his poems aloud. This was a great source of cheer to people who habitually suffered from "despondency." On May 29, 1891, he wrote to one of its leaders, J. W. Wallace, that he was "badly prostrated, horrible torpidity" but went on to say, "I guess I have a good deal of the feeling of Epictetus & stoicism—or tried to have. They are specially needed in a rich & luxurious, & even scientific age. But I am clear that I include & allow & probably teach some things stoicism would frown upon & discard. One's pulses & marrow are not *democratic & natural* for nothing."

[1997]

LINCOLN: THE ALMIGHTY HAS HIS OWN PURPOSES

———•◆•———

I claim not to have controlled events, but confess plainly that events have controlled me. Now, at the end of three years' struggle the nation's condition is not what either party, or any man, devised, or expected. God alone can claim it.

Lincoln to Albert G. Hodges (April 4, 1864)

On March 4, 1865, Abraham Lincoln for the second time took the oath of office as president of the United States. As was the custom then, he was sworn in after delivering his inaugural address. On taking the oath, he kissed the open Bible. After the ceremony, Chief Justice Chase presented the Bible to Mrs. Lincoln and pointed to the pencil-marked verses kissed by the president, Isaiah 5:27–28:

> None shall be weary nor stumble among them; none shall slumber nor sleep; neither shall the girdle of their loins be loosed, nor the latchet of their shoes be broken.
>
> Whose arrows are sharp, and all their bows bent, their horses' hoofs shall be counted like flint, and their wheels like the whirlwind.

On this day Lincoln delivered the most remarkable inaugural address in our history—the only one that has ever reflected literary genius. Its last paragraph, beginning, "With malice toward none; with charity for all," is universally famous, but the heart of the address is the long preceding paragraph, which concludes (perhaps to the surprise of Lincoln himself, the firm rationalist in all things) in open wonder that perhaps, after all, God's hand could be seen settling "the slavery question."

There was good reason for the leader of a "Union" broken by three years of civil war—the North called it "the Great Rebellion" and the Confederacy "the War for Southern Independence"—not to be weary or stumble or sleep, but to be ready for battle with arrows sharp and bows strung. The previous November, Lincoln had been reelected, despite widespread disapproval of emancipation and bitterness that the war was taking so long. Lincoln had made sure that soldiers in the field would get to vote. He had triumphed over the dismissed head of the Army of the Potomac, George B. McClellan, whose Democratic Party platform, which McClellan had repudiated, advocated negotiations with the South leading to a compromise peace. There would have been no end to slavery in the foreseeable future.

Lincoln had for a long time expected defeat in the 1864 election. A series of smashing Union victories kept him in the White House despite the lack of sure national support for the Emancipation Proclamation or the hundred thousand ex-slaves in the Union army and navy. In March, Grant—at last a general "who fights," Lincoln rejoiced—had been made general-in-chief. In September, Sherman had captured Atlanta, going on to the sea to capture Savannah in December, and early the next year would rip the Confederacy apart as he stormed into the Carolinas. Sheridan in September and October triumphed in the Shenandoah Valley at Winchester, Fisher's Hill, and Cedar Creek. [But] it was not until the end of 1865 that the Thirteenth Amendment would finally be ratified, giving legal assurance to the long-tortured race that "neither slavery nor involuntary servitude . . . shall exist within the United States."

Victory was in the air, after three heartbreak years of frustration, incompetence, and defeat which must have made Lincoln grit his teeth as he was successively let down by McClellan, McDowell, Burnside, Hooker, and how many other generals quickly shown up by Lee, Jackson, Johnston, and Nathan Bedford Forrest. Sherman thought Forrest the most remarkable man to come out of the fighting.

Still, on March 4, 1865, despite anger among Radical Republicans in Congress because Lincoln was so eager to get states like Louisiana back in the Union with only 10 percent of the people professing loyalty, Lincoln was confident enough to say that "the progress of our arms, upon which all else chiefly depends, is as well known to the public as to myself; and it is, I trust, reasonably satisfactory and encouraging to all. With high hope for the future, no prediction in regard to it is ventured."

Lee was to surrender to Grant at Appomattox Court House on April 9. In masses too great to be resisted by their dispersed masters, the slaves had been voting for freedom with their feet. The South was soon to think of itself not as a defeated army but as a martyred civilization "baptized in blood," a cause made forever sacred by the struggle it had put up on its own soil against greater numbers and resources. Antislavery opinion might feel, in the words of Ulysses Grant, that slavery was "the worst cause for which men ever fought." The inextinguishable need of the master class to dominate showed itself in a furious hatred of the ex-slaves. In two years the Ku Klux Klan would form in Tennessee under the leadership of the same Nathan Bedford Forrest whose troops had massacred black Union soldiers at Fort Pillow. By sheer force of circumstances, the war to end "the Great Rebellion"—Lincoln's official policy—had become a second American revolution leading to the end of slavery. Lincoln's prime aim was to save the Union, "with or without slavery." In the first years of the war he had no more anticipated a holy war for human freedom than most Union soldiers expected or desired. Yet without the Civil War, slavery might have continued into the twentieth century. The Southern cause became so desperate that some Confederate leaders proposed arming the slaves. Lincoln responded that any slave who fought to preserve slavery deserved to be a slave.

Revisionist historians, far removed in time and spirit from the struggle for emancipation, like to worry the facts leading up to the Civil War in order to show that human slavery was not the root cause of the war. Even when academics allow that by the 1850s the agitation over slavery had become the prime disturbance of American life, "wiser heads" could somehow have fashioned some compromise or other that would have settled the matter without war. Ultimately, said the Lincoln expert David Herbert Donald in *Lincoln Reconsidered*, the problem was "an excess of democracy."

Abraham Lincoln knew better. As he said in the second inaugural, "One-eighth of the whole population were colored slaves, not distributed generally over the Union, but localized in the Southern part of it. These slaves constituted a peculiar and powerful interest. All knew that this interest was, some-how, the cause of the war."

The Lincolns in Kentucky had nothing but the ground they cleared; they were utterly removed from slaves and slave owners. They crossed the Ohio into southern Indiana, said George Dangerfield, with the "irremediable status of poor whites. . . . Ten years later, Thomas Lincoln heard the call of the Illinois prairies, and he and his family crossed the Wabash and the Sangamon. Their struggles and tragedies were those of all but the most fortunate migrants."

Lincoln grew up with the country, passing one frontier after another into the American heartland and finally settling in Springfield. As a constantly tested young man in pioneer territory with barely a month's formal schooling, self-educated, dependent on the hardest physical labor for the slightest claim to a better life, he was as much at home with American beginnings as Thomas Jefferson. Parson Mason Weems's life of George Washington was no fable to someone for whom the American Revolution was as holy as the creation. Lincoln's zeal for the Union over everything else was at the root of his political opposition to the extension of slavery, of his war policy, of his loyalty to the "republican system" in general, and of his concern for the American future. Confederate vice president Alexander Stephens, who knew Lincoln when they were both in Congress, said that Lincoln's feeling for the Union amounted to "religious mysticism." That recognizes the passion Lincoln brought to the subject. What is really interesting about it is Stephens's wonder at something so far removed from his own willingness as a slaveholder to destroy the coun-try in order to protect his property rights in human beings.

Lincoln was not a sanguine man by nature, nor did he ever lose the melan-choly and superstitious belief in "omens" that afflicted life on the frontier. He was a restlessly ambitious self-made man, a political animal to his fingertips who found himself in the law. That was his salvation, his career, his creed. Its name was reason, a faculty that relieved him of useless emotional upheavals and kept him stable, superior to the mob spirit of the frontier. Above all, rea-son linked him to his idol, Thomas Jefferson, and to the Revolution that was fading in the minds around him.

In his early address, 1838, to the Young Men's Lyceum of Springfield, he said that "the pillars of the temple of liberty . . . must fall, unless we, their descendants, supply their places with other pillars, hewn from the solid quarry of sober reason. Passion has helped us; but can do so no more. It will in future be our enemy. Reason, cold, calculating, unimpassioned reason, must furnish all the materials for our future support and defence."

As a young man, creating himself out of the few books available to him, Lincoln came to trust his own mind. The hysterical religious revivals that relieved the loneliness of the frontier had no effect on him, especially when roaring young men assured their audience that each person could ensure his own salvation. Neither did the "Free-Will" or Separate Baptists his parents joined when his mother was still alive, nor the Pigeon Baptist Church to which his father and stepmother subscribed. He was just not interested in any partic- ular creed; nothing he ever said on man in relation to God reminds one of Emerson's faith that man in himself is religious enough. Something of the Calvinism so natural to the hardships of the frontier clung to the churchless and fatalistic Lincoln—nothing was assured in this life, and everything good in it was a surprise, a gift—the only hint that there may yet be a Providence. For a long time he held to "the doctrine of necessity"—no one came to his own views freely. As president, he patiently endured hatred and threats of vio- lence that he considered inevitable to his severe sense of life as well as to his position. But everything had to be tested by his own mind. Beyond that—the shadows and, "This too will pass."

Lincoln, for all his theoretical loyalty to Jefferson, was far removed from the abstractions of the Virginia gentry who first wrote the laws. He made another idol of "the great compromiser" Henry Clay and became a highly suc- cessful lawyer for the dominant railroad in Illinois. He was prudent enough to be a Whig, that party of complacent successes divided by slavery that eventu- ally vanished into the new Republican Party. The law, operating in oral argu- ment and written documents, was Lincoln's mature schoolroom and helped to form the cogency and directness of his writing. His law associate Leonard Swett said after Lincoln's death that

> his whole life was a calculation of the law of forces and ultimate results. He believed the results toward which certain causes tended; he did not believe that those results would be materially hastened or impelled. . . . He believed from the first, I think, that the agitation of

slavery would produce its overthrow, and he acted upon the result as though it were present from the beginning.

Lincoln's partner William H. Herndon described Lincoln's perceptions as "slow, cold, clear, and exact." It has often been noted that he had "a country-man's mind." He was slow to make it up, but tenacious once he had made it up.

His fierce rationalism can also be seen as a reaction to the violence always surrounding blacks. The same man who when rejected by a woman could describe himself as "the most miserable man living" had no trouble standing up to ruffians. The speech to the Young Men's Lyceum in Springfield calling for "reason, cold, calculating, unimpassioned reason," also showed him deeply affected by attacks on blacks in free Illinois.

So in the debates with Senator Douglas that made him nationally famous, he easily made an appeal from one self-made man to others for the justice due free white labor. Lincoln, despite his one informal use of "nigger," would not stoop to the demagoguery that allowed Douglas, all too alert to the prejudices of his audience in southern Illinois, to horrify it with the news that Frederick Douglass, the runaway slave who had become the leading black abolitionist, had actually been seen riding in a carriage with a white woman.

Lincoln repeated the Free-Soil case from town to town in the seven debates with Douglas. Slavery was wrong, morally and humanly wrong, and imprisoned masters along with their slaves. As Jefferson had feared, it was as disturbing as "a firebell in the night." Lincoln charged that Douglas, along with a majority of the Supreme Court under Taney and accommodating Northern Democratic presidents Pierce and Buchanan, were conspiring to make the whole country safe for slavery.

Douglas won the Senate race, but Lincoln's was substantially the majority view in the North. Many (perhaps most) Northerners were as indifferent to slavery and abolitionist zeal as they were to the defense of slavery based on Scripture put up by Southern clergymen. They could not be indifferent to the South's determined effort, decade after decade, to nationalize its "peculiar institution." This, which the South believed to be the only way of safeguarding slavery, was the ultimate cause of the Civil War.

As president, Lincoln resisted the attack on Fort Sumter by calling for 75,000 troops. But as early as his special July 4, 1861, message to Congress, he said that the war to save the Union would establish a future in freedom for all:

This is essentially a People's contest. On the side of the Union, it is a struggle for maintaining in the world, that form, and substance of government, whose leading object is, to elevate the condition of men—to lift artificial weights from all shoulders—to clear the paths of laudable pursuit for all—to afford all, an unfettered start, and a fair chance, in the race of life.

At Gettysburg he transcended the war to proclaim a "new birth of freedom." Saying "*we* are met, *we* have come to dedicate ... *we* can not dedicate, *we* can not consecrate, *we* can not hallow," he ended by perceptibly raising his tone when he came to the word *people*—"government of the *people*, by the *people*, for the *people*." Karl Marx in his articles on the war for *The New York Tribune*, the young Henrik Ibsen in his furious elegy on the murder of Lincoln (for which he blamed the kings and potentates of Europe)—both understood, with Lincoln, that the victory of liberal democracy in America could be the supreme event of the century. "Thanks to all," Lincoln was to write in August 1863 after Grant's victory at Vicksburg cleared the Mississippi. (This to a man from Illinois who opposed the Emancipation Proclamation.) "The Father of Waters again goes unvexed to the sea.... Thanks to all. For the great republic—for the principle it lives by, and keeps alive—for man's vast future—thanks to all."

By March 4, 1865, with slavery disintegrating and the South going to capitulate in just one month, the president of the United States, reviewing the course of "the great contest," found it natural, at last, to declare for himself how utterly wrong and sinful he thought the whole system of slavery. To say this as president was to put many things behind him—not least his failure early in the war to countenance the immediate emancipation of slaves in the Confederate territory under their control won by Union generals Hunter and Fremont. This was the influence of New England, when, as Henry Adams remembered of the "dark days of 1856," "Concord glowed with pure light." But Lincoln was too worried about the border states remaining in the Union to agree with abolitionist and Transcendentalist New England ministers who theologized the war as God's own justice and demanded immediate and total emancipation. (They went to the White House to tell Lincoln they were carrying this message from God Himself. Lincoln replied, "Don't you think, gentlemen, He might have spoken first to *me*?") And of course the

Emancipation Proclamation granted freedom only to slaves whose masters were in rebellion.

[....]

Lincoln was so avid a politician that one of his law partners said his ambition gave him no rest. He grew up entirely apart from blacks and as a rising lawyer and public figure had no social reason to feel kinship—not many whites did, not even the New England abolitionists who had Frederick Douglass speak on their platform. Lincoln had learned early to restrain his feelings about the misery he had seen. He once wrote to his proslavery friend Joshua Speed, "I hate to see the poor creatures hunted down, and caught and carried back to their stripes, and unrewarded toils; but I bite my lip and keep quiet." He reminded Speed that years before, traveling from Louisville to St. Louis, they had seen slaves "shackled together with irons. That sight was a continual torment to me; and I see something like it every time I touch the Ohio, or any slave border."

Debating with Douglas for the Senate in 1858, Lincoln was outraged by Douglas's "declared indifference" to slavery. The trouble was not just Douglas's expediency, the folly of believing that "a house divided" *could* stand, but Douglas's "covert real zeal for the spread of slavery." Lincoln's passion on the subject here marks the moral leadership from the White House on the race question which seems to have died with him. Imagine any of our recent presidents breaking out like this:

> I hate it because of the monstrous injustice of slavery itself. I hate it because it deprives our republican example of its just influence in the world—enables the enemies of free institutions, with plausibility, to taunt us as hypocrites—causes the real friends of freedom to doubt our sincerity, and especially because it causes so many good men among ourselves into an open war with the very fundamental principles of civil liberty—criticizing the Declaration of Independence and insisting that there is no right principle of action but *self*-interest.

In a time when Southerners mocked the statement that "all men are created equal" in the Declaration of Independence as "absurd, contrary to fact," Lincoln's only counter to this, his supreme emblem of reason, was to go back to what was self-evident.

Lincoln's belief in the rationality of the law helps us to understand the nonconformity of his religious views. Then, as now, a majority of Americans professed belief in God, went to church, and, whether they knew or admitted it, surely thought of their church as a way of belonging and surviving in a violently divided society.

Lincoln never joined any organized church. His law partner in Springfield William H. Herndon saw him reading such Enlightenment skeptics as Voltaire, Tom Paine, and Count Volney—the latter thought morality the only point of religion. Whatever his indifference to frontier revival meetings and the primitive Baptist churches his parents attended, Lincoln's perfect confidence in his own mind (emotionally he was a depressive; as president he dreamed of his own death and state funeral) explains his religious independence.

Lincoln had been right to fear, in his first debate with Douglas on August 21, 1858, that "there is no peaceful extinction of slavery in prospect for us." Seven years later, when he stood in front of the Capitol to deliver his second inaugural, all his positing of the issue on the territories alone, all general hopes for compromise with the South, had become ancient history. The most dramatic thing about the second inaugural, what makes its historical candor so surprising against the usual official rhetoric, is that it says modern history in America begins with and because of the Civil War. Lincoln can now say openly that "the Negro" is the issue of the time and slavery the cause of the Civil War.

Of course this same "Negro" is still just an object, exists entirely within the context of slavery, and is as much a symbol to Lincoln as he is to everyone else. For all politicians, as for most American citizens, he is never an individual human person. But through the impassioned biblical evocations of the second inaugural, [the abstraction] has been moved from the political struggle over the territories between North and South to the condemnation of slavery itself. Such condemnation could arise only from principles already known to a Christian nation thanks to the one text most Americans regarded as the abiding interpretation of their existence.

The Bible was still an essential personal resource for this generation of Americans. South and North each found in the Bible justification for its struggle, its own self-declared holiness. Never again in American history would

there be so much honest, deeply felt invocation of God's purpose in supporting one or the other side. Everything so long festering in the American heart
over the need to believe that God does intervene in history—everything that
was to be threatened after the war by the idea of nature as a self-operating
mechanism—now flamed out with all the passion of war itself. The Bible was
still a bridge between life and death. The Christian promise of salvation
offered the one testimony to which people had access that there is "surely" a
life beyond this one, a judgment superior to the earthly judgment. And
this was burningly proved by the sacrifice of life itself, as shown by the
unprecedented, once improbable determination of hundreds of thousands of
Americans to mutilate and destroy one another because of loyalties that North
and South believed to have the sanction of the Almighty Father, Creator of the
Universe, who between 1861 and 1865 was still sitting in judgment on each individual creature.

More than one American was now remembering the Book of Numbers:
"Would to God all the Lord's people were prophets." John Brown's body lay
a-mould'ring in the grave, but his soul went marching on. Was not the terrible
war a carrying out of what Brown in his last letter from Charlestown Prison,
December 2, 1859, had defined as the "active" principle of religion "pure and
undefiled"? Were there vengeful antislavery and black soldiers who approvingly
remembered that in bleeding Kansas, Brown had justified taking out and
killing proslavery people because "without the shedding of blood there is no
remission of sins"?

Sin? Harriet Beecher Stowe had represented the "pure" conscience of abo-
litionism when she had written in Uncle Tom's Cabin, "What is peculiar to slavery, and distinguishes it from free servitude, is evil, and only evil, and that
continually." On the next page she added, "The great object of the author in
writing has been to bring this subject of slavery, as a moral and religious question, before the minds of all those who profess to be followers of Christ, in
this country." But Southern preachers, poets, politicians, and editors had no
trouble defending slavery by the New as well as Old Testament, and in this
they were not simply rationalizing their economic interests and social structure. They, too, were loyal to a religious tradition. They, too, were believers.
"Sin" was a critical issue of the time, on both sides of the slavery question.
The appeal to righteousness and the sense of moral guilt were more vehement

and impassioned than anything Germans expressed over Auschwitz, Russians over the Gulag, Americans over the "wasting" of peasant hamlets in Vietnam.

But when before the war—impossible then to imagine so terrible a civil war—had any national leader, not just some wild and vehement William Lloyd Garrison publicly tearing up the Constitution and professing that he was speaking for God's own truth in its simplicity and power—when had it been possible for any national leader, much less the president himself, to call slavery an offense against God and to suggest that the war was God's own punishment of those who had profited from the pain and exploitation of their slaves?

The age of *belief* reaches its culmination in the second inaugural, but with a subtlety and humility that make words from a war president on this public occasion all the more astonishing.

Lincoln begins calmly, almost wearily, reviewing the struggle over slavery that had inevitably ended in war. He is magnanimous enough to say, despite the South Carolina "fire-eaters" who opened the war by firing on Fort Sumter, "All dreaded it—all sought to avert it." Without mentioning the threats to himself, he recalls the dangers under which he had delivered the first inaugural in 1861, describes insurgent agents in Washington "seeking to *destroy* the Union without war—seeking to dissolve the Union, and divide effects, by negotiation. Both parties deprecated war; but one of them would *make* war rather than let the nation survive; and the other would *accept* war rather than let it perish. And the war came." It came, Lincoln says categorically, because one-eighth of the whole population were colored slaves. These slaves constituted

> a peculiar and powerful interest. All knew that this interest was, somehow, the cause of the war. To strengthen, perpetuate, and extend this interest was the object for which the insurgents would rend the Union, even by war; while the government claimed no right to do more than to restrict the territorial enlargement of it.

After this forthright summary of how the war came (Southerners still insist the issue was one of states' rights), Lincoln notes, "Neither party expected for the war, the magnitude, or the duration, which it has already attained. Neither anticipated that the *cause* of the conflict might cease with, or even before, the conflict itself should cease. Each looked for an easier triumph." To which he added a perfect description of the war—of all great wars—"and a result less fundamental and astounding."

Suddenly we move from the surprise and havoc of war to what—in 1865—was still central to any invocation of God—God as the one true judge, who alone makes the final judgment:

> Each looked for an easier triumph, and a result less fundamental and astounding. Both read the same Bible, and pray to the same God; and each invokes His aid against the other. It may seem strange that any man should dare to ask a just God's assistance in wringing their bread from the sweat of other men's faces; but let us judge not that we be not judged. The prayers of both could not be answered; that of neither has been answered fully. The Almighty has his own purposes.

No president before Lincoln had thought it imperative to discuss a divisive social issue in a religious context, and this with such passion and tribulation. Never before had America been in a war whose immediate effects were so "fundamental and astounding." The general sorrow of the war brought to a peak of intensity not seen before or after a whole people's trust in God. Never again would a consensus in America reach such depths of religious urgency.

God was not yet dead in 1865, nor was He yet entirely identified with what Puritans, who thought the divine mystery more interesting than petty behavior, called "the filthy rags of righteousness." He was the presence and the destiny, the ever-living God of religious seekers and zealots, absolutists of the spirit. The greatest of them led His disciples to pray that the Father's will may yet be done on earth, as it is in heaven. He was the God not of correct behavior but of fire in the hearts of men.

Like all honest men on the subject who value their freedom from orthodoxy, Lincoln had had his doubts about the very existence of God. But he was now president of the United States in the most terrifying crisis. It was up to him to unite his country morally as well as in war. He was carrying it all on his shoulders, aware at every excruciating moment that the country could survive only by the sacrifice of hundreds of thousands of young men.

In a little more than a month after his inauguration, April 14, Good Friday, he would be shot to death by a mad actor who had been driven to frenzy at hearing Lincoln in his last speech, April 11, envision the possibility of Negro suffrage. Lincoln never got over the superstitions of the primitive frontier. He had witnessed the violence that never leaves American life. His life had been threatened by Confederate partisans as he had made his way to Washington to take office. It would not have seemed strange to him, who had sent so many other men to death, that he might have to give up his own life.

"This mighty scourge of war" had made him more truly a man of sorrows than this haunted man had been before. But it had liberated him from his pre-war compromises and his enforced declaration that he claimed no right to do more about slavery than restrict the territorial enlargement of it. He had said that "the great body of the Northern people do crucify their feelings in order to maintain their loyalty to the Constitution and the nation." Belabored on all sides in the first years of war for seeming "vacillating," he was now able to speak out with a passionate clarity of heart and mind when so many doubts had been burned away by the emergence of Grant.

Lincoln now had the freedom to say about Southerners praying for the continuance of slavery, "It may seem strange that any men should *dare* to ask a just God's assistance in wringing their bread from the sweat of other men's faces." Lincoln the flatboatman, carpenter, cabin builder, Indian fighter, farmer, hunter, rail-splitter had known a good deal more about sweat than the leading Southern Presbyterian divine, the Reverend James Henley Thornwell, who said that slaves were *lucky* to have been "redeemed from the *bondage* of barbarism and sin."

Lincoln's opposite number, President Jefferson Davis of the Confederate States of America, a West Point graduate and a Mississippi slaveholder, had in early proclamations asked Southerners to observe days of humiliation and prayer in full confidence that "it hath pleased Almighty God, the Sovereign Disposer of events, to protect and defend the Confederate States hitherto in their conflict with their enemies, and to be unto them a shield."

The seemingly built-in religiosity of the South comes through to us, almost amusingly, in the fundamentalism of that expert killer General Thomas Jonathan Jackson—the immortal Stonewall—who in battle cried "Kill them! Kill them!" but who was not sure it was proper to fight on the Sabbath.

General Edward Porter Alexander, head of Confederate artillery, is hard on Jackson in his memoirs *Fighting for the Confederacy*. Alexander bitterly criticizes him for his action at the Seven Days' Battles (June 26–July 2, 1862). Alexander emphasizes Jackson's "incredible slackness, and delay, and hanging back, which . . . decidedly slackened his own exertions, with the result that General Lee's victory was shorn of the capture of McClellan's entire army."

> The question naturally arises, what was the matter with him? . . . For myself, I think that the one defect in General Jackson's character was his religious beliefs. He believed with absolute faith, in a personal God. . . . It is customary to say that "Providence did not intend that we should win." But Providence did not care a row of pins about it. If it did, it was a very unintelligent Providence not to bring the business to a close—the close it wanted—in less than four years of most terrible and bloody war. . . . It was a serious incubus upon us that during the whole war our president and many of our generals really and actually believed that there *was* this mysterious Providence always hovering over the field . . . and that prayers and piety might win its favor from day to day.
>
> We had the right to fight, but our fight was against what might be called a Darwinian development—or an adaptation to changed and changing conditions.

By the time he wrote this, the irreverent general of artillery did not have to say that the South in defeat recouped itself religiously as "the Religion of the Lost Cause, Baptized in Blood." This creed became a favorite way of preserving, in its own eyes, the godliness of the South.

By contrast, Lincoln the supremely self-made man, the assiduous politician whose ambition knew no rest, had learned in war all too much about the limitations of the human will. His doubts accorded with his sense of a universe not made exclusively for man's self-interest. He was interestingly unlike the divines, South and North, who were perfectly assured that God spoke to them and acted entirely in their behalf. He said in his address that he found particularly "strange" whatever upheld human bondage. In humility he quoted Matthew 7:1: "But let us judge not that we be not judged." He concluded his third paragraph: "The prayers of both could not be answered: that of neither has been answered fully."

In his torturing responsibility to the nation, to the future of democratic government in the world, Lincoln had come through a terrible experience to submit to a power higher and greater than anything his political ambition had prepared him for. Now he felt himself responsible before God for whatever he did and said to guide the nation.

The most compelling sentence to me of the second inaugural is the one that leads to the essence of the speech in the fourth paragraph. There is a troubled searching here of God's will, a startling admission by a man who was as self-trusting in religion as he was in law and the art of writing. *The Almighty Has His Own Purposes.* And it is all he has to say with any confidence about God's will.

He then turns to what he *is* sure of—the sinfulness of slavery. He draws on Matthew 18:7: "Woe unto the world because of offences! for it must needs be that offences come; but woe to that man by whom the offence cometh!" Jesus is here speaking of offenses against children. It is typical of Lincoln's literary acumen as well as his sense of urgency that he seized on the word *offences*—so much more striking than *temptations* or *hindrances* in post–King James translations—to launch into a passage so awesome, a great public cry from the heart:

> If we shall suppose that American slavery is one of those offences which, in the providence of God, must needs come, but which, having continued through His appointed time, He now wills to remove, and that he gives to both North and South this terrible war, as the woe due to those by whom the offence came, shall we discern therein any departure from those divine attributes which the believers in a Living God always ascribe to Him? Fondly do we hope—fervently do we pray—that this mighty scourge of war may speedily pass away. Yet, if God wills that it continue, until all the wealth piled by the bondman's two hundred and fifty years of unrequited toil shall be sunk, and until every drop of blood drawn with the lash, shall be paid by another drawn with the sword, as was said three thousand years ago, so still must be said "the judgments of the Lord, are true and righteous altogether."

This is extraordinary, but so long buried in official marble with other American scriptures that unless its conditionals are noted, one is likely to miss the religious hesitation in it, Lincoln's actual reserve. "Let us suppose," he says in effect, that slavery is an offense that God inexplicably allowed into human history. Let us even suppose that he allowed just so much time for it. To suppose anything like this is actually to suppose a very peculiar God. But since it all happened as described, and believers hold God accountable for all things, one can only yield to the enigma of having such a God at all. It is clear that the terrible war has overwhelmed the Lincoln who identified himself as the man of reason. It has brought him to his knees, so to speak, in heartbreaking awareness of the restrictions imposed by a mystery so encompassing it can only be called "God." Lincoln could find no other word for it.

On April 4, 1864, writing to a Kentuckian who was troubled by the enlistment of ex-slaves in the Union forces, Lincoln explained how his views of slavery had evolved to the point where he now fully approved the enlistment of 130,000. He had always been naturally antislavery, quoting himself: "If slavery is not wrong, nothing is wrong." But as president he initially felt that he had "no unrestricted right to act officially upon this judgment and feeling." Early in the war, he had not allowed Generals Fremont and Hunter to free slaves under their control. He had permitted measures, clearly unconstitutional, to become lawful so as to preserve the country. Nothing was so imperative as to avoid the wreck of government, country, and Constitution altogether. Since the border states, like Kentucky, had declined his proposal for compensated emancipation, he had no choice but that of "laying a strong hand upon the colored element." Those who objected to these soldiers, seamen, and laborers could not now, in the same breath, claim to support the Union. Lincoln went on:

> I attempt no compliment to my own sagacity. I claim not to have controlled events, but confess plainly that events have controlled me. Now, at the end of three years' struggle, the nation's condition is not what either party, or what any man, devised or expected. God alone can claim it. If God now wills the removal of a great wrong, and wills also that we of the North as well as you of the South, will pay fairly for our complicity in that wrong, impartial history will find therein new cause to attest and revere the justice and goodness of God. Yours truly, Abraham Lincoln.

Lincoln's God was born of war. It would not have survived without him, since only Lincoln understood Him. Lincoln had nothing to say about Jesus as redeemer and intervener in this life. What was personal to Lincoln was a sense of divinity wrested from the many contradictions in human effort. God came to him through a certain exhaustion. Faith was still deep and intense enough to allow doubt and survive it. The sense of Providence during the Civil War— there was still no alternative—was of a kind we cannot now fully take in.

In Lincoln's own "fiery trial" we see a refusal to "know" God and to see Him directing all one's hopes and ambitions in life. What we have in the second inaugural is religiously tentative, like our own effort to say that there is no peace. We live on a precipice.

The close of the second inaugural—charity for all and malice toward none—is memorable because it is noble and surprising to come out of so ghastly a war. But nothing to my mind is so worth repeating as the veritable outcry earlier over the iniquity of slavery: "Yet, if God wills that it continue, until all the wealth piled by the bondman's two hundred and fifty years of unrequited toil shall be sunk, and until every drop of blood drawn with the lash shall be paid by another drawn with the sword, as was said three thousand years ago, so still it must be said 'the judgments of the Lord, are true and righteous altogether.' "

To the New York political boss Thurlow Weed, who had complimented him on the address, Lincoln on March 14 admitted, "I expect it to wear as well as—perhaps better than—anything I have produced; but I believe it is not immediately popular. Men are not flattered by being shown that there has been a difference of purpose between the Almighty and them. To deny it, however, in this case, is to deny that there is a God governing the world. It is a truth which I thought needed to be told; and as whatever of humiliation there is in it, falls most directly on myself, I thought others might afford for me to tell it."

The North triumphed, leaving behind it such idealism as Lincoln, Harriet Beecher Stowe, Julia Ward Howe, and abolitionists like the two younger brothers of William and Henry James (both wounded in the war) had contributed to the Union cause. The crass triumphalism in which the war ended for the North, plus the intoxication of riches, the emergence of a scientific culture, and the settling of the West abetted the erosion of religious sentiment among writers and scholars. Skeptical veterans of the war like Oliver Wendell Holmes Jr. and Ambrose Bierce were ironic about a society in which a John D. Rockefeller righteously declared, "God gave me my money."

The triumphant North needed proof of its saintliness, and found it in the consecration of Abraham Lincoln. The civil religion that came out of the war turned America itself into a sacred object and ritual and demanded that America be its own religion—and that everybody had to believe in it. The Lincoln who never joined the Church became the god of a godless religion. Under the smug Republican administration of Calvin Coolidge, a great temple in Washington was built around a statue of Lincoln seated on a throne. Now the people truly had someone eternally to worship.

Lincoln had been assassinated on a Good Friday. The overwrought sermons that followed on Easter Sunday of course turned the dead president into an American Christ. His body went home to Springfield on a journey that stopped in city after city so that Lincoln could lie in state over and over again.

> *Coffin that passes through lanes and streets,*
> *Through day and night with the great cloud darkening the land,*
> *With the pomp of the inloop'd flags, with the cities draped in black,*
> *With the show of the States themselves as of crape-veil'd women standing,*
> *With processions long and winding and the flambeaus of the night,*
> *With the countless torches lit, with the silent sea of faces and the unbared heads,*
> *With the waiting depot, the arriving coffin, and the sombre faces.*

His body, thought safely interred in Springfield, was briefly stolen, bringing more associations with the Christ who did not remain in His tomb. Lincoln had become the divine Son he never publicly addressed. A Lincoln never less than kindly was imposed on every association with the Civil War.

A visitor to Gettysburg notes that with the exception of the Gettysburg Address, there is no explanation of how the war came about, no mention of slavery. But on display are swords in profusion, cannons, rifles. Robert E. Lee in a small diorama is shown holding the reins of his beloved horse Traveller and comforting the survivors of Pickett's charge. This does not exactly get to the substance of what Lincoln called a new birth of freedom.

A century and a half later it is possible to say that religion and America as a religion are in the minds of many people synonymous. Lincoln said America was a proposition. Religion was to him a matter of the most intensely private conviction. Did he suspect that a wholly politicized religion would yet become everything to many Americans? It was different during the agitation over slavery and the outbreak of fratricidal slaughter. A great many people were certain that they lived and died overseen by God, for purposes instilled in them by God. One cannot think of the long, long story of black bondage and the war that ended it without a shiver of awe. It is the one chapter in American life that brings us back to biblical history.

[1997]

EMILY DICKINSON:
CALLED BACK

———◆———

Emily Dickinson died in Amherst on May 15, 1886. A few days before, she had written her Norcross cousins, "Called back," and this phrase is on her stone in the Dickinson family plot.

Called back. Whatever the faith that this old-fashioned phrase may seem to express, it is more typical of Emily Dickinson's verbal economy than of her religion. No one who reads far into the 1,775 poems that Thomas H. Johnson has edited with such scrupulousness and literary intelligence in *The Complete Poems of Emily Dickinson* (substantially the same text as the definitive three-volume edition Mr. Johnson prepared for the Harvard University Press in 1955, but without the variants for each poem) can miss the fact that Emily Dickinson was not sure of what being "called back" could mean. In poem after poem she expressed, in her odd blend of heartbreaking precision and girlish winsomeness, the basic experience, in the face of death, of our fear, our awe, our longing—and above all, of our human vulnerability, of the limit that is our portion. It is this sense of our actuality, this vision without certainty, this dwelling only on our possibility, that makes her poems so awesome and so witty, for she likes to catch things exactly, and implicitly expresses her delight in hitting the target.

I cannot dance upon my Toes—
No Man instructed me—
But oftentimes, among my mind,
A glee possesseth me. . . .

Until recently, however, it was exactly this quality of precision, bringing home the felt sensation, that in many instances her editors missed or blurred or omitted. The reason for this is a tragic-comic tale of genius in a provincial setting.

During her lifetime, Emily Dickinson had only seven poems published— all of them appeared anonymously and, as Mr. Johnson has said, almost surreptitiously. Each of them had in some way been changed and damaged by Victorian editors who distrusted her originality. Her only contact with the "literary world" had been the Boston critic Thomas Wentworth Higginson, to whom she had written in 1862 for guidance, and who advised her with a kindly obtuseness that did not make the seclusive Emily less lonely. After her death, in helping to edit the first volume of her poems (1890), he changed many lines in order to make them immediately acceptable. One mass of Emily Dickinson's poems, almost nine hundred of them, had been discovered by her sister Lavinia only after her death, and most of them, as Mr. Johnson explains in his introduction to the Harvard Press edition of the poems, were in different stages of composition and sewn together in little packets. No one in her immediate circle had guessed at Emily's productivity, and the discovery of a major poet by no means rejoiced everyone she had loved. When her sister Lavinia went for help to their brother Austin's wife, Sue, who had been Emily's special friend, Sue sulkily sat on the poems until Lavinia went to the wife of an Amherst College astronomer, Mrs. Mildred Todd, who with Higginson's help put out a first selection of the poems in 1890.

Slowly, as Emily Dickinson's unexpectedly large reputation came home to Amherst, a contest over manuscripts began. The parties were Sue's daughter, Martha Dickinson Bianchi, who with Alfred Leete Hampson issued several editions of her aunt's poetry, and Mrs. Todd and *her* daughter, Millicent Todd Bingham. Eventually, Mrs. Bianchi's share was bought up and donated to Harvard, while the Todd-Bingham interests, so to speak, were transferred to Amherst College. Surely there is a new version of Henry James's *The Aspern*

Papers in this tale. Even now, although Mr. Johnson was able to gather all the poems together for this great edition, rival claims persist.

[....]

I like Emily Dickinson's dashes. I am glad that Mr. Johnson has put them back. If that is the way she wrote, that is the way she wrote. The dashes have a light fierceness; they set the rhythm of her thinking. And in this great poem of Death's taking a lady out for a drive, the dashes help to create that "shudder of awe" that Goethe thought was man's only proper response to life and death. It is her ability to make us shudder that is Emily Dickinson's greatest achievement. No wonder that where some nineteenth-century American writers seem great, she is merely deep. "Deep" is not "great," for she does not have Whitman's scope, his ability to make us think of his poetry as the instrument of the world process. On the other hand, greatness of a certain kind—greatness of subject, of vision, of voice—which we associate with Emerson and Whitman and Melville, has been so much more frequent than deepness that we rarely notice such a distinction. We do not even know that it can exist. The chief quality of our greatest writers is that each of them brings a wholly new world into being: each is the prophet of a new consciousness, virtually the teacher of a new religion. Their virtues are always rebelliousness, independence, self-sufficiency.

But the originality of a new religious teaching, though it can be electrifying in its power to change our minds, to make us see the world with new eyes, is not the only literary virtue. As literature, Whitman and Emerson and Thoreau do not have the texture constantly to engage and to surprise us, to uncover distinctions and to reveal new subtleties. Emily Dickinson does. She does not create a new world, as Whitman does; she gives us the range of this one.

Perhaps the quality that so fascinates me in her work is only the inherent quality of poetry itself, which with every word, stroke on stroke, establishes the poet's inner consciousness as our true world. It may be that in this country we have had all too little poetry (as opposed to declamation in the last century and fine word-painting in this), and so are constantly surprised by the precision of feeling, the depth of sound, that are found in so great a beginning as

Because I could not stop for Death—
He kindly stopped for me—

The Carriage held but just Ourselves—
And Immortality.

But surely the great quality of this poem, on the surface so painfully witty, so ironically demure, is that it remains enigmatic. The poem describes Death calling for a lady, and the journey they take, although described with touching brief glimpses of the world fast vanishing from her consciousness, remains mysterious and incommunicable. The horses' heads were toward Eternity; there is no going back. We can no longer see behind us, yet what Eternity itself is we cannot say.

To write of death with this wonder, this openness, this overwhelming communication of its *strangeness*—this is to show respect for the lords of life and death. This respect is what true poetry lives with, not with the armed fist of the perpetual rebel. But to know the limits is to engage subtlety and irony and humor; it is to write with a constant wariness of the gods. Emerson thought he had licked the problem of the gods by replacing worship with personal imagination. Thoreau, whose whole work is a mystic's quest for certainty, drove his entreaty into those overcharged single sentences that represent his artistic achievement. Whitman hoped that on occasion he might be mistaken for a god. Melville, who loved the myth of Prometheus, insisted on his antagonism to the gods. But all these are attitudes, whistlings in the dark, sharply in contrast with Emily Dickinson's provisional, ironic, catch-as-catch-can struggle with her own fears. She gave as her primary reason for writing poetry—"I had a terror—since September—I could tell to none—and so I sing, as the Boy does by the Burying Grounds—because I am afraid." Perhaps she was thinking of the love she had never had, the pain of separation that can be like death, that is a death. So many of her poems are about death that the word, in her poems, finally becomes the symbol and the effect of all separation. In the great poem that I have been discussing, death is a journey out of the known world; it is a gradual separation from the light. Yet the tone of the poem on the surface is playful, even coy. The emotional charge of the poem, the mysterious sense of submission that it leaves us with, lies in the contrast between the whimsicality of language and the mystery of the destination even after the journey is over. There is even a particular achievement in identifying a Victorian lady's submission and weakness with the human condition!

And I had put away
My labor and my leisure too,
For His Civility—

With the next stanza (the third), the sense of the passage, of the slow separation from life that absorbed her in so many poems, is borne home to us in significant images of human struggle:

We passed the School, where Children strove
At Recess—in the Ring—

and of the ebbing world:

We passed the Fields of Gazing Grain—
We passed the Setting Sun—

The sense of increasing cold, the gradual passage toward death, the lady's finding herself inadequately dressed and armed against the hill of death—this reaches its unforgettable apogee in the revelation:

Since then—'tis Centuries—and yet
Feels shorter than the Day
I first surmised the Horses' Heads
Were toward Eternity—
We slowly drove—He knew no haste

This last image catches first the drawn-out sense of intimation, and then the shock of irrevocability that is our strongest sense of death. When one thinks of how many human beings have tried to get around this fact, and how few have succeeded in expressing it, we have a sudden sense of the most that human beings can know and feel. We are "with it," as they say, all the way. We have a sense of the human soul stretched to the farthest, of valor encompassing the most that it can know.

[1961]

CREATURES OF CIRCUMSTANCE:
MARK TWAIN

———◆———

Only an American would have seen in a single lifetime the growth of
the whole tragedy of civilization from the primitive forest clearing.
—*Bernard Shaw to Hamlin Garland, 1904*

I went right along, not fixing up any particular plan, but just trusting
to Providence to put the right words in my mouth when the time
came; for I'd noticed that Providence always did put the right words
in my mouth, if I left it alone.
—*Mark Twain*, Huckleberry Finn

All I wanted was to go somewheres; all I wanted was a change.
—*Mark Twain*, Huckleberry Finn

[. . . .]

Henry James is supposed to have said that only primitive people could
enjoy Mark Twain. Mark Twain was always more popular in England than
James, who was not popular there at all. He was a favorite on the Continent,
where James would never have an audience. Of course "delicious poor dear old
M.T.," as James condescended after their one meeting, was no more "primitive" than James himself. He was intensely respectful—for himself—of all
Victorian amenities. But growing up with the country, as James never did,
absorbing its unrest, its extremes of poverty and wealth, its crudest lust for
power and position, he naturally identified himself with the many Americans
who were forever fighting it out, just barely keeping their heads above water.
James gave primacy to his own impressions; this made Europe sacred as the
favorite source of his impressions. Mark Twain's first book, *The Innocents Abroad*

(1869), typically took him to Europe and other holy places as a destroyer, the "American vandal."

These two major storytelling talents of a time and place when realistic fiction began to dominate our literature did not feel that *they* were living in the same time or place. They could not read each other. Mark Twain said he would rather be "damned to John Bunyan's heaven" than have to read *The Bostonians,* conceivably the one James novel he might have attempted for its satire on respectable New England. But as he confessed to Kipling, he did not read fiction at all; he preferred biography and history, *fact* books. The genius of fiction and the waywardness of nineteenth-century America permitted James and Mark Twain to make contraries of storytelling, of form, of literature itself, while retaining their parity as individualists.

In the end both came to what James called "the imagination of disaster"— James because his conservative "tradition," sacred Europe, was as corrupt as anything else; Mark Twain because nothing failed him like success. But disasters were only the outer shell of capitalism, the great God of chance, the Balzac novel of grandeur and decline that every ambitious nineteenth-century soul lived through. James, who was to say that the starting point of all his work was "loneliness," tried to find in society imaginatively considered what he despaired of finding in lasting affection. Mark Twain came to say that "the greater the love, the greater the tragedy." Even the women in his family were too frail to support his demand for constant assurance; wife and daughters sickened, then died on him.

But James and Mark Twain were certainly Americans of their time and place. Both began life under the rule of overwhelmingly religious fathers: James became indifferent to organized religion, Mark Twain hostile. Both were wanderers from earliest age; both were significantly without the conventionalizing university stamp that our bravest speculative minds—Whitman, Melville, Dickinson—were also free of. Both became preeminent literary figures very early, always with *some* audience for James, an eager one for Mark Twain, and were indefatigable producers into their seventies. Both were star writers for the new magazines that made fiction a going concern in their time. Yet both were increasingly idiosyncratic and uneasy in relation to the mainstream of fiction in English; both felt in old age that their audiences had not kept up with their originality and independent force. Both, despite their great success in society, their attraction (Mark Twain's was magnetic) for the great and powerful, ended up American isolates like Hawthorne, Melville, Dickinson, Whitman.

Mark Twain's harshly Calvinist father died broke when his younger son was twelve, leaving with him a searing memory of having to look at his father's corpse—no doubt because it exposed the ultimate humiliation of the human body. He was a wandering printer in his teens, a newspaperman, a silver miner, an editor, a correspondent, a professional humorist, and finally, after a practical and respectable Victorian marriage, a newspaper owner, property owner, and best-seller on the subscription system. This fabulous American career, representing America to itself, made Mark Twain the legendary example of what his friend William Dean Howells called the post–Civil War type—"the man who has risen." Unlike the general type, Mark Twain became the man who saw through the pretenses of society. The frontier, Howells said, made Mark Twain more "the creature of circumstances than the Anglo-American type." The frontier broke up all cultural traditions even when it wanted to respect them; it was derisive of the consolations of religion even when it retained the church as an institution and a social control; it *lived* the survival of the fittest; it naturally venerated the profit motive, the predatory character, the rich strike, and the eventual domination by monopoly. It took violence as the proof of manhood, made a cult of woman, the "good" woman, at a time—as you never learn from Mark Twain—when whoring as well as boozing and gambling were the chief distractions from prospecting. The frontier, having no tradition, worked on images of the past like acid.

It also created the picturesque figure of the liar, the deceiving teller of tales, the professional hoodwinker of the innocents back East. The West became an idyll even when—sometimes because—its inescapable savagery could not be concealed. It became a fundamental article of romance for some new realists. His assiduously pleasing friend Howells, from the old Western Reserve (Ohio) but long since merged into Boston, adored "Clemens" (the two were always "Clemens" and "Howells" to each other) because the western environment seemed to stick to him. Howells said he never tired, even when he wished to sleep, watching his friend lounge through hotel rooms in the long nightgown he preferred and telling the story of his life, "the inexhaustible, the fairy, the Arabian nights story, which I could never tire of even when it began to be told again."

[. . . .]

Mark Twain's world was all personal, disjointed, accidental. He was indeed, as Howells said, the "creature of circumstances." And so were his characters, which made them creatures of chance in a world more skeptical than had been seen before in the literature of "God's own country." "Circumstances" made Mark Twain, and the shock and fascination of them in succession gave the airy tone to his work. His genius lay in accumulating episodes; he turned life into a stream of facts and pictures—comic, unpredictable, exaggerated, wild—without overall meaning, without ideology, without religion.

From the beginning, Mark Twain's real subject—against a landscape of unlimited expectations and constant humbling—was the human being as animal nature, human cussedness taken raw, single traits magnified as fun, pretense, burlesque, spectacle, and violence. He took from the blatant demonstrativeness of frontier humor its central image of man undomesticated, removed from his traditional surroundings—a stranger wandering into a thin and shifting settlement of other strangers, then plunging into a dizzying succession of experiences always "new."

Mark Twain is the ancestor of all that twentieth-century fiction of southern poverty, meanness, and estrangement that was out of step with American moralism and pious abstractionism. The characters are generally low, and there is no attempt to make them less so. Southern characters just *lived*, without ostensible purpose, sometimes in mud everlasting, as do the "Arkansaw" characters in that "little one-horse town in a big bend"—chapter 21 of *Huckleberry Finn*—where Colonel Sherburn will shoot down poor, miserable Boggs. This is the poor white's South before (and after) the Civil War, not the plantation house from which Colonel Sherburn scorned the mob.

All the streets and lanes was just mud; they warn't nothing else *but* mud—mud as black as tar, and nigh about a foot deep in some places; and two or three inches deep in *all* the places. The hogs loafed and grunted around, everywheres. You'd see a muddy sow and a litter of pigs come lazying along the street and whollop herself down in the way, where folks had to walk around her, and she'd stretch out, and shut her eyes, and wave her ears, whilst the pigs was milking her, and look as happy as if she was on salary. And pretty soon you'd hear a loafer sing out, "hi! *so* boy! sick him, Tige!" and away the sow would go, squealing most horrible, with a dog or two swinging to each ear,

and three or four dozen more a-coming; and then you would see all
the loafers get up—and watch the thing out of sight, and laugh at the
fun and look grateful for the noise. Then they'd settle back again till
there was a dog-fight. There couldn't anything wake them up all over,
and make them happy all over, like a dog-fight—unless it might be
putting turpentine on a stray dog and setting fire to him, or tying a
tin pan to his tail and see him run himself to death.

[....]

Where did Mark Twain learn to write like that? To catch on paper, as he did
in speech, the exact cadence of words as they fall within the mind? Of course
the South produced great talkers, and like so many of its vehement personalities up to and including Lyndon Johnson, they knew how to apply pressure
on people.* Mark Twain must have learned very early that the mouth must
always be ready. The celebrated funnyman began as a bookish, sensitive,
undersized, violently moody youngster who learned how to defend himself,
then—like Tom Sawyer—to command a situation by throwing in occult references, interspersing a string of words between himself and every bit of trouble at hand.

The special "trick," the infallible trigger-quick snap and emphasis on the
right word, was something more distinct, and purer, than the traditional gift of
gab. Mark Twain's instinct is for the sentence, the thunderclap of surprise
essential to the monologist—an effect usually more suited to the short poem,
which must be all style, than to prose fiction. He knew, as Robert Frost was
boastfully to put it, that "a sentence is a sound on which other sounds called
words may be strung." A sentence in Mark Twain, as in Frost, is above all a
right sound. Hemingway, for all his homage to *Huckleberry Finn* as the initiator
of modern American writing, was a rhetorician who brought an ironic and
brutal simplicity to a style not "natural" like Mark Twain's but ostentatiously
reduced. Hemingway (like Thoreau) does not try to capture the spoken sound
of a sentence. You can sense him checking his own spontaneity as he writes.
He is a painter, a whittler, not a listener. Henry James, carrying his wholly
mental English to the farthest periphery of consciousness, somehow managed
not to stumble even when he composed in rhythms that were not only removed

---

*"You have to be able to dominate the existence that you characterize. That is why I write about
people who are more or less primitive." Flannery O'Connor to a friend, September 30, 1966.

from ordinary speech but were inconceivable from anyone but Henry James. Frost could have been speaking for Mark Twain when he wrote in a letter, "The vital thing, then, to consider in all composition is the ACTION of the voice,—sound—posturing, gesture. . . . Why was a friend so much more effective than a piece of paper in drawing the living sentences out of me? . . . I can't keep up any interest in sentences that don't SHAPE *on some speaking tone* of voice."

Some speaking tone of voice became the everyday voice of Mark Twain as he wrote. And what he heard in himself was often mimicry. The *edge* in people's voices, their littlest emphases and explosions, was something he could never resist putting down. They were the little "snags," in the mouth as on the river, the clots natural to speech before it floods on. Of course he knew from steamboat days, having had to memorize everything on the Mississippi, how to make words reproduce the river—"and by and by you could see a streak on the water which you know by the look of the streak that there's a snag there in a swift current which breaks on it and makes that streak look that way." But much of the line in a character's mouth is mimicry of every quantity of sound Mark Twain got down from someone's speech. "The streets was full, and everybody was excited." "The place to buy canoes is off of rafts laying up at shore. But we didn't see no rafts laying up so we went along during three hours and more." Mark Twain's often shrewish voice can be heard in Colonel Sherburn's scorn of the mob flocking up to his gate to lynch him after he has contemptuously murdered Boggs. The all-assertive inflections, the complacent self-reference, the unsparing *absoluteness* of every ad-hominem shot, is straight from the repertoire of southern vocal dueling, public insult: "The idea of *you* lynching anybody! It's amusing. The idea of you thinking you had pluck enough to lynch a *man!* . . . Do I know you? I know you clear through. I was born and raised in the South, and I've lived in the North; so I know the average all around. The average man's a coward."

The pleasure we share in all this assertiveness is the pleasure of command—to command attention, to command the crowd. Mark Twain was sometimes "radical" when things went against him; he was no egalitarian. It is the eternal ego power of Tom Sawyer, that nonstop performer, that the old Mark Twain came to recognize in another show-off, Theodore Roosevelt, and heartily detested. No doubt with something of a twinge, for in old age, when he resembled King Lear more than he did Tom Sawyer, he called himself "an old derelict" and "God's fool." But the everlasting type, the genius of the ever-ready verbal topping, is Tom Sawyer. Tom, so prompt to trick and direct others, is clearly one version of what saved his alter ego, Mark Twain; the boy makes his way and always has his way by words alone. What pleasured Mark Twain most about youth—and this is the genius of Huck Finn, who is also no mean talker and a ready deceiver—is its capacity for first impressions, the aspect of discovery. Mark Twain's fellow Missourian T. S. Eliot, reading *Huckleberry Finn* in late middle age for the first time, noticed that the adult in Mark Twain was boyish, "and only the boyish side adult." The boy seems to have learned very early in life how to "handle" adults as well as the boy gang with words. His "angelic," decidedly mature, easily suffering wife sighingly called him "Youth."

[. . . .]

When Mark Twain turned to *The Adventures of Huckleberry Finn* after finishing *The Adventures of Tom Sawyer* in 1876, he clearly meant to write another "boy's book" in the light comic tone that for the most part had carried Tom and his friends in St. Petersburg from one escapade to another. Despite the dread, the fear-soaked superstitions, and the violent deaths described in *Tom Sawyer*, the book is a comedy and in tone benign and more than a shade condescending to boys who, when all is said and done, are merely boys. Mark Twain had become a wealthy and ultra-respectable member of the best society in Hartford by the time he sat down to re-create his own boyhood in *Tom Sawyer*—minus his own religious fear and loneliness. His benevolence toward childhood and boyhood is a little smug. Mark Twain undertook more than he anticipated when he turned to *Huckleberry Finn.* By an instinct that opened the book to greatness, he wrote Huck's story in the first person and so at many crucial places in the book *became* Huck. Yet the facetious "Notice" facing the opening page is only one of many indications that *Huckleberry Finn* was intended to be just a sequel to *Tom Sawyer:*

> Persons attempting to find a motive in this narrative will be prosecuted; persons attempting to find a moral in it will be banished; persons attempting to find a plot in it will be shot.

From the moment Mark Twain began to describe things as Huck would see them, and to make of Huck's vernacular a language resource of the most captivating shrewdness, realism, and stoical humor, Mark Twain was almost against his will forced to go deeper into his own imaginative sense than he had ever gone before. Odd as it may seem, he was compelled—in this one book— to become a master novelist.

He had not been a novelist at all before writing *Tom Sawyer*; obviously everything having to do with his early life in Hannibal recharged him and opened not only the gates of memory and imagination but also his unexpected ability to write close, sustained narrative. Writing in the first person became the deliverance of Mark Twain. Still, given his training in one vernacular style after another during his days as a frontier humorist, it was not in itself exceptional for him to impersonate a fourteen-year-old vagabond, the son of the town drunk, who hates being "adopted": "The Widow Douglas, she took me for her son, and allowed she would sivilize me; but it was rough living in the house all the time, considering how dismal regular and decent the widow was in all her ways."

What made the difference between this and just another humorous "oral delivery" was that Mark Twain had fallen completely into Huck's style and Huck's soul. (There were to be passages in which Huck became Mark Twain.) Smart-alecky and sometimes mechanically facetious as Mark Twain was when he first assumed Huck's voice, winking at the reader as he presented Huck's ignorance of religion, of polite language, of "sivilized" ways, Mark Twain would soon be committed to a great subject—Huck the runaway from his father and Jim the slave running away from Miss Watson, going down the river, hoping to enter the Ohio River and freedom. Freedom from respectable ways for Huck, freedom from slavery for Jim: the quest is eternal even though they miss the Ohio River in the dark and keep going South. In the last third of the book they return to the purely boyish world of Tom Sawyer, with Tom the everlasting kid, prankster, brat, forcing a Jim who was really free all the time (as only Tom knows) to be a "prisoner" on the Phelps farm.

The quest for freedom is eternal because Huck and Jim have nothing in this world but that quest. Mark Twain the ultra-success in Hartford had returned to what he once knew, most feared, and what always excited his imagination most—the Mississippi Valley world at its human bottom, the world of the totally powerless and unsettled. He, too, remained something of a vagrant, a drifter; in old age he called himself a "derelict." He would never, despite appearances, be content with his celebrated position in life; like Huck at the end of this book, he wanted "to light out for the Territory ahead of the rest."

Huckleberry Finn is above all a novel of low company—of people who are so far down in the social scale that they can get along only by their wits. In 1885 the Concord Public Library excluded *Huckleberry Finn*. It was not altogether mistaken when it complained that the humor was "coarse" and that the substance was "rough, coarse, and inelegant, dealing with a series of experiences not elevating, the whole book being more suited to the slums than to intelligent, respectable people." The wonderful satire in chapter 17 on the genteel way of life in the Grangerford family would not be possible without Huck's unpreparedness for such a way of life; the hilarious Victorian sentimentality is put into true perspective by Huck, the anguished observer of the murderous feud between the Grangerfords and the Shepherdsons.

Huck has *nothing* but his wits. As he says about himself, "I go a good deal by instinct." The society along the river is class-conscious, but the classes cannot help knowing each other and entering into each other's lives. In chapters 24–29 the awful Duke and Dauphin enter into the family of the dead Peter Wilks, pretending to be its English branch, and the fact that they do not talk "educated," but make the most ridiculous mistakes, does not alert the family until it is almost too late. From time to time Huck temporarily attaches himself to plain middle-class folks like Mrs. Judith Loftus; in chapter 11, when he disguises himself as a girl, it is his sex rather than his low speech that gives him away.

Huck certainly gets around. He can be pals with Tom Sawyer and be taken in hand by Judge Thatcher, the Widow Douglas, and Miss Watson; he convinces Mrs. Judith Loftus that he did grow up in the country; in chapter 13, he steals the canoe attached to the foundering *Walter Scott* and so helps to send the robbers caught on the boat to their deaths; he can play the servant to professional con men like the Duke and Dauphin, who at successive times masquerade as actors, medicine men, and Englishmen.

In a great novel of society—which *Huckleberry Finn* so acidly turns out to be whenever Huck and Jim go ashore—what counts is the reality behind the appearance. That reality, though sometimes naively misinterpreted by Huck (but only for a self-deluded moment), depends always on Huck's inexperience. Nothing could be more devastating as social satire than the Victorian gingerbread and sentimental mourning described absolutely "straight" by the homeless and admiring Huck. All this turns into a hideous bloodbath as a consequence of Huck's ingenuous help to the lovelorn couple from feuding families. To go from the Grangerford parlor to the riverbank where Huck covers the heads of the Grangerford boys slain in the insane feud is to travel a social epic. Only the classic "poor white," Huck, goes the whole route—as the onlooker that Mark Twain remained in his heart.

The riverbank scene ends on one of those recurrent escapes that make up the story line of *Huckleberry Finn*—"I tramped off in a hurry for the crick, and crowded through the willows, red-hot to jump aboard and get out of that awful country." Huck has to keep running from "quality" folks like the Grangerfords, the Wilkses, the murdering "awful proud" Colonel Sherburn. He "weren't particular"; he just wants to go "somewheres." He chooses to *stay* low company, as his father does. Vagrancy is his first freedom. He does not even choose to go traipsing down the Mississippi with Jim, who just happens to be on Jackson's Island when Huck gets there. The novel is one happening after another; Huck happens to fall in with a runaway slave instead of living by the book with Tom Sawyer. As Pap Finn chooses the mud, so Huck chooses the river. Or did the river in fact choose him?

Thanks to the everlasting river, the "monstrous big river," the always unpredictable river, Huck and Jim on their raft float into a tough American world. It is full of hard characters, crooks, confidence men, kindly widows, and starchy spinsters who in good Mark Twain fashion never seem to be sexually involved with anyone; slave owners and slave hunters who can never be expected to regard Jim as anything but a piece of property; pretty young girls for whom Huck's highest accolade is that they have "the most sand"—grit and courage, the power to disbelieve and defy the lying elders around them. The church is fundamental to these people, but their religion emphasizes duty to God rather than brotherhood for the outcast and the slave. They are hard without knowing it, for they are hysterically self-protective. They are a human island in the midst of a great emptiness.

So Huck, not yet fourteen, has to struggle for a knowledge of adult society without which he will not survive. In *Tom Sawyer* children and adults lived in parallel worlds without menacing each other; in *Huckleberry Finn,* as in real life, children and their elders are in conflict. A middle-class boy like Tom Sawyer has to "win" a game in order to triumph over his inevitable defeats in later life. Huck has to survive now. He has to win over Pap Finn's meanness and the Widow Douglas's strictness; over Tom Sawyer's boyish silliness and Jim's constant terror that he may be caught; over the murderous robbers on the *Walter Scott* and even the protectiveness of Mrs. Judith Loftus; over the horrible arrogance of Colonel Sherburn and the lynch mob foolishly crowding Colonel Sherburn's door; over the greediness of the "King" and the cool cynicism of the Duke.

Huck on the river, becoming a part of the river, making the river one of the principal characters, reminds us of the genesis of *Tom Sawyer* and *Huckleberry Finn*. Mark Twain recalled in *Old Times on the Mississippi* that he had had to learn the whole river in order to become a pilot. Huck has to be the unresting pilot of his life and Jim's; he must become the American Ulysses in order to survive. This is why from time to time he can lie back and take in the beauty and wonder of the scene, as in the glorious description of sunrise on the Mississippi that opens chapter 19. This chapter significantly has the book's meanest characters, the Duke and Dauphin, coming aboard. Think of a boy Huck's age struggling against a father who wants to keep him down, who tries to rob him, and who beats him and keeps him locked up. Whereupon our Ulysses contrives his own "death" and gets away with it after making as many preparations for his deception and escape as a spy going into enemy country. No wonder he is always on "thin ice," or as he says in one of his best descriptions of flight, "I was kind of a hub of a wheel."

There, in the struggle of a boy to establish himself over hostile powers, in the discovery of menace when confronting life on one's own terms—there is the true meaning of a "boy's book"; it explains why boys can read *The Adventures of Huckleberry Finn* as boys and then grow up to read it as an epic of life that adults can identify with. The great epic, the tale of the wandering hero triumphing over circumstances—this is the stuff of literature that a boy is nearest to, since every initiation into the manhood he seeks must take the form of triumphing over an obstacle. Whether he is planning to deceive his father into thinking he is dead, scaring off slave hunters with stories of smallpox on their raft, or (in the last ten chapters) submitting to Tom Sawyer's games and thus subjecting poor Jim to real imprisonment, the hero of this book is still only a boy. This proximity to both real danger and made-up danger is how life appears to a boy, who must steal from the adult world the power, but also the fun, that he needs in order to keep feeling like a boy. Even though he must trick this world, lie to it, outwit it, he is a boy in his conventional attitudes. The Wilks girl had "the most sand" you ever did see in a girl, and the Grangerford house was the splendidest.

Huck does not have the easy out of pretending to despise a middle-class world whose love comes his way without his seeking it. Nor does love from people he has just met mean as much to him as his own measure of people. He is attachable, but not for long; adoptable, but he will not admit liking this. You remember his boyish inexperience when you see how much he values, in the sunrise along the river and in the circus into which he has sneaked, the beauty and "splendidness" the world has kept in store for him. The nature of the life experience, as the story of a boy always brings out, is that we just pass through and are soon different from what we thought we were; are soon gone. Life is a series of incommensurable moments, and it is wise to enjoy them; one minute the Grangerford boys are bloody dead along the river, and the next morning or so, "two or three days and nights went by; I reckon I might say they swum by, they slid along so quiet and smooth and lovely."

Pap Finn in delirium tremens cries out to the Angel of Death, "Oh, let a poor devil alone!" This expresses the real struggle, against underlying despair, that Mark Twain admitted for the first time in *Huckleberry Finn*, before he savagely settled into the despair of his old age. The river that "holds" the book in its grasp is full of menace as well as an unreal floating peace. For the most part, traveling the river is a struggle, a wariness, even when Huck is temporarily on land. In the marvelous and somehow central scene in which Huck methodically arranges his "death" and then, worn out, prepares to "catch a few winks," he is still a river rat who feels himself pursued at every turn.

From the very beginning of their flight, Huck and Jim are in ecstasies whenever they are safe for a while. Early in the book, when Huck watches the townspeople shooting off a cannon to raise his "body" from the bottom, he says with an audible easing of his breath, "I knowed I was all right now. Nobody else would come a-hunting after me." Just treading on a stick and breaking it "made me feel like a person had cut one of my breaths in two and I only got half, and the short half, too." A boy is up against forces bigger than himself, the greatest of which can be his inexperience. So he has to play "smart." But the smarter the boy, the more fatalistic he is; he knows who runs things. Wary of people, Huck weaves his way in and out of so many hazards and dangers that we love him for the dangers he has passed. He is our Ulysses, he has come through. Yet coming up from the bottom, he has none of Tom Sawyer's foolish pride; the "going" for this boy has become life itself, and eventually there is no place for him to go except back to Tom Sawyer's fun and games.

The sense of danger is the living context of the book's famous style, the matchless ease and directness of Huck's language. Huck and Jim are forever warding off trouble, escaping from trouble, resting from trouble—then, by words, putting a "spell" on trouble. Jim is always getting lost and being found; Huck is always inventing stories and playing imaginary people in order to get out of scrapes before they occur. As Jim in his ignorance is made to play the fool, so Huck in the full power of his cleverness is made to play the con man. They need all the parts they can get. They live at the edge of a society that is not prepared to accept either one of them; they are constantly in trouble, and it is real trouble, not "prejudice," that menaces Jim. Although Mark Twain often plays to the gallery when he mocks the iniquity of slavery from the complacent perspective of Connecticut in the 1880s, the feeling that Huck and Jim attain for each other is now deservedly the most famous side of the book. For once, black and white actually love each other because they are in the same fix. "Dah you goes, de ole true Huck; de on'y white gentleman dat ever kep' his promise to old Jim."

But we never forget what the hard American world around them is like and why they are both in flight. For people who are penniless, harried, in real danger of death, vigilance alone gives a kind of magical power to a life over which "mudsills" and slaves have no power. The superstitions Huck and Jim share are all they have to call on against the alien forces of nature. Equally effective, a kind of superstition as well, is the spell they put on things by arranging them in strict order. Although Huck sometimes becomes Mark Twain when Mark wants to satirize old-time property "rights" in slaves, Mark sinks into Huck when, in the crucial scene preparing his getaway, Huck doggedly lists everything he has, everything he is taking with him, everything he knows—in order to shore himself against danger.

It must have been this scene in chapter 7 of *Huckleberry Finn* that so deeply drew Ernest Hemingway to the book. All modern American writing, he said in *Green Hills of Africa*, comes out of *Huckleberry Finn*. He called the much-disputed end of the book "cheating," but he recognized his affinity with the book as a whole. Hemingway surely came to his famous "plain" style through his compulsion to say about certain objects, only this is real; this is real; and my emotion connects them. In Hemingway's great and perhaps most revealing story, "Big Two-Hearted River," the suffering mind of the war veteran Nick Adams seeks an accustomed sense of familiarity from the stream he fished before the war. He then puts his catch away between ferns, layer by layer, with a frantic deliberateness. So Huck preparing his getaway in chapter 7 tells us:

> I took the sack of corn meal and took it to where the canoe was hid, and shoved the vines and branches apart and put it in; then I done the same with the side of bacon; then the whisky jug; I took all the coffee and sugar there was, and all the ammunition; I took the wadding; I took the bucket and gourd, I took a dipper and a tin cup, and my own saw and two blankets, and the skillet and the coffee-pot. I took fish-lines and matches and other things—everything that was worth a cent. I cleaned out the place. I wanted an axe, but there wasn't any, only the one out at the wood pile, and I knowed why I was going to leave that. I fetched out the gun, and now I was done.

The boy without anything to his name finally has something to carry away. Taking the full inventory of his possessions is a ritual that Huck goes through whenever he is in danger and about to hunt up a new place to "hide." This element of necessity can be the most moving side of the book. It "explains" the unique freshness of the style as much as anything can. A writer finds his needed style, his true style, in the discovery of a book's hidden subject, its "figure in the carpet." Here is a book which is an absolute marvel of style, but in which, by a greater marvel, life is not reduced to style and is certainly not confused with style. Huck Finn's voice has many sides, but fundamentally it is the voice of a boy-man up to his ears in life, tumbling from danger to danger, negotiating with people, and fighting back at things as necessity commands. The sense of necessity that only bottom dogs know is what gives such unmediated, unintellectualized beauty to the style. Mark Twain, fully for the first time, knew how to let life carry out its own rhythm. The interesting thing is that he did not particularly intend to do this. When he took the book up again several years after he had written chapter 16, planning to describe the comedy and horror of the Grangerfords' existence, he was tougher on the society along the river than he had ever expected to be. For starting with chapter 17 he had to describe the folly of "quality" folk like the Grangerfords, the inhuman arrogance of Colonel Sherburn, and the stupidity and loutishness of "ordinary" plain people.

Mark Twain's fascinated loathing extends to the whiskey-sodden towns-people who egg on poor old Boggs as he stumbles about, foolishly threatening Colonel Sherburn. Because that imperious man murders Boggs, Mark Twain can disgorge himself of his own exasperation with "ordinary" Americans by describing the crowd around the dying man:

> There was considerable jawing back, so I slid out, thinking maybe there was going to be trouble. The streets was full, and everybody was excited. Everybody that seen the shooting was telling how it hap-pened, and there was a big crowd packed around each one of these fel-lows, stretching their necks and listening. One long lanky man, with long hair and a big white fur stove-pipe hat on the back of his head, and a crooked-handled cane, marked out the places on the ground where Boggs stood, and where Sherburn stood, and the people fol-lowing him around from one place t'other and watching everything he done, and bobbing their heads to show they understood, and stoop-ing a little and resting their hands on their thighs to watch him mark the places on the ground with his cane; and then he stood up straight and stiff where Sherburn had stood, frowning and having his hat-brim down over his eyes, and sung out, "Boggs!" and then fetched his cane down slow to a level, and says "Bang!" staggered backwards, says "Bang!" again, and fell down flat on his back. The people that had seen the thing said he done it perfect; said it was just exactly the way it all happened. Then as much as a dozen people got out their bottles and treated him.

The famous speech by Colonel Sherburn after the murder ridicules the crowd that has come to lynch him. The speech is wonderful in its lordly con-tempt for the townspeople, but of course it is not Sherburn but Mark Twain who is telling the crowd off. The crowd admiringly watching the man in the "big white fur stove-pipe hat" act out the killing is Mark Twain at his best. In this pitiless scene, one of the most powerful blows ever directed at the compla-cency of democracy in America, life becomes farce without ceasing to be horror. The grotesqueness of the human animal has put life to the final test of our acceptance. And we accept it. The absurdity and savagery that Mark Twain captured in this scene proved more difficult to accept when, no longer young and now humiliated by near-bankruptcy, he found himself face-to-face with a driving, imperial America that was harsher than anything he had known on the frontier.

[1984]

WILLIAM AND HENRY JAMES: OUR PASSION IS OUR TASK

———•◆•———

... the method of narration by interminable elaboration of suggestive reference (I don't know what to call it, but you know what I mean) goes against the grain of all my own impulses in writing; and yet in spite of it all, there is a brilliancy and cleanness of effect, and in this book especially a high-toned social atmosphere that are unique and extraordinary.... But why won't you, just to please Brother, sit down and write a new book, with no twilight or mustiness in the plot, with great vigor and decisiveness in the action, no fencing in the dialogue, no psychological commentaries, and absolute straightness in the style? ...

I mean ... to try to produce some uncanny form of thing, in fiction, that will gratify you, as Brother—but let me say, dear William, that I shall greatly be humiliated, if you *do* like it, and thereby lump it, in your affection, with things of the current age, that I have heard you express admiration for and that I would sooner descend to a dishonoured grave than have written.... I'm always sorry when I hear of your reading anything of mine, and always hope you won't—you seem to me so constitutionally unable to "enjoy" it.... how far apart and to what different ends we have had to work out (very naturally and properly!) our respective intellectual lives.

Thus William James to Henry James on the publication of *The Golden Bowl* in 1905, and the latter's unusually sharp reply to the older brother whom he adored—and could barely read. There is always an obtrusive irony in honoring the Jameses together: they could never fully honor or, after a certain point, really understand each other. This was something that both recognized and that William almost enjoyed. They were always seeking to gratify each other, "as Brother," for the Jameses loved each other as passionately as they debated their differences, and delighted in each other's careers. Never as in the James family, indeed, was so little envy or indifference brought to so many conflicting intellectual ambitions, and never was so much fraternity brought to so little mutual understanding. How deeply the elder James delighted in his genius sons, though he could only, from his vast intimacy with God, look down on both science and art as frivolously incomplete! How ready William always was to read each of Henry's essays and novels as it came along, so quick with eager brotherly praise, so ready to define Henry's subtlest triumphs and to miss them! How much Henry stood in awe of William, showered him with adulation, professed himself a "pragmatist," and resented it when William forgot to send even a technical monograph!

Yet though their devotion to each other was profound, their essential antipathy of spirit went deeper still. But antipathy is not the word: there was only a kind of loving non-recognition. Similar as they were in their studies of human consciousness, in raising to an ideal end the operative supremacy and moral serenity of an individual "center of revelation," they could only smile to each other across the grooves in which each had his temperament. Henry at least knew his failure to recognize the design unfolded in William's empiricism, where William so genially slid over the symbolic design stamped on Henry's every effort, praised him for his "high-toned social atmosphere," patronized him, and missed that need to *use* the novel as a medium of inquiry that cut Henry's career off from the Anglo-American fiction of his generation. Henry was always an isolated figure in the philosophic James household, where William was its reigning active heir, the versatile young naturalist who spoke in his father's hearty voice even when he revolted against his father's foggy theology, the naturalist in a scientific era whose interests drew him everywhere.

William could at least follow Henry's works and comment on them (he commented on everything)—praise the early style or deplore the later, admire a character and confer a judgment. When William's first book, the great *Psychology*, appeared in 1890, Henry could only fidget in embarrassment and complain that he was too absorbed properly to appreciate "your mighty and magnificent book, which requires a stretch of leisure and an absence of 'crisis' in one's own egotistical little existence." Or, later, say of *A Pluralistic Universe* that he had read it "with enchantment, with pride, and almost with comprehension. It may sustain and inspire you a little to know that I'm *with* you, all along the line.... Thank the powers—that is, thank *yours*—for a relevant and assimilable and referable philosophy.... Your present volume seems to me exquisitely and adorably cumulative...."

There it was always: William's thought was "adorable," but Henry was too absorbed. Henry had always been absorbed, where William's mind opened outwards to all the world from his father's notations on Swedenborg to psychical research, from Kant to William Jennings Bryan; Henry was absorbed in making novels. William tried to be an artist and a chemist, went to Brazil with Agassiz to collect fishes, took an M.D. between periods of almost suicidal depression, debated endlessly with his opponents and loved them all, learned psychology by teaching it, wrote letters to all the cranks about their manias, gravitated into philosophy, fought against imperialism; Henry went on making novels. He made novels as he had made his first critical essays, his famous "impressions" and the enduring myth of England he absorbed from his childhood reading *Punch:* by storing and molding what he had, and by never taking in anything he would not use. They had tried to make a lawyer out of him, they tried to teach him some elementary facts of science; Henry went on collecting impressions—impressions of Italy and of the pictures he found in Italy (Emerson loved these), impressions of Newport, Paris, Geneva and Saratoga; impressions of the mourned cousin, Mary Temple, whose face was the face of Milly Theale, Maggie Verver, and Isabel Archer. The only culture he had was literature and pictures, and the only literature he sought was the nineteenth-century novel—he did not care even for poetry; but he had a mission and his mind and life composed a single order of desire: he made novels.

To the other Jameses Henry was always the marvelous unknown child who sat quietly alone, dreaming pictures and studying novels, and always bewilderingly content with his own mind. He seemed so little to adhere to anything except his own tropisms of taste; he had no "message," no positive belief or apparent need of one. William, on the other hand, was racked until he could find an ontology as plastic as life and true of every last thing in it; and he ran excitedly through all the disciplines, rejecting, disputing, extracting, until he could square the "irreducible facts" with the highest fact of his own nature. To Henry he might have said what their father had said to Emerson: "Oh, you man without a handle! shall one never be able to help himself out of you, according to his needs, and be dependent only upon your fitful tippings-up?" William always needed a handle; and he could use one only by reacting against something. What he principally reacted against was his father. Henry drew from the elder James by enclosing himself in the independence the father preached; he did not react against his father's theology, he was indifferent to it. William, however, was too much like his father in combativeness and vivacious curiosity to reproduce anything but his temperament. Nothing could have seemed more lethal to him than his father's glacial metaphysics, poetic as many of its elements were. The elder James had escaped the dreariness of Calvinism—its belief in a kind of haphazard criminality of human nature—by nailing the human mind and will to the dreariness of a perpetual mysticism. The world was now joy, where Calvin's had been the fear of fate; but the only release allowed man was submission; the only hope a projected union with God. Utopian socialist though he fancied himself, he saw the natural world only as a medium of communication with supernatural truth. Thought was reduced to the labored ecstasy of extracting mystic "secrets"; man lived in an automatic effort at revelation.

Nothing was more alien to William than any belief which bound man to something not in his particular nature and experience. In his biological theory of mind the mind was not a mere faculty, as the soul was not a region; it was an effect and transmission of consciousness, and purposive; the endlessly probing antennae of the whole human organism, and the exercise of it. All of a man's life was engaged in his thought or spoke or hid in it; the mind did not "receive" ideas, it shaped them in seeking adaptability; it sought ends. Yet what was so significant in William's psychology, often condemned as "literary," was that it buttressed in moral philosophy a theory of knowledge. Though he was almost the first American to establish psychological studies in the laboratory, he was always impatient with laboratory psychology and a mere corpus of facts. What he was getting at, as in his pragmatism, was not only a more elastic sense of reality, a more honest and imaginative perception that all life and thought begin in discrete individuals and are shaped by their differences, but a need to show that what was not a real experience to an individual had no existence that one could name and take account of.

To the merely bookish, who would rather intone their knowledge than be shaped by it; to the merely devout, who would rather worship their God than be transformed by Him; to the formal logicians and contented monists, for whom the world's disorder and depths are so easily sacrificed, William James has always seemed loose or even vulgar because he preached that an idea has meaning only as it is expressed in action and experience. That he was so misunderstood is partly James's own fault, since he *would* speak of "the cash-value" of an idea in his characteristic attempt to reach the minds even of those for whom cash-value was the only value. But it is largely the fault of ourselves and our personal culture, since the rarest thing in it is still moral imagination. For what James was leading to in his pragmatism—once it had served as a theory of knowledge—was moral in the classic sense of conduct, moral in the enduring sense of the order and use of a human life. Tell me, he seemed always to be saying to those who were so content with ideas rather than with thinking, with metaphysics rather than with morality, what is it you *know*, what is it that is changed in you or by you, when you have achieved your certainty or knowledge? What is it you live by, appreciably, when you have proved that something is true? James knew well enough, and could formulate the ends and satisfactions of his opponents better than many of them could; but that was only incidental to his essential aim. Knowledge is for men that they may live—and men may live for ideal ends. So is the monist happy in his all-enveloping unity, the rationalist in his ideal symmetry, the mystic in his visions. And all of these exist, said James; all of these must be taken into our account of the human experience and the demands of our nature. But do not confuse, he went on, your individual need of certainty with the illusion that some supra-human order is ascertained by it; do not confuse your use of reason—and delight in it—with the illusion that what cannot be named or verified by rationalism does not exist.

To say this is not to forget how treacherous James's ideal of the provisional can be, and that he is particularly dissatisfying when he merely brings us to the borders of moral philosophy. He triumphed by disproving all the cults and systems which ignored the shaping power of man's individuality, by threshing his way through pre-scientific myths and post-scientific arrogance. But like so many American naturalistic thinkers, he took a certain necessary definition of the good life for granted (or confused it with the Elysian fields of the Harvard Department of Philosophy?); whereas it is the unrelenting consciousness of it that is most lacking. Yet what is most important here is that the great particular for him, as for all the Jameses, was the human self, and that out of it they made all their universals (though it is always a question what Henry's universals were). For the elder James the center of existence was the self that seeks to know God and to be sublimated in Him; William's theory of knowledge began with the knowing mind that *initiates* the ideas to which the test of experience is to be applied; Henry found his technical—and moral—triumph in the central Jamesian intelligence which sifts the experience of all the other characters and organizes them. This, had William not so clearly pined for Stevenson when he read Henry's novels, he might have recognized as Henry's "handle." For in an age when all the materials through which William was running so eagerly demanded large positive answers, wholesale reconstructions, and a worldview, Henry had quietly and stubbornly reproduced his father's mystical integrity in the integrity of the observing self. The novel for him was to be *histoire morale*, a branch of history that sought the close textures and hidden lights of painting; but the highest morality was not so much in the story as it was in the exercise of the creative principle behind it.

That devotion to a creative principle was the great epic of Henry's integrity, as everything he ever sought or wrote was a commentary on it. In most writers their works exemplify their ambition; Henry's were about his ambition, as they were, in one sense, only his ambition written large. Just as William's vision always came back to a loose sea of empiricism in which man could hold on only to himself, so Henry's was to define and to fill out the moral history of composition. His theory of art was not preparatory to a manipulation of experience; it *was* his experience. His interest was fixed on writing about the symbolic devotion of writing, as so many of his stories were of writers (but only of depressed or unsuccessful writers: there was no "dramatic process" in the surface of success). And the central Jamesian intelligence, in all his disguises as "the foreground observer," "the center of revelation," the artist planning his effects, the critic "remounting the stream of composition," was always sifting and commenting in turn. "The private history of any sincere work," he wrote once, "looms large with its own completeness"; it was his symbol of man's completeness. He studied his novels endlessly as he wrote them, corrected them endlessly when they were published, wrote a preface to each in which he summarized the history of its composition, defined his every intent and use of means, speculated on the general principles they illustrated, and at the end, as he hinted to Grace Norton, might have written a preface to the prefaces, commenting on *them* in turn. Secretions within secretions, knowingness within knowingness: out of so self-driven an integrity, as out of the intense interior life of his characters, there could be grasped the central fact of the effort, the search, the aura of devotion, that gave meaning to the artist's life and form to his work. And always the thread remained firmly in the artist's hand, pulling it back to himself—the story of Henry James was the story of Henry James writing his novels.

Life for both always returned to the central self. Significantly, it was always the richness of their personal nature that distinguished all the Jameses, and the overflow of life in them that gave them their vascular styles. Ralph Barton Perry says of the elder James that he felt his visions so intensely, and had so many together, that he had to get them all out at once. The elder James was always running over, laughing at himself for it, and never stopped running over. Like William, he had so many possible thoughts about so many things; and he had the James exuberance (the seed *was* Irish) that always ran so high in them despite the unending family history of illness. Superficially, of course, no two styles would seem to be so different as William's and Henry's: the one so careful to be spontaneous, the other so spontaneously labored; the one so informal in its wisdom, flinging witticisms, philosophical jargon, homeliness, and hearty German abstractions about with a seeming carelessness, protesting doubt at every point, yet probing with angelic friendliness in all the blocks of the human mind; the other so *made* a style, solemnly and deliciously musical, reverberating with all the tones of all the books Henry had ever read, forever sliding into cozy French idioms, shyly offering the commonest spoken expressions in quotation marks—Henry always sought to be friendly. Yet both were great spoken styles, intimate and with an immense range of tone: the only difference being that William talked to friendly Harvard seniors and Henry later dictated to his secretary. What no one has ever said enough about Henry's style, of course, is that it was the family style become molten: like all the Jameses, he wrote instinctively out of his amplitude. He gushed in his letters and he gushed in his novels, but there was always the James motor power behind him, their terrible need to seize and define everything within their range. And more, there was that "blague and benignity" in his style that Ezra Pound caught: the tricky interior changes of pace, the slow mandarin whisperings, the adjectives that opened all vistas for him like great bronze doors, the extraordinary *soundings* he could make with words, and, covering them all, always his deceiving gentleness, the ceremonial diffidence, and his sudden barbs and winks.

To think of their styles is to be aware of the great innocence that was in all the Jameses, an innocence of personal spirit if not of moral perception. Financially secure, encouraged by their father to be different and uncontrolled, even to be without a profession, both ranged at will in what was still the household age of modern thought—a period when the security of their society encouraged those first studies in the naturalism of the psyche and a voracious interior life. The only revolution either could envision was in new ways of knowing; and it is significant that William led the way to "the stream of consciousness." They all had the natural outpouring that came with innocence, the innocence that trusted in all the data of their inquiry, took the social forms for granted, and based life upon the integrity of the observing self. "In self-trust are all the virtues comprehended." It was the Emersonian faith of their culture, in all its genteelism and instinctive trust in individuality. Just as the elder James's theology committed man, as it were, to be a recording angel, to seek the necessary revelation and inscribe it, so they were all recording angels, much as William said of Henry that under all his "rich sea-weeds" and "rigid barnacles and things" he cared only for making novels. Life was here and now, in all that system of relations between minds in which experience immediately consists; man *studied* it. The highest aim, somehow, was to be an author. But there is no very great sense of tragedy in any of them (compare them with the Adamses), no sense of that world process which is something more than William's metaphysical novelty and pluralism; the great depths of life are not in them.

In a time like our own, when men are so lost in themselves because they are so lost from each other, the Jamesian integrity can seem small comfort to us. We can take no social form for granted; we cannot possess or be possessed by those explorations in human consciousness which only parallel—or at best reveal—our quest for security. To say this is not to make a judgment on the Jameses, but to define our predicament. Our enforced sense of evil has nothing so creative in it as their innocence; and their legacy is still most precious for its symbolic integrity, its trust in mind, its superiority to our "failure of nerve." Even Henry James's greatest contributions to human pleasure and self-comprehension, or his insistence on the integrity of a work of art, are less important now than the emblem his pride raises before us. Even William's full devotion to realism, his imaginative projection of complexity, are less important to us now than the respect he breeds in us for all the forms of reality and our necessary understanding of them. And it is this which is now most visible in them and most important to us: the simplicity of their respect for life and the intensity of their elucidation of it. They both worked in that period of modern history when the trust of man in his power to know was at its highest, when the revolution of modern political democracy, science, and materialism carried along even those who were skeptical of the idea of progress. And if we feel at times that they are even greater than their thought, more far-ranging than the forms that contain them, it is because they burned with that indestructible zeal we need so badly to recover—the zeal that cannot blind men to illusion, but must always rise above it, the zeal that cries that life does have a meaning: we seek to know.

In one of those exquisite stories, "The Middle Years," in which Henry James was always writing out the lesson of his own loneliness and neglect in the story of the celebrated writer neglected and misunderstood by those nearest him, the writer cries on his deathbed: "It *is* glory—to have been tested, to have had our little quality, and cast our little spell." "You're a great success!" his young attendant assures him. And Dencombe replies, wearily, but with mounting exaltation: "We work in the dark—we do what we can—we give what we have. Our doubt is our passion, and our passion is our task."

[1955]

THE DEATH OF THE PAST: HENRY ADAMS AND T. S. ELIOT

———— • ◆ • ————

I will show you fear in a handful of dust.
—*T. S. Eliot*, The Waste Land

It was 1918 and America was at war again. In his great house on Lafayette Square just across from the White House—for forty years the square had been his favorite lookout on the presidents he joyfully despised—Henry Adams felt that as a survivor of the nineteenth century's "drama of human improvement," as a student of what he called History's mad acceleration into "chaos," he had come to the most dramatic moment of all. History in his century had replaced religion as the first drama of human existence. History had long been the greatest possible subject to his madly speculative mind. "That wonderful century," as the codiscoverer of natural selection Alfred Russel Wallace had called it, "the century of progress" hailed by Leopold of Belgium when he took over the Congo, had ended at last. As usual, Henry Adams was there to pick up the pieces.

He was eighty years old in February 1918, and he would be dead in March. Since his stroke six years before, he could write hardly anything but his wickedly brilliant letters relating Washington political gossip and the tendency of History to fulfill the sourest prophecies of Henry Adams. But surrounded by his Japanese vases, a great Turner, his color print of Blake's *Nebuchadnezzar Eating Grass*, his choice French impressionist works resting on chairs built to accommodate his tiny figure (he was just a little over five feet tall), his great library, and the Adams family portraits in one of the twin houses built for him and his friend John Hay by his Harvard classmate H. H. Richardson, Adams spent voluptuous hours listening to the beautiful young Aileen Tone singing the medieval French chansons to which he was still determined to find the original words. She was the last of those honorary nieces whom he hired for their excellent French, their pleasing voices, and a disposition (marked among bright young women in Washington) to admire without limit the flashing mind and prodigious interests of this fierce little old man who was venomous to everyone but a few friends yet was strangely fascinating to many. Elizabeth Cameron, the young wife of the Pennsylvania senator and political boss Don Cameron, had become his favorite woman in the world. But even she confessed, "It is a curious faculty you Adamses have of inspiring terror; it must be because you are frightened yourself and communicate it."

After his wife's tragic death in 1885 her real nieces had attended him. As they had grown away, his determination to discover words for the medieval chansons led him to France for seven months every year. How pleasant it was to bring together his passion for the medieval and his delight in handsome, witty, elegantly well bred young women competent to assist his researches and to enjoy his wittily abrasive views of his degenerate country. He was a great appreciator of Woman—never more so than after Marian's death, when he needled his friends at dinner by announcing the superiority of every woman present to her husband. For all his contemptuous ways and doomsday notions, Adams had a gift for friendship that singled out the wives of his friends the secretary of state, the British ambassador, the chairman of the Senate Foreign Relations Committee. No one in the rough-mannered new century would ever approach Adams's ingratiating way of sharing with intimates a mind alarmingly superior. "There is something voluptuous in meaning well." He had no friends who were not leaders of American society and enterprise, drivers of the "powerhouse." He liked to tell them to their faces that they lacked passion. But he was too special a case—privately wealthy, obsessively exclusive, the wholly intellectual spectator of a power in which he did not share—not to know that he was an oddity in America's governing class. A senator from Wisconsin—on the floor of the Senate!—had called him a begonia.

How much did he mean his public idolatry of women? How much did he mean anything he said after Marian—"Clover"—took her life thirty-three years before? For a scholar who had virtually founded the modern historical seminar at Harvard in the 1870s, a superb critical intelligence with a particular instinct for smelling out established untruths in American history, Henry Adams had certainly become a genius, or devil, at mystifying his friends. When his *Education* was finally released to the public after his death, he continued to mystify those he most fascinated.

This unbearably proud descendant of two of the most famous public men in American history now made a point of putting his best self into letters. He had burned his diaries and his letters to Marian after her death. *The Education of Henry Adams*, begun in 1903, completed in 1907, privately printed in just one hundred copies, and sent out, as he put it with his usual mock deference, "to the persons interested, for their assent, correction, or suggestion," would make him famous, ultimately an American classic. Mark Twain said of his *Autobiography* (unlike the *Education* it was not a work of art but a tormented man's garrulity) that "only dead men tell the truth." Dead men do not tell the truth in the *Education*. Adams was not interested in telling the "truth" about himself—whatever that was. His aim was to present himself as History.

Like the economic swashbucklers of his generation—Rockefeller, Morgan, Whitney, Carnegie—Adams said, "The public be damned." He said it often. His contempt for what his brother Brooks called "the degradation of the democratic dogma" was absolute. He was snobbishly pleased because he had had to pay Scribner's to publish his nine-volume *History of the United States of America During the Administrations of Thomas Jefferson and James Madison*. Such was the fate of the exceptional historian with a private income in a literary market dominated by mere novelists of the new American middle class.

How provocative and contemptuous Adams was in publishing his own pseudonovels. *Democracy* (1880), a satire on Washington society, was issued anonymously. *Esther* (1884), a story of New York society and his particular friends the artist John La Farge and the geologist Clarence King, was published under a feminine pseudonym. Adams encouraged rumors that his friend John Hay, and possibly others, had written each of the romans à clef. His favorite pose was to stay behind the scenes. Even when elected president of the American Historical Association in 1894, he managed to avoid delivering his presidential address, "The Tendency of History," by addressing it from Mexico. President Charles William Eliot of Harvard was exasperated by Adams's refusal to appear in person for an honorary degree. He thought

Adams an overrated man and was the only one among Adams's hundred "friends" to return his copy of the privately printed *Education.*

Yet this immensely private, proud, unfathomably touchy person—"angelic porcupine" his friends called him—was the most public recluse in Washington. Living in his famous house opposite the president's, he knew everybody who in his considered opinion was worth knowing. He had been the closest friend of Secretary of State Hay during the McKinley and Roosevelt administrations and was supposed to have been Hay's secret adviser. Compared with grandfather John Quincy Adams and great-grandfather John Adams, Henry was just a rich eccentric scholar with mystifying interests in everything from Paleolithic art to the craze for a "science" of history. But this most superior and forbidding person so easy to dislike was Washington's most informed political gossip. Through the friends he had made in England during the Civil War as private secretary to his father the American minister, through his family connections and his all-important friends in politics, science, and literature, he was an informed and informing intelligence office. He had learned very early that Washington "usually had more to do with compromise than anything else." This made society interesting. No other American intellectual of the time was so much at the center of things while pretending to despise it. And he was at the heart of Washington power without any official position whatever.

Even as he approached eighty, Adams had a special grasp of the old century's struggles among the European powers, a grasp that after he took us into the war those struggles led to, Adams's fellow historian Woodrow Wilson was the last to admit. As usual, with his sharp intuitions of historical "acceleration" (his favorite theme), Adams expressed approval of nothing but the working out of a blind process. The nineteenth century was the "century of hope," Alfred North Whitehead was to say, because it invented invention. The release of new productive forces was almost beyond calculation. Adams was spellbound by inventions like the famous dynamo he virtually "prayed" to at the Paris Exposition of 1900. But he was less interested in their social use than he was in the emergence of new forces. At eighty he had lived long enough to see "a new universe of winged bipeds ... British airplanes sailing up and down under my windows at all hours." That was not progress, just a new item to weigh in the scale of history.

In his "scientific" theory of history Adams emphasized the "law" of acceleration and the tendency of modern societies to go mad under the pressure of multiplicity. He grandly took the second law of thermodynamics to mean that in industrialized society, entropy signified a hemorrhaging of vital energy. The centralization vital to modern technology and politics would crack. He had long prophesied an uncontrollable explosion of energy expanding to reach the whole planet and likely to tamper with it. He was a better guesser than most Victorian prophets because he suspected that the system's call for ever more power was uncontainable, but it hid a death wish. America of the nineteenth century, the America that had made nonsense of the "eighteenth-century" Adams tradition of political reason in control of a wholly new society, now stood in Adams's mind for mechanical energy alone. It was *the* powerhouse. In 1917, with the once-provincial colonies about to rescue the British Empire—but not for long and certainly not for Britain's sake—Adams saw what he had guessed in England during the Civil War: "Our good country the United States is left to a career that is positively unlimited except by the powers of the imagination." That "Maryland school-master type" Woodrow Wilson, whom Adams hardly bothered to despise (Adams's own circle hated Wilson to the point of frenzy), was morally overwhelmed by this power. Wilson talked nonsense about saving for democracy a world that for the most part had never known democracy.

> We shall fight for the things which we have always carried nearest to our hearts,—for democracy, for the right of those who submit to authority to have a voice in their own governments, for the rights and liberties of small nations, for a universal dominion or right by such a concert of free peoples as shall bring peace and safety to all nations and make the world itself at last free.

Wilson wept over the young men he sent out to die and trusted that the worst war in history would end war forever. Bad as William II sputtering *Gott mit uns*, Wilson was overheard at Paris saying, "If I didn't think God was behind me, I couldn't go on. . . ." For his own reasons Adams had gloated over Wilson's call to war. He had long sought a great Atlantic alliance. "It is really a joy," he wrote to an English friend, "to feel that we have established one great idea even though we have pulled the stars out of their courses to do it."

The war itself did not move him one way or another. All his life this perfect spectator had studied war and narrated war; he had supposed himself, from his family intimacy with power, capable of calculating the direction of war and the future of national power. The habit of "exclusion," which he said he had learned as a literary style at Harvard (it was in fact a family trait), had become his only style for life and thought. If Henry Adams felt anything in particular about the 116,708 Americans who were to die in the war, he left no word. The greatest American historian of his crucial century, the most versatile imagination among American scholar-historians, would have agreed with Randolph Bourne (had he bothered to hear of Randolph Bourne) that "war is the health of the state." He would not even have noticed Bourne's lonely protest against America-in-the-war; it was not in Adams's character or in his philosophy to worry over the two thousand prosecutions under Section 3 of the Espionage Act.

On the other hand, Henry James's hysterical espousal of England must have seemed to Adams uninformed. Settled in England since 1876, James, in gratitude for "Europe" as the best vantage point for fiction, had taken England as the dream country of his eloquent heart and mind. In 1914 James almost died of shock, but before he did die in 1916 he became a British subject in order to show that *he* was in the war. On the outbreak of war he wrote to Howard Sturgis:

> The plunge of civilization into this abyss of blood and darkness by the wanton feat of those two infamous autocrats is a thing that so gives away the whole long age during which we have supposed the world to have been, with whatever abatement, gradually bettering, that to have to take it all now for what the treacherous years were all the while really making for and *meaning* is too tragic for any words.

He was to wish he had not lived on "into this unspeakable give-away of the whole fool's paradise of our past." This idealization of England, this total surprise that great-power rivalry could lead to war, would have made Adams laugh his death's-head cackle. Henry James may have had the "imagination of disaster," as he claimed; the lasting disaster of the war was beyond his comprehension. Thomas Hardy, in his notes to *The Dynasts* on August 1914, wrote, "The human race is to be shown as one great network or tissue which quivers in every part when one point is shaken, like a spider's web if touched." That was more to the point of 1914, that onset of all our woe, when crowds in London and Berlin shouted "We want war! We want war!" D. H. Lawrence described the enthusiasm for war as "sensational delight posing as pious idealism."

Had Adams lived into the 1920s, he might have been able to read "Gerontion," the imaginary monologue of "an old man" composed by a thirty-year-old poet from St. Louis, now living in England, who had scornfully reviewed *The Education of Henry Adams* and then borrowed images from it for his poem. Unlikely as it is to imagine Adams recognizing his connection with the poem, he was certainly—like Eliot—another figure wasted by history in which he had played no part.

> *Here I am, an old man in a dry month,*
> *Being read to by a boy, waiting for rain.*
> *I was neither at the hot gates*
> *Nor fought in the warm rain*
> *Nor knee deep in the salt marsh, heaving a cutlass,*
> *Bitten by flies, fought.*
> *My house is a decayed house,*
> *And the jew squats on the window sill, the owner,*
> *Spawned in some estaminet of Antwerp,*
> *Blistered in Brussels, patched and peeled in London.*

With his deadly gleefulness Adams once noted that he and his even more catastrophe-minded younger brother Brooks had discussed "the total failure of the universe, as usual, and especially of our own country, which seems to afford even more satisfaction." If there was no war, he wrote just before the war, the Middle West, all "stomach, but no nervous center,—no brains— would overwhelm America like an enormous polyp." War, he had argued, was necessary in order to institute "an Atlantic system," including Germany, from the Rocky Mountains to the Elbe, since this was "the energy center of the world." And the war, or at least a future war, might well be against a still-disorganized Russia before it was able to industrialize Siberia. When Adams reached England from France safely in August 1914, Bernard Berenson congratulated him: "I trust that you are satisfied at last that all your pessimistic hopes have been fulfilled."

Adams was not disheartened by the outbreak of hostilities. Henry James in Rye, on the Channel coast, constantly looked toward France as though he could share the war. Edmund Gosse:

> The anguish of his execration became almost the howl of some ani-
> mal, of a lion of the forest with the arrow in his flank, when the
> Germans wrecked Rheims Cathedral. He gazed and gazed over the
> sea southeast and fancied that he saw the flicker of the flames. He ate
> and drank, he talked and walked and thought, he slept and waked and
> lived and breathed only the War.

Yet no less than James, and no less than the thirty-year-old expatriate from St. Louis who had been prevented by the war, by his marriage to a distraught Englishwoman, and by his own growing "aboulie" from sailing home to defend his Harvard dissertation on the philosophy of F. H. Bradley, Adams plainly projected his solitariness, his sexual sorrow, and his special dryness of heart and mockery onto a world at war. It had fulfilled all his anticipations of what nineteenth-century power struggles could lead to. He was a man so totally acid, embittered, enraged, that his dislike of the contemporary world had become a kind of ecstasy. In the 1890s he had thundered to his adored Elizabeth Cameron:

> I expect troubled times for many years to come. On all sides, espe-
> cially in Europe and Asia, the world is getting awful rickety. In our
> country we shall follow more or less the path of the world outside.
> For my own part, hating vindictively, as I do, our whole fabric and
> conception of society, against which my little life has squeaked protest
> from its birth, and will yell protest till its death, I shall be glad to see
> the whole thing utterly destroyed and wiped away.

Adams once confessed that his "instinct was blighted from babyhood." Yet as much as the expatriate Eliot, fifty years his junior, this gifted, equally anti-democratic American was to make his grateful audience in the twenties (when at last it heard of Henry Adams) think of the current world as a wasteland.

Adams the great historical dramatist was the widowed husband of a highly charged, acidly witty Boston patrician, Marian Hooper Adams, a gifted pioneer photographer. At the age of forty-two, on December 6, 1885, a Sunday morning "when all believers were safe in church," she drank the cyanide she kept for developing her pictures.

There is no reason to believe that Marian Hooper Adams, [un]like Vivien Haigh-Wood Eliot, was in any way marred by a husband's sexual difficulties. We do not know as much about Henry Adams as we have learned about the gifted, troubled poet who wrote "The Love Song of J. Alfred Prufrock" before his marriage, "Gerontion" and *The Waste Land* after it. Adams, who felt that he had "finished my dinner" at forty-seven, when Marian died, had objective reasons, a great historian's expert reasons, for distrusting the modern age. He was another modernist who found a public only after the First World War confirmed his long-seated belief that the modern world was meaningless, insane, out of control. But unlike Yeats, Lawrence, Eliot, and Pound, Adams's ostensible subject *is* the historical process. His particular hope—dismissing every other—was to make a "science" of history. This was conjectured by a remarkable literary imagination that, he admitted, relied on images, not facts. Adams's real theme, like that of Eliot and all the great modernists, was the agony of change, the fear of the masses, the longing for an absolute. Long before he wrote the last sentence of the *Education*, Adams knew that if he and his like returned to the twentieth century, they would not "find a world that sensitive and timid natures could regard without a shudder." More and more indeed, the best were to lack all conviction, the worst to be full of a passionate intensity.

Adams omitted his wife from the book of his life. He concentrated on history as the mere acceleration of mechanical forces, ending in their uncontrollable dispersion. He was obsessed by the accumulation and centralization of power as the underlying theme of American history. But as though he had anticipated the nuclear age, he was also spellbound by the possibility of total destruction. His personal bitterness fed his malicious reading of History. The nineteenth century had given Western man—democratic, capitalist, "scientific" man—an unparalleled sense of power. In midcentury America, Whitman asserted in *Democratic Vistas* (1871), "It seems as if the Almighty had spread before this nation charts of imperial destinies, dazzling as the sun . . . making old history a dwarf." Adams's unhappy prophecy was that power stayed in the "powerhouse." So much centralization could not last. What Adams was saying below his breath, of course, was that power might prove suicidal because man could not be trusted. If History was always on his mind, suicide was never far away. A less cosmic version of so much disappearance, randomness, and destruction was Adams's writing near the end of his life, "All one has cared about has been a few women, and they have worried one more than falling empires."

Adams was fascinated by force, that prime image of nineteenth-century physics. In his own life, horribly as mechanical progress excited him, he knew no force more powerful than what he called Woman. Woman was outside and superior to the money-making routine of men. Woman was the virgin figure, the "goddess" in Adams's mythology, who in the Middle Ages was what the dynamo was now. (The American had incorporated the dynamo into himself.) Woman was the great exception to the materialist society, and Marian was the magnetic pull on Adams's "posthumous" existence from her death in 1885 to his in 1918. The image and terror of her death were to last long after the fact. Marian Adams's death by her own hand was to become the supreme instance in Adams's life of the "force" that can be exerted by a personal compulsion. All we know is that her love for her long-widowed father was more pressing than her love for her husband. When Dr. Hooper, to whom she wrote a full account of her doings every Sunday morning, died, she died with him. She bowed under this yoke and Adams bowed to the force of her necessity. Necessity, in good positivist style, was to become the theme of the last sections of his *History of the United States*. For Adams, sex was indeed to become "the sacred fount," the mysterious source of energy. Just as "Clover" became the all-disposing but especially all-forgiving Virgin in *Mont-Saint-Michel and Chartres*, so the *Education* projected her as Woman, a main force in history. The mysterious hooded figure he had Saint-Gaudens design over her (and later his) famous tomb in Rock Creek Cemetery is more a female figure than a male one.

In chapter 21 of the *Education*, "Twenty Years After (1892)," Adams pointedly takes up his life after Marian's death without saying a word about her. In "The Dynamo and the Virgin (1900)" he introduces the succession of force figures that dominated his historical imagination.

> . . . he turned from the Virgin to the Dynamo as though he were a
> Branly coherer. On one side, at the Louvre and at Chartres, . . . was
> the highest energy ever known to man . . . yet this energy was

unknown to the American mind. An American Virgin would never dare command; an American Venus would never dare exist.

> . . . The idea survived only as art. . . . Adams began to ponder, asking himself whether he knew of any American artist who had ever insisted on the power of sex, as every classic had always done; but he could think only of Walt Whitman. . . . All the rest had used sex for sentiment, never for force. . . . Society regarded this victory over sex as its greatest triumph.

This victory symbolized to Adams the repressive spirit of modern capitalism. What he did not say (current religion bored him) was that so much propriety, so much conscious virtue on the part of America's upper classes, had replaced every possible tinge of supernatural religion. "God" was really "dead." What replaced Him was the immortality of Art. The nineteenth-century antagonists of progress who came to be considered modernists by the twentieth century can be identified by their belief, as Henry James put it to H. G. Wells, that "art *makes* life, makes interest, makes importance." Literature is the only life that has pattern, shape, meaning, the only life that may last; literature and art—this was Adams's reason for writing *Mont-Saint-Michel and Chartres*—are what religion leaves behind it. Only through literature is History embodied and the divine law recalled. To Henry Adams, as to all the House of Adams, History was still the first art.

Henry Adams had no respect for the new realistic fiction produced by his generation. To John Hay he was to write with easy superiority that "James knows almost nothing of women but the mere outside; he never had a wife. . . . Howells . . . cannot deal with gentlemen and ladies; he always slips up." In his manifesto "The Art of Fiction" (1884) James had hailed the novelist as succeeding to the "sacred office" of the historian. Although Adams never spoke of himself as an "artist," the Adamses, writers all (none of them was such a writer as Henry), accepted the ability to write as if it went with the offices they held and their command of intellectual and political history. Henry Adams never had to say that he was in command of his art, which in the United States was still called History.

Intellectual authority had belonged to historians because the writing of history was associated with the keeping of political tradition. Historians in America were part of the history they lived to write, they were men of the world, the political world. It would not have occurred to Parkman, Prescott, Bancroft, or Adams that the work of such wild men as Poe and Melville, beggarly romancers, might be more lasting than that of historians. Marian Adams said of Henry James that it is "not that he bites off more than he chaws but that he chaws more than he bites off." James seemed to Adams to be setting the scene and arranging his effects with studied effort, to have *trained* himself to look at society through the eyes of the great European novelists of manners.

By the end of the First World War, when Henry Adams died and his *Education* came alive, History had ceased to be the narrative art that it had been to the nineteenth century. History as some Great Tradition, History as Intellectual Authority had become as much a Great Ruin as religion. This was certainly the idea of William Butler Yeats, T. S. Eliot, Ezra Pound, D. H. Lawrence, the Ernest Hemingway whose first important work was called simply *In Our Time*. Modernist literature would picture history exclusively as a Great Fall.

The young Henry James, afraid that a new country could not give a novelist the rich settings that old Europe did, had said apropos of Nathaniel Hawthorne that it takes a good deal of history to produce a little literature. Forty years later Eliot was writing in "Gerontion" that "History has many cunning passages," and would soon discount [it] in the name of tradition. History was an immense panorama of futility and anarchy. Tradition was religion. The self would not suffice.

> *I have seen the moment of my greatness flicker,*
> *And I have seen the eternal Footman hold my coat, and snicker,*
> *And in short, I was afraid.*

In 1919 the thirty-one-year-old Eliot, caught by the war in England and happy to stay there, reviewed *The Education of Henry Adams* under the head, "A Sceptical Patrician." Eliot was unimpressed by the book, scornful of the man. He already had the sharply cutting air of critical authority that would please conservatives like Paul Elmer More. More could not understand why Eliot's poetry was so newfangled, so different from his prose. Eliot's reply: poetry deals with the world as it is. Eliot's severity as a critic was already a bit of an act, necessary to the postwar skepticism that would welcome as the very voice of itself Eliot's dislike of nineteenth-century sentiment.

The authoritative manner was also necessary to his secret despair as he wrote in a mosaic style and with gallows humor the poetry of a world more absurd than himself. Like Henry Adams, Eliot liked to deceive and mock the public. Nothing would have seemed more ridiculous to Eliot than Whitman's romantic democracy: "The soul of the largest and wealthiest and proudest nation may well go half-way to meet that of its poets." The poet in the modern world was damned. Damnation showed in the manic kaleidoscope of moods in "Prufrock," the desperate playfulness which is itself mimicked in stray couplets that tease the ear with their mock chords, as if forced from a hurdy-gurdy. The "indecisions" and "revisions" end on a helpless blank.

> *When I am pinned and wriggling on the wall,*
> *Then how should I begin*
> *And when I am formulated, sprawling on a pin,*
> *To spit out all the butt-ends of my days and ways?*
> *And how should I presume?*

When one considers Eliot's real emotions, and forgets the stern lawgiver who was soon to hypnotize English studies, it is touching to read Eliot's confession in *On Poetry and Poets* (1957) that he could not bear to reread his critical prose. To More's complaint that his poetry and criticism were disturbingly different, he replied that criticism describes the world as it should be.

The 1919 review of *The Education of Henry Adams* is insolent, clever, destructive. Eliot in America could never have written with such lordliness. No wonder the extraordinary lament of the "old man" of "Gerontion" reads like a cry from the soul of Henry Adams as much as it does one from the young Eliot, so quick to cry in "Prufrock" (1917), "I grow old ... I grow old. . . ."

Why, unless he recognized himself in Adams and in Adams's own painful sense of tradition, did Eliot find him so unimpressive? But of course Adams *was* American history, and Eliot was trying to discharge himself of America.

He was much more refined than the equivalent Englishman, and had less vitality, though a remarkably restless curiosity, eager but unsensu-

ous.... And his very American curiosity was directed and misdi-
rected by two New England characteristics: conscientiousness and
scepticism.

Here is precisely what makes the book, as an "autobiography,"
wholly different from any European autobiography worth reading.
Adams is perpetually busy with himself.... But Adams is superla-
tively modest, diffident.... Conscience told him that one must be a
learner all one's life, and as he had the financial means to gratify his
conscience, he did so. This is conspicuously a Puritan inheritance....
Still, there are always others whose conscience lays upon them the
heavy burden of self-improvement. They are usually sensitive people,
and they want to do something great; dogged by the shadow of self-
conscious incompetence, they are predestined failures....

Wherever this man stepped, the ground did not simply give way,
it flew into *particles*.... He was seeking for education, with the wings
of a beautiful but ineffectual conscience beating vainly in a vacuum
jar. He found, at best, two or three friends, notably the great John
Hay, who had been engaged in settling the problems of China and
Cuba and Manchuria. Adams yearned for unity, and found it, after a
fashion, by writing a book on the thirteenth century.

The Erinyes which drove him madly through seventy years of
search for education—the search for what, upon a lower plane, is
called culture—left him much as he was born: well-bred, intelligent,
and uneducated.

Eliot grasped, and was appalled by, Adams's preoccupation with self. This
preoccupation haunted Eliot emotionally: the prisoner in his cell was to
declare the highest aim of literature an escape from emotions and personality;
escape from the self became the great theme of a religious striving that was
more striving and cultural piety than it was belief.

Because I do not hope to turn again
Because I do not hope
Because I do not hope to turn

. . .

(Why should the agèd eagle stretch its wings?)

...

And I pray that I may forget
These matters that with myself I too much discuss
Too much explain
Because I do not hope to turn again

The prisoner in his self was even the subject of Eliot's doctoral thesis on F. H. Bradley's *Appearance and Reality*, and Bradley would be quoted in the notes to *The Waste Land* as a gloss on lines 411–17:

. . . I have heard the key
Turn in the door once and turn once only
We think of the key, each in his prison
Thinking of the key, each confirms a prison
Only at nightfall, aethereal rumours
Revive for a moment a broken Coriolanus

What provoked Eliot most in his review of the *Education* was his recognition that Adams's "scepticism" was his own. It was a despair of the modern world mounting to the "horror" of Mr. Kurtz as he finds himself in the heart of darkness. The children of the founding fathers are deracinated, besieged.

Signs are taken for wonders. "We would see a sign!"
The word within a word, unable to speak a word,
Swaddled with darkness. In the juvescence of the year
Came Christ the tiger

In depraved May, dogwood and chestnut, flowering judas,
To be eaten, to be divided, to be drunk
Among whispers . . .

Does the prisoner in his self know how alone he is? Henry Adams would certainly have recognized himself as "a broken Coriolanus." The descendants of Puritans now adored the Middle Ages. The leadership of their country had long since passed the Adamses by. Eliot in England, who on the appropriate date wore a white rose in memory of Richard III, also bewailed John Quincy

Adams's having had to yield the White House to Andrew Jackson. Adams the self-dramatizing "failure" became a terrible and terrifying old man who liked, as he said, to discuss the total failure of the universe. Eliot would have found superfluous Adams's "dynamic theory of history." But since Eliot was interested in history only as tradition, he would have agreed that the supposed dynamics of history lead to chaos, the dispersion of energy trailing out between the stars.

The center will not hold. "Hail nothing full of nothing, nothing is with thee," is Hemingway's lampoon at the end of "A Clean, Well-Lighted Place." A real or rhetorical bitterness would soon be the norm. But where was the primal fault—in the supposed absence of deity, in the revolt of the masses, in the eclipse of authority, in democracy itself? Or was it, horror of horrors, in the primal scene? As Adams said (and it was one of the more sincere sentences he ever wrote), "All one has cared about has been a few women, and they have worried one more than falling empires." Sex after the war would become a divine energy that would not suffer connection with other divinities. The Puritans had once insisted on a connection. The young Eliot lampooned Boston gentility, but "Prufrock" demonstrated the brilliant effect of repression. Adams and Eliot had excellent reasons not to free themselves of the New England virtue that was their pride, their minutest discrimination, their ability to pass judgment on the millions they despised.

The prisoner in his self, the self-exiled Coriolanus, is there because he chooses to be there. He is different from his pitiful age. The price he pays is sexual martyrdom, a familiar Christian forfeit, a distrust of woman that trembles through every reference by Eliot to a woman's hair.

> *A woman drew her long black hair out tight*
> *And fiddled whisper music on those strings*
> *And bats with baby faces in the violet light*
> *Whistled, and beat their wings*
> *And crawled head downward down a blackened wall*

It was a distrust that Adams also felt in his grief, in his guilt as a husband, and it resonated in his dinner-party glorification of Woman.

Sexual desolation is not hostile to wit and eloquence. Henry James was amazed by the power of self-revelation Adams displayed in old age. The young Eliot never wrote better than in "Prufrock," "Gerontion," *The Waste Land, The*

Hollow Men. He was to show himself sublimely eloquent in the poem leading to his conversion, *Ash-Wednesday*, and in the *Four Quartets* that closed his career with so many golden assurances.

> *And all shall be well and*
> *All manner of thing shall be well*
> *When the tongues of flame are in-folded*
> *Into the crowned knot of fire*
> *And the fire and the rose are one.*

One sometimes regrets the elder statesman who replaced mad but enduring Prufrock.

Eliot's famous assumption of "impersonality" was necessary to his early provocations in the absurdist style of Laforgue and Corbière, the harsh tensions of the Jacobean dramatists and the metaphysical poets. Baudelaire called drugs artificial paradises. (Eliot's favorite writers rather specialized in artificial hells.) In view of the sexual tragedy hidden within *The Waste Land* and its emphasis on dryness, it was certainly a great act that Eliot put up in the unrelieved gravity of his critical pronouncements. Finally, however, he admitted of the poem, misread by a generation with his encouragement, "To me it was only the relief of a personal and highly insignificant grouse against life; it is just a piece of rhythmical grumbling." The grouse was not insignificant, and Eliot's magnificent rhythmical sense, essential to his emotional power over the reader, expresses more than "grumbling." But equally resonant of Eliot's distrustful political soul was his famous early saying, "Poetry is not a turning loose of emotion, but an escape from emotion; it is not the expression of personality, but an escape from personality." It is only too clear why Eliot added, ". . . of course, only those who have personality and emotions know what it means to want to escape from these things." Other people do not suffer as we do.

Eliot sought at first to "escape" by turning many tortured fragments into scenes that positively drugged us as they flashed across an interior memory we discovered to be our own. The heap of broken images, the "little voices," as he brilliantly called them, showed us the refrain of buried words beating against the public world. The musicality was insidious but totally captivating as the phrases echoed and varied themselves. Here was a tour de force that depended on the shock effect of discontinuity without letup. "The thousand sordid images / Of which your soul was constituted," his great lines in "Preludes," came through in a haunting aura of music. Like Stravinsky, Eliot knew how to jar the reader with a force that made connection with the reader's own life. When Eliot said in disparagement of Henry Adams that "it is the sensuous contributor to the intelligence that makes the difference," he was referring to his own poetic strategy. He knew how to borrow for sensuous contribution even when he reversed what he borrowed.

In chapter 18 of the *Education*, "Free Fight (1860–1870)," Adams begins:

> The old New Englander was apt to be a solitary animal, but the young New Englander was sometimes human. Judge Hoar brought his son Sam to Washington, and Sam Hoar loved largely and well. He taught Adams the charm of Washington spring. Education for education, none ever compared with the delight of this. The Potomac and its tributaries squandered beauty. Rock Creek was as wild as the Rocky Mountains. Here and there a negro log cabin alone disturbed the dogwood and the judas-tree, the azalea and the laurel. The tulip and the chestnut gave no sense of struggle against a stingy nature. The soft, full outlines of the landscape carried no hidden horror of glaciers in its bosom. The brooding heat of the profligate vegetation; the cool charm of the running water; the terrific splendor of the June thunder-gust in the deep and solitary woods, were all sensual, animal, elemental. No European spring had shown him the same intermix-ture of delicate grace and passionate depravity that marked the Maryland May. He loved it too much, as though it were Greek and half human.

In "Gerontion," published in *Poems* (1920), Adams's excited roaming became

> *In depraved May, dogwood and chestnut, flowering judas,*
> *To be eaten, to be divided, to be drunk*
> *Among whispers; by Mr. Silvero*
> *With caressing hands, at Limoges*
> *Who walked all night in the next room . . .*

Later the speaker complains, in some of Eliot's most wonderfully shaped and affecting lines,

> *I have lost my passion: why should I need to keep it*
> *Since what is kept must be adulterated?*
> *I have lost my sight, smell, hearing, taste and touch:*
> *How should I use them for your closer contact?*

The judas-tree became a favorite symbol of betrayal, and "Gerontion" himself an image not only of aged impotence and despair but of the difficulty, perhaps the impossibility, of reaching Christ the Savior rather than Christ the tiger, whose terrible force leaped out at us "in the juvescence of the year," in "depraved May." "Gerontion" is a wonderfully effective and penetrating poem in Eliot's most clamorous, stricken early style. It does not matter that he made ominous those images in Adams that were joyful with "passionate depravity." It is funny to read Eliot's final dig at Adams in his review of the *Education:* "There is nothing to indicate that Adams's senses either flowered or fruited; he remains a little Paul Dombey asking questions." Adams, remembering "the dogwood and the judas-tree, the azalea and the laurel," showed that his senses had indeed flowered and fruited in the primitive nature that once surrounded Washington.

Eliot was thirty-one when he wrote his poem, as was Adams when he exulted in the Washington spring of 1869. The Adams whom Eliot reviewed with so much distaste could only have been the speaker in "Gerontion." What a transference that would have been between these Puritans born half a century apart who yet were artistically two ends of the same thought. Both suffered the inaccessibility of God. That is the deepest strain in "Gerontion": it is easier for God to devour us than for us to partake of Him in a seemly spirit. Nowhere in Eliot is the God for whose eclipse he blames the modern world real and apparent to Eliot himself; it is religion, not faith, that will give him assurance, and religion will be valued for the "culture" it leaves. Eliot admitted that he was as ready to become a Buddhist as a Christian after the turmoil leading to *The Waste Land,* a poem that ends in Buddhist imperatives and the Upanishad cry for peace. Adams in *Mont-Saint-Michel and Chartres,* as in his poem "Buddha and Brahma," shows the same pluralism—religion is culture rather than belief, religion is literature that attests the unbelief Adams never denied and was even sardonically proud of. History is the only master! Eliot, even as a Harvard undergraduate studying Oriental religion, always sought something "higher."

Adams, citing Whitman as the only American artist "who had ever insisted on the power of sex," omitted to say that Whitman found democratic America the correlative of his sensuous energy. Whitman the old believer, the "sweet democratic despot," thought of democracy itself as a form of sex. It went without saying that sex was a form of democracy. Adams and Eliot emphasized the defeat of both. But what makes "Gerontion" so impressive is that in the speaker's privation one does hear worlds revolving, one does see the stars. The *Education* astonished postwar readers by revealing a sense of the "failure" of America, bitterly insisted on by Adams, that the best-placed Americans were feeling. This would soon be interpreted as the *modern* failure. Eliot in "Gerontion" made his war-besotted generation see history as nothing but human depravity:

> *After such knowledge, what forgiveness? Think now*
> *History has many cunning passages, contrived corridors*
> *And issues, deceives with whispering ambitions,*
> *Guides us by vanities.*

The disconnection between the self and the modern world was not as general as Adams and Eliot said it was. It was in themselves as men and artists, refined to the point of pain by their need to embrace an absolute. An unmoved mover—Dynamo or Virgin!—was just a literary idea to their indifferent contemporaries. They saw themselves as the embodiment of history in a world rushing to the death of the past.

What made Adams and Eliot great—and kept them solitary—was their ability to hear in their minds those "little voices" that they made others hear in a work of art. One hears these voices in the *Education*, in *Mont-Saint-Michel and Chartres*, and in Adams's extraordinary letters from Boston to Tokyo, Washington to Palermo, London and Paris to Samoa. Although Adams had once presumed to make a science of history, it was the art of history he was best at—history as the actual appearance and complication of mankind; history as manner, pretense, personal ambition, and undying hatred. These voices made a revolution in poetry when they were heard in "The Love Song of

J. Alfred Prufrock." They were to dominate the generation that recognized itself in *The Waste Land*.

Our buried feelings, even in their humiliated state, can make the triumph of literature. Poetry, Rilke said, is the past that breaks out in our hearts. "Poetry" in the largest sense—the personal voice that Emerson inaugurated as a national tradition—became in Adams and Eliot a form of submission rather than the revolution in human affairs that Emerson identified with America. We must decipher what history has made of us. This can become a way of despair, as it was in Adams, who reversed the belief in progress that had established the House of Adams, and in Eliot, who in England mourned the last of the Plantagenets as though America had killed off the Middle Ages—which indeed it had. Too respectful and submissive a sense of tradition brought Henry Adams to lament the "unity" of the Middle Ages falling into the "multiplicity" of the terrible nineteenth and twentieth centuries, and it brought Eliot to the beautiful articulation that was his genius:

> . . . De Bailhache, Fresca, Mrs. Cammel, whirled
> Beyond the circuit of the shuddering Bear
> In fractured atoms. Gull against the wind, in the windy straits
> Of Belle Isle, or running on the Horn,
> White feathers in the snow, the Gulf claims,
> And an old man driven by the Trades
> To a sleepy corner.
>   Tenants of the house,
> Thoughts of a dry brain in a dry season.

Yet mere suspension in the universe, these wonderful images of a power greater than ourselves that makes for anonymity, owed something to the reversal of the "century of hope" with which American literature had begun in an age of faith, at the hands of Ralph Waldo Emerson.

[1984]

VII

—— ◆ ——

THE LITERARY LIFE

EDMUND WILSON
AT WELLFLEET

———•◆•———

[. . . .]

"Joan's beach" was a riot. The great beach was replaced every afternoon by the great society. Each year Joan's weathered old beach hut sank more abjectly into the sand while around it rose the mercilessly stylized avant-garde house of a wealthy Leninist from Philadelphia. A leathery old man with a shaven head and showing off a powerful chest, a man who looked just as photographically virile as the old Picasso, walked with emphatic strides to the "nudies' beach." In the great clown tradition of the good old American summertime, pliant young girls in striped tank suits and Huck Finn country straw hats sat in the lotus position practicing yoga. The ocean gamboled, young men dived into rollers and then hopped up and down in the water waiting for a wave to carry them back to shore. Down the beach couples lay about open, free, and friendly as if they had just made the happiest love. Red Japanese kites with long tails bobbed up and down wheeled by the screams of the children on the cliffs.

In the midst of all this Edmund Wilson was hoarsely at the center of everyone's attention, sometimes forced against his will into the usual gossip and polemic. He sat without ease; he scooped up a handful of sand and let it drift slowly through his half-clenched fist as people running out of the water gathered around him only to run back into the water. So many staring, giggling, and deadly scrutinizers, guessing that he was "someone," made him nervous, but he unhappily sat on, unable to make his escape. So he talked. He talked as if he were reluctant to talk but too stubborn to stop. He talked as if talking were a physical difficulty forced upon him by a disagreeable world. But it was one he had learned to use for his own purposes, and even with cunning, in short, shy, killing observations. Then, looking as if he had just heard himself for the first time, he would throw his head back in a loud whinnying laugh.

He talked about what he was reading and writing. He talked, as he wrote, from current preoccupations only. His talk was as formal as his writing. He invariably led off with a topic. He had been reading this new thing of Sartre's, and had to say that the fellow was not as big a windbag as he had been led to believe. He liked the man's big French radical schemes. This Allegro man and his brazen but not uninteresting guesses on the mysterious principles and practices of the Essenes. An irritable rejoinder to Gilbert Seldes, who had been telling a story about getting tight with T. S. Eliot in the twenties. Gilbert had the date wrong. A new book about our animal aggressive tradition. Everything the new young anthropologists were telling him he had known from Darwin. He was still a nineteenth-century mechanist and materialist: "We must simply get along without religion." As for T. S. Eliot, he had the story in his notebook *and* the exact date. Had you by any chance looked into Swinburne's novels? The amusing structure of the Hungarian language, which he was just then learning? "My dear boy," he had greeted me on the beach the week before, "have I given you my lecture on Hungarian? No? Then sit down and listen." There was also this new book on magic. He was very proud of his magician's lore and often set out to do tricks that did not always succeed. He was too distracted. At Rachel's birthday party one summer, he came with his equipment and disappeared into the lean-to searching for newspapers he said he needed for his act. Time passed, no Edmund. We looked in and found him absorbedly reading one of the newspapers.

Everything alive to him was alive as words, had to find its exact finicky representation in every single trace of his experience and of his reading. Much of the day and often late into the night, he sat in his great big study in the old house just off Route 6. He sat there with the stuffed owl that he hated, with the sets of Scott and Dickens that had come down to him from Wilsons and Kimballs and Mathers like the gold-topped cane and the family pictures he could never stop studying. Just outside the study was the great Delphin set of the Latin and Greek classics in their heavy striped bindings. Inside the study were the books he used for each book, like the many-volumed Michelet he had needed for *To the Finland Station*.

There were several desks in that study, and he moved from one to the other as he worked now on one book, now on another. He wrote always by hand, in his elegant and peremptory script, and there were as many projects going on at once as in a Renaissance painter's workshop. Everything in the household revolved around his day's work and the regimen needed to accomplish it. He had his own record player in that room, his own bathroom just a few steps down from his study, his own bedroom when he wanted it in this separate suite of rooms. Out on Route 6 cars screeched on their way to and from Provincetown, the pleasure place; girls with streaming hair bicycled past in halters and shorts. But inside the study that was deep inside the house off the main highway, Edmund Wilson—protected by his tall beautiful European wife, Elena—sat writing at one desk or another, reading in one language or another, eagerly waiting for Elena to bring the mail back so that he could get still more reading matter and letters to answer.

He lived to read and write. Each new language—after the Latin, Greek, French, and Italian he had learned at school, the Russian, German, and Hebrew he had acquired mostly by himself, the Hungarian he was now so proud of, the Yiddish he typically attempted from grammars after he had learned the Hebrew alphabet—was a "love affair," he once said to me, with some subtle new syntax to love. He laughed at academic specialists with their proprietary talk of "my field"—more usually, in modern American, "my area." One of his favorite antagonists was a scholar who was always pressing him to read Cervantes. (Spanish, for some reason, never interested Wilson.) "Elena and I have been attempting *Don Quixote*," he once calculatedly told him, "and I have to admit that we find it just a mite dull." The other turned pale and stood up, shaking: "Harvard thinks differently!"

Yet what Wilson wrote dealt so much with the plight of personality, his fascination with his own family, his need to involve himself with other people, that one could see in his every sentence the extraordinary effort he put out, by words alone, to free himself from bookish solitude. Life was one elaborately constructed sentence after another, and he had been sentenced to the sentence.

The formality of sentence structure even on the beach, like the aloofness of his manner when you were drinking and gossiping with him in his own house, was like nothing any of us would ever see again. Ponderously shy, abrupt, exact, and exacting, he was matter-of-fact in a style of old-fashioned American hardness. He could be massive, unyielding on the smallest matters. Why did I always feel that I had to shout in order to reach him? There was that famous distraction, the great bald dome thinking away, arranging its sentences, even as he talked to you. But of course he made no easy splash of talk to swim in, as the rest of us did at the many cocktail parties. To depart from the question he had set was to find yourself addressing questions to the air.

He was tyrannically correct with himself and officiously correct about everybody else. The correct word, the unquestionable historical detail were professional matters. Competence was the only right relation to others. He worked from fragments and etudes in his notebook; short flights were the natural span of his intellectual imagination. But he had also absorbed from his passion for grammar (and no doubt his long solitude; he was an only child, with a deaf mother and a neurasthenic father) some un-American patience and thoroughness. He knew nothing else so well as how to make a book. He made books out of his intellectual satires against intellectuals, out of the light verse he sent his friends at Christmas, out of his *New Yorker* book reviews, out of his hatred of Robert Moses's high-handed urban renewal, out of his compassion for Indians, out of his typical belief (based on early holidays there) that Canada represented a better, uncorrupted version of his now too big and too powerful country, out of his aversion to the endless bookkeeping forced on American taxpayers by the Internal Revenue Service. This somehow turned into a book against the cold war.

Wilson made books out of virtually everything that crossed his mind. But certain subjects (especially American, nineteenth-century, related to the Civil War and the Gilded Age) never just *crossed* that mind. They stayed there, decade after decade, to be used as articles after they had first been sketched in his notebook-journal. Then they got rewritten for his books and would be rewritten again for new editions of these books. What he knew he knew; what he read he remembered; what he had seen of San Diego or Jerusalem or Odessa stayed with him forever. No one else I knew had so much patience with his own writing, his own impressions, the stories he told and retold from notebook to article to book to the next meeting in his living room. He could recast his own writing—and yours—with the same air of easily inhabiting the world by words alone. No one else I know had the same impulse to correct and rewrite everybody else. He once returned from lunch to *The New Yorker,* saw on someone's table a proof of my review of his book *The Shores of Light,* and quietly changed a date in it.

He could be hilarious in his retentiveness, his obstinacy, his intense personal relation to any book or subject that he liked very much or disliked very much. Discussing *The Scarlet Letter* (a book that as a literary modernist he easily disliked because it belonged to the American schoolroom or too much to his own past: on his mother's side he was descended from the Mathers), he was angrily asked by a young professor of American studies, "May I ask when you last read the book?" "Nineteen fifteen," Wilson said breezily.

Later, relaxed on the beach after the crowd had gone to a cocktail party at a psycho-historian's (it was to begin as a memorial service on the anniversary of Hiroshima, and one could see trailing up from the beach a procession of shoeless intellectuals, the ladies in fashionable white outfits, carrying candles), Wilson was rosy with scotch and full of his special belief in conspiracies. Getting liberated as crowd, bottle, and day dwindled, he said, with the caustic smile he reserved for anxiously Americanized and patriotic Jewish intellectuals, "Bobby Kennedy knows who *really* killed his brother—and is not telling." "Edmund, you're going overboard, the way you did in that preface!" He leaned back on his sand hill with perfect confidence. "My dear boy, you mustn't discount my legal background."

My legal background! He meant Edmund Wilson Sr., one of the best lawyers of his day in New Jersey, at one time attorney general of the state and, though a Republican, invited by Woodrow Wilson to join his cabinet in 1913. Edmund Jr. seemed to trace his own tics, quirks, and obsessions to his father, who was a passionate admirer of Lincoln the lawyer. (The tragedy of Lincoln runs through *Patriotic Gore* as the tragedy of the superior man in America.) The father identified with Lincoln the melancholic. Though a lawyer for the Pennsylvania Railroad and able to give his less finicky relatives advice about the stock market, Wilson Sr. would not buy a share of stock. He regarded stock transactions as a form of gambling. Like many brilliant men of his generation, he thought his own life a forfeit to the big-business spirit in America.

He became a "nervous invalid," a total hypochondriac; his professional career yielded to his concern with his own symptoms. His wife, a heartier type, not "intellectual," went deaf under the strain of her husband's breakdown.

Edmund Wilson knew he was "odd," and was always looking into his ancestry for the sources of his own obsessions as well as the intellectual interests plainly derived from the many preachers, lawyers, doctors behind him. He wrote about his parents and grandparents: "The fact was that I knew almost nobody else. I knew they had their doubts about me, and that in order to prove myself I should have to show that a writer could become a successful professional." T. S. Matthews, who had known Wilson on *The New Republic*, liked to say that Wilson's parents had once bought him a baseball suit—but that he had gone on reading even after he had put on the suit. As a writer, he had indeed proved himself thirty years before with *Axel's Castle*. But despite his many books since and his long record of production, he had become with increasing insistence a kind of self-proclaimed outsider to the "America I see depicted in *Life* magazine." He liked in the 1960s to say, in the sight of so many "sophisticated" academicians, that "old fogeyism" was creeping in. He now made a point of stating—boasting?—of how little money he had accumulated. Thanks to his worrisome income-tax case, he was in financial trouble virtually to the very end of his life in 1972. *The Cold War and the Income Tax* was, however, a bit of political afterthought when he was nailed by the government for neglecting to pay his taxes. He was just too distracted even to sign the returns that his wife prepared for them. But when the government attached much of his income and heavily fined him, it became a point of defiance with him, as against the swollen crazily prosperous sixties, *not* to have amassed much money and to be, in the good old American style, "agin the government." My friend Peter Shaw wrote that in the sixties every typical product of America (including the student rebellion) "lacked modesty of scale." Edmund Wilson was certainly not "modest"; but he did enjoy being out of scale with the rest of the country.

At several periods in his life, he noted in his journal, he had felt impelled to write protests against various officials of the United States government; he first wrote one as a sergeant in the A.E.F. Medical Corps. As if he were now one of his own forebears, he lived in two "old-fashioned country towns," Wellfleet, Massachusetts, and Talcottville, New York; he depended on a small income from one of his few relatives who had gone into business; he did not drive a car or use a typewriter; he did not teach, give lectures, join honorary societies that asked to honor him. When he at last accepted the Emerson-Thoreau Medal of the American Academy of Arts and Sciences, he explained that he must refuse to make a speech and insisted on reading his translation of Pushkin's *The Bronze Horseman.* When he accepted the MacDowell medal, he terrified the chairman by rolling the medal between his palms to show that he could make it disappear.

He would not play the game. Every year he became ceremonially more difficult, seemingly more perverse, more alienated from what President Johnson called "the Great Society," from the endless American sociability, from the "successful career" that American writers strive for as thirstily as professors and oil executives. Of course he had authority, and how proudly he could use it. To ward off the many people who want something from a "name," he had a postcard printed up on which it was noted (with a check against the appropriate box) that Edmund Wilson does not read manuscripts for strangers; does not write articles or books to order; does not write forewords or introductions; does not make statements for publicity purposes; does not do any kind of editorial work, judge literary contests, give interviews, broadcast or appear on television; does not answer questionnaires, contribute to or take part in symposiums. And so on!

As the contrast deepened each year between Wilson and the "America I see depicted in *Life* magazine," his concern with right words and standards seemed to become more intense, his irritation with sloppiness and misuse even more pronounced, his sense of his own intellectual honor loftier and yet more anguished. The old radical was becoming the old curmudgeon.

Behind Wilson's ever more pressing urge to make order of his life by words, behind the obsessive journal-keeper feeding on the one book he never had to give up writing—a day as its own subject, its only expressive task—there was some patrician belief that through style everything, even in his disordered country, would yet fall into place. He had always been a fussy corrector of everything he read. Now the authority derived from his sound education, from his many books and almost "bewildering" interests, from being *Edmund Wilson,* became as necessary as the articulation of the bones to the movement of the body. This insistence on "correctness"—as of a judge or minister or national leader in the days when a few solitary geniuses molded American culture—became basic to the sense of his role in American life. Let the young and the newer stocks have their pretentious social science theories and academic careers and ridiculous "New Criticism"! He was the last American man of letters, the great anachronism—and not without mischief.

Wilson now depended on "style" in an aristocratic-political sense more familiar to English universities and the House of Commons than to American intellectuals. He seemed to read the young writers with more attention than they read themselves, and loved to point out to a writer his misuse of a word and some error in detail. "Trotsky was killed not with a pickax but with an ice ax. You made the same mistake in your last book." Sometimes the pressure to write well was so grinding that, as one noticed when the notebooks began to be published, there was not a picture seen but just the effort to make one. Writers his too concrete mind could not grasp—Blake, Kafka—he dismissed with a wave of his hand. What he understood he understood.

There was a kind of political majesty to all this. Behind the pressing personal urge to correctness, I saw the moral significance of "right words" to Wilson's class—the professional gentry of lawyers, preachers, educators, scientists, which from the time of New England's clerical oligarchs had remained the sustaining class of American intellectual life. Despite all these eager beavers from the newer stocks, the few figures with the most unquestioned influence still represented—and often in the person of Edmund Wilson himself—the old American clerisy. These were still the policy makers, while imitative critics spoke haughtily of "irrelevant texture" in Shakespeare. Was the intellect in America to be banished to the new mass universities? The true thinkers were the policy makers behind the scenes who, no matter how many billions heaped up by the old robber barons they gave out as heads of the great foundations, were as detached as Henry Adams from the unctuous propaganda of American business.

Wilson thus seemed the one man of letters in the American tradition who still represented the traditional American caste of professional diplomats like George Kennan, judges like Oliver Wendell Holmes and Learned Hand, scholars who were lawgivers like Noah Webster. No wonder that *Patriotic Gore*, our American Plutarch, ended on Justice Holmes, as it began with Harriet Beecher Stowe and that most superior intellect, Abraham Lincoln. Such men and women were "the capable," as Sinclair Lewis (a doctor's son) had admiringly called the lonely doctors, philosophic lawyers, and scientists who in their work resist the bitch goddess that William James (another doctor) had called

American success. Though business ruled the roost and money was more important to everybody, it was "the capable," who came from a long tradition of professional concern, who still kept up for others the standards Edmund Wilson grew up with.

The chief expression all this took was the bitter polemic he wrote in 1962 to preface the long-delayed *Patriotic Gore.* It had taken him fifteen years to put the book together from a lifetime of reading and absorption in the literature of the Civil War. In the summer of 1962 his bitterness against the American state took the form of a preface that was really an effort to deny the love of the American past and his belief in American moral heroism that made the book itself so moving.

Like so much else in his work, *Patriotic Gore* also took off from family history. One of his earliest memories seems to have been of the original two-volume set of General Grant's memoirs, published by Mark Twain (and sold by subscription to all good Americans) as a service to the strange man who had crushed the South but as president had proved a disaster both to the nation and to himself. After leaving the White House he went bankrupt, was cheated of his own money, and, dying of cancer, he undertook the *Personal Memoirs* at Mark Twain's urging in order to provide for his family.

Wilson, so deep in "all that Civil War stuff" that the enchanted reader could not help following him at every turn of the great narrative, nevertheless opened his book with a preface that read as if composed to drive off anyone still holding the illusion that the Civil War was historically necessary. As if the title (from "Maryland, My Maryland") were not surly and sarcastic enough, Wilson compared the Northern "refusal to grant the South its independence" (certainly an unhistorical way of putting it) to the Soviet suppression in 1956 of the Hungarian revolt. The history of the United States was nothing but a big-power drive. The United States had been an aggressor against the Indians, against the Mexicans, against the South. "The institution of slavery, which the Northern states had by this time got rid of, thus supplied the militant Union North with the rabble-rousing moral issue which is necessary in every modern war to make the conflict appear as a melodrama.... The North's determination to preserve the Union was simply the form that the power drive now took...."

"I am trying," Wilson claimed, "to remove the whole subject from the plane of morality and to give an objective account of the expansion of the

United States." This was hardly Wilson's forte. The value of his book, of course, lay in its intense biographical method. Wilson was no more at ease in "objective" history than he was in removing any subject "from the plane of morality." His main text, so assiduous in tracing every detail of character and intelligence in his main figures, was full of the most obvious gratitude for what they had contributed to the eradication of slavery and the preservation of the country. But on and on Wilson went in his preface, ticking off Pearl Harbor as Roosevelt's doing ("... it has been argued, to me quite convincingly, that this act was foreseen by our government and—in order to make our antagonists strike the first blow—deliberately not forestalled at a time when a Japanese delegation was attempting to negotiate peace"), ticking off Hiroshima, ticking off our postwar belligerence toward Russia, ticking off our preparations for bacteriological and biological warfare. The United States, it seemed, had obstructed Castro's Socialist revolution, thus forcing him to seek support from the Communists. (Castro was himself to give the lie to this in acknowledging his long Communist background.) But Wilson was in such a state about any and all wars fought by the United States that he was wild enough to write that though Jews had strong reasons for fighting Hitler, it was wrong of them to support the war, since "the extermination of six million Jews was already very far advanced by the time the United States took action."

Wilson then excused the southern resistance to the civil-rights movement on the grounds that southerners "have never entirely recognized the authority of the Washington government." This was as mistaken in fact as it was foolish in theory. The South was the most militaristic section of the country and had been enthusiastic for war against Spain in 1898, against Germany in 1917, Korea in 1950. Southerners in the 1840s had led the attack against Mexico and had wanted to annex Cuba. Lincoln had said over and over what the North knew to be the simple truth: it was the South's attempt to foist the slave system on the free territories that led to the Civil War.

Wilson's bitterness on the subject of America's "power drive" of course represented the despair of many Americans as their government vainly attempted to "contain" the whole world against communism. The government since 1941 had become too autonomous and powerful. But Wilson, very much like Thoreau in his own passionate political essays against the American state, made no effort to prove his case; he just helped himself out with caustic images taken from his reading on the power drives of animals. There was little in that preface one could deal with as historical evidence. It was a series of defiant assertions in the old American style: government is not to be trusted! Many younger Americans were soon to feel this, but they had radical solutions for still *more* government, Leninist style, that Wilson laughed at.

A question naturally emerged. Why, if Wilson felt bitter about the Civil War and about American history in general, should he want to spend fifteen years on this book? To which the only possible answer was another question. Why, if he *said* he felt that way about the Civil War, should he have written such an extraordinary book around it?

For *Patriotic Gore* is a great book. It was the greatest single performance of Wilson's unique career as a man of letters (and contained in passing the most profound considerations on literature in America I had ever read). It made the passion that went into the war, and into the disillusion that followed it, more affecting than any other contemporary book on this greatest of national American experiences. It had in particular a fullness of historical atmosphere, a sensitivity to the great personages of the vital writers and leaders, that made the reader see Mrs. Stowe, Lincoln, Grant, Sherman, and the others as commanding figures in a great American epic. Though Abraham Lincoln "examined the mechanical devices that were brought to him in the years of his Presidency and is reported to have understood them, he does not seem to have been much impressed by the development of machinery in America or even much interested in it." Grant, dying of cancer of the throat, dictated his *Personal Memoirs* until it became impossible to use his voice. "Humiliated, bankrupt and voiceless, on the very threshold of death, sleepless at night and sitting up in a chair as if he were still in the field and could not risk losing touch with developments, he relived his old campaigns."

There, in the heroes, the writers, the sensitive consciences, the faithful diarists of the conflict, was Edmund Wilson's own story. There was no real social history in this book of studies in the literature of the Civil War, no grasp of the real social issues and movements behind the war and nineteenth-century America. History to the "old radical" was still, as it had been to Emerson, biography.

As the sixties darkened into war, and he became increasingly ill, his sense of himself, of his necessary authority, became more pronounced and more tragic. At a party in Ed O'Connor's house in the Wellfleet woods, Wilson, drunk and defiant, said, laughing, that the FBI would be suspicious of him.

"I've been married four times!" As he stumbled out of the party and down the stairs, the consort of the famous historian who was so proud of knowing exactly who was who on *la plage des intellectuels* said throatily, "Really, shouldn't someone look after the poor old man?"

[1978]

HANNAH ARENDT:
THE BURDEN OF OUR TIME

———•◆•———

I met Hannah Arendt in 1946, at a dinner party given for Rabbi Leo Baeck by Elliot Cohen, the editor of *Commentary*. It was that long ago. She was a handsome, vivacious forty-year-old woman who was to charm me and others, by no means unerotically, because her interest in her new country, and for literature in English, became as much a part of her as her accent and her passion for discussing Plato, Kant, Nietzsche, Kafka, even Duns Scotus, as if they all lived with her and her strenuous husband, Heinrich Bluecher, in the shabby roominghouse on West Ninety-fifth Street.

No less than the Bluechers, I felt that Hitler's war had not ended. The "Holocaust" (no one yet called it that) as the ultimate horror of the Nazi regime's twelve years so dominated every conversation with them that I was not surprised to learn that Hannah was writing a book on totalitarianism. In the first edition of *The Origins of Totalitarianism* (1951) the book's thesis was credited entirely to the unpublished philosophy of Bluecher. Bluecher, an extraordinarily mental creature, an insatiable orator in his living room on the great thinkers was incapable of writing for publication, whether in German or English. He made up for this by shouting philosophy at you in the sweetest kind of way. He was given to fantasy and exaggeration, noble lies about his military knowledge (he had been a teenage recruit in the Kaiser's army) and his relationship to the family of Marshal Bluecher. As a Protestant and independent German radical married to a Jew, he impressed me most by his concern and even identification with Jews. Nothing had so unhinged me from my old "progressive" beliefs as the destruction of the Jews.

It sometimes seemed to me that Hannah and Heinrich were not only close to but enclosed by what Churchill had called "the worst episode in human history." The reverberations of the Nazi experience would never cease. And in the immediate postwar years Hannah impressed me every time I saw her by her stalwart Jewishness, her independent commitment to a Jewish homeland, her directorship of an organization devoted to restoring to devastated Jewish communities the religious and cultural treasures stolen by the Nazis. As a refugee in Paris after 1933 she had worked for the Youth Aliyah trying to get children into Palestine.

Intellectually, like many another Jewish thinker, she was indifferent to Judaism; she had been much more influenced by Christian thought and by what she canonized all her life—philosophy as a daily activity. She had written a famous doctoral dissertation under Karl Jaspers at Heidelberg on St. Augustine's concept of love, and never tired of quoting her favorite maxim from Augustine, "Love means: I want you to be." Her conversation, unlike Bluecher's, was so much from what she had written or was planning to write that, reading her again for this piece, I distinctly heard her "You must think what you are doing"—a refrain in her conversation and her books until it became her reason for dismissing Eichmann as just an unthinking nonentity— she owed to her philosophic training and especially to the gruff but pliant voice repeating her favorite themes and quotations.

In those early years after the war, before she became the first woman professor at Princeton, a powerful presence at Chicago, Berkeley, etc., her astonishing expressiveness as an expounder was already inseparable from her charm as a woman. This expressiveness, physical and tangible, was for me her greatest attribute. She was too reverential about the great thinkers to claim "originality" in philosophy itself; her distinctive procedure, which she must have learned in German seminars, was to circle round and round the great names, performing a "critique" in their name when she disowned a traditional position. Even in the kitchen she sailed into the airiest flights of German speculation. In the early days this took the form, ironically, of abjuring what

Santayana had called "egotism" in German philosophy in favor of politics, the public realm, the Greek tradition of the polis.

This was ironic because though she had shifted from the supposed unworldliness of German philosophy (Heidegger the sometime Nazi was the most telling current example) to political thought, and during the *Origins of Totalitarianism* period constantly cited Montesquieu and Tocqueville, her interest (as Sheldon Wolin has pointed out)* turned but to be more in Nietzschean prejudices about the "elite" and the "mob" than in the kind of empirical observations with which Tocqueville had filled his great book on the revolutionary spectacle of "democracy in America."

The Origins, for me, is the book of hers most concentrated on its subject and relatively undistracted by the spectacular theorizing of Heidegger, Husserl, Jaspers, Bultmann that never ceased to haunt her, but it still was more about "origins" than about German and Russian society. Even the harshly brilliant structure she built up in her last chapters on the parallels between the Hitler-Stalin bureaucracies, their arbitrary use of exclusion and terror, the central importance of the police, seems to me now, rereading the book, a stupendous literary idea, like the structure of Dante's Hell. There is not a reference to the actualities of czarist society.

I still think that her thesis was right and that "total domination" (a clearer term than "totalitarianism") is exactly what Stalinism and Hitlerism had in common. But Lenin, the real author of the one-party state, does not figure in her book because the Russia that formed Lenin does not figure there. The fascination of *The Origins* is in Arendt's unremarked gift of concentrated literary force—the last chapters are overwhelming, apocalyptic. But she attained this force through her severe logic. The book hammers out the exclusive theory of totalitarianism with which she started and to which her selected phenomena had to fit. So no other book on the subject had such an impact. With her you knew where you were. Totalitarianism was the "burden of our time."

Hannah Arendt was indeed (on one side of her) a grand and incessant theorist. She was also a complex temperament who, in her East Prussian severity with other people's weaknesses and disagreements, always had sharp put-

---

New York Review of Books, October 26, 1978.

downs for theories and persons she disliked. Her theorizing and her "imperiousness," as Elisabeth Young-Bruehl puts it in her admiring, extraordinarily full, and on the whole dependable biography, did not prevent her from being a femme fatale, though she would have been puzzled by the compliment. The trouble she had with the wives of some American admirers she never ascribed to anything but their lack of parity with their more congenial husbands. Despite her scorn for such feminist tracts as Simone de Beauvoir's *The Second Sex*, I doubt that she had any more interest in feminism, pro or contra, than did Immanuel Kant. Her "heroes" certainly included women of her own moral stamp, like Rosa Luxemburg. Many women, responding to her own gift for friendship, became positive addicts of Arendt.

As a student she had, as Young-Bruehl reveals, an affair with Heidegger, and never got over it. She was proposed to by such eminences as Leo Strauss, W. H. Auden, Hans Morgenthau, and was vainly propositioned by the Austrian novelist Hermann Broch: "Let me be the exception, Hermann." At her funeral her hard-boiled publisher William Jovanovich startled everyone by breaking down for a second and crying, "I loved her fiercely!" Her first husband, Gunther Stern (later Anders), once heard me talking at a party about Hannah, and interrupted to say, "I wish to thank you for speaking so well of my ex-wife, Hannah Arendt." When I reported this to Hannah, she took it as a matter of course and came out with a tribute to their spiritual education in Weimar days—their training in *Erkenntnis* as mutual recognition. She and Bluecher were positively intoxicated with each other. She identified him so much with herself that she had him buried from a Jewish funeral chapel.

Heidegger, with his belief in "thinking" as an autonomous activity, influenced her far more than did her father-figure Jaspers, whose style she privately thought prolix. Emerson (whose admirer Nietzsche laughed that he had been too much influenced by German philosophy) was smugly sure that "so long as a man thinks, he is free." Heidegger believed that "thinking" (apparently only philosophers and poets have ever done it) seeks meaning, not knowledge. To find meaning, one must take up a stance toward the universe, whereas knowledge seeks to possess some portion of it. Knowledge, as in science, is too limited. As "truth," a special prejudice of our science-dominated minds, it is too easily confirmable and therefore transient in interest. Heidegger as philosopher drew heavily on the pre-Socratics and on a poet like Hölderlin for his image of true philosophizing. He was consciously "archaic"; Arendt's final excuse for his Nazifying was that he was "primeval." Both would have agreed with that most Germanic saying of Rilke's, "Poetry is the past that breaks out in our hearts."

Poetry as a spell from the past was part of Heidegger's appeal for Arendt, who wrote a plaintive, stricken kind of lyric verse and who naturally saw poetry as central to her philosopher's ability to wonder at the phenomenal world. What Heidegger emphasized as *Denken* was really revelation—perfectly poised attentiveness to what is "concealed." This encouraged and intensified in Arendt the connection between thinking as dialogue with oneself and her natural sense of solitude. She had grown up fatherless; even before she became a refugee and "homelessness" played a dominating role in her sense of herself as exceptional and a "pariah," she adhered to a German tradition of exalted solitude that her many fierce interchanges in America never diminished.

The sense of freedom central to her political theory depended on a person's ability to think for thinking's sake. "Thinking" as a positive ideal, as a way of closing in on any subject without surrendering to its worldly repute, became her way of independence as well as a constant goad to her untiring intelligence. Her intellectual self-confidence went hand in hand with a candid "loneliness in this world" to which she always managed to give a philosophical and even theological aura. This was the foundation of her free religious concern rather than belief. No one was ever more contemptuous of "psychology"; she never mentioned Freud's name without a laugh. In her own occasional moments of emotional distress, she could be not just appealing but Antigone-like in her struggle with herself. She was lofty about other people's conflicts and involvements—especially when these became so hopelessly personal that they could not "think" as a way of solving them themselves.

All this gave Arendt an unceasing seriousness of tone and inflexibility of judgment fundamental to the tragic vision of our age behind everything she wrote. The resentment *Eichmann in Jerusalem* raised among some intellectuals just brought out the feelings many of them had stifled when they read *The Origins of Totalitarianism*. Before there was "the banality of evil" there was "radical evil."

It is the appearance of some radical evil, previously unknown to us, that puts an end to the notion of developments and transformations of qualities. Here, there are neither political nor historical nor simply moral standards but, at the most, the realization that something seems to be involved in modern politics that actually should never be involved in politics as we used to understand it, namely all or nothing. . . .

The fear of "parting" that was so fundamental to her emotional temperament became the "break with tradition" in philosophy and politics. "Loneliness" (carefully discriminated from the necessary solitude of "thinking") she ascribed to the atomized and estranged masses whose helpless anger gave opportunity to the enslaving Nazis. Her overpowering sense of loss, the strain of remembering golden Weimar days on the cluttered, steamy Upper West Side (from the windows of her new apartment on Morningside Drive she could see a park it was suicide to enter) made for more than the usual refugee fret; she had to come to terms with Adenauer as well as Hitler, Nixon as well as the John Adams whom she venerated, rather too didactically for American ears, as a maker of America's "glorious beginnings." As a convert to political theory from German idealism, she had to confront and explain so many phenomena that she emerged as an authority in the country that as a good European (like Freud) she once despised but had come to love—for the tradition of political freedom in the oldest written constitution in the Western world.

Ambivalence stayed a central fact of her existence and her teaching. On the one hand, as she defiantly told a German audience when she became a great favorite and prizewinner over there, "I am a German Jewess thrown out by Hitler." On the other hand, it was up to her and what she (like Heidegger) unattractively called her "peer group" to put the tradition together again.

This conflict between the Jew and the German was exactly in line with the amazing creativity of Jews in the German language, from Moses Mendelssohn to Heine, Marx, Freud, Kafka up to her friends Walter Benjamin and Hermann Broch. The locus classicus is Arendt's almost tormentedly autobiographical biography *Rahel Varnhagen: The Life of a Jewess.* Varnhagen (1771–1833), married to a German nobleman, was born Rahel Levin, the daughter of a Jewish dealer in gold. She kept a famous salon, and figured as a reigning symbol of "universalism" while the Enlightenment in Germany still permitted such an easy exchange between a "Jewess" and Goethe, Schleiermacher, Fichte, Chamisso, Brentano, Wilhelm, and Alexander von Humboldt. The tension that pervades *Rahel Varnhagen* often sounds desperate. Rahel, an extraordinarily attractive personality who sometimes felt she had sold out and admitted at the end of her life that she was finally glad she had been born Jewish, was nevertheless—like her troubled biographer Hannah Arendt—interested in everything concerning Jewish "identity" and status, but not the old religion.

Marx's father had him baptized; Heine converted in order to enter society; Freud, much as he depended on Jewish society in Vienna when the respectable world abhorred him, conveniently dismissed all religion as "illusion." Kafka, who like his fervent admirer Hannah Arendt was studiously respectful of Jewish cultural tradition and even of Yiddish, was no more a religious Jew than she was. He told his Gentile admirer Gustav Janouch, "He who has faith cannot talk about it; he who has no faith should not talk about it."

Those born to Jewish Orthodoxy usually leave it behind in order to become independently creative. The achievement of the most famous modern Jews is so clearly in violation of the Law that the emergence on the world scene of individual *Ostjuden* (the last to break away) came very late. The Israeli scholar Jacob Talmon used to say that this was the tragedy of Zionism: it came so late. German Jews were "liberated" from religion earlier than other Jews, partly as a reaction to the enthusiasm for free inquiry in German philosophy and literature. Even "the greatest Jewish scholar of our time," Gershom Scholem, the principal authority on Jewish mysticism, was not a practicing Jew. The ultra-Orthodox, I am informed, tend to shy away from discussion of the Holocaust. As my student David Zuger said, "It's too recent."

The young Karl Marx asserted that the proletariat was to carry out the mission of German philosophy. Hannah Arendt, a traditionalist who found no tradition for her Judaism, was much influenced by the spirit of the Gospels, not by Christian belief. The first edition of *The Origins of Totalitarianism* ended with resounding consolation from St. Paul in the prison at Acre—"Therefore do yourselves no harm; for we are all here."

I was not surprised, when *Eichmann in Jerusalem* appeared, to see her scorn for the Israeli prosecutor Hausner as a "Galician Jew," a "ghetto type." I had often enough heard her on "little Jews," and though she once confessed to a German friend in my hearing, with a great air of disclosure, that she had one Russian grandfather, I never knew until I read Young-Bruehl's excellently informative biography that her mother's family were in fact Russian Jews and that the Jews of Königsberg (now Kaliningrad) were predominantly Russian.

If Hitler had not brought both German and Russian Jews to the same pit, German-Jewish fear and resentment of their Eastern brethren might have remained the same fear of Jewish Orthodoxy (equivalent to inferior social status). Chaim Weizmann (himself no believer) was stupefied by the complacency with which some parvenus identified themselves as "Germans of the Mosaic persuasion." Rabbi Leo Baeck, so firm in his Jewish belief that he called Zionism "a crutch I don't need," was, long before the Eichmann book in which she called him "the Jewish Führer," not someone she admired.

Arendt's respect for herself as a Jew involved not the slightest respect for the synagogue. And since the synagogue as the foundation of Jewish community life necessitated "leadership," her charge in the Eichmann book that many in the Judenrat had collaborated with the Nazis really had its foundation not in her better understanding that the condemned Jews were politically helpless but in her scorn for Jewish "leaders." (One of the many disgusting attacks against Jacobo Timerman by the new Jewish right is that he flouted "Jewish leadership.") Arendt herself, following the French critic of the Jewish establishment Bernard Lazare, believed in being a "pariah" rather than a "parvenu." Of course she found it easier to think of herself as a "pariah" (totally independent) when intellectual America resounded with her name than she would have to find herself a "pariah" in Treblinka.

Her scorn for Jewish religious practice led her to ignore features of Jewish passivity that would have explained the Jewish political weakness she lamented at the opening of *The Origins*. The Jehovah's Witnesses who were so impervious to Nazi assaults in the camps were not so different from the many Jewish Orthodox who believed that they were dying for *kiddush ha-Shem*, the sanctification of the Name. In the "God-intoxicated" depths of traditional Judaism, in the religious separateness that was thrown back on the Jews and was by no means unwanted, lay much of what Arendt excoriated as opportunism. The Jews being assembled for death by the Nazis were God's "pariahs"—made so by their uncertain relation to an all-sovereign God who was their only raison d'être.

Eichmann in Jerusalem was a journalistic coup, a masterful—but often arrogantly tendentious—assemblage of evidence. Arendt had become an extraordinary literary performer in English. The tone, as Gershom Scholem told her in a famous reproach, was heartless. Since in my experience she could not take criticism, I was not surprised when she began her unsatisfactory reply by addressing Scholem by his old German name, Gerhardt.

The "banality of evil" thesis followed from Arendt's now favorite idea that mere bureaucrats, dreadfully "normal" functionaries like an Eichmann, did not "think" what they were doing and were to the philosopher's taste—boring. This was appalling German intellectual swank. It has not become less injurious to "thinking." Many a journalist and television commentator refers to the "banality of evil" with a confidence that makes one sick.

Arendt herself disproved the "banality" thesis when she opened her book by criticizing the prosecutor's attempt to make Eichmann's devilish character the explanation of his deeds. As she said, the defendant in a murder trial especially is to be judged not by his "character" but by his deeds. There is nothing "banal" about the "extermination" (as the world has come to call it) of 6 million Jews. The Holocaust, "Death as God" Saul Bellow called it in *Herzog*, should not have aroused so much idle chatter on the part of Jewish intellectuals, whether as useless explanation, bad literature, or phony theology. No doubt the dreadfully irrelevant literature proves nothing more than what Arendt rightfully attacked as political weakness. From which she was certainly not exempt.

I cannot leave it at that. "You must think what you are doing" is a piece of wholly unpolitical Heideggerian elitism that hardly applies to mass politics and condemned people. As Young-Bruehl shows, Arendt could be inconsistent to an extreme. In conversation during the McCarthy period, her political judgments were catastrophic; her considered retrospect on the astonishing degradation of America in recent years—no one said anything better during the bicentennial about the American situation than her reflections in these pages, "Home to Roost"*—was properly acerb and even tragic in tone. Her political instinct was unerring against those who, like Sidney Hook, still called themselves socialist but were always so much more interested in foreign policy against Russia that they overlooked or excused depredations at home. On the influence of those she called ex-Communists rather than "former" Communists, those who have made a career

---

*New York Review of Books, June 26, 1975.

of having once been Communists, she called the turn very early in the fifties. This was when the former Trotskyist Irving Kristol called for the restriction of civil liberties. His ascent after that did not surprise her in the least.

Never having been a leftist, she ignored the necessity of having a "line." She believed in "revolutionary councils," supported enthusiastically Churchill's denunciation of the "iron curtain," adored Rosa Luxemburg in lofty unconcern for Rosa's revolutionary Marxism, paid no attention to her beloved John Adams's little tyrannies in office. "Freedom and justice" said it all for her—a party of one. It would have amazed her to read the misleading review of Young-Bruehl's book by Peter Berger in *The New York Times Book Review*, with its attempt to make her out as an exponent of the German left. She was in fact roundly criticized as a reactionary by the German teachers to whom she lectured. On many current issues her positions were determinedly moral rather than political, quirky rather than "sensible" in the liberal (or rightist) American style: they were not to be anticipated even by her.

But what made her exceptional indeed, especially when seen against the mingled success and fright that marked so many American Jews in the postwar years, intellectuals and "leaders" alike, was what I will always think of as her intellectual love of God, her belief in gratitude for our gift of being. A less fancy way of saying this: many modern Jews are religiously frustrated; she was not willing to be. While she discounted Judaism, and was often impatient with Jews, she did so out of spiritual need. Many who speak in the name of the Jews and even of the Holocaust seemed to her just hungry for importance— and, what is poignant, for identity.

I do not think for a moment that Hannah Arendt knew the solution to Jewish history. Perhaps there is no solution so long as the religious crisis goes unremarked. But what made Hannah Arendt's name a specter and a bugaboo to many, an everlasting consolation to a few, is that she invested her expressiveness (this was the impact of her experience, her personality, her "love of the world," all more than "thinking") in the conviction that there has been a "break" in human history. She lived this. That there has been a "break," that we live in truly "dark times," no one confronted by her was allowed to doubt. Arendt's greatest value, her distinct example, was that she could not accept this break, as most of us do.

[1982]

THE DIRECTNESS OF
JOSEPHINE HERBST

———•◆•———

This tribute to Josephine Herbst was read at a memorial service held at St. Luke's Chapel in New York on February 18, 1969.

There are people who knew Josie longer than I did, and are better qualified to speak of her, and for her many friends, than I am. I met her early in 1950, a time when she had already endured many disappointments as a writer and as an American radical, and when she was already caught up in the long, hard struggle for survival that was to end only in the early hours of January 28. The nineteen years in which I knew her were years of great poverty, great isolation, often of humiliating frustration and silence. So I cannot speak, as others could directly, of the spunky and brilliantly independent girl from Sioux City who typically enough went off to Berkeley for an A.B. as if college were a romantic adventure—and, the year after, took the lifelong adventure that was already herself to New York, where she read for George Jean Nathan and H. L. Mencken on *The Smart Set* and began to form those friendships with writers for which she had, unlike many writers, a special and enduring genius.

Nor can I speak directly here of her creative beginnings—of how, in 1921 she went to Europe, as so many writers of her marvelous generation did, without quite knowing how she would live, yet typically got right into the heat of things, political and literary, in Weimar Germany. I cannot speak here directly of Josie in the twenties, when she was so much a part of the new American writing that was emerging in Paris with her friend Hemingway, or of Josie in the early thirties, when she found expression for all her burning old-fashioned American idealism in identifying herself with, in being right on the spot as a correspondent to report, what then still seemed the old-fashioned Russian idealism, the Negro boys from Scottsboro, the struggling farmers from her native Iowa. She was with Dreiser and Dos Passos when they went down to investigate the terror against the striking Kentucky miners, with the Cuban peasants during the 1935 general strike, with the first victims of Hitler's terror in those years of the thirties, before the war, when apparently it took a socialist experience and imagination to guess the potential horror of what so many bourgeois German Jews could not.

In 1937 Josie was, of course, in Spain to cover the Spanish Civil War—and she was really there, steeped in the life of the frontline villages and, typically enough, getting desperately needed rations for her fellow correspondents in the Hotel Florída from her always well stocked friend Hemingway, from whose room the smell of frying bacon and other goodies would drive less fortunate writers crazy. And during the Second World War, Josie, who needed the job desperately, was of course fired from the OWI, then busily mobilizing American opinion against fascism, for having been a premature anti-fascist.

As I say, I did not know her then—I met her only in 1950, when her books were all out of print, when she was out of a job, out of cash, out of fashion, and might have been out of a home if it hadn't been for that blessed stone house in Erwinna—surely one of the few writers' residences in Bucks County still dependent on an outhouse. Pauline Pfeiffer, Hemingway's second wife, said to me in Key West, talking about Josie's plight with a shudder—"A woman shouldn't be that poor." But she was, and every friend of Josie's knows how tough it was for her up to the end.

Yet—and this is what I have come here to say—I have never known in my life any other writer who was so solid, so joyous, so giving, who was able to take difficulties so much in her stride, and, who even when she was getting pretty old and sick, made you see that flaming girl from Sioux City and Berkeley and New York, Germany and Russia and Cuba and Spain, who was always getting mad about injustice and pompous stupidity, always radiating that marvelous sense of physical space and human possibility that was the gift of the Middle West to so many writers of her generation.

Josie, who could easily get mad and also make you see the fun of getting mad, got mad always in behalf of other people. I was enchanted to read in Carlos Baker's forthcoming biography of Hemingway that one day in that romantic long ago, when Josie and her husband, John Herrmann, went fishing with Hemingway off the Keys, Hemingway lost his temper at John for not getting enough ice to keep their catch fresh, and kept grousing at him until Josie broke in: "Hem, if you don't stop, I'll take your pistol and shoot you." Hemingway, who was so fond of Josie that he later gave her one of his manuscripts, was properly impressed.

Josie had many gifts—she was a natural writer, an expressive lyricist of human emotion and of landscape, a firm and canny observer in her novels of every human snare, an extraordinarily warm, loving woman who could express her love for her friends in letters that were as direct and overflowing as the warmth of her voice and the spontaneity of her soul. On Saturday morning, January 25, she said two sentences that so impressed Dr. Fries that she entered it in Josie's medical chart. "I want you to give a final message to my friends. Tell them that I do not repent, that I love life unto eternity, love and life."

When I think of what I loved and valued most in her, as someone in whom the writer and woman were so intermingled, it comes down to this directness, this particular old-fashioned straightness of her every attitude, that exploded out of her, often laughingly, as if Josie Herbst were the shortest distance between two points. This directness was an old-fashioned political attitude in America, it was once our politics, and Josie suffered its loss; it was an old-fashioned morality: you must speak out, now; it was her old-fashioned freedom and her beautiful strength. She was so full of existence, of politics and nature and literature and friendship, that her letters, her incomparable letters, the kind of letters people never even think of writing anymore, were an explosion of directness. You received everything on her mind and heart, and it was the gift of her, direct—

Friday morning, Erwinna, Pa., July 7, 1950—

A tiny yellow duck broke loose from its mother and waddled down the hill to my back door—then began a loud squawk in terror and fearful recognition that it was lost, lost. I got it in my hand and it settled down at once—I could have held it like that forever until we both perished, two ninnies in bliss together while the world fell apart. I called up the farm, they came with a truck as if the duck were a cow to be transported only in a huge affair and took it away. I loved it madly—Russell writes Scribner's may do the Bartram book and that Hastings House are bastards. It will work out. I am glad to think of you with friends away from New York. Here it was divinely cool last night . . . a late big moon and before that a night thick with fireflies. Some stars are pale green. Some icy blue and there are some as red as my barn.

And on she went for a whole solid single-spaced page, ending—"When one wants grapes, one goes to the poor. They will be willing to rob the birds but they will share with you, share and share alike. They will even love you for your need and shelter you in their arms, hasta revista, Josie."

But alas, we won't.

[1969]

SAVING MY SOUL AT THE PLAZA

———•◆•———

To my surprise, "The Committee for the Free World, Midge Decter Executive Secretary," invited me to attend its conference on "Our Country and Our Culture," February 12–13, at the Plaza Hotel in New York. Admission, $50. I confess that whenever I see a piece of print reading "The Committee for the Free World, Midge Decter Executive Secretary," I laugh. I'm reminded of a young reporter, who was granted an interview in the Oval Office with President Lyndon Johnson, and so exasperated Johnson by his bumbling questions that the great man, rising to his full 6 feet $3^1/_2$ inches, sputtered in indignation: "How can you ask a chickenshit question like that of the Head of the Free World?"

For all the contemptuousness and rigidity of the views I first observed years ago at a Dalton School PTA meeting, Midge Decter's easy laughter still persuades me that in *this* "neoconservative" there is a cynic waiting to be let out. Although she surprised me by going public to excoriate homosexuality, liberated women, and Protestant clergymen foolish enough to worry over Lebanese children without a roof over their heads, I confess to affection for Midge. I cannot resist her smile of worldly experience. When I called her to accept the invitation, admitting that I was surprised to be asked, she cheerfully said: "It's not too late to save your soul."

The Committee for the Free World is not exactly a committee, though I am sure it is run like one by the local presidium, drawn largely from *Commentary's* staff and writers, whose struggle against international communism earned the committee a grant (in 1981) of $100,000 in Mellon money from the Carthage Foundation in Pittsburgh. The Committee is the latest and most aggressive of those bodies of former leftist intellectuals, in the tradition of the Congress for Cultural Freedom, which, concentrating on the danger of communism abroad and at home, still consider themselves an avant-garde of sorts. Unlike the American Committee for Cultural Freedom, however, which fell apart in dissension over McCarthyism because many members still considered themselves liberals, radicals, democratic socialists, and would not wish to become fellow travelers of Senator Taft, James Burnham, William F. Buckley Jr., and *tutti quanti*, the Committee for the Free World is a straightforward rightist organization— for former liberals and former leftists.

This avant-garde has personal and political ties with the Reagan administration, can always be depended upon to support Begin and to ignore much of what goes on in South Africa. It is part of that astonishingly wide "conservative" network in America represented by Social Democrats USA, Freedom House, the current United States delegation to the United Nations, the magazines *Commentary, The National Review, The American Spectator, The New Criterion, Mainstream, The American Scholar,* and *The Public Interest,* the Hoover Institution on War, Revolution, and Peace, Georgetown University's Center for Strategic and International Studies, the Heritage Foundation, the American Enterprise Institute for Public Policy Research, the evangelists behind the Moral Majority, the defense contractors behind the American Security Council, libertarians opposed to gun control, the groups in favor of capital punishment and opposed to abortion, the "Right to Work" lobby—and, of course, Senator Jesse Helms's Congressional Club. This last was described by *The Wall Street Journal* as "a unique political conglomerate, the best-known and possibly the largest political fund-raiser on the national scale"; it has such offshoots as the American Family Institute, the Institute on Money and Inflation, the Institution on Religion and Democracy.

We live in a time of many reversals; it is undoubtedly true, as Henry Steele Commager suggested long before Reagan became president, that if the Bill of Rights were submitted to Congress today it would not pass. The twentieth century may yet be remembered for uniting, right to left, in hatred of the Enlightenment. As always, political intellectuals and cultural bureaucrats think they are moving history when they are only changing "positions." You are old, you ex-hopefuls, and your hair has become very white; and yet you incessantly stand on your head—do you think, at your age, it is right? Still, the "conservative consensus" that so excited William Safire and Norman Podhoretz at Reagan's election, though its vision of America resembles that of a defense contractor, seems more powerful than it really is partly because of the idiocy of the extreme left, the general disenchantment with radicalism, the weakness of the labor movement.

Some far-right foundations oiled with Texas money will not support organizations in which Jews are prominent, no matter how "anticommunist" they are. In any event, good relations between conservatives and the Reagan administration are not always predictable. A recent Heritage Foundation report attacking affirmative action was mostly written by government employees. Helping to found the Committee on the Present Danger, a former incarnation of the Committee for the Free World, did not save Eugene V. Rostow from being fired as head of the Arms Control and Disarmament Agency. Norman Podhoretz, who evidently believed that *Commentary* had provided the intellectual momentum for Reagan's victory in 1980, was not made head of the International Communications Agency, a post he had reportedly been given reason to expect.

Still, "neoconservativism" itself is so successful an employment agency for right thinkers that one becomes quickly accustomed to the news that *Commentary*'s contributors are associated with the Georgetown Center for Strategic and International Studies, the Hoover Institution, the American Enterprise Institute, etc., etc. And it was no surprise that Dr. William Bennett, director of the National Endowment for the Humanities, was scheduled as the guest speaker for the committee's lunch, although the snowstorm that weekend prevented his appearance. Dr. Bennett, a Harvard Law School graduate who prefers academic administration to the law, was assistant to President John Silber of Boston University and assistant director to the late Charles Frankel at the National Humanities Center. Despite his association with such an old-fashioned liberal as Frankel, Dr. Bennett is undoubtedly a genuine conservative and not a convert. But he has appointed to the advisory board of the NEH a genuine neoconservative, Professor Gertrude Himmelfarb. One of the favorite

theses of this distinguished specialist in nineteenth-century England, so comforting to those who have recently made it in the United States, is that poverty,
even in Victorian England (and despite the wealth of its documentation), was
the delusion of upper-class types who were getting sensitive.

Before Dr. Bennett was finally named to head the endowment, Reagan
nominated a Texas university expert on William Faulkner whose decisive contribution to our period was the disclosure that Abraham Lincoln had violated
due process when he drew up the Emancipation Proclamation. We must be
grateful to Irving Kristol for helping to stop that particular appointment,
which would have made for some strange political bedfellows indeed. But how
far Irving Kristol, the "godfather" of the neoconservatives, as he was acclaimed
at the Plaza conference, has traveled from the streets of Williamsburg, a
Trotskyist alcove at City College, and a job on *Commentary* (when its editors
and contributors still could contradict one another) that he should know well
enough the views of a Confederate zealot to relieve the administration of
embarrassment.

Kristol, until very recently Henry Luce Professor of Urban Values at New
York University, now the university's professor of social theory in the economics department, is also the editor of *The Public Interest*, an adviser to conservative
congressmen, a recent guest at the White House, and a board member of several American corporations. Unlike novelists, poets, and ordinary scholars,
whose work does not easily lend itself to support by an ideological pressure
group, the intellectuals who depend on the cold war for their careers find not
only safety in numbers but the assurance of worldly progress. The solidarity
they display on every question of opinion! The last time I wrote for
Commentary, an assistant keeper of the flame struggled for an hour on the long-
distance line to Notre Dame, where I was then teaching, to persuade me to
take out a derisive description of Richard Nixon.

The blizzard made it impossible for me to get to the Plaza in time to hear the
main presentation on "Politics and the Arts" by Hilton Kramer. Kramer was
also absent, but in the discussion period the meeting heard from Joseph
Epstein, the editor of *The American Scholar*, the organ of the Phi Beta Kappa
associations and a journal never known for any political position, until Epstein
started publishing views resembling those of Kramer, his old colleague on the
New Leader, once the official organ of the American Socialist Party. Indeed,

Epstein's observations at the conference, summarized by *The New York Times* of February 14, might have been written by Kramer himself:

> Something odd has happened to American literary culture in recent years. Suddenly American literature, contemporary American literature, seems rather lackluster, a bit beside the point, less than first rate, even though American political power is still great. Why?
>
> To think the worst of our society—against a superabundance of evidence to the contrary—gives the self-dramatizing American literary imagination a background against which to dramatize itself. And the contemporary literary scene is rife with writers whose chief stock in the trade of ideas is a fairly crude sort of anti-Americanism.

This formula—"writers whose chief stock in the trade of ideas is a fairly crude sort of anti-Americanism"—led, I was told, to discussion of strategy at the Plaza. How are right-thinking people to turn the American novel around? Of course, to raise the question suggests Zhdanovism, agitprop, or what Soviet literary orthodoxy constantly demands of the "shock troops of literature": "Bring our literature into line with Soviet progress!" But there were no novelists, poets, critics, or philosophers at the conference to provide the media communicators present with elementary distinctions between the realms of art and "American political power." Being at the Plaza, Scott Fitzgerald's favorite oasis in his favorite city, I remembered an observation in his notebooks. "Art inevitably grows out of a period when, in general, the artist admires his own nation and wants to win its approval. This fact is not altered by the circumstance that his work may take the form of satire. . . ." Satire was a closed subject to the Plaza patriots so aggrieved by what only intellectual thugs used to denounce as "anti-Americanism." When I mentioned the Plaza scene in *The Great Gatsby* to one middle-aged "discussant," he looked at me suspiciously and said, "What's a Gatsby?"

As art critic of the *Times* Hilton Kramer was a heavy stylist who seemed to be keeping his opinions under tight restraint, while outside the *Times's* art columns he became more interesting as he became politically more shrill, deploring, for example, the sinister connection between homosexuality and radicalism. He made a point of this in reviewing Martin Green's *Children of the Sun*. Evidently a new outlet was needed, *The New Criterion*, and for this Kramer and his publisher managed to obtain half a million dollars (in all) from the John M. Olin Foundation, the Smith Richardson Foundation, the Scaife Family Charitable Trust, and the Carthage Foundation (also mainly supported by Richard Mellon Scaife).

The New Criterion takes its name, of course, from T. S. Eliot's *The Criterion* (1922–1939). Eliot was able to found *The Criterion* in 1922 because that was the year that *The Waste Land* established him as the most provocative but influential poet-critic of the modernist movement. It was considered an organ of the most austere and distinguished European opinion—along with the *Nouvelle Revue Française, La Revue des Deux Mondes, Die Deutsche Rundschau,* and Benedetto Croce's *La Critica.* Eliot said that poetry deals with the world as it is, criticism with the world as it should be. He saw the world descending into chaos because of its lack of respect for spiritual truth and religious authority; he was also a marvelous *working* critic who wrote and inspired unforgettable observations on the practice of art.

Few of Eliot's contributors went as far as he did when, with his curious political ingenuousness, he wrote in *The Criterion* supporting the ultra-royalist and anti-Semitic Action Française and wrote that if he had to choose, he would elect fascism over communism. (Eliot voted Labour in 1945 and disavowed the Page-Barbour Lectures of 1933, *After Strange Gods,* in which he declared that "reasons of race and religion combine to make any large number of free-thinking Jews undesirable.") Eliot gave *The Criterion* its authority, and its modest costs were supplied by Eliot's employer, the publishing firm of Faber and Faber. Far from being in any way jingoistic or "patriotic" in the hectoring style favored by former leftists who have changed nothing but their opponents, Eliot above all sought to found a "European" consciousness. With the outbreak of war in 1939, Eliot gave up *The Criterion.*

The New Criterion, supported in part by the John M. Olin Foundation, has its editorial offices at 460 Park Avenue in the office of the Olin Corporation, which in 1982 had revenues of $2.2 billion and is currently number 195 on *Fortune's* list of the top 500 companies. More than half of the Olin Corporation's business is in chemicals. It owns the license for the manufacture of Winchester rifles. Some of its many products are small-caliber ammunition, pool chemicals, skis, carpet padding, copper for the U.S. Mint, brass, cellophane, cigarette paper. A literary and art review whose editorial column preaches the virtue of something called "democratic capitalism" (no further discriminations are made) must be one of the more modest investments of Olin money.

One political passion behind Eliot's *Criterion* was resentment of what Henry James, describing his own native's return in *The American Scene,* lamented as "the inconceivable alien." Eliot said that American history came to an end with the accession of Andrew Jackson. Each year, on the anniversary of Richard III's defeat and death at Bosworth Field, he wore a white rose. Like many of us in America today, Hilton Kramer is descended from "the inconceivable alien." We are not Anglo-Catholic or royalist, and we have learned that even T. S. Eliot was not as orthodox in literary or political opinion as he wanted to be. History does move. Our tradition is a pluralistic, democratic America, with its constitutional prescription of mixed powers, intellectual freedom, and some ineradicable awareness that this buoyant and exciting society still rides cruelly over millions. There has been no stronger American tradition than the struggle for a just society.

The political passion behind *The New Criterion,* at least in its first issues, seems mostly to be resentment of intellectuals who think differently from Hilton Kramer. The 1960s may be over for most of its young people but they are not over for Kramer, who views most of our cultural defects as survivals of a defunct radicalism. Introducing *The New Criterion* in September 1982, Kramer announced that "most of what is written" in American journals pretending to criticism "is either hopelessly ignorant, deliberately obscurantist, commercially compromised, or politically motivated.... Criticism at every level...has almost everywhere degenerated into one or another form of ideology or publicity or some pernicious combination of the two...." Example? The innuendo in Dore Ashton's *American Art Since 1945* that the Philip Morris Company would have censored Hans Eisler's parody of Schönberg's *Pierrot Lunaire,* in a concert the company sponsored to accompany the Guggenheim Museum's exhibition of German Expressionism, had the company "only known" what was going on. Kramer indignantly rejects such thoughts about American corporations, but wants to know why it is wrong and even sinister "for corporate patrons of the arts to evince the least curiosity about the social implications of the artistic programs they are invited to sponsor." Another example: left-wing criticism by two English art historians of John Rewald's *Post-Impressionism,* the present "cult status" of the Marxist critic John Berger, the sad case of Lucy Lippard, who in the seventies "fell victim to the radical whirlwind." Hilton

Kramer has detected a "radical whirlwind" in Mrs. Thatcher's England and Mr. Reagan's America, countries where heavy unemployment has counterproduced a growing fatalism and despair.

I had no idea that the left had retained so much power in the Reagan epoch; and, in fact, when such an independent critic as Ada Louise Huxtable writes in *The New Criterion*, she attacks the grotesque corporate buildings that are ruining Madison Avenue two blocks away from the Olin Corporation's offices. It remains to be seen whether anything will be said in *The New Criterion* about the self-satisfied ignorance that is so much a product of the mechanisms and mechanistic thinking that dominate "communications" in every field.

Perhaps it will. In his own writing, Kramer's "new" criterion for appraising what happens on the American scene is mainly whether it can be linked not to the actualities of American society but to anti-Americanism. Since "anti-Americanism" can no longer be identified with being soft on communism (no one in his senses now being soft on communism), it consists of being critical of American business. Yet as editor, it must be said, Kramer publishes sober pieces on art, music, and cultural history that go their own way. It is a positive relief to find Frederick Crews writing in the current issue, "There is no need to attach sinister importance to the strange political tenor of [Leslie] Fiedler's latest criticism."

The Albert Schweitzer Professor of the Humanities Emeritus at Columbia, Robert Nisbet, also missed the first session, where he was to give one of the main talks, on "The University and its Discontents." This was read to the panel and, according to the *Times*, Nisbet cited polls among students at the Columbia Graduate School of Journalism showing that 75 percent of the students believed the United States exploited and impoverished third world countries and that 89 percent felt the primary aim of American foreign policy was to advance private business. "It is in this light," Nisbet said, "that I expect to see a new mass movement arise during the next few years comparable to the Greens in West Germany."

Nisbet is an academic Tory whose recent book, *Prejudices*, from which excerpts appeared in *Commentary*, displays a closed view of a modern world in which actual politics and social forces play no part at all. He sees our chief problem as the bureaucratic omnipresent state, which has eliminated or minimized all those institutions that once intervened between state power and the individual—family, community, religion—in order to inform and protect the citizen, and that provide him with the culture, freedom, and opportunity for responsible opinion and free decision.

It is somehow supposed that this revocation of personal and community rights occurred almost wholly under the baleful influence of the great totalitarian ideologue Rousseau. No one who knows American life outside the university could agree that this "revocation" exists in the summary terms Professor Nisbet asserts. But modern history to Professor Nisbet is a closed circle of ideas, the wrong ideas. Society, the actual spectrum of human difference and people's mingled lives, with all the strange beliefs and resentments that keep them going, does not come into it. Nisbet is charming, witty, and writes in a style of civilized regret for everything that has taken place since the French Revolution.

Whenever he goes to history itself for actual documentation, his theoretical frame eludes genuine crises and conflicts. In the style of Jeane Kirkpatrick, who not only accommodated herself to "authoritarian" states but came to like them, Professor Nisbet praises Elizabethan England as an example of the superior literature and art that came into being under "authoritarian" regimes as ways of circumventing the censor. Thus to align Shakespeare's England with South Africa, Chile, Argentina, Bolivia, etc., should puzzle writers in exile from these "authoritarian" countries. How was Shakespeare able to please the "authorities," while Nadine Gordimer and other talented writers from South Africa and South America can't? A poor joke, as Professor Nisbet's versions of actual history often are.

But his absence left a hole in the conference; he supplies to neoconservative publications the necessary tone of deep thought and cultural pessimism, without ruffling anyone's political ambitions, although his idea of social history is innocent to the point of farce. In a discussion of "Covetousness" in *Prejudices* his principal example is academics competing for endowed chairs. Compared with neoconservatives, though, Professor Nisbet is no more than an old-fashioned conservative with a longing for "the traditional community, which alone is the source and sustenance of birth, marriage, and death." He is, very properly, outraged by what he calls the "shameless culture." That is just the word for it— "anti-American" as that makes Professor Nisbet. But how odd that under "Effrontery" his principal examples (names not given, but everyone who came of age in the sixties will be able to identify them) should be the university president who, having insisted on a yacht and a private jet, fled from bandoliered blacks, a former secretary of defense "who ... helped to instigate the longest, costliest, and most unsuccessful war in United States history, winning renown for his computerized body counts"; and "the astronomer-impresario" who on television is "in constant incantation of the great god science and in equally constant anathema of all religious impulse."

Professor Nisbet might have found examples of "effrontery" and "the shameless culture" closer to home. Example: Professor Irving Kristol's paper on "The Responsibility of the Press," the main event of the conference's closing session. His thesis: the media are in the hands of an "educated minority," who do not reflect the sane views of the populace. Plato had it wrong when he said that "democratic man" is guided by passion and antinomianism. Kristol: "The debasements of democracy appear only among the educated. They are dedicated to the destruction of the civilization they have inherited."

Yet this "educated minority," according to Kristol, is recruited mostly from journalism schools, which represent the *fourth* level of mind in American education. (The fifth is schools of education.) I doubt myself that much can be said for the journalism schools, but I had forgotten how much of an Anglophile Kristol became when he was co-editor of *Encounter.* "The only journal in the English-speaking world worthy of respect," he said, "is *The Economist.*" *The Economist* alone interprets events from "the point of view of those who take responsibility for governing, those destined to govern." In America, by contrast, journalism's only goal is one adversary to the established order, its aim (again I quote him word for word) "to destroy all authority."

Such reflections from the point of view of those responsible "for governing" may have been to the point when Kristol dined at the White House on January 19, although one doubts he mentioned Plato to the president. According to the *Times* story, the guests were summoned because "the president is reaching out for advice." On leaving, Professor Kristol told the press:

The President certainly did not look besieged. He was the same as he's always been the few times I've seen him—very relaxed, very pleasant, and amiable. The evening was informal. The President did not take the lead. There was really no effort in any systematic way to canvass anything.

There was the same relaxed and cheerful tone in Professor Kristol's scorn at the Plaza for those who object to the "squeal rule," which until it was blocked on February 14 by a federal district judge, required federally supported family-planning clinics to notify parents when minors received prescriptions for contraceptives. This is known as "getting government off our backs." The judge stressed that the "squeal rule" "contradicts and subverts the intent of Congress," which provided funds to combat "the problems of teenage pregnancy." With the contempt of a nineteenth-century Tory backbencher deriding Irish rebels, Professor Kristol strongly defended the "squeal rule." As evidence of the imbecility of television and the debasement of moral standards in our society, he cited the thirteen-year-old who (back turned) was presented on television as someone "sexually active" and therefore in need of contraceptive devices. Thirteen years old and already a tramp! Kristol could not contain his laughter as he dismissed this thirteen-year-old degenerate as the sort of person liberals worry about. Television had called her "sexually active." Warming to his topic, Kristol called her a "sexual activist."

The audience roared. It roared again when John O'Sullivan, an Irish journalist who writes in the British press, reported such unanimity in Britain for the Falkland war that misguided grumblers in Fleet Street were denounced as "traitors." The Plaza neoconservatives, united by the Red Menace, also seemed united behind the Ten Commandments. O'Sullivan solemnly advocated them to the assembled, along with a special warning against abortion and adultery. He denounced "those elite groups favorable to adultery" and explained that "antiwar attitudes now current spring from the hedonism rampant in our society."

I was delighted to see so much enthusiasm for the Seventh Commandment, but was less delighted by Mr. O'Sullivan when he defended the *New York Post* on the grounds that it features "transsexual murders" because Rupert Murdoch is outraged by vile sexual practices, and that the real reason such features are disliked is that the paper keeps to a right-wing editorial line. None of the neoconservatives present, many of whom must see the *Post*'s display of gore and sexual crimes every day, raised a doubt or put in a word for "our culture."

Michael A. Ledeen is senior fellow in international affairs at Georgetown University's Center for Strategic and International Studies. He was formerly editor of the *Washington Quarterly* and for a year and a half a member of the State Department. Eliot in *The Waste Land* described

> *One of the low on whom assurance sits*
> *As a silk hat on a Bradford millionaire.*

But that millionaire was a wallflower compared with Mr. Ledeen, "an expert on terrorism," an intellectual who obviously feels responsibility for governing and on whom assurance sits like a halo. He sputtered, he glowed with self-assurance when he denounced the stupidity and worse of *The Washington Post* in exaggerating the Watergate scandal. But principally he explained, in Jeane Kirkpatrick fashion, that "liberals present Central America in terms of a nineteenth-century Marxist model."

Clearly the Nicaragua that was once owned by President Somoza and his family presents not the slightest resemblance to the outdated Marxist scheme of things—even when Somoza, irritated by subversion, had his own people bombed. Nor is there any resemblance to nineteenth-century fables of social oppression in the activity of Roberto D'Aubuisson. As Mr. Ledeen pronounced his scorn for the wrongheadedness with which so many Americans view authority in Central and South America, I thought of what Gabríel Garcia Márquez said in Stockholm last December on receiving the Nobel Prize about "the unearthly tidings of Latin America, that boundless realm of haunted men and historic women, whose unending obstinacy blurs into legend":

> There have been five wars and seventeen military coups; there emerged a diabolic dictator who is carrying out, in God's name, the first Latin American ethnocide of our time. In the meantime, 20 million Latin American children died before the age of one—more than have been born in Europe since 1970. Those missing because of repression number nearly 120,000, which is as if no one could account for all the inhabitants of Upsala. Numerous women arrested while pregnant have given birth in Argentine prisons, yet nobody knows the whereabouts and identity of their children, who were furtively adopted or sent to an orphanage by order of the military authorities. Because

they tried to change this state of things, nearly 200,000 men and women have died throughout the continent, and over 100,000 have lost their lives in three small and ill-fated countries of Central America: Nicaragua, El Salvador, and Guatemala. If this had happened in the United States, the corresponding figure would be that of 1,600,000 violent deaths in four years.

For Ledeen, I suppose, all these figures can be put aside because García Márquez is pro-Castro and neglects to mention *his* repressions—as he should.

The panel on the press and the two-day conference on "Our Country and Our Culture" were summed up by Norman Podhoretz, who expressed his surprise that previous speakers—on the arts, the universities, the press—had generally sounded so "gloomy." For himself, Podhoretz radiated confidence in the success of the neoconservative cause. "We are surrounded by lynch mobs just barely restrained," but "our work has not been in vain. We are a political community now. The resonance of what we do is greater than ever. . . . There are more of us around than there were ten years ago. . . . We are the dominant faction within the world of ideas—the most influential—the most powerful. . . . By now the liberal culture has to appease *us*. . . . People like us made Reagan's victory, which had been considered unthinkable."

Few intellectuals still uphold the power of ideas, Podhoretz explained. He quoted Professor Gertrude Himmelfarb's derisive comment: the liberal culture just supinely believes that "history is something that happens to us." He, Podhoretz, believes "in *nothing* but ideas." And because of this faith in ideas and "our ability to persuade people by fearless advocacy and concentrated argument, we were able to establish our power by doing things in a certain way."

Just "how right we were" in warning the United States of the Soviet menace was demonstrated by the Soviet invasion of Afghanistan—as if the dangers of Soviet expansionism have not been evident since the Baltic countries were swallowed up by 1940 and have not been the great preoccupation of American politics since the end of World War II. Another example: *Time's* cover story of February 14 on the KGB, which would not have been possible without the steady warnings by *Commentary* on the subject. Henry Anatole Grunwald, the editor in chief of *Time*, mildly objected to this and was heard suggesting that *Time* was not without resources of its own.

Podhoretz counseled his congregation not to be dismayed. "Events have come to our rescue, which is why we were able to prevail. . . ." Still, ". . . We have a very long way to go in the shaping of a national consensus. . . ."

As Podhoretz wound up the conference in a tone of voice that brooked no disagreement, no hint of an alternative, I thought back to that less militant time when Podhoretz, though still a "liberal" and a fervent opponent of the war in Asia (he quoted Eisenhower on how such a war could never be won), said to me about his accession to the editorship of *Commentary:* "I never knew power could be so pleasant." But mostly I wondered what had led this ambitious man to such delusion about his importance, to so much paranoia about the "liberal enemy," to so much heartlessness in a world where the evidence of wretchedness on the streets of New York north and west of the Plaza would once have been enough to jar someone who had grown up in the Brownsville section of Brooklyn.

Scott Fitzgerald said that the mark of a first-class mind is the ability to hold opposing ideas in the mind at the same time. Norman Podhoretz's "success" lies in his inability to hold not opposing but varying ideas in his mind at the same time. In summing up the conference, Podhoretz assured his audience that "partisanship is the only way to establish a cause," that neutrality in intellectual opinion is as absurd and dangerous as neutralism between America and Russia. He more than suggested, as he has in his recent publications, that those who are not with Norman Podhoretz are acting like dupes—if not worse—of the KGB.

In a cover story in *Harper's* magazine for January, Podhoretz stated without any fear of contradiction that if George Orwell were alive today he would be a neoconservative. Emphasizing the obvious parallels in *1984* between "Oceania" and Stalin's Russia, and Orwell's attested hatred of totalitarianism, Orwell's contempt for the literary and intellectual left—Orwell's deriding of the "pansy left" was as vociferous as Midge Decter's in her *Commentary* article "The Boys on the Beach"—Podhoretz assured *Harper's* readers that Orwell would easily have given up his old concern for the English working class and, like Podhoretz and the Committee for the Free World, have concentrated his political energies entirely on the present danger from communism.

Podhoretz omitted one of Orwell's main concerns about totalitarianism: it despises neutrality and objective truth. *1984*, with its vision of Newspeak, of the destruction of the past and the incessant rewriting of history, represents

Orwell's most anguished feeling that objective truth is the prime condition of our existence. But he saw truth as an ideal, truth even as our most deeply personal claim on life, as dying out of our world.

Orwell was certainly right. At a meeting last month of Jewish establishment figures troubled about Begin, Sharon, and Lebanon, I heard two distinguished lawyers say, in defense of their own qualified protest against the practices of the Begin regime, that in the political world "the" truth is untenable, that we must be resigned to something like a lawyer's advocacy. And as the Plaza conference was breaking up, a *Commentary* writer on Jewish matters to whom I mentioned my horror of the behavior of Begin and Sharon told me that she did not even accept the Israeli commission of inquiry's condemnation of Sharon, that she could not feel indignation about the grenade thrown into the crowd supporting the commission of inquiry, which killed one person and wounded several more. Jews have always "disagreed with each other." She ended by expressing high scorn for those who still think that there is a "center" from which to discuss *anything* about Israel. From such reflections am I to find salvation for my soul.

[1983]

VIII

—•◆•—

SUMMING UP

A PARADE IN THE RAIN

————— • ◆ • —————

Well over 40,000 books were published in the United States last year. No one can blame *The New York Times Book Review, The New Republic, The New York Review of Books*, certainly not the fragmentary book supplements indifferently included by Sunday newspapers in Chicago, Washington, San Francisco, for commenting on few of these books and for listing just a handful. Editors and reviewers have their own tastes; New York sophisticates are not more likely to see, much less to discuss, a book of western history published by the University of Montana Press than *Penthouse, Hustler, Screw*, etc., are to publish a serious review of some new edition of Sigmund Freud.

Like so much in American life, the book world is big, busy, commercial, driven; not likely to be too aware of its compulsiveness, special interests, many blinders. If complaints are made adjacent to the publishing world, they are made by a few writers and still independent publishers about the increasing domination of the trade by toy companies in the margarine trust. If complaints are made about the state of American writing, they are usually aired in small academic quarterlies by "experimental" writers whose most notable trait, as Edmund Wilson said of Cyril Connolly, is "that whether it's peace or war, Cyril complains it keeps him from writing."

So much in American cultural life now depends on money from the government, the conglomerates, the foundations, that I could reel off examples of commercialization and stop in perfect satisfaction. In good populist fashion I could locate in the big money the prime reason why there are so few real bookstores left even in New York that the Columbia University bookstore is now another Barnes and Noble supermarket featuring paperbacks and best sellers. Nor can we forget the unequaled oppression suffered by upper-bourgeois and professional women with tenured husbands who have rallied to the support of Marilyn French's *The Women's Room* (2.7 million in paperback), and Judy Blume's *Wifey* (3.5 million). Judith Krantz three months before the March 9 publication of *Princess Daisy* earned nearly $5 million. I open a press release about Erich Segal's "new blockbuster," ten years after *Love Story, Man, Woman and Child*, to learn the publication plans for this story of a loving marriage on the brink of tragedy: 200,000 copies on the first printing, $200,000 initial advertising budget. The book is already a Literary Guild alternate, a Doubleday Book Club selection, a Family Circle excerpt. Foreign-language rights have been sold for "record figures" to France, Germany, Italy, Denmark, Portugal, Spain.

Which goes to show you—what? Nothing we do not already know about "the feminine readers who control the destinies of so many novels," as Harpers noted on declining *Sister Carrie* in 1900, nothing new about the lure of the big buck in publishing as in academia, the meat business, the David Merrick business. Do any of these stray items explain why you will almost never see a grown-up man in business carrying even a best-seller? Why college students are obliged to "explicate" James Joyce and Ezra Pound without knowing where a sentence should end—or begin? Why American publishers are so ruthless about remaindering their books? Why the paperback industry, pulping books the second they cease to be "blockbusters," resembles nothing so much as the meat factory in Upton Sinclair's *The Jungle*?

The million-dollar advances and earnings, the money-mindedness that leaves its grease stain on every discussion of a "popular" book (and of a markedly unpopular one)—these, along with the widespread contempt for politics, the breakdown of intellectual authority that gives every sexual and ethnic faction the brief authority of anger, are not just symptoms of some profound cultural malaise—they are the malaise. The malaise is the new book supermarkets that will give no earnest young reader a chance to discover anything unexpected; the magazines and book supplements that accept "cultural comment" only when written in a snappy prose whose function is to startle the reader rather than to inform him; the English departments featuring the triumph of "deconstructionism" over some helpless poem—and this to captive audiences of graduate students whose only chance to get an assistantship at Upper Wyoming State and to mark 300 themes a week is to imitate this fictitious superiority of "creative" critics over the poems they discuss.

Our literary culture is in the same disarray as our politics and its replacement by mob-mindedness. Factionalism rules the roost; the most desperate ignorance and cruelty have to be heard out with respect; ideologies are as rampant as cancer cures. New wars of religion are upon us, and intolerance rules. This country is going through the profound inner crisis that Marx and Henry Adams foretold: the technology of the future is already here and has outrun our existing social and economic relations. "The history of an epoch," said Einstein, "is the history of its instruments." Frightened of our instruments, yet increasingly dependent on them, we live intellectually from crisis to crisis, hand to mouth. We have no believable goals for our society or for ourselves. If books are more and more produced simply as commodities, just like the movies, it is because books even for the minuscule number of Americans that regularly buy them tend to be diet books, self-help books, information manuals, almanacs, thrillers.

Of course film has largely usurped the inevitability of narrative that used to belong to the novel. But as that peculiarly incisive novelist, V. S. Naipaul, says in a wonderful essay on Conrad,

> More and more today, writers' myths are about the writers themselves: the work has become less obtrusive. The great societies that produced the great novels of the past have cracked. . . . The novel as a form no longer carries conviction. Experimentation, not aimed at the real difficulties, has corrupted response. The novelist, like the painter, no longer recognizes his interpretive function; he seeks to go beyond it; and his audience diminishes. And so the world we inhabit, which is always new, goes by unexamined, made ordinary by the camera, unmeditated on; and there is no one to awaken us to a sense of true wonder.

To be sure, there are many good and even valuable books that sell—even by scholars who seek to define our crises and awkwardly chart the inhuman future. Scholarly university presses can at least overlook some, not all, of the terrors of the marketplace and have written a bright chapter in our book history. More good and bad books are published than ever; there are more real and quack publishers; as there are more readers, more "successful" personalities to celebrate in our popular magazines, more facts on file.

When I think of the influence on American life of our two greatest literary periods—the 1850s and the 1920s—of Emerson, Thoreau, Twain, Dreiser, Mencken, Hemingway, Fitzgerald, Faulkner, Edmund Wilson—my complaint is not just that the good books have so little lasting reverberation, but that our many splendid talents don't have the scope in which to exercise influence. They seem to be part of the drift instead of exercising some mastery.

What is ominous about our literary state is that so much is accepted as ad hoc, temporary, spasmodic—and so has to be "sensational" in order to show some effect. American writing—featuring so many "generation crises," leaping off the front pages with personality stars who are such for a month, fiction written from any sexual or ethnic complaint—resembles a parade in the rain. Nothing lasts. I am not so foolhardy as to pretend that I know what lasts— that I can analyze to the depths what has no depth. Scott Fitzgerald, as his friend Edmund Wilson laughed, couldn't spell. Fitzgerald has lasted. He predicted it, for "the stamp that goes into my books so that people can read it blind like Braille." Whatever the stamp is that made *Gatsby* last for all its plotfulness, *An American Tragedy* for all its barbaric epithets, *The Sound and the Fury* for all its obsessive family matter, Frost for all his sententiousness, Stevens for all his contemplative coldness, I am quite sure that most of our leading novelists and poets just now do not have it.

One reason may be the inability to imagine the full impact of the technological storm on our mental life. Tom Wolfe is a very clever journalist, as audience-minded as a strip teaser, and has written his most serious book, about the astronauts, in *The Right Stuff.* I am properly impressed with all his research, his sense of what is new and urgent about the condition of being an astronaut; I recognize the effort of his highly pepped-up prose to convey the danger, the thrill, above all the science, of being an astronaut. Wolfe knows what is going on in the remotest air fields and space stations; his style captures the razzmatazz, the "spritz," as stand-up comics used to call it, the frenetic flow and delirium of a special way of flying, talking, living.

But from the title down, all *The Right Stuff* says about the inner world of astronauts is that they have to show the "right stuff"—to be the super elite that so few can join. Wolfe is satisfied to show how the men—and their wives—respond to this unusual pressure, show some extra manliness. Even when we grant that this world is entirely new to everyone, especially to the astronauts, the psychology of the book is military. We suspect that human beings in solitude and danger are more complex than this, and above all less chatty. Wolfe is an understandably conceited fellow with this big story and we respond to his assurance. But the only motivations he can explore are those that the astronauts officially know.

The rocket world, like everything excessive and super-mechanic laid on us just now, may be too serious a subject for journalists to dress up as literature. Wolfe can hardly be blamed if he thinks "literature" is old-fashioned. Only a journalist has the drive, the obstinacy, the encouragement from his publisher to do a book like *The Right Stuff.* The most ambitious imaginative work to deal with technology in our lives, Thomas Pynchon's *Gravity's Rainbow,* significantly became just another item in the academic department of "absurdity." Pynchon, unlike most literary fellows, at least majored in science, which may be why, like the cultural historian Jacques Barzun, he looks on science as "the great entertainment." Pynchon may just be a promising candidate for immortality because he is able to infuriate American big shots incapable of thinking an inch beyond their personal importance. The writer's advisory committee to the Pulitzer Prizes, which recommended *Gravity's Rainbow* for the fiction prize in 1974, was overruled rudely by a *Wall Street Journal* editor higher up on the Pulitzer totem pole; no fiction prize was awarded that year. He explained with some irritation, that he couldn't even read the damned thing.

We are reminded of the glorious days when *Moby-Dick* was proclaimed a book "for bedlam," *Huckleberry Finn* "fit only for the slums," *The Waste Land* "a hoax." After all, John S. Sumner and the Society for the Suppression of Vice managed to make even Dreiser's *The Genius* interesting by suppressing it. Nothing is now suppressible or censorable. Our literary thinking is so much geared to the hourly crisis that vulgarities like Joseph Heller's *Good as Gold* are indulged because *Catch-22* became a byword for our anxious belief that nothing works. All is irrational. The fatalism of the man in the street, that perennial victim, has at last been matched by the cynicism of what are called "top intellectuals." So much alienation from American life is understandable—after all, what is a system for if it is not to satisfy us without limit? But when our precious alienation becomes abrasive at the expense of every bourgeois but ourselves, it becomes just another piece of American claptrap.

Since the future is plainly here, and we cannot understand all it is doing to us—even that may not be the point that some far-off generation will know about us—it may just be the mysticism of knowledge that so much nescience confronts us with. "It is because so much happens," Joe Christmas's grandmother lamented in *Light in August.* "Too much happens." We are no longer sure just where all this is happening. So a whole dimension of present literature is occupied by nostalgia.

Although there is a marked decline in history courses, in the sense of the past, history has become the sense of crisis, of a civilization in decline, of what one might well call the evaporation of history. Too many zigzag lines on our historical graphs lead on the one hand to instant history, on the other to the idealization of the frontier, the John Wayne syndrome so weepily exploited by Joan Didion in nicely simple books like *Slouching Towards Bethlehem.* Nothing historical exists now for its own sake. Our sense of history is entirely contemporary, as witness Barbara Tuchman's *A Distant Mirror,* which is not about the distant Middle Ages but about the chain of wars that, along with technology as a form of aggression rushing out of two terrible wars, has so clearly subdued our minds.

The writer's problem is that we are locked into "today"—conceptually, superconsciously. We cannot see beyond the whirlwind of change in which we spin round and round like the lovers in Dante's hell whose greatest pain was to remember past happiness, and so could not blame their temptation. We are waiting on history to carry us to some next stage of consciousness as once people waited on God to accomplish just that. But books are not written by history. You have to be strong in the legs to write, said Henry Thoreau. That was spiritual self-confidence.

Yet there is no country in the world with the buoyancy, the inborn sense of freedom, the explosive amount of universal material that we present to the world as the great modern experiment—and feel in ourselves. It is our very disorder and factionalism, the fact that so many Americans have nothing in common but their living on this continent, even the violence and insecurity endemic in our shifting American lives, that in the past produced writers who were famous—for having nothing in common with each other. American disorder is our strength as well as our dismay. But what we never felt before, never, never! was the sense that nothing is so real to us as ourselves, that there is so little to respect, that we have so few dreams.

[1980]

TO BE A CRITIC

———— ·◆· ————

Forty and more years ago, when I began practicing this peculiar trade of criticism, I had the good fortune to fall in love with a then unfashionable subject, American literature. I say "fall in love with," not "specialize in," for it never occurred to me to devote myself exclusively to this literature. There was not enough of it, yet what there was would still have been too much for me even if I had had the patience to give up everything else for it.

I certainly did not want to do that. I was under no illusion that American literature was more significant than English or French or Russian literature, or that it could be understood in itself apart from English its mother tongue, English its mother literature, its connections with German literature at the beginning of the nineteenth century and with French and Russian literature at the end of it. To devote oneself exclusively to American literature would have seemed to me a confession of mediocrity. And in any event literature, or at least some of the literature of Western man, was practically all the culture I had. It composed for me, in T. S. Eliot's phrase, a simultaneous order. It included such writers as America never had: all the great dramatists; great novelists of manners who were also among the most profound critics of human nature, like Tolstoy; great poets of the sensuous life—Villon, Shakespeare himself, Goethe, Baudelaire; great philosophic and critical spirits who were knife blades opening up the imagination—Montaigne, Rousseau, Voltaire, Diderot, Nietzsche.

So it was not in fond illusion that American writing was food enough for the mind that I settled down to practice some criticism of it. I fell in love with it because in a sense this literature was mine—I felt part of it and at home with it. I reacted with intellectual affection to the tone of certain American writers—I was charmed and stimulated and satisfied by certain American books because I felt that I really understood them. I felt, as the French have learned to say about certain moral problems, *authentic* in my critical reactions to certain American writers. I seemed to know what they were talking about; I thought I recognized what they were aiming at; I liked the voices in which they spoke. I was at home with certain texts; I responded with intellectual kinship and pleasure. I knew the modulations of their language; I could see their landscapes. And very important indeed, I shared much of their belief in the ideal freedom and power of the self, in the political and social visions of radical democracy. I felt I had started from the same human base and was accompanying some writers to the same imaginative goal.

Behind all these friendly and interested reactions was the fact that my judgment was real to me, too real to distrust. I felt free to like what I liked, not to like what I didn't, and to support my critical reactions by formulating aesthetic reasons. It was easier forty and more years ago to feel this pleasant confidence in one's critical judgment, for American literature was still in the making, and the best writers and critics rather condescended to it. If you settled down to it with any passion, you realized that you were eccentric and were making claims for writers that no distinguished mind would look at for a moment. In those days the total approval now extended to Henry James (even as a political mind) was by no means shared by everyone. Criticism was still a matter of individual knowledge and taste, not a way of introducing students to literature; people still thought they could learn more about life from a good story than from the most brilliant exegesis of the story. So I was left, in delicious isolation, to read books that no one else had looked at in years, to have reactions that were wild but which I didn't know enough to tame—to be, without shame, what in those days was considered the absolute second choice and consolation prize: a critic.

"Criticism" is just a word, but critics are very real if their opinions are real to themselves. A critic lives in a buzz of culture and in a vast exchange of opinions like everyone else. Being a critic, dedicated to opinion, he often sets too much store by other people's opinions. If you tell him that *King Lear* is an unbelievable play, full of rant and uncontrolled opinions, he will not ignore you, as a poet would, but will in his own mind figure out what it is in *King Lear* that would allow a presumably good head to think such a thing. A critic deals in considerations about art, not in life as drama, not in the psychic situation that an imaginative writer sees everywhere he goes. A critic is more naturally considerate of opinions than a novelist; his world is made up of opinions. For him literature is not himself seeking to put the widest amount of experience into dramatic consciousness; it is literature, many literatures, many writers, books, forms, styles, traditions—all of which add to the burden on him of other people's opinions; he takes off from them. No critic is ever one by himself; criticism takes place in society, it is a dialogue with the past and one's contemporaries. The circle of examples and tradition and opinions draws tighter and tighter around the critic trying to add something useful and honest to the many libraries that have put him into being.

Nevertheless, a critic is someone whose reactions to a work of art are so real as to be binding on himself and meaningful to others; he will use, not imitate, the learning and insight of other people. The critic is someone whose reactions are so authentic to himself as to become, above all else, *interesting* for others because illuminative of their own unconscious experience in the presence of art. By reactions I mean the ability to take pleasure in what is good, to recognize in the concrete instance the classical truth of those aesthetic laws that are so few and incontrovertible, yet meaningful only in the practice of art and in profound critical response to art.

What is "personal" is what is most deeply experienced by the whole person of the critic. Taste cannot be, and should not be, made so "objective" that opinions become simply right or wrong. The value of a particular work in criticism never depends on the critic's *position* alone. In our day critical fashion tyrannizes over many innocent minds. But it does not follow that a book attacking Henry James derives any necessary merit from opposition to the vast herd of sophisticates who hold that James is the last word in the English novel, which in their experience he may well be. A good critic can uphold any reasonable opinion, if only he will *hold* it and engage himself with the work of art that inspired him to it. Jean-Paul Sartre may not convince us in his essays on Dos

Passos and Faulkner that Dos Passos is so bold in technique as to be the greatest twentieth-century novelist, that Faulkner is so traditionalist in his thinking as to kill the future for his characters. But Sartre engages *U.S.A.* and *The Sound and the Fury* with an understanding and conviction that make his own critical thinking in these essays an experience to us—Dos Passos and Faulkner have already been great experiences to Sartre.

What counts is that the critic should be really involved with a work; that we should follow the track of his curiosity into it just as long and as passionately as may be necessary. This follows from what I call being-at-home-with-a-text, from feeling in one's bones that one knows what the work is about, that one knows the tone of voice in which the writer speaks, that one is present, oneself all present, at every stage. Criticism exists, after all, because the critic has an intense and meaningful experience of a work. And if he doesn't, why pretend that he does? Why bother, if what one is doing is not intensely real to oneself?

This is the first condition, not of "criticism" but of being a critic. When I read Shakespeare, I am dazzled by the speed and force of his mind. But I also know when I read him that there is something fundamental about Shakespeare that I do not truly understand. I do not mean that Shakespeare's characters use expressions that have to be explained. Historical matter can be learned. But even if I were immensely learned, I would not feel that I understand Shakespeare for myself—which is all the fun and all the use of being a critic. Many people have written importantly *around* Shakespeare without convincing me that they understand him for themselves. Most readers are in fact uneasy with Shakespeare, which is why the silly snobbish question of who wrote his plays rages in every generation. Shakespeare is the unknown whom even the greatest critics, like Johnson and Goethe, have redrawn in the character most suitable to themselves. Perhaps only John Keats, because he was a virtuoso of language like Shakespeare, saw him "whole." In the famous letter of October 27, 1818, he wrote in clairvoyant excitement that "the poetical Character ... is not itself—it has no self—it is everything and nothing. ... It has as much delight in conceiving an Iago as an Imogen. ... A Poet is the most unpoetical of anything in existence; because he has no Identity—he is continually infor[ming] and filling some other Body. ..."

These orphic revelations make a dependable guide to the subtle and mischievous imagination that bars our full understanding. Keats, at least, mastered Shakespeare's protean mind; because in his own way he duplicates Shakespeare's sense of language, he is confident that his own reaction of wild delight is also a path to new knowledge. Keats does not preach Shakespeare the romantic, Shakespeare the monarchist, Shakespeare the cynic, as so many other critics have done. It is not Shakespeare's *opinions* that impress Keats; it is his pure poetic intelligence that in turn becomes each character it can create and takes its force from each dramatic event. Shakespeare discovered Keats to himself. The Shakespeare text, which is a chore to students and an intellectual maze to scholars, was to Keats a release, of the kind that Herman Melville was later to find in Nathaniel Hawthorne: "For genius, all over the world, stands hand in hand with genius, and one shock of recognition runs the whole circle round."

Keats *knew* Shakespeare as only one great poet knows another, can imitate him without really knowing the other's language. To know, not just to know about, is the highest aim of criticism, and depends on sensibility intellectually cultivated, on the most urgent instinct for aesthetic achievements and distinctions. Of course, one great writer talking about another can be subjective and may well seem tendentious to a later generation. But the condition of being-at-home-with-a-text that I am setting forth here as crucial to criticism, the reality compelling response, is important because it risks being fallible. To be a critic, nothing else is so important as the ability to stand one's ground alone. This gets more important as criticism gets more standardized and institutionalized, as the critic gets more absorbed in literary theory rather than in the imaginations who are his raison d'être. The more abstractions we deal with, the more we look for proof; since this is not possible in literature, we look for confirmation from other persons. This now usually means the captive audience of half-literate students.

Criticism is a branch of literature, not of science. Like any form of literary expression, criticism can satisfy nothing but our sense of imaginative truth: its judgments operate only within our inner sense, and depend on our taste and culture. Critical statements are not binding on everyone, as are proofs of scientific truth. Keats on Shakespeare, Melville on Hawthorne, are operating within a realm that most people have never heard of, and which does not touch on their lives in the slightest. Literature operates significantly only on exceptional individuals fortunate enough to afford the luxury of pleasing their imaginations. "I went far enough to please my imagination," said Thoreau. Criticism operates on even a smaller number. If Keats's reaction to Shakespeare seems more "personal" than a scientist's findings can ever be, that is because literature exists only in the realm of minds, and takes its sanction from laws of art that are understood only in relation to the human mind.

Keats is one of the few writers on Shakespeare who help me to read *him* and not just to read about him. Shakespeare is entirely real to Keats, and so Keats makes Shakespeare less unreal to me. That is what I look for in a critic—his use to me; I can use critics whose general point of view is outrageous to me, but who in specific matters have this capacity for making a writer real and a text real. A useful critic is someone who has already begun to use a text in a significant personal way, who is not in doubt about his fundamental reaction, who is not arbitrary but is convinced, in his reading of Shakespeare (or Dos Passos), that he knows what there is to know. Of course, this is not enough for the ages; only the greatest critics survive, for as Johnson said, they raise opinion to knowledge. These are the lawgivers of art, and there are very few of them—far fewer, it turns out, than there are original minds in science. But opinion in criticism, if held at a level deep enough to become interesting, can vivify our sense of what writing is all about and may even excite us to write in new ways. If I ever make an anthology of criticism, it will be called *The Useful Critic*, and will feature only writings that have helped me.

It would come from all sources, and would be an odd mixture indeed. The conversation of Johnson, Goethe, Auden. An early criticism of Vladimir Nabokov by Isaac Babel. The art criticism of Baudelaire, the music criticism of Nietzsche. A few lines from Whitman, interviewed by Horace Traubel, on Emerson's essential genius as a "critic or diagnoser." Marx on Balzac, showing how important it is for "revolutionaries" to respect genius on any side. Emerson on "The Poet," because this rhapsody is the most eloquent and uncompromising revelation of the artist as hero who stands behind his prophetic writings. William James delighting in Emerson, William James curtly correcting Henry Adams's attempts to apply "science" to history. Melville's magnificent praise of his as yet unmet friend in "Hawthorne and His Mosses," because it shows in every free and flowing line of praise how Hawthorne's insistence on becoming a storyteller in Calvinist New England could help another genius to recognize himself. Henry James's preface to *The*

Portrait of a Lady, not because it reveals the "laws" of any art but James's own, but because James's art is founded on the celebration of civilized beauty with which this preface begins.

Among twentieth-century critics in English, my anthology would include (poets make my favorite critics; they have the most intense personal consciousness of art) Eliot on Pascal, D. H. Lawrence on Hardy, Randall Jarrell on Frost, Conrad Aiken on Faulkner, Wallace Stevens for his general reflections on intellectual nobility, Robert Penn Warren on Conrad. It would include V. S. Pritchett, because he is a genius at truly *literary* journalism, and for any of dozens of appreciations of the English and European novel, but especially for his essays on the comic novel; Edmund Wilson, for many illuminations of different literatures, but especially for the observations on American style in *Patriotic Gore.*

This list could go on, just as personally, to include A. C. Bradley, whom in my unfashionable way I still deeply admire on Shakespeare; Erich Auerbach, the great German refugee scholar, whose *Mimesis*, on the representation of reality in Western literature, is the most useful contemporary work in criticism that I own. I can never turn to Auerbach on Homer or Montaigne or even Shakespeare without being enlightened in the deepest and most active way. My anthology would include Lessing on the contrast of actor and audience; Whitehead on Shelley; Erich Heller, for his moving intellectual sympathies with Nietzsche, Rilke, Thomas Mann; Joseph Frank for his work on Dostoevsky.

My list would *not* include academics whose sense of their own authority has never instructed or even provoked me. What I ask of a critic is that he usefully show the impact on his own consciousness of another's artistic power. If the critic cannot reveal to others the power of art in his own life, he cannot say anything useful or even humane in its interest. He will scrawl, however learnedly, arbitrary comments on the text.

Literary thought starts in the most intimate, the closest possible touch with subject matter, not critical method. To be absorbed, to be involved at every point with the implications of a subject, is to see the text in context, and this alone turns the mind back ever more freshly to the rest. Literary thought means to me reaction to a unique act. The *force* of the act breaks up something already existent and "makes new." A book is not just the precious lifeblood of a master spirit; it has consequences in many minds as well as origins in many minds. It *connects* in all sorts of unspoken ways; then it becomes the act of a particular culture; and as an image of a particular time turns the past into the present. From text to text the aroused reader, the true critic, lives in *all* these time-worlds, space-worlds, dream-worlds.

2

To be a critic, to exercise thought on the literature of a developing culture, means that one wants to influence and not just to show that the flowers entombed in a certain well-wrought urn had never been moved into the light. The critic should be an agent of change, moving from concrete—even physical—reactions into unexpected realizations of all that may be embedded in a writer's unique force. No critic, alive to his subject matter rather than to a critical formula, comes to close grips with a text without changing a reader's mind. The experience of literature can be, it used to be, a particularly concentrated and driving force for transforming a person's life. There can be a reorientation to the physical, mental, and political universe in the writer's mind. One shares a new universe, if ever so briefly. Even when our minds drift on to other mental universes, we ourselves have been altered in unsuspected ways.

But of course this may be absurd just now. We live in a period when literature provides information, has no influence moral or political compared with the visual power of television, films, advertising, the screaming headline. So it is also an age—if only in the universities—of endless theorizing about what literature cryptically is. The emphasis is on the "reader" (meaning the critic, not the common reader). The critic becomes the central figure in every "creative" transaction. Language as such contains the intrinsic authority once ascribed to individual talent; "text replaces voice." But not without the fond belief, typical of critical intelligence rather than of creative power, that what a "strong" poet is really thinking about when he writes a poem is supplanting his predecessors.

3

The connection between illiteracy (or even anti-literature) in the mass and critical theory in the universities, between the atrocity of best-sellerdom and what Coleridge called the multiplication of secondary distinctions is ignored.

These are political phenomena, but criticism today battens on the increasing evidence of political chaos. Consider the futility of any teacher in the 1980s invoking what Eliot in a famous passage called "the historical sense":

> [This] we may call nearly indispensable to anyone who would continue to be a poet beyond his twenty-fifth year; and the historical sense involves a perception, not only of the pastness of the past, but of its presence; the historical sense compels a man to write not merely with his own generation in his bones, but with a feeling that the whole of the literature of Europe from Homer and within the whole of the literature of his own country has a simultaneous existence and composes a simultaneous order.

I grew up with the historical sense; it was a sign that history had a discernible pattern and might even have a manifest end. Whether the writer was a Christian like Eliot, a transcendental novelist like Proust, a mythologist like Joyce, or a radical critic in the Hazlitt tradition like Orwell, the historical sense seemed as natural as a sense of time. The last great writer among us to believe this was Jean-Paul Sartre, for whom philosophy came down to a contest between being and nothingness, between man as the creator and embodiment of value and a universe that does not exist without man. Sartre the philosopher, critic, novelist, dramatist, polemicist, veered over the postwar years toward a more and more revolutionary contempt for existing institutions; he expressed more than anyone else—in a generation of radical writers often demoralized by Communism, the God That Failed—the will to remain faithful to the perennial dream of revolution in France. There the radical intellectuals write the best books, but the bourgeoisie and the bureaucracy never relinquish the actual power. Revolution traditionally remains the intellectuals' imaginary paradise.

The more the actual oppressiveness of Communism finally came through to this class (Solzhenitsyn's *The Gulag Archipelago* turned around many left intellectuals), the more Sartre, despite his anguish over the suppression of the Hungarian Revolution, *tried* to remain faithful to his fundamental idea. All value is embodied in revolutionary change, transferring vital being to new elements in society. The author of such works essential to our time as *L'Etre et le néant, La Nausée, Huis Clos, Les Séquestrés d'Altona*, had already shown himself an innovative critic in his *Baudelaire* and in three volumes of essays with the perfect Sartrean title of *Situations*. His uniquely objective memoir of childhood, *Les Mots*, his research into Flaubert, *L'Idiot de la famille*, showed again that the most trenchant studies of the nature of literature, of the reason for its power, are made by philosophers.

Sartre's blend of existentialist psychoanalysis, his unrelenting scorn for French bourgeois life (that cradle of their best authors) could not conceal his own increasingly exasperated culture revolution. He did his best to get arrested, rejected his Nobel Prize. But the French do not arrest their most famous authors even when they make a point of hawking some inflammatory leftist paper. De Gaulle, then president, noted that the French had arrested François Villon and it hadn't helped.

But after Sartre, socialism as the secular religion of the intellectuals lost its punch. The continuing practice in every café and classroom of *le discours* (whether or not the subject requires so much impersonation of intelligence) has often survived belief, conviction. Sainte-Beuve said that in France one remains Catholic after one has ceased to be Christian. With the dissipation of classic leftism there became prominent in the newly technological and modernized France a more ironic and neutral intellectual—the essayist Roland Barthes, the philosopher Jacques Derrida, the psychoanalyst Jacques Lacan. They stimulated that ever-present audience in France for an intellectual formula that upsets convention, for the necessarily literary [idea] that has shock value promising a new way of seeing things.

France in this period significantly became a center of advanced technique, of discoveries in molecular biology and linguistics, which had been a tradition since Ferdinand de Saussure. The New Wave in fiction produced nothing lasting, but it had a significantly close association with film. The prominent new literary theorists, whether structuralists like Lévi-Strauss or poststructuralists like Derrida, were experts in literary form, writers bound to the scientific idea that language has an innate structure and authority all its own that has more effect on the individual writer than the writer has on it. The universal structures of language, the fact that comparative study always shows more resemblances between languages than contrasts, was as a scientific observation held to be superior to the romantic cult of individual genius and the supposedly discredited phenomena of inspiration.

The appeal of [this] literary theory was that it was a wholly new, more "scientific" form that also became literature. It upheld the impersonal authority of what the French like to call *litérarité*, the "literariness" in discourse itself. The poet's touch was not always necessary to turn words into literature, but the critic was necessary to explain that language itself was more interesting than the poet who used it.

With the New Criticism, the critic in the university had become an authority rather than a mere interpreter. Contemporary literature had somehow come to take all preceding literature under its wing, but it was always the next line in a contemporary poem that had to be explained by some Great Big Explicator to students who had no Latin, no French, no German, had never read the Bible, knew Oedipus as a character in Freud. Mencken said that nobody ever went broke underestimating the American audience. Modernism became the favorite dish in the English department just when the best minds tended to go elsewhere and what was required of an English major was not that he know how little the great English novels resemble Henry James's but that he make obedient sounds of comprehension and addiction about works so packed with learning as *The Waste Land* and Pound's *Cantos*.

Nevertheless, the New Criticism soon took a backseat to advanced literary theory. This was easy, because the habit of reading, reading for yourself, reading indifferent to fashion and ideology, reading because it is at least one way of puzzling out your life and the world's, was becoming more and more difficult to practice. There emanates from the many new authorities over our lives a real censorship; there is also—"also"?—a staggering indifference to reading insofar as reading itself still represents some personal determination to change habits of seeing and thinking. No bibliomaniac today can honestly affirm that reading maketh the whole man—that literature represents *any* force of change equal to technology, political violence, insurrection, war, or to films, television, the endless reversals of images, to proclamation and visual threat. Change is so incessant that the individual secretly torn apart by its flux is no longer under the old Sartrean illusion of the self moving beyond itself while retaining its metaphysical unity—but instead is losing identity. That identity once seemed the very grounds of life. We see now that it rested on the twin pillars of religion and capitalism, which have survived as institutions, not objects of respect. Change is beyond our present categories, even when they are about nothing else.

4

I grew up as what my old teacher and friend Mark Van Doren called a "private reader." Nothing in the world was so delightful, my own pleasure principle, as taking more and more books every day out of the public library—an institution then open every other day. I spent the better part of every day reading; I lived to read. There were never enough books for this—never words enough to describe the transformations taking place in me as I read. The private experience of books, as Saul Bellow once put it in a beautiful essay, was some unknown person's "sealed treasure." There was that in me, reading myself into the writing of my first book year after year at the golden tables in room 315 above Forty-second Street, that was an experience of human advancement and liberation too subtle to be shared. Only writing about it, an act of criticism, confronting a text, could express some of the pent-up thinking involved in absorbing, moving with all those black marks on paper.

And what did one read for? Why so *much*? Because it was understood, as Isaac Babel put it in the title of a story, that "you must know everything." If reading was not indiscriminate and omnivorous, endlessly exploratory, seeking knowledge at every turn and from the most neglected of books as well as the most famous, what was it?

It was their orthodoxy—by which I understood their limitation largely to poetry and only to a certain kind of lyric poetry—that made me shy away from the New Criticism. I felt that everyone had a right to read in his/her own way and to admire just what had given one the greatest pleasure. It was absurd to think that what Henry James called "form" was more essential than what James's own adored Balzac knew as the human comedy. It was absurd of James, who knew nothing about it, to call the great Russian novelists "loose and baggy monsters." It was absurd of F. R. Leavis to leave Dickens out of the "great tradition" of the English novel—absurd of R. P. Blackmur, the most brilliant and elusive of the New Critics, to put down Frost as easily as he put down Cummings—absurd, when Eliot became in effect literary dictator, to read Donne and Marvell as if Keats and Whitman had never existed.

What I most objected to in the New Criticism was that the act of criticism became a star performance, annihilating earlier performers—not so much advancing knowledge as impressing students. Students took the severity of their master's voice as another excuse for not reading beyond the assignment. And what was assigned was not just Brooks and Warren, but a certain mildewed way of looking at the world that I found ludicrously uninformed, as when Cleanth Brooks informed an audience that Emerson was responsible for Hitler. When I began to teach regularly in the fifties, I was staggered by the medievalism of my students: they knew just a few chosen texts, and all the rest was commentary by brilliant critics whose *names* you had only to mention for everyone to recognize that you had consulted Authority.

The real success of the New Criticism was not in the realm of ideas or taste, but in teaching our blissfully uneducated students and children "how to read." I had not realized that a movement against illiteracy could be considered a movement in criticism. Then taste shifted from the untimely classicism of the New Criticism. The counterculture adored the Freudian critique of repression, pan-sexual poets like Whitman. The well-wrought urn was bombed by cultural terrorists (one even became president of the Modern Language Association) who could have shouted with Goering, "When I hear the word *culture* I reach for my revolver." The private reader in old-fashioned solitude confronting a text had to yield to the public clamor, to the thundering simultaneity of film, television, advertising, political atrocity. Nihilism, posing as revolution, exulted in the post-humanist observation of Jean-Luc Godard—"We are interested only in process. Form and content are process." On the murder of the Israeli athletes at the Munich Olympics, Godard pronounced: "The Palestinians were right with their basics, but not their external conditions. They didn't realize the world was just watching a looking-machine—the television—and the killings didn't have the effect they wanted." A will-o'-the-wisp was strenuously pursued at our best universities by the exasperated children of the bourgeoisie. Not the text counted but, in good anarchist style, The Act.

The Act was many things now in the revolutionary consciousness of the alienated young. It was Action painting, where as one especially observant critic noticed, the idea was "to fuck up the painting." It was populism of the most frenzied antinomian sort: all cultures are equal, especially if some of them have no culture. It was what a marginal group proudly asserted as Camp, and what Susan Sontag in *Against Interpretation* held up as the necessary erotics of art. A certain diffuse and even vicarious eroticism indulged in the fable of the everlasting Id—to which Ego, that Victorian patriarchal self so marked among chauvinistic males, had to yield. Outmoded Freud had hoped for the reverse.

Meanwhile, any real advance intellectually was taking place not in imaginative literature, but in structuralism and in its growing perception of the real unity of cultures based on universal identity. There was developing in France and there would soon emerge in the United States more evidence that what really fascinated literary theory was the innate creativity of language itself.

The romantic Transcendentalist Emerson had guessed that language is "fossil poetry," that words alone, contracting their expressive history, exert the appeal that gets the poet to listen and obey. Emerson was an orphic mind and soul, and foretells the curious religiosity behind our present view of language. Hegel thought that the World-Spirit moved to some inherent destiny through gifted individuals. Just now literary theorists (a different breed from students of linguistics) celebrate language as itself more the real author of some text than the individual author.

My prime requirement for a critic has always been sureness of touch, the firmest possible contact with the subject in hand (which can be not just a particular text but one moving *through* the text into a whole series of contextual relationships). This requires the necessary separation between the private reader and his book. The current breakdown of traditional political relationships, as well as the way in which films and television (Godard's "looking-machine") absorb us into the process itself, show that a clearly defined subject matter becomes more and more remote and even unnecessary to literary theory.

Harold Bloom is a prodigy of learning, memory, exegesis. We owe him a great deal for bringing the English romantics—especially Blake and Shelley—back into critical favor after the Eliot dictatorship fell. Bloom's early books are wonderfully stimulating—not least because his sense of Jewish tradition has benefited from Gershom Scholem's re-creation of Jewish mystical tradition. There is a frustration of religion in Bloom that excitedly finds expression in English romanticism; as Whitehead said, romanticism is spilled religion. But under the spell of Freud's "family romance," Bloom has cultivated ideas of the necessary rivalry between poets, of the necessary "misreading" of long-established texts, that totally mistake the critic's power and responsibility. Bloom, essentially orphic in his pronouncements, is attempting to make of the universal spirit-in-time-and-space-as-the-genius-of-poetry (this was German orphic romanticism) something that will enable *him* to slip into it as a kind of poet.

I have observed Bloom lecture; I have been in the audience of eager but baffled note-takers as he examines a poem like Wallace Stevens's "Sea Surface Full of Clouds" and piles so many allusions to other writers onto it that the audience is not so much enlightened as intimidated. It may be essential to Harold Bloom that his audience not know quite what he is talking about. In his contribution to *Deconstruction and Criticism*, "The Breaking of Form," he comes out with this:

> Angus Fletcher, in his studies of Spenser, Milton, Coleridge, and Crane, has been developing a liminal poetics or new rhetoric of thresholds, and I follow Fletcher both in my notion of the topoi or "crossings" as images of voice, and in my account of the final revisionary apophrades or reversed belatedness, which is akin to the classical trope of *metalepsis* or transumption and to the Freudian "negating" (*Verneinung*) with its dialectical interplay of the defenses, projection and introjection. I will re-expound and freshly develop these Fletcherian ideas in the reading of Ashbery that follows.

This staggering pronouncement reminds me of Ross Chambers in *Critical Inquiry* (Winter issue, 1979):

> The structuralist revolution, or more precisely the trend towards linguistic analysis of texts manifesting the so-called poetic function of language, has immeasurably increased our understanding of the types of relationships, paradigmatic and syntagmatic, which constitute the *"literarité"* of texts. But it has necessarily left out of account those relationships which, because they are hierarchical, do not so easily admit of contrastive analysis in terms of binary equivalences; these are the "interpreting relationships" which exist between a specific segment of discourse within a text and the text as a whole.
>
> If such is the duplicity of commentary, then interpretation only compounds the problem by further contextualizing the intratextual contextualization! Literature, in some ways, is like a gift which comes with its price tag attached in the form of commentary—and to which, through interpretation, we endlessly strive to restore the value it has, for that very reason, lost.

Everyone who "teaches" literature now knows that there are fewer and fewer private readers among students, still fewer each year who would understand the old-culture dream of wanting to "know everything." There seem to be practically none who will say to the critical "performance" of Harold Bloom that it is now all personal myth-making, barbarously and self-hallucinatingly arcane and, to impress innocent students, a form of aggrandizement.

On the other hand, is there another way just now, in and out of the universities, to make students respect "literature"? Of keeping the subject serious under the onslaught of all in this disruptive period that keeps a private reader from his old dream that by thinking in new ways he will yet help others to rethink the world? That rethinking, new ways of seeing past our outworn connection with the world, must be the silent force behind our reading?

For many people just now, the private reader asserting his own thinking as a sufficient act may not seem enough. There are just too many forces against him. There always are. Those forces were never stronger than when Nadezhda Mandelstam memorized her husband's work in order to keep it alive. When Solzhenitsyn was arrested for writing a private letter and in the Gulag had to write whole plays and essays in his mind, apportioning the words there by the bricks he once had to lay in the prison camp. When Andrey Sinyavsky, arrested for writing his defiance of "Socialist Realism," had to explain to a Soviet judge in defense of his fellow prisoner Yuri Daniel that a character's speeches are not to be identified with the personal views of the author.

Sinyavsky is out of Russia now, like Joseph Brodsky, Vasily Aksyonov, Anatoly Gladilin, Viktor Nekrasov. Aksyonov in New York: "Sometimes I think it is not a tragedy, that it is our duty as writers now in the West to try to restore the links between Russian culture and Western culture, to prove we haven't become people without any spiritual life."

The forces in Latin America were never more depressing, endlessly cruel and fanatical when such writers as Garcia Márquez, Jose Donoso, Vargas Llosa, Carlos Fuentes, Márcio Souza, Julio Cortázar—émigrés all—dazzled the outside world with the centuries of solitude their Latin America represents. Exiles. I think of Naipaul, for me the greatest contemporary novelist in English, as I think of Conrad; of Nabokov; of Nelly Sachs driven to the edge of madness by the Holocaust but at the edge of sanity writing her best poems in Sweden; of Samuel Beckett deciding to write in French; of Elias Canetti sticking to German (wherever he lives). When is the true writer and the creative deed *not* wrung out of oppression and the most freezing solitude? Freud escaped to England, described himself as "an island of pain in a sea of indifference." Just now the primary task of the critic may be not only to expound the deed but to demonstrate its continuity, resisting every imaginable threat and emptiness.

But to do this requires a sense of the radical insufficiency of language itself. Language is not a god. Flaubert, describing Rodolphe tiring of Emma Bovary's passionate protestations: "Because lips libertine and venal had murmured such words to him, he believed but little in the candor of hers; he thought that exaggerated speeches hiding mediocre affections must be discounted;—as if the fullness of the soul did not sometimes overflow into the emptiest metaphors, since no one can ever give the exact measure of his needs, nor of his conceptions, nor of his sorrows; for human speech is like a cracked kettle, on which we hammer out tunes to make bears dance when we long to touch the stars to tears."

[1981]

APPENDIX

———•◆•———

I. HOME IS WHERE ONE STARTS FROM

"The Kitchen," from "The Kitchen," *A Walker in the City* (New York: Harcourt, Brace & World, 1951), pp. 64–71.

" 'Beyond!'," from "The Block and Beyond," ibid., pp. 95–99, 104–8.

"Mrs. Solovey," from "The Block and Beyond," ibid., pp. 115–31.

"Yeshua," from "Summer: The Way to Highland Park," ibid., pp. 158–63.

II. THE LITERARY LIFE

"Brownsville: 1931," from *A Walker in the City* (New York: Harcourt, Brace & World, 1951), pp. 146–52.

"The New Republic: 1934," from "1934," ibid., pp. 15–20.

"At V. F. Calverton's: 1936," from "1936," ibid., pp. 61–62, 65–76.

III. THE AGE OF REALISM

"Preface to *On Native Grounds*," from *On Native Grounds* (New York: Harcourt, Brace and Co., 1942), pp. vii–xii.

"The Opening Struggle for Realism," from ibid., pp. 3–12.

"Two Educations: Edith Wharton and Theodore Dreiser," from ibid., pp. 73–90.

"An Insurgent Scholar: Thorstein Veblen," from "Some Insurgent Scholars," ibid., pp. 131–41.

"The New Realism: Sherwood Anderson and Sinclair Lewis," from ibid., 207–11; 213–17; 218–25.

"Willa Cather's Elegy," from "Elegy and Satire: Willa Cather and Ellen Glasgow," ibid., pp. 247, 249–257.

"All the Lost Generations: F. Scott Fitzgerald, E. E. Cummings, Ernest Hemingway, and John Dos Passos," from "Into the Thirties: All the Lost Generations," ibid., pp. 312–59.

IV. THE LITERARY LIFE

"Provincetown, 1940: Bertram Wolfe, Mary McCarthy, Philip Rahv," from *Starting Out in the Thirties* (New York: Vintage, 1980), pp. 151–55.

"Mary McCarthy and Philip Rahv," from "1940," *Starting Out in the Thirties* (New York: Vintage Books, 1980), pp. 155–61.

"Delmore Schwartz," from "Words," *New York Jew* (Syracuse, N.Y.: Syracuse University Press, 1996), pp. 23–24, 24–25, 25–26.

"Saul Bellow and Lionel Trilling," from "Midtown and the Village," ibid., pp. 40–47.

V. CONTEMPORARIES

"The Fascination and Terror of Ezra Pound," from *The New York Review of Books* (March 13, 1986), 15–19, 20–24.

"William Faulkner: *The Sound and the Fury*," from *An American Procession* (New York: Alfred A. Knopf, 1984), pp. 345–56.

"Southern Isolates: Flannery O'Connor and Walker Percy," from "The Secret of the South," *Bright Book of Life* (New York: Delta Books, 1974), pp. 54–67.

"Arthur Schlesinger, Jr.: The Historian at the Center," from *Contemporaries* (Boston: Little, Brown, 1962), pp. 415–21.

"President Kennedy and Other Intellectuals," from ibid., pp. 447–65.

"Professional Observers: Cheever, Salinger, and Updike," from "Professional Observers: Cozzens to Updike," *Bright Book of Life* (Notre Dame, Ind.: University of Notre Dame Press, 1973), pp. 110–24.

"The Earthly City of the Jews: Bellow, Malamud, and Roth," from "The Earthly City of the Jews: Bellow to Singer," ibid., pp. 127–49.

"The Imagination of Fact: From Capote to Mailer," from ibid., pp. 209–20; 236–41.

"The Single Voice of Ralph Ellison" from "Absurdity as a Contemporary Style," ibid., pp. 245–55.

"Two Cassandras: Joan Didion and Joyce Carol Oates," from "Cassandras: Porter to Oates," ibid., 189–98, 198–205.

"James Wright: The Gift of Feeling," from *New York Times Book Review* (July 20, 1980), pp. 27–30.

VI. DEPARTED FRIENDS

"The Intoxicating Sense of Possibility: Thomas Jefferson at Monticello," from "New Worlds," *A Writer's America* (New York: Alfred A. Knopf, 1988), pp. 9–12, 14–15.

"Emerson: The Priest Departs, the Divine Literatus Comes," from *An American Procession* (New York: Alfred A. Knopf, 1984), pp. 32–41.

"Thoreau and American Power," from "A Lover and His Guilty Land," ibid., pp. 71–80.

"Hawthorne: The Ghost Sense" from *New York Review of Books* (October 24, 1968).

" 'Melville Is Dwelling Somewhere in New York,' " ibid., pp. 137–60.

"Walt Whitman: I Am The Man," from *God and the American Writer* (New York: Vintage Books, 1988), pp. 107–19.

"Lincoln: The Almighty Has His Own Purposes," from ibid., pp. 120–26, 130–41.

"Emily Dickinson: Called Back," from *Contemporaries* (Boston: Little, Brown, 1962), pp. 50–52, 53–56.

"Creatures of Circumstance: Mark Twain," from *An American Procession* (New York: Alfred A. Knopf, 1984), pp. 184–86, 189–93; 202–10.

"William and Henry James: Our Passion Is Our Task," from *The Inmost Leaf* (New York: Harvest/ HBJ Books, 1955), pp. 9–20.

"The Death of the Past: Henry Adams and T. S. Eliot," from "Epilogue," *An American Procession*, op. cit., pp. 3–21.

VII: THE LITERARY LIFE

"Edmund Wilson at Wellfleet," from "Growing Up in the Sixties," *New York Jew* (New York: Alfred A. Knopf, 1978), pp. 239–49.

"Hannah Arendt: The Burden of Our Time," from "Woman in a Dark Time," *The New York Review of Books* (June 24, 1982).

"The Directness of Josephine Herbst," from a tribute delivered at Josephine Herbst's memorial service, February 18, 1969.

"Saving My Soul at the Plaza," from *The New York Review of Books* (March 31, 1983), pp. 38–42.

VIII: SUMMING UP

"American Writing Now," from *The New Republic* (October 18, 1980), pp. 27–30.

"To Be a Critic," from *Contemporaries* (New York: Horizon Press, 1982), pp. 3–18.

INDEX